T0301538

# THE SMS BLACKWELL HANDBOOK OF ORGANIZATIONAL CAPABILITIES

## Strategic Management Society Book Series

The Strategic Management Society Book Series is a cooperative effort between the Strategic Management Society and Blackwell Publishers. The purpose of the series is to present information on cutting-edge concepts and topics in strategic management theory and practice. The books emphasize building and maintaining bridges between strategic management theory and practice. The work published in these books generates and tests new theories of strategic management. Additionally, work published in this series demonstrates how to learn, understand, and apply these theories in practice. The content of the series represents the newest critical thinking in the field of strategic management. As a result, these books provide valuable knowledge for strategic management scholars, consultants, and executives.

### Published

*Strategic Entrepreneurship: Creating a New Mindset*
Edited by Michael A. Hitt, R. Duane Ireland, S. Michael Camp, and Donald L. Sexton

*Creating Value: Winners in the New Business Environment*
Edited by Michael A. Hitt, Raphael Amit, Charles Lucier, and Robert D. Nixon

*Strategic Process: Shaping the Contours of the Field*
Edited by Bala Chakravarthy, Günter Müller-Stewens, Peter Lorange, and Christoph Lechner

*The SMS Blackwell Handbook of Organizational Capabilities*
Edited by Constance E. Helfat

# The SMS Blackwell Handbook of Organizational Capabilities

Emergence, Development, and Change

Edited by

Constance E. Helfat

Blackwell
Publishing

350 Main Street, Malden, MA 02148-5018, USA
108 Cowley Road, Oxford OX4 1JF, UK
550 Swanston Street, Carlton, Victoria 3053, Australia

First published 2003 by Blackwell Publishing Ltd

*Library of Congress Cataloging-in-Publication Data has been applied for*

ISBN 1-4051-0304-3 (hardback)

A CIP catalogue record for this book is available from the British Library.

Set in 10 on 12 pt Galliard
by Ace Filmsetting Ltd, Frome, Somerset


For further information on
Blackwell Publishing, visit our website:
http://www.blackwellpublishing.com

# Contents

## Part II   Incremental Development and Change

## Part III   Dealing with Radical Change

# Contributors

*Jay B. Barney*, The Ohio State University
*Iain M. Cockburn*, Boston University
*Wesley M. Cohen*, Duke University
*Giovanni Dosi*, St Anna School of Advanced Studies
*Kathleen M. Eisenhardt*, Stanford University
*Sydney Finkelstein*, Dartmouth College
*Giovanni Gavetti*, Harvard University
*Constance E. Helfat*, Dartmouth College
*Rebecca M. Henderson*, Massachusetts Institute of Technology
*Mike Hobday*, University of Sussex
*Daniel Holbrook*, Marshall University
*David A. Hounshell*, Carnegie Mellon University
*Samina Karim*, Boston University
*Steven Klepper*, Carnegie Mellon University
*Bruce Kogut*, Insead
*Richard N. Langlois*, University of Connecticut
*Theresa K. Lant*, New York University
*Daniel A. Levinthal*, University of Pennsylvania
*Franco Malerba*, Bocconi University
*Jeffrey A. Martin*, University of Texas at Austin
*Luigi Marengo*, University of Trento
*Will Mitchell*, Duke University
*Richard Nelson*, Columbia University
*Luigi Orsenigo*, University of Brescia and Bocconi University
*Keith Pavitt*, University of Sussex
*James Brian Quinn*, Dartmouth College
*Daniel M. G. Raff*, University of Pennysylvania
*Ruth S. Raubitschek*, United States Department of Justice
*Richard S. Rosenbloom*, Harvard University
*Kenneth L. Simons*, University of London
*Harbir Singh*, University of Pennysylvania
*W. Edward Steinmueller*, University of Sussex
*Scott Stern*, Northwestern University
*Mary Tripsas*, Harvard University
*Steven M. Usselman*, Georgia Institute of Technology
*Birger Wernerfelt*, Massachusetts Institute of Technology
*Sidney G. Winter*, University of Pennsylvania

# Acknowledgements

This book grew out of a conference on the Evolution of Firm Capabilities, held in September 1999 at the Tuck School of Business at Dartmouth College. Scholars in strategic management, economics, business history, organization theory, and management of technology came together to examine how the resources and capabilities of organizations emerge, develop, and change over time. This book would not have been possible without the contributions of many of those scholars and their colleagues. The book also would not have been possible without the financial support of the conference by the Tuck School of Business at Dartmouth and the Consortium on Competitiveness and Cooperation (the latter via funding from the Alfred P. Sloan Foundation). Many people, too numerous to name here, provided support and encouragement along the way. I owe a particular debt, however, to Dick Nelson for suggesting the conference in the first place, and for his support and that of Sid Winter throughout this process. The support of Dan Schendel and Mike Hitt of the Strategic Management Society (SMS) also made it possible to include this book in the SMS book series.

Constance E. Helfat

The editors and publishers gratefully acknowledge the following for permission to reproduce the copyright material:
"Dominance by birthright: entry of prior radio producers and competitive ramifications in the U.S. television receiver industry." *Strategic Management Journal.* Steven Klepper and Kenneth L. Simons, © 2000. Reproduced by permission of John Wiley & Sons Limited.
"The nature, sources, and consequences of firm differences in the early history of the semiconductor industry." *Strategic Management Journal.* Daniel Holbrook, Wesley M. Cohen, David A. Hounshell, and Steven Klepper, © 2000. Reproduced by permission of John Wiley & Sons Limited.
"Superstores and the evolution of firm capabilities in American bookselling." *Strategic Management Journal.* Daniel M. G. Raff, © 2000. Reproduced by permission of John Wiley & Sons Limited.

"Product sequencing: co-evolution of knowledge, capabilities, and products." *Strategic Management Journal*. Constance E. Helfat and Ruth S. Raubitschek, © 2000. Reproduced by permission of John Wiley & Sons Limited.

"Path-dependent and path-breaking change: reconfiguring business resources following acquisitions in the U.S. medical sector, 1978–1995." *Strategic Management Journal*. Samina Karim and Will Mitchell, © 2000. Reproduced by permission of John Wiley & Sons Limited.

"The satisficing principle in capability learning. *"Strategic Management Journal*. Sidney G. Winter, © 2000. Reproduced by permission of John Wiley & Sons Limited.

"Untangling the origins of competitive advantage." *Strategic Management Journal*. Iain M. Cockburn, Rebecca M. Henderson, and Scott Stern, © 2000. Reproduced by permission of John Wiley & Sons Limited.

"Strategy and circumstance: the response of American firms to Japanese competition in semiconductors, 1980–1995." *Strategic Management Journal*. Richard N. Langlois and W. Edward Steinmuller, © 2000. Reproduced by permission of John Wiley & Sons Limited.

"Dynamic capabilities: what are they?" *Strategic Management Journal*. Kathleen M. Eisenhardt and Jeffrey A. Martin, © 2000. Reproduced by permission of John Wiley & Sons Limited.

"Leadership, capabilities, and technological change: the transformation of NCR in the electronic era." *Strategic Management Journal*. Richard S. Rosenbloom, © 2000. Reproduced by permission of John Wiley & Sons Limited.

"Capabilities, cognition, and inertia: evidence from digital imaging." *Strategic Management Journal*. Mary Tripsas and Giovanni Gavetti, © 2000. Reproduced by permission of John Wiley & Sons Limited.

# CHAPTER ONE

# Stylized Facts Regarding the Evolution of Organizational Resources and Capabilities

## Constance E. Helfat

## Introduction

The resources and capabilities of firms have commanded the increasing attention of scholars and practitioners. This area of inquiry has had an enormous impact on the field of strategic management, has played an important role in allied fields such as human resource management, international business, and technology management, and has made inroads into industrial organization economics and organization theory. As work has proceeded, we have learned that we cannot fully understand the nature and impact of firm resources and capabilities without understanding the underlying dynamics of how they emerge, develop, and change over time. This handbook therefore focuses on the evolution of firm resources and capabilities. The chapters include theoretical and empirical contributions that together enhance our understanding of resource and capability accumulation and reconfiguration within firms.

How do the resources and capabilities of organizations emerge, develop, and change over time? This one question itself contains three separate questions regarding how resources and capabilities first emerge, then develop, and then change, as well as questions regarding linkages between these phenomena. In raising these questions, we must confront some critical issues. Here I focus on two of these issues: (1) adaptation of resources and capabilities over time, and (2) heterogeneity of organizational resources and capabilities during the lifecycle of an industry. As explained shortly, the extent of heterogeneity may change over time in a manner that depends on the extent to which resources and capabilities adapt over time. But first, some definitions are in order.

The terms "resources" and "capabilities" mean different things to different people. In what follows, an organizational resource refers to an asset or input to production (tangible or intangible) that the organization owns, controls, or has access to on a semi-permanent basis. An organizational capability refers to an organizational ability to perform a coordinated task, utilizing organizational resources, for the purpose of achieving a particular end result. Firms may differ in the utility and effectiveness of their resources and capabilities.

A focus on the evolution of resources and capabilities implies that history matters. For example, historical antecedents at the inception of an industry may affect the subsequent evolution of the firms and their resources. In addition, the ability of organizational resources and capabilities to adapt over time has important consequences for the success and failure of firms and of entire industries. Therefore, it is important to ask whether organizational resources and capabilities alter from their initial state in any meaningful fashion. If resources and capabilities do change over time, then we can ask whether they become relatively more or less heterogeneous over time and how the evolution of diversity affects firms and society.

The theoretical straw man for the first question regarding adaptation of resources and capabilities derives from population ecology (Hannan and Freeman, 1989), which in its strong form holds that firms are inert. By implication, resources and capabilities do not change over time. Any heterogeneity of resources and capabilities within an industry simply reflects the degree of heterogeneity at the time of founding. Other theories such as evolutionary economics (Nelson and Winter, 1982) take a more balanced view: although as a first-order approximation firms tend to behave as they have in the past, their routines and capabilities also adapt and change. From this perspective, we then can ask whether, and to what extent, resources and capabilities within an industry become more similar to or different from one another over time.

## Stylized Facts

If resources and capabilities are inert, the whole question of their evolution is moot. Evidence presented here and elsewhere, however, suggests that resources and capabilities do evolve and change over time. The more interesting issue has to do with the circumstances under which firms can or cannot change, as well as the extent and nature of any changes in resources and capabilities. Research in this handbook suggests that the following "stylized facts" may characterize the evolution of resources and capabilities. While future research may change these "facts" and will almost certainly add to them, the following candidates for stylized facts provide a starting point for further analysis:

*Market entry*

1  Entrants to a new industry have heterogeneous sets of resources and capabilities, determined in part by the past histories of the firms and their founders.
2  The success of entrants in a new industry depends in part on the extent to which pre-existing resources and capabilities of firms or their founders carry over.

*Adaptation and change*

3  Organizational resources and capabilities can and do change over time. Firms are not inert.
4  Evolution of organizational resources and capabilities is history dependent. Past history constrains change in resources and capabilities.

*Heterogeneity*

5   The evolution of heterogeneity in organizational resources and capabilities within
    an industry depends on the initial degree of heterogeneity and on the particular
    history-dependent paths taken by resources and capabilities as they evolve.
6   Broad similarities in the resources and capabilities that firms possess within an in-
    dustry coexist with important heterogeneity between firms that does not converge
    quickly over time.

In what follows, I explain how the research in this book supports these propositions. I
also elaborate on several themes that recur in many of the chapters. These themes
include: the co-evolution of organizational resources and capabilities with organizational form, products, and market structure; managerial cognition as an influence on,
and consequence of, resource and capability evolution; the importance of dynamic
capabilities and learning; the role of geographic location and social networks in the
evolution of resources and capabilities; and the impact of public policies.

The handbook is organized according to a time line of resource and capability evolution: emergence within an industry; incremental development and change; and adaptation in response to major technological and market changes. These three aspects
of capability evolution overlap. For example, in order to understand the longer-term
consequences of conditions surrounding the emergence of resources and capabilities,
we must trace how resources and capabilities develop and change over time. Additionally, the ability of organizations to adapt to radical technological or market change
depends in part on their history up to that point. Each chapter in this volume, however, is placed in one of the three portions of the time line that is a primary focus of the
research.

This handbook brings together scholars of strategic management, economics, history, organizational theory, international business, and management of technology.
The book contributes to research within each of these fields, as well as to inter-discipli-
nary research on the evolution of resources, capabilities, and organizations. Many of
the contributions in this volume are full-blown research chapters, some accompanied
by comments of discussants. Other contributions are shorter commentaries on streams
of research that highlight key issues for future work on the evolution of resources and
capabilities.

## Topics of Research

Before explaining how the evidence in the chapters supports the stylized facts outlined
above, I first briefly summarize the topics covered in the handbook. This collection of
research begins with three empirical studies of the emergence of resources and capabilities within industries, and its impact on the success or failure of firms. In a study of
the US television industry, Klepper and Simons show that the pre-entry experience of
radio firms affected their likelihood of entry into the new industry, as well as the amount
of innovation and rate of exit from the industry. Holbrook, Cohen, Hounshell, and
Klepper expand the analysis of pre-entry experience to include the prior experience of

founders of new firms, and examine four firms that entered the early semiconductor industry. Raff also deals with market entry and the role of founders, in a comparison of the evolution of two major booksellers that together created the superstore segment of the US book retailing market. In an accompanying commentary, Pavitt compares and contrasts these studies.

Three shorter comments on streams of research add to the analysis of the emergence of resources and capabilities. First, Levinthal makes a new distinction between "strong form" and "weak form" imprinting when firms are founded. Then Kogut analyzes the emergence of organizational capabilities within networks of firms, and Lant focuses on capabilities directed toward gaining legitimacy for firms in a new industry.

The next set of chapters deals with incremental development and change in resources and capabilities. First, Wernerfelt develops a mathematical model in which minor errors by firms over time lead to heterogeneity of firm resources. Next Malerba, Nelson, Orsenigo, and Winter use a "history friendly" economic model to analyze the evolution of firm competencies in the computer industry over time, including the impact of public policies. Dosi, Hobday, and Marengo then analyze the co-evolution of problem-solving capabilities and organizational form in the context of the design of complex product systems. Next Helfat and Raubitschek develop a conceptual model of the co-evolution of organizational knowledge, capabilities, and products, illustrated by histories of three Japanese electronics companies. In a related study, Karim and Mitchell study acquisitions as a way to reconfigure the resources and capabilities of both acquiring and acquired firms, and analyze acquisitions in the US medical sector.

Several commentaries build on the foregoing analyses of capability development and change. Quinn's comment on the Helfat and Raubitscheck and Karim and Mitchell chapters deals with the relationship between outsourcing and the evolution of capabilities. Singh then examines relational capabilities that enable firms to gain access to new resources and knowledge through alliances, while Pavitt focuses on the ability of large firms to adapt and change through their innovative routines. Finally, Barney makes the broader point that the analysis of resources and capabilities can usefully be thought of as part of evolutionary economics.

The last several chapters in the handbook deal with adaptation of capabilities in response to major technological and market change. Cockburn, Henderson, and Stern analyze the impact of the pre-existing positions of firms, as well as firm response to the environment, on the adoption of new science-driven drug discovery techniques in the pharmaceutical industry. Langlois and Steinmueller examine the competition that US semiconductor firms encountered from Japanese firms in DRAMs during the 1980s, and the response of the US firms. Then Eisenhardt and Martin analyze dynamic capabilities associated with specific activities such as new product development that can help firms survive and prosper when faced with changing technologies and markets.

Underlying any adaptation in capabilities is what Winter terms "capability learning." In his chapter, Winter analyzes the processes that govern the start, stopping, and re-ignition of capability learning. Once an initial learning process ends, an organizational crisis may re-ignite learning through a change in an organization's aspiration level. The chapters by Rosenbloom and by Tripsas and Gavetti deal with attempts to re-ignite learning where the success of these attempts depended on the abilities and cognition of senior executives. Rosenbloom traces the ultimately successful efforts of NCR to adapt to the introduction of electronics in the business equipment industry, in contrast to Polaroid's failure in the market for digital imaging documented by Tripsas and Gavetti. Commentary by Usselman focuses on the impact of upper management on the evolution of organizational capabilities.

The final two comments on streams of research also deal with learning and dynamic capabilities when companies are faced with change. Finkelstein focuses on the capability of learning from major corporate mistakes, illustrated by Motorola's cellular phone business. Barney then concludes by arguing that dynamic capabilities are themselves firm resources that can be subjected to the same sort of analysis as other resources and capabilities.

## Stylized Facts and the Evidence

The research just described contains conceptual grounding as well as empirical support for the stylized facts proposed earlier. In what follows, I explain how the various chapters support each of the stylized facts.

### Market entry

Entry into a market may come from new firms or from established firms that already participate in other industries. Several of the chapters analyze aspects of entry, including but not limited to the chapters dealing with the emergence of capabilities in Part I of this handbook.

The chapters provide conceptual grounding for the first proposed stylized fact that entrants into new industries have heterogeneous capabilities. Winter, for example, points out that organizational aspirations affect the heterogeneity of capabilities. In Winter's model, aspirations regulate organizational investments in learning, and therefore partially determine new capabilities that emerge. As a result, heterogeneity in initial aspirations contributes to heterogeneity in firm capabilities.

Kogut then analyzes resources and capabilities directly, noting that differences in the geographic location and network of firms at founding leads to heterogeneity of resources. Barney observes in his discussion of evolutionary economics and resource-based theory that the concept of variation in evolutionary theory further underpins the heterogeneity of firms upon founding. Finally, Helfat and Raubitschek, in an analysis of new product introduction and market entry, incorporate the second stylized fact that the success of entry depends on the extent to which a firm's pre-existing capabilities carry over to the new market.

Several of the chapters also provide empirical support for these two proposed stylized facts. Klepper and Simons demonstrate that entrants into the new U.S. television industry differed in their prior business experience. Moreover, the firms whose technological and market knowledge carried over best to the new industry were most successful. Similarly, the analysis by Holbrook et al. of four firms in the US semiconductor industry shows that the firms entered the industry in order to exploit their differential knowledge and connections developed from past activities. The most successful of these firms, Motorola, had prior business experience that enabled the company to adapt to the conditions of the new industry.

Raff provides further evidence regarding heterogeneity of capabilities and market entry. Raff documents how the two firms that created the superstore segment of the bookselling industry, Borders and Barnes & Noble, began with very different approaches to the business, and developed very different capabilities in line with these approaches. Finally, Lant shows that at the inception of the new media "industry" in New York, individual firms differed in their pre-existing and newly acquired social capital, which they could leverage to develop legitimacy for themselves and the industry.

### Adaptation and change

The next stylized facts suggest that firm capabilities can and do change, but in a manner constrained by and dependent on their past history. A number of the chapters provide theoretical support for these propositions. In Wernerfelt's model, the resource base of the firm evolves through minor errors that alter the existing resource base. Helfat and Raubitschek propose that "core" and "integrative" knowledge change via systems of learning that depend on existing organizational knowledge and products. The model of Malerba et al. also includes learning from experience, such as in R&D. Singh further notes that knowledge accumulation and codification of experience is critical for development of an effective relational capability. And in Winter's model, events that produce an up-tick in aspirations re-ignite "overt" organizational learning that leads to changes in capabilities. Aspirations also adapt to experience and outcomes: an organization's prior experience influences ideas about what can be learned. More generally, Levinthal notes that even "weak" form organizational imprinting implies that an organization's initial state constrains change. Eisenhardt and Martin add that the capability to adapt and change evolves via path dependence in the form of specific mechanisms for learning, such as repeated practice, codification of experience, and learning from past mistakes. Finkelstein suggests that organizations require institutionalized processes that enable them to learn from major mistakes.

A great deal of evidence in this handbook supports the twin stylized facts that firm capabilities do change over time, but in a constrained manner. Raff shows that the book superstores developed new capabilities and merchandising approaches to meet evolving business needs, but in a manner constrained by each firm's initial business approach and evolving asset base. Karim and Mitchell find that companies use acquisitions to alter their capabilities, extending their pre-existing capabilities incrementally and, less frequently, moving in new directions. Helfat and Raubitschek find a similar pattern of internal company alteration in core technological knowledge by Japanese electronics companies. As the companies expanded into new product lines, they often built on existing capabilities and sometimes changed them in more fundamental ways. Dosi, Hobday, and Marengo also provide evidence of reconfiguration of non-routine activities to improve organizational learning by producers of high-technology customized capital goods.

With regard to the ability of firms to adapt to radical technological or market change, not surprisingly, much of the evidence points to the difficulty of change. The chapter in this collection that suggests the greatest difficulty of organizational change is that of

Klepper and Simons. In this study, the prior experience of firms at the time of entry into the new US television industry predicts survival and market shares much later on. Along the same lines, Holbrook et al. show that the pre-entry experience of the semi-conductor firms limited their strategic visions in a manner that persisted over time, often making change difficult. This study also documents, however, that the initial strategic mindset of one of the firms helped the company to adapt to changing market conditions.

Tripsas and Gavetti extend the analysis of strategic mindset and managerial cognition in their study of Polaroid's entry into the digital imaging market. Although the prior cognition of senior management helped the firm to develop new technological capabilities in digital imaging, Polaroid failed to achieve market success because the company stuck with its old and inappropriate business model. Similarly, Finkelstein's analysis of Motorola shows that despite the fact that the firm had patents and R&D related to digital cellular phones, the company stumbled when senior management misjudged the pace of market change from analog to digital phones.

With regard to the role of management, Rosenbloom's study of NCR has somewhat more optimistic implications for the capacity of organizations to change. Although NCR initially and unsuccessfully sought to adapt to the new era of electronics in an incremental manner, new management with more revolutionary ideas took charge in response to a crisis. The firm eventually returned to its pre-eminent position, aided by its pre-existing reputation and strong customer relationships.

Two other studies provide yet more evidence of historically constrained organizational change in response to radical changes in technologies and markets. Cockburn, Henderson, and Stern show that the extent to which individual pharmaceutical firms pursued science-driven drug discovery depended on the extent to which each firm initially used this approach in the 1960s. All of the firms, however, did eventually adopt this approach to drug discovery. Similarly, Langlois and Steinmueller show that firms in the US semiconductor industry were able to improve their manufacturing capabilities when challenged by Japanese companies. Here too, history mattered: the recovery of US firms hinged importantly on their pre-existing design-intensive innovative capabilities in higher margin chips. More generally, Pavitt notes that companies need to adapt not only their technologies, but also their organizational practices, when faced with technological and market change.

## Heterogeneity of capabilities within industries

Having established that resources and capabilities can and do change, I next examine changes over time in the heterogeneity of firm resources and capabilities within an industry. As discussed earlier, evidence in this handbook shows that entrants to a new industry have heterogeneous resources and capabilities. Evidence in this book also pertains to the issue of whether and how the initial degree of heterogeneity in an industry changes over time. As next explained, the evidence supports the proposed stylized facts that evolution of heterogeneity in resources and capabilities is path dependent, and that broad similarities in resources and capabilities coexist with important heterogeneity between firms that does not converge quickly over time.

Before examining the empirical evidence regarding the evolution of heterogeneity, it is helpful to briefly highlight relevant theoretical and conceptual contributions in this book. Wernerfelt shows that small deviations in firms' initial resource bases can lead to persistent differences between firms over time. Levinthal points out that local search by firms through a complex space of alternate organizational forms implies that a firm's starting position affects, but does not fully determine, where the firm ends up. Helfat and Raubitschek further note that firms may not be able to exploit all future options embedded in their initial positions, and therefore may place different "bets" when developing capabilities and products. The outcomes of these bets, including an element of randomness or luck as highlighted by Barney, may yield new options and paths of knowledge creation that differ between firms. Additionally, Winter shows that heterogeneity in performance aspirations and aspiration adjustment leads to heterogeneity in capability development over time.

The empirical evidence in several of the chapters demonstrates a path-dependent link between the initial heterogeneity of resources and capabilities in an industry and subsequent evolution. Klepper and Simons show that although entrants in the early US television industry differed in their resources and capabilities, only a subset of the firms survived a shakeout. The survivors had more homogenous capabilities than did the original set of entrants, in part due to the similarity of pre-entry experience among the surviving firms that helped them to prosper. Raff also documents differences in the business approaches of the superstore booksellers. In this case, initial heterogeneity in the capabilities of the two firms increased over time, as the firms built on their past success to develop very different sets of capabilities and resources. Raff's work also documents how, despite broad similarities in the sorts of capabilities required to succeed as a book superstore, the nature of these capabilities differed a great deal between the firms.

Langlois and Steinmueller provide additional evidence regarding the impact of initial heterogeneity of resources and capabilities on subsequent evolution in an industry. When Japanese semiconductor companies challenged US firms in DRAMs, the US and Japanese companies had very different strengths, rooted in different capabilities developed early on to meet different patterns of end-use demand. Although the capabilities of the firms in the two countries became more similar over time, especially in manufacturing, they nevertheless remained strongly differentiated. Cockburn, Henderson, and Stern also document the slow diffusion of capabilities with regard to science-based drug discovery in the pharmaceutical industry. As a result of slow diffusion, heterogeneity of drug discovery practices persisted for a long period of time, with the rate of adoption affected by heterogeneity in firm location and other pre-existing firm-specific attributes.

Finally, Eisenhardt and Martin observe more generally that dynamic capabilities often have common features associated with "best practice" across firms, such as the need for cross-functional integration between research and manufacturing in product development. The specific features of such capabilities, however, may vary between firms. As Pavitt notes, evidence shows that firms differ in the organizational practices that link technological capabilities to products and markets. Singh further observes that firms differ systematically in their ability to manage alliances, as a result of differences in managerial understanding of the sources of alliance success and in the alliance management processes that firms employ.

In summary, theory and evidence in this handbook suggest that the evolution of heterogeneity in resources and capabilities depends on the starting point. Because resources and capabilities often change slowly, initial heterogeneity may persist. Over time, however, imitation and diffusion of resources and capabilities may decrease the initial heterogeneity. Reduced heterogeneity also can result from an industry shakeout, where the surviving firms have similar sets of resources. Differences between firms in their resources and capabilities, however, also may persist and even increase over time in a more forgiving environment.

## Recurring Themes

Beyond the stylized facts just discussed, many themes recur in the chapters. One important theme concerns the way in which differences in geographic location shape the initial resources and capabilities of firms in an industry, as well as their subsequent evolution (see especially Kogut, Lant, Langlois and Steinmueller, as well as the discussion of Japanese and American television firms in Klepper and Simons). Because geographic location has a large impact on the initial resources and capabilities of firms, and because resources and capabilities evolve in a history-dependent manner, the impact of geographic location persists. Although capabilities may become more similar over time as firms from different geographic locations compete against one another, the evidence suggests that convergence is slow and substantial heterogeneity between firms based on geographic location persists.

A second theme regarding what might be called "collective" capabilities is related to the topic of geographic location. Lant, Kogut, and Singh point to the importance of social capital and relationships between firms, often embedded in networks of relationships that are specific to geographic locales. The initial composition of these networks, along with the social capital embedded in them, affects the subsequent evolution of the networks and of the resources to which these networks provide access.

Another theme deals with the importance of managerial cognition or mindset (see especially Tripsas and Gavetti; Holbrook et al.; Rosenbloom). Initial managerial cognition shapes the emergence and development of resources and capabilities, and persistence in managerial cognition shapes subsequent attempts to alter resources and capabilities. Like heterogeneity in geographic location, heterogeneity in managerial cognition may persist over time.

A fourth theme involves the co-evolution of resources and capabilities with other factors, including products (Helfat and Raubitschek; Langlois and Steinmueller; Malerba et al.; Raff; Wernerfelt), organization (Cockburn, Henderson, and Stern; Dosi, Hobday, and Marengo; Pavitt), aspirations (Winter), and market structure (Klepper and Simons; Malerba et al.). Firms gain knowledge in the process of creating, making, and selling products that augments current capabilities and provides new options for future development of capabilities and products. At the same time, past capability and product trajectories constrain future options. The organizational structure and processes of the firm also strongly affect the ability to develop, utilize, and alter resources and capabilities over time. The same holds for aspirations, which regulate learning. Finally, market structure depends in part on the resources and capabilities of firms. For example, when a shakeout occurs because some firms lack the resources needed for survival, an industry becomes much more concentrated, as in the work of Klepper and Simons.

An important aspect of this co-evolution, and of capability evolution more generally, concerns learning and "dynamic" capabilities that build, integrate, and reconfigure resources and capabilities (Teece, Pisano, and Shuen, 1997). Most of the chapters deal with this subject in some manner. Here I note two aspects of learning and change not often studied in research on dynamic capabilities. First, as Rosenbloom's study of NCR so clearly demonstrates, leadership at the top of an organization is an essential element of dynamic capability. NCR did not have a culture of learning, but as a result of effective leadership that reconfigured firm resources wisely, the company ultimately survived and prospered. Secondly, as Winter explains, aspirations regulate learning and the efforts of organizations to change. This fundamental point has been largely overlooked in the literature on resources and capabilities. It also is consistent with the evidence in this volume regarding the impact of crises in spurring companies to change, presumably by changing aspirations.

A final theme concerns the impact of public policy on the evolution of capabilities (see especially Holbrook et al. and Malerba et al.). Since public policies tend to vary by geographic location, the importance of geography takes on added significance. Public policy also can affect the diversity of entrants to an industry, and therefore affects the heterogeneity of resources and capabilities both initially and as the industry evolves. Holbrook et al. highlight the importance of encouraging diversity in the resources and capabilities of competitors, especially entrants, because greater diversity may yield better technologies and products. Malerba et al. find that encouraging diversity of entry may increase the extent of subsequent competition. Hence, public policy at the inception of an industry has important consequences for society in general. Once again, history matters.

## Conclusion

The range of issues analyzed in this handbook points to the promise of research on the evolution of resources and capabilities. The evidence presented here supports the six proposed stylized facts of capability evolution, all of which highlight the history dependent nature of organizational resources and capabilities. The contributions in this volume also raise questions to investigate in future work on the dynamics and evolution of organizational resources and capabilities (see also Dosi, Nelson, and Winter, 2000). Such research has implications for many topics that often are studied without reference to the resources and capabilities of individual firms and their histories. The chapters in this book have begun to deal with these topics, which include market entry, market structure, industry evolution, competition, technological change, diffusion of innovation, investments, and public policy. There is, of course, much more to do. We have a myriad of opportunities for future research.

## References

Dosi, G., Nelson R. R., and S. G. Winter (eds) (2000) *The Nature and Dynamics of Organizational Capabilities.* New York: Oxford University Press.

Hannan, M. and Freeman, J. (1989) *Organizational Ecology.* Cambridge, MA: Harvard University Press.

Nelson, R. R. and Winter, S. G. (1982) *An Evolutionary Theory of Economic Change.* Cambridge, MA: Harvard University Press.

Teece, D. J., Pisano, G., and Shuen, A. (1997) Dynamic capabilities and strategic management. *Strategic Management Journal*, 18, 509–34.

# Emergence of Resources and Capabilities

# CHAPTER TWO

# Dominance by Birthright: Entry of Prior Radio Producers and Competitive Ramifications in the US Television Receiver Industry

## Steven Klepper and Kenneth L. Simons

## Introduction

Entry plays a central role in nearly all industry economists' models of industrial competition. Equilibrium is assumed to be brought about by a pool of potential entrants, ready to enter if incumbent firms earn excessive profits. If an unlimited pool of such potential entrants, each with capabilities comparable to incumbent firms, is assumed to exist, then in the long run economic profits are driven to zero. Where these firms come from and where they get their capabilities is not generally considered in such models; all that is important is that a sufficient number of them exist to drive economic profits to zero. This perspective stands in sharp contrast to the business strategist's conception of industrial competition. Strategists assume that firms are fundamentally different. They exhort firms to identify and exploit their core capabilities, which can be the source of persistent economic profits. But where do these capabilities come from? Do firms possess them when they initially enter industries? If so, then entrants will differ in the threat they pose to incumbents, and entry will no longer insure that economic profits are driven to zero over time. Indeed, the very notion of an equilibrium in which all firms earn zero economic profits would no longer be so compelling.

In light of the importance of entry in models of industrial competition, it is surprising how little industry economists and strategists know about where entrants come from and how their backgrounds affect their fates. The few studies that consider all the entrants into an industry and analyze how their backgrounds affect their market share and survival over the industry's evolution are not reassuring about conventional models. They suggest that firm histories do have a substantial effect on firm performance (Lane, 1989; Mitchell, 1991; Carroll et al., 1996). Whether the effects of pre-entry experience dissipate or persist over time and exactly how the backgrounds of entrants condition their performance is less clear. Even less is known about what effect, if any, heterogeneity among entrants has on the nature of competition and the market structure of industries.

This paper explores how prior experience conditions entry, firm performance, and the evolution of market structure in one industry, television receivers, where considerable information could be collected about an important class of potential entrants – firms that produced radios prior to the start of the TV receiver industry. This is a particularly interesting group of firms because radio producers dominated the TV industry even though they accounted for a minority of entrants. Moreover, the TV receiver industry has drawn a lot of attention from researchers, particularly doctoral students, due to the sharp shakeout of producers it experienced and the eventual demise of all US TV producers when the industry was besieged by international competition (Datta, 1971; Levy, 1981; Willard, 1982; LaFrance, 1985; Wooster, 1986). This has left in its wake considerable information to draw upon to understand the nature of competition in the industry and to analyze how the background of entrants affected their performance and the evolution of the industry.

We exploit various sources to construct a comprehensive data base on TV and radio producers. We identify every producer of televisions, its date of entry and exit, any ownership changes it underwent, and its periodic market share. We compile a list of all firms that produced radios in the few years before the start of the television industry. For each, we determine the number of years it produced radios, its size, the type of radios it produced, and whether it entered the TV receiver industry. This enables us to analyze how radio producers' backgrounds affected entry into the TV industry and the extent of heterogeneity among the radio entrants. We also use the information to analyze how experience in radios affected firm market shares and firm exit rates over the different eras of competition in the TV industry. Furthermore, we exploit a list of major TV product innovations and construct a list of early TV process innovations to explore the pathways by which radio experience influenced firm performance.

A model of the evolution of a new industry developed by Klepper (1996, 1999) is used to generate hypotheses concerning how radio experience conditioned entry, firm performance, and the evolution of market structure in the TV industry. The model emphasizes the role of innovation and heterogeneity among entrants in contributing to a shakeout and the evolution of an oligopolistic market structure. Firms with more relevant experience are conjectured to have superior abilities to manage R&D in the new industry. This provides them with a competitive advantage that persists over time due to a process of increasing returns that enables the most qualified early entrants to dominate the new industry. R&D is the source of the increasing returns because larger firms have greater output over which they can apply, and thus profit from, their innovations. The model yields a number of implications about how pre-entry experience affects entry and firm performance that we use to structure our empirical analysis. We also use the model to speculate on how the pre-entry characteristics of the most successful television producers made the industry ultimately so vulnerable to international competition.

Our findings indicate that among firms producing radios, those with the most relevant experience entered the television industry. On average, these firms entered earlier, survived longer, and had larger market shares than nonradio producers. Indeed, no nonradio producer ever captured a significant share of the television market. Not only did the radio firms have distinctive advantages over the other entrants, but among these firms the larger ones survived longer and captured a greater share of the market. The hazard rates of the radio producers, especially the larger ones, were not only lower during the early years of the industry but also when the pace of technological change picked up during the commercialization of color television and later when the industry was besieged by international competition. The model implicates innovation as the source of the persistent advantage of the radio firms. Consistent with the model, our findings indicate that nonradio entrants did little innovation and the larger radio producers thoroughly dominated both product and process innovation, which appears to have contributed significantly to their greater longevity and ultimate dominance of the US industry.

The paper is organized as follows. In the next section we review the evolution of competition in the television set industry, focusing especially on the role played by the radio producers. In the following section we use the model of industry evolution in Klepper (1999) to structure how pre-entry radio experience is expected to influence firm entry, innovation, survival, and market structure. Next, we present the empirical analysis. In the following section we discuss alternative explanations for our findings and speculate on why the leading US producers of televisions proved so vulnerable to international competition. We also consider the extent to which other industries have evolved similarly to televisions and the implications of our findings for modeling competition in new industries. In the last section, we offer concluding remarks.

## Radio Producers and the Evolution of the Television Receiver Industry[1]

While many individuals contributed to the development of television, Vladimir Zworykin and Philo Farnsworth are the acknowledged pioneers of the industry. Zworykin began his research in the US at Westinghouse and continued it at RCA when RCA took over the radio research of GE and Westinghouse, two of its parents. By the late 1930s RCA had developed a commercially viable monochrome television system on which it had taken out many patents. Farnsworth's work was initially privately financed, and later Farnsworth Television and Radio Corporation was formed to exploit Farnsworth's patents and to produce radios.

Technical standards for monochrome broadcasting were agreed to by the emerging industry and adopted by the Federal Communications Commission (FCC) in 1941, but World War II delayed commercial broadcasting and the sale of receivers until 1946. Subsequently RCA and CBS engaged in a battle over color broadcasting standards that was eventually won by RCA in 1953. Demand for television receivers was great after World War II, and annual sales of monochrome receivers reached nearly 3 million sets in 1949 and over 7 million sets in 1950. As an increasing fraction of US homes were equipped with television sets, annual sales of monochrome receivers did not subsequently rise much above 7 million sets. Color receivers were introduced in 1954, but their high price, poor quality, and limited color broadcasts kept sales down until 1964, when approximately 1.4 million color sets were sold. Subsequently color sales increased sharply to nearly 6 million sets in 1968, after which growth slowed as sales rose to approximately 11 million sets in 1980.

A flood of firms entered the industry after commercial broadcasting began, similar
to the radio receiver industry following the craze that broke out after the initiation of
radio broadcasting by Westinghouse and the *Detroit Daily News* in 1920. The annual
number of entrants, exits, and firms over the period 1947–89 based on periodic listings in the trade publication *Television Factbook* is plotted in figure 2.1.[2] In 1947, 31
firms were listed as producers. Entry was rapid initially: the number of producers rose
by 45 to 76 in 1948, 59 firms entered in 1949, and entry remained high for the next
four years, with an additional 44 firms entering in 1950–3. Subsequently entry dropped
sharply, averaging one firm per year through the end of the series in 1989. The number
of firms peaked at 92 in 1951, after which there was a sharp shakeout in the number of
producers. By 1958 only 38 firms were left in the industry, and this declined further to
15 in 1974, which is the year before Japanese firms initiated (limited) manufacturing
in the US Although figure 2.1 indicates that further exit of US producers was largely
offset by foreign firms initiating manufacturing in the US, the Japanese industry also
experienced a shakeout and the combined number of US and Japanese firms continued to decline.

Through 1989 a total of 177 US firms entered the industry, many of which came

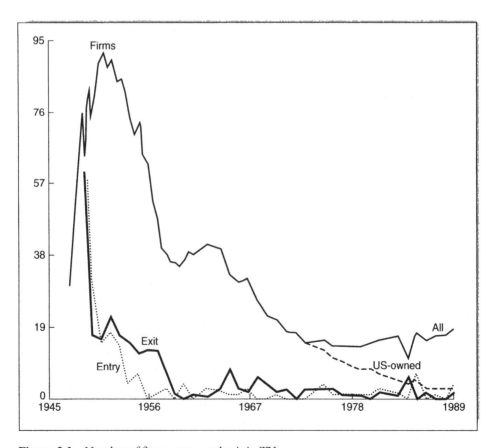

**Figure 2.1**   Number of firms, entry, and exit in TVs

from the radio industry. According to listings in the marketing journal *Thomas' Register of American Manufacturers*, Volumes 1945–8, 53 of the entrants were radio producers. Among the 16 largest radio producers in 1940 listed in table 2.1, 14 entered the industry. These firms quickly came to dominate the television industry. RCA was the early leader. Following its radio policies, it liberally licensed its patents in a pool, provided technical assistance to its licensees, and sold picture tubes liberally to all manufacturers of sets, and after 1958 made all its patents freely available to US firms to settle various antitrust suits. As in radios, this contributed to a decline in RCA's market share and it was eventually displaced by Zenith as the sales leader in both monochrome and color sets. The four-firm US concentration ratio over the period 1948–80 varied from 41 percent to 63 percent in monochrome sets and 57 percent to 73 percent in color sets, with RCA and Zenith generally accounting for 40–59 percent of sales, qualifying the industry as an oligopoly (LaFrance, 1985: 158). Other leading firms included GE, Philco, Emerson, Admiral, Motorola, Magnavox, and Sylvania (with subsidiary Colonial), all of which were radio producers.[3]

Similar to radios, the rise in sales of television receivers over time was driven by improvements in quality and reliability and by large reductions in price. The quality of sets was improved greatly through innovations in picture tubes and tuning. After the development of monochrome sets, the most significant TV innovation was the shadow mask tube developed by RCA, which was the basis for the color system approved by the FCC. Process innovation improved the reliability of sets and greatly lowered their price. Over the period 1958–80 labor productivity in the combined radio and TV industry increased by an average of approximately 5 percent per year, with real TV prices declining at a comparable rate. Many early process innovations were developed by the radio entrants

**Table 2.1** Sixteen large radio producers in 1940

| Firm | Sales in 1940 (thousands) |
| --- | --- |
| Radio Corp. of America | 1700 |
| Philco Corp. | 1675 |
| Zenith Radio & Phonograph Corp. | 1050 |
| Emerson Radio & Phonograph Corp. | 1050 |
| Galvin Mfg. Corp. (Motorola) | 950 |
| Colonial Radio Corp. | 650 |
| Belmont Radio Corp. | 550 |
| Noblitt Sparks Industries Inc. | 400 |
| Crosley Corp. | 350 |
| General Electric Co. | 350 |
| Simplex Radio Corp. | 250 |
| Stewart-Warner Corp. | 250 |
| Electrical Research Laboratories | 250 |
| Wells-Gardner Co. | 200 |
| Farnsworth Television & Radio Corp. | 100 |
| Sparks-Withington Co. | 100 |
| All other producers | 1584 |

*Source*: MacLaurin (1949: 146).

under the direction of their experienced radio engineers.[4] Later process advances were heavily driven by solid-state developments, which made it possible to develop more precise and reliable circuitry using a greater number of circuit elements. Solid-state developments also led to a long progression of improvements in manufacturing efficiency as firms steadily streamlined production through automation.

The advent of solid-state electronics provided an opening for initially Japanese and later other foreign firms to enter the television industry. Up to 1965 imports of television sets were negligible, but subsequently Japanese firms began exporting to the US all solid-state monochrome sets, a market in which US firms had lost interest. These sets were marketed through chains such as Sears Roebuck and K-Mart that handled their own distribution. It was not long before Japanese exports expanded into color sets, which were generally cheaper and of better quality than US sets. The Japanese firms were consistently ahead of the US firms in the move to solid-state components and then integrated circuits, which helped them lead US firms in the development of automated manufacturing methods. As imports mounted in the United States after 1970, US firms that remained in the industry largely moved their operations to Taiwan, Korea, and Mexico to exploit lower labor costs. The Japanese firms also moved to Taiwan and Korea. Later, Korean and Taiwanese firms, some of which had been nurtured by US and Japanese partners, entered the industry, and they and some of the Japanese firms initiated limited manufacturing in the US to counter import restrictions. The move offshore did not stem the exit of US producers, and by 1989 RCA had exited the industry and only three US firms were left. The last of these firms, Zenith, sold out to Goldstar of Korea in 1995.

## Model of Industry Evolution

In this section, we lay out the basics of the model developed in Klepper (1999) to account for shakeouts and the evolution of an oligopolistic market structure. The model yields implications regarding entry, firm survival, and innovation. These are reviewed and used to develop hypotheses regarding the types of radio producers that entered the TV industry and the effects of their backgrounds on innovation and survival.

### The model

The model depicts the evolution of a new industry. Time is defined in discrete periods $t = 1, 2, \ldots$, where period 1 is the start of the industry. In each period, it is assumed that a new group of potential entrants to the industry arises. Potential entrants can be preexisting firms producing related products. They can also be individuals with the requisite organizational skills and knowledge to start a new firm. It is assumed that potential entrants differ in their capabilities, where the key capability in the model is their ability to manage R&D. This capability is subsumed in a single parameter, denoted as a, which scales the productivity of the firm's R&D efforts. Potential entrants are assumed to be able to assess their abilities to manage TV and R&D and hence $a_i$ is assumed to be known prior to entry. It is also assumed to be fixed over time.

The productivity of the firm's R&D plays a key role in determining its average cost of production, which is modeled as

$$c_{it} = c_t - a_i g(r_{it}) + \varepsilon_{it}$$

where $c_{it}$ is firm i's average cost in period t, $c_t$ is a cost component common to all firms in period t, $r_{it}$ is firm i's spending on R&D in period t, $\varepsilon_{it} \geq 0$ is a random cost shock to firm i in period t, and as noted above $a_i$ calibrates the productivity of the firm's R&D efforts. In each period, it is assumed that new opportunities for innovation arise. For simplicity, all innovations are assumed to lower average cost. The extent of the reduction in average cost from innovation is determined by the amount of R&D the firm conducts, $r_{it}$, and productivity of its R&D, $a_i$. The function $g(r_{it})$ is assumed to be such that $g'(r_{it}) > 0$ and $g''(r_{it}) < 0$ for all $r_{it} > 0$ to reflect diminishing returns to R&D. All patented innovations are assumed to be licensed and instantly available to all firms and all nonpatented innovations are assumed to be costlessly imitated with a lag, which is assumed to be one period. This is modeled as $c_t = c_{t-1} - l_t - max_i\{a_i g(r_{it-1})\}$, where $l_t$ is the reduction in average cost associated with patented innovations[5] and $max_i\{a_i g(r_{it-1})\}$ is the largest cost decrease from nonpatented innovation realized among all firms in period t − 1. Last, $\varepsilon_{it}$ is a random cost shock that causes the firm's average cost to exceed its minimum possible value in period t. Cost shocks arise from factors such as difficulties in imitating the leading firm's unpatented innovations, unanticipated capital shortages, lax management, etc. It is assumed that cost shocks are independent across periods and thus last for only one period.

In each period, firms are assumed to retain their customers from the prior period, but if they want to expand they must incur a cost of growth of $m(\Delta q_{it})$, where $\Delta q_{it}$ is the growth in the firm's output and $m'(\Delta q_{it}) \geq 0$ and $m''(\Delta q_{it}) \geq 0$ for all $\Delta q_{it} \geq 0$ to reflect increasing marginal costs of growth. This cost of growth applies to entrants as well as incumbents and thus determines their size at entry.[6] For simplicity, it is assumed that the industry demand curve is fixed over time and that all firms are price takers, so that in each period the price $p_t$ clears the market.

Firms in the industry in period t choose $r_{it}$ and $\Delta q_{it}$ to maximize $\Pi_{it}$, their profits in period t before the realization of the cost shock $\varepsilon_{it}$:

$$\Pi_{it} = [p_t - c_t + a_i g(r_{it})] (q_{it-1} + \Delta q_{it}) - r_{it} - m(\Delta q_{it}).$$

Potential entrants in period t enter iff $\Pi_{it}{}^* \geq 0$ and incumbents in period t − 1 remain in the industry iff $\Pi_{it}{}^* \geq 0$, where $\Pi_{it}{}^*$ is the maximum possible profits of firm i in period t. Furthermore, it is assumed that if a firm incurs a sufficiently large cost shock in period t then it also exits. This is modeled by assuming that if $\varepsilon_{it} > p_t - c_t + a_i g(r_{it})$, in which case the firm would incur losses from production in period t, then the firm disbands its R&D operation and permanently exits the industry.

## Implications of the model

Klepper (1999) derives a number of implications of the model. In each period, larger firms invest more in R&D since the total profit from R&D, which equals the reduction in average cost times the firm's output, is scaled by the firm's output. Furthermore, in every period firms expand until the marginal cost of growth equals their profit per unit of output. The firm's profit per unit of output is determined by its investment in R&D and its R&D productivity. Therefore, larger firms and firms with greater R&D productivity have greater profit margins and thus expand faster. Consequently, among firms that entered in the same period, firms with greater R&D productivity conduct more R&D and are always larger and more profitable than firms with lower R&D productivity. Furthermore, among firms with the same R&D productivity, firms that entered earlier start growing earlier and are thus always larger and more profitable than later entrants.

Expansion of incumbents over time and (initially) entry causes the total output of the industry to rise over time and $p_t - c_t$, the average price-cost margin of firms that do no R&D, to decline over time. When $p_t - c_t$ is high initially, the minimum R&D productivity required for entry to be profitable is low and a range of firms in terms of their R&D productivity enter. As $p_t - c_t$ falls over time, the minimum $a_i$ needed for entry to be profitable rises. Eventually entry becomes unprofitable even for firms with the greatest R&D productivity, at which point entry ceases.

The decline in $p_t - c_t$ also causes the profits of incumbents to decline over time. This is partially offset by the rise in firm R&D over time that occurs as firms grow, which lowers firm average costs. In every period, incumbents that experience a sufficiently large cost shock exit. Incumbents also exit when $p_t - c_t$ falls sufficiently that they cannot earn positive profits even if they produce at their minimum possible cost. The latest entrants with the lowest R&D productivity are always the least profitable and thus the most vulnerable to exit. Thus, even after entry ceases, firms exit, with the latest entrants with the lowest R&D productivity expected to exit first. This causes the number of firms to decline steadily over time, resulting in a shakeout. It also causes the earliest entrants with the greatest R&D productivity to take over an increasing share of the industry's output, which contributes to the evolution of an oligopolistic market structure.

Thus, the model predicts that over time firm profit margins decline, entry eventually ceases and a shakeout occurs, and the industry evolves to be an oligopoly. This corresponds to what occurred in the TV industry. As such, the model passes an initial hurdle of being able to account for the key market structure developments in TVs. We now use it to gain further insights into the main issues of the paper, namely how experience in radio production would be expected to influence entry into the TV industry and how heterogeneity among entrants in terms of their radio experience would be expected to influence firm performance.

In the model, entry and firm performance depend on two factors, both of which are assumed to be determined independently of the new industry: the R&D productivity of potential entrants, and the time they gain the ability to enter. Both are influenced by the experiences of potential entrants prior to entering the new industry. Experience in radio production prior to the start of the TV industry is an example of the type of pre-entry experience that would be expected to influence both a potential entrant's TV R&D productivity and also when it became a potential entrant. Radio producers were well positioned early to learn about technological developments in TVs, which were driven by two prominent firms in the radio industry, RCA and Farnsworth. Many had also been in business for some time and thus had well-developed organizations and access to capital to use to mobilize their efforts in TVs. Both factors qualified radio producers as early potential entrants. They also had experience in R&D and distribution that was likely to be useful in managing R&D in TVs. In particular, firms that produced radios for use in the home, primarily for entertainment, had accumulated considerable information about improving and marketing radios that was likely to be useful for TVs, whose principal market was also home entertainment. Indeed, it was noted earlier that (home) radio producers that entered the TV industry used their experienced radio engineers to direct their production-oriented R&D in TVs. It is exactly this kind of research that was not patentable and that in the model distinguishes the firms in terms of their costs (patented innovations were widely licensed and thus available to all firms on similar terms).

It thus seems plausible that firms with experience producing home radios would have a higher R&D productivity in TVs and also qualify earlier as a potential entrant. In the model, firms have no uncertainty about their own prospects or those of the industry, and these two factors completely determine whether and when they enter. Of course, considerable uncertainty prevailed when the TV industry began, but nonetheless it seems reasonable to assume that firms had some awareness of their own prospects and those of the industry. Thus, among firms producing radios prior to the start of the TV industry, it would be expected that their perceived R&D productivity in TVs would vary according to the extent of their experience producing home radios. Since potential entrants with greater perceived R&D productivity would have greater expected profits, this suggests the following hypothesis:

> Hypothesis 1: Among firms producing radios prior to the start of the TV industry, the greater their experience producing radios, particularly for home entertainment, then the greater the likelihood of entry into the TV industry.

Furthermore, if firms producing radios prior to the start of the TV industry already had the relevant experience to become TV producers, and hence were among the earliest potential entrants, then those that entered would enter earlier than other entrants. This is stated as Hypothesis 2:

> Hypothesis 2: Among all firms that entered the TV industry, firms with (home) radio experience prior to the start of the TV industry would enter earlier.

The model provides an indirect way to probe these conjectures further and also to generate hypotheses concerning firm performance. The model predicts that in each period, firms' R&D productivity must exceed a threshold for entry to be profitable and entrants will vary in their R&D productivity. Some, notably entrants without radio experience, might on average be closer to the minimum R&D productivity required for entry to be profitable. Entrants with less experience in (home) radios might have a higher average R&D productivity than nonradio entrants but a lower average R&D productivity than the entrants with the most experience producing (home) radios. Among firms entering at the same time, their R&D productivity determines their profitability and in turn their hazard of exit and market share at any given moment. This suggests the following hypothesis:

Hypothesis 3: Among firms entering at the same time, their initial hazard will be lower and their market share larger the greater their experience producing (home) radios.

Note that to the extent potential entrants correctly anticipate the productivity of their efforts in TVs, Hypotheses 1 and 3 imply that the same factors that influence entry among firms producing radios prior to the start of the TV industry should also influence their longevity and market shares.

Hypothesis 3 is framed in terms of the *initial* hazard and market shares of contemporaneous entrants, suggesting that the predicted ordering might not hold as the entrants aged. It holds at young ages because the average R&D productivity of the entrants differs according to their experiences in home radios. Over time, though, the least productive entrants would be more likely to exit, which could cause the average productivity of surviving entrants with different amounts of radio experience to converge. This possibility is illustrated in panel a of figure 2.2. Let the upper curve denote the distribution of R&D productivity for entrants with experience producing radios and the lower curve be the distribution for entrants with no radio experience, and let m denote the minimum R&D productivity required for entry to be profitable. The main difference in the two distributions is at the lower end. A relatively high fraction of the entrants without radio experience have an R&D productivity close to or equal to m, whereas very few of the entrants with radio experience have an R&D productivity close to m. In contrast, the distributions overlap at the high end and the maximum R&D productivity for both groups of firms is equal. Over time, as the entrants with the lowest R&D productivity exit first, the average R&D productivity of the two groups will tend to converge, causing the hazards and market shares of the two groups of survivors to converge. Alternatively, suppose, as in panel b of figure 2.2, that the maximum R&D productivity of the entrants with radio experience exceeds that of the entrants without radio experience. As the firms with the lowest R&D productivity tend to exit over time, the average R&D productivity would continue to be greater for the surviving radio than nonradio entrants and their hazards and market shares would not converge. This implies the following corollary to Hypothesis 3:

Corollary: Among firms entering at the same time, experience producing (home) radios may influence firm hazards and market shares not only initially but also at later stages of evolution of the industry.

The next hypothesis concerns the causal process by which the background of entrants affects their hazard. Holding time of entry constant, the model predicts that firms with greater R&D productivity will do more R&D, which coupled with their greater R&D productivity implies they will account for more innovation than firms with lower R&D productivity. Indeed, this is the basis for why firms with greater experience producing radios are expected to have a lower hazard and greater market share. This implies the following hypothesis:

Hypothesis 4: Among firms that entered at the same time, the amount of innovation they generate per year will be larger the greater their experience producing (home) radios.

If indeed innovation is the key determinant of a firm's hazard, as the model predicts, then introducing measures of innovation and R&D per firm into an econometric hazard model should reduce the influence of firm backgrounds on the hazard. This is stated as Hypothesis 5:

> Hypothesis 5: If controls are introduced for firm rates of innovation, then the effect of experience producing (home) radios on the hazard should decline.

## Empirical Analysis

To probe the hypotheses, we first need to identify the firms producing radios prior to the start of the television industry. Our list of radio producers is based on *Thomas' Register of American Manufacturers. Thomas' Register* lists radio producers under the category, "Radio Apparatus: Complete Sets, Outfits, etc." We include in our sample all 265 firms listed in this category in the 1945–8 volumes of *Thomas' Register*, which list producers in 1944–7. The listings in the *Television Factbook* indicate that 56 of the 265 firms entered the TV industry.[7]

For each of the 265 firms, we measure its radio experience on three dimensions. The first is based on its size. Larger radio producers were heavily involved in production engineering. Consequently, we expected the larger firms to be more experienced at R&D. For each radio producer, we measured its size according to its capitalization, as reported in the 1948 volume of *Thomas' Register*.[8] *Thomas' Register* classified each radio producer into one of 12 capitalization categories, with firms of unknown capitalization placed in a separate category. The categories in which the radio producers were classified are reported in table 2.2. The number of radio producers and the percentage that entered the TV industry in each category is also reported. The top category is open ended, including all firms with a capitalization of over $1 million. Not surprisingly, perhaps, the entry rate is greatest for firms in this category. Accordingly, one measure we use of the firm's experience is a 1–0 dummy variable equal to 1 for the

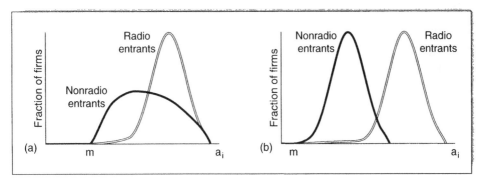

**Figure 2.2**  Alternative distributions of capability for radio and nonradio entrants
(a) Identical maximum capability for radio and nonradio entrants. (b) Higher maximum capability for radio vs. nonradio entrants.

58 firms with a capitalization in the top, 4A category. The other 207 firms are treated as the (omitted) reference group.[9]

The second measure of experience reflects the types of radios each firm produced. *Thomas' Register* has a brief description for the majority of radio firms indicating the type of radios they produced. We divided these descriptions into 11 categories. They are listed in table 2.3 along with the number of firms and percentage that entered TVs in each category. The first category, home radios, includes firms with descriptions such as "home," "household receiver," or "combination with phonograph." We interpreted all of these firms as producing radios for the home. The second category includes descriptions indicating receivers, but not designating whether they were for home use. We suspect these firms also largely produced radios for the home, and this is supported by their comparability with home radio producers in the fraction entering TVs. The third category includes firms without any description, suggesting that they typically produced (home) radios which required no further explanation. The other categories are quite different. The largest, radios for aircraft, marine, police, and military, connotes a radio designed primarily for communication rather than home entertainment. This applies as well to the category, communications, 2-way. The miscellaneous category includes firms making custom equipment, special purpose equipment, unassembled sets, and sets for exports, and the commercial category includes firms making coin-operated, hotel, and centralized radios. These all seem quite different from home radios. Accordingly, we constructed two 1–0 dummy variables to reflect the type of radios firms produced. The first, which we label home, equals 1 for the 79 firms in either of the first two categories. The second, which we label unknown, equals 1 for the 65 firms in the third category without any description. The other 121 firms are treated as the (omitted) reference group.

The last measure of experience equals the number of years the firms produced radios. For each firm we used prior volumes of *Thomas' Register* to ascertain when it was first listed in the category, "Radio Apparatus: Complete Sets, Outfits, etc.," which was started in the 1922 volume. We subtracted this year from the last year it was listed in

**Table 2.2** Number of radio producers and TV entry rate for alternative size categories

| Capitalization category (Thomas' Code) | Number of radio producers | % entering TV production |
|---|---|---|
| Over $1 million (4A) | 58 | 44.8 |
| $500,000–$1 million (3A) | 23 | 21.7 |
| $300,000–$500,000 (2A) | 12 | 25.0 |
| $100,000–$300,000 (A) | 57 | 15.8 |
| $50,000–$100,000 (B) | 24 | 8.3 |
| $25,000–$50,000 (C) | 10 | 0.0 |
| $10,000–$25,000 (D) | 10 | 10.0 |
| $5,000–$10,000 (E) | 3 | 0.0 |
| $2,500–$5,000 (F) | 1 | 0.0 |
| Unknown (X) | 67 | 14.9 |
| All radio producers | 265 | 21.1 |

**Table 2.3** Number of radio producers and TV entry rate for alternative product categories

| Product type category | Number of radio producers | % entering TV production |
|---|---|---|
| Home radios | 63 | 49.2 |
| Receivers | 16 | 31.3 |
| No special type indicated | 65 | 21.5 |
| Portable, compact, miniature | 7 | 14.3 |
| Automobile | 1 | 0.0 |
| Communications, 2-way | 13 | 15.4 |
| Transmitters and receivers | 6 | 0.0 |
| Aircraft, marine, police, military | 46 | 4.3 |
| Commercial | 10 | 0.0 |
| Experimental radios or R&D | 5 | 0.0 |
| Miscellaneous | 33 | 3.0 |
| All radio producers | 265 | 21.1 |

1944–7 to measure its years of experience. This variable took on values ranging from 0 to 25, with a mean and median of 6.6 and 4 respectively.

**Entry**

We begin by testing Hypotheses 1 and 2 concerning entry of the radio producers into the TV industry. To test Hypothesis 1, we estimated a logit model of the probability of TV entry for the 265 radio producers. The independent variables are the 4A size dummy, the home and unknown radio type dummies, and the years of radio production variable. Maximum likelihood estimates for the model are reported in table 2.4. All the coefficient estimates are positive, substantial, and significant at conventional levels, indicating that all three elements of experience increased the probability of radio firms entering the TV industry. The log odds ratio of entry relative to not entering was 0.111 greater for each additional year of production of radios, 1.348 greater for firms with a 4A capitalization, and 3.041 and 2.313 greater for firms in the home and unknown radio type categories. Among the firms that entered, their years of experience varied from 0 to 25 with a mean of 11.8, 47.4 percent were in the 4A category, and 89.5 percent were in the home or unknown radio type category. If the firms in the unknown radio type category are assumed to be home radio producers, the results indicate that nearly all the entrants were home radio producers. Moreover, two of the remaining six, Westinghouse and Sparks-Withington, were well-known home radio producers.[10] Thus, one notable result of the initial analysis is that few, if any, nonhome radio producers entered the TV industry, suggesting that home radio experience was a virtual necessity for a radio producer to be able to compete in the TV industry.

We probed our specification further by first adding a 1–0 dummy for firms with capitalization in the second highest, 3A category. Its coefficient estimate was positive, consistent with the estimate of the 4A dummy, but it was not significant at conventional levels. Second, we divided the years of experience into two variables based on whether firms were in the 4A size category or not. This enabled us to test whether

**Table 2.4** Logit model for TV set entry

| Variable | Coefficient estimate (S.E.) | |
| --- | --- | --- |
| Constant | —4.619*** | (0.607) |
| Capitalization over $1 million | 1.348*** | (0.420) |
| Home radio producer | 3.041*** | (0.568) |
| Unknown-type producer | 2.313*** | (0.612) |
| Years of radio experience | 0.111*** | (0.025) |
| Log likelihood | —91.739*** | |
| N | 265 | |

†p < 0.10; *p < 0.05; **p < 0.01; ***p < 0.001 (one-tailed).

years of experience might just be a proxy for size among the firms in the top, open-ended 4A size category. The estimates for both groups of firms were significantly different from zero and not significantly different from each other, suggesting that the influence of years of experience on entry was not due to size.

Hypothesis 2 conjectures that (home) radio experience conditions not only the decision to enter but also the speed of entry. We tested this by estimating a model for the annual hazard of entry for all 176 entrants into TVs over the period 1946–89.[11] We used the Cox proportional hazards model, which specifies the hazard of entry of firm i in year t as $h_{it} = f(t)\exp(\beta' x_i)$, where $h_{it}$ is the probability of firm entry in year t for firms that have not yet entered by year t, $f(t)$ is a function of time which allows the hazard of entry to change as the industry evolves, $x$ is a vector of variables expected to shift the hazard of entry proportionally in each year, and $\beta$ is a vector of coefficients. In the Cox model, $f(t)$ is such that the hazard is allowed to take on its best-fitting value each year, and attention focuses on the estimates of the coefficients. We include in the vector $x$ three variables: the 4A size dummy, the years of radio production variable, and a dummy variable equal to 1 for entrants that produced radios in the years 1945–8. We do not attempt to distinguish the radio producers in terms of the types of radios they produced since nearly all of them seem to have produced home radios.[12] Accordingly, we interpret the radio dummy as measuring the effects of experience in producing home radios.

Maximum-likelihood estimates of the model computed using Stata are reported in table 2.5. All three estimates are positive, indicating that each element of experience contributed to earlier entry, with the radio and size 4A coefficient significant at the 0.05 level and years of radio production significant at the 0.10 level (one-tailed). Being a (home) radio producer increased the probability of entry by 73.8 percent per year, being a size 4A radio producer increased it further by 95.0 percent per year, and each additional year of radio experience increased the probability by 2.2 percent per year.[13] These findings support the hypothesis that radio firms were well positioned to enter early, with larger radio producers and secondarily ones that had produced radios longer seemingly having a greater incentive to enter earlier. The estimates of the effects of radio size and years of production are consistent with both factors conditioning the profitability of entry, thereby enhancing incentives for earlier entry.

**Table 2.5** Cox proportional hazard model for TV set entry

| Variable | Coefficient estimate (S.E.) | |
| --- | --- | --- |
| Radio producer | 0.553* | (0.267) |
| Capitalization over $1 million | 0.668* | (0.292) |
| Years of radio experience | 0.022† | (0.017) |
| Log partial likelihood | —744.196 | |
| N | 176 | |

†p < 0.10; *p < 0.05; **p < 0.01; ***p < 0.001 (one-tailed).

### Survival and market share

If experience in producing radios affects the probability and timing of entry via its effects on the profitability of entry, then the same experience factors that influenced entry should also affect the performance of TV entrants, as reflected in Hypothesis 3 and its corollary. We explore this first by estimating a model for the hazard of exit of TV entrants. We begin again using the Cox proportional hazard model, where the dependent variable is now the hazard of a firm exiting the industry in year t assuming it has survived up to year t. We include the 1–0 radio dummy, the 4A size dummy, and the years producing radios as independent variables. Hypothesis 3 is framed in terms of firms entering at the same time. We saw above that radio firms entered disproportionately early. Thus, if we include all TV entrants in our estimation of the hazard, we risk that radio experience could simply proxy for time of entry, which is also expected to condition the hazard. To avoid this complication, we estimate the model using only the 134 firms that entered TVs by 1951.[14] Firms that were acquired by other TV producers were treated as censored exits.[15]

The estimates of the model are reported in the first column of table 2.6. All of the coefficient estimates are negative, as predicted, indicating that greater radio experience lowered the hazard of exit. The estimated effects of the radio and 4A dummy are both substantial and significant at conventional levels, with being a radio producer lowering the annual hazard by 59.5 percent and being a 4A producer lowering it further by 59.6 percent. The estimate of experience implies a reduction in the hazard of 1.1 percent per year for each year of experience, although the estimate is small relative to its standard error and is not significant at conventional levels.

In the second column of table 2.6 we probe the corollary to Hypothesis 3. We drop the insignificant experience variable and generalize the hazard model to allow the radio and size dummy variables to affect the hazard differently in the periods 1948–54, 1955–64, and 1965–89.[16] The first period pertains exclusively to the era of monochrome television, the second corresponds to the period when color TV was introduced but color sales were few, and the third period corresponds to when color TV was successful and international competition became intense. The estimates indicate that the effects of experience were not confined to the early years of the industry but persisted strongly over time. All the coefficient estimates are negative, and the estimates are largest absolutely in the last period, when they are also statistically significant. Prior radio experience decreased the

**Table 2.6** Cox proportional hazard model for TV set exit (standard errors in parentheses)

| Variable | 1 | | 2 | |
|---|---|---|---|---|
| Radio producer | —0.904** | (0.327) | | |
| in 1948–54 | | | —1.196*** | (0.359) |
| in 1955–64 | | | —0.455 | (0.418) |
| in 1965–89 | | | —2.797** | (1.126) |
| Capitalization over $1 million | —0.906** | (0.374) | | |
| in 1948–54 | | | —0.867† | (0.601) |
| in 1955–64 | | | —0.900† | (0.558) |
| in 1965–89 | | | —1.156* | (0.680) |
| Years of radio experience | —0.011 | (0.022) | | |
| Log partial likelihood | —449.853 | | —446.589 | |
| N | 134 | | 134 | |

†p < 0.10; *p < 0.05; **p < 0.01; ***p < 0.001 (one-tailed).

annual hazard by an estimated 69.8 percent, 36.5 percent, and 93.9 percent in the three respective periods, with yet a further estimated reduction of 58.0 percent, 59.4 percent, and 68.5 percent for the 4A radio producers. Based on the reasoning in the theory behind the corollary to Hypothesis 3, the findings suggest that radio experience conferred distinctive competitive advantages that could not be compensated by other types of experience.

Further insight into the role of experience on the hazard over time can be gleaned from figure 2.3. A moving average of the annual hazard is computed for three classes of firms: entrants without radio experience (the top curve), less than size 4A radio entrants (the middle curve), and 4A radio entrants.[17] The hazards of all three groups of firms fell around the mid-1950s when the technological frontier temporarily stalled as consumers rejected color TVs, but subsequently the hazards of the nonradio and smaller radio firms increased as the hazards of the larger radio producers stayed roughly constant. Thus, radio experience exerted a substantial effect on the hazard throughout the 40 or so years of the industry that we analyze.

We also test the effect of radio experience on firm market shares by estimating three regressions relating firm TV market shares in 1951–3, 1959–60, and 1970 to the same three experience variables used in the hazard analysis. Data on monochrome market shares for 1951–3 and 1959–60 are from the *Look* Appliance Survey, as reported in Datta (1971: 25). Data for 1970 pertain to color TVs and are from Wooster (1986: 106–107). The relatively small firms with unreported market shares were assigned average values of the market share not allocated to specific firms. Only the firms surviving in each year were included in the analysis, and the log of market share was used to reduce skewness. Since market share data were available only for a few leading producers, almost all of which were 4A prior radio producers, the radio dummy proved inestimable and the analysis simply compares 4A radio producers versus all other firms combined. The firms with market share data have disparate years of radio production, which enabled us to include the years of radio production variable in each regression. The estimates of the regressions are reported in table 2.7.

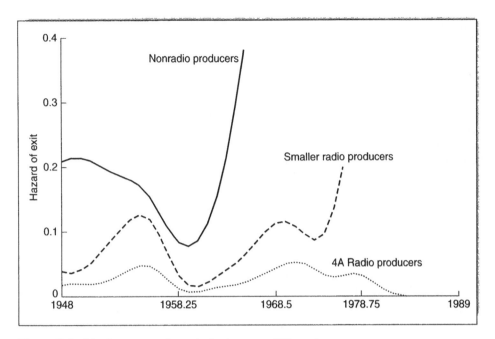

**Figure 2.3**    Moving average hazard of exit among TV producers

The coefficient estimates for the 4A dummy and for years of radio production are positive in each regression, indicating that radio experience increased firm market shares at all three times. The estimates indicate that the main predictor of TV market share is the 4A radio-size dummy. This reflects the fact that with the exception of DuMont Laboratories in 1951–3 and Olympic Radio and Television in 1960, both of which had relatively small market shares, and Motorola in all three periods, all the firms with the largest market shares were 4A radio producers, which conveys the extent to which the US TV industry was dominated by the leading radio producers. Indeed, the estimated coefficient for 4A radio producers is consistently large, and is significant at the 0.001 and 0.05 levels (one-tailed) respectively in the first two periods. Only in the final period, when there were only 16 producers, is the 4A dummy insignificant (if only the 4A dummy is included it is marginally significant at the 0.10 level one-tailed).

**Innovation and survival**

Hypotheses 4 and 5 probe the mechanism by which radio experience influenced firm performance, featuring the role played by innovation. To test these hypotheses, we need data on the innovations introduced by each firm. Such data are difficult to compile. We found one series on major product innovation through 1979 compiled by Levy (1981) based on interviews with TV executives. Each innovation is dated and attributed to one or more firms. Since we could find no

**Table 2.7** OLS models for log of TV set market share at consecutive times (standard errors in parentheses)

| Variable | Dependent variable: market share in | | |
|---|---|---|---|
| | *1951–3* | *1959–60* | *1970* |
| Constant | —1.352*** | —0.746* | —0.485 |
| | (0.136) | (0.296) | (0.844) |
| Capitalization | 0.943*** | 1.011* | 0.959 |
| over $1 million | (0.295) | (0.489) | (0.901) |
| Years of radio | 0.016 | 0.035† | 0.023 |
| experience | (0.015) | (0.026) | (0.051) |
| $R^2$ | 0.235 | 0.329 | 0.131 |
| N | 83 | 32 | 16 |

†$p < 0.10$; *$p < 0.05$; **$p < 0.01$; ***$p < 0.001$ (one-tailed).

substantial list of process innovations identified with firms and dates, we constructed our own list by using the *Industrial Arts Index* (later *Applied Science and Technology Index*) to look up trade articles related to TV set manufacturing and then examining the articles to find references to new methods in TV set production.[18] Each innovation identified was classified according to its date and manufacturer(s) involved and was given a 1–7 point subjective estimate of its impact on manufacturing costs. We focus on the years through 1957 when considerable numbers of articles about TV set process innovation were published. These measures of innovation are necessarily crude, but nonetheless should capture some of the key innovative differences across firms.[19]

To test Hypothesis 4, we computed separate annual rates of product and process innovation for nonradio producers, less than size 4A radio producers, and 4A radio producers.[20] They are reported in table 2.8. Firms with radio production experience had much higher rates of innovation than nonradio producers, and among the radio producers the larger ones had the greatest innovation rates. For product innovation, the mean of producers' annual number of innovations was 0 for the nonradio producers, 0.011 for the smaller radio producers, and 0.039 for the larger radio producers.[21] For process innovation, the mean rate of innovation was 0.082, 0.180, and 0.670 for the nonradio, smaller radio, and larger radio firms. The patterns are similar when process innovation rates are weighted according to the rankings of the innovations. The statistical significance of these patterns is tested using Wilcoxon's (1945) nonparametric rank-sum test, which tests whether two distributions are different. The test indicates that five of the six inter-group differences, all except the larger versus smaller prior radio producers for product innovation, are significant at the 0.05 level or lower. Thus, radio producers, especially the larger ones, were more innovative than nonradio producers.

To test Hypothesis 5, we reestimated the equation for the hazard of exit including variables measuring firm innovation rates in addition to the radio and size dummies. We combined the product and process innovations data to compute an overall rate of innovation for each firm over the period 1948–79. We also use an

**Table 2.8** Innovations per firm per year by prior radio production and radio size

| Type of TV set producers | Product innovation | Process innovation |
|---|---|---|
| Non-radio (N = 81) | 0.000 | 0.082 |
| Radio small (N = 28) | 0.011 | 0.180 |
| Radio large (N = 25) | 0.039 | 0.670 |

Statistical significance p-values (Wilcoxon rank-sum test)

| Types | Product innovation | Process innovation |
|---|---|---|
| Radio large vs. non-radio | 0.000 | 0.000 |
| Radio small vs. non-radio | 0.016 | 0.001 |
| Radio large vs. radio small | 0.155 | 0.038 |

Product innovation from 1948 to 1979. Process innovation from 1948 to 1957.

additional measure of innovation based on a classification developed by Willard (1982) for the 19 principal color TV producers that he analyzed. Each firm was assigned a rating of 0 to 3 based on expert opinion regarding its commitment to innovation. We included this rating and a second dummy variable equal to 1 for firms not rated by Willard, which presumably were the least committed to innovation among the producers in the color era. The estimates of this model are reported in table 2.9.

We first report estimates of the model with just the radio and 4A dummies in column 1 and then add the innovation variables in column 2.[22] Both innovation variables have a substantial impact on the hazard, with the first significant at the 0.05 level and the second significant at the 0.10 level (one-tailed). The innovation rate variable has a standard deviation of 0.85, so a one standard deviation increase in the innovation rate is estimated to yield a 43.0 percent decrease in the annual hazard. An increase of one point in Willard's innovation ranking is estimated to lower the annual hazard by 59.4 percent. These effects are large, especially when the effects cumulate over a number of years.

Consistent with Hypothesis 5, adding the innovation variables to the statistical model causes the coefficient estimates of the radio and 4A dummies to fall (absolutely). The coefficient estimate of the radio dummy drops 14 percent from —1.010 to —0.872, and the coefficient estimate of the 4A dummy drops 54 percent from —0.968 to —0.446. Given the crude nature of the innovation variables, this provides substantial support for Hypothesis 5.[23]

We report the estimates of one further model in the last column of table 2.9. Willard also rated firms' distribution systems on a 0 to 3 point scale. We added this variable to the model to test whether the innovation variables might have been proxying for distributional factors and also to assess the effect of firm distribution networks on the hazard. The coefficient estimates of the innovation variables are hardly affected, suggesting that innovation was an important determinant of the hazard in its own right. Moreover, the coefficient estimate of the distribution variable is positive, suggesting that if anything firms with more extensive distribution networks had higher hazards, though the coefficient estimate on the distribution variable is insignificant.

**Table 2.9** Effects of prior radio experience, innovation, and distribution on TV producers' exit

| Variable | 1 | | 2 | | 3 | |
|---|---|---|---|---|---|---|
| Radio producer | —1.010*** | (0.251) | —0.872*** | (0.255) | —0.843*** | (0.256) |
| Capitalization over $1M | —0.968** | (0.353) | —0.446 | (0.360) | —0.516† | (0.378) |
| Innovation rate | | | —0.666* | (0.308) | —0.704* | (0.319) |
| Willard innovation | | | —0.901† | (0.590) | —1.164* | (0.700) |
| Willard distribution | | | | | 0.441 | (0.631) |
| Willard no data | | | 1.836* | (0.983) | 2.181* | (1.101) |
| Log partial likelihood | —449.975 | | —438.463 | | —438.210 | |
| N | 134 | | 134 | | 134 | |

†p < 0.10; *p < 0.05; **p < 0.01; ***p < 0.001 (one-tailed).

## Discussion

Our findings suggest there was great heterogeneity among TV entrants that was related to their performance. About one-third had experience producing radios before TVs. Nearly all of these firms produced radios for home entertainment, and they tended to be larger and to have produced radios longer than radio producers that did not enter the TV industry. Radio producers in general, and the larger and more experienced ones in particular, entered earlier than other firms, and they dominated the industry throughout its history. Nearly all the leading TV producers had been large radio producers, and radio producers, especially the larger ones, consistently had a lower hazard than other entrants throughout the evolution of the industry. Virtually all the major TV product and process innovations were developed by the radio producers, especially the larger ones, and this appears to have been an important element of their success. In summary, the background of firms in terms of their experience in the radio industry had a profound effect on entry and performance, with the most established home radio producers dominating the TV industry throughout its history.

Our findings provide some insight into the nature of the process governing entry. Among the radio producers, the ones with more experience relevant to TVs were more likely to enter and to enter earlier than firms without radio experience. Mitchell (1989) and Lane (1989) also found that firms with more experience producing related products were more likely to enter new diagnostic imaging markets and the ATM industry respectively, though they were not generally among the earliest entrants. The TV industry was atypical, though, in that it was characterized by far less uncertainty than the average new product by the time it got started following World War II. The technology was commercially feasible even before the War and it was widely available through licensing and sale from RCA, the industry leader, which may help explain the quick entry of the experienced radio producers.[24] Perhaps most interestingly, the same factors governing entry for the radio producers also affected their performance. Producers of (home) radios survived longer and developed more innovations than nonradio entrants, and the larger radio producers and secondarily the ones that had produced radios longer captured the largest market shares, survived the longest, and were the most innovative. This suggests that when making their entry decision, potential entrants were able to anticipate some of the factors that would influence their performance. On the other hand, years of radio production was a considerably stronger predictor of entry than performance, suggesting a la Jovanovic's (1982) model of industry evolution that radio entrants needed to enter to discover fully how their background would affect their capabilities in the TV industry.

Our findings also provide discriminating evidence on the nature of the advantages conferred by prior experience in related products. Lane (1989), Mitchell (1991), and Carroll et al. (1996) found that entrants in ATMs, diagnostic imaging products, and autos with experience in related products outperformed other entrants. Carroll et al. (1996) attributed the advantages of experienced automobile entrants to having established decision-making structures and greater access to capital. They conjectured these advantages were greatest when firms were young, and consistent with this they found that certain types of experience had their greatest effect on the hazards of automobile entrants at young ages. In diagnostic imaging products, Mitchell (1989) found that incumbent firms with direct distribution networks were more likely to enter new imaging subfields, presumably because their distribution networks provided them with a competitive advantage over *de novo* entrants. Lane (1989) appealed to learning by doing as the source of the advantage of experienced cash handling, security, and computer firms in the ATM industry. Our findings suggest that these were not the primary ways that experience enhanced the performance of radio producers. In contrast to Carroll et al., producing radios and being a larger radio producer had at least as great an effect on firm hazards at later stages of evolution of the industry, when TV producers were older. Regarding distribution networks, radio producers did sell TVs through their radio distributors, which may have imparted an initial advantage, but TV firm distribution networks had little effect on the hazard during the later evolution of the industry.[25] Last, learning is generally thought to be driven by cumulative experience, typically measured by total cumulative output and years of production, yet the total number of years of radio production was only a weak determinant of performance among the radio entrants. Our findings point to innovation as the source of the advantage of the more experienced firms. A number of the radio entrants used their experienced radio engineers to direct their process-oriented innovation in TVs, and the radio entrants, particularly the larger ones, totally dominated innovation in TVs, which appears to have contributed to their greater longevity.

Klepper's model stresses the importance of both innovation and heterogeneity among entrants in explaining the shakeout and oligopolistic market structure that emerged in TVs. Our findings have largely been consistent with the model. Moreover, a number of other patterns are supportive of the model. At the outset of the industry, firm rates of return on investment were high, enabling a wide range of firms in terms of their capabilities to enter the industry. Over time, though, competition caused firm rates of return to decline sharply, inducing firms to exit. As Wooster (1986: 150) notes, the continuing high rate of innovation spurred by semiconductor developments put great pressure on the smaller firms, who could not justify the costs of innovation because they lacked a large enough output over which to spread the costs. Only the largest US

TV producers, nearly all of whom had been large radio producers, were able to withstand these pressures, and in the end even they succumbed. All of these patterns resonate with Klepper's model.

There are other explanations for shakeouts, but they accord less closely with our findings. In the theories of Utterback and Suárez (1993) and Jovanovic and MacDonald (1994) major technological developments[26] alter the basis of competition, causing a shakeout by making entry more difficult and forcing out of the industry firms less able to adapt to the new environment. Neither theory predicts that the pre-entry backgrounds of entrants will affect their survival during the shakeout and thus neither theory can address our most salient findings. Indeed, the recent conceptualization of the dominant design theory in Christensen, Suárez, and Utterback (1998) suggests that pre-entry experience would be disadvantageous because it would wed firms to technologies ultimately rendered obsolete by the emergence of a dominant design. Moreover, both theories suggest a rise in hazard rates with the onset of the shakeout and then a convergence in the hazard rates of different types of firms as the shakeout proceeds (Klepper and Simons, 1999). There was no indication of a rise in hazard rates after the start of the shakeout in TVs (Klepper and Simons, 1999) and the only indication of a convergence in the hazard rates of radio and nonradio firms after the start of the shakeout was short lived.

Our findings and explanation for the shakeout in TVs also provide a way of understanding the ultimate demise of all the US TV producers. In hindsight, it appears that the US firms were beaten at their own game. The leading Japanese firms were also radio producers. Indeed, they pioneered solid-state radios. They accounted for most of radio imports in the US, which by 1964 accounted for 64 percent of the US market (Wooster, 1986: 40). Furthermore, they were nurtured by Japanese industrial policies: tariffs and restrictions on foreign direct investment limited foreign competition, MITI negotiated favorable technology licenses for all firms collectively, R&D and exports were subsidized, and preferential access to capital was provided (Wooster, 1986). By the 1970s Japan's top five firms were of comparable or greater size than the two largest US firms, Zenith and RCA (Wooster, 1986: 151–152). According to Klepper's model, this provided them with a greater incentive to innovate than all the US producers except RCA and Zenith, and their greater experience with semiconductors provided them with an innovative advantage over RCA and Zenith. This would help explain why in the era of intense international competition the Japanese firms were more willing than the US firms to engage in the costly investments in innovation needed to exploit developments in semiconductors, and why the US firms pursued a more gradual approach to innovation than the Japanese firms involving greater reliance on manual labor in low-wage countries (Wooster, 1986: 142).[27]

While pre-entry experience was valuable not only in TVs but also diagnostic imaging products, ATMs, and autos, and no doubt in other industries as well (cf. Klepper, 1999), there have been well publicized instances in which prior experience has seemingly been a handicap in dealing with technical advance (Tushman and Anderson, 1986; Henderson and Clark, 1990; Christensen and Rosenbloom, 1995). This raises the specter that the importance of pre-entry experience in a new industry may depend on the nature of the industry's technology. A recent dissertation on the evolution of the laser industry (Sleeper, 1998) provides an intriguing counterexample to the television industry. The laser industry is over 30 years old and still has not experienced a shakeout. Moreover, experienced and inexperienced firms have had comparable hazards, largely due to the unusually low hazard of *de novo* entrants that were started by employees of incumbent laser producers. This may have to do with the nature of technological change in lasers. For most lasers, the production process is simple and production engineering is not terribly important, which may limit the value of prior experience in related products. Furthermore, many innovations in lasers involve creating new types of lasers that open up new uses and thus appeal to new users of lasers. The returns to such efforts depend only on the number of new customers the firm can attract and do not depend on its pre-innovation output, thus undermining an important advantage that incumbents have in Klepper's model. Thus, even if prior experience provides a firm with an initial advantage, any greater growth it induces will not provide the firm with a continuing advantage, as it would if firm size conditioned the returns from subsequent innovations. Thus, the importance of pre-entry experience both for firm survival and the evolution of a new industry's market structure may depend on the nature of technological change in the new industry, a topic which warrants further study.

## Conclusion

Entrants into the TV industry were diverse. A minority had experience producing radios, which set them apart from the rest of the industry. It enabled them to dominate innovation, which in turn contributed to their overall dominance of the TV industry. The diversity of entrants coupled with continual technological change also appears to have shaped the way the market structure of the TV industry evolved.

While the TV industry is just a single case study, it is hardly an isolated one. It raises many fundamental questions. For one, if the experiences of preexisting firms affect their performance in new industries, do the experiences of founders play a similar role for *de novo* firms? Eisenhardt and Schoonhoven's (1990) findings for semiconductors and Sleeper's (1998) for lasers suggests they do, but little is known about these issues. More generally, if preexisting and *de novo* firms draw upon their prior experiences to innovate and compete in new industries, what role do extramarket institutions play in imparting the experiences they draw upon? The success of the Japanese TV producers attests to the potential effect that government policy can have on the capabilities of firms. If indeed extramarket institutions play a key role in shaping firm capabilities, then it behooves us to consider how these institutions can best be designed to play this role.

The way the TV industry evolved also questions the usefulness of models of industrial competition predicated on free entry. Such models presume that all firms are equally capable, which hardly does justice to the diversity that prevailed in the TV industry. Such models also typically embrace the idea of an equilibrium brought about by free entry. This does not resonate well with the prolonged shakeout of producers that occurred in the TV industry.

The evolution of the TV industry has been studied from many angles, but little has been made of the dominance of the industry by experienced radio producers. Our analysis of this dominance raised a host of fundamental questions. Hopefully our findings will go a long way toward providing an answer, at least based on one industry, to the questions raised by Richard Nelson (1991) in the title of his incisive essay, "Why do firms differ, and how does it matter?"

## Acknowledgements

We thank Keith Pavitt, Richard Rosenbloom, Peter Thompson and participants in the 1999 Dartmouth Conference on the Evolution of Firm Capabilities. Klepper gratefully acknowledges support from the Economics Program of the National Science Foundation, grant no. SBR-9600041.

## Notes

1   The main sources used to compile the information in this section are MacLaurin (1949), Datta (1971), Levy (1981), Willard (1982), and Wooster (1986).
2   We determined firms' dates of entry into and exit from TV set production during 1947–89, the period in which the *Factbook* published lists of producers, by examining the lists in each edition and recording the names of all TV set manufacturers and the dates when they were listed as producers. Only the main and most reliable list from the *Factbook* was used, with the exception of several makers of self-assembly TV kits which were included to ensure comparability of the data over time. Mergers and acquisitions were recorded based on information in Datta (1971), Levy (1981), Willard (1982), LaFrance (1985), and Teitelman (1994), and for purposes of figure 1 the smaller producer was treated as exiting whenever two TV producers came under single ownership. Also in figure 1, the number of firms is indicated for each volume of the *Factbook*, but entries and exits are summed across quarterly or biannual volumes published in early years of the *Factbook*. For 1947, a count of 31 firms was used based on a reference in the 17 January 1948 issue of *Television Digest and FM Reports* (p. 1) to Supplement 57, which listed TV set manufacturers (the supplement itself could not be obtained despite the publisher's kind efforts).
3   Also prominent were Sears Roebuck and Montgomery Ward, which sold television sets that were manufactured for them by other firms under their own brand names.
4   See, for example, *Electronics* (1947, 1958), DeCola (1948), *Tele-Tech* (1948a, 1948b, 1948c, 1949, 1950, 1951), *Factory, Management and Maintenance* (1950a, 1950b), Osbahr (1951), Lord (1953), *Modern Packaging* (1955), and Plesser (1959). Many revealing articles about the television manufacturing process can be found in the journals cited here, particularly *Electronics*.
5   Licensed innovations will yield reductions in average cost to licensees if the licensor cannot fully appropriate the value of the innovations through licensing.
6   Entrants in period t have no output prior to entry and thus enter at size $\Delta q_{it}$.
7   One radio producer entered television manufacture by acquisition, in 1949. Since it was ambiguous whether the firm should be considered a true entrant in its own right, it was excluded from the samples of radio and television producers.
8   If a firm in our sample was not still listed as a radio producer in the 1948 volume of *Thomas' Register*, we used its capitalization as of the last volume of *Thomas' Register* in which it was listed as a radio producer. We also checked every radio producer that entered the TV industry and found that each had the same capitalization at the time it entered as in the 1948

volume of *Thomas' Register*, so that our measure reflected its size as of its entry into the TV industry.

9    The capitalization categorization is based on the firm's total assets and thus measures not just its size in radios. For most of the firms, though, radios were their dominant product, so our measure would largely be expected to reflect the size of the firm's radio investment. To probe this, we examined the classifications of the 16 firms in table 2.1 listed as the leading radio producers in 1940. All but two were classified in the top, 4A capitalization category, with the other two in the next category, suggesting a close correspondence between a firm's overall size and its size in radios. We also developed a measure of firm size in radios based on the listing in table 2.1, with unlisted firms assigned the average sales of firms outside the listed group. This variable performed similarly to our dummy for capitalization in the top 4A category, suggesting the 4A dummy largely reflected the firm's size in radios.

10   Westinghouse had an ambiguous description that prevented it from being classified as a home radio producer.

11   The sample period ends in 1989 because the *Television Factbook*, which is our source for data on TV producers, did not publish lists of TV producers after the edition copyrighted in 1989. Its first list was for 1948, and we used information from the 1945–8 monthly issues of the accompanying trade journal, *Television Digest and FM Reports*, to backdate the listing to 1946. Foreign firms entering US production were excluded.

12   We experimented by including in our analyses the home dummy, which distinguishes the firms that we were most confident produced home radios from the group without any description (the unknown category) and the other six producers. Its coefficient estimate was always small relative to its standard error (although generally positively associated with firm performance), suggesting that the radio entrants did not differ much, if at all, in terms of their production of home radios.

13   To illustrate how these figures are computed, the coefficient estimate of the radio dummy is 0.553, which implies that the hazard of entry for a radio producer is $\exp(0.553) = 1.738$ times the hazard of a nonradio producer, all else equal. Hence radio production increases the hazard of entry by 73.8 percent.

14   The estimates were similar when all firms were included.

15   We also estimated the model treating acquisitions as ordinary exits, which had little effect on the estimates.

16   We also estimated the model including the experience variable, and as expected its coefficient estimate for each period was small and insignificant.

17   For each year t in figure 2.3, weighted average numbers of exits and firms were computed using all years with available data within ±10 years. Weights proportional to a Gaussian distribution with mean t and a standard deviation of 2 years were used, and the weighted number of exits was divided by the weighted number of firms. This approach yields nonparametric estimates of the hazard that avoid major year-to-year fluctuations in raw annual figures.

18   Of approximately 210 relevant indexed articles, 198 were obtained and analyzed, yielding a list of 264 process innovations by US firms. Where multiple firms were credited with an innovation, credit was divided evenly among the firms. While large firms may have received more attention from the trade journals, which could impart a bias to the lists, all firms had incentives to report their innovations. Employees in small as well as large firms were given financial incentives by trade journals to write in with details of process improvements, and manufacturing process articles were a source of considerable prestige for engineers and firms.

19   More information about the measures of product and process innovation is in Klepper and Simons (1997).

20   Given that years of radio production does not lend itself to a comparable treatment and its coefficient estimate was small relative to its standard error in the hazard analyses, we focus just on these three groups.
21   For both product and process innovations, the annual rate of innovation for each firm was computed by summing its number of innovations and dividing by the number of years it was a TV set producer for which innovations data were available. The mean innovation rate for each group was computed as the average of the annual innovation rate among firms in the group. As in the survival and market share analyses, the data pertain to entrants by 1951, although the findings are similar using all entrants.
22   As before, the years of radio production variable is excluded. Similar conclusions are reached if it is included.
23   Adding a firm innovation rate variable to the market share regressions of table 7 has a similar effect. Innovation rates are computed using only years preceding each set of market share data, and entrants in 1951 are excluded in the first regression. The 4A size coefficient drops 19 percent, 53 percent, and 7 percent using market share in 1951-3, 1959-60, and 1970 respectively. Thus, the innovation variable explained much of the market share differences that had been attributed to size. Willard's innovation variables, which pertain only to years from 1960 onward, were excluded.
24   There were also many firms producing radios, and TVs were destined to compete with radios, both factors that Mitchell (1989) found sped up entry into new diagnostic imaging products.
25   Moreover, Datta (1971) investigated the importance of marketing during the early, monochrome years of the industry and found that firm marketing efforts and advertising had little effect on survival and growth. Television firms could also market through the chain stores, obviating the need for a distribution network. Indeed, this was the way the Japanese firms broke into the US market, which further suggests that distribution networks provided little advantage during the later evolution of the industry.
26   In Utterback and Suárez the development is the emergence of a dominant design and in Jovanovic and MacDonald it is a major invention developed outside the industry.
27   It cannot explain, though, why earlier the US firms were slow to adopt solid state developments, crystallized by an advertising campaign from 1968 to 1973 conducted by Zenith to promote its hand-wired sets over those produced using solid state components.

## References

Carroll, G. R., Bigelow, L. S., Seidel, M. D. L., and Tsai, L. B. 1996. The fates of *de novo* and *de alio* producers in the American automobile industry 1885–1981. *Strategic Management Journal*, Summer Special Issue 17: 117–137.

Christensen, C. M., and Rosenbloom, R. R. 1995. Explaining the attacker's advantage: technological paradigms, organizational dynamics, and the value network. *Research Policy* 24: 233–257.

Christensen, C. M., Suárez F. F., and Utterback, J. M. 1998. Strategies for survival in fast-changing industries. *Management Science* 44: S-207–220.

Datta, Y. 1971. Corporate strategy and performance of firms in the U.S. television set industry. Ph.D. dissertation, State University of New York at Buffalo.

DeCola, R. 1948. Monitoring scope for television production lines. *Tele-Tech* February: 40–41.

Eisenhardt, K. M., and Schoonhoven, C. B. 1990. Organizational growth: linking founding team, strategy, environment, and growth among U.S. semiconductor ventures, 1978–1988. *Administrative Science Quarterly* 35: 504–529.

*Electronics* 1947. Television production line, October, 132–134.

*Electronics* 1958. Mechanizing equipment assembly. Engineering issue, 24 October, 82–84.

*Factory Management and Maintenance* 1950a. Laid out for low-cost handling, 108 (March): 70–73.

*Factory Management and Maintenance* 1950b. These ideas pay off 14 to 1, 108 (August): 101–103.

Henderson, R., and Clark, K. 1990. Architectural innovation: the reconfiguration of existing product technologies and the failure of established firms. *Administrative Science Quarterly* 35: 9–30.

Jovanovic, B. 1982. Selection and the evolution of industry. *Econometrica* 50: 649–670.

Jovanovic, B, and MacDonald, G. 1994. The life cycle of a competitive industry. *Journal of Political Economy* 102: 322–347.

Klepper, S. 1996. Entry, exit, growth, and innovation over the product life cycle. *American Economic Review* 86: 562–583.

Klepper, S. 1999. Firm survival and the evolution of oligopoly. Working paper, Carnegie Mellon University.

Klepper, S., and Simons, K. L. 1997. Technological extinctions of industrial firms: an enquiry into their nature and causes. *Industrial and Corporate Change* 6: 379–460.

Klepper, S., and Simons, K. L. 1999. Industry shakeouts and technological change. Working paper, Carnegie Mellon University.

LaFrance, V. 1985. The United States television receiver industry: United States versus Japan, 1960–1980. Ph.D. dissertation, Pennsylvania State University.

Lane, S. J. 1989. Entry and industry evolution in the ATM manufacturers' market. Ph.D. dissertation, Stanford University.

Levy, J. 1981. Diffusion of technology patterns of international trade: the case of television receivers. Ph.D. dissertation, Yale University.

Lord, K. M. 1953. Mechanized dip soldering. *Electronics* June: 130–137.

MacLaurin, W. R. 1949. *Invention and Innovation in the Radio Industry.* Macmillan: New York.

Mitchell, W. 1989. Whether and when? Probability and timing of incumbents' entry into emerging industrial subfields. *Administrative Sciences Quarterly* 34: 208–230.

Mitchell, W. 1991. Dual clocks: entry order influences on incumbent and newcomer market share and survival when specialized assets retain their value. *Strategic Management Journal* 12(2): 85–100.

*Modern Packaging* 1955. Parts by the reel, August: 100–101, 186–188.

Nelson, R. R. 1991. Why do firms differ, and how does it matter? *Strategic Management Journal*, Winter Special Issue 12: 61–74.

Osbahr, B. F. 1951. Production aids in television receiver manufacture. *Tele-Tech* April: 42–43, 83.

Plesser, E. W. 1959. Simple machines, too, build TV sets. *American Machinist* 19 October: 160–163.

Sleeper, S. D. 1998. The role of firm capabilities in the evolution of the laser industry: the making of a high-tech market. Ph.D. dissertation, Carnegie Mellon University.

Teitelman, R. 1994. *Profits of Science.* Basic Books: New York.

*Tele-Tech* 1948a. Conveyer and test systems speed TV set assembly, March: 36–38.

*Tele-Tech* 1948b. TV receiver and parts assembly techniques, October: 32–35.

*Tele-Tech* 1948c. Television engineering and manufacturing at Philco, November: 61–94.

*Tele-Tech* 1949. DuMont opens largest TV assembly plant, October: 24–25.

*Tele-Tech* 1950. Test equipment in TV receiver manufacture (first of a series) September: 35, 77–79.

*Tele-Tech* 1951. Test equipment in TV receiver manufacture (second of a series), April: 30–32, 76–81.

Tushman, M. L. and Anderson. P. 1986. Technological discontinuities and organizational environments. *Administrative Science Quarterly* 31: 439–465.

Utterback, J. and Suárez, F. 1993. Innovation, competition, and industry structure. *Research Policy* 22: 1–21.

Wilcoxon, F. 1945. Individual comparisons by ranking methods. *Biometrics* 1: 80–83.

Willard, G. E. 1982. A comparison of survivors and nonsurvivors under conditions of large-scale withdrawal in the U.S. color television set industry. Ph.D. dissertation, Purdue University.

Wooster, J. H. 1986. Industrial policy and international competitiveness: a case study of U.S.–Japanese competition in the television receiver manufacturing industry. Ph.D. dissertation, University of Massachusetts.

# CHAPTER THREE

# The Nature, Sources, and Consequences of Firm Differences in the Early History of the Semiconductor Industry

Daniel Holbrook, Wesley M. Cohen, David A. Hounshell, and Steven Klepper

## Introduction

Corporate strategy is centrally concerned with the characteristics of firms that condition performance. Related notions of firm capabilities, core competences, dynamic capabilities, and intangible assets have been invoked to help firms identify their unique, inimitable qualities and devise a business strategy to exploit them (cf. Rumelt, Schendel, and Teece, 1994). Spurred by policy and theoretical concerns and access to establishment census data, economists have also examined intraindustry firm differences, focusing on profitability and behaviors such as entry, exit, innovation, and advertising (e.g., Ravenscraft, 1983; Schmalensee, 1985; Mueller, 1986; Rumelt, 1991; Cohen and Klepper, 1992; Geroski, 1995; Jensen and McGuckin, 1997; Caves, 1998). Economists have found firm behavior and performance to be quite heterogeneous, although robust findings have not yet emerged on the sources of the heterogeneity. The strategy literature is also voluble on the sources of within-industry differences in performance, but it too does not offer robust findings.

In this paper, we step back from both the management and economics literatures on intraindustry firm differences to consider some basic questions. For example, how do firms in an industry differ, and how do the differences affect behavior and performance? What are the sources of the differences? How are they influenced by managers' decisions? These issues are relevant to scholars of management in their attempts to prescribe what firms need to do to achieve superior performance. While economists tend to be more concerned with the performance of industries as a whole than individual firms, differences in the products and problems that firms work on may also affect the long-run performance of industries. They also raise questions about whether markets, left to themselves, are likely to spawn a socially desirable degree of firm heterogeneity.

However fundamental, these questions concerning firm differences are not easy to address. We thought it possible to make some limited headway by exploiting the detail and richness of a recent historical study of the experiences, activities, and performance of four firms in the early semiconductor industry (Holbrook, 1999). The firms include: Sprague Electric Company, a producer of electronic components; Motorola Incorporated, a manufacturer of telecommunications equipment and systems; Shockley Semiconductor Laboratories, a start-up created by a co-recipient of the Nobel prize in physics for the invention of the transistor; and Fairchild Semiconductor Corporation, also a new firm set up by eight defectors from Shockley. These firms were chosen based on the availability of data and their diverse backgrounds and fates. Shockley failed relatively quickly. Sprague prospered for a time and made important contributions to technical advance before it exited. At first immensely successful, Fairchild contributed innovations of great importance and, when it stalled, several of its founders and employees left to form many of the firms that populate the industry today. Motorola steadily expanded its operations in semiconductors and continues to prosper, though even it has faced major challenges at several junctures.

Using archives, interviews, published and unpublished accounts by insiders, and secondary sources, we reconstruct the backgrounds of the four firms and how they addressed the challenges they faced during the early years of rapid technological change in the semiconductor industry. We examine the firms' perceptions of opportunities in the industry, their capabilities, decision-making processes, and the technical and business choices they made. We use this examination to reflect on hypotheses regarding the nature and role of firm capabilities developed by scholars of management and economics. We also analyze the impact of firm differences on the rate of technical advance for the industry, a central concern of industrial organization scholars working from an evolutionary perspective (e.g., Nelson, 1991).

For each of the firms, we provide highly condensed versions of the histories presented in Holbrook (1999).[1] These histories delimit the questions we address. We lay out these questions in the next section. We then recount the origins of the semiconductor industry and present the four firm histories. In the following section, we use the firm histories to reflect on the questions raised. In the last section, we discuss the implications of our reflections for firm strategy and public policy.

## Literature and Theory

The nature, sources, and consequences of firm differences within industries have been addressed at some length – and in greatest detail – in the recent strategy literature. In this section, we briefly review some of the key hypotheses and insights from this and related literatures. Our review is selective, guided by the questions we can address based on the firm histories.

We begin by examining the conditions associated with the entry of the four firms into the industry. While conventional economics is silent regarding the particular features of firms that motivate entry into an industry, the strategy literature's resource-based view of the firm stresses the importance of pre-existing know-how, often termed "intangible assets," in guiding what firms do. This suggests that firms entered the semiconductor industry at least partly to leverage their know-how, which for established firms refers to know-how previously developed for purposes that did not anticipate the emergence of the semiconductor industry. Similarly, *de novo* firms might be envisioned as entering to leverage assets that their principals previously assembled. This raises questions about whether the pre-entry assets of pre-existing and *de novo* firms – especially know-how – explain the timing of entry, initial market positioning and product mix, and the range of options, both perceived and truly available, to entrants at the time of entry.

If existing know-how influenced firms' entry decisions, did it also influence the firms' subsequent behavior and performance? Did it affect the types of R&D projects they undertook as well as the particular products they produced? Once again, conventional economics postulates little link between firm characteristics and either R&D decisions or product market strategy. Some guidance, however, is provided by evolutionary theories. They conceive of firms as repositories of competence that imply a pattern of specialization by entrants (Nelson, 1991).

If different types of expertise lead firms to enter an industry and subsequently produce different kinds of products and work on different problems, what kinds of expertise are important: Substantive expertise embodied in human and physical capital? Different styles of management learned from prior experience? And how precisely do expertise and the firms' (or their principals' in the case of *de novo* firms) prior experience influence and differentiate their perceptions about the future of semiconductor technology and products? Evolutionary theories, once again, focus on understanding firm competencies, and particularly the unique histories that generate them.

To be able to describe the nature and sources of firm differences, it is useful to understand, in the language of Nelson and Winter (1982), where the key knowledge resides within the firm that affects its operational and more forward-looking decisions. It is also important to understand how that knowledge is used. One possibility suggested throughout the management literature (e.g., Barney, 1994) and consistent with the conventional economic view of firms as unitary actors is that top management possesses this knowledge. What, however, is this key knowledge? Chandler (1962) underscores the importance of management in setting the strategic direction of the firm and internally allocating the firm's resources to achieve its goals. For managers responsible for units with multiple functions, it is also essential to know-how to achieve cross-functional coordination and integration (Chandler, 1962; Iansiti, 1998).

Alternatively, the bureaucratic politics model conceives of firms as composed of individuals and groups distinguished by their goals, interests, and power, with key decisions the outcome of a bargaining process among different coalitions (cf. Allison, 1971; Barney, 1994: 64). Relatedly, in the principal – agent literature firms are thought of as nexuses of contracts mediating the interests of parties with different objectives and knowledge (Holmstrom and Tirole, 1989). Evolutionary theories of the firm offer yet a different perspective. These theories not only conceive of the role of top management as being limited, but view firms' choices as largely the outcome of historically determined routines (Nelson and Winter, 1982; Winter, 1988; Nelson, 1991). These different conceptions of decision-making within the firm call into question the role of top management and whether decision-making itself is deliberative or largely follows trajectories conditioned by past practice.

As semiconductor technology evolved and markets developed, firms had to make decisions about both their current and future products, processes, and capabilities. However these decisions were made, did perceptions of key decision-makers change over time to keep pace with changes in the industry? Did key managers recognize that at times their firms needed to change directions in significant ways? If so, were the firms constrained in making those changes and why? Did the firms understand the limits on their abilities to change? The answers to these questions are important if we are to understand how firm differences evolved in the industry. Among them, understanding the limitations on change is especially important.

One factor that can limit firms' ability to change is the inability to acquire key human and physical assets. The resource-based view of the firm stresses how tacitness can limit the marketability of key resources and also make them difficult to imitate. The ability of firms to change also depends on whether they can acquire and use extramural know-how and information. Related notions of absorptive capacity (Cohen and Levinthal, 1990), competency traps (Levitt and March, 1988), and core rigidities (Leonard-Barton, 1994) all suggest that the existing know-how of firms may constrain their ability to exploit new information and even recognize what information is worth exploiting (Cohen and Levinthal, 1994).

Another factor that may limit the ability of firms to change is ambiguous feedback from the environment. Some settings are sufficiently complex and uncertain that it is not possible even retrospectively to understand the basis for firm success (Rumelt et al., 1994: 226). Competition may also limit the ability of firms to change. Ghemawat (1991) emphasizes the importance of commitments, suggesting that if firms delay pursuing key technological developments they can be preempted by rivals that have already captured the relevant market. Relatedly, Klepper (1996) and Sutton (1998) develop models in which R&D competition dictates a concentrated market structure, which suggests that firms may be foreclosed from pursuing a broad research agenda if they delay too long.

If the past actions of firms distinguish their future efforts, can we think of these actions as coalescing in the form of capabilities? A key building block in the strategy literature is the concept of core capabilities; firms are presumed to be different and are advised to exploit their distinctive "core" capabilities to succeed (e.g., Prahalad and Hamel, 1990; Andrews, 1971; Porter, 1980). This assumes core capabilities are hard to change and hence distinguish firms in an enduring way. If indeed firms can be usefully thought of as having capabilities that confer competitive advantage because they are hard to imitate, what are these capabilities composed of? Are they based on "intangible" assets that involve tacit know-how and are difficult to imitate and purchase, as stressed in the resource-based view of the firm? Are the key capabilities of firms anything more than some specific know-how in a well-defined domain, or are they the ability to change over time, as stressed in Teece et al.'s (1997) dynamic capabilities theory? If Teece et al's argument is correct, then successful firms' key capabilities would be expected to change as the environment and technology evolve (cf. Fujimoto, 1999).

Finally, diversity among firms may have implications for social welfare as well as firm strategy. Rumelt et al. (1994: 44) crystallize this issue in the form of the following question: "Is the search for rents based on resource heterogeneity contrary to public welfare, or does it act in the public's welfare?" The evolutionary literature (e.g., Nelson and Winter, 1982) and the literature on R&D spillovers (e.g., Griliches, 1991) suggest that social benefits could be realized in two reinforcing ways. Through the competitive struggle, only the "best" performing technologies survive, and the greater the number of firms advancing the technology in different ways, the better will be the surviving best technology. Simply, the best technology selected is likely to be better the broader the field upon which the market can act (Nelson, 1982). Another way diversity can enhance technological progress is through complementarities that commonly exist in rivals' R&D activities (cf. Levin and Reiss, 1984; Cohen and Malerba, 1994). In such a setting, R&D spillovers can increase the productivity of each firm's R&D, making the "best" surviving technology even better still. For spillovers to be realized, however, information has to flow across firms through various conduits, including the movement of engineering personnel, informal information exchanges, publication of firm R&D findings, and licensing. These conjectures raise a number of questions that in a technologically turbulent industry such as semiconductors are best applied to R&D and other technological activities. Did the firms conduct R&D on different problems, or when they worked on the same problems, did they pursue different approaches to solve them? To the extent that their R&D efforts differed, were the differences related to the firms' backgrounds and histories? Did the "best" technologies survive, and were the best technologies improved by virtue of more actors working on different things? Did information channels exist that conveyed information about the R&D activities and findings of rivals, and did the productivity of the firms' R&D improve as a consequence?

We return to these questions after the histories of the four firms are related.

## The History of Semiconductor Research and the Firm Histories

In this section, we first provide background concerning the origins of the semiconductor industry. This provides a context for the firm histories which follow.

The semiconductor industry, as we know it today, traces its origins most clearly to the invention of the point-contact transistor at Bell Labs in late 1947 and the subsequent licensing of this invention and its immediate follow-on, the junction transistor, by Bell Labs beginning in 1951. Semiconductors had been objects of study – and much puzzlement – since the nineteenth century. The term refers to a class of materials that perform somewhere between an electrical conductor and an electrical insulator; hence the term, "*semi*conductor." Although many researchers sought fundamental understanding of this class of materials, such knowledge eluded them well into the twentieth century. Indeed, the commercial *application* of semiconductors preceded their fundamental understanding by a generation.

The advent of commercial radio in the early 1920s, emerging principally from the activities of amateurs, brought semiconductors into the world of commerce in the form of the crystal detector used in low-end radio receivers. These semiconductor crystals performed as a diode – an active circuit element that rectifies alternating current radio waves – thereby allowing them to be detected and heard through an earphone. Only with the emergence of quantum theory and its application to the solid state of matter in the late 1920s and early 1930s did researchers – including the very best physicists and physical chemists in the world – begin to understand semiconductor phenomena.

Radio's enormous growth during the interwar years, coupled with the burgeoning growth of long-distance telephony and other forms of telecommunications, made the development of a satisfactory semiconductor theory all the more important for the research community. The invention and development of the vacuum tube diode and vacuum tube triode in the first two decades of the twentieth century provided the basis for this spectacular growth. But vacuum tubes proved to be lacking owing to their burning out, their heat generation, and their limited electronic characteristics (signal gain, noise, and frequency range).

World War II provided the vital context in which intensive and wide-ranging semiconductor research and development would be done in the United States to address the shortcomings of vacuum tubes. Significant progress occurred through the coordinated efforts of the Office of Scientific Research and Development, involving university researchers and a number of industrial firms, including Western Electric, the manufacturing arm of AT&T and sibling of Bell Labs. At war's end, however, Bell Labs' research director Mervin Kelly, believing that semiconductor science and technology constituted an enormous frontier, organized a new fundamental research program in semiconductors for the postwar era. Led by physicist William Shockley, who had taught informal seminars on semiconductor theory at Bell Labs during the 1930s, the program involved a number of physicists, materials specialists, and electrical engineers. It soon led to significant advances in semiconductor theory (especially the role of holes, or minority carriers) and the invention of the point-contact transistor on December 23, 1947. Shockley subsequently invented the junction transistor, the patent for which was issued only days after the end of an important symposium in which Bell Labs began to transfer its research findings and inventions to would-be entrants in the new industry of semiconductor electronic device manufacture (Riordan and Hoddeson, 1997).

Because of its parent company AT&T's agreement with the US Justice Department's Antitrust Division, Bell Labs offered licenses to any interested party willing to meet its upfront fee of $25,000 (for which credit would be given against future unit-based royalties). Its principal mechanism of technology transfer *vis-à-vis* the transistor was the quickly famous "Transistor Technology Symposium" of 1951 and its sequel of 1952. By the end of the first 5-day symposium, licensees and the technical and procurement arms of the US military services had gained access to a vast amount of formally *codified* knowledge about transistors, including their design, characteristics of operation, and the factors of design that influenced those characteristics and the basic materials from which they were constructed. In its 1952 symposium, AT&T conveyed information about the manufacturing techniques – many of them informal and depending on *tacit* knowledge – employed at Western Electric's point-contact transistor plant in Allentown, Pennsylvania. Owing to Shockley's invention of the superior junction transistor, however, many of those techniques were rapidly becoming obsolete.

With the exception of Fairchild, each of the firms considered in the present paper had representatives who attended the Bell transistor symposia. Each of these representatives, just as each of these firms, brought different sets of organizational capabilities to the manufacture of transistors and different experiences in the electronics industry. Their principals also held different views as to how important mastery of both the codified knowledge of semiconductor theory and the tacit knowledge inherent in transistor manufacture would be to their firms' success with the new technology. The histories of these firms are related in the order in which they entered into semiconductor production: Sprague first, followed by Motorola, Shockley, and Fairchild.

## Sprague Electric

Sprague Electric, founded in 1928 by Robert C. (R. C.) Sprague, manufactured capacitors and other electronic components. The company supplied components to several important World War II research and development programs and emerged from the war enlarged and with an ongoing relationship with the military. The company's postwar research, mostly funded by the military, focused on printed circuits, ceramic-coated wires, and ceramic- and plastic-molded capacitors, which enhanced capabilities it acquired and strengthened during the war (Sprague Electric Annual Report, 1949). The military conveyed its enthusiasm for the transistor to defense contractors, Sprague included. Representatives from the firm were invited to attend both the 1951 military-sponsored Bell Laboratories transistor symposium, and the 1952 version for early transistor licensees. In the latter year Sprague also hired a new head scientist, Kurt Lehovec, to run the company's semiconductor research. Lehovec had worked at the Army Electronics Laboratory at Fort Monmouth, where he was an administrator of the 1949 Bell Labs/Joint Services transistor development contract. Lehovec began the company's foray into semiconductors by designing and building refining, crystal growing, and other process equipment (Lehovec, telephone conversation, April 16, 1995).

Impatient with R&D progress, in 1954 Sprague Electric licensed Philco's electrochemical transistor, which was manufactured using a highly mechanized production process. The Philco transistor was a natural fit for Sprague. Sprague's capacitor production employed electrochemical processes and Sprague had considerable experience making small electronic components and in the mechanization of production (Sprague Electric Annual Report, 1954: 10–11). The Philco manufacturing process chemically eroded a thin spot in the middle of a small piece of germanium and then electroplated it with indium to provide the transistor action. At the time, the Philco transistor was the highest-frequency transistor available. This characteristic suited military applications and computer makers, Sprague Electric's main customers, particularly well (Sprague Electric Annual Report, 1956: 12). Sprague built its ongoing development programs around the electrochemical device. In spite of reservations about the Philco device, Lehovec worked to improve the production process, especially in such areas as growing and refining germanium crystals (Lehovec, unpublished: 29–30).

By the mid-1950s Sprague's Research and Engineering Division included over 300 researchers. The great majority of them, however, focused on capacitor research, with the semiconductor efforts much smaller. In 1956 Sprague Electric hired an entire team from Philco to take charge of Sprague's new transistor plant in Concord, New Hampshire, which opened in 1957 (Sprague, 1993). The new plant introduced geographic distance between R&D and production, rendering their coordination difficult. R. C. Sprague, not adequately knowledgeable in semiconductor science, controlled the firm's research policy "with a rigid hand," frequently taking issue with the head of R&D, frustrating the company's development of adequate semiconductor-related expertise (Sprague, interview, 1 November 1994). He also headed the firm's "Fourth Decade Committee" responsible for long-range research and development planning (Sprague, 1993: 75).

Under pressure from military demand for smaller, more reliable circuits, the company turned explicitly to problems of miniaturization (Sprague, interview, 1 November 1994; Kleiman, 1966: 31–68). Relying on its existing capabilities, Sprague produced two ceramic-substrate hybrid circuits. These used printed wiring and passive components with electrochemical transistors attached later. The company had long experience in producing the passive elements of such circuits; hybrids seemed a small step. In spite of late 1950s developments using silicon instead of germanium and photolithography rather than electro-chemistry to make transistors, Sprague Electric stuck with its ceramic-based hybrid circuits until well into the 1960s, trying to capitalize on its historical expertise.

Kurt Lehovec, the company's chief scientist, worked on improving the electrochemical technology, proposing improved production techniques (Lehovec, unpublished: 29–30). Inspired by a 1958 conference where he heard a paper suggesting new complex circuit applications, he thought that such circuits could be made from conjoined transistors. Realizing that they would need to be electrically isolated from each other, Lehovec developed, and later patented, a method to do so (Lehovec, unpublished: 39). This patent ( 3,029,366, issued April 10, 1962), which outlined a method of using diodes to block current from flowing between adjacent transistors, later proved crucial to making monolithic integrated circuits.

The shift in the industry to silicon-based devices coincided with the geographical shift of the semiconductor industry from the East Coast to Northern California. Sprague's location made it difficult to tap into the information networks beginning to spring up among the innovative firms in what is now known as Silicon Valley. The company's existing ties were with East Coast companies and universities – ties that Sprague's research manager later recalled "provided precious little know-how" (Sprague, 1993: 70).

R. C.'s son, John Sprague, a Stanford Ph.D. in semiconductor physics, joined the family firm in the late 1950s. Rapidly assuming a prominent role in Sprague's research agenda, he focused the firm's efforts on gaining leading-edge semiconductor knowledge. The planar process, invented at Fairchild Semiconductor in 1958, was proving extremely useful in making transistors economically. John Sprague realized the importance of this new technique. His semiconductor team was small, six researchers to start, with the bulk of the firm's R&D focused on capacitors, the company's main business and one under attack by changing technologies and new competitors (Sprague, 1993). Sprague's planar R&D program struggled, hampered by its small size and the complex demands of the new technology. The early 1960s addition of the planar monolithic integrated circuit compounded the problem.

By 1963, Sprague Electric was the sole supplier of electrochemical transistors, a profitable position, but one that thwarted attempts to move away from the increasingly obsolete technology (Braun and MacDonald, 1982: 145). In 1962 R. C. Sprague, hoping for faster R&D progress, hired an entire team of researchers from Westinghouse, where they had been working on silicon planar devices. Though they were able to get planar devices into production in Concord, their presence and success exacerbated the rift between the R&D lab and production. John Sprague, seeking to eliminate this chasm, moved all semiconductor R&D to the firm's new Worcester, Massachusetts, plant (Sprague Electric Annual Report, 1968: 6). Many of the employees there promptly left, not wanting to work under an R&D person (Sprague, interview, 1 November 1994).

Though the firm produced transistors and later monolithic integrated circuits, it never gained significant market share. Losses plagued the firm from the late 1960s into the following decade. John Sprague increased its semiconductor R&D program throughout the 1960s, but the company's financial situation could not sustain the needed efforts. In the 1970s the firm was sold to conglomerates twice, finally dissolving in the mid-80s.

### Motorola incorporated

Paul Galvin founded the Galvin Manufacturing Corporation in 1928. The company first produced a battery eliminator for home radios, then complete radio sets, including the "Motorola," the first practical car radio. (Petrakis, 1991: 20–91). The 1930s brought relative prosperity to the firm. In the run-up to World War II, Galvin's engineers produced prototypes of the Walkie-Talkie, a crystal controlled two-way radio considerably smaller than existing Army units. Initially cautious, the Army ordered large numbers of the units after mid-1941 (Petrakis, 1991: 140–144). The company's reputation for building rugged equipment, first gained for its mobile radios, proved essential for the military market and strengthened the company's relationship with the armed forces after the war.

In the 1930s Galvin had hired Daniel Noble, an engineering professor and radio consultant, as the company's Director of Research (Noble, 1964: 6; Petrakis, 1991: 146). Noble was intelligent, opinionated, and highly driven to apply his learning. Galvin and Noble would remain the main influences on the company for several decades.

After the war Motorola (the name adopted in 1947) continued to serve the military and commercial radio and television markets. At that time the firm's main capabilities lay in printed circuits, ceramic substrates, and electronic system design and manufacture. Dan Noble, who gained exposure to the new semiconductor arts while representing Motorola at the MIT Radiation Laboratory and at Harvard's Radio Frequency Laboratory during the war, insisted that the company build a foundation in this new field (Noble, 1977: 18). In 1948 he chose Phoenix, Arizona, for a new research lab's location. Noble intended the lab to focus on military-sponsored research and to supply "a window on the world of electronic research" (Noble, 1974: 1). At least two company representatives attended the 1951 Bell Labs Transistor symposium at the invitation of the military (AT&T Archives, 1951: 10). The firm apparently did not send anyone to the 1952 symposium, though by that time it had acquired a transistor license.

The semiconductor division's management was skilled in semiconductor science and technology. The R&D lab, which expanded from 40 staffers at its founding to over 800 five years later in 1954, focused not on new discoveries, but on taking "new technology which was coming along somewhere else and .l.l. making it work" (Taylor, 1985: 30). Its main customer was Motorola's equipment divisions, and it focused on power devices, rectifiers in particular, for radios and other electronic equipment. This emphasis provided the technical background for the firm's later move into automotive electronics, which paid off hugely when the company developed the first practical rectifier for automobile use, allowing alternators to replace troublesome generators. To facilitate coordination between research and production, Galvin and Noble mandated close and constant communications between the semiconductor unit and the systems divisions (Weisz, 1985: 17–18).

In the late 1950s the firm decided to expand into the commercial semiconductor market. Motorola had invested in a broad semiconductor R&D program to serve its internal needs; by the mid-1950s, though, the company's internal consumption alone could not support the Phoenix R&D efforts. Noble and Galvin further stressed that the company's expertise would only be an advantage if it entered the commercial field soon (Petrakis, 1991: 215–218). To stay current with customer demands the company broadened its research program further and hired individuals and teams of individuals from other companies including Western Electric, Hoffman Electric, and Bell Telephone Laboratories (DaCosta, n.d.: 36; Ackerman, n.d.: 9–10). By these means the Phoenix facility established a base of expertise in both diffused and alloy transistors. Motorola acquired a license from RCA for alloy transistors, a device suited to audio and power applications. Motorola also acquired scientific and technical information from other sources, particularly Bell Labs (Taylor, 1985: 30).

By the late 1950s enlarged production had weakened the coordination between R&D and production. To counter this trend, in 1958 Noble hired Les Hogan, a Harvard physics professor, as manager of the semiconductor division. Hogan broke up the existing organizational structure and replaced it with product groups with responsibility for both R&D and production (Taylor, 1985: 18). These changes "tended to sacrifice even more the development of really novel and new technology" (Taylor, 1985: 37). He also maintained Motorola's wide-ranging R&D efforts that supported both the equipment divisions and other commercial customers.

Like Sprague and most other electronics companies, Motorola was greatly influenced by its work for the military. The emphasis on size and reliability compelled the company to address miniaturization. Dan Noble had long emphasized the usefulness of hybrid circuits because they took advantage of Motorola's existing areas of expertise and used proven components and production techniques (Noble, 1954: 4). Long experience with printed circuits, ceramic materials, and the design of rugged circuits made hybrids a good fit for Motorola. Further, hybrid technology's reliability, relatively low price, and suitability for both Motorola's internal needs and its main customers recommended it to Motorola management (Hogan, 1961: 3). By the end of the 1950s, however, responding to technological developments elsewhere and to continued military demand for small, complex circuits, Motorola semiconductor research included work on less conservative approaches to integration like thin film and monolithic devices and circuits (Motorola, Inc., 1960: 1).

Motorola struggled with monolithic integrated circuits, whose complexities demanded mastery of a wide range of interrelated production and testing technologies

(Lesk, interview by M. H. Petrakis, June 13, 1989: 12). Like Sprague, Motorola was hampered by its geographic isolation from the new Northern California semiconductor center with its extensive channels of information exchange. This led the Semiconductor Division's research manager to bemoan the "inbred" nature of the laboratory (Welty, 1989: 9). Further, Motorola's corporate research connections were with companies no longer on the technological frontier, such as RCA and Bell Labs (*Business Week*, 1962: 116; Golding, 1971: 51). These links could not provide the knowledge needed to move into monolithic integrated circuits, retarding Motorola's progress in that area.

The company's struggles with monolithic ICs did not prevent it from making important contributions to the development of those devices. In 1962, for example, the Air Force supported a $3 million project in Phoenix devoted to developing better techniques for producing thin films of metals and other materials, an area in which Motorola already had expertise from its extensive prior experience in printed circuits and in which it made lasting contributions to monolithic semiconductor technology (Miller, 1962: 85–95).

The company's investment in a broad research agenda, supported by the company's commercial, automotive, and military equipment divisions, and its ability to maintain that agenda over a long period of time, nonetheless enabled it to prosper eventually in the new technology. By the end of the 1960s Motorola had captured a significant portion of the IC market (Tilton, 1971: 69).[2] In the following decade it became a major force, becoming one of the largest manufacturers of computer chips in the world, a position it maintains today.

## Shockley Semiconductor Laboratories

Shockley Semiconductor Laboratories was founded by William Shockley, one of the inventors of the transistor, and perhaps the pre-eminent semiconductor physicist of his day. Educated at Cal Tech and MIT, upon graduation in 1936 Shockley joined Bell Labs and became part of a new research group pursuing basic research in solid state physics (Hoddeson, 1977: 28). The war took Shockley away from Bell Labs. He worked on submarine warfare tactics, applying new operations research techniques, and consulted on radar training programs to optimize bombing accuracy (Baxter, 1946: 405–6). Shockley thus established a close relationship with the military which lasted throughout his subsequent career, including membership on the Department of Defense Research and Development Board and ongoing consulting relationships with all of the military branches.

Shockley played a mainly theoretical role in the 1947 invention of the transistor (Hoddeson, 1981: 68). Wanting to "play a more significant personal role" in transistor development, Shockley almost immediately emerged with the ideas that yielded his most important patent, that for the junction transistor (Shockley, 1976: 599). Shockley also assumed an important role in the dissemination of semiconductor knowledge. His role in Bell Labs transistor symposia and his 1950 book *Electrons and Holes in Semiconductors*, which clarified the theory of transistor action, elevated him to the top of his field and provided him extensive and lasting contacts throughout the academic and industrial semiconductor community (Shockley, 1950); Hoddeson, 1977: 25–26). In

1955 Shockley took a leave of absence from Bell Labs for the purpose of "investigating various opportunities" (Shockley, 1955).[3]

Shockley found backing for his venture from Arnold Beckman, founder of Beckman Instruments and a fellow Cal Tech graduate. Shockley moved into rented space in Palo Alto, California, and recruited employees for his company. His preeminence in solid state physics and broad and deep connections with the academic world allowed Shockley to secure the brightest young semiconductor scientists and engineers available, including some from his previous employer, Bell Labs. In 1956 the company employed 37 staff, 12 with Ph.D.s Only four employees, however, were "mechanical designers and production men" (Shockley, 1956). One year later, the research staff was 34 (Shockley, 1957a); 2 years after that, the production force was 20 and the research staff twice that, out of a total employment of just over 100 (Dimmick, 1959).

Shockley initially planned to make a double-diffused silicon transistor, a device invented at Bell Labs but which had not yielded to production. He could not, however, sustain this focus. Instead, he instituted a secret project on which a small number of his researchers worked (Moore, interview with D. Holbrook, February 23, 1994). Here for the first time in his commercial career Shockley's personal version of "not invented here" syndrome emerges. His initial plan required the use of techniques developed by others; the secret project would be his conception alone and would repeat the scientific triumph of his junction transistor. In 1957 Shockley totally dropped the diffused silicon transistor, replacing it with efforts to develop a four-layer diode, a device of his own invention.

For the remainder of his tenure with the firm, Shockley promoted his four-layer diode. Almost immediately this emphasis drove away eight of his most talented employees to found their own firm, Fairchild Semiconductor. Initially attracted to Shockley by the prospect of working on the cutting edge of semiconductor technology, these men grew frustrated with the lack of emphasis on production. The "traitorous eight," as Shockley called them, included Robert Noyce and Gordon Moore, who later founded Intel. The prominence of the four-layer diode reflects Shockley's lack of emphasis on producing devices suited for the existing market. Shockley, primarily a theoretician, saw production as subsidiary to research. Theory, however, was no longer the most important aspect of semiconductor technology. Production required mechanical and engineering skills and a willingness to proceed without scientific understanding. Shockley's education and experience hindered his recognition of this fact. His choices of cooperative programs revealed this approach. His company would do the research while production would be farmed out.

Three years after founding the firm, Shockley summarized its position as still "in a building-up stage" and "consuming capital rather than making profits" (Shockley, 1958). Ignoring strong currents in the industry, Shockley's company made no efforts to produce miniature circuits, choosing instead to promote the four-layer diode as "actually the first solid circuit produced in the electronic field" (Biesle, 1959). By 1960 the company still had no appreciable sales (Shockley, 1957b). Beckman, tired of the venture, sold the company to Clevite Corporation, an Ohio-based firm with existing interests in semiconductors. Shockley largely removed himself from the company, focusing on his new teaching position at Stanford University and consulting with the military services. In 1964 Clevite sold the firm to IT&T, which dissolved it in 1967.

## Fairchild Semiconductor

The eight ex-Shockley researchers who founded Fairchild Semiconductor initially offered themselves as a team to a number of firms but then decided to form their own company. With financial backing from Fairchild Camera and Instrument Company, a New York-based firm, they set up shop in Mountain View, California, in 1957 (Malone, 1985; Braun and MacDonald, 1982: 72). Convinced that the silicon diffused transistor, a more stable device than the germanium transistor, would be warmly received in the market, the company's late 1950s activities were of two main types: designing and modifying processing equipment and mastering the intricacies of the required production processes. The technology demanded a diverse set of compatible and complementary skills that by chance and design collectively the eight largely possessed (Moore, interview with D. Holbrook, 23 February 1994; Malone, 1985: 90). At Shockley Semiconductor Labs the Fairchild eight had gained valuable technical skills and insight into silicon technology, as well as skills in designing and making various pieces of process equipment. They decided to pursue the double-diffused silicon mesa transistor (Moore, interview with D. Holbrook, 23 February 1994) and put the device into production a few months after founding the company.

The mesa transistor used a photolithographic production process that involved masking the silicon wafer surface with a layer of silicon oxide. Experimenting with this layer, Jean Hoerni, Fairchild's theoretician, invented the planar process in 1958. Instead of removing the oxide layer, Hoerni left it on the wafer surface, leaving the resulting transistors with a flat profile (hence the name) and giving them greater electrical stability. This process not only simplified production somewhat, but also produced more reliable transistors, and thus fostered mass production of transistors. Making planar transistors required the development of several interrelated sets of skills, including oxide masking and diffusion, mask making and photolithographic techniques, and metallization. Fairchild's research and development program for the following years aimed to tap the potential of the silicon/silicon oxide system.

Robert Noyce's invention of the monolithic integrated circuit in 1959 followed from Hoerni's planar process. Rather than cutting the wafer into individual transistors and then combining them into circuits, why not, Noyce reasoned, make multi-transistor circuits on a wafer (Noyce, 1977: 63–9; Wolff, 1976: 50–1). The oxide layer provided a surface for depositing fine metallic lines to connect the transistors into a circuit. Extending the planar process in this way made the monolithic IC practical, and provided the company with an early lead in what soon proved to be the dominant approach to integrating circuits. Fairchild's earlier success making and selling silicon transistors gave it the resources for the research needed to bring the IC to market.

By 1960 the company's R&D laboratory employed 400 researchers, the majority of whom were involved in developmental work rather than basic scientific research. The research laboratory was organized into functional areas, most of which focused on a specific part of the production process (Holbrook, 1999: 361–363). This close coordination of production and research brought problems to the fore, and allowed comparatively easy progress to be made in solving them. Gordon Moore and Victor Grinich, the directors of research and of engineering, gave researchers a great deal of autonomy.[4] The technical managers were all expert in semiconductor science and technology. By capitalizing on a diversity of technical and scientific opinions within the firm, Fairchild's management style allowed it to tackle and solve various technical problems with relative ease.

The company's research and development was guided by what Noyce called the theory of least knowledge (Moore, interview with D. Holbrook, 23 February 1994). When confronted with a problem, the first step was to take an educated guess at a solution. If it worked, no further research was needed. If it did not, then more research was performed and the next potential solution tried. Fairchild research placed little emphasis on basic research, eschewing scientific understanding in favor of pragmatic results. At times, of course, intractable problems demanded scientific understanding, and Fairchild made important contributions in some cases, but much of the knowledge generated at Fairchild was tacit, based on the specific experiences and exigencies of the company's production lines.

Between 1960 and 1966 Fairchild's increasingly powerful position in the industry and its growing reputation for superior research attracted attention throughout the industry, which in turn invoked two-way flows of information. Fairchild laboratory reports mention some 71 firms either supplying or receiving information during this period.[5] The expansion and prosperity of the semiconductor industry, however, also led employees to leave for greener pastures, "spinning off" their own firms.

Expansion also eroded the close relationship between R&D and production. The company established production facilities away from its Northern California R&D labs for reasons of labor availability and costs, making it increasingly difficult to continue the close coordination of research and production (Moore, interview with D. Holbrook, 23 February 1994; Bassett, 1998: 230). Though Fairchild prospered in the first half of the 1960s and its research lab continued to produce leading-edge research results, the firm's production capability and new product output began to lag its competitors, and the firm lost market share. The problems discouraged Robert Noyce, who left Fairchild in 1967 with Gordon Moore and their colleague Andrew Grove to form Intel Corporation. Les Hogan from Motorola was hired to take over the firm. Though he enjoyed some success at Fairchild, the company was beset by new competition and new technologies in which it was behind (Malone, 1985: 124–127). Fairchild was sold to the French conglomerate Schlumberger in 1979 and again to National Semiconductor in 1986.

## Reflections on the Firm Histories

In this section, we use the firm histories to reflect on the questions raised earlier. Our reflections are organized into six areas corresponding to the questions: entry, market segmentation and positioning, knowledge and decision-making, limits on change, core capabilities, and diversity.

### Entry and the sources of firm differences

Why did firms enter the emergent semiconductor industry? All four firms entered to exploit knowledge and connections developed from past activities. We consider in turn the motives for entry of Sprague, Motorola, Shockley, and Fairchild.

An incumbent firm in the electronic components industry, Sprague saw dual opportunities in the manufacture of transistors. First, as a leading supplier of capacitors to
the telecommunications and electronics industry, Sprague's executives expected that
transistors would transform these industries, including the way they would use the
firm's capacitors. Thus, the firm had to know something about transistors just to remain in business. But Sprague believed that its manufacturing know-how – ability to
achieve high-volume production of reliable electronic circuit components – and its
design knowledge – ability to design new and often proprietary circuit components –
positioned it well to enter the transistor business. Doing so would not only buttress its
existing product line, but it would also allow the company to exploit the close relationship the firm had developed with the military, which was both a major customer of its
components and also a major funder of electronics R&D (especially in semiconductors). The military had chosen Sprague to be among the small number of firms to
attend Bell Laboratories' first Transistor Technology Symposium; thus it had early
access to Bell Labs' technology, and AT&T's consent decree assured that Sprague
would have continued access to Bell Labs' deep knowledge of semiconductors, including product design and process know-how.

Motorola had a history similar to Sprague's in that it was an experienced firm in the
electronics industry. It also had developed an important relationship with the military
and was recognized by the services for its rugged telecommunications equipment.
Thanks to its record, it was similarly well positioned to access Bell Labs' early discoveries. Like Sprague, it also had knowledge of nonmilitary electronics, but as a systems
and end-product manufacturer, it had superior knowledge on this front.

Shockley entered the industry with four considerable assets. First, he possessed the
reputation as the most knowledgeable theorist of semiconductors in the United States,
if not the world. Second, he was the inventor of record of the junction transistor,
which, employing his deep understanding of semiconductor phenomena, he had swiftly
invented after his Bell Labs' colleagues Bardeen and Brattain had invented the point-
contact transistor. Third, he had a close relationship with the military. This relationship had been fostered beginning in World War II when, using newly developed methods
in operations research, he had helped to optimize strategic bombing programs. His
interaction with the military had grown after the war when he became a member of the
Research and Development Board of the Department of Defense. Indeed, he was
regarded as an "insider" by the military, and his fame as a transistor inventor made his
connection with the military all the more valuable. Fourth, he was intimately connected with Bell Labs. Both he and his backers assumed that his access to Bell Labs
gave him real advantages far beyond those of any Bell licensee. Yet, unlike Sprague and
Motorola, he lacked the base of customers and the associated marketing and manufacturing experience of those firms. But he clearly believed that this deficiency was compensated by his prowess as a theoretical researcher, his reputation as an inventor, and
his connections to the research community, which he exploited in recruiting an obviously top-flight staff.

Fairchild was the least well positioned of the four firms with respect to the market,
but benefited from Shockley's astute judgement of talent and the experiences of its
founders at Shockley Labs. The major (anti-)lesson they learned at Shockley was the
necessity of keeping a sharp focus on getting a marketable product out the door.

Fairchild's eight founders were a talented group with broad skills. While at Shockley, they also acquired valuable technical skills in the design and production of processing equipment and valuable insights into silicon technology which, once they left Shockley, enabled them to develop quickly a marketable transistor. So, although they did not have direct up-market experience, they possessed excellent scientific and technical knowledge and newly developed production skills, which positioned them extremely well for the emerging market.

To the degree that the distinctive experiences of the four firms conferred intangible assets, they support the resource-based view of the firm that firms enter new areas to exploit intangible assets initially developed for other purposes. Note that this conclusion holds both for the two pre-existing electronics producers and the two new firms, with the relevant experience for the new firms being the experience of their founders. Although the new firms did not themselves have organizational histories, their founders (e.g., Shockley and the staff he recruited) had histories from which they drew and which, to a large extent, helped to shape their respective paths.

## Market segmentation and positioning

The initial products of the firms and the problems they worked on were directly related to their distinctive histories before entering the semiconductor industry. The key here is to understand what conditioned each firm's top managers' view or understanding of how to make money with semiconductors (i.e., what products to make for which markets) and what was necessary to get there (i.e., how to employ both human capital and equipment). These views were conditioned not only by their prior experience but also by their perceptions of scientific advance, technological change, and future uses of the technology.

Sprague believed that its manufacturing expertise would distinguish it in the semiconductor industry. Accordingly, it was content to license the technology it initially employed from Philco, which used a technology related to the technology Sprague used for capacitors and which yielded high-frequency transistors prized by the military both for their telecommunications applications and for use in computers. Motorola, reflecting its production of audio "system" products and military products, limited its initial transistors to power devices suitable for radio and other communications equipment. This early emphasis on power devices further conditioned its subsequent application of semiconductors to automotive applications (i.e., rectifiers for alternators). Its heritage as an automotive radio producer and its experience in military applications of radios also conditioned it to focus semiconductor research on devices for its mobile communications equipment. Shockley concentrated on a device of his own invention, the four-layer diode, reflecting his confidence in his abilities as a theoretical physicist to develop important new devices, as he had done at Bell Labs. He was averse to mere imitation and to mere improvement of prior technology through small changes in configuration or manufacturing process improvement. He focused attention on inventing novel products, which led him to contract out development and production to other firms, matters he considered beneath his status. He specialized in research, which he perceived to be his comparative advantage. Novelty came at the expense of reduction to practice. On the basis of their experience at Shockley and their broad expertise, the founders of Fairchild focused initially on silicon transistors, which they were convinced would prove to be superior owing to their stability at higher temperatures. They also focused initially on the double-diffused mesa transistor on which they had worked at Shockley (and which he later abandoned), reflecting their commitment to developing devices that could be produced and marketed. Their commitment to silicon and to the mesa transistor conditioned their development of the planar process, which in turn, as Robert Noyce staunchly maintained, led them inevitably to the integrated circuit.

After their initial specializations, the evolution of the firms' portfolios of products and research problems continued to be influenced by the customers they served and their historical production expertise. Inevitably, firm behavior was also influenced by their successes and failures. Both Sprague and Motorola focused on discrete devices and hybrid circuits, reflecting the demands of their customers for discrete devices. Both firms produced discrete devices for radio and TV applications, and both firms produced circuits for computer makers, who initially favored reliable circuits of the hybrid type. Sprague's considerable expertise in ceramic circuits and its developing expertise in printed circuit boards led them to favor hybrid circuits. Motorola had long been pragmatically oriented toward producible devices and had developed great expertise in printed circuit technology, which favored the more conservative hybrid circuits in their efforts to miniaturize circuits. In both instances, specialization in hybrid circuits seemed to have slowed the efforts of both Sprague and Motorola to produce integrated circuits. Shockley remained committed over time to novel devices of his own invention given his theoretical orientation and egocentricity, both of which were reinforced by receipt of the Nobel Prize. Fairchild's focus on production and R&D serving production led it to focus on all aspects of production, which contrasted with Sprague and Motorola, both of which tended to acquire production personnel and equipment as well as to license technology for production from other firms. As its leaders came to understand more intimately the challenges of production and the opportunities available to the firm from a deeper understanding of its associated problems, the more this understanding conditioned their behavior in terms of the company's R&D program. They committed greater resources to process research while not abandoning work on product development.

Thus, the firms specialized according to their substantive technical knowledge and, for the two pre-existing firms, the types of customers they had serviced prior to semiconductors. No firm appears to have systematically scanned a wide range of possibilities and then made their choices based on a systematic comparison of the alternatives. Nor did any firm consider the actions of rivals with a view toward strategic preemption or matching in the marketplace. Rather, each followed an initial and subsequent course, acting almost instinctively to capitalize on their past experiences. Thus we find – at least tentatively – that the resource-based view of the firm seems to hold and that, upon finer-grain analysis, many of the conjectures from evolutionary theories of the firm seem to hold as well. In all cases, the "strategic vision" of the firms' founders was limited by their past experience; these bounded visions tended to persist and to make a difference over a long period of time.

### Knowledge and decision-making

As stressed in a section above, differing states of knowledge about semiconductors, manufacturing, and markets help to explain firm decision-making at the time of entry and conditioned subsequent firm performance. But knowledge continued to be a vital, if less-than-tangible, asset in firm behavior, especially as it conditioned executive-level decision-making. The sources of knowledge, the flow of knowledge within the firms, and the locations within the firms where the truly "key" knowledge resided appear to have been important to the long-run performance of all four firms.

The experiences of all four firms underscore the close coordination between R&D and production that was needed to make technological advances. In order for firms to improve their production capabilities, research was required on many different aspects of production, and in order to develop new devices firms had to develop new production skills, based in part on the production and application of new knowledge. This was perhaps most apparent in Fairchild. Its success stemmed largely from its ability to improve simultaneously multiple aspects of the production process. This ability rested squarely – at least in its heyday – on the ability of its key managers to produce new knowledge in their functional areas, to share that knowledge across functions, and, critically, to use that knowledge irrespective of where it was generated. Fairchild's two major technological breakthroughs, the planar process and the integrated circuit, grew out of its close coordination between R&D and production. The tensions palpable at Sprague and Motorola, where R&D and production were conducted in separate geographic locations, and the defection from Shockley of the eight founders of Fairchild due to Shockley's lack of emphasis on production in research and his frequent secretive research projects within his small organization, are matters of historical record. The differential performance of these firms clearly points to the interrelatedness of the knowledge generated in R&D and production as well as the need for close coordination between the two activities and sources of knowledge.

The ability of the firms to coordinate R&D and production was perhaps the most important determinant of their success over time. While top management was the final arbiter on all decisions involving the coordination of R&D and production in all four firms, the success of the firms in coordinating R&D and production was largely based on the structures top management set up to facilitate the coordination. Fairchild represented the extreme in which R&D efforts, in the firm's early years, were decentralized according to each functional area of production and in which R&D and production were carried out together in each area by teams responsible for both activities. This cross-functional coordination not only contributed to Fairchild's great early commercial success, but it also led to Fairchild's two major breakthroughs: the planar process and integrated circuits. When the firm grew large and geographically dispersed and when R&D had become highly centralized and an end in itself, this type of coordination broke down, contributing to Fairchild's decline – at least in two of the founders' minds. (Those founders, incidentally, left Fairchild to found Intel, where they deliberately banned any kind of research being done except on the factory floor.)

In Motorola, top management dictated frequent contacts and exchanges between production and R&D personnel located at different establishments. When this was not sufficient, Hogan was brought in to reorganize Motorola's efforts along the lines of (early) Fairchild in order to achieve closer coordination between R&D and production. Notably, Motorola was the only one of the four firms to survive and prosper for a prolonged period. Coordination of R&D and production at Sprague was carried out more via a top-down process in which a long-range planning committee, dominated by the firm's founder, R. C. Sprague, made the strategic decisions. R. C. Sprague's narrow orientation, reflecting his background in production and his relative ignorance of solid state physics, frequently led him to overrule the R&D director. Though it succeeded to some degree in the early transistor industry, Sprague was not able to adapt to developments brought on by the integrated circuit until it was too late.

Shockley was the ultimate in a top-down management style in which he resisted efforts by the eight defectors and his financier to focus the company's activities on production process rather than product innovation. Consequently, Shockley Labs never produced a commercially successful product in spite of the founder's definitive knowledge of semiconductor physics and his record as the inventor of the junction transistor.

Our four case histories, although not fully representative of the entire industry, underscore the critical role of top management in identifying what knowledge was critical for firm success, creating structures in which that knowledge could be secured, and then coordinating the flow of that knowledge across functions. Thus, one of the key points for understanding differences across the firms is not simply where the key operational knowledge resided within the firm, but where top management believed it to reside and how they tried to combine it.

The importance of cross-functional integration is consistent with Chandler's (1962) view of the role of top management in industrial firms and is subsequently highlighted by Iansiti (1998) in his examination of product development in the computer industry. Chandler emphasizes the importance of top managers in coordinating the different functional areas of corporations. This coordinating role that we observe as being critical in semiconductors is different from both the nexus-of-contracts view of the firm in economics and the bounded role of management in evolutionary theories. The need for coordination between R&D and production resonates with the emphasis in the nexus-of-contracts view of the firm as involving different units, each with their own knowledge and interests. However, the importance of top management in achieving effective coordination attests to the inability of purely contractual specifications to limit the tensions between R&D and other functions and to channel those tensions into creative activity bounded by pragmatism. Moreover, that this role was performed so differently and effectively in the different firms suggests it involved not only managerial discretion but also great skill.

The role of top management in coordinating R&D and production is also different from top management's role in setting broad strategic parameters for decision-makers as emphasized in the evolutionary view of the firm. In the semiconductor industry, however, the knowledge intensity of product design and process control meant that to be effective in setting strategic direction top managers had to possess this knowledge and then act on it. Fairchild is the best example here. In the case of Motorola, however, top management recognized its own limitations but compensated by deftly involving more knowledgeable personnel in R&D, manufacturing, and marketing in charting the strategic direction of the company. In Motorola's case, cross-functional coordination could also generate effective strategy.

## Limits on change

The semiconductor industry changed markedly in the period covered by our firm histories. How did the key decision-makers perceive changes in the industry as they occurred? In turn, did they perceive the need for their firms to change, and given these perceptions, how precisely did they formulate such needs? When they formulated a strategy of change, were they constrained in carrying out this strategy? Our four histories offer a remarkable spectrum of phenomena *vis-à-vis* change over time. The pattern for each is reasonably clear, but of course we are working from imperfect information in all four cases so our observations are tentative.

With the exception of Shockley Labs, which never progressed very far, leaders in the firms recognized changes in the industry and attempted to change considerably over time. Both Sprague and Motorola sought to broaden the types of semiconductor devices they produced. In Sprague this occurred when John Sprague entered the firm. Motorola recognized early on the need to broaden its technology to justify its broad-based R&D effort in semiconductors, which it felt was necessary to keep up with advances. Both firms also attempted to master integrated circuit technology when the advantages of monolithic circuits over their hybrid approaches became apparent. Fairchild was one of the two leaders in silicon semiconductor devices, but, late in our period, when it fell on hard times, Fairchild's leaders attempted to change by bringing in Hogan from Motorola to right itself. The record indicates, though, that all three firms had difficulty changing. With the exception of evolutionary economics, the various theories discussed earlier allow firm leaders to recognize that change is necessary, but they offer markedly different views on constraints on change.

Change largely involved keeping up with a rapidly moving technological frontier. Much technological knowledge is tacit, and it has been conjectured in the resource-based view of the firm that such knowledge is difficult to acquire in the market, making it difficult to keep up with rapid technological advance. The record on this score is mixed. Up to the era of integrated circuits, Sprague, Motorola, and Shockley all were able to purchase information that was largely tacit; all three firms were able to hire individuals and even teams of individuals with important technological knowledge from Bell Labs, RCA, GE, and other firms. They were also able to hire key people from academia. They also acquired equipment and technology licenses from similar firms. For a while, this enabled them to stay abreast of technological developments in the industry.

But the invention and development of integrated circuits brought about changed conditions in the industry. As the pioneer of the integrated circuit, Fairchild sensed little need for change. Indeed, from the time of their defection from Shockley, Fairchild's founders sensed that they were on the right path of semiconductor development. Their approach to technological change was to do more of what they were doing and to figure out how to do it better. The development of the mesa transistor and the planar process at Fairchild quickened their arrival at the next major milestone in the industry, necessitating no fundamental change within their organization or their approach to the technology and the industry. Rather, Fairchild forced change on its competitors.

Both Sprague and Motorola tried to master integrated circuit technology, and both encountered formidable problems. The record is brief but suggests that both Sprague and Motorola found that producing an integrated circuit required far more tacit knowledge than had been required with prior technological advances. Furthermore, there were many interrelated technological advances involved in integrating circuits, all of which had to be mastered. Although perhaps some of the requisite knowledge could be purchased in disembodied or embodied form, it appears that much could not, and without complete mastery of all the interrelated aspects of integrated circuit technology, the firms had difficulty.

Another reason for the greater difficulties Sprague, Motorola, and Shockley encountered in changing over time was that their sources of information were becoming increasingly obsolete. All but Fairchild were connected to Bell Labs, RCA, and other eastern electronics firms that increasingly were not at the technological frontier of the industry. After about 1953 or 1954, Bell Labs was no longer at the technological frontier owing to its comparatively limited application of semiconductors in the Bell system, especially *vis-à-vis* miniaturization. Continued reliance on Bell and other eastern firms attenuated the knowledge Sprague, Motorola, and Shockley received about technical and market-related developments, which appears to have handicapped them. Had they been better connected to firms at the technological frontier, perhaps they would have been able to purchase the tacit knowledge they needed to keep up with developments in integrated circuits.

Despite its acknowledged difficulties, Motorola was eventually able to master integrated circuit technology and prosper, whereas Sprague was not (Shockley did not try). A definitive explanation for these outcomes is impossible, but the record is suggestive. One possible explanation is that Motorola committed early to a broad R&D program, whereas by the time Sprague realized the importance of such a commitment it was too late. For example, at the time that John Sprague joined the firm, the firm had done little research on many of the basic processes fundamental to monolithic chip production (specifically Sprague had done little on diffusion, mesa transistors, and planar technology). Although Sprague did increase its R&D expenditures substantially in the integrated circuit era, it never seemed to generate enough sales to yield sufficient profits to cover its R&D expenditures. In contrast, early on Motorola recognized the need for a sufficiently large sales base to be able to support the broad-based R&D it thought necessary to keep up with technical advances. It chose to produce a much wider range of semiconductor devices than required to service its own needs and to market its full line aggressively. This strategy provided considerable profits and resources to support R&D in areas that proved to be critical in the manufacture of integrated circuits. Fairchild, of course, committed early to a very broad R&D program that was key to its success. Thus, early commitments may have played an important role in the success of Fairchild and ultimately Motorola and in limiting the ability of Sprague to change.

Neither Fairchild nor Motorola, though, appear to have made their commitments to preempt rivals. Fairchild's broad R&D program was driven by its emphasis on mastering production problems and arriving at consistency of product and process – factors that account for both its initial and continued successes. As Robert Noyce later argued, Fairchild's early commitment set it on a trajectory that led to the integrated circuit. This trajectory was so fecund and the firm's commitment was so extensive that Fairchild later could not change course (away from the bipolar elements of their integrated circuits and toward the MOS design); hence Noyce, Moore, and Grove found it easier to leave Fairchild and establish Intel than to change Fairchild. Motorola's strategy for change was aimed internally, not for any preemptive purposes; it sought to rationalize its own R&D efforts, which required a larger sales base than its own needs could generate. The importance of having sufficient sales to justify a large R&D program is consistent with the models of Klepper (1996), Cohen and Klepper (1996), and Sutton (1998). In these models, firms need to have a large enough output over which to apply their innovations in order to generate sufficient profits to cover the costs of their R&D. This imperative limits the number of firms that ultimately can survive and maintain a broad R&D program, making early commitment particularly important for long-term survival.

## Core capabilities

If a firm's entry and continued profitability in an industry are conditioned by such intangibles as know-how, access to scientific and engineering networks, and other forms of tacit knowledge, can we think of these things joining with the past actions of firms to constitute something called "core capabilities"? Our histories speak, at least modestly, to this question. Each of the firms had intangible assets, in the form of distinctive expertise and connections, which they exploited in choosing their products and the problems on which they worked. The histories suggest that these intangible assets were beneficial but were not generally sufficient to provide enduring profits. Sprague, for example, was able to use its prior experiences initially to earn substantial profits in semiconductors, but eventually its intangible assets proved to limit its ability to adapt. Fairchild's initial intangible assets also proved initially to be extraordinarily valuable, but as the firm grew its top management's efforts to coordinate R&D and production faded and Fairchild declined. Only Motorola was able to sustain its success. Thus, consistent with the dynamic capabilities theory, the most important capabilities are ones that enable a firm to adapt to technological and market change over time, and only Motorola appears to have possessed these capabilities.

What explains Motorola's "dynamic capabilities" (Teece et al., 1997) or "evolutionary learning capability" (Fujimoto, 1999)? The history of Motorola speaks only softly to this question and sometimes with mixed messages. We offer two of them here in an attempt to identify the key factors that shape the dynamic capabilities of firms. One message centers on the skill of managers in coordinating R&D, production, and marketing. Motorola's managers appear to have been quick to observe changes in the environment and were willing to change their firm's course when it was deemed necessary to survive in such a changed environment. We have already underscored the importance of Motorola's size and scope in helping to make such change possible. Yet another message, not necessarily contradictory to the first, and consistent with an important role for preexisting knowledge and experience in affecting expectations (Cohen and Levinthal, 1994), is that Motorola's strong position and technological leadership in the upstream market for semiconductors – mobile telecommunications, consumer electronics, etc. – put it in an excellent position to monitor, forecast, and adapt to change in the market for semiconductors. Other firms in the industry, of course, were fully comparable to Motorola in this respect. Our histories do not encompass those firms, however, and thus our reflections on dynamic capabilities remain limited at best.

### Diversity

The four semiconductor firms we examined developed and produced different sets of products and employed different manufacturing methods. They also often conducted R&D on different facets of semiconductor technology, and, even when their R&D efforts were dedicated to the same goals, they often adopted different approaches. While the four firms surely differentiated themselves to reap profit, the record suggests that the differences across these firms also accelerated the pace of technological change in the semiconductor industry and, in the process, yielded social benefits.

Different forms of diversity confer different kinds of social benefits. At the most obvious level is the diversity that stems from firms specializing in different products for buyers with different needs and tastes. Clearly, the more options that can be offered to such buyers, the greater their overall welfare. Diversity can even be beneficial when firms produce competing variants of the same product. Even if only one is ultimately selected, the more variants the better the expected quality of the winner. But, in many instances, there is also a borrowing of features from the losers which improve further the selected winner. Similar arguments apply to R&D. When firms work on competing approaches to solving the same technical problem, it is reasonable to conjecture that the more approaches explored, the better the quality of the outcome (Nelson, 1982). When firms work on different problems, advancing distinct facets of a technology, they can build upon one another's findings as long as the requisite information flows across firms, yielding complementarities that accelerate the pace of technical advance (Holbrook, 1995).

The kind of diversity associated with firm specialization was evident from the outset of the semiconductor industry. The four firms began by producing different products based on different materials and production methods that serviced different types of customers. Upon entry Sprague pursued germanium transistors, worked on improving production processes such as materials refining and crystal growing, and, on the basis of Philco's patent, developed high-frequency transistors for computer makers. Motorola entered with the objective of manufacturing silicon devices and soon arrived at the design of new products for a broad range of applications, including power rectifiers for the automotive and other industries and transistors for audio applications and mobile communications. Though Motorola also contributed to production process development, its most significant contribution in the early phase of the industry was in widening the scope of silicon transistors in the market. Fairchild's founders made the production of practical silicon devices its highest priority and devoted their principal efforts to reducing uncertainty and variability in every step of the manufacturing process. Pursuing this strategy led to their focus on the mesa transistor and the invention of the planar process, which when pushed to this approach's ultimate logic led to the monolithic idea – the integrated circuit. Shockley directed all his organization's efforts to the development of novel devices in which he could claim authorship.

The firms not only specialized but also competed, both by producing variants of the same product and attempting to address the same technical challenges in different ways in their R&D, largely reflecting their distinctive skills and expertise. Although this type of diversity did not address different customer needs and eventually was winnowed out through competition, it nonetheless also seems to have contributed to social welfare. In some cases, the firms developed complementary innovations, which collectively contributed to greater advance than any one firm alone was capable of achieving. We suspect as well that by having multiple firms work on the same problem it also raised the chances of any particular type of advance being realized. Consider, for example, one of the most important advances achieved in the early years of the industry, the miniaturization of circuits.

The impetus to miniaturize electronic circuits came from the armed services. Each branch thought reductions in size and energy consumption were imperative to advancing its weapons systems and thus increasing national security, a major concern throughout the Cold War. To the degree that firms in the incipient semiconductor industry targeted military markets for their products and derived R&D funds via contracts from the military services, miniaturization modulated their strategy and firm behavior, at least in part. But not all firms solely targeted military markets. This alone ensured diversity of approaches to miniaturization. Moreover, even the firms that worked for the military tended to pursue different approaches to miniaturization, reflecting that each service ran its own miniaturization program and each service's R&D program managers hedged their bets by pursuing a range of approaches to miniaturization. Thus, in spite of the pursuit of a common objective, diversity was the order of the day.

Conditioned as they were to military markets, both Motorola and Sprague pursued hybrid circuit R&D, which involved mounting discrete transistors on ceramic substrates on which printed circuits and passive components had been deposited. This approach exploited both firms' existing skills in materials and processes, but the two firms pursued very different approaches to the realization of hybrid circuits, owing especially to their very different "initial conditions" at the time of entry in the semiconductor industry. Motorola possessed far greater upstream knowledge of circuits given that it was the dominant manufacturer of mobile communications equipment. It approached miniaturized hybrid circuits from a very pragmatic position, reflecting a realistic assessment of its capabilities and its R&D leader's philosophy ("Our motto has been *Profit* first, then progress of the revolutionary kind."). Consequently, its initial approach was to incorporate discrete transistors, which it had begun to make, into standardized modules based on printed circuits (a technology that Motorola had mastered in high-volume production). But Motorola's experience with its equipment in the field also led it to put a premium on ruggedness in its circuits, thus conditioning how it approached component protection, insertion, and soldering in printed circuit boards. Hedging its bets, Motorola also simultaneously pursued a less conservative miniaturization research program in thin film circuits, which sought to deposit both passive and active circuit elements on a substrate in thin layers. Like Motorola, Sprague pursued the conservative technology of hybrid circuits owing to its experience as a passive circuit element supplier to the military. This experience conditioned its leaders to think of electronic circuits as collections of distinct elements that were assembled into a whole rather than as something whose elements could be integrated. It placed far less emphasis on ruggedness, and it did not pursue as aggressively the building-block approach inherent in Motorola's pursuit of modularity.

Shockley exhibited no interest whatsoever in miniaturization.[6] Certainly Shockley was aware of military wants and needs. He had been, after all, a member of the Pentagon's Research and Development Board, and once he decided to establish his own company, he traded heavily on his connections to military R&D organizations. But catering to the military did not provide Shockley with enough room to pursue the kinds of novel innovations that he perceived as his comparative advantage and that would satisfy his ego.

Fairchild's "traitorous eight," as the history shows quite clearly, sought to get a product out the door as soon as possible, a product that would exhibit consistency of performance characteristics, something that its principal customer (initially the military services) also valued. Fairchild focused on transistor manufacture, especially mastery of processes that determined quality, reliability, and uniformity of product. When pushed to its logical extreme, the company's invention of the planar process of making silicon diffused mesa transistors led one of its founders, Robert Noyce, to ask why so much time was devoted to cutting transistors out of a silicon slab and then packing them individually only for them to be laboriously soldered into circuits when they could be simply wired together with other photolithographically deposited circuit elements (e.g., resistors and capacitors) to achieve an integrated circuit. Without its internal development of great skill and know-how in diffusion methods (whose lineage goes back through Shockley Laboratories to Bell Labs) and especially in oxide masking techniques, Fairchild could not have succeeded in realizing the idea of the integrated circuit.

Although not explicitly discussed in the firm histories, Texas Instrument's efforts in the nascent semiconductor industry suggest some additional observations about the role of diversity. TI is universally credited with the production of the first silicon junction transistor, which it first publicly demonstrated in May 1954. The key to TI's success in this endeavor stemmed in large measure from the work of Gordon Teal, a former Bell Labs researcher whose ideas about producing pure, single-crystal semiconductor materials were rejected for a long time within Bell Labs (including by the leader of Bell Labs' semiconductor research program, William Shockley). Thus constraints imposed by Bell Labs' managers became opportunities for differentiation at TI. Given that TI's major market strategy was to meet military demand, its semiconductor research program was also heavily influenced by the services' goal of miniaturization. This objective manifested in TI's recruitment of Jack Kilby from a small electronics firm located in Milwaukee, where he had worked on hybrid circuits. He was assigned specifically to work on the miniaturization problem; disenchanted with hybrids, his solution was the integrated circuit. Kilby realized in practice his ideas for integration before Noyce did at Fairchild, although, following a long, bruising patent fight, the two are almost universally regarded as co-inventors of the integrated circuit. Noyce and Fairchild were in a far better position to manufacture integrated circuits with superior methods because of Fairchild's earlier development of and commitment to the mesa transistor and the planar process.[7]

The two firms' routes to the integrated circuit differed significantly. These differences mattered and even conditioned the two firms' behavior after their respective patent documents became known to each other, owing both to the initial conditions that prevailed at the time of the firms' entry and to their different paths pursued following entry. For example, the two firms approached the packaging of their integrated circuits in fundamentally different ways, stemming in part from differences in the fabrication of the chips themselves. Though the two firms arrived at, loosely speaking, the same spot, their trajectories carried them in different directions very soon after their brush with one another.

The achievement of miniaturization via the integrated circuit suggests how diversity characterized by competing approaches to the same goal can contribute to technical advance. The history of miniaturization also illustrates how diversity contributed to technical advance by making available different but complementary – rather than competing – technologies. This was clearly observed in the unintended contribution to the integrated circuit made by Sprague and Motorola, which ironically grew out of their failed attempts to achieve miniaturization through hybrid circuit development. Most notably, Sprague's Kurt Lehovec's patent covering diode isolation of conjoined transistors was critical to successful integration of active elements on a semiconductor monolith. Every firm making monolithic ICs used Lehovec's patent, which Sprague widely licensed. It was, however, the product of Lehovec's individual talents as an inventor and researcher rather than the result of specific organizational expertise at Sprague. Motorola's substantial experience with printed circuit technology definitely fed back into the industry's drive toward the monolithic approach in that it had mastered the photodeposition of thin metallic layers on substrates. These techniques were vital in connecting the circuit elements laid down on a single slab of silicon.

Thus, firms such as Fairchild and TI that devoted their miniaturization efforts to monolithic circuits contributed different kinds of innovations, and others such as Sprague and Motorola that worked on other approaches were also able to contribute to the monolithic approach. Diverse approaches to semiconductor product design outside the miniaturization project similarly fueled a number of other technological advances in the industry that fed back into the monolithic approach. Most notable among these approaches is the MOS (metal-oxide-silicon) transistor, which gave the industry the "gate" that is now fundamental to the microprocessor (Bassett, 1998). As one research manager at Bell Labs commented on his organization's huge giveaway of the transistor and the formalized knowledge that lay behind it, the opportunities for semiconductor electronics were far, far greater than Bell Labs and the Bell system could reasonably fully exploit. Diversity ensured that much of the opportunity space presented by the transistor's invention was both fully explored and aggressively exploited.

While the different backgrounds of the firms led them to make different choices, which appear to have enhanced social welfare in a number of ways, it is important to recognize how various features of the environment supported or even nurtured their diversity. One key feature of the environment supporting the industry's diversity was uncertainty regarding the most fruitful directions for advancing product and process technology. The environment was also characterized by a rapid evolution and differentiation of user needs as well as uncertainty regarding those needs and associated applications. Government also played a direct role in supporting the semiconductor industry's diversity, particularly through procurement policies that represented a series of different and sometimes competing bets on everything ranging from the most fundamental features of the technology to specific applications.

Key features of the environment also enabled those differences to contribute to social welfare. It almost goes without saying that a system of for-profit market capitalism that selects superior products, processes and, in turn, firms, was key to the realization of the impact of diversity on technical advance. Furthermore, the technical advances achieved in the semiconductor industry from the joining of the knowledge emerging from different firms' R&D efforts could only be realized in an environment supporting a relatively unencumbered flow of information across firms. The miniaturization project, for example, was characterized by enormous information flows across firms and suppliers. Military R&D program officers often played critical roles in spreading information, seeking as they did to make the most of their hedged bets. Licensing, publications, and professional society conferences devoted to miniaturization also insured the flow of information about the varied approaches to miniaturization. More generally, antitrust and intellectual property policies that encouraged the liberal licensing of technology (illustrated most saliently by AT&T's liberal licensing of the fundamental transistor technology) were also essential to the rich flow of information. Intellectual property policy also did not impede knowledge outflows that resulted from the formation of spin-offs and the mobility of personnel.[8] Indeed, Fairchild itself epitomized the importance of an easy flow of information to the realization of the benefits of diversity. The firm's contributions clearly depended on the ability of frustrated employees with a different vision from their employer's to start their own firm and subsequently develop innovative products and manufacturing methods that greatly enhanced social welfare.

## Implications for Strategy and Policy

The foregoing case studies, although clearly limited, suggest important differences across firms. Two broad differences appear to have mattered, particularly for the performance of individual firms and, to a more limited extent, for the industry as a whole. First, firms differed considerably in their technological goals. Even when different firms' goals corresponded, they pursued those goals in significantly different ways. These differences appear clearly in the R&D activities of the firms, and they accrued over time. Second – and important for individual firm performance but perhaps less significant for the industry – firms differed in the ability of their top managers to integrate the activities and information flows across the different functional areas of R&D, manufacturing, and sales.

The cases suggest that the sources of these differences stemmed from the pre-entry and early post-entry experiences of the firms (i.e., Motorola and Sprague) or their principals (i.e., at Shockley and Fairchild). These experiences had lasting effects on both what firms perceived to be worth doing and on their ability to do it. They included each firm's prior development and application of specific technologies; their established and often geographically proximate networks of information from rivals, other firms (e.g., AT&T), and buyers (including government); and their leaders' or founders' management practices and related perceptions of the knowledge required to succeed and how that knowledge should be marshaled.

The effects of these experiences endured during the period we examined not because the firms did not see the need for change, but because, when a need for change was recognized, as in the case of Sprague, they found change difficult. Constraints on change stemmed in part from an inability to secure the necessary kind of expertise and to integrate it across functions sufficiently rapidly to remain at the technological frontier. This is especially evident in the drive toward miniaturization that blossomed in the invention of the integrated circuit. Motorola stands as the singular case of successful change. That success probably stemmed from its technological and financial ability and willingness to place a broad range of early bets in the form of a diverse range of R&D activities, as well as from its knowledge of prospective applications that came from its upstream integration into end-user markets. Motorola gained the expertise to move quickly as the market for integrated circuits took off; its internal demand and strong links to government buyers allowed it to dedicate sufficient resources to achieve its objectives and also to update dynamically its bets on the technology's future applications.

We are struck in these cases by the relative absence of the sort of decision-making process, commonly assumed by economists, that would lead firms to converge rapidly to some similar set of R&D and production activities. The firms we studied seldom, if ever, deliberated over a range of technological and business options and then selected a particular path. Even when they were somewhat deliberative, they were typically too constrained by past events and existing capabilities to depart substantially from past practice. In our firms' decision-making, we see relatively little attention dedicated to monitoring – no less matching or preempting – competitors. The firms were too focused on their own challenges to look up. Thus, the nature of their decision-making limited convergence in their R&D and production.

Although a study of four firms in a single industry considerably limits what can be inferred for business strategy and public policy, the experience of Sprague, Motorola, Shockley, and Fairchild and the semiconductor industry provide some narrow basis for informed speculation. Our study suggests that differences across the four firms affected their individual performance and survival. For example, Shockley's belief that a strong patent position was key to success, and his associated inattention to the market and production, seemed to have doomed him. Sprague's late embrace of integrated circuit technology and weak links to key information sources as the technology evolved undermined its long-run viability. Fairchild, in contrast, arrived on the scene with the right configuration of technical expertise and management practices. This happy combination of scientific and technical knowledge, engineering skills, and organizational instincts about the need for cross-functional integration yielded early dramatic success – at least for a short period. As both its manufacturing and research organizations built their own distinctive capabilities and cultures, Fairchild gradually lost its distinctive ability to integrate manufacturing and R&D. The firm also lacked the ability to retain key personnel as the external demand for their individual capabilities lured them away. Motorola's deep experience in government and private sector applications of the electronics technology positioned it well.

To say that firm differences mattered, and even arrive at some coarse understanding of what firms in this industry needed to know or have in order to succeed does not, however, yield clear prescriptions for strategy and business policy. Our analysis is necessarily *ex post*; we know things that top management did not and could not readily discern *ex ante* due to the enormous uncertainties and complexity that surrounded the rapidly evolving technology of semiconductors, their applications, and the nature and strength of final demand. Given *ex ante* uncertainty, one would then be tempted to believe in the wisdom of Motorola's nurturing of what we might now call "dynamic capabilities," that is, the ability to learn and change. Even that prescription is too glib and benefits unduly from our knowledge of how things turned out. Motorola put those pieces in place largely because it already spanned a broad range of functional areas, and possessed strong links across R&D, manufacturing, and the end-product markets. So, a bit like Fairchild early on, its ability to succeed was at least partly conditioned by what it brought to the party, that is, what it was doing prior to the emergence of the semiconductor industry; in other words, luck mattered.

In light of *ex ante* uncertainty, perhaps the only prescriptions one can make are that firms should both try to understand where an industry is going and develop an objective understanding of their own capabilities as well as the constraints on changing those capabilities. But this prescription is rather too facile as well if one accepts the possibility that it is actually difficult to do any of those things, even to understand the firm's own capabilities. If top management could do these things, though, it is not even clear that the firm should exploit its core competencies or try to change them. The best course of action may be to recognize limits and act accordingly. Arguably, this is one way to interpret what Noyce, Moore, and Grove did when they left Fairchild to form Intel, and what Intel did subsequently when it exited from the memory chip market decades later (cf. Burgelman, 1994). Indeed, Sprague and Shockley's benefactor, Beckman, would have likely profited from early exits.

Although mainly nihilistic implications for business strategy emerge from our limited study, its implications for public policy are a bit more constructive. It appears that, at least in the formative stage of a technologically turbulent and advancing industry, the industry as a whole benefited from the differences that existed across firms, particularly differences in their R&D activities. We have highlighted how differences in *ex ante* and early post-entry experiences of firms and their principals conditioned these differences in R&D activities. Rivalry among the technical units of the various service branches of the U.S. military and the different needs of other customers in the market for electronic components also played roles in creating diversity in technological approaches and capabilities. Via licensing and less formal channels, Motorola, for example, benefited from the early efforts of Sprague. Fairchild of course benefited from the spillover of technical know-how from Shockley, and all the firms of course benefited from the work of Shockley and his colleagues while they were at Bell Labs. More generally, the dominant technology of integrated circuits that eventually emerged embodied the findings of the broad range of firms that worked on miniaturization – beyond the four that we examined, including firms that survived as well as those that exited. In the early semiconductor industry, the existence of multiple firms distinguished by their capabilities and orientations enhanced the rate of technical advance of the industry as a whole.

This one case would suggest that, at least in the case of emergent or technologically active industries, government should consider adopting policies that foster diversity. Examples of such might include antitrust policies that protect entry, subsidies to startups, or support of university or government research that might directly spawn or support a broad range of diverse R&D activity within an industry. In the case of the semiconductor industry, policies such as the forced licensing of AT&T's transistor technology and multiple military service pursuit of miniaturization, as well as tolerance for employee mobility across competitors, had this effect. More generally, there is no reason to believe that, in the absence of these policies, the rate of technical advance achieved in the semiconductor industry would have been as great.

## Acknowledgement

We thank the US Small Business Administration for financial support.

## Notes

1  Less condensed histories are contained in a longer version of the paper presented at the conference on the evolution of firm capabilities at Dartmouth, September 1999. This version of the paper is available from the authors.
2  In 1967 Motorola's share of the IC market was estimated at 12 percent, roughly a third of Fairchild's, and half of TI's (Tilton, 1971: 66).
3  According to a scientist who later worked for him, Shockley said that "he had seen his name often enough in *Physical Review*; he now wanted to see it in the headlines of the *Wall Street Journal*" (Queisser, 1988: 82).
4  Moore, interview with D. Holbrook (23 February 1994): "[M]y inclination was to give the people that were doing [research] a fair amount of flexibility, thinking they knew best."
5  This was tallied from Fairchild Progress Reports between January 1, 1960, and November 1, 1966. SA 88–095.
6  Perhaps this reflected a kind of mindset that pervaded his former employer, Bell Laboratories. Although Bell Labs responded to the needs of the military in many different ways, its leaders demonstrated little interest in what later became known as integration. They seem to have been content with discrete circuit components which could be substituted for vacuum tubes in their vast telephone switching network. In making this substitution of transistors for vacuum tubes, Bell Labs and its AT&T cousin Western Electric put a premium on reliability and performance rather than on saving space and energy; the Bell system had already amortized its vast telephone exchanges and repeater stations, and it had incorporated energy costs into its rate base.
7  As Noyce later said, "We were in a position at Fairchild where we had, because of the particular way we had decided to make transistors by leaving an oxide layer on top of them, one more element than everybody else did to built into the package to make the integrated circuit, and that happened to be the one that worked' (Braun and MacDonald, 1982: 89).
8  Mowery and Nelson (1999: 380) support this point when they state, "In semiconductors, a combination of historical accident and US government policy resulted in a relatively weak intellectual property rights environment for most of the first three decades of the US industry's development. This environment was conducive to high levels of cross-licensing and entry by new firms, which contributed to rapid growth and innovation."

# References

Ackerman, C. Interview with Jack Saddler. Motorola, Inc. Corporate Archives, Motorola Museum of Electronics: Schamburg, IL; 9–10.

Allison, G. 1971. *Essence of Decision*. Little, Brown: Boston. MA.

Andrews, K. R. 1971. *The Concept of Corporate Strategy*. Dow–Jones Irwin: Homewood, IL.

AT&T Archives. 1951. Transistor symposium, list of guests. September 17, 1951, 11|04 02, p. 10.

Barney, J. B. 1994. Beyond individual metaphors in understanding how firms behave: a comment on game theory and prospect theory models of firm behavior. In *Fundamental Issues in Strategy*, Rumelt, R. P. Schendel, D. E. Teece, D. J. (eds). Harvard Business School. Press: Boston, MA; 55–69.

Bassett, R. K. 1998. New technology, new people, new organizations: the rise of the MOS transistor, 1945–1975. Ph.D. dissertation, Princeton University.

Baxter, III, J. P. 1946. *Scientists Against Time*. Little, Brown: Boston, MA.

Biesle, S. C. 1959. Memo to H. Schuler, January 23, Stanford University Special Collections, Palo Alto, CA: SA 90–117: 13/8.

Braun, E. and MacDonald, S. 1982. *Revolution in Miniature: The History and Impact of Semiconductor Electronics*. 2nd edn, Cambridge University Press: Cambridge, UK.

Burgelman, R. A. 1994. Fading memories: a process theory of strategic business exit in dynamic environments. *Administrative Science Quarterly* 39: 24–56.

*Business Week* 1962. Business Week, May 5, p. 116.

Caves, R. E. 1998. Industrial organization and new findings on the turnover and mobility of firms. *Journal of Economic Literature* 36(4): 1947–1982.

Chandler, A. D. Jr. 1962. *Strategy and Structure: Chapters in the History of the Industrial Enterprise*. MIT Press: Cambridge, MA.

Cohen, W. M. and Klepper, S. 1992. The anatomy of industry R&D distributions. *American Economic Review* 82: 773–788.

Cohen, W. M. and Klepper, S. 1996. A reprise of size and R&D. *Economic Journal* 106(437): 925–951.

Cohen, W. M. and Levinthal, D. A. 1990. Absorptive capacity: a new perspective on learning and innovation. *Administrative Science Quarterly* 35: 128–152.

Cohen, W. M. and Levinthal, D. A. 1994. Fortune favors the prepared firm. *Management Science* 40: 227–251.

Cohen, W. M. and Malerba, F. 1994. Is the tendency to variation a chief cause of progress? Mimeo, Carnegie Mellon University.

DaCosta, H. Interview with Jack Saddler. Motorola Museum of Electronics: Schamburg, IL; pp. 16, 36.

Dimmick, W. F. 1959. Memo to William Shockley, April 1, 1959, Stanford University Special Collections, Palo Alto, CA, SA 90–117, 14/5.

Fujimoto, T. 1999. *The Evolution of a Manufacturing System at Toyota*. Oxford University Press: New York.

Geroski, P. A. 1995. What do we know about entry? *International Journal of Industrial Organization* 13(4): 421–440.

Ghemawat, P. 1991. *Commitment, the Dynamic of Strategy*. Free Press: New York.

Golding, A. 1971. The semiconductor industry in Britain and the United States: a case study in innovation, growth and the diffusion of technology. D.Phil. dissertation, University of Sussex.

Griliches, Z. 1991. The search for R&D spillovers. NBER, working paper no. 3768.

Hoddeson, L. 1977. The roots of solid-state research at Bell Labs. *Physics Today* 30(3): 23–30.

Hoddeson, L. 1981. The discovery of the point-contact transistor. *Historical Studies in the Physical Sciences* 12(1): 41–76.

Hogan, O. L. 1961. Final draft of C. L. Hogan's speech. Motorola, Inc. Corporate Archives, Motorola Museum of Electronics: Schamburg, IL; p. 3.

Holbrook, D. 1995. Government support of the semiconductor industry: diverse approaches and information flows. *Business and Economic History* 24(2): 133–168.

Holbrook, D. 1999. Technical diversity and technological change in the American semiconductor industry, 1952–1965. Ph.D. dissertation, Carnegie Mellon University.

Holmstrom, B. R. and Tirole, J. 1989. The theory of the firm. In *Handbook of Industrial Organization*, Schmalensee R., Willig, R. D. (eds). North-Holland: Amsterdam; 63–133.

Iansiti, M. 1998. *Technology Integration*. Harvard Business School Press: Boston, MA.

Jensen, J. B. and McGuckin, R. H. 1997. Firm performance and evolution: empirical regularities in the US microdata. *Industrial and Corporate Change* 6(1): 25–47.

Kleiman, H. 1966. The integrated circuit: a case study of product innovation in the electronics industry. DBA dissertation, George Washington University.

Klepper, S. 1996. Entry, exit, growth, and innovation over the product life cycle. *American Economic Review* 86(3): 562–583.

Leonard-Barton, D. 1994. Core capabilities and core rigidities: a paradox in managing new product development. *Strategic Management Journal*, Summer Special Issue 13: 111–125.

Levin, R. C. and Reiss, P. C. 1984. Tests of a Schumpeterian model of R&D and market structure. In *R&D, Patents and Productivity*, Griliches, Z (ed). University of Chicago Press for the NBER: Chicago, IL; 175–202.

Levitt, B. and March, J. G. 1988. Organizational learning. *Annual Review of Sociology* 14: 319–340.

Malone, M. 1985. *The Big Score: The Billion Dollar Story of Silicon Valley*. Doubleday: Garden City, NJ.

Miller, B. 1962. Motorola investigates compatible circuits. *Aviation Week* 76(2): 85–95.

Motorola, Inc. 1960. Annual Report, Motorola, Inc. Corporate Archives, Motorola Museum of Electronics: Schamburg, IL.

Mowery, D. C. and Nelson, R. R. 1999. Explaining industrial leadership. In *Sources of Industrial Leadership*, Mowery, DC, Nelson, RR (eds). Cambridge University Press: Cambridge, MA; 359–382.

Mueller, D. C. 1986. *Profits in the Long Run*. Cambridge University Press: Cambridge, UK.

Nelson, R. R. 1982. The role of knowledge in R&D efficiency. *Quarterly Journal of Economics* 97: 453–470.

Nelson, R. R. 1991. Why do firms differ, and how does it matter? *Strategic Management Journal*, Winter Special Issue 12: 61–74.

Nelson, R. R. and Winter, S. G. 1982. *An Evolutionary Theory of Economic Change*. Harvard University Press: Cambridge, MA.

Noble, D. 1954. Familiar tune, familiar theme. *Motorola Engineering Bulletin* 2(4): 4.

Noble, D. 1964. Memo, Daniel Noble to Mark Harry Petrakis. (Motorola, Inc. Corporate Archives, Motorola Museum of Electronics: Schaumburg, IL; Box 7B, Folder 17, June 22, 1964), 6–8, 10.

Noble, D. 1974. Memo from Daniel E. Noble on "History of Motorola in Phoenix. (Motorola, Inc. Corporate Archives, Motorola Museum of Electronics: Schaumburg, IL.; Box 7B, Folder 17, February 7, 1974) 1–3.

Noble, D. 1977. Some of my Motorola activities: personal reference notes for Motorola archives. (Motorola, Inc. Corporate Archives, Motorola Museum of Electronics: Schaumburg, IL; Box 7, Folder 38, August 15, 1977), pp. 2, 18.

Noyce, R. 1977. Microelectronics. *Scientific American* 237(3): 63–69.

Petrakis, H. M. 1991. *The Founder's Touch: The Life of Paul Galvin of Motorola.* 3rd edn, J. G. Ferguson Publishing, Motorola University Press: Chicago, IL.

Porter, M. E. 1980. *Competitive Strategy: Techniques for Analyzing Industries and Competitors.* Free Press: New York.

Prahalad, C. K. and Hamel, G. 1990. The core competences of the corporation. *Harvard Business Review* 68(3): 79–91.

Queisser, H. 1988. *The Conquest of the Microchip: Science and Business in the Silicon Age.* (transl. Crawford-Burkhardt, D. Harvard University Press: Cambridge, MA: 82–84.

Ravenscraft, D. J. 1983. Structure-profit relationships at the line of business and industry level. *Review of Economics and Statistics* 65: 22–31.

Riordan, M. and Hoddeson, L. 1997. *Crystal Fire: The Birth of the Information Age.* W. W. Norton: New York.

Rumelt, R. P. 1991. How much does industry matter? *Strategic Management Journal* 12(3): 167–185.

Rumelt, R. P., Schendel, D. E., and Teece, D. J. (eds). 1994. *Fundamental Issues in Strategy.* Harvard Business School Press: Boston, MA.

Schmalensee, R. 1985. Do markets matter much? *American Economics Review* 75: 341–351.

Shockley, W. 1950. *Electrons and Holes in Semiconductors, with Applications to Transistor Electronics* (reprinted 1976). Robert E. Krieger: New York.

Shockley, W. 1955. Letter to M. J. Kelly (8 September 1955) Stanford University Special Collections, Palo Alto, CA: SA 90–117, 13/13.

Shockley, W. 1956. Letter to Mr. Francis Donaldson (28 November 1956) Stanford University Special Collections, Palo Alto, CA: SA 90–117, 13/12.

Shockley, W. 1957a. Memo to Duryea, Beckman Instruments (1 March 1957) Stanford University Special Collections. Palo Alto, CA: SA 90–117, 14/8.

Shockley, W. 1957b. Memo "Senior staff, May 1957" SA 90–117, 14/8.

Shockley, W. 1958. Letter to S. Clark Beise (9 July 1958) Stanford University Special Collections, Palo Alto, CA: SA 90–117, 13/8.

Shockley, W. 1976. The path to the conception of the junction transistor. *IEEE Transactions on Electron Devices*, EN-23(7): 597–620.

Sprague Electric Annual Reports. 1948–1978. Special collections, Harvard Graduate School of Business, Boston, MA.

Sprague, J. L. 1993. *Revitalizing U.S. Electronics: Lessons from Japan.* Butterworth-Heinemann: Boston, MA.

Sutton, J. 1998. *Technology and Market Structure.* MIT Press: Cambridge, MA.

Taylor, W. 1985. Interview by David Grayson Allen, (Motorola, Inc. Corporate Archives Motorola Museum of Electronics: Schaumburg, IL; January, 22, 1985) 16–18, 24, 30, 37.

Teece, D., Pisano, G., and Shuen, A. 1997. Dynamic capabilities and strategic management. *Strategic Management Journal* 18(7): 509–533.

Tilton, J. 1971. *International Diffusion of Technologies: The Case of Semiconductors.* Brookings Institution: Washington, DC.

Weisz, W. 1985. Interview by David Grayson Allen. Motorola, Inc. Corporate Archives, Motorola Museum of Electronics: Schaumburg, IL; February 26, 1985 pp. 8–19.

Welty, J. 1989. Interview by Mark Harry Petrakis. Motorola, Inc. Corporate Archives, Motorola Museum of Electronics: Schaumburg, IL; June 13, 1989, p. 9.

Winter, S. G. 1988. On Coase, competence, and the corporation. *Journal of Law, Economics, and Organization* 4: 163–180.

Wolff, M. F. 1976. The genesis of the integrated circuit. *IEEE Spectrum* August: 45–53.

# CHAPTER FOUR

# Superstores and the Evolution of Firm Capabilities in American Bookselling

## Daniel M. G. Raff

### Introduction

Our images of the colonial America usually involve a relatively primitive economy with relatively low levels of per capita income, no factories and generally low levels of technology in the cities and towns, and much of the population engaged, in isolated places and for long and terribly demanding hours, in agriculture. Yet the colonists were predominantly people of the word, and there was a flourishing trade in publishing and bookselling from a very early date (Tebbel, 1972). The book trade has been with us ever since.

The distribution part of the industry has since undergone tremendous change, not least in the latter decades of the twentieth century. It was in that period that chain stores became a dominant force in retail bookselling. This proceeded in two phases. During the first, the stores of the chain companies were of roughly the same size as those of the independents. The principal nonorganizational difference between the two was locational: the independents were predominantly sited in central business districts and the shopping streets of towns, while the chain stores were predominantly to be found in suburban and regional malls. In the second phase, the chain stores became an order of magnitude larger than the modal independent (on a wide variety of metrics) and began to seem in the breadth of their merchandising more like libraries than shops.

The subject of this paper is the second of these transitions: the emergence of the so-called superstores. The phenomenon is striking. In 1975, there were no bookstores with anything like these characteristics anywhere in the United States outside of a few large cities and at most a handful of university towns. At the close of the century, they are a commonplace of the urban and suburban landscape. The natural interest of the book-selling business to academics entirely aside, one might reasonably wonder when, how, and why this came about. This interest is only heightened by the diffusion in other lines of retail trade of apparently similar formats (generically known as category-killers). This paper lays out the history in books, with a focus on the evolution of the capabilities required to sustain the new formats and operations.

The paper takes the form of a clinical study. There are no formal hypotheses and there are certainly no formal tests. Rather, the paper follows the early lifecourses of the only two firms that mattered quantitatively and attempts to expose, in an intellectually disciplined way, the opportunities which were recognized, the challenges which then presented themselves, and the responses as they evolved. This may seem to represent more modest progress in knowledge than the usual positivist empirical work puts on offer. But the approach exposes issues and relationships which are obscure in the standard statistical data and may be worthy of thought.

The heart of the paper is narrative, but narratives always have ideas in the background. The ideas in the background here are those of the resource-based view of the firm (Wernerfelt, 1984; Barney, 1986, 1991; Peteraf, 1993) and of evolutionary economics (Nelson and Winter, 1982). Special attention is therefore paid to the processes by which firms conduct their businesses, to the influence these processes have on what makes particular firms differ in profitable ways, and ultimately to the influences these competitively valuable differences can exercise on the development trajectories of the firms in question.

The basic finding is simple. There are two major book superstore chains. The stores look superficially very similar. They are certainly very different, in many very similar ways, from the format they displaced. But the commonalities mask striking differences in approach, apparently quite stable, rooted in the initial resources of the two companies and the natural trajectories for developing and exploiting the resources.

Because of the prominence of the firms the paper focuses on, some of the developments discussed below have been the subject of articles in widely read newspapers such as the *New York Times* and the *Wall Street Journal* and in various magazines. These accounts are generally well written, but they are equally generally unhelpful in understanding the issues of interest here. The evidentiary basis of the paper does not overlap with them. The paper is instead based on extensive interviewing among industry participants (both at the retail level and upstream of it), personal investigation of many facilities (both of the focal firms and of specific competitors), and a detailed reading of the trade press over the entire period. The retail interviewing included individuals who were principal actors (that is, executives with operating responsibilities and experience) in the focal firms both at the time of the events in question and later and also principal actors in carefully selected competitor firms (some in their positions at the time of the events in question and all with close knowledge of the events.) The focus of the interviews was on business systems and on the circumstances of and thinking behind key strategic decisions. Relative to the widely read accounts, this is novel.

## The Origins and Early Development of Borders

Thomas and Louis Borders grew up in Louisville, Kentucky. Thomas went to college at Notre Dame, Louis to the University of Michigan. Thomas went on to Michigan for an MA in English literature. Louis went east to MIT, continuing to study mathematics though shifting his focus from the pure to the applied side. After a brief period abroad, Thomas returned to Ann Arbor. Louis dropped out of MIT and joined his brother.

Life in Ann Arbor was dominated by the University of Michigan – nearly half the town's population was either employed by the university or enrolled in it. The university was one of the two or three most prominent public universities in the United States. Its faculty numbered more than 3,000 and was famous for advanced research activities. The student body of nearly 25,000 studied at an undergraduate college and a breathtakingly broad complement of graduate and professional schools. All of these people spent a great deal of their time reading. A great deal of what they read was books. Louisville had not been a great book town, but both Borders brothers had from a young age developed a keen interest in books. It had only grown over time. Contemplating what to do with their lives and where to do it, it had seemed to the Borders brothers that there might be a living to be made in Ann Arbor in the book trade.

They started a used bookstore in the late 1960s. That business is generally both frustrating and unexciting. It is frustrating because the good acquisitions sell quickly and the bad ones stay, just another volume on the shelf to the browsing customer but an increasingly conspicuous mistake, and an increasing burden on working capital, to the bookseller. To do well, a used bookstore owner needs to be constantly replenishing the good acquisitions, and to do that from Ann Arbor in those days would have required a burdensome amount of travel. At the high end, the business is about buying and selling collectible objects rather than texts the customer will enjoy actually reading – a perversely unintellectual relationship with the objects of sale, some thought. It is also a business in which the stock turns over perhaps once a year on average. Opportunities to make decisions – correct or mistaken – were infrequent. The Borders brothers were young. It just wasn't the right life.

As the shine wore off the idea of selling used books, the brothers began to contemplate a different business model. There were at the time roughly a dozen bookstores selling new books in Ann Arbor and its immediate vicinity. Appendix 4.1 lists the bookstores and characterizes their stock as of the time when the Borders brothers opened their first retail store. About half of these, and all of the relatively large ones, were literally across one street or another from the central core of the university. Almost all the stores were very close. Most of these sold texts and other assigned books, a more or less modest selection of other books, school supplies, pennants, and clothing with a university logo. The merchandising of the nonassigned books was generally either narrow or dull. But the university community was large, diverse, curious about books, and naturally acclimatized to buying them. The Borders brothers sensed tremendous unmet demand and no real competition.

"We just wanted to run a good bookstore," Thomas Borders has remarked. Goodness in this context meant variety – the breadth of the offerings. The focus was to be on the customer. Ann Arbor had many intellectually adventurous book buyers; and the idea was to offer them a very broad selection of unusually interesting books, whatever those might be. The brothers consciously refrained from focusing on a specific product segment such as academic books. The notion of offering no trade books seemed perverse as well as condescending. Their basic idea dictated a much wider range than that.

Borders was hardly the first bookstore to focus on a very specific local customer base. Successful independent bookstores like Cody's in Berkeley and the Seminary Coop in Hyde Park have long built their trade on an intimate knowledge of the wants of their communities. But the Borders brothers pursued this strategy much more comprehensively and went far further with their solutions.

At the time, important features of many bookstores' operations did not seem to have been organized to please or tempt the customers, still less to maximize the ultimate profits. Consider the most salient example in Ann Arbor's part of the country. Even in the great Kroch's and Brentano's store in the Loop in Chicago, the largest bookstore in the Midwest in that period, books were within broad categories generally shelved by publisher. This made the instruction "Find me four Jane Austin novels" something of a challenge and certainly time-consuming for the customers. It also made keeping track of Jane Austen sales relative to Henry James sales difficult. The people it made life easy for were in the channels of distribution. They were allowed to behave as rack jobbers, just like the people who keep the shelves for chips and sodas in convenience stores such as 7–11s fully stocked. This system was very convenient for their doing their own inventory checks and making suggestions about optimizing their own offerings. The Borders brothers instead sought to think through how the bookstore itself ought to present its offerings if its objective was to make finding and opening up books, and contemplating buying them, easy and attractive. The Borders brothers thus wanted to work backwards from desired outcome towards operations, always keeping the perspective of the customer.

Thomas and Louis began their retail operations in 1971 by leasing a 2,000-square foot storefront on the main commercial street running near the campus. Thin and deep, it was a good shape for a bookstore intent upon drawing customers in. The brothers found, without particularly looking, that the incremental value of adding titles was strongly positive; and so they added more and more. With their growing breadth of offerings, they increasingly felt the need to monitor their holdings systematically. So Louis wrote a relatively simple computer program to track inventory. The program and its successors became more and more sophisticated over time as more efficient approaches and greater functionality were added.

At first the programs simply tracked what stock they had on hand. This was not a small feat in itself. By the time they began to outgrow the site, their computing demands obliged them to rent time on an IBM System 3 mainframe and to run the program at night.

Assortment breadth continued to grow and the business continued to prosper. The Borders brothers had in fact discovered an unmet need. A site of 11,000 square feet spread out over two floors, attractively situated on the same street, became available. At first, the second floor was used only for operations. But bookcases displaying merchandise kept encroaching into that space and attracting customers who bought the books. Gradually the bookcases won. The brothers rented warehouse and back-office space in a lower-rent district. By this stage, a printout of their inventory, which they laboriously generated on a dot-matrix printer every 2 weeks, ran roughly a thousand pages. Each book in stock had a control card – essentially half an IBM punch card – in it; and when the book sold, these were collected at the cash register and forwarded reasonably promptly to data processing. So Borders could in principle keep its inventories more or less in real time by monitoring the flows in and out, in the process establishing sales records by stock-keeping unit in the process.

The people who made the selections of what to put on the shelves were called "buyers" and were roughly half a dozen in number. Indeed, they were buyers just as the word was used in the early days of department stores (Hower, 1943). They had managerial responsibilities in that they made merchandising decisions. But they also worked on the sales floor, sometimes rang up sales, spoke casually with customers, and even listened in as customers talked or thought out loud about what items they wanted but found unavailable. The buyers' most valuable attribute wasn't particularly their youth (some stayed 20 years) or their ability personally to draw customers into the store but rather their knowledge of both the tastes of the Ann Arbor population which might be enticed into considering books in their category and of the books these potential customers might be offered.

This knowledge could not be used in an abstract, frictionless setting. The order cycle was quite lengthy in the early 1970s. Borders would sell a book on Day 1 and know this fact informally through a review of the control cards in the store on Day 2. But at that stage the business couldn't support the fixed costs of a back-office staff large enough to confirm details and make up order forms every day or to deal with the inevitably more numerous incoming shipments and all the checking and correspondence associated with each arrival. The company kept the fixed costs of leasing computer time down by running the inventory program and sending out the orders only at intervals. Once an order form was actually filled out, the order went into the mail. Once it arrived at the publisher (which it did almost all of the time), the question of meshing with the publisher's fulfillment cycle arose. Then there was the shipper, and the actual shipping. It might, in those days, be Day 85 or Day 92 – 12 or 13 weeks after Day 1 – before the replacement actually arrived.

Demand conditions could easily have changed over such an interim. Indeed, Louis Borders noticed, they might have changed favorably as well as unfavorably. Some books had a pronounced appeal but to a sharply limited group of customers, and some held a markedly seasonal attraction. But some had a large latent clientele and sold chiefly on reviews, recommendations, and word-of-mouth. It was very desirable for the buyers to have whatever assistance might be available in forecasting what demand for a particular title would be. This became particularly valuable as the number of new books published each year grew vigorously. As Louis's inventory software grew increasingly sophisticated, it came to incorporate increasingly subtle decision support information and increasingly subtle characterizations of what individual books (i.e., stock-keeping units) were like.

The software actually developed in discrete stages. Upgrades and other unavoidable changes in hardware and system software necessitated application software revision. A stable platform might have led to slow and relatively continuous change. But the computers, as well as the business, evolved in bursts.

The first system went into use not long after 1971. This was the card-based system for tracking on-hand inventories. It covered the single store. It incorporated no notion of a purchase order: the card was generated when the book arrived. Because time on the mainframe was in fact fairly expensive, the program was run only at intervals. So the brothers in fact went for extended periods not knowing what their stock was.

The second phase went into use ca. 1974. This could distinguish incoming books from those on hand, a capability useful both for buyers and for anyone dealing with customers. This generation of the software was in fact capable of running several stores so long as there was only one warehouse or distribution center. More important at that stage, it had forecasting capabilities – linear regressions, in effect. The calculations were not very complex; but they were a very far cry from the system at Kroch and Brentano's.

Later versions followed rapidly. They exploited the emerging bar-coding and scanner technology (Brown, 1997). They could handle a more complex network of distribution centers and stores. Even more important as time passed, the software grew much more sophisticated in its forecasting capabilities. For as the company's scale grew, the merchandising process became an increasingly intolerable burden on the established buyers. It took years to develop new buyers with the skills and knowledge the company wanted, and the old ones increasingly desperately needed help. So the ultimate phase of software development was an expert system. The fundamental design principle was that any information about a book the buyer would use in making a decision should be codified and put into the data base – details of subject, quality, intellectual level, sales history, seasonality, ties to other books through author and subject, and so forth. The software amounted to a toolbox of predictive tools. Despite the breadth of merchandising, the system was soon doing 70 percent of the buys, and that number was rising.

Behind all this was an idea as simple and as powerful, with the late twentieth-century decline in information-capture and -processing costs, as Henry Ford's notion of "any color the customer wants so long as it is black" had been earlier in the century (Nevins, 1954). Shelf space appeared to be the bookseller's main commercial constraint. Unsold books could, after all, be sent back to the publishers for an extended period if they remained in good condition and if the bookstore paid the freight and stood the packing and working capital costs. The Borders brothers thought they could "make money selling one copy each of $7.95 books" (late 1970s dollars – the reference is to new books at list prices) if they and their associates could use the shelf space efficiently by choosing the books intelligently and getting very good at knowing when they had chosen wrong. Doing this effectively involved complex considerations far beyond the powers of intuition of even the most gifted buyers. Systematic information about what sales to expect, with what temporal pattern, and systematic tools for analyzing these facts were of the greatest value. The ultimate constraint in their business model was buyer knowledge and decision-making capacity. Shelf space was most valuable when its owner had a good idea of what to put on it.

It naturally struck the Borders brothers that their expertise at getting the right books would be helped by shortening the fulfillment cycle time. They did what they could on that front without resorting to premium delivery services. They went from mailing the publishers typed-out order forms to submitting computer punch cards and began moving toward the bar code and phone-line communication of the late 1980s and 1990s. In all of this they were typically 2–3 years ahead of their competitors. But anticipating demand remained the innovation of central importance. By the time the software had a name – the Book Inventory System – it had absorbed a very substantial amount of retailing history, both aggregated and broken down by localities – and recognized 10,000 distinct subject categories.

## Development of the Company

The Borders brothers were thus succeeding in delivering the service they wanted, supporting an unusually broad inventory; and they were making money doing it. Few independent bookstores could do this, because few dealt with small and stable enough communities that the owners or buyers could personally know all the customers and their preferences. The Book Inventory System was the key to the Borders brothers' success.

The brothers wanted to propagate the consumer experience they were delivering – more people should have access to good bookstores. They also wanted to make some money from the software asset they had created.

One possible way of doing this was to sell or lease the services of the Book Inventory System, customizing the data as appropriate. The more ambitious version of this which they found most attractive involved bundling the Book Inventory System with warehousing and supply chain management. But for any of these to be practical, the Borders brothers would also need to find interested and qualified booksellers who wanted the services. These did not have to be owners of established independent bookstores, though the brothers thought that many of these people might be interested. The brothers imagined there were many cities which could support their sort of store but had no substantial independent bookseller in place. The simple part of what was required to take advantage of the opportunity thus involved actual or potential control of an attractive site and the ability to mobilize enough in the way of capital and bank commitments for leases, fixtures, and inventory and other working capital needs (say, $300,000 in all) in timely fashion.

Field research revealed that there were candidate store sites, though fewer obviously outstanding ones than the brothers had initially imagined. Independent bookstore owners with a drive to run a Borders-type store were scarcer still, unfortunately, and those among them who could raise the money required were a very small number. But even those initially showed real ambivalence about the Book Inventory System. Picking books was what they did. Knowing their customers was what they got paid for. To rely upon the Book Inventory System would be, they felt, to undermine the central sources of satisfaction in their work. The brothers found some customers. But they increasingly felt this was not where the money was.

So they turned, in the mid-1980s, to the other obvious approach to capitalizing the value of its software asset: they began expanding their own retail reach. The first new store was in Birmingham, Michigan, an upper middle-class suburb of Detroit; and this worked well. The next was in Atlanta, but the location was not good and the store did not do well. The next was in Indianapolis, and this was again a success. As this initiative proceeded and successes began to accumulate, running the business on a day-to-day basis became more complex. At the same time, strategy was becoming more important. It became clear that some experienced managerial assistance was in order if they were to continue to expand, and Robert DiRomualdo, a prominent consumer goods retailing executive, was head-hunted in 1988. He threw himself into organization and expansion efforts. The successful stores were soon as far-flung from Ann Arbor as Philadelphia and as prominently sited as, in Philadelphia, roughly a block down the main shopping street letting onto Rittenhouse Square.

The store systems developed in ways quite distinct from the merchandise selection. The distribution infrastructure improved to the point that 90 percent of trade inventory arriving from publishers was processed in company-owned facilities within 48 hours for shipment to the stores. New stores were larger than they had been – now averaging nearly 28,000 square feet and on the order of 150,000 titles – and this offered great scope for the Book Inventory System. (Typical mall stores and independents were in the 3000–5000-square foot range, typically stocking 10,000–25,000 titles. But the mall stores, in particular, were selling convenience: they were not intended to be a destination.) The company also developed a distinctive, attractive, and inviting fixturing for the stores. Borders furnished the shelf areas with comfortable chairs for browsers as well as nooks for them to browse in.

The company hired (using a screening process which was unusually rigorous for the industry) and trained a store staff of young, well-educated employees who were interested in books. These employees were paid well relative to prevailing wages, were given a monthly book-buying credit in addition to their wages, and were given the opportunity to invest in the company unusually early in their term of employment. The level of their motivation was visibly very high.

Layout designers made it easy for customers to have the staff consult a data base about what books were in stock, what books were out of stock but on order, and what books could be special ordered. When the books were in stock, the staff member escorted the customer to the book and was instructed not to leave the scene before physically placing the book in the customer's hands. Buying remained centralized in Ann Arbor, but input was systematically solicited from the stores, and store-level staff had direct and meaningful input into Book Inventory System forecasting exercises.

The stores also began to incorporate coffee bars and café tables at which potential customers could read or simply sit and talk with friends. An unusually broad selection of magazines and out-of-town (and even overseas) newspapers were kept in stock. Performance areas in which authors could make appearances and in which both they and local groups could give readings or concerts were set aside. The stores began to deploy a staff person to manage the calendar of such events full time. This was particularly important for generating traffic in a business that had traditionally been highly seasonal, with most of the profits traditionally being made in the fourth quarter of the year. In addition, store hours increased. Monday-through-Saturday hours of 9 a.m. to 11 p.m. and Sunday hours from 9 a.m. to 9 p.m. were standard. In the Rittenhouse Square neighborhood, for example, this made the store the late-evening and lazy Sunday destination of choice.

These initiatives complemented one another and, equally, the unusually diverse selection of titles. In terms of broad categories, the merchandising was more valuable for the investment in staffing and sales routines, coffee bars and ancillary activities to draw the right sort of potential customers into the stores, and layout, furniture, and fixturing designed to encourage such individuals to start reading books they might want to buy. The same was true in all permutations. The stores became a shopping destination, even for potential customers who might respond well to the selection but would not have sought it out. Revenues rose, comparable-store sales rose smartly, and profitability improved.

## Barnes & Noble

Leonard Riggio came to New York University as a night school undergraduate in the mid-1960s. He took a day job in the campus bookstore to pay his bills. He started at the university as an engineering major but soon shifted over to business. His time at the campus bookstore was equally focused and brisk. He began in an entry-level job, was promoted rapidly, and within several years had become merchandise manager.

College bookstores at that time were generally owned and operated by their school. The basic mission was the timely provision of textbooks. Profit was not a primary consideration; nor was the breadth or even the intellectual excitement in the nontextbook book offerings; nor was the usefulness or attractiveness to the customers of the nonbook offerings. The whole bookstore operation was generally understood to be a support function for the specific academic programs of the institution, not the provision of service to the customers who bought the books or anything else. It was not very much like retailing.

Riggio increasingly felt that he would do things differently, and better, were he running the store. He had two main ideas. The first was that a higher level of service would generate both customer loyalty and improved sales. As a slogan, this came down to "Put the book into the student's hands," which seemed radical enough; but Riggio could see that it had much broader implications – for the selection of books to be offered, the ways in which they were displayed, the speed and effort with which special orders were to be pursued, and for many other aspects of operations. The other idea was that fast cashiering was also desirable: both the student and the store would be better off if paying for the book involved minimal delays. It seemed to Riggio that traditional college bookstore methods offered an easy commercial target.

The undergraduate engineer was morphing into the dropout entrepreneur. In 1965, Riggio borrowed the $5,000 he needed to get started. He had to scrape to find it – some came from credit cards, some from relatives, some even from Household Finance. His initial venture was a textbook store just off the campus on Waverly Place. The location was good, his ideas were well received, and he managed the store aggressively. He tried to know the regular customers by name. He cashed checks. He monitored the shelf inventory personally. He would drive in his station wagon to make pickups from New York area distributors when necessary. Occasionally, when a book was needed urgently and was unavailable in the channels, he would buy it retail from a competitor and take whatever margin he could get. The clientele liked what the store delivered, and the store prospered.

Riggio was ambitious, and he looked for a way to grow. He took on other college bookstores in the New York area and succeeded in making them profitable. The margins on the books were generally fixed and the usual lease terms involved a fixed percentage of sales going to the institution. So he focused his attention elsewhere. Payroll usually bulked large among the other expenses. Much of the money was typically spent on record keeping, buying, and other administrative activities he could more cheaply centralize. Increasingly, he also thought about how the floorspace was being used. The margins on clothing, cosmetics, and even used textbooks were more attractive than those on new books. Incremental changes paid off handsomely. He took on more and more college stores, farther and farther afield; but he began to look for something more than incremental expansion through contracts to run other people's stores.

An opportunity soon presented itself. The earliest predecessor to Barnes & Noble, Inc. had begun doing business in 1874. By the 1960s, it had interests in many branches of the book trade but derived most of its revenue from textbook sales. Its main retail venue was a large store and storage space on the east side of Fifth Avenue at 18th Street, about three-quarters of a mile north of Riggio's store and the NYU neighborhood on the way to midtown. But the firm had fallen on evil days. When John Barnes died in 1969, no other family members were available to take the company on; and its retail and wholesale businesses were sold to Amtel, a retailing conglomerate. By 1971, however, Amtel had concluded that the business as well as the family was in longterm decline and put it on the block. This seemed like a major opportunity, and Riggio again borrowed money. The 29-year-old bought the floundering company in 1971 for $1.2 million.

The Fifth Avenue store certainly enhanced Riggio's textbook business, but he was beginning to have bigger ideas still; and he now had 42,000 square feet of store and storage space in the world's most central business district to play with. He kept on with the college stores. He began, taking advantage of the Barnes & Noble legacy, a wholesale operation, buying used books on nearly 150 campuses for resale. But chiefly he began to focus on retailing.

Riggio had a concept for his retailing initiative: the store would sell education as well as (if not indeed more than) entertainment. Merchandising of popular nonfiction and how-to books expanded radically relative to the trade stores of the day. He stocked relatively little fiction in hardcover and all of that heavily discounted to draw in customers. There was generous merchandising of discount paperbacks, but the discounts were much smaller. The location was accessible and the store organization helpful to the unaccompanied customer – the usual broad categories were broken down into many more signed subcategories. Customers responded well to the new approach.

Starting in 1972, a more radical innovation took shape. Riggio leased increasingly large spaces across Fifth Avenue from the main store – at one stage in excess of (an incremental) 40,000 square feet – and devoted them single-mindedly to off-price sales. The recently published books were sold at heavy discounts, the remainders and used books even cheaper. The range ran from 40 percent to 90 percent. "If you paid full price," the advertisements ran, "you didn't get it at Barnes & Noble." The space was large, the stock immense, and the spirit that of a supermarket. Best-seller lists in effect advertised sales. Shopping carts were available on the way in. "Pile 'em high and let 'em fly" was a motto.

Riggio was more formal in tone speaking to a reporter for the main bookselling trade paper in 1976 but the same spirit shows through:

> These are everyday people who have shopping behaviors similar to people we see in shopping centers across the country. The best way to reach them is by everyday sound merchandising. We've taken the stuffiness out of a bookstore . . . [We] give customers a feeling that they are being treated as customers, not as potential scholars. (Freilich, 1976: 72)

Many of the customers in the Annex and in all bookstores, the article went on quoting him, have no intention of reading the books they buy. They buy them as shelf fillers, in order to project images of themselves through their collections. We see people returning week after week to the Annex and buying 10–15 books. (Freilich, 1976: 73)

It must be said that the books did sell.

The company began opening branches. Some were specifically modeled after the Sales Annex, others were general trade bookstores. All were in the Northeast, and all sold all their books at a discount. Best-sellers and selected advertised titles were offered at 33 percent off. The other hardcovers were for sale at 15 percent. Selected paperbacks were offered at 20 percent and the rest went at 10 percent.

By 1986, there were 33 of these stores, mostly in the Northeast. The company's ability to dispose of remainders had been enhanced by its early acquisition of Marlboro Books, a remainder and mail-order house. The college division had continued to flourish and by now had contracts on 142 campuses. The company had also added a division servicing 153 book departments in drug stores and supermarkets, a rack-jobbing business for mass-market paperbacks.

At that time, there were two major national chains of bookstores (with well in excess of 1000 outlets between them) and a number of regional chains. The national chains were owned by department store holding companies – Walden-books by Los Angeles-based Carter-Hawley-Hale and B. Dalton by Minneapolis-based Dayton-Hudson – and had gotten big riding the growth of suburban malls (in which department stores were generally anchor tenants) and the growing population of educated, relatively affluent people. The chain bookstores averaged in the 3,000–4,000-square foot range, stocking roughly 30,000 titles (including magazines) on average. The mall stores were originally able to exploit the mall foot traffic and to price for convenience rather than having to use price to attract customers. Business had, between this fact and the demographics, boomed in the 1970s. But the national chains could not be insensitive to their competitive environment; and as the regional chains – many of which were discount houses – grew, pricing pressure increased. The summer of 1985 was bad, the Christmas season of 1985 and the winter of 1986 brutal. Revenues and gross margins suffered badly. Only companies which were organized for this sort of competition had any chance of surviving.

Late in 1986, Dayton-Hudson concluded that the growth prospects of B. Dalton division were not adequate under its own management and decided to shop it. Riggio felt like the Pac-Man as he contemplated adding a national network of 798 stores which had grossed $538 million the previous year to his $225 million company, but it seemed to him that the next step up for his company was clearly to go national. One of the two national companies was for sale and he became determined to bid. The key financing was raised from a Dutch retailer, Vendex, which owned a shareholding in Barnes & Noble and trusted Riggio implicitly. There was competition for the property, but Riggio returned to New York with the deal.

Becoming a national retailer in name was the easy part. Many aspects of running a business so much larger than it had been were initially challenging to his management team, and it was 2–3 years before the learning tapered off. The scale of operations magnified the costs of mistakes, when they happened, and the inevitable occasional simple bad luck. There was more. For example, real estate operations in general and the evolving economics of mall leasing in particular were unfamiliar and early sources of difficulty. As the Barnes & Noble executives mastered the problems, however, performance improved. Many Dalton back-office functions were ultimately relocated to New York and were reengineered in the process. Scale economies were enhanced and absolute headcounts fell. Indeed, there was, overall, a steady focus on centralization and economies of scale – in distribution infrastructure, buyer expenses, terms on the stock, and advertising as well as in financial and administrative functions – wherever they could be found.

The Dalton inventory management software was better than what Barnes & Noble had, and it was far better suited to a network so much larger and inevitably more complex. But it was still relatively crude. The Dalton system had been introduced in 1966 and had been often modified but never rewritten or superseded. It was a model stock system with automatic reordering. The buyers, with some limited input from store managers regarding best-sellers and regional titles, chose the books and set the models, just as they always had. The software could generate statistics – for individual titles and for roughly 100 categories, it could report total sales and sales by individual stores, and by stores sorted into six broad groups by annual sales, and overall. But it had no forecasting capability. Overall, the system was basically one of static equilibrium with sporadic – and analytically essentially unassisted – human interventions. In a striking contrast to the Borders view, one buying executive told *Publishers Weekly* that at Dalton, "[i]t is the buyers who make the computer a valuable tool" (Maryles, 1977: 126).

Oddly enough, the increasing size of the company relative to the other customers of publishers did not have massive direct effects on the prices it paid for books – the discount schedules topped out at order numbers which were small relative to the company's orders for, say, national best-sellers. But there were other possibilities for accommodation. A very large customer could get away with paying more slowly than a smaller one could. There were also shadowy areas in returns – the trade privilege concerned books which were not shopworn or otherwise damaged, and perhaps the books the chains shipped back were not scrutinized so carefully. Perhaps invoice disputes were settled more amicably or at least in a fashion less costly in terms of time and direct expense. Cooperative advertising funds (i.e., funds for advertising both the book and the place to buy it) may have been available on easier terms.

The company's basic competitive thrust continued to be selling off-price books and discounting, and there could be no doubt it was better placed to pursue this after the acquisition than it had been before. Competition, on the other hand, was heating up. Crown Books was especially worrying. The regional chain had started in Washington, DC in the late 1970s. It was run by a Harvard Business School-educated son of a family that owned a successful drug store chain. Crown sold a narrow selection of books at sharp discounts in 3,000–6,000-square foot outlets with no-frills fixturing sited in shopping malls. This made it difficult for competing chains, never mind independents, to profitably stock slow-moving titles and indeed, any titles being ordered in one's, two's, and three's.

Crown clearly aspired to a national expansion and had become a notable source of pressure on B. Dalton's pricing and profits prior to the sale. Crown's eyes at one point settled on Bookstop, another regional firm (at that stage operating in Texas, Florida, and California). The Bookstop stores were even larger, at 9,000–10,000 square feet; but that was not by itself the most interesting thing about them. The Bookstop entrepreneurs had the idea that they could use their space (and so much space) most efficiently if they developed a clear customer base and knew what those customers wanted. So they offered all their books at 10 percent off, but offered another 10 percent to "members." Membership cost $7 and involved showing a membership card at the sales register in a way that enabled Bookstop to track the member's interests. The software was unsophisticated – and in the event, the information was used for little more than compiling mailing lists and candidate expansion sites – but the concept was a step up on Dalton's. Crown's interest in Bookstop (in which it already owned a 20 percent stake) became pronounced. Riggio got on an airplane to Texas with a lawyer saying that he wasn't coming home until he'd bought the company. He stayed until he prevailed.

The puzzle to the trade in all of this was how operators could profitably fill the shelves of such large (and larger and larger) stores in the suburbs. Barnes & Noble had discovered surprisingly large appetites for information, for cheap best-sellers, and just for cheap books. They now found that the more people were offered, the more they wanted. People came and bought. Even special orders went up distinctly, albeit less than proportionately to revenue.

The ambience of these stores was not upmarket, however, and certainly not reminiscent of an independent bookstore. The merchandising was not designed to cater to scholarly or at that time even particularly to literary tastes. The prime virtue of inventory, from management's perspective, was that it sell quickly. The person at the register ran the register, and was selected because he or she had seemed likely to be good at it.

As time passed, there were some marginal adjustments to the approach. Riggio acquired the trade name, hallowed in American literary history, of Scribner's; he also bought the Doubleday trade name and the small chain of stores that came with it. The point of both purchases was to have a wider variety of brands to offer upscale mall developers.

The industry changed significantly over the course of the 1980s. The chains had expanded, roughly doubling the number of their outlets. Many independents had folded as the malls continued to divert Main Street traffic, though mall growth subsequently slowed. Department stores had virtually abandoned the bookselling field. But the biggest change from Barnes & Noble's perspective came in 1989, when the company first built free-standing stores comparable in size to the new, large Borders stores.

The Barnes & Noble business model was different from that of Borders, however. It was a Ferrari shell, unkind industry commentators said, with a VW engine. Barnes & Noble sought to have a large selection but still had no sophisticated software for customizing it to local populations and to the ebbs and flows of their tastes. The staff were neither selected, trained, nor motivated to interact with customers as the Borders staff were. There was wood paneling in the stores; there were chairs; and there was coffee. The stores were a place where customers wanting to forget about the world for a little while could stay. Discounts on backlist titles eased. But the primary allure remained the advertised prices and the high-volume items – these were critical, in Riggio's view, to building traffic.

Hardcovers were offered at a minimum of 10 percent off list price, best-sellers at 30 percent off. (The chain's costs were still relatively low – the old reasons remained, and they were a larger customer now.) Barnes & Noble superstores offered much larger selections than independents and mall-based bookstores, but the merchandising still tended, relative to Borders, to mass market items. The company also kept substantial inventories of individual items relative to Borders. Much more floor space was devoted to very heavily discounted – though to the bookseller disproportionately inexpensive – publishers' overstocks. Barnes & Noble also published and sold out-of-copyright classics and reference works, in attractive hardcover editions, under its own imprint. The target was 10 percent of sales. Again, these were cheap to stock, in this case because the content was free and the incremental cost of the hardcover binding was in fact small. The books could be priced very inexpensively compared to recently published works and still be priced very profitably. All in all, Barnes & Noble continued to seek its profits from low costs and high volume.

Barnes & Noble was large and ambitious, potentially a force to be reckoned with. Riggio opened eight superstores the first year, 27 the next, 58 the year after. There was no sign of stopping – he clearly envisaged a major shift and a very large chain of superstores. The collision came when Barnes & Noble set out aggressively to lease precisely the sort of sites Borders sought.

## Stability of a Sort

The growing geographical diffusion of the superstore model represented a major change in American book retailing. But the increasing administrative burdens and the necessity of fully national scale if a contest with Barnes & Noble was truly in prospect made the Borders brothers' work at Borders, Inc. increasingly different, and more burdensome, than it had been. This time, the new life looked less attractive. In 1992, the Borders brothers prepared for a public offering but then sold the company, on attractive terms, to Kmart Corporation, a national retailing company headquartered in the Detroit suburb of Troy, Michigan. Kmart had previously purchased Waldenbooks, the other predominantly mall-based chain of traditionally sized, merchandised, and managed bookstores besides B. Dalton; but the Kmart managers had begun to think that the future lay in a different approach. Despite the Borders growth, it certainly remained different: according to the public offering document, sales of hardcover best-sellers remained a strikingly small percentage of company retail sales in fiscal 1991 (Borders, 1992).

Barnes & Noble attempted an initial public offering of stock in 1992 but withdrew it when investors seemed uneasy about the company's debt levels and the prospects of the superstore model. The following year saw steady expansion of the superstore business and sales per square foot. The trend in average ticket size numbers also pleased the analysts. The company said it expected half its revenue to come from the new model stores by the end of the following fiscal year, and the transaction went ahead successfully in 1993. The 1993 prospectus indicated that Barnes & Noble had developed a proprietary inventory management information system. The system still (see appendix 4.2) had much more limited functionality than the Borders system, but Borders-style functionality was not at the heart of the business model the prospectus described.

In 1995, Kmart sold its bookselling operations to a group of divisional executives. The new company then conducted its own IPO to raise capital to operate as an independent company on a national scale.

In 1996, i.e., once the IPOs were done, Barnes & Noble operated 431 superstores and the Borders Group 157. The Annual Reports gave total sales of $2.45 billion and $1.96 billion respectively. (Note that these numbers include mall chains and other sources as well as the superstores. But most of the features of the business models under discussion would have had some spillover effects.) Barnes & Noble had a higher stock turn, but the ratio of net earnings to total revenue was twice as high at Borders. Both firms discounted many new books, and each earned handsome margins on its café sales. But the basic shopping experience in the two sets of stores remained differentiated roughly as it had been (see appendix 4.3). The models were, after all, continuing to work. Indeed, in 1996 Barnes & Noble commanded a share of the market for all bookstores (including trade, college, religious, and chain store sales) of 19.5 percent and Borders 15.6 percent, for a total between the two superstore groups of 35.1. The year before, the total had been 32.1. The year after, it would be 40.3.

## Discussion

The superstores are all very different from the mall stores as these existed and from most of the independents. As a group, in this contrast, they seem very much the same. They were large and often free-standing. They were inviting places to tarry and read, not, apparently, mere venues for sales. Their assortments were, relatively speaking, overwhelmingly broad. They sold best-sellers, and some other books, at substantial discounts. They offered ancillary services, such as cafés, and ancillary activities, such as readings and discussion groups.

Yet behind these similarities – beneath the surface of the stores – the two chains represented quite different approaches to retailing and required quite different capabilities. The focus of Borders was on assortment; and software to optimize this was at the heart of the business. Barnes & Noble's focus was on price and thus on infrastructure and practices to promote volume. These two chains' capabilities originated and developed in distinctive ways, the one oriented around information and the other more directly reaching for scale. Ambitions may have preceded capabilities, but the capabilities preceded, and seem to have driven, actual strategies: the original differences were still visible a decade later. To the extent that the strategies ultimately converged to any significant extent, that convergence happened only incrementally and relatively late in the day. This was an equilibrium in which the superficial homogeneity disguised variety under the skin.

The Borders history lends itself easily to interpretation in terms of the resource-based view of the firm. To reiterate, the important fact about the company that emerges from the history given here is not that it sold books or that it offered a wide variety of books in large and handsome or well-sited stores, and still less that the core of its retail capability lay in a base of sales skills in its staff. The core of its capability was, rather, software and an evolving statistical history of local purchases. The company made money by leveraging the software – in effect, by selling software services. The resistance of many independent bookstore owners to buying the services is only one of the many details lending credence to this interpretation. (Indeed, my colleague Sidney Winter remarked, the resistance of the independents seems to underscore the point that the unavailability of the requisite information technology was not the sole consideration in the way of a Borders-type innovator.)

Much of the Borders history concerns the development of routines and capabilities complementary to the software. The instructions to the floor staff about what to do after looking up book information in the computer data base is a very direct example, but the employment of people to schedule school poetry readings and the like is not far off. Post Milgrom and Roberts (1990), this pattern seems only natural. In the history as I have recounted it, the company was dazzlingly effective at accessing complementary assets. The difficulty with most of them lay less in creating them than in thinking of them. This observation emphasizes the value retailing perspective which DiRomualdo brought to the firm's management. It may be an example of the constraining effects of established routines.

On the other hand, the idea that powerful complementarities inevitably drive organizational inertia seems, on this account, overdrawn. The complementarities in the ultimate system may indeed be robust. But that system emerged only over time, a consequence of a series of decisions made in specific contexts – a series of incremental adaptations and changes. It is evident by example that the company did not take the only possible profitable path.

One could dynamize this resource-based view of Borders by developing the evolutionary perspective on its history more explicitly. One can discern in the basic business five distinct activities routines for executing which can have powerful interconnections and complementarities. These activities are organizing the book stock (both the process and the resulting physical pattern), tracking the inventory, estimating demand at the level of titles, ordering new stock, and fulfilling the orders. There was a widely diffused set of routines to carry out these functions. The Borders firm was an innovator, initially with a valuable new idea about how to track the inventory. The crudest initial version was facilitated by recent improvements in information technology, and the idea's full flowering was supported by information technology's subsequent development. The innovation regarding inventory extended easily into an innovation in demand estimation and into ordering. These raised the rewards for innovating in stock organization as well. All these made the costs and constraints imposed by the traditional approach to fulfillment even more apparent, so the innovator took that on as well.

There are a number of salient features in this account. The complementarities are powerful when the system is static and sometimes of even greater value when the system is itself changed: in this case, the value of the (historically) later innovations depends on the implementation of earlier ones. The constantly accumulating sales history enhances the value of all of them. The underlying innovations are all basically informational and replication emerges as the preferred strategy for appropriating their value. The diffusion of the superior technique puts market pressure on the stalwarts of the old technique and is a major force in their decline. But the superior technique does not diffuse by imitation and free entry. The genes, to put matters back into evolutionary perspective, descend because the mutations embodying them survive and flourish.

Barnes & Noble represents a different mutation (albeit one with a somewhat similar phenotype). Its superstores arose from different preconditions, rooted in far more traditional retailing economics; and in the company's development, it faced a different set of problems. That the solutions which emerged and the complementarities which were ultimately exploited were different should not be surprising. Yet there were powerful and persistent complementarities; and their value only grew over time. As the sales history record grows richer, it is not surprising that merchandising grows somewhat broader; but it is equally unsurprising, given the complementaries, that convergence remains incomplete. Scale economies being at the core of Barnes & Noble's approach, the company's replication strategy does not seem odd. The diffusion of its technique in the population puts a different pressure on the independents – not only can potential customers purchase relatively esoteric books at Borders rather than having to order them, but the customers can purchase popular titles cheaply due to Barnes & Noble. The independents, whose fixed costs are more of a burden to them than the chains' were, cannot fight back effectively.

In all of this, one sees familiar (Nelson, 1991) themes. The market imposes only loose constraints: profitable firms in a given industry can differ in performance-relevant ways. These differences arise partly from free new choices but partly from past choices, that is, from the firm's history. When firms do choose, they do not necessarily know all the alternatives which will emerge, never mind the consequences of the particular alternatives before them. Core capabilities seem to be very persistent (though whether the costs of changing them are direct or opportunity costs is less clear). Firms which are wise, or lucky, in the capabilities they develop relative to the competitive environment in which they do and will operate prosper.

In this fashion did a new format for bookselling emerge. Not long after this paper's narrative ends, there was a new evolutionary event: the rise of Amazon.com. (Sahlman and Katz, 1999). That and its sequellae represent a related subject. But it is a complex one, requiring a careful treatment of its own.

## Appendix 4.1 1971–1972 Book Trade Directory (Excerpt)

Lists of Publishers and Booksellers
Helaine MacKeigan, Editor
(Bowker: New York)

Ann Arbor – 67,340. Area code 313

| | |
|---|---|
| Blue Front Store, 701 Packard St. (48104) | Paperbacks |
| Ray E. Collins, owner | |
| Centicore Bookshop, 336 Maynard St. (48108) | General |
| 665–2604 | |
| (Br: 1229 S. University Ave. (48104)) | |
| P.M. Wyman, mgr. | |
| art, for lang (fr, ger, rus, sp), hb, juv, papbks, scholarly | |
| art sup, frames, graphic art, prints | |
| Circle Bookshop, Inc., 215 S. State St. (48108) | Metaphysical |
| 769–1583 | |

R. S. Erlwine & J. C. Sullivan, owners
hb, papbks (hp), meta (occult, astrology, eastern rel, mysticism)
Concordia Lutheran Jr. College Book-Store, 4090 Geddes Rd. (48105)          College
Myrtle Schafter, mgr.
Follett's Michigan Book Store, 322 S. State St. (48108)          College General
662–6594
Follett Corp., Chicago, owner; Robert F. Graham, mgr.
hb, papbks, text-c
coll. sup
Hadcock Music House, 314 S. Thayer, Box 1267 (48106)          Special
E. Hadcock, owner
hb, mus, papbks, text-c
Logos Bookstore, 611 Church St. (48104)          Religion
661–4563
Inter-Varsity Christian Fellowship, owner
Jim Carlson, mgr. & buyer
hb, juv, papbks, rel-c, p, rental
ch & SS sup, gifts, gr CDs, rel per, rec
Bob Marshall's Book Shop, 211 S. State St. (48108)          General
663–5624
Robert F. Marshall, owner; Rose Marion Blake, mgr; Donald Wilcox,
buyer
art, hb, juv, papbks, rel-c, j, p
Overbeck Bookstore, 1216 S. University Ave. (48104)          College
663–9333
E. C. Overbeck, owner
hb, juv, law, med
staty
Slater's, Inc., 336 S. State St. (48108)          College General
662–4543
Florence C. Slater, owner; George Coons, mgr; Dean McLaughlin,
buyer;
Winifred Martin, juv. buyer
hb, juv, papbks, text-c
art & col sup, per staty
Student Book Service, 1215 S. University Ave. (48104)          College General
761–0700
Fred Shure, owner
art, for lang, hb, papbks
col sup
Ulrich's Book Store, 549 E. University Ave. (48104)          College General
NO 2–3201
Fred Ulrich, owner; Ernie Bundy, Howard Baker & D. O. Brown,
buyers;
Martha Jump, juv buyer
hb, juv, med, papbks, text-c, s
art & col sup
Wahr's University Book Store, 316 S. State St. (48108)          College
662–5669.
Leo E. Hallen, mgr.

## Appendix 4.2  Excerpt from "Prospectus: 8,235,000 Shares, Barnes and Noble Inc.," (September 27, 1993)

Strategy:

. . .

Business:

. . .

*Completing Installation of Proprietary Inventory Management Information System.* The Company has developed a proprietary inventory management information system, WINGS, which the Company believes increases store productivity by allowing for increased operating efficiency and improved customer service. WINGS provides bookselling personnel with on-line inventory information regarding in-stock availability and shelf location. WINGS enables store personnel to (i) place book orders directly with wholesalers through direct electronic data interchanges, allowing customization of inventory and efficient restocking of fast-selling titles, (ii) provide convenient and efficient service for customers with special requests or orders, and (iii) increase the speed and accuracy of receiving merchandise and processing returns and point-of-sale transactions. WINGS is currently used by the Company in all of its superstores and approximately 100 of its mall bookstores, with installation in its other mall stores to be completed during 1994.

## Appendix 4.3  Superstores on the Main Line: November, 1999

Borders and Barnes & Noble operate superstores on Philadelphia's Main Line six-tenths of a mile apart in Bryn Mawr, Pennsylvania. The following observations from a site visit one evening in early November, 1999, speak to the point in the text.

There were two distinctive features to the areas near the stores' entrances. The first concerned the displays of newly published books. The numbers broke down as follows.

|  | *Borders* | *Barnes & Noble* |
|---|---|---|
| Total titles | 541 | 270 |
| of which: | | |
| Non-fiction | 297 | 42 |
| Biography | 65 | 37 |
| Fiction | 179 | 191 |

The Barnes & Noble fiction section included significantly more mysteries and upmarket romances (e.g., Danielle Steele).

Equally striking was the amount (and proportion) of floor space devoted to remaindered books. Barnes & Noble devoted roughly five times the space to this that Borders did. The floor space was on the main floor, adjacent to the newly published books, the cash registers, and one of the two doors. This is prime territory.

The number of volumes in the general fiction shelves may be proxied by the offerings for writers with surnames beginning with a single letter of the alphabet. The selections under the letter "M" had the following features.

|  | *Borders* | *Barnes & Noble* |
|---|---|---|
| Total volumes | 1,056 | 1,153 |
| Duplicates | 173 | 453 |

| | | |
|---|---|---|
| Distinct titles | 883 | 700 |

A more detailed look at a nonfiction category highlighted the differences. Under "German History" the following could be observed.

| | Borders | Barnes & Noble |
|---|---|---|
| Total volumes | 195 | 106 |
| Distinct titles | 186 | 81 |
| Hardcover titles | 40 | 19 |

(The hardcover titles tend to be more current. All features of this table are robust to the exclusion of coffee table books about Hitler, the Second World War, etc.)

Given these facts, it is perhaps not surprising that Borders had twice as many computer terminals – offering shelf locations for books in the store, in-stock positions for all their local stores and distribution centers, and ordering information for books not in stock in any of these – than Barnes & Noble did.

## Acknowledgements

The original version of this essay was presented at the CCC/Tuck Conference on the Evolution of Firm Capabilities in Hanover NH, September 25–26, 1999. I thank the Wharton School's Reginald Jones Center, Center for Leadership Studies, and Emerging Technologies Program and the NBER/Sloan Foundation Program in Industrial Technology and Productivity for research support. I am grateful to a large number of industry participants and commentators for their candid thoughts and reflections. (Most of these interviews were conducted in confidence and are therefore not cited directly in the text. The interview notes will be deposited in the Archives of the University of Pennsylvania Library with access available to qualified scholars.) My academic colleagues George Day, Constance Helfat, Daniel Levinthal, Keith Pavitt, Sidney Winter, and the late Zvi Griliches gave many helpful comments. The discussions with Helfat and Winter were especially sustained, penetrating, and influential in my thinking. Jay Haverty and Wendy Tao gave excellent research assistance. I alone am responsible for the content.

## References

Barney, J. 1986. Strategic factor markets: expectations, luck, and business strategy. *Management Science* 32: 1231–1241.

Barney, J. 1991. Firm resources and sustained competitive advantage. *Journal of Management* 17: 99–120.

Borders, Inc. 1992. (August 12) Form S-1 Registration Statement. Securities and Exchange Commission: Washington, DC.

Brown, S. 1997. *Revolution at the Checkout Counter: The Explosion of the Bar Code*. Harvard University Press: Cambridge, MA.

Freilich, L. 1976. Barnes and Noble: the book superstore – of course, of course. *Publishers*

*Weekly* January 19: 71–73.

Hower, R. 1943. *History of Macys of New York 1858–1919: Chapters in the Evolution of the Department Store.* Harvard University Press: Cambridge, MA.

Maryles, D. 1977. B. Dalton, with 350 outlets due by 1979, views its bookselling future with rosy optimism. *Publishers Weekly* September 19: 126–129.

Milgrom, P. and Roberts, J. 1990. The economics of modern manufacturing. *American Economic Review* 80: 511–528.

Nelson, R. 1991. Why do firms differ, and how does it matter? *Strategic Management Journal,* Winter Special Issue 12: 61–74.

Nelson, R. and Winter, S. 1982. *An Evolutionary Theory of Economic Growth.* Harvard University Press: Cambridge, MA.

Nevins, A. 1954. *Ford: The Times, the Man, the Company.* Scribner's: New York.

Peteraf, M. 1993. The cornerstones of competitive advantage: a resource-based view. *Strategic Management Journal* 14(3): 179–191.

Sahlman, W. and Katz, L. 1999. Amazon.com: going public. Harvard Business School Publishing Case 899003.

Tebbel, J. 1972. *A History of Book Publishing in the United States, I: The Creation of an Industry 1630–1865.* Bowker: New York.

Wernerfelt, B. 1984. A resource-based view of the firm. *Strategic Management Journal* 5(2): 171–180.

# CHAPTER FIVE

# Commentary on Chapters by Klepper and Simons, by Holbrook et al., and by Raff

## Keith Pavitt

The chapters by Klepper and Simons and by Holbrooke et al. both analyze the dynamics of firms that developed and produced major innovations: television and semiconductors. Raff analyzes the place of radical technological change in a user industry: information and communication technology (ICT) in bookselling. Klepper and Simons rely heavily on quantitative analysis, and both Holbrooke et al. and Raff on historical narrative. All describe what happened with the benefit of hindsight. All confirm the importance of firm-specific capabilities in competitive performance, but with important differences in nature and outcome. I shall stress here the interactions of corporate technological competencies with organizational practices.

The Klepper and Simons chapter could usefully tell us more about the competencies that enabled radio firms to succeed better than others in the TV market. Explanations in terms of size and R&D are not enough, since firms in other industries – like chemicals and automobiles – were also big and spent heavily on R&D, but were not successful in the TV market; indeed, it is likely that most – if not all – of them did not even try to enter it. This is because technological proximity[1] is an important factor influencing the capacity to enter. The narrative discussion in the chapters suggests that radio firms turned out to have core technological competencies for TV, because they were using the same knowledge base (i.e. physics and what was then called electrical engineering). In addition, the move from radio to TV required no major changes in organizational practices.[2] The same consumer market was being served. External linkages to the same bodies of knowledge, the same component suppliers and the same communications infrastructure were of central importance. Internal linkages between product design and mass production remained key.

The contrast with semiconductors is striking. It turned out that the success of incumbent firms would have required major additions to their technological competencies and networks (i.e. quantum physics), the ability to form effective linkages between product design and a very demanding production technology, and learning about major new classes of customers (i.e. computer firms and the military, in addition to radio firms).

In bookselling, the situation was very different. Like machinery in manufacturing,

ICT has turned out to be a relatively cheap but pervasive technology, diffused by specialized suppliers.³ It has therefore become what practitioners call a "background" or "enabling" technology (i.e. broadly available to all competitors, but essential for efficient design, manufacture and delivery of corporate products), rather than a "core" or "critical" technology (i.e. central to corporate competitiveness; distinctive and difficult to imitate). ICT has therefore been mobilized to reinforce other distinctive corporate advantages: quality and variety in the provision of books in Borders, large volumes and low costs in Barnes & Noble. More generally, background technologies do not create a distinctive and sustainable competitive advantage, but they can have major effects on corporate organization and industry performance. This creates a puzzle for those analytical frameworks that stress the central importance of sustainable advantage (e.g. Barney, 1991; Porter, 1996).

I have consciously said that various competencies "turned out" to be critical to competitive success. We cannot assume that the paths following the development and adoption of major new technologies are clearly signposted beforehand. Firms are constrained in their movements by their past, and trajectories appear clear after the event, but the essential features of revolutions are difficult to identify when they are happening.

There are therefore no simple recipes for managers, nor for industrial economists. Depending on the characteristics of each major technological shift, either incumbents or entrants may win, competitive advantage may be sustainable or not, and it is much easier to be wise after the event than beforehand. Taken together, the papers suggest that a better understanding of the evolution of capabilities requires greater empirical and analytical depth in notions of innovative "routines" and, more specifically, of the coevolution of technology, organization, and markets. Many of the elements that should be included in such analysis are touched upon in the three chapters and the comments above. In empirical analysis, we should exploit the growing opportunities for bibliometric analysis, in addition to the invaluable contributions of business historians. And in our analytical frameworks, we should remember the central importance given to the nature of the technological knowledge base in the writings of Rosenberg (1974), Nelson and Winter (1977), Dosi (1982), Freeman (1984), and Abernathy and Clark (1985).

Finally, we should remember that firms and their capabilities are influenced by the environments in which they operate. Klepper and Simons mention in particular the positive influence of Japanese industrial policies on the competitive position of Japanese TV producers. I would like to propose more studies of the influence of US federal policies on the emergence and exploitation of US capabilities in IT and biotechnology. One story (very influential outside the USA) is that the central features are entrepreneurship, flexibility, risk capital and the like. Another, emerging more recently from historical studies, shows the importance of federal funding of basic capabilities by the NIH and DARPA.⁴ Which should we foreign observers take more seriously?

## Notes

1  Or "relatedness": see Rumelt (1974). See also Patel and Pavitt (1997).
2  On the links between technology and organizational practices, see Pavitt (1998).

3   See Rosenberg (1963).
4   See Computer Science and Telecommunications Board (1999).

# References

Abernathy, W. and Clark, K. (1985) Mapping the winds of creative destruction, *Research Policy*, 14, 3–22

Barney, J. (1991) Firm resources and sustained competitive advantage. *Journal of Management*, 17, 99–120.

Computer Science and Telecommunications Board (1999) *Funding a Revolution: Government Support for Computing Research*. Washington, D.C.: National Research Council, National Academy Press.

Dosi, G. (1982) Technological paradigms and technological trajectories: a suggested interpretation of the determinants and directions of technical change. *Research Policy*, 11, 147–62.

Freeman, C. (1984) Prometheus unbound, *Futures*, 16, 495–507.

Nelson, R. and Winter, S. (1977) In search of a useful theory of innovation, *Research Policy*, 6, 36–76.

Patel, P. and Pavitt, K. (1997) The technological competencies of the world's largest firms: complex and path-dependent but not much variety, *Research Policy*, 26, 141–56.

Pavitt, K. (1998) Technologies, products and organization in the innovating firm: what Adam Smith tells us and Joseph Schumpeter doesn't, *Industrial and Corporate Change*, 7, 433–52.

Porter, M. (1996) What is strategy?, *Harvard Business Review*. November–December, 61–78.

Rosenberg, N. (1963) Technological change in the machine tool industry, *Journal of Economic History*, 23, 414–43.

Rosenberg, N. (1974) Science innovation and economic growth, *Economic Journal*, 84, 333.

Rumelt, R. (1974) *Strategy, Structure and Economic Performance*. Cambridge, MA: Graduate School of Business Administration, Harvard University.

# CHAPTER SIX

# Imprinting and the Evolution of Firm Capabilities

## Daniel A. Levinthal

I've been asked to address the question of imprinting in the context of a book on the emergence of capabilities. This may strike some as an oxymoron. This perception has some truth, but only a partial truth. I suggest that we consider two interpretations of imprinting – a strong form that precludes ideas of adaptation and change and a weak form that incorporates notions of change but views these change processes as constrained and guided by an organization's initial state. These latter ideas generally are understood as path dependence.

Before examining the possible interpretations of the notion of imprinting, it is worth considering the source of this idea. Imprinting was introduced to the management literature, more precisely the literature on organizational sociology, by Stinchcombe (1965). At one time, Coase's (1937) work was referred to as oft cited but little read. That sobriquet no longer seems fitting for Coase, but Stinchcombe's classic work on organizational sociology is a prime candidate for such a title.

The primary agenda of his far-ranging essay is to explore the diversity of organizational forms.[1] Stinchcombe (1965: 143) notes a "correlation between the time in history that a particular type of organization was invented and the social structure of organization of that type at the present time." Stinchcombe suggests that this empirical observation follows from three distinct properties. First, organizations are born in waves. For instance, the early part of the nineteenth century saw the birth of large cohorts of textile firms; the mid-1800s saw the birth of a large number of men's fraternal organizations. Stinchcombe cites Schumpeter as providing a technologically based rationale for the former sort of wave of foundings, but notes the later sort of wave of foundings suggests that social dynamics that are broader than merely economic ones are at work as well.

However, the fact that organization populations tend to be founded in relatively close temporal order doesn't in and of itself suggest anything about the diversity in organizational forms in such populations. The second element in the argument is the suggestion that organizations at founding tend to reflect the modes of organizing prevalent at that time, due to a mixture of the technical requirements of their purpose and the social structure at the time of their birth. With regard to the social structure, the critical elements for Stinchcombe are the ways different societies and societies at different points in time allocate political power, wealth, and the organization of labor markets.

The third, and final, element of the argument, and the piece that is most central to the concerns of this book, is the supposition that organizational forms are relatively stable across time. Who sustains traditional practices? Which actors' interests become vested? Selznick's (1957) work on institutionalization processes provides the primary answer. To achieve its technical objectives, an organization makes external and internal commitments, including the socialization of individuals and the allocation of power. As an outcome of such efforts, ideologies are elaborated that justify the power distribution and roles. Such actions, however, "not only mobilize social forces for present purposes . . . [they] also infuse the resulting structure with value, to make it an 'institution' rather than a dispensable technical device."[2]

Thus, Stinchcombe makes an argument for imprinting at a point in time, an organization's birth, and the persistence of this imprinting on organizational forms. Stinchcombe's work enjoyed a revival of interest as a result of its centrality in Hannan and Freeman's (1989) arguments concerning structural inertia and the liability of newness. While stemming from Stinchcombe's work, Hannan and Freeman offer a somewhat different emphasis. Stability in form, for them, stems from the importance of reliable, or predictable performance of organizations across time. Reliability is argued to be a prime basis of selection pressure.

Strong form imprinting arguments have played an important role in population ecology research. Furthermore, the boundary conditions concerning what properties of an organization are in fact subject to such inertial forces has been a source of considerable empirical research (Singh, House, and Tucker, 1986; Haveman, 1992; Kraatz and Zajac, 1993). For the most part, this work does not concern itself with society's imprinting force; rather, research tends to take an organization's form as given and considers the question of its persistence across time.

Weak form imprinting arguments suggest that current organizational forms bear some legacy of the form at founding, but need not be characterized by that founding form. One process consistent with such an argument is that of local search through a complex space of alternate organizational forms (Levinthal, 1997). The notion of an organizational form suggests some mutually consistent set of structures – employment structure, technical production of goods or service, authority structure and so on. If in fact these elements of structure are interdependent in their contribution to overall organizational fitness, then the set of possible forms will comprise a "rugged fitness landscape" (Kauffman, 1993; Levinthal, 1997). Certain constellations of policies will be associated with relatively high levels of performance. Deviations from such a constellation that lead to an inconsistent set of structures will prove dysfunctional. At the same time, there is likely to exist a number of effective constellations of choices or, expressed more technically, local peaks in a fitness landscape.

Imprinting results in such a setting as long as organizations' search for superior forms is, to some degree, local. Even with local search, an organization will come to identify a reasonably consistent set of policy choices. However, the set that the organization identifies, the local peak that it discovers, is dependent upon the organization's starting position in the landscape. In contrast, if search processes are global and an organization can identify the entire set of possibilities, then there would be no such path dependence or imprinting effect. It is the conjunction of local search and, in turn, path dependence that leads to imprinting.

Gavetti and Levinthal (2000) broaden the conceptualization of search for alternate forms to include not only processes of local, experimental search but to include as well actors' imperfect cognitive representations of the actual fitness landscape. Actors are able to think intelligently about distant points in the fitness landscape and, in that sense, are not constrained by the initial substantiation of their organizational form. However, an actor's particular representation still provides cognitive blinders that guide initial choices and thereby seed and constrain subsequent efforts at experiential search. Gavetti's follow-on work with Tripsas (Tripsas and Gavetti, 2000) illustrates the power of this cognitive imprinting in the context of Polaroid's efforts to pursue the opportunity posed by digital imaging.

A more rationalistic account of path dependence may stem from the dual assumptions of interdependence among policy choices and the inflexibility of policy choices across time. Some commitments may not be readily reversed, whether investments in specialized physical assets (Williamson, 1975; Ghemawat, 1991) or administrative choices, such as the structures of employment relationships. These commitments will constrain and influence the choice of temporally flexible policy choices with which they are interdependent (Ghemawat and Levinthal, 1999).

As one relaxes the bounds of rationality on choice and action, one moves from stronger to weaker forms of imprinting. However, what is perhaps more striking, unless one entertains fantasies of frictionless worlds, imprinting, at least in its weaker forms, remains. Imprinting plays a central role in our efforts to understand the heterogeneity in firms' capabilities. Whether through local search, cognitive frames, or past commitments, prior states of a "system" constrain and guide the movement to future states. Such a "weak form" view of imprinting by no means implies that the firm is inert. It merely implies that firms have a history and that the shadow of that history persists.

## Notes

1   A side agenda item for Stinchcombe is an idea for which this essay is most often cited – the notion of liability of newness.
2   Some modest self-reflection on change efforts at our home academic units can make this abstract argument more vivid.

## References

Coase, R. (1937) The nature of the firm *Economica*, 4, 386–405.
Gavetti, G. and Levinthal, D. (2000) Looking forward and looking backward: cognitive and experiential search, *Administrative Science*.
Ghemawat, P. (1991) *Commitment*. New York: Free Press.
Ghemawat, P. and Levinthal, D. (1999) Choice structure, business strategy and performance: a generalized NK-simulation approach. Working paper.
Hannan, M. and Freeman, J. (1989). *Organizational Ecology*. Cambridge, MA: Harvard University Press.

Haveman, H. (1992) Between a rock and hard place: organizational change and performance under conditions of fundamental environmental transformation, *Administrative Science Quarterly*, 37, 48–75.

Kraatz, M. and Zajac, E. (1993) A diametric forces model of strategic change: assessing the antecedents and consequences of restructuring in the higher education industry, *Strategic Management Journal*, 14, 83–102.

Levinthal, D. (1997) Adaptation on rugged landscapes, *Management Science*, 43, 934–50.

Selznick, P. (1957) *Leadership in Administration*. Evanston IL: Row Peterson.

Singh, J., House, R., and Tucker, D. (1986) Organizational change and organizational mortality, *Administrative Science Quarterly*, 31, 587–611.

Stinchcombe, A. (1965) Social structure and organizations In J. March (ed.), *Handbook of Organizations*. Chicago, IL: Rand McNally.

Tripas, M. and Gavetti, G. (2000) Capabilities, cognition, and inertia: evidence from digital imaging, *Strategic Management Journal*, 21 (10–11): 1147–62.

Williamson, O. (1975) *Markets and Hierarchies*. New York: Free Press.

# CHAPTER SEVEN

# Imprinting or Emergence, Structure or Rules, or Why Dirty Dancing Is Always Better When You Are More Than Two

## Bruce Kogut

It is one of the dimensions of being a professor in a business school with which one has to make do. The dilemma of teaching MBAs is how to teach well to them and to teach ideas that you believe to be theoretically sound, empirically verified. Invariably, one succeeds at this endeavor. After all, there are theories, there are empirical facts, and there is even intersection between these two realms.

The other day I presented the claim that there are no dyads, but only triads. A student's jaw dropped, and then he began to laugh to himself. He had a hard time to control himself. Others joined in; apparently, the claim triggered thoughts of a day-time soap opera. The next picture I showed is displayed as figure 7.1. I would not say it was mass hysteria, but something close to it. I was afraid that this experience would destroy forever my love for this figure. It has not, it says something too important for what I think we should be thinking about.

We should be thinking about the rules that speak in the ears of managers as they make their decisions. These rules include sometimes "accept projects that have positive net present values." They also include such rules as "if you have a technology with externalities and the market is young, partner with many firms to establish your technology as a standard." And they also might include rules of a more sociological or even political nature, such as "don't upset state-owned enterprises." The structure that we observe reflects these emergent rules.

But the structure also constrains. Even if you have a rule to partner in order to establish your technology as a standard, you may not be able to implement this rule if there are no partners left, or if all proximate partners are working on another technology. Structure emerges from rules, but structure then influences subsequent behavior in its own right.

These rather vague notions have a few concrete implications that are worthwhile to think about. Consider the following:

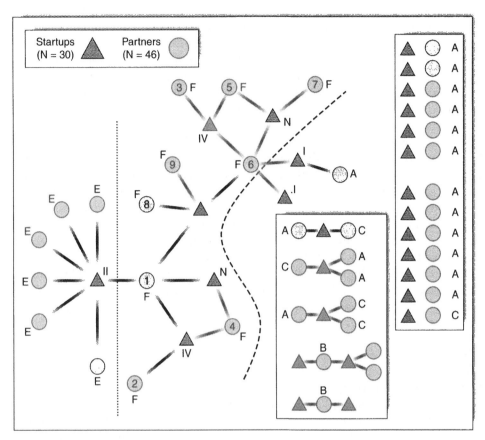

**Figure 7.1** Biotechnology

1   The work on imprinting usually cites Stinchcombe's (1965) magisterial article on stratification and its effect on organizations. This claim is easily validated just by looking across countries and noticing how organizations reflect their country conditions. Since organizational capabilities do not easily change, Stinchcombe's hypothesis implies that the capabilities of firms are strongly influenced by their institutional and political origins of birth. This observation led me once to hit upon my favorite title "The importance of being inert: country imprinting and international competition" (Kogut, 1992a). The Stinchcombe claim is that context matters, and this context is prescribed within institutional and social borders. I like to illustrate this claim by the following proposition. Consider an urn filled with balls upon which are written the strategies of all the firms in the world. Forecast the strategy of the firm of the ball to be drawn at random and write down the strength of your belief in its accuracy. Now, let me tell you the country of origin of the firm (and, for those of you who are protesting, we will partial out sectoral influences). Has not your confidence increased? The delta in your belief is our introspective confirmation of Stinchcombe's conjecture. And we did this even without running a random component analysis.

2    For people in strategy, the resource view starts with a few articles in the 1980s. This is probably not serendipitous. This was the period when Japanese competition presented American and European firms with the challenge that they had to improve quality and time to the market, that is they had to learn new organizational skills. This historical context was not lost on those who study international competition in historical perspective, for there is a stunning pattern in the cyclical rise and fall of particular countries. Many have associated this pattern with technologies. The evidence does not speak strongly to this hypothesis. Others, such as Richard Nelson and Gavin Wright (1992), and myself (Kogut, 1992b), have argued that these patterns are best explained by organizational innovations that are specific to particular regional and national locations. They are circumscribed within these borders because institutions, politics, and culture matter. Strategy has been slow to understand this claim. Only recently have some voices started to think about sources outside the firm. This observation is only remarkable in strategy because the focus is on firm rents and the assumption is that rents can only be earned by resources specific to a firm. Yet, these resources themselves are concatenations of the networks (e.g. labor, material, educational) external to the firm. Surely, firms differ in their design principles, and in the facility by which these resources are combined and managed. Still the external context matters for the provision of the basic materials, as well as for determining the conditions of competition and demand.

3    Stinchcombe's claim is that institutional context influences not only the provision of external resources, but also the way in which firms organize these resources. Germany has holding companies, and its firms are organized into divisions, with worker co-determination at the top, and work councils on the floor. DiMaggio and Powell (1983) addressed the puzzle how to explain this within-country homogeneity. They suggest firms are coerced to do this (Germany requires co-determination), they respond to normative expectations (Germany supports a "social economy"), or to mimetic influences (prestigious German firms adopted this practice, so will I). DiMaggio and Powell summarize these homogenizing forces under the label of "isomorphism," that is, organizations are similarly constituted in organizational fields. They posit then firms are products of social forces. This perspective is echoed in Podolny's (1993) work on status effects found in networks, or in Gulati and Gargiulo's (1999) claim that networks in one industry replicate the pattern in another network. These seem like similar arguments but they are quite different. Podolny measures status as a "structural" construct, such as the centrality of an actor in a citation network. The claim is this structural variable influences subsequently the network to stabilize around these patterns. Gulati's and Gargiulo's argument is, as is almost all the literature on diffusion of firm practices (e.g. poison pills, multidivisional structure), about dyadic relations between nodes. IBM and Sun partner in semiconductors, and they partner in software. This argument predicts who the nodes will be in a relational network. It does not predict the structure of the network. It tells us where relationships come from, not where network structure comes from. It can't predict, for example, that relationships in biotechnology will be dispersed, and alliances in microprocessors will reveal a star structure. From my studies with Gordon Walker and others (Kogut, Walker, and Kim, 1992c; Walker, Kogut, and Shan, 1997), we know that these industries look this way. Of course, all of this does not

matter if you don't think that position and structure are important to a firm's strategic opportunities and resources. If you are of this opinion, then don't try out this argument on all the small software firms that grunted and groaned about Microsoft, while they all rode its standard.

4   The problem of isomorphism is that it assumes that whatever a firm is isomorphic to, already exists. How did this all start? In my thinking, it starts with a few constraints and coercive mechanisms, such as the state saying "you must have work councils." No wonder so many studies have found the influence of state on human resource practices. But this should be the start of the analysis, not the end. (It may not be the start if we want to ask about the strategies pursued by firms and other actors to induce the state to enact coercively.) I would then consider at least two competing sources of variation: technology and social construction. Certain technologies display, for example, network externalities that foster standard races. In these races, alliances will be important, and hence firms will race to partner. If "tipping" points are reached, then a few stars will be created, whereby a couple of firms (or less) will be central. The government will have views on whether one star is a good idea, and here the constraint of anti-trust might matter. However, I would also look at the Podolny prestige effects, whereby cooperation is also influenced by social stratification. Business groups might avoid each other, small firms might be shunned by banks. Stinchcombe has returned, no longer as an isomorphic slam-dunk, but as a rule that influences the decisions of firms with whom and whether to partner. The network *emerges* from this combination of technological, social, and coercive elements.

5   Strategies in emergent settings are a worthy subject of study, but I wish to arrive at one more conclusion. We have stated that firms' capabilities reside partially on the resources external to them. We have noted that networks emerge in response to technological and social influences, and the social influences (if not the technological ones as well) will surely differ by countries. Does this variation in network structure matter to the performance of firms? We don't have many statistical studies on this question, but there are many qualitative studies. I think the answer is yes. If asked, how much does it matter, I would wager sometimes a lot. I am thinking, for example, of Dyer's (1996) studies on how supplier relationships are a source of advantage to Toyota.

Let me summarize the above discussion by posing what I believe to be an emergent research program. This program looks at capabilities as they develop over time. These capabilities are not just specific to firms, but to networks in which firms are located. The intellectual challenge is to understand how these networks form dynamically over time and in response to what factors. I have suggested that one way to view this formation is the competition among rules, some which are fixed, that guide the decisions of firms. Those rules that proliferate stochastically determine the structure of the network. This structure, in turn, both inhibits the strategic choices of firms, and also provides differential capabilities to them depending upon their location in this structure.

There are some implicit questions in this approach that are related to past research. For example, monopoly power has often been measured by the number of competitors. Most studies show that this power drops quickly with the number of competitors.

Network structure is not simply the number of firms, or the density of the industry. Structure means that a network can be summarized by global statistics, but also that individual firm strategies are influenced by its local environment.

Let's make this clearer. Burt (1992, 1997) proposes to measure this local structure by the degree of closure ("structural holes"). He shows in many studies that firms occupying such holes enjoy rents. These results ask why are they sustained? The answer to this question is not clear, because we don't have a theory of how networks are formed in the first place and how structure endures. These issues deserve more attention.

Granovetter (1995) looks more at global statistics regarding path lengths. Path lengths are useful for understanding the speed of diffusion, and they were empirically measured in this context. His claim is that innovation is promoted by searching distantly from one's local position, regardless of how closed it is. He has a theory of innovation, Burt has a theory of rent abstraction.

These lines of inquiry suggest that strategy should think more abstractly about the structural properties of an industry. These properties reflect technological and social rules. They suggest heterogeneity among firms may be attributed to variations in position in a differentiated network. These variations reflect different access to capabilities in this network (e.g. supplier chains) and different abilities to abstract rents or to identify innovations.

This merging of social stratification as revealed in network formation and the strategies of firms as determined by "rules" (e.g. abstract rents) represents a vast terrain of inquiry. It breaks the solipsistic argument of unique resources determining profits, when unique is defined as what others don't have. It returns the focus to understanding position as arising out of "quality" of a firm (its prestige, its technological record) and to its structural position in the network. Resources, capabilities, structure all matter but in a curiously new way. Isn't it marvelous what a bit of historical attention to cross-country and cross-industry variations can suggest? If only I can get that student to get his mind down to business.

## References

Burt, R. S. (1992) *Structural Holes: The Social Structure of Competition*. Cambridge, MA: Harvard University Press.

Burt, R. S. (1997) The contingent value of social capital, *Administrative Science Quarterly*, 42, 339–65.

DiMaggio, P. J. and Powell, W. W. (1983) The iron cage revisited: institutional isomorphism and collective rationality in organizational fields, *American Sociological Review*, 48, 147–60.

Dyer, J. H. (1996) Does governance matter? Keiretsu alliances and asset specificity as sources of Japanese competitive advantage, *Organization Science*, 7, 649–66.

Granovetter, M. (1995) *Getting a Job: A Study of Contacts and Careers*. Chicago: University of Chicago Press, 2nd edn.

Gulati, R. and Gargiulo, M. (1999) Where do interorganizational networks come from?, *American Journal of Sociology*, 104, 1439–93.

Kogut, B. (1992a) The importance of being inert: country imprinting and international competition. In S. Ghoshal and E. Westney (eds), *Organization Theory and the Multinational*

*Corporation*. New York: Macmillan.

Kogut, B. (1992b) National organizing principles of work and the erstwhile dominance of the American multinational corporation, *Industrial and Corporate Change*, 1, 285–326.

Kogut, B. Walker, G., and Kim, D. J. (1992) Cooperation and entry induction as an extension of technological rivalry, *Research Policy*, 24, 77–95.

Nelson, R. and Wright, G. (1992) The rise and fall of American technological leadership: the postwar era in historical perspective, *Journal of Economic Literature*, 30, 1931–64.

Podolny, J. M. (1993) A status-based model of market competition, *American Journal of Sociology*, 98, 829–72.

Stinchcombe, A. L. (1965) Social structures and organizations. In J. G. March (ed.), *Handbook of Organizations*, Chicago: Rand-McNally 142–93.

Walker, G., Kogut, B., and Weijian Shan, W. (1997) Social capital, structural holes, and the formation of an industry network, *Organization Science*, 8, 109–25.

Watts, D. (1999) *Small Worlds: The Dynamics of Networks Between Order and Randomness*. Princeton: Princeton University Press.

# CHAPTER EIGHT

# Strategic Capabilities in Emerging Fields: Navigating Ambiguity, Leveraging Social Capital, and Creating Identity in Silicon Alley

## Theresa K. Lant

New firms struggling to accumulate resources face challenges to their survival that exceed those of firms that already have resource endowments. These challenges include a liability of newness (Stinchcombe, 1965; Singh and Lumsden, 1990) and a liability of smallness (Aldrich and Auster, 1986; Bruderl et al., 1992). New ventures typically start with few resources, and are at a high risk of early failure (Aldrich, 1999). Entrepreneurs' resource endowments may be limited to their own human, financial, and social capital; they must be capable of attracting these resources from their environment. Resource holders such as investors, customers, and potential employees perceive investments of their resources in these new ventures as highly risky. Nascent firms lack a history of interaction with stakeholders; they have not had the opportunity to develop reputational capital. Reputation is developed through interactions with stakeholders and via the circulation of information about the firm among stakeholders (Deephouse, 2000; Fombrun, 1996; Rindova and Fombrun, 1999).

The challenges of survival for new firms in *emerging industries* are increased well beyond those of new firms in established industries. Not only must entrepreneurs convince resource holders that their firm is worthy of investment, they must also work to establish resource holder confidence in the emerging industry of which they are a part. Aldrich and Fiol (1994) and Aldrich (1999) have argued that entrepreneurs working to establish new industries must establish legitimacy for their industry as well as their individual businesses.

> Without widespread knowledge and understanding of their activity, entrepreneurs may have difficulty maintaining the support of key constituencies. Potential customers, suppliers, and sources of financial resources may not fully understand the nature of the new venture, and potential employees may view jobs in the new population with a mixture of skepticism and distrust. To succeed, founders must find strategies to raise the level of public knowledge about a new activity to the point where it is taken for granted. (Aldrich, 1999: 231)

Thus, entrepreneurs in emerging industries must create cognitive legitimacy for new types of businesses, products, or services. "Cognitive legitimacy refers to the spread of knowledge about a new venture .l.l. One can assess cognitive legitimacy by measuring the level of public knowledge about an activity" (Aldrich and Fiol, 1994: 648).

The idea that entrepreneurs do something "different" than managers is widely accepted, but not well understood. Upon deeper reflection, the argument that entrepreneurs "create legitimacy" has profound implications for the way we think about "competitive capabilities." Entrepreneurs in emerging industries must engage in collective action that helps to develop the legitimacy of their emerging fields of business (Mezias and Kuperman, 2000). In doing so they play an active role in *creating* their emerging environment. In such a context, before firms in emerging industries can attract financial and human resources, they must obtain the attention and legitimacy resources that are the inputs to the process of developing reputational capital.

In emerging economic sectors, market segments and the boundaries of competition are not yet established. Entrepreneurial actors play key roles in the evolution of industry roles and structures. What types of capabilities facilitate the creation of cognitive legitimacy in emerging fields? What are the capabilities that enable entrepreneurs to legitimize new technologies, markets, and ways of doing business? In order to explore the question of capabilities in emerging fields, I draw on my observations of a nascent regional agglomeration, called Silicon Alley. My observations of the entrepreneurial actors in this field suggest that they are engaged in a process of trying to make sense of who they are, what their product or service offerings are, what the potential market is, and with whom they should form relationships. The capabilities that appear to be important in developing cognitive legitimacy include: the ability to navigate and structure ambiguous environments; the ability to exercise social capital, and the ability to create and sustain an identity that is simultaneously unique and credible (see figure 8.1).

## Description of Silicon Alley

*Silicon Alley* is a regional agglomeration of firms, located in the New York metropolitan area, engaged in new media businesses. The term new media refers to the combination of "elements of computing technology, telecommunications, and content to create products and services which can be used interactively by consumers and busi-

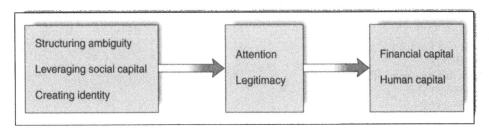

**Figure 8.1** Capabilities for attracting attention, legitimacy, and capital

ness users" (PriceWaterhouseCoopers, 2000). This regional sector began to emerge in New York City in the early 1990s. New media employment in the New York area grew from approximately 28,000 FTEs in 1992 to almost 250,00 FTEs in 1999. New media positions increased 40 percent per year between 1997 and 1999. Total New York area payroll in new media grew 55 percent annually since 1995, from $1.4 billion to $8.31 billion in 1999 (PriceWaterhouseCoopers, 2000). The total number of companies engaged in new media has grown 25 percent annually from about 4,000 in 1996 to approximately 8,500 in 1999. Total gross revenues increased 53 percent from $2 billion in 1996 to nearly $17 billion in 1999 (see table 8.1). This growth in new media in New York is being driven by entrepreneurial activity. According to a Coopers & Lybrand/New York New Media Association study, in 1996, 89 percent of new media entities in New York were privately held, and over half had annual payrolls of less than $300,000. Sixty-three percent had revenues under $1 million, 18 percent had revenues between $1 and $5 million, and only 19 percent had revenues over $5 million. In 1999, a PriceWaterhouseCoopers/New York New Media Association Study stated that 70 percent of the 8,500 companies reported revenues under $1 million. Twenty-one percent had revenues between $1 and $5 million, and 9 percent had revenues over $5 million. Since 1997, $6 billion in venture and IPO funding has been raised. The number of firms receiving venture capital rose from 32 in 1998 (average deal $8.1 million) to 110 in 1999 (average deal $11.5 million). The number of IPOs in the region rose from 8 in 1998 (average capital raised $32.5 million) to 41 in 1999 (average capital raised $85.1 million).

## Capability 1: Structuring Ambiguous Environments

In order to attract resources to their nascent firms, entrepreneurs must make sense of their businesses for resource holders. Resource holders need to understand the potential market that the firm will serve, the value of the product or service that the firm will provide, and the nature of competition that the firm will face. In emerging industries,

**Table 8.1** Growth in New York new media, 1996–1999

|  | 1996 | 1997 | 1999 |
| --- | --- | --- | --- |
| No. of new media "entities" | 4,250 | 5,000 | 8,500 |
| FTEs | 71K (in NYC 24K) | 106K (NYC 56K) | 250K (NYC 138K) |
| Total revenue | $3.8 billion | $5.7 billion | $16.8 billion |
| Privately held (%) | 89 | 83 | Approx. 95 |
| Revenues less than 1 million (%) | 63 | 83 | 70 |
| Revenues between 1–5 million (%) | 18 | 12 | 21 |
| Revenues over 5 million (%) | 19 | 5 | 9 |

Information obtained from Price WaterhouseCoopers NYNMA surveys.

there is a great deal of ambiguity with respect to all of these factors. Pollock and Rindova (2001) refer to the uncertainty of investors as being due to a lack of "organizing structures." An organizing structure would include such things as categories of products. Research on information processing has demonstrated that such organizing structures are necessary for information comprehension (Fiske and Taylor, 1984). Resource holders will not provide their resources to businesses that they do not understand. Once an industry has matured and the positions of competitors have evolved, then investors and customers alike come to understand that, for example, Dell and Gateway are competitors in the personal computer market. Customers understand the product category and can compare the competitors on features of their product.

In emerging industries, the nature and value of products and services are not understood. It is often unclear how one firm's product compares with another, or if two firms are even competing in the same product category. This is because both the nature of products and their potential value is in flux; the relative positions of firms offering these evolving products are also evolving. A well-known example of such ambiguity and the evolution of product/service definitions can be seen in the way firms that emerged as Internet search engines have added features such as information categorization, content agglomeration, and email over time. Potential customers and competitors experienced significant uncertainty regarding the nature and value of these services, how to use them, and which firms should be considered direct competitors.

Entrepreneurial actors worked to create organizing structures around product/service categories in a number of ways. For instance, a communiqué from the organizer of Silicon Alley '98, a conference on New York New Media, states that "many of the companies [participating in the conference] are not yet categorized .|.|. if your company is one of them please let me know which category you would like to be listed under (commerce, content, interactive, agency, etc.)" (Calacanis, 1998). The New York New Media Association (the local non-profit industry association) also helped create such structures by asking members to identify themselves within various categories, which evolved over time, and then organizing their membership directories according to the categories.

The ability to create structure in the ambiguous environment of Silicon Alley can be seen in the "real time" categorization processes around product/service offerings. Early in the life of Silicon Alley, the number of major business categories listed by the New York New Media Association was 15 (1997 Directory). These categories were derived from the prior industries in which NYNMA members were employed, including film, publishing, and broadcasting. Even the category of digital media had its origins in CD-ROM games and educational materials. Within these major categories were numerous sub-categories. Most are derived from lines of business that predate the Internet. By 2001, the number of major business categories had increased to 18; more significantly, the new categories, web casting, e-commerce, and audio, were categories created specifically for Internet-enabled capabilities that had not existed before. Sub-categories increased overall by 12; several of these additions represent new technologies or capabilities, such as DVD and B2B e-commerce. Others, however, appear to represent the movement of traditional services into the new media marketplace, such as architects and temporary staffing services. This categorization process appears to "borrow" structure and meaning from categories in established industries that already carry meaning for resource holders. Then, new categories are added as the unfamiliar products and services start to connote something meaningful. The number and complexity of categories begins to increase through this structuring process. Resource holders come to understand the meaning of new categories through the association between old, familiar categories and new, unfamiliar ones.

The ability to create meaning and order under conditions of ambiguity is touted as a strategic capability. Organizations trying to get a piece of the action in new media attempt to leverage this ability. Coopers and Lybrand's New Media Group was one of the first consulting firms to focus attention and resources on new media. Very early in the evolution of Silicon Alley one of their advertisements states: "Some Do. Sum Don't. We Do. New Media. WE GET IT." Similarly, one of the first law firms to start representing new media firms in New York City claims "Here is what New Media looked like to investors just a few years ago (a person looking through opaque glasses). Then we made it make sense." A public relations firm proclaims "Even Your Mother Doesn't Know What the Hell You Do . . . We'll Explain it to Her . . . and Everyone Else." Early movers in sense-giving activity gain attention and legitimacy by providing meaning and order for resource holders, thus reducing their sense of uncertainty.

## Capability 2: Creating and Leveraging Social Capital

Actors in this emerging field come from a wide variety of professional backgrounds and industries, including advertising, graphic design, publishing, digital technology, software development, visual and performing arts, and journalism. Initially, there were few network connections among individuals in different professional groups. From a structural holes perspective (Burt, 1997) this affords significant opportunity for bridging structural holes, a form of entrepreneurial arbitrage.

In this process of trying to simultaneously create and make sense of this new arena of social and economic activity, interaction among actors across "firms" is as important and pervasive as interaction among actors within firms. Often the purpose of these connections is to gain financial resources, knowledge resources, or legitimacy (Aldrich and Fiol, 1994). Sometimes the purpose of relationships is unclear. There is a drive to make connections; perhaps creating options for the future. There are many examples of events and settings whose purpose is to provide the opportunity to make these connections. "Cybersuds," sponsored by the New York New Media Association (NYNMA), is "a chance to meet people from the regional new media community in a casual atmosphere – exchange ideas, business opportunities, and gossip" (NYNMA communiqué, 1998). Participants would include diverse groups ranging from young "would-be" artists from the East Village to representatives from New York consulting, law, and venture capital firms. A local monthly publication, the *Silicon Alley Reporter*, has a regular column entitled "Digital DimSum" which reports on planned and unplanned events in which players in this field are found interacting and playing together.

Professional boundaries and definitions defined by traditional media and traditional industries started falling away as interaction among players from different arenas increased. Images of converging, shifting and blurring boundaries of interaction among actors with different backgrounds are exemplified by advertisements for the Silicon Alley 1998 conference, which looks like a Venn diagram, and for New York's Information Technology Center at 55 Broad Street, which calls itself the "Global Community Sandbox."

Entrepreneurial actors leverage their social capital by bridging structural holes, creating opportunity for themselves and others, and becoming more central to network interactions and the flow of information. For example, in a feature article in *Wired Magazine* the editor of the *Silicon Alley Reporter* (a start-up magazine dedicated to reporting on news in Silicon Alley) is described as a central network broker. "VC's and money-starved executives alike use him as a human search engine for lucrative deals. It's not just that he's a magazine editor. The *Silicon Alley Reporter* has become to Calacanis what the pole is to a stripper – a means of orienting the show. People come to Jason Calacanis because he's a connector" (*Wired*, 7/99). Calacanis did not come to the "show" endowed with much social capital (or financial & human capital either). He leveraged his friendship ties with a group of early Silicon Alley entrepreneurs, founded a newsletter in which he reported on their activities, and over the course of several months became a major media "voice" for Silicon Alley entrepreneurs.

Another example of leveraging social capital is the case of Bill Rudin, a younger member of the powerful Rudin real estate family in New York City. Young Mr Rudin was aware of the growing number of Internet entrepreneurs in his social circle. His family owned the former headquarters of bankrupt Drexel Burnham Lambert in lower Manhattan. Through his social connections he recognized an opportunity; through his family connections he had the means to seize an opportunity. When the Guiliani administration formed the New York Information Technology District Commission and the Lower Manhattan Revitalization Plan, a project dedicated to modernizing the former Drexel building became feasible. Rudin convinced his father and uncle to accept the risky project, which became the New York Information Technology Center at 55 Broad Street (aka the Global Community Sandbox). Rudin had to leverage his social capital once again in order to convince new media business tenants to move to his building. During Silicon Alley's emergence, the lower Manhattan financial district was suffering from a local recession and high vacancy rates. New media entrepreneurs preferred to be in Soho, Greenwich Village, and the Flatiron districts, where they perceived their social and business networks to be denser and yield more opportunity. Rudin's first tenant was CD retailer N2K (since acquired by CDNow); once this prominent tenant was signed, it became easier to obtain subsequent tenants. Number 55 Broad Street is now a major center for new media and new technology firms, education, and conferences.

## Capability 3: Creating a Unique and Credible Identity

A key group in the emerging New York new media community has been called the "Early True Believers." They are "the closest thing Silicon Alley has to an indigenous population .l.l. they're brainy math-and-music types with impressive liberal-arts educations, mostly upper-crust backgrounds, and birthdays in or around 1966" (*New York Magazine*, 3/6/00). They would hold social networking events called

"CyberSlacker parties" (*New York Magazine*, 3/6/00). Many of the friends and attendees are the founders of Silicon Alley firms such as MTVi, Feed, Razorfish, Pseudo.com, StockObjects, Nerve, and the *Silicon Alley Reporter*. Beyond social networking, these entrepreneurial actors moved quickly to spread the word about the possibilities for new media business and about how and why New York was both different and "the place to be" for new media. They brought with them a sense of their own social identity, and tried to influence the character of New York new media to be consistent with this identity. They used several vehicles to spread the word. One vehicle was to sponsor and organize "events" – conferences, seminars, and parties that would draw both "true believers" and newcomers together. Thus, social networking appears to serve a collective identity function as well as an information arbitrage function.

The manner in which information is communicated by the media also influences the perceived "identity" of Silicon Alley. Much of what is written focuses on what makes New York new media distinctive. The editor of the *Silicon Alley Reporter* is the Alley's self-proclaimed evangelist. He uses his "bully pulpit" to influence the identity of the new emerging NY media environment. "A bunch of granola eating hippies from San Francisco were going to dictate the most powerful medium of all time? Give me a break. I'll tell you who's going to dictate the most powerful medium of all time – New Yorkers and people in Los Angeles, because they've always dictated what's happened to big mediums" (Shiftonline, 6/11/99). On his editorial page, the editor of the *Silicon Alley Reporter* states:

> Ten years from now people will laugh when they read about all the attention given to the browser wars. Give me a break, is Seinfeld funnier on a Sony TV rather than a JVC? New York and Los Angeles are becoming the driving force in the Internet Industry for a very simple reason: they are the talent and media capitals of the world. Sure, content and community are going to take longer to play out than the tools to make them. Right now, LA and NYC may be on the bottom of the food chain by the Red Herring's and Upside's standards because we don't have the immediate revenues that make myopic venture capitalists drool. But there's no place on the food chain I'd rather be. Would you rather have made the camera that shot "Citizen Kane," or make "Citizen Kane? (*Silicon Alley Reporter*, April, 1998: 3).

These identity-creation communications appear to be aimed at establishing what Brewer (1991) calls "optimal distinctiveness" of social identity. Participants in New York new media seek to be both distinctive and legitimate. Being seen as a legitimate business is critical in order to obtain resources from the environment. However, in order to compete effectively with other new firms for these resources, one must stand out in the crowed. These attempts to be both unique and credible can be seen in the juxtaposition of images in new media advertising. One advertisement shows a man in a suit surfing across the recognizable financial district skyline of lower Manhattan. This firm is attempting to be seen as wacky, nimble, Internet savvy, but also one that fits in with the established financial community. Another firm places itself at the crossroads of "Wired" and "Wall Street;" again, a demonstration that the firm "gets" the Internet, but is well placed in the financial community.

## Conclusion

The firms in Silicon Alley have and will suffer the liabilities of smallness and newness. Many will survive, however, either as independent entities or as parts of merged organizations. My observations suggest that the three capabilities – the ability to navigate and structure ambiguous environments; the ability to exercise social capital, and the ability to create and sustain an identity that is simultaneously unique and credible – are exercised actively during the emergence of the industries that constitute new media. If my predictions are correct, the firms most likely to survive will be those who exercised these capabilities most effectively.

## Acknowledgement

Based on a presentation at the Conference on the Evolution of Firm Capabilities: Emergence, Development, and Change, Tuck School of Business. I would like to thank Constance Helfat for organizing the conference and for her support and suggestions with respect to this chapter.

## References

Aldrich, H. E., (1999) *Organizations Evolving*. London: Sage Publications.
Aldrich, H. E. and Auster, E. (1986) Even dwarfs start small. In B. M. Staw and L. L. Cummings (eds), *Research on Organizational Behavior*, Vol. 8. Greenwich, CT: JAI Press, 165–98.
Aldrich, H. E. and Fiol, C. M. (1994) Fools rush in? The institutional context of industry creation, *Academy of Management Review*, 19(4), 645–70.
Brewer, M. (1991) The social self: on being the same and different at the same time, *PSPB*, 17, 475–82.
Bruderl, J., Preisendorfer, P., and Ziegler, R. (1992) Survival chances of newly founded business organizations, *American Sociological Review*, 57(2), 227–42.
Burt, R. (1997) The contingent value of social capital, *Administrative Science Quarterly*, 42, 339–65.
Calacanis, J. M. (1998) SA98 Update! E-mail communiqué, February, 12.
Deephouse, D. L. (2000) Media reputation as a strategic resource: an integration of mass communication and resource-based theories, *Journal of Management*, 26, 1091–112.
Fiske, S. T. and Taylor, S. E. (1984) *Social Cognition*. Reading: Addison Wesley
Fombrun, C. (1996) *Reputation: Realizing Value from the Corporate Image*. Boston: Harvard Business Press.
Garud, R. and Lant, T. (1998) Navigating Silicon Alley: kaleidoscopic experiences. Working paper.
Lant, T. K. and Baum, J. (1995) Cognitive sources of socially constructed competitive groups: examples from the Manhattan hotel-industry. In W. R. Scott and C. Sorenson (eds.), *The Institutional Construction of Organizations*. Thousand Oaks, CA: Sage.
Mezias, S. J. and Kuperman, J. (2000) The community dynamics of enterpreneurship: the birth of the American film industry, 1895–1929, *Journal of Business Venturing*, 16, 209–33.
*New York Magazine*, 3/6/00.
Pollock, T. and Rindova, V. (2001) How buzz works: an examination of the role of media

reported information in the IPO market. Working paper.

Porac, J. F. and Thomas, H. (1990) Taxonomic mental models in competitor definition, *Academy of Management Review*, 15, 224–40.

Porac, J. F., Thomas, H., and Baden-Fuller, C. (1989) Competitive groups as cognitive communities: the case of Scottish knitwear manufacturers, *Journal of Management Studies*, 26, 397–416.

Reger, R. K. and Huff, A. S. (1993) Strategic groups: a cognitive perspective, *Strategic Management Journal*, 14, 103–24.

Rindova, V. and Fombrun, C. (1999). Constructing competitive advantage: the role of firm-constituent interactions, *Strategic Management Journal*, 20 (8), 691–710.

Shiftonline, June 11, 1999.

*Silicon Alley Reporter*, April 1998: p. 3.

Singh, J. and Lumsden, (1990) Theory and research in organizational ecology. *Annual Review of Sociology*, 16, 161–95.

Stinchcombe, A. (1965). Social structure and organizations, In J. G. March (ed.), *Handbook of Organizations*. Chicago, IL: Rand McNally, 142–93.

Weick, K. (1979) *The Social Psychology of Organizing*. New York: Random House.

White, H. W. (1981) Where do markets come from? *American Journal of Sociology*, 83, 517–47.

*Wired*, 7/99.

# Part II

# Incremental Development and Change

# CHAPTER NINE

# Why Do Firms Tend to Become Different?

## Birger Wernerfelt

## Introduction

A central lesson to emerge since the early 1980s of research in management is that a firm's strategy has to be rooted in its unique properties. Unless a firm is already different, it is hard to prescribe a path to sustainable above-average profits. This makes management theory look simultaneously good and bad. The good part is that firms, in fact, *are different* from each other. So the theory is relevant. The bad part is that we have a very poor understanding of how and why firms *become different* (Rumelt et al. 1991; Nelson, 1991: Helfat, 2000).

One explanation is that a firm will want to differentiate from an identical competitor in order to reduce competition. However, this does not explain who gets the more attractive position, or what prevents other firms from entering and driving down profits. Another class of stories, which include evolutionary economics (Nelson and Winter, 1982), population ecology (Hannon and Freeman, 1989), and various other uses of genetic analogies, is that firms are different because bounded rationality prevents them from becoming identical. Some management theorists look at this as unsatisfactory, because we believe that management matters in the sense that firms try to, and generally succeed in, doing the right things.

The present chapter presents a theory that combines elements of competitive differentiation with some bounded rationality. The argument is one in which competitive pressures cause a small deviation from rationality to snowball into a major deviation in the growth path of the firm. In two steps, the argument is that: (1) An initial error produces, in the firm's resource stock, a change that hurts in the execution of the current strategy, but helps in the execution of another strategy. (2) This puts the firm at a competitive disadvantage that it can escape by changing its strategy. The overall argument is consistent with D'Aunno, et al.'s (2000) view that both institutional and market forces contribute to organizational change. The idea that a missed step in the resource development process can have long-term consequences has some similarity with Cohen and Levinthal's claim that "lack of investment in an area of expertise early on may foreclose the future development of a technical capability in the area" (1990: 128).

Another feature of the proposed theory is that it operates on an essential function of the firm; the reporting of information to management. This links it to a theory of the firm, ensures that it applies to all firms, and fits well with informal accounts suggesting that most differences between firms are organizational, having to do with what groups of employees do and do well. We do not mean to imply that the mechanism proposed here is the only source of firm heterogeneity. Other explanations, such as the existence of past irreversible investments in physical assets (Sutton, 1991; Ghemawat, 1991), no doubt play a role in several cases.

Most of the chapter will be devoted to what we will call the "reporting error" version of the argument. The premise is that employees can report only a minor fraction of the available information to management, and that management's information constitutes a resources. So a reporting error will cause a slight misfit between a firm's resources and its product-market strategy. More importantly, a reporting error will put the firm at a competitive disadvantage relative to competitors who have not suffered such setbacks. So the firm finds itself with incentives to tweak its strategy away from competition and in the direction of its resources. Over time, this firm would acquire more resources to support the new strategy. The next time it suffers a reporting error, it would therefore not be an option to revert to the original strategy. Competition forces the firm further and further away and it becomes increasingly different from its original competitors. If many employees report a lot of information per period over a large number of periods, the chances of such bifurcating errors could be large.

**Example**

Because the preceding may seem a bit abstract and far-fetched, we will now offer a fictional and simplified, but still more specific example.

Consider two providers of executive education, who initially follow identical product-market strategies. In order for the firms to keep the content of their courses up to date, their employees collect information from students and instructors. Suppose now that an employee meets a customer, who is interested in more quantitative course content than the majority of the market. If this customer is particularly convincing, the employee may submit a report that gives "too much" detail about the type of quantitative course content customers want, and too little detail about what other customers want. One could now tell a reasonable story about management itself being misled by this report. However, assume that management understands that the report does not cover the wants of representative customers. Even so, compared to competition, management knows less about what non-quantitative course content is desired, but more about the quantitative content. So it is not unreasonable to predict that the firm will offer a slightly more quantitative course than its competitor.

This product differentiation leads to a decline in competition and the beginnings of market segmentation. To be really effective in its niche, the firm has to learn more about the market for quantitative courses, and perhaps differentiate its offerings more sharply from those of the competitor. When the next error occurs, the only attractive changes in the strategy will take the firm even further away from competition. So over time, it will collect different information, build up different resources, and offer a different product.

## Plan of the chapter

In the next section, we develop the intuition behind the "reporting error" version of the argument in more detail. In order to convince skeptics that the argument is logically consistent, we then present a formal economic model of the process. To make clear that the reporting error story is just an example, albeit an important one, we end the chapter by describing several other cases in which errors can produce heterogeneity.

## Intuition

In this section, we will go through several steps to make the argument at an intuitive level.

### The Informational Implications of Specialization

It is not necessary to argue that modern society is characterized by a lot of division of labor. This is the *raison d'être* of all economies. We want to make the more rarely argued point that specialization of task implies specialization of information (Simon, 1976: 238; Polanyi, 1962). Agents learn about their environments, and as they perform different tasks, they learn different things. An R&D manager will tend to learn more about his area than somebody else's and a sales person will generally be the local expert on her district. Two trading partners, who may or may not be in the same firm, will tend to learn different things about the environment. So while specialization of task obviously implies a need for coordination, it also endows agents with heterogeneous information. Management can coordinate better if more of this information is taken into account, and the values of different pieces of information depend on the direction of coordination, that is the product-market strategy.

The above is just a new way of saying what we already know; that there is a relationship between organizational design and strategy. Every product-market strategy creates different demands for different pieces of information, and implies an ideal set of reporting rules. Similarly, a particular set of reporting rules provides management with a specific subset of the feasible information. The current and accumulated information available to management is in turn a resource that supports a specific strategy better than others. *We can therefore think of strategies and reporting rules as pairs. If one changes, so should the other.*

### When do we have firms?

The need for ongoing adaptation to changes in the environment takes center stage in the adjustment-cost theory of the firm (Wernerfelt, 1997). The theory relies on the costs of adapting a trading relationship to new circumstances. (1) If the need for adaptation arises very infrequently, the players may negotiate changes on an as-needed basis. A house renovation is an example of this type of arrangement. (2) If the number of possible changes is very small, the players can refer to an ex ante agreed upon price, and change without any extra negotiation. This is, for example, what happens if you decide to ask for extra services at the hairdresser. (3) If frequent and diverse changes are needed, the above solutions do not work well, but a hierarchical relationship, or a firm, may. That is, in exchange for an average payment and the right to quit, one player may agree to let the other decide on the changes. The relationship between a manager and a secretary is an example of this.

The theory then implies that firms are used when diverse, high-frequency adjustments are needed: exactly when large amounts of new information have to reach management. So upward reporting of information is an essential property of firms. As evidence of the importance of communication, recall that *it is common to define someone's place in a firm by "who they report to,"* rather than by their productive role.

Fortunately, the firm often gives employees good incentives to communicate. While agents in an arm's length relationship may withhold information from each other in order to protect their bargaining positions, the upfront negotiation in the firm implies that there is less reason to withhold information there (Wernerfelt, 2001). Consistent with this, empirical studies have shown that there is more communication within, than between, firms (Tushman, 1978; Simester and Knez, 2002). Conversely, Monteverde (1995) demonstrated that activities demanding more cross-functional communication are more likely to be performed inside the firm.

### What information gets reported to management?

If all information could be reported to management, they could in theory coordinate the team perfectly. However, this is not possible. Nor is it possible for management to tell employees exactly what information to report. On the assumption that information can be put into classes, the best management can do is to formulate rules asking for reports on certain classes of information. As noted above, management wants the rules to result in information that supports execution of its product-market strategy. Once the rules are formulated, individual employees have to decide how to apply them.

Both formulation and application of reporting rules are very complex tasks because only a tiny fraction of the employees' information can be reported to, and used by, management. Furthermore, the reporting choices are made under highly imperfect information. Management has to base its requests on judgements about what classes of information will prove important, and employees have to make guesses about whether trends are merely local or of broader importance. So while it is possible that management and employees can find the ex ante optimal set of reporting decisions, it is not unreasonable to predict occasional mistakes.

### Why do different firms choose to focus on different information?

As noted above, we could also phrase this question as "why do firms have different resources?" or "why do firms pursue different strategies?" While there undoubtedly are many reasons for this, we want to think of ex ante identical firms that diverge because of seemingly innocuous errors in the reporting of information. In order to minimize the role of bounded rationality in the argument, we will assume that only one player errs, and that the error is short-lived. For simplicity, this can be thought of as a single error in a discrete time setting.

It is likely that most reporting errors have relatively minor impacts on firm performance. However, because one piece of information often aids in the interpretation or use of another, a missing report tends to reduce the value of other, correctly reported, information. This complementarity works both within and between time periods. For example, a missed report on an object ("the state of $x_1$ at time t") may make a another report on a related topic ("the state of $x_2$ at time t") or a later report on the same object ("the state of $x_1$ at time t+1") less valuable. In this way, an error can cause more widespread damage.

*There are two forces through which such damage can cause a firm to change its strategy and reporting rules. There is a resource effect and a competitive effect.* First, based on the mistaken report and the damage, the firm has (ever so little) additional information and "expertise" in a new area, but fewer than expected resources in the old product-market area. Using resource-based logic, it may thus make sense to build on the expertise and tweak the strategy towards the new resources. Second, because competitors now have relatively more expertise in the original product-market area, they can be expected to exploit their newfound advantages and amplify the differences. This makes the new area even more attractive because the firm can avoid competition from similar, but stronger, rivals.

If the new area suggested by the reporting error is sufficiently attractive, the two above effects may cause the firm to change its strategy and hence its future reporting practices. Over time, the attractiveness of the original strategy will decrease as the novel expertise accumulates. The next time it suffers a reporting error, it would therefore not be an option to revert to the original strategy. Competition forces the firm further and further away and it becomes increasingly different from its original competitors. In this way, a small deviation from the optimal reporting path can lead to a much larger deviation over time. So a population of homogeneous firms, with a small proclivity to make reporting errors, can over time develop quite different kinds of expertise, and thus become heterogeneous.

## Model

In this section, we will formalize the above intuition in a mathematical model. This is done for the skeptics.

### Modeling philosophy

The modeling follows the "low fat" philosophy that is very common in economics, but less so in the strategy field. The idea is to keep the model as simple as possible, such that the reader can readily identify the conditions that are sufficient for the results. This means that many realistic factors are omitted because they are not necessary.

In the present setting, this is most dramatically seen in the modeling of employees' local environments and the set of feasible messages. The idea is that these environments are so rich that only a coarse sketch of their information content can be reported to the central manager. This is modeled by assuming that reports are limited to just one, out of many possible, dimensions in each period. As a result, we get a very simple, but obviously not realistic, picture of the relative magnitudes.

Some of the simplifying assumptions are not completely innocuous. A good example of this is the parameter values. We choose to look at an error that leads the firm to an inferior, but acceptable, strategy. Many other parameter values will not yield divergence. However, because the models are so stylized, we are not really interested in showing when one does and doesn't get divergence – just that some errors can make it happen.

We will first look at a case in which each firm has only one employee, and then go on to the more complicated case with more employees.

### The local environments

We assume initially that each firm has one employee, who learns about developments in a large number of areas. New information arrives in each area in each period. So an employee receives a large number of sequences, each of which contains information about trends in different aspects of consumer tastes or technologies. For simplicity, we assume that there is a one-to-one correspondence between sequences and strategies, in the sense that each sequence helps a firm keep a specific strategy in sync with the times. Bearing in mind that the firms initially pursue the same strategy, we assume that this strategy requires that the sequence $x(t)$, x(t+1), x(t+2), etc. gets reported to management. To put a label on the first reporting mistake, we use y() to represent a specific different sequence. In any given period, x(t) and y(t) are i.i.d. draws from a zero-mean distribution with variance $\sigma^2$. Being exceedingly abstract, we will say that a firm can execute the product-market strategy $X$ perfectly in period $t$ by setting the control variable $Dx(t)=2x(t-1)+x(t-2)$. Similarly, a firm can perfectly execute the $\Upsilon$ strategy in period $t$ if it sets $Dy(t)=2y(t-1)+y(t-2)$. This formulation captures the ideas, (1) that information has value beyond the current period, (2) that the value of different pieces of information depends on the firm's strategy, and (3) that strategy and reporting rules go together.

### Organizational processes

Each firm has one manager, who in each period formulates and implements the product-market strategy that the firm will follow. The manager and the employee cannot be the same person, making it necessary that the latter report to the former. However, in each period, the employee can inform the manager of only one sequence. This captures, in a very crude way, the idea that the employee is unable to report everything he knows about his local environment.

To keep the model simple, and to clarify the impact of the bound on communication, we assume that a firm can not execute more than one product-market strategy in any given period, and that it cannot reliably get information on one strategy while executing another.

## Competition

We look at two identical firms, $a$ and $b$, and imagine that they compete on quantity. We use $Q_{xa}(t)$ to denote firm $a$'s period $t$ sales if it follows the product-market strategy $X$, while $Q_{ya}(t)$ is its sales if it follows the $Y$ strategy. Similarly, $Q_{xb}(t)$ and $Q_{yb}(t)$ are firm $b$'s period $t$ sales with these two alternative strategies. We will use $D_{xa}(t)$ and $D_{ya}(t)$, respectively, to denote how firm $a$ executes whatever strategy it chooses in period $t$. Analogously, if firm $b$ follows the $X$ strategy in period $t$, $D_{xb}(t)$ describes its execution, while if it chooses strategy $Y$, $D_{yb}(t)$ is its period $t$ execution. We assume that firm $a$'s price with the $X$ strategy is given by

$$P_{xa}(t) = \mu_x - [D_{xa}(t) - 2x(t-1) - x(t-2)]^2 - v[Q_{xa}(t) + Q_{xb}(t)], \tag{1}$$

where $\mu$ and $v$ are positive. This formulation captures three reasonable premises, each of which is essential for the argument.

1  There is more demand for the firm's products if the strategy reflects the state of the environment. This is here modeled as $2x(t-1) + x(t-2)$.
2  There is less competition between firms using different strategies. This is modeled as an extreme case in which firms using the $X$ strategy are completely unaffected by anything done by firms following the $Y$ strategy.
3  Competition leads to lower prices.

Reflecting the assumption that the firms initially are identical, firm $b$'s price with the $X$ strategy is determined symmetrically by

$$Pxb(t) = \mu_x - [D_{xb}(t) - 2x(t-1) - x(t-2)]^2 - v[Q_{xa}(t) + Q_{xb}(t)]. \tag{2}$$

Of course, if a firm does not follow the $X$ strategy, its $Qx$ is zero, and the other firm is a monopolist.

In parallel to the above, we assume that the prices for the $Y$ strategy are

$$P_{ya}(t) = \mu_y - [D_{ya}(t) - 2y(t-1) - y(t-2)]^2 - v[Q_{ya}(t) + Q_{yb}(t)], \text{ and} \tag{3}$$
$$P_{yb}(t) = \mu_y - [D_{yb}(t) - 2y(t-1) - y(t-2)]^2 - v[Q_{ya}(t) + Q_{yb}(t)], \tag{4}$$

We will denote the unit costs of firms following the $X$ and $Y$ strategies by $c_x$ and $c_y$, respectively. So the attractiveness of the two strategies differ only by $\mu_x - \mu_y$ and $c_y - c_x$.

## Equilibrium when both firms follow the X strategy

We first look at the case in which both firms use the $X$ strategy, and both managers are perfectly informed about the $x()$ sequence, such that they can set $D_{xa}(t) = 2x(t-1) + x(t-2)$ and $D_{xb}(t) = 2x(t-1) + x(t-2)$. In this scenario, firm $a$ will select $Q_{xa}(t)$ to maximize the expected value of its profits. Dropping time arguments and assuming that unit costs are $c_x$, firm $a$'s profits are $[P_{xa} - c_x]Q_{xa}$. Firm $b$ will aim to maximize the expectation of $[P_{xb}- c_x]Q_{xb}$. We assume that the firms do not observe each other's executions (the $D$'s) before selecting quantities. Using that $D_{xa} = 2x(t-1) + x(t-2)$ and $D_{xb} = 2x(t-1) + x(t-2)$, the first order conditions are

$$\mu_x - c_x - vQ_{xb}{}^* - 2\,vQ_{xa}{}^*=0, \text{ and} \qquad (5)$$
$$\mu_x - c_x - vQ_{xa}{}^* - 2\,vQ_{xb}{}^*=0. \qquad (6)$$

In equilibrium, $Q_{xa}{}^* = Q_{xb}{}^* = [\mu_x - c_x]/3\,v$, and bôth firms make profits of

$$(\mu_x - c_x - v2[\mu_x - c_x]/3\,v)\,\mu_x - c_y/3v =[\mu_x - c_x]^2/9\,v \qquad (7)$$

per period.

## One firms follows the $\Upsilon$ strategy

By reasoning identical to that used above (or really just by relabeling), we see that if both firms follow the $\Upsilon$ strategy, they will each make per period profits of $[\mu_y - c_y]2/9\,v$. We will assume that $\mu_x - c_x > \mu_y - c_y$, the $X$ strategy is more attractive than the $\Upsilon$ strategy. So if both firms use in the $\Upsilon$ strategy, they will earn less than if they both use the $X$ strategy.

However, it is possible than a firm could do better by being a "monopolist" in the $\Upsilon$ strategy than by competing with the $X$ strategy. To check this, we note that firm $a$, if it pursues the $\Upsilon$ strategy while firm $b$ pursues the $X$ strategy, would maximize the expectation of $[P_{ya} - c_y]Q_{ya}$. If its manager is perfectly informed about the $y()$ sequence, she can set $D_{ya} = 2y(t - 1) + y(t - 2)$, and the first order condition is

$$[\mu_y - c_y]- 2\,vQ_{ya}{}^*=0. \qquad (8)$$

This gives profits of

$$(\mu_y - c_y - v[\mu_y - c_y]/2\,v)\,[\mu_y - c_y]/2\,v = [\mu_y - c_y]^2/4\,v. \qquad (9)$$

Comparison with (7), the "duopoly" profits from the $X$ strategy, we see that the firm makes higher profits in the former scenario if

$$[\mu_y - c_y]<2[\mu_x - c_x]/3. \qquad (10)$$

In the following, we will be looking at cases in which (10) holds. Without this assumption, the firms would prefer to become heterogeneous simply in order to avoid competition. Since we are trying to evaluate a different explanation for the same phenomenon, we will want to neutralize the purely competitive argument. So between perfect information scenarios, we assume that both firms would prefer to follow the $X$ strategy, in spite of the fact that they have to compete with each other.

## A reporting error

Let us therefore start with a situation in which both firms follow the $X$ strategy and intend to keep their managers perfectly informed about the $x()$ sequence. Suppose now that an error occurs in firm $a$ at time $t - 1$, such that the manager receives $y(t - 1)$ instead of $x(t - 1)$. Should the firm switch to the $Y$ strategy in period $t$ and thereafter?

If firm $a$ switches to the $Y$ strategy, its manager does not know $y(t - 2)$, so she has to set $D_{ya}(t) = 2y(t - 1) + Ey(t - 2) = 2y(t - 1)$, and

$$E\ [D_{ya}(t) - 2y(t - 1) - y(t - 2)]^2 = \sigma^2. \tag{11}$$

The ignorance leads to an inferior execution, and lower demand as modeled in (3). On the other hand, if firm $a$ decides to stay with the $X$ strategy, the manager does not know $x(t - 1)$ and has to set $D_{xa}(t) = 2Ex(t - 1) + x(t - 2) = x(t - 2)$, and

$$E\ [D_{xa}(t) - 2x(t - 1) - x(t - 2)]^2 = 4\sigma^2. \tag{12}$$

So in period $t$ alone, firm $a$'s resources, the knowledge of $x(t - 2)$ and $y(t - 1)$, are a better fit for the $X$ strategy, because more recent information is more valuable. However, two additional factors favor a switch. First, there is a competitive effect: while firm $a$ has no competitor if it switches to the $Y$ strategy, firm $b$ will exploit $a$'s weakness if it stays with the $X$ strategy. Second, there is a resource effect: while $x(t–2)$ will cease to be of value in period $t + 1$, $y(t - 1)$ will favor the $Y$ strategy for one more period.

To see the implications of these effects, we first assume that firm $a$ stays with the $X$ strategy. Since firm $b$ does not observe the execution $D_{xa}(t)$ before setting its quantity, we make the conservative assumption that it will not know that firm $a$'s manager did not learn $x(t - 1)$. We will furthermore assume that firm $b$ competes as if the probability of such a mistake is very, very low. For simplicity, we set it to zero. So $Q_{xb}{}^*(t) = [\mu_x -c_x]/3\,v$, and the first order condition for $Q_{xa}{}^*(t)$ will be

$$\mu_x-c_x-4\sigma^2 - vQ_{xb}{}^*(t)-2\,vQ_{xa}{}^*(t)=0 \tag{13}$$

In equilibrium,

$$Q_{xa}{}^*(t) = [\mu_x-c_x]/3v-2\,\sigma^2/v, \text{ and} \tag{14}$$

firm $a$'s profits in period $t$ are therefore

$$[\mu_x-c_x-4\sigma^2- (2\mu_x-2c_x-6\sigma^2)/3]\ [\mu_x - c_x - 6\sigma^2]/3\,v = [\mu_x-c_x-6\sigma^2]^2/9\,v \tag{15}$$

If on the other hand firm $a$ switches to the $Y$ strategy, we can use (8) to see that its quantity in period $t$ will be

$$Q_{ya}{}^*(t) = (\mu_y-c_y-\sigma^2)/2\,v, \tag{16}$$

While profits in period $t$ are

$$[\mu_y - c_y - \sigma^2]^2 / 4 \, v. \tag{17}$$

Comparing (17) and (19), we see that the presence of the competitor using the $X$ strategy makes the ignorance more costly there. Firm $b$ is able to exploit its competitive advantage.

The final difference between firm $a$'s situation in the two strategies is that the information $y(t-1)$ will be valuable also in period $t + 1$, while $x(t-2)$ will not. So if firm $a$ switches to the $Y$ strategy and its manager receives $y(t)$, (9) tells us that it earns a profit of $[\mu_y - c_y]^2 / 4 \, v$ in period $t + 1$. If it stays with the $X$ strategy and its manager receives $x(t)$, firm $b$ will know, from observing the inferior execution $D_{xa}(t) = x(t-2)$, that firm $a$'s manager did not receive $x(t - 1)$. So while firm $b$'s first order condition is (6), $a$'s first order condition in period $t + 1$ is

$$\mu_x - c_x - \sigma^2 - vQ_{xb}{}^*(t + 1) - 2 \, vQ_{xa}{}^*(t + 1) > = 0, \tag{18}$$

and in equilibrium

$$Q_{xa}{}^*(t + 1) = (\mu_x - c_x - 2\,\sigma^2)/3 \, v, \text{ and} \tag{19}$$
$$Q_{xb}{}^*(t + 1) = (\mu_x - c_x + \sigma^2)/3 \, v. \tag{20}$$

Firm $a$'s profits in period $t + 1$ are therefore

$$[\mu_x - c_x - \sigma^2 - (2\mu_x - 2c_x - \sigma^2)/3] \, [\mu_x - c_x - 2\sigma^2] / 3v = [\mu_x - c_x - 2\sigma^2]^2 / 9v. \tag{21}$$

So the two reasons why a reporting error makes the $Y$ strategy more attractive to firm $a$, are that its resources are a better fit in periods $t$ and $t+1$, and that it becomes competitively disadvantaged if it stays with the $X$ strategy.

To look at the combined implications of this, we assume that firm $a$ discounts future profits by the factor $\delta < 1$ per period. The net present value of switching to the $Y$ strategy is

$$[\mu_y - c_y - \sigma^2]^2 / 4 \, v + \delta[\mu_y - c_y]^2 / 4v + [\delta^2 / 1 - \delta][\mu_y - c_y]^2 / 4v, \tag{22}$$

while the net present value of staying with the $X$ strategy is

$$[\mu_x - c_x - 6\sigma^2]^2 / 9v + \delta[\mu_x - c_x - 2\sigma^2]^2 / 9v + [\delta^2 / 1 - \delta][\mu_x - c_x]^2 / 9v. \tag{23}$$

Comparing, we see that (22) may be larger than (23) even if $[\mu_y - c_y] < 2[\mu_x - c_x]/3$. For example, if $\mu_x - c_x = 31$, $\mu_y - c_y = 20$, $v = 1$, $\sigma^2 = 5$, and $\delta = 1/2$, then the value of (22) is $56.25 + 50 + 50 = 156.25$, while (23) is $1/9 + 441/18 + 961/18 = 702/9 = 78$. So this example shows that *a single reporting error may cause a firm to permanently switch from the ex ante more attractive X strategy to the Y strategy.*

If the firm later suffers another reporting error, say getting $z(T)$ instead of $y(T)$, it may well be that $[\mu_z - c_z]$ is too small to justify a further change in strategy. However, it seems reasonable to expect that some later errors will be sufficiently attractive to produce further changes in the firm's strategy. While we have not described the "distances" between $X$, $Y$, and other strategies, it seems reasonable to conjecture that the differentiation process explained above will result in increasing differences.

**Extension: several employees**

The above result was driven by two forces: the fact that the mistaken report has value in periods $t$ and $t+1$, and the fact that the error puts the firm at a competitive disadvantage if it presses on with the original strategy. In the case where several employees report correctly, the first factor works against bifurcation, but the second may still make it the optimal response. In addition, the presence of more employees increases the potential for errors. We will now change the model to look at this.

We assume that each firm has $n$ employees, each of whom observes a different aspect of the $x$ and $y$ sequences. Specifically, employee $i = 1, 2, \ldots, n$, observes $x_i(t)$ and $y_i(t)$, but can only report on one of these. We assume that the reports are complementary in the sense that a manager only knows $x(t)$ if all the firm's salesmen report on their $x_i(t)$'s, and similarly only knows $y(t)$ if all the firm's salesmen report on their $y_i(t)$'s.

Suppose now that the firms are competing on the basis of the $X$ strategies, but that one of firm $a$'s employees erroneously report $y_i(t-1)$. If the firm stays with the $X$ strategy, its period $t$ profits in periods $t$, $t+1$, and $t+2$ are given by (15), (21), and (7). So the net present value is again that expressed in (23). If the firm switches to the $Y$ strategy, its period $t$ profits will be

$$[\mu_y - c_y - 4\sigma^2]^2/4v, \tag{24}$$

while its profits in periods $t+1$ and $t+2$ are those in (17) and (9). Consequently, the net present value is

$$[\mu_y - c_y - 4\sigma^2]^2/4v + \delta[\mu_y - c_y - \sigma^2]^2/4v + [\delta^2/1-\delta][\mu_y - c_y]^2/4v \tag{25}$$

Using the same numerical example as before, the value of (25) is $0 + 28.125 + 50 = 78.125$. Recalling that the value of (23) is 78, we see that the firm also in this case should switch to the $Y$ strategy. As illustrated by this example, *the chance that an individual reporting error will cause the firm to change is smaller when there are more employees. On the other hand, we would expect more errors in firms with more employees.*

## Broader Versions

We have chosen to lead with the "reporting error" version of the argument, because reporting is an essential activity in firms, and because it is easy to formalize. However, the theory should apply to a much wider set of activities inside firms. The purpose of the present section is to go through several other examples of the story. The key aspect in all of these examples is that *an error produces, in the firm's resource stock, a change that hurts in the execution of the current strategy, but helps in the execution of another strategy.* Once understood, the point is rather simple, so we will very briefly describe possible results of several accidental deviations from intended actions.

*Incorrect time allocation*

If an R&D employee or a salesperson spends what is ex ante "too much" time on a lead, it may hurt the execution of the current strategy in terms of costs and timeliness. However, the allocation may ex post yield valuable information (discovering aspertame).

*Too low quality*

If an employee does "too bad" a job on some aspect of a product or service, it will hurt the firm's reputation in its current market, but perhaps suggest future designs that could be targeted at different segments.

*Too high quality*

In the opposite case, where the employee does a job that is "too good," current costs will increase, but the error may reveal information that can be used to enhance the quality of future offerings.

*Components that do not fit*

Suppose that an employee, by mistake, produces a component that does not fit with those produced by his colleagues. This will hurt the firm's ability to deliver on time in the original market, and at the same time gives it some production experience that could be used to make different designs.

## Summary

We have tried to offer a new explanation for the existence of persistent differences between firms. The basic idea is that a minor error can snowball into a major deviation. Compared to other explanations of the same phenomenon, the theory has the pleasant property that a very small amount of bounded rationality, followed by perfectly rational behavior and competitive pressure, can produce the effect. Two further attractive properties of the explanation are that (i) it is rooted in essential properties of the firm and therefore applies to all firms, and (ii) that it is based on a theory of the firm, and thus relates the RBV to a broader body of theory.

## References

Cohen, W. M. and Levinthal, D. A. (1990) Absorptive capacity: a new perspective on learning and innovation, *Administrative Science Quarterly*, 35 (1), 128–52.

D'Aunno, T., Succi, M., and Alexander, J. A. (2000) The role of institutional and market forces in divergent organizational change, *Administrative Science Quarterly*, 45 (4), 679–703.

Ghemawat, P. (1991) *Commitment*, New York, NY: The Free Press.

Hannon, M. T. and Freeman, J. (1989) *Organizational Ecology*, Cambridge, MA: Harvard University Press.

Helfat, C. E. (ed.) (2000) The evolution of firm capabilities, *Strategic Management Journal*, 21, special issue (10–11).

Monteverde, K. (1995) Technical dialog as an incentive for vertical integration in the semiconductor industry, *Management Science*, 41 (10), 1624–38.

Nelson, R. R. (1991) Why do firms differ and how does it matter? *Strategic Management Journal*, 12 (Winter), 61–74.

Nelson, R. R., and Winter, S. G. (1982) *An Evolutionary Theory of Economic Change*, Cambridge, MA: Harvard University Press.

Polanyi, M. (1962) *Personal Knowledge: Towards a Post-critical Philosophy*, New York, NY, Harper and Row.

Rumelt, R. P., Schendel, D., and Teece, D. J. (1991) Strategic management and economics, *Strategic Management Journal*, 12 (Winter), 5–30.

Simester, D. I. and Knez, M. (2002) Direct and indirect bargaining costs and the scope of the firm, *Journal of Business*, 75 (2), 283–304.

Simon, H. A. (1976) *Administrative Behavior*, New York, NY: The Free Press, 3rd edn.

Sutton, J. (1991) *Sunk Costs and Market Structure*, Cambridge, MA: MIT Press.

Tushman, M. L. (1978) Technical communication in R&D laboratories: the impact of project work characteristic, *Academy of Management Journal*, 21 (4), 624–45.

Wernerfelt, B. (1997) On the nature and scope of the firm: an adjustment–cost theory, *Journal of Business*, 70 (4), 489–514.

Wernerfelt, B. (2001) Indirect adjustment–costs in firms and markets, manuscript, MIT. Available at SSRN as abstract 258374.

# CHAPTER TEN

# Firm Capabilities and Competition and Industrial Policies in a "History Friendly" Model of the Evolution of the Computer Industry

Franco Malerba, Richard Nelson, Luigi Orsenigo, and Sidney G. Winter

## Introduction

Since the early 1990s industrial organization economists and scholars of business organization have come to recognize more clearly than before the often very great differences among competing firms in the capabilities they have to do various things, and the central role these capability differences play in determining the winners and losers in industrial competition. A number of scholars writing and teaching in the field of business strategy have argued that a central aspect of a firm's thinking about strategy ought to be the kinds of capabilities it needs in order to succeed in competition, and effective ways to develop or acquire those capabilities. Increasingly it is being recognized and argued that the key capabilities in question often are dynamic capabilities, capabilities that enable a firm to continue to innovate effectively and to take advantage of its continuing innovation.

This view of relevant firm capabilities, and the appropriate focus of strategic thinking in firms, clearly does not apply to firms in all industries. But it does seem right for firms in industries where innovation is a central aspect of competition. This view of competition, of course, is "Schumpeterian." And industrial organization economists increasingly have come to recognize that Schumpeter's theory of what competition is all about is much more appropriate than neoclassical views of competition in a wide range of industries, where R&D spending is significant.

They also have come to recognize that in such industries the phenomena of first mover advantage, or dynamic increasing returns more generally, may be very important. Firms that initially get a lead may be able to push off from that early lead to establish a position that is close to unchallengeable. Dynamic increasing returns may exist on the "supply side," as firms that get an early lead in product design and a large early share of the market can use their revenues to invest in more R&D than their competitors, and increase the advantages that their products hold over those of competitors. There also may be dynamic increasing returns on the demand side, if old customers tend to return to their original suppliers for their next purchases, or if there are bandwagon effects. Under these conditions, competitive process may relatively quickly destroy competitive industry structure. This problem of course, raises some major issues of public policy in the field of anti-trust, and in other areas.

In this chapter, we explore some problems that industrial policy faces in industries characterized by dynamic increasing returns on the basis of a "history friendly model" of the evolution of the computer industry.

The "history friendly" models[1] we are developing are models that attempt to formalize the verbal appreciative theories about the major factors explaining the particular pattern of evolution of an industry or technology put forth by empirical scholars of that industry. Thus these models tend to incorporate more industry-specific details than is customary of models built by economists. Since the logic of many verbal explanations for particular patterns of industry and technology evolution, or coevolution, involves non-linear dynamics, our history friendly models take the form of simulation models.

But while the early models we are building are tailored to particular industries, we are interested as well in generalizations that can be made that cut across industries, and in identifying key clusters of structural variables that seem naturally to group industries. Thus our research program is very much in the spirit of traditional industrial organization. And while to date our focus has been largely on trying to understand observed patterns, we also are very much interested in what these models can tell us about the efficacy of economic policies.

Our first history friendly models have been about the evolution of the computer industry and computer technology. Here, virtually all appreciative theoretic accounts have highlighted dynamic increasing returns of one form or another. While different authors have placed the emphasis in different places, our own analysis, which was sharpened greatly by our building and running a formal model, shows clearly that at least two different kinds of dynamic increasing returns play key roles in the history of the industry. One is increasing returns in a firm's efforts to advance its product and process technologies. Firms that are initially successful learn from their past successes and, because technological success generally leads to greater sales and profits, have the funds to further expand their R&D efforts. The other is increasing returns on the marketing side. For a variety of reasons, customers who buy a particular brand of computer one time, tend, other things equal, to buy that same brand when they expand their capacity or replace their old equipment. However, this latter tendency was much stronger in the era of mainframe computers than in the era of personal computers, to anticipate the history that we will go on to recount briefly.

The result of these dynamic forces was, of course, the rise of IBM as a near monopolist in mainframes. On the other hand, IBM was not able to transfer its monopoly position to personal computers. Our simulation models suggest that, given the structure of dynamic increasing returns, this pattern was nearly inevitable (although the way IBM entered the PC market certainly militated against its achieving a durable market dominating position there). If IBM had not reached dominance in mainframes, some other firm would. The interactive operation of those two different kinds of dynamic increas-

ing returns virtually guaranteed that a dominant firm would emerge. And that a dominant firm would have had trouble extending its monopoly into PCs because of the
absence there of a strong customer lock-in effect.

Could public policies have changed these patterns? This is the question we explore
here. We do not address directly issues related to the desirability of industrial policy.
Rather, we examine the efficacy problems that policy faces in dynamic environments.
How does policy affect industry structure over the course of industry evolution? Is the
timing of the intervention important? Do policy interventions have indirect and perhaps unintended consequences on different markets at different times?

We focus on three sets of policies: anti-trust, interventions aiming at supporting
the entry of new firms in the industry, and public procurement of totally new products. The reasons for examining anti-trust are straightforward. It is commonly considered to be the main instrument to curb monopoly power and in the history of the
computer industry the discussion on the actions of anti-trust authorities figure prominently.

The focus on interventions favoring the entry of new firms stems from the recognition of the crucial role of entrants in spurring competition, in opening up new markets
and in generating new technologies. Lack of new entrants is often considered to be
one of the possible explanations of the failure of the European industry to compete
successfully with the USA in the computer industry as well as in other high technology
industries. More generally, policies supporting entry have become one of the favored
tools of industrial policies in Europe, both for promoting industrial growth and for
raising market contestability.

Finally, in the history of high technology industries, public procurement in favor of
firms developing totally new products (particularly in the United States) has been
quite relevant in fostering high rates of technical change.

However, it is a legitimate question to ask whether and to what extent such policies
can be successful in industries characterized by dynamic increasing returns, especially if
the dynamic returns are generated by multiple sources. Are either anti-trust or the
promotion of entry sufficient to contrast the emergence of a monopoly? How big
should the interventions be and at what time should they act? To anticipate some of
our results, if strong dynamic increasing returns are operative, both through technological capabilities and through customer tendency to stick with a brand, the results of
our simulations show that there is little that anti-trust and entry policy could have
done to avert the rise of a dominant firm in mainframes. On the other hand, public
procurement played a role in affecting market structure and concentration. However,
if the customer lock-in effect had been smaller, either by chance or through policies
that discouraged efforts of firms to lock in their customers, the situation concerning
anti-trust and entry support might have been somewhat different. In the first place,
even in the absence of anti-trust or entry encouraging policies, market concentration
would have been lower, albeit a dominant firm would emerge anyhow. Second, antitrust and entry encouraging polices would have been more effective in assuring that
concentration would decrease. The leading firm would continue to dominate the market, but its relative power would be reduced.

The chapter is organized as follows. We briefly discuss the history of the computer
industry. Next we present the model and examine history replicating simulations, be-

fore comparing the effects of alternative – extremely stylized – policy interventions. Finally, we draw some conclusions.

## The Evolution of the Computer Industry and Competition Policy

Given space constraints, we can recount only a stylized history of computer technology and the computer industry, drawing from Flamm (1988), Langlois (1990), Bresnahan and Greenstein (1999), and especially Bresnahan and Malerba (1999).

The history of the computer shows continuous improvements in machines that serve particular groups of users, punctuated from time to time by the introduction of significant new component technologies which not only permit the needs of existing users to be met better, but also open up the possibility of designing machines that serve new classes of users whose needs could not be met using older technology. In the United States these punctuations were associated with the entry into the industry of new firms, and these new firms almost always were the first to venture into the new market. However, this happened to a significant lesser degree in Europe, and hardly at all in Japan.

The evolution of the industry divides rather naturally into four periods. The first began with the early experimentation with computers which culminated in designs sufficiently attractive to induce their purchase by large firms with massive computation tasks, as well as by scientific laboratories. This opened the era of the mainframe computer. The second era began with the introduction of integrated circuits and the development of minicomputers. The third era is that of the personal computer, made possible by the invention of the microprocessor. We now are in the era of networked PCs and the increasing use of the Internet.

During World War II and the years just after, governments in several countries funded a number of projects with the aim of developing computers useful for governmental purposes. In the late 1940s and early 1950s a number of companies, in Europe as well as in the United States, began investing their own funds hoping to develop a computer sufficiently attractive to win the market of scientific laboratories, large firms, and other organizations who had large-scale computation needs. The early 1950s saw the entry into the industry of IBM – then a major punched-card and tabulating machinery company, but with significant capabilities in electronic computing derived in good part from government R&D contracts – and the rest of the Bunch (Burrows, Univac Rand, NCR, Control Data, Honeywell), as well as GE and RCA. These companies differed in the strategies they took, and in their success in developing machines that would sell at a profit. By 1954, with the introduction of the 650, IBM began to pull ahead of the Bunch, and with the introduction of the 1401 in 1960, came to dominate the world market for accounting machines.

IBM dominated not only in the American market, but also in Europe, and Japan. A small-scale domestic industry was able to hold on in Europe, and later in Japan, only by virtue of a combination of government subsidy, a guaranteed government market, and protection. Component technology improved greatly during the the mainframe era, and transistors gradually replaced vacuum tubes as the basic circuit elements. These developments enabled significant improvements in mainframe performance, and some reduction in cost. In the early 1960s IBM introduced its 360 family of models, and seized an even larger share of the mainframe market.

The invention and development of the integrated circuit enabled even further improvements in mainframe computers and also reduced barriers to entry in the mainframe industry, thus stimulating the entry of new competitors to IBM. However, integrated circuits not only permitted large computers to be made even more powerful. They opened the possibility of designing computers that had a considerable amount of power, but could be produced at a much lower cost than mainframes. DEC's PDP8, the first minicomputer, was produced in 1965. Minicomputers opened up a new demand class which had not been tapped by mainframes, which included medium-sized research laboratories, manufacturing firms, and some small businesses.

In the United States new firms, like DEC were the first into the new minicomputer market; these new firms seized and held a significant share of that market. IBM lagged in getting into minicomputers, and never achieved there the dominance it achieved in the mainframe market. While the availability of integrated circuits provided an opportunity for European and Japanese firms to get into the minicomputer market, as in the earlier case with mainframes, firms in Europe and Japan lagged. American firms took a considerable fraction of the minicomputer market in Europe and Japan, and domestic firms held on there only through a combination of subsidy, and protection.

The introduction of the microprocessor marked another punctuation in the history of the industry. Microprocessors enabled significant improvements in mainframe and minicomputer designs. However, their most important impact was to permit the design of reasonably powerful computers that could be produced at quite low costs. Personal computers opened up a new demand class which had not been touched by mainframes and minicomputers: small firms, and personal users.

As in the case of minicomputers, in the United States new firms entered the industry aiming to serve the new personal computer (PC) market: these included prominently specialized PC design and manufacturing firms (such as Apple, Commodore, Tandy, and Compaq). Established mainframe and minicomputer producers were slow in seeing the new market and the needs of users in that market. Interestingly, when IBM did get into PCs, it did so with external alliances: Microsoft for operating systems software, and Intel for microprocessors. IBM did manage to seize a significant fraction of the personal computer market, but was never as dominant there as it had been in mainframes. And, of course, in recent years IBM's share in PCs has eroded significantly.

A striking characteristic of the firms producing personal computers is that they are primarily assemblers, buying most of their components on the open market. Also, most of the software for personal computers is developed and supplied by software specialists. This is in sharp contrast with mainframe production, particularly in the early and middle stages of the industry. Thus IBM not only designed and produced most of the critical components for its mainframes, but also wrote most of the basic software. For a time, IBM also designed and produced a significant fraction of the integrated circuits that were employed in its mainframes. In minicomputers there was, from the beginning, more vertical specialization than in mainframe production, with most minicomputer companies buying their integrated circuits, and a number of other key components, on the open market. But personal computers have seen even more vertical disintegration.

As noted, the advent of personal computers led, in the United States, to the birth of a number of new firms, several of which turned out to be very successful. Just as in the case of minicomputers, in Europe and Japan in contrast few firms entered. And, except where there was heavy government protection or subsidy, American firms have come to dominate foreign markets for personal computers.

There are many interesting challenges for history-friendly modeling in the history recounted above. In a previous paper (Malerba et al., 1999), we analyzed the pattern of development of industry structure. A second challenge is provided by the progressive vertical disintegration of the computer industry, and in particular by the sharp increase in specialization that has marked the era of personal computers. Still a third challenge is to explain the significant differences between the United States on the one hand, and Europe and Japan on the other, with respect to the ability of new firms to take advantage of "competence destroying" technological changes.

In this chapter we focus on a somewhat different issue. We discuss some problems concerning the conduct and the effects of alternative policy interventions which have or might have influenced the evolution of the computer industry. The policy interventions that will be discussed concern anti-trust and entry support. On the contrary we will not discuss military policy, which was quite relevant in the early history of the industry. As far as antitrust policies are concerned, during all the history of the industry they were anti-IBM both in the Unites States and Europe. In the United States antitrust policies forced IBM to unbundle mainframe hardware from software and to behave less aggressively with respect to Amdahl and PCMs. In Europe on the contrary they were highly tolerant of national champions in their anti-IBM role. Entry support policies have been at the center of the policy debate, particularly in Europe, because entry has played a major role in the history of the industry. This debate has discussed how to foster entry in order to improve national competitiveness and, to a lesser extent, to increase competition within concentrated segments such as mainframes.

Before discussing these policies, we are going to present the basic structure of the model.

## The Model

Here we lay out the basic model. Given the nature of complex simulation models, it is impossible to present all the details of all the equations, without befuddling the reader and obscuring the basic logic of the model. We have tried, therefore, to lay out in transparent form what we regard as the gist of the model. Interested readers may obtain a full copy of the simulation model by writing to the authors.

### The topography

In this model we consider a single stylized episode of the sort under consideration. At the start of the episode, there is a single component technology, which we will call "transistor" technology, which has the promise of enabling useful computers. Later, a new component technology, which we will call "microprocessors," comes into exist-ence. The potential purchasers of computers value two attributes. One is the "per-formance" of the computer. The other is its price, or "cheapness." The desirability of any computer design can be summarized in terms of how it rates in those two dimen-sions of Lancaster attribute space. By a useful computer we mean one that meets thresh-old requirements of potential purchasers. There is more on this later.

Each of the component technologies is associated with outer limits on what com-puters incorporating them can achieve in the two relevant dimensions. For analytic convenience, we have treated those technological constraints as defining a rectangular box. Thus in figure 10.1 the two boxes depict the set of technological characteristics that potentially can be achieved in computers designed around transistor, and micro-processor, component technologies. Note that the use of microprocessors permits computers to be designed that are better than transistor-based computers regarding both performance and cheapness. However, the most dramatic improvement that is permitted by the incorporation of microprocessors lies in that of cheapness.

Those outer limits of what is feasible under the two technologies are "potentials." The potential is not achievable, however, without significant investment of resources in research and development, and requires learning from experience. The first efforts of a new firm trying to design a computer using transistors, or (later) microprocessors, will only be able to achieve a design characterized by point Z (for zero experience). We will specify later the dynamics of design improvement built into the model.

On the demand side, there are two quite separate groups of potential customers. One group, which we will call "large firms" greatly values "performance" and wants to buy "mainframes." The second group, which we will call "individuals, or small users" has less need for high performance but values "cheapness." They provide a potential market for "personal computers," or PCs.

Each of our two user groups requires a minimum level of performance, and cheap-ness, before they can be enticed to buy any computers at all. Once threshold character-

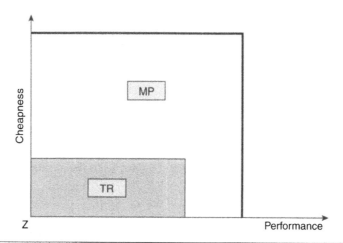

**Figure 10.1** Technological characteristics that can be achieved in computers designed around transistor, and microprocessor, component technologies

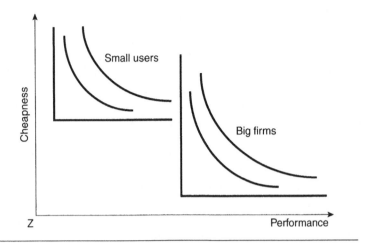

**Figure 10.2** Preferences of "big firms" and "small users" respectively

istics are reached, the value that customers place on a computer design is an increasing function of its performance, and its cheapness. In figure 10.2 we depict the preferences of "big firms" and "small users" respectively. The difference in the demands of the two user groups, that we specified above, is reflected in both the difference in threshold requirements, and in the indifference curves.

If one overlays figure 10.1 on figure 10.2, one can note that even if computers achieve the outer limits permitted by transistor technology, the threshold requirements of small users will not be met. Thus the design of computers that can successfully enter the personal computer market depends on the availability of microprocessors.

The "indifference curves" of figure 10.2 depict designs of equal value or "merit" in the eyes of the two customer groups. We assume that higher computer merit translates into more computers bought by customers. We shall develop the details later.

The above discussion indicates clearly some of the broad outlines of what one would expect to see in a simulated industry history, and also points to some of the matters that need to be treated in specification of the dynamics. Assuming that there is some way that firms can obtain funds, computer technology will start out at Z. Over time, and with R&D spending, computer designs will improve until ultimately they crack through the threshold requirements of the "mainframe market." Then firms that have achieved threshold-meeting designs, will begin to make sales. As computers improve, sales will grow. The introduction of microprocessors will open the potential of meeting mainframe demands even better, and of designing machines that will sell on the PC market. Firms that try to pursue those possibilities will need some funding in order to do that because, initially at least, no one will buy their wares. However, ultimately one would expect that microprocessor computers would take over the mainframe market, and be able to tap the new PC market.

We now turn to explicit dynamics.

### Innovation dynamics, firms' finance, R&D, advertising, and pricing decisions

When transistors, and later microprocessors, come into existence, firms have to learn how to design effective computers using these new components. Firms gradually develop competence in using the new technology as a result of the R&D investments they make, and the experience they accumulate. Our model of firm learning is meant to capture significant elements of the "dynamic competence" theory of the firm that has been developed by Winter (1987), Dosi and Marengo (1993), and Teece, Pisano, and Shuen (1992).

In the model, firms are represented by sets of technological and marketing competencies that are accumulated over time, and by rules of action. The local competencies in the model are design capabilities: by building incrementally on their past achievements and by accumulating experience, engineers produce successive generations of computers with superior cost/performance attributes. Other actions reflected in the model of the firm concern the pricing of products, R&D and advertising expenditures, the adoption of new technologies and diversification into new markets. There is no explicit representation of production per se, or of investments in capacity. It is assumed that the requisite production capabilities can be hired at a price per computer that reflects the "cheapness" attribute of the design.

Our model also is designed to incorporate the fact that in this industry, and in a number of others, a considerable period may go by after a firm starts trying to operate in a new technology before it is able to sell any product, if it ever achieves that. At the start it must have external financing.

Thus at the beginning of our episode, with the introduction of transistors, we assume that there are a number of firms, endowed by "venture capitalists" with an initial budget to spend on R&D, who hope to exploit the new technological opportunities. All firms start with the same initial design capabilities, depicted by Z in figure 10.1, and perhaps interpretable as the design characteristics that have been achieved by experimental computers that are in the public domain. Firms start off with different, randomly selected initial budgets, IB, which are used to finance an R&D project, the length of which is fixed and equal for all firms. During this initial time, in each period firms spend a constant fraction of their budget on R&D. If the funds are exhausted before a marketable design is achieved, firms exit.[2]

Design outcomes are influenced by firm-specific strategies represented by choices of search direction in the capabilities space, but also by latent technological opportunities. Firms are born with different, randomly selected trajectories of technological improvement along the two technological dimensions, costs and performance. In order to capture – in an extreme form – the notion that competencies cannot be changed rapidly and costlessly, in the model it is assumed that this trajectory is firm-specific and time-invariant. Thus, after the initial period, the firms in the industry will be doing different things, and will be achieving computer designs of different characteristics.

As firms spend on R&D, they accumulate technical competencies. Technical progress is represented in the model as a change in a computer design along the two technical dimensions, generated by the application of these firm-specific competencies. Technical competencies are represented as a stock that grows over time as a result of R&D expenditures. One can think of competencies as reflecting the shared experience of two types of "engineers": cost-oriented and performance-oriented engineers. Their mix is defined by the technological trajectory that characterizes each firm. As time goes by, firms hire new engineers, maintaining constant at any period the proportion between the two types and hence the trajectory of advance.[3]

In each period $t$, R&D expenditures, $R_t$, are used to pay the stock of engineers of last period, $R_{t-1}$. For each of the two design dimensions, if the share of total R&D allocated to one particular type of engineers is $R_{it} > R^i_{t-1}$, then the surplus is invested in hiring new engineers, at a given cost $c_{eng}$ per engineer Conversely, if $R^i_t < R^i_{t-1}$, then 10% of the engineers is fired. If $R^i_t < 0.9\ R^i_{t-1}$, the budget $B$ is used to pay for the difference.

From period to period, the quality of the design that a company is able to achieve in each relevant dimension – performance and cheapness – improves according to the following equation:[4]

$$\text{change } X_i = a_0(R_i)^{a1}\ (T_j)^{a2}\ (L_i - X_i)^{a3}e \tag{1}$$

The first variable, $R$, is the firm's R&D expenditure aimed at achieving design improvements of a particular sort, where $i = 1$ denotes performance and $i = 2$ denotes cheapness. That expenditure allows the firm to maintain a given stock of engineers dedicated to advancing computer design in the two relevant dimensions. That expenditure, in turn, is a constant fraction of its period-by-period R&D expenditures in total. The fraction reflects the firm's "bet" as to the most useful direction to proceed. As we noted, a firm's total R&D expenditure per period is a constant fraction of the total funds lent to it by its venture capital financiers. After that initial loan is drawn down, a firm either has achieved a commercially viable design, or it is out of business.

The second variable, $T$, is the number of periods that the firm has been working with a particular technology, in this case transistors. For all firms that start with a technology at the same time, this second variable will be the same. However, when later in this exposition we begin to describe the evolution of computers employing microprocessor technology, firms will differ regarding the times when they get into that technology, and thus in that technology there will be differences across firms in this experience variable.

The third variable in the equation, $L_i - X_i$, is distance of the achieved design to the frontier. As what is achieved comes closer and closer to the limits of what is achievable, a given R&D expenditure will achieve less and less further progress. There is also a random element to what a firms achieves, $e$.

As indicated, if a firm runs through its initial loan before it achieves a marketable product, it simply fails. However, if a firm manages to push its design into the region where customers are buying, it is a new ball game. Now funds from revenues can be invested in R&D and in marketing.

Profits, $\pi$ are calculated in each period t as:

$$\pi_t = Mp - Mk, \tag{2}$$

where $M$ is the number of computers sold, $p$ is the computer price and $k$ is production cost of a single computer.

Production costs, k, are determined by the technical progress function. Price is obtained by adding a mark-up, μ, to costs:

$$p = k (1 + \mu) \tag{3}$$

The mark-up, μ, is initially set equal for all firms, but it then grows over time as a function of the market share that has been achieved. In other words, as firms gain monopoly power, they (partly) exploit it by charging prices above marginal costs. Specifically:

$$\mu = 0.1 + 0.1 \ m \tag{4}$$

where m is the firm's market share.

The gross margin over production costs is used to cover several things. Firms start to spend a constant fraction σ (15 per cent for all firms in this version of the model) of their profits in each period to pay back their debt $Dt$ to investors – that is to say, the initial budget capitalized at the current interest rate, $r$, until the debt has been fully paid back. What is left is used to invest in R&D and in advertising.

R&D expenditures, $R_t$, are simply determined as a constant fraction, φ, of what is left of gross profits, $\pi_t$, after the repayment of the initial budget.

$$R_t = \phi \ \pi_t (1 - \sigma) \tag{5}$$

The variable φ is time-invariant and firm-specific, although in the simulations of this chapter its value has been set equal for all firms.

Advertising expenditures are considered in a very similar way to R and D expenditures, in that they produce marketing competencies that are accumulated over time. If firms do not invest, their advertising capabilities deteriorate over time – and hence the size of the advertising expenditures effect decreases, for any given amount of expenditure. Moreover, it is assumed that the effect of advertising on sales follows a logistic curve. Specifically, the model first computes advertising expenditures, $A^*$:

$$A^*_t = \delta \ \pi_t (1 - \sigma) \tag{6}$$

Then, this value is divided by a number that defines the amount of advertising expenditures beyond which the elasticity of sales to advertising is equal to zero (i.e. the asymptote of the logistic curve). This ratio is then inserted into a logistic curve to yield the value of the variable A in the demand equation (see equation 7).

The excess gross profits after debt repayment, R&D expenditures, and advertising is invested in an account, $B_t$, that yields the interest rate, $r$, in each period and is treated in this model as "reserves." These reserves will enter the model in an important way for transistor firms who have survived into the era when microprocessors have become available as an alternative component technology. We will consider what happens then when we consider transition dynamics.

## Market dynamics

An essential feature of the computer market is the existence of differentiated products and different market segments. The model incorporates some of these features of the demand side of the industry.

The industry is composed of different types of users who have different needs regarding the characteristics of computers. Moreover, demand behavior is influenced by informational considerations and by the advertising efforts of producers, as well as by the actual utility of alternatives presented. "Comparison shopping" is limited. Some customers may purchase computers that are far from the best on the market at the time, simply because, viewed in isolation, those computers are worth the asking price. Finally, bandwagon and brand loyalty effects may play an important role in determining the performance of individual firms.

First of all, the demand for computers is expressed as a demand for specific product characteristics in a Lancasterian vein. Let p be the price charged for a specific computer, then denote "cheapness" by $X_1$ $(= 1/p = 1/k(1+\mu))$, and "performance" by $X_2$.

Computers are demanded by two different user groups, identified as "big firms" and "individuals". They constitute, respectively, the mainframe market and the personal computer market. The choice of these two particular groups of users is due to the fact that mainframes have been mostly used by big firms, while personal computers have been sold for personal uses (at home or at work). These users differ in their threshold requirements for the attributes of cheapness and performance, with individuals having more stringent minimum requirements for cheapness but less stringent requirements for performance than do big firms. The market activity of each type is represented by independent purchasing decisions by a large number of "submarkets" of that type. Submarket buying behavior reflects the fact that computers are durable goods that deliver services over a period of time, and the demand facing producers is a demand for replacements or increments to the stock of such durables.

The number of submarkets in each main market (mainframes and PCs) is a parameter of the model. Individual sub-markets buy computers if they don't have one – either because they have never bought one before or because of breakdowns. Computers have a finite life and surely break down after $\tau$ periods. The model keeps track of the average age, $G$, of the computers held by each submarket. In each period, a fraction $G/\tau$ of the submarkets experiences computer breakdowns and becomes ready to buy new computers. Moreover, submarkets buy computers if they "see" the supply: when there are only few firms in the market, individual submarkets may not purchase any computers. The probability of buying a computer is equal to one if there are at least $S$ firms selling in the marketplace. When there are only $n < S$ firms, the probability decreases proportionally.

A simple formulation of consumer preferences is the following. Consider a particular group of consumers. Define $M$ as the "level" of utility associated with a computer with particular attributes. Then, the utility of a computer with cheapness $X_1 = 1/p$ and performance $X_2$ for the user class s is given by a Cobb–Douglas function with the arguments that measure the extent to which threshold requirements have been exceeded rather than the raw values of cheapness and performance themselves:

$$M = b_0 \, (X_1 - X_1 \min)^{b1}(X_2 - X_2 \min)^{b2} \tag{7}$$

where $b_0$ is a scale parameter, and $X_1 \min$ and $X_2 \min$ are the threshold levels for cheapness and performance. If threshold requirements are not met, $M = 0$. The sum of the exponents in the utility function operates like a sort of generalized demand elasticity reflecting performance as well as price.

Consider now some number of customer groups, say two. Let the (integer) number of computers of a particular character that potentially would be purchased by a specific group of customers (if no other competing products were offered in the market) correspond to the level of utility, $M$. In other words, the greater the "merit" of a machine, the greater the number of machines that will be purchased. This way, the utility function has a cardinal interpretation and is treated heuristically as a demand curve.

After some time, some firms will succeed in achieving a computer design that satisfies the minimum thresholds required by consumers in the mainframe market and will start selling their product on the market. At the beginning, the market is small, both because the utility delivered by computers is low (the industry is in its infancy and technology has not yet progressed very much) and because many consumers may not even perceive that these products are available (or they may not even realize that computers might be useful to them). As the quality of computers increases and as more and more firms enter the market, total demand grows as a consequence of both an increase in the number of consumers and an increase in the number of computers purchased by individual groups of customers.

If there is more than one kind of computer that meets threshold requirements, our analysis of demand involves variables other than M. The appreciative story put forth by many scholars of the history of the industry to account for the sustained dominance of IBM in the mainframe market includes concepts like bandwagon effects or brand loyalty (or lock-in), and advertising. Thus history friendly modeling needs to bring these in.

Customers select different computer designs as a function of their relative utility, $M_i$, as it results from the specific mix of price and performance characteristics. However, various informational constraints, like bandwagon and brand-loyalty effects, affect customer behavior. These are captured in a compact formulation by the effect of the variables measuring the firms' market shares and advertising.

The probability, $P_i$, that any submarket (individual computer buyer or group of them) will purchase a particular computer, $i$, is as follows.

$$P_i = c_0(M_i)^{c1} \, (m_i + d_1)^{c2}(A_i + d_2)^{c3} \tag{8}$$

$c_0$ is specified so that the sum of the probabilities adds to one. As noted, $M$ denotes the "merit" of a computer; $m$ is the market share, in terms of the fraction of total sales revenues accounted for by that computer. Note that the market share variable can be interpreted either in terms of a bandwagon effect, or a (probabilistic) lock-in of customers who previously had bought machines of a particular brand. The $d_1$ assures that computers that have just broken into the market, and have no prior sales, can attract some sales. $A$ is the advertising expenditures of the firm producing the computer. The

$d_2$ performs here a similar role to $d_1$ for firms that have just broken into the market and have not yet invested in advertising.

Given that customers in a particular submarket buy a particular computer, $M$ is the number they buy. Note the following. First, if there is only one computer that meets threshold requirements, each submarket will buy it with probability 1, and will buy $M$ units of it, as we asserted (assumed) earlier. Second, assume that there is more than one computer that passes the threshold. If $c1$ is very high, and $c2$ and $c3$ are very low, virtually all the customers will buy the computer with the highest merit score. On the other hand, if $c1$ is relatively low, or $c2$ and $c3$ are high, a higher merit computer may be "out sold" by a rival computer that has the higher existing market share, or which has been advertised more intensively, or both.

In the absence of the bandwagon/brand loyalty effect and of advertising, the demand module would behave similarly to a standard demand curve. Demand would converge to "best value for the money," although in the limit a positive probability of survival for inferior computers always remains. Convergence is faster the higher is the parameter $c_1$. The consideration of brand loyalty and of the bandwagon effect changes this picture quite drastically, introducing inertia and forms of increasing returns.

### Competition between the technologies, with "locked-in" firms

Within this model, after a number of periods have gone by, and after a number of transistor firms have successfully entered the mainframe market, microprocessors come into existence. A number of new firms start out at point "Z" in figure 10.1, with funding provided by venture capitalists, just as previously new firms had started out at that point using transistor technology. Some of these firms will fail before they get into a market. Others may succeed.

Notice that while existing transistor firms provide no "barrier to entry" for microprocessor firms who have aimed their trajectory toward the personal computer, or PC, market, the existence of established transistor firms in the mainframe market creates a significant barrier to entry. First of all, if a microprocessor firm achieves a design that meets threshold requirements in the mainframe market, that computer is in competition with existing transistor-based computers that already have achieved higher than threshold quality levels. Second, the extant transistor mainframe producers have acquired positive market share, and have engaged in significant advertising, and that further disadvantages a newcomer. It is an open question within this model whether a new microprocessor firm can survive in the mainframe market. If not, and if extant transistor firms cannot or do not switch over to making mainframes out of microprocessors, the potential in the mainframe market afforded by microprocessor technology never will be realized.

In fact, we know that microprocessor firms did enter the mainframe market, but did not fare well there, in part because extant mainframe firms themselves adopted microprocessor technologies. Further, some of those old mainframe firms, IBM in particular, then used microprocessor technology to try to enter the PC market. Thus there are two different kinds of transitional dynamics that need to be built into this model, if it is to be "history friendly." First, we must enable firms that originally are using one technology to switch over to another. Second, we must enable firms who are in one market to try to diversify into the other.

## Transition dynamics

We noted above our desire to capture in our model a number of aspects of the new understandings about dynamic firm competencies, and competence "lock-ins." We have built into the model that firm competencies are "cumulative" with today's design efforts building on what was achieved yesterday. Firms tend to get better and better at the particular things they are doing. On the other hand, it is clear that firms often have a good deal of difficulty when they try to do significantly new things. Thus Tushman and Anderson (1986), and Henderson and Clark (1990), have documented the difficulty that firms often have in coping when the best technologies underlying their products change significantly. Quite often extant firms cannot switch over rapidly enough to counter the efforts of new firms using the new technology. Christensen and Rosenbloom (1994) have put a spotlight on similar difficulties that extant firms have had in recognizing new markets when they opened up.

In our model, existing transistor-based mainframe firms are able to switch over to microprocessor technology for use in their mainframe designs, but this may be time consuming and costly for them. It is new firms that do the initial work of advancing computer design using microprocessors. The probability that an extant transistor firm will try to switch over is a function of two variables. The first is how far along microprocessor computer designs have been pushed. The second is the closeness of a transistor firm to the technological possibility frontier defined by transistor technology. The former clearly is a signal to extant firms that "there is a potentially powerful new technology out there, and we may be in trouble if we don't adopt it." The latter is an indication that "we can't get much further if we keep on pushing along the same road."

If an old transistor firm decides to switch over, it faces one significant disadvantage, but also has an advantage. The disadvantage is that the experience that got it to the forefront of transistor technology (recall equation 1) counts for little or nothing if it shifts over to microprocessor technology. Thus in its first efforts in microprocessor computer design, it will achieve only about the average for extant microprocessor-based mainframe firms. Further, it must incur a once and for all switchover cost in order to start designing, producing, and marketing microprocessor based mainframes. However, extant transistor firms have the advantage of large R&D budgets which, with a cost, they can switch over to working with the new technology, and a stock of accumulated earnings on which they can draw to cover any transition costs.

In sum, the adoption of the new technology takes place in two steps. First, a firm must "perceive" microprocessors technology. Perception is a stochastic process that depends on the current technological position of the potential adopter in relation to the technological frontier in transistors and on the progress realized by the new technology:

$$Pr_{perc} = [Z_i^g + Z_{mp}^{h}/2]^\lambda \tag{9}$$

where $P_{perc}$ is the probability of perceiving microprocessors technology, $Z_i$ is the fraction of the transistors technological frontier covered by firm i, and $Z_{mp}$ is the fraction of the microprocessors frontier covered by the best-practice microprocessors firm. The parameter λ measures the general difficulty of perceiving the new technology.

Once firms have perceived the possibility of adoption, they have to invest in order to acquire the new technology. Adoption costs ($C_{ad}$) entail a fixed cost, $F_{ad}$, equal for all firms, and the payment of a fraction $q$ of firms' accumulated budget, linked to factors like the training of engineers and the like. Thus,

$$C_{ad} = F_{ad} + q\, B_t \tag{10}$$

Firms whose budget does not cover the fixed costs or whose profit rate is negative cannot adopt microprocessors. Moreover, the competence-destroying nature of the new technology is captured by the notion that adoption implies that the experience accumulated on the old technology counts now much less. In the model, experience (T) is reduced by a factor which is a parameter of the model.

Once firms have adopted the new technology, they have access to the new technological frontier and can innovate faster. However, they maintain their original trajectory.

Once an old transistor mainframe firm has switched over to microprocessor technology, it is potentially open to diversify by designing and trying to sell computers on the PC market. Diversification can take place only after the adoption of microprocessors. The incentive for diversification is a function of the size of the PC market, defined in terms of the number of computers sold, as compared to the mainframe market. Specifically, diversification becomes possible when the ratio between the size of the PC market and the size of the mainframe market is bigger than a threshold value, which is a parameter of the model.

The firms' old design trajectory will, in general, not be a good one to pursue if it wants to diversify into PCs. As noted, IBM diversified by setting up an entirely new division, and that is what we assume about diversification of mainframe producers into the PC market in this model. The parent company founds a new division trying to exploit the available competencies specific to PCs, rather than to apply its own competencies to the new market.

The new division inherits from the parent company a fraction of the budget, of technical capabilities and advertising capabilities. The size of these fractions are all parameters of the model. The position of the new division in the design space is determined as the average merit of design prevailing in the PC market at the time diversification occurs. In other words, the parent company exploits "public knowledge" in the PC market and partly "imitates" PC firms. The technical progress trajectory (i.e. the mix of engineers of the two types) is randomly recalculated. After birth, the new division behaves exactly as a new entrant, with independent products and profits and budget.

The new divisional firm faces the disadvantage that there already are firms selling in the PC market, with designs that already exceed thresholds, positive market shares, established advertising budgets, and experience in the PC market. However, the new divisional firm does have the advantage of being able to dip into the "deep pockets" and resources of its mother firm, which can switch over to PCs a sizeable fraction of its extant R and D and advertising budgets. After the initial infusion of resources, the new PC branch firm is on its own.

## History Replicating and History Divergent Simulations

This model is able to "replicate" the industry history, with a parameter setting that reflects the basic key assumptions that economists who have studied the computer industry suggested were behind the pattern that happened. We call this parameter setting the "standard set." The details of the simulations are discussed in a previous paper and, for reasons of space, we do not discuss them here again (Malerba et al., 1999).

A dominant transistor-based firm (IBM) emerged relatively quickly in the mainframe market. That firm held on to its large share of the market, even when new microprocessor firms entered that market and challenged it. Part of the reason the dominant firm held on is that it shifted over to microprocessor technology in a relatively timely manner. That firm then entered the PC market, and gained a non-trivial, but not a dominant share.

The key factors that led to this pattern were assumed to be the following. First, the early buyers of IBM equipment tended to feel themselves "locked in" to IBM for upgrades, extensions, and renewal of their computer capacity, largely because of specialized software. This made entry of new firms difficult. In terms of our model, a firm that has a high market share in mainframes will, because of that, attract a significant share of new purchases. Second, by the time the new technology came along, computer design under the old technology was reasonably advanced, and the leader, IBM, responded to the availability of new technology pretty rapidly. In terms of our model, soon after the first microprocessor firms enter the mainframe market, the dominant transistor firm in that market switches over to microprocessors. Third, IBM's massive resources enabled it quickly to mount an R&D and advertising effort sufficient for it to catch up with the earlier entrants into the PC market. However, because the PCs produced by a number of other companies were compatible with the software used by IBM PCs, there was no specific lock-in to IBM. And within the class of IBM compatibles, customers were quite sensitive to the merit of the computers being offered, particularly to price. In terms of our model, in the PC market the coefficient on quality was high, and the coefficient on specific market share was low.

After a "history friendly" replication base case had been achieved, we modified the value of the parameters we identified as corresponding to the fundamental causal factors of the observed history, in order to see if those changes produced quite different patterns of evolution. Thus, we reduced the coefficient on market share in the demand equations for mainframes, to see if this would damp down the tendency of a dominant firm to emerge, and hold on in the face of new stringent competition. Second, firms using microprocessor technology entered the mainframe market earlier, before a dominant firm had emerged. Third, transistor firms were more sluggish in shifting over to microprocessors, and it was more costly for them to do so. Fourth, demand in the PC market was more sensitive to advertising, and less sensitive to computer quality, so that a deep-pockets company diversifying into PCs from mainframes had a chance of quickly grabbing a large share of the PC market. Results of the simulations were consistent with our expectations.

Being satisfied that the structure and the parametrization of the model capture the

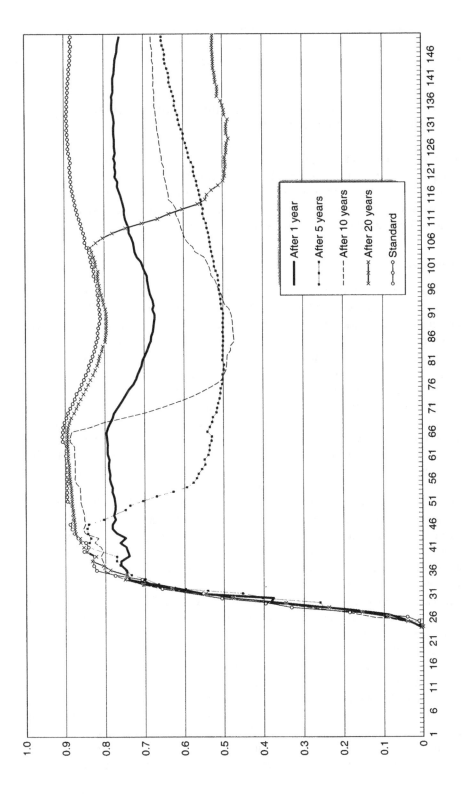

**Figure 10.3** Antitrust: Herfindahl in mainframe market

basic logic behind the evolution of the computer industry, we are now confident to use this apparatus to carry on further experiments and counterfactuals to analyze the problems and the effects of alternative policy interventions.

## Competition and Industrial Policies in Dynamic Markets: Anti-trust, Entry Support, and Public Procurement

In this chapter two broad groups of policies are going to be discussed: antitrust and entry support. Anti-trust policies have the aim of reducing the high level of concentration in the market, while entry-support policies have the objective to increase contestability and variety. We will examine them in their effects on market concentration, price, and technological change. Results refer to 100 runs.

### Anti-trust policies

In our model anti-trust authority (AA) intervenes when the monopolist reaches a share of 75 per cent of the market.[5] It acts by breaking the monopolist in two. The two new firms originating from the old monopolists have half the size and resources of the previous monopolist: budget, engineers, cumulated marketing expenditures (and thus also bandwagon effect). They maintain however the same position in terms of product attributes (cheapness and performance), experience and technology of the previous monopolist.[6] The two new firms differ only in terms of trajectory: one of the two has the monopolist trajectory, the other a trajectory chosen at random.[7]

We have tested a very rapid AA intervention or a very late one. In one case antitrust intervenes very soon, 1 year after the first firm has reached a share of 75 per cent of the market. This is a very unrealistic run, because most of the time AA breaks the first entrant. But we have used it as an extreme case. In other cases AA intervention is not immediate (5 years), late (10 years) or very late (20 years).

Results are shown in figure 10.3 for the mainframe market, where the Herfindahl indexes for the various cases are compared. When AA intervenes extremely early, the market becomes concentrated again very soon, and remains so, albeit at a lower level than for the standard case. From the two firms resulting from antitrust intervention one will emerge again as a monopolist, because it will benefit from increasing returns and lock-ins at the demand level.

In the case of not immediate AA intervention (5 years), all the firms have already entered the market but they are still small in terms of size. The break up of the largest firm has the effect of making firms more similar in terms of size and resources, so that the emergence of a monopolist takes more time and the Herfindahl index reaches at the end of the simulation a medium to high level (between 0.6 and 0.7). On the contrary if the AA intervenes late (10 years), the monopolist has already reached a certain size and the two new firms resulting from the intervention are already rather large with respect to the other competitors: therefore, one of the two new large firms will gain the leadership and the market will tend toward concentration, with a final level of the Herfindahl index higher than in the previous case. Finally, if the intervention occurs too late (20 years) the market will be divided into two oligopolists, which will not profit any more from the possibility of gaining market leadership because increasing returns are limited (technological opportunities are almost all depleted).

These results show the relevance of the timing of the intervention in dynamic markets. It makes a big difference whether AA intervenes too early or too late. In dynamic markets, it is important to consider whether all the potential players have already entered the market or not, firms are of small size or large size, and increasing returns have started to fade away. In case AA intervenes too early and increasing returns are still quite high, after the intervention the few players in the market generate a situation quite similar to the initial one. On the contrary, if AA intervenes too late, with limited increasing returns, the market will remain divided between two large firms.

Another interesting result of our model is the effect on the second market (PC) of an antitrust intervention in the first market (mainframes). As one can see from figure 10.4, as a consequence of the AA intervention in the first market, the level of concentration in the second market decreases. The reasons are basically two. When antitrust acts very early or early, and large mainframe firms are able to regenerate their advantages, two mainframe firms instead of one diversify in the PC market: the market leader and a second firm that has gained some considerable market share. Thus the PC market will be shared by a greater number of large firms, both new microprocessor firms and mainframes firms, and concentration will decrease. In case antitrust acts too late, only one firm will diversify in the other market as in the standard case. Its size however will be very small and the overall level of concentration in the PC market will decrease.

The trends in performance and prices (not reported here) do not show significant differences over time between the standard case and the antitrust interventions. Here static efficiency considerations related to the breaking of the monopolist allow for lower prices (due to the lower mark-up). However static considerations are compensated by a more limited increase in cheapness (or moving down the learning curve) and in performance due to the smaller size and the reduced R&D budget.

Finally, we have tested the effects of antitrust when one of the two sources of increasing returns characterizing the mainframe segment – lock-ins at the demand level – is not present (figure 10.5). In order to do that we have put the exponent on market share equal to zero in the demand equation. In this case the Herfindahl index in mainframes decreases, although not significantly, because of the working of the effects of increasing returns on the R&D side. Interestingly enough, antitrust effects are significant and show a similar pattern (although at a lower level) as the ones in figure 10.3, with one difference. Once broken, in most case concentration tends to remain at the same level and not to pick up again, as in the case with demand lock-ins.

### Entry support

In our model the support for entry with the aim of increasing the degree of contestability and variety in the market is done in three broad ways. The first concerns the support for the exploration (pre-market) phase of existing firms; the second the support of small firms in the post-entry phase; the third the increase in the number of firms in the market.

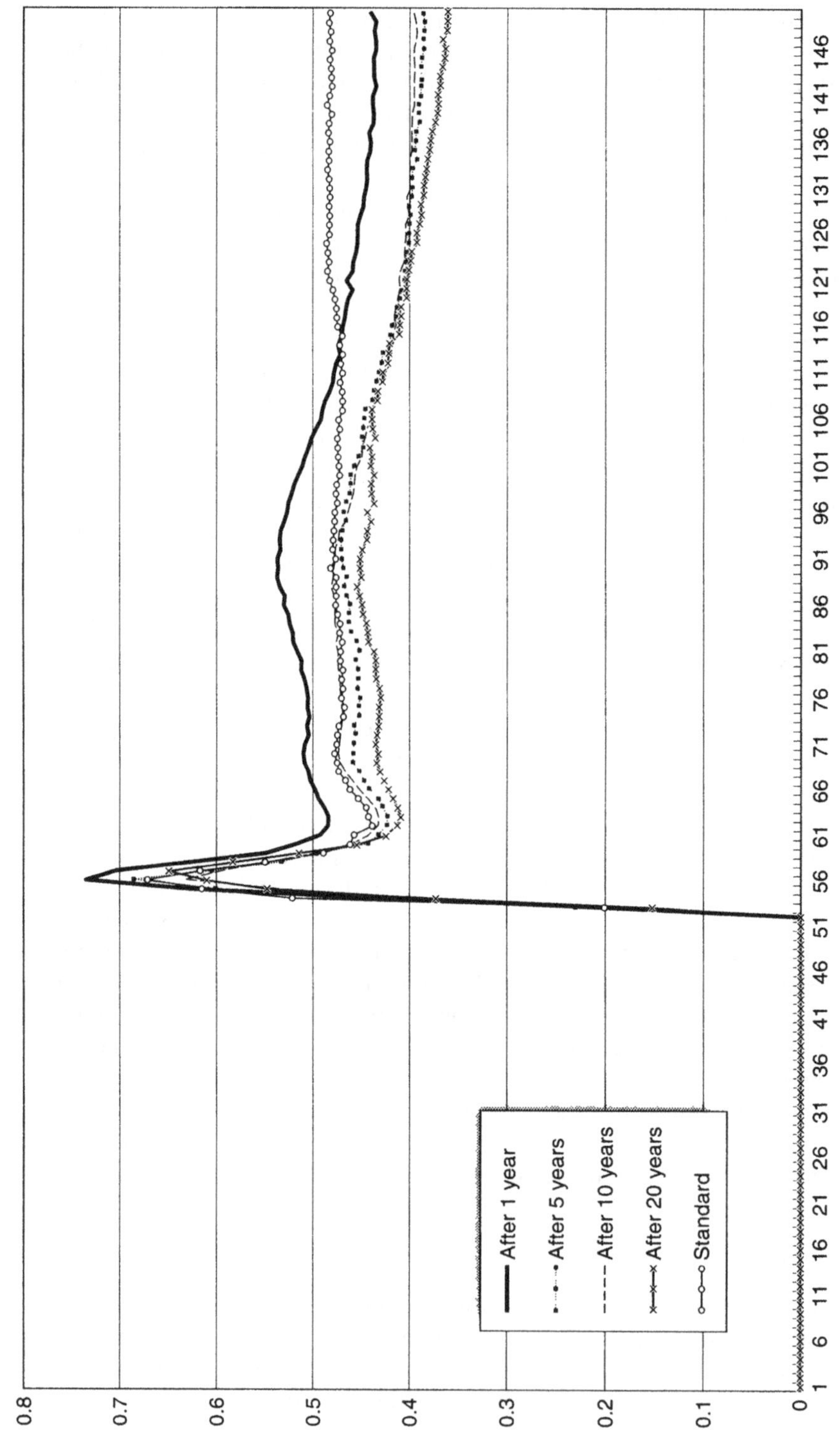

**Figure 10.4** Antitrust: Herfindahl in PC market

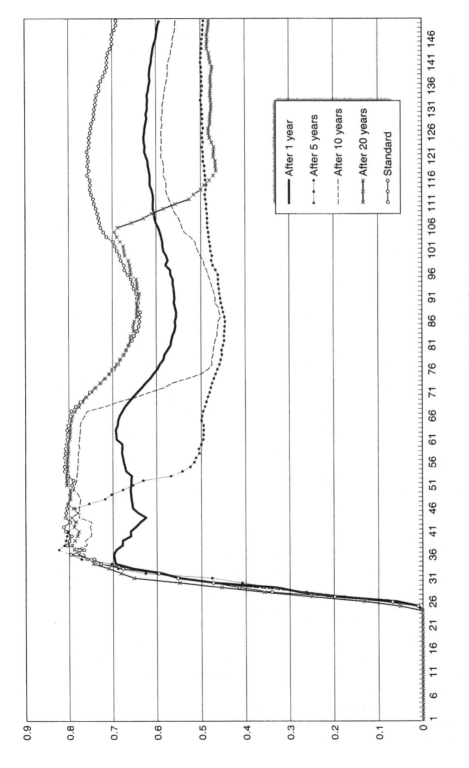

**Figure 10.5** Antitrust: Herfindahl in mainframe market (no demand lock-in in mainframe)

*Support for the exploration by firms*
First, government policy may support exploration. In our runs, support is given first to all first generation (transistors) firms (six in total) or only to firms with a small budget and later to all second generation (microprocessor) firms (twenty in total) or only to firms with a small budget. Total support is calculated in terms of share of the total initial budget of firms.[8] In this case 30% of the total initial budget of firms is divided among either all firms or the smaller ones. To each firm a share proportional to its budget is assigned.

Results show that, as far as concentration is concerned, no major difference with the standard case exist for the mainframe market (which remain highly concentrated: see figure 10.6, where only the support for the exploration of small firms is shown). For the second generation firms, exploration support increases the entry of microprocessor firms into the mainframe market (with little effect on the concentration level in that market). However the greater number of (microprocessor) mainframes firms now leads to a greater number of diversifiers into the PC market. Thus the Herfindahl in PC market decreases because of that figure 10.7.

*Support for the post-entry survival of new small firms*
An alternative policy may be related to the support of new firms that just entered the market and that may lack resources and capabilities. The government may support either all firms except the leader or only the small firms (in figures 10.6 and 10.7 we have shown only this second case). Again, 30 per cent of the total initial budget of firms is distributed among the entrants. The total support is again proportional to its size in terms of market share. The government gives half of the budget in the first quarter of the first year, then a fourth of support in the first quarter of the second year and the last fourth in the first quarter of the second year.

This type of policy is totally ineffective in mainframes: concentration does not decrease (see figure 10.6). The explanation is that in this case support is given to firms that were already in the market and losing. Given the strong increasing returns in the market, this is not enough to counterbalance the dominance of the leader. In the PC market, concentration is again lower than in the standard case, because of the greater number of diversifying firms from the mainframe market.

*Support for the creation of new firms*
Third, a set of policies may concern the support for the creation of totally new firms (in the form of public funding of new risky initiatives), in order to increase competition and the variety of approaches and trajectories. Here again the same amount of money (30 per cent of the total initial budget of firms) is given to two firms, without the requirement to be given back to the venture capitalists as in the standard case.

As figure 10.6 shows, the creation of two new firms in mainframes decreases somewhat the concentration in the mainframe market. The major effects however are on the PC market (see figure 10.7). The support to the two new microprocessor firms is a significant one: the initial budget of the 20 microprocessor firms is concentrated in two new large firms. Thus initially the Herfindahl index in the PC market rises. It then decreases and goes to a level even lower than the standard one, when the greater number of diversifying mainframe firms enters the PC market.

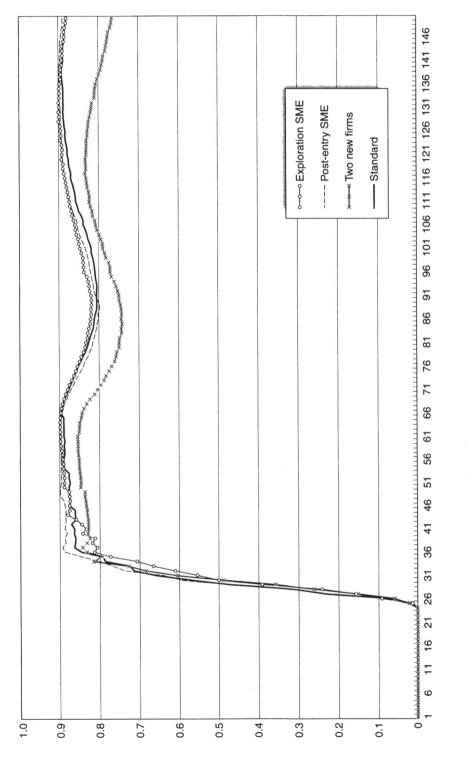

**Figure 10.6** Herfindahl in mainframe market (30% funding)

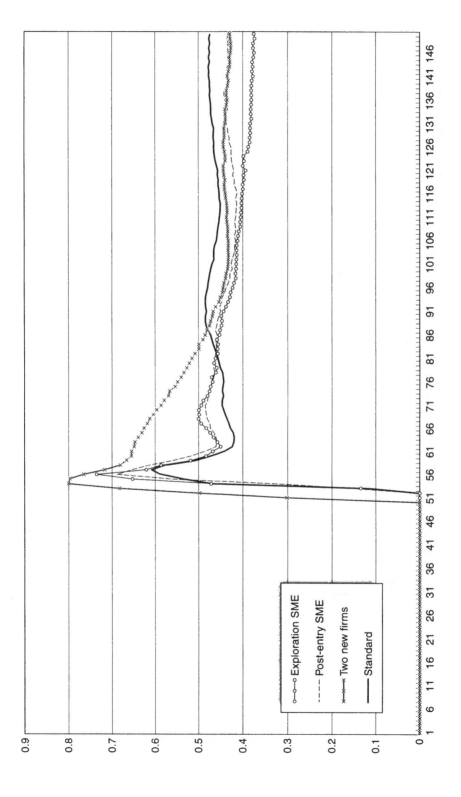

**Figure 10.7** Herfindahl in PC market (30% funding)

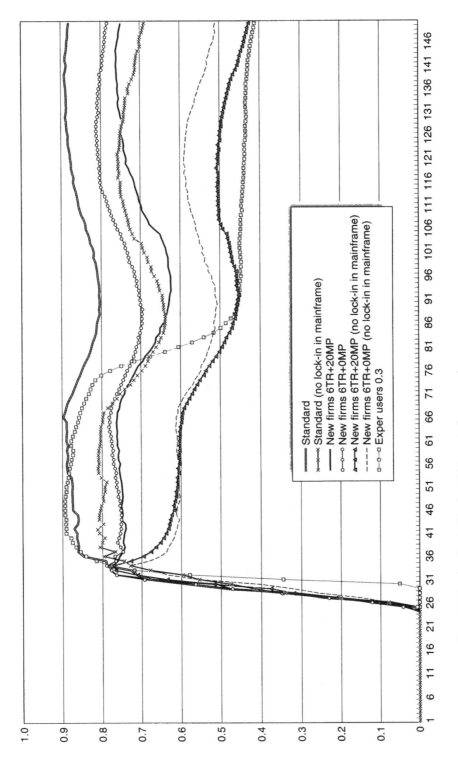

Legend:
- Standard
- Standard (no lock-in in mainframe)
- New firms 6TR+20MP
- New firms 6TR+0MP
- New firms 6TR+20MP (no lock-in in mainframe)
- New firms 6TR+0MP (no lock-in in mainframe)
- Exper users 0.3

**Figure 10.8** New firms (100% funding): Herfindahl in mainframe market

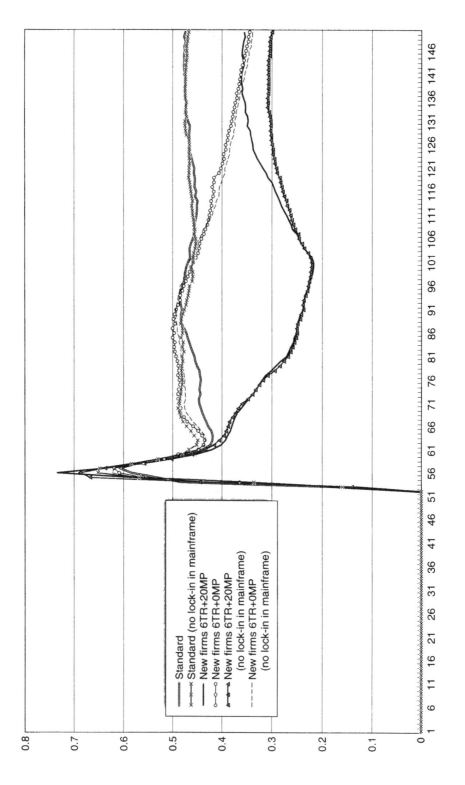

**Figure 10.9** New firms (100% funding): Herfindahl in PC market

*Alternative runs on antitrust and entry support policies*

Given the unsatisfactory results of antitrust and entry support policies in terms of reducing concentration in the mainframe market, other types of simulations have been run.

The first set of simulations regards policies that aim to *greatly increase the number of new entrants*, in order to increase the variety of approaches. Thus the simulation keeps the same amount of support (30 per cent of the total initial budget) but increases the number of firms created with that support (4 or 6 transistor firms). Results (not reported here) show no change in concentration from the standard case.

Also, the *coupling of the two policies* (antitrust and entry support) is not more successful than the use of a single type of policy. In fact in a second set of simulations, we have tested an antitrust intervention coupled with the creation of new firms or the support of new entrants. Results (not reported here) do not show major differences with the cases discussed above.

In a third group of simulations we have envisaged an *exceptionally big intervention*, reaching 100% of the total initial budget of firms (instead of 30 per cent). In one set of simulation runs we studied the effect of a support of the creation of only 6 new transistor firms. In a second set of runs, support was given to 6 new transistor firms and 20 new microprocessor firms. Results (Figures 10.8 and 10.9) show some decrease in the Hefindahl index in mainframes, and a considerable decrease in the Herfindahl index in PC.

Finally, we have explored the role of policy in an environment *with less strong increasing returns*. We have maintained increasing returns at the R&D level, but not at the demand level in the mainframe market, by setting the exponent of the market share in the demand equation equal to zero. As one could imagine, the standard simulation shows a lower level of concentration in the mainframe market. Then we have analyzed the effects of the same type of policy interventions discussed above (support of 30 per cent of the total initial budget). Results in figures 10.10 and 10.11 show some reductions in the concentration in mainframes and PC markets. These reductions are not considerable however. Finally, we have introduced the strong type of intervention (support of 100% of the total initial budget for the creation of several new firms) just discussed above. In this case, the runs regarding the policy interventions show a much lower level of concentration (see Figures 10.8 and 10.9). In addition, policies in the mainframe market are more effective in decreasing the level of concentration than in the standard case of strong increasing returns. While significantly diminished however, concentration does not go below 0.4, even in the case of 6 new transistor firms and 20 microprocessor firms.

## Public procurement of new products

The government may act also as a customer who likes experimenting with new technologies in established markets and therefore likes buying those products that incorporate the new technology. The government may buy totally new products not deterred from that experimentation simply because the quality of the new products is not up to that which they had been buying.

In our simulations, the government buys the new microprocessor-based mainframes

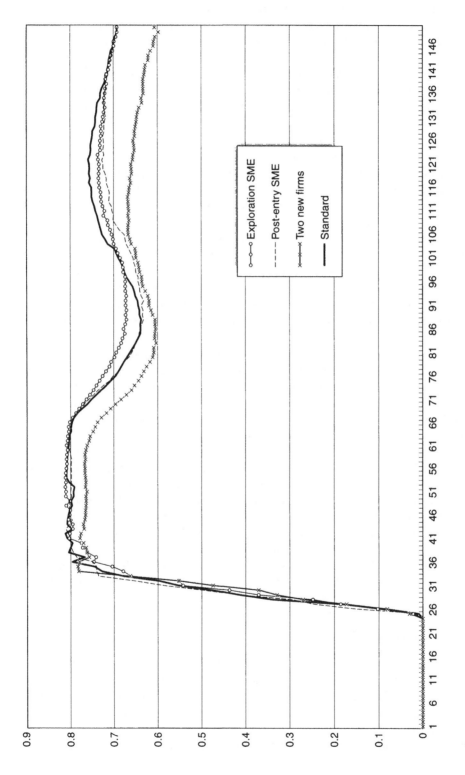

**Figure 10.10** Herfindahl in mainframe market (30% funding) (no demand lock-in in mainframe)

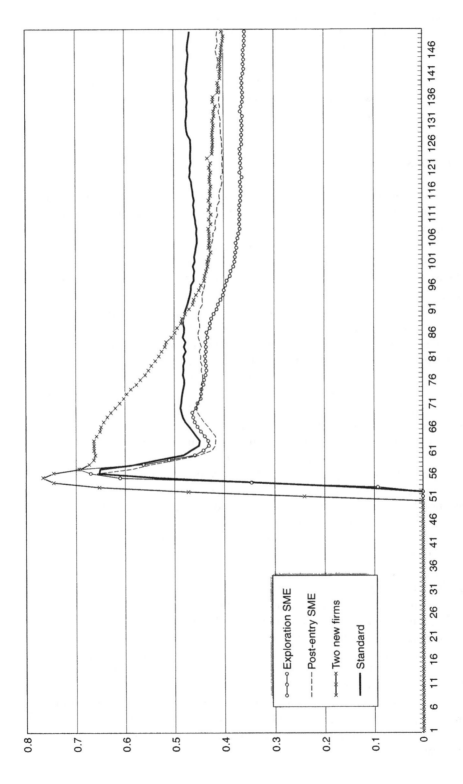

**Figure 10.11** Herfindahl in PC market (30% funding) (no demand lock-in in PC)

and acts as a large group of customers (30 per cent of the market) who like experimenting and buy products with the new technology. In this case the new microprocessor technology takes off rapidly, both in terms of new firms producing mainframes with the new technology and of established firms eventually adopting the new technology. But the new firms with the new technology are also able to take a dominant position in the market, and concentration in the mainframe market is significantly reduced. (see figure 10.8)

## Conclusions

The results of the simulations suggest some rather "provocative" conclusions. First, in strongly cumulative markets, where there are strong dynamic increasing returns, there is obviously a strong tendency towards concentration and some sort of "natural monopoly." Our main result is that it is extremely difficult to contrast this tendency. In most of our simulations, policy interventions are ineffective in significantly modifying the degree of concentration. Only very big and focused interventions have a chance to be effective. Even when one source of increasing returns is taken away, concentration and a market leader emerge and policy intervention, albeit more successful than in the other case, is not able to break down the dominant firm and to significantly reduce concentration. Only policies of public procurement in which the government plays the role of experimental user constitutes a fundamental mechanism allowing the growth and survival of new firms with new promising technologies that would have otherwise faced a difficult time in a different context.

Second, the reason for this "policy ineffectiveness" of antitrust and entry support policies lies in the strongly cumulative nature of the market. Small initial advantages tend to grow bigger over time and catching up is almost impossible. Leaders do not only have a "static" advantage: they run faster than laggards. Thus, policies of the kind of antitrust and entry support are somehow designed toward "leveling the playing field." But this is not sufficient. In order to get results, some form of "positive discrimination" may be necessary. That is to say, policies should make competitors able to run (much) faster than the monopolist, and not just remove static disadvantages. This is what public procurement in favour of highly innovative products (thus having a high potential for improvement with respect to existing products) does.

Third, our simulations suggest that there is actually almost no difference in terms of technological progress and prices between more concentrated and more competitive situations. In our model, the classical Schumpeterian trade-off does not practically exist. In terms of our (admittedly extremely rough) measures of "welfare," there are no specific reasons to favor monopoly or competition. This does not necessarily imply that monopoly should not be contrasted. If anything, the implication might be the opposite. We should not be too worried to contrast monopoly on the basis of the "Schumpeterian trade-off."

This is even more the case, if competition had additional virtues. For example, one might dislike monopoly on grounds different from purely "efficiency" considerations, but simply on more political bases: large concentrations of power are not desirable in a democratic society. Closer to the nature of this chapter – and obviously in an evolutionary perspective – one of the main virtues of competition is likely to reside in its ability to generate novelty, e.g. entirely new products or processes or major technological discontinuities. In its present form, our model captures it through the role played by public procurement targeted to products embodying a totally new technology and supplied by firms that enter the mainframe market on the basis of the technological discontinuity associated to the appearance of microprocessors. In this case public policy is able to affect market structure and significantly decrease concentration.

## Acknowledgement

Luca Giorcelli, Luca Berga and Christian Garavaglia provided an invaluable contribution to the development of the model. Alessandro Politano also helped in the testing of the model. Support from the Italian National Research Council (CNR) and from Bocconi University (Basic Research Program) is gratefully acknowledged. An anonymous referee has provided helpful suggestions. This chapter draws from the paper "Competition and industrial policies in a history friendly model of the computer industry," *International Journal of Industrial* Organization, 2001.

## Notes

1   These models are in the tradition of evolutionary models (Nelson–Winter, 1982; Nelson, 1995).
2   Albeit different in basic concepts, structure and overall framework, this part of the model is similar to the Jovanovic (1982) model. First start with an uncertain environment and only learn through experience – trial and error in the market – if this endowment is valuable or not. We are grateful to a referee for showing us this point.
3   As we will see later, the assumption that technical competencies grow over time is valid only within a given market and technology. With the emergence of a new technology or a new market, the accumulated competencies of existing firms decay in various ways.
4   We use log linear equations whenever plausible because most economists have a good feel for their behavior and their quirks. Also, while in most cases the behavior being specified obviously relates to particular firms, to avoid clutter we do not denote that specifically.
5   Given the feature of our model, the 75 per cent share could be set higher or lower without changing the nature of the intervention. In fact, the monopolist in a few years reaches a share between 85 per cent and 90 per cent of the mainframe market and does not fall below it in the course of the whole simulation.
6   In a simulation, we have halved the monopolists in two but have maintained the overall endogenous bandwagon effect to one of the two new firms. Of course, the firm that have the bandwagon effect very rapidly regain a monopolistic position. This interesting result points to the fact that an antitrust intervention that aims just to break in two the R&D and the size of the monopolist, without paying attention to bandwagon effects in a market with high lock-ins, is doomed to certain failure.
7   In another set of simulations, we have created two new firms with exactly the same trajectory. Results do not differ from the new random trajectory case.
8   In a series of runs the government supports firms' R&D expenditures instead of the budget. Results have not changed significantly.

## References

Bresnahan T. F. and Greenstein, S. (1999) Technological competition and the structure of the computer industry, *Journal of Industrial Economics*, 47, 1–40.

Bresnahan T. F. and Malerba, F. (1999) Industrial dynamics and the evolution of firms' and nations' competitive capabilities in the world computer industry. In D. Mowery and R. Nelson (eds) *The Sources of Industrial Leadership*. Cambridge: Cambridge University Press

Christensen, R. (1994) Technological discontinuities, organizational capabilities, and strategic commitments, *Industrial and Corporate Change*, 3, 655–86.

Dosi, G. and Marengo, L. (1993) Some elements of an evolutionary theory of organizational competence. In R. W. England (ed.), *Evolutionary Concepts on Contemporary Economics*. Ann Arbor: University of Michigan Press.

Flamm, K. (1988) *Creating the Computer*. Washington, DC: Brookings Institution.

Jovanovic, B. (1982). Selection and the evolution of industry, *Econometrica*, 50(2), 649–70.

Henderson, R. and Clark, K. B. (1990) Architectural innovation: the reconfiguration of existing product technologies and the failure of established firms, *Administrative Sciences Quarterly*, 35, 9–30.

Langlois, R. N. (1990) Creating external capabilities: innovation and vertical disintegration in the microcomputer industry, *Business and Economic History*, 19, 93–102.

Malerba, F., Nelson, R., Orsenigo, L., and Winter, S. (1999) History friendly models of industry evolution: the computer industry, *Industrial and Corporate Change*, 1, 3–41.

Nelson, R. (1994) The co-evolution of technology, industrial structure, and supporting institutions. *Industrial and Corporate Change*, 47–63.

Nelson R. (1995) Recent evolutionary theorizing about economic change, *Journal of Economic Literature*, 23 (March), 48–90.

Nelson, R. and Winter, S. (1982) *An Evolutionary Theory of Economic Change*. Cambridge, MA: Harvard University Press.

Teece, D. J., Pisano, G., and Shuen, A. (1992) *Dynamic capabilities and strategic management*. Working paper, Haas School of Management, University of California at Bekeley.

Tushman, M. L. and Anderson, P. (1986) Technological discontinuities and organizational enviroments, *Administrative Science Quarterly*, 31, 439–56.

Winter, S. (1987) Knowledge and competence as strategic assets. In Teece, D. J. (ed.), *The Competitive Challenge*. Cambridge, MA: Ballinger, 159–84.

# CHAPTER ELEVEN

# Problem-solving Behaviors, Organizational Forms, and the Complexity of Tasks

## Giovanni Dosi, Mike Hobday, and Luigi Marengo

### Introduction

The dominant form of analysis of organizational behaviors and structures, closely drawing from mainstream economics, takes a rather extreme agency approach, seeking to identify the most efficient incentive mechanisms for the coordination of decisions. However, such an incentive-based approach adopts the highly dubious assumption that both the structures for problem-solving and the necessary search heuristics (e.g. "rules of thumb" for decision-making) exist, unproblematically, from the outset. Here and throughout the chapter, the term "problem-solving" includes all the acts undertaken by individuals and groups within economic organizations (firms) to resolve organizational and technological problems and to conceptualize, design, test, and build products and processes.

In the case of most firms – new and incumbent ones – facing market and technological uncertainty, what one could call the "problem-free" assumption is profoundly unrealistic and assumes away the difficulty of constructing a theory to explain the co-evolution of problem-solving knowledge and organizational arrangements in firms. In turn, this demands some basic analytical tools to examine how firms deploy and match problem-solving activities with governance arrangements.[1] This is especially important where tasks are inherently complex and non-routine in nature and where many possible problem-solving and organizational solutions are possible.

The first purpose of this chapter is to outline an evolutionary framework for analyzing how problem-solving knowledge in firms co-evolves with organizational forms in complex task environments. These characteristics apply to most activities performed by new high technology firms and to the many functions in larger established corporations which are non-routine and non-codifiable by nature, including strategy formulation, R&D, marketing, distribution channel management, new product design, process engineering, human resource development and supply chain management.[2]

The second and complementary aim is to operationalize the evolutionary view of how firms as knowledge repositories cope with complex, non-routine tasks by evolving appropriate structures to deal with them. The practical application of the approach considers one important class of economic activity, which represents an extreme case of product and task complexity, namely the production of complex products and systems (or "CoPS"), including high cost, tailored capital goods, systems constructs, and services.[3] Because each new product tends to be different and because production involves feedback loops from later to early stages (and other unpredictable, "emerging" properties), highly innovative non-functional organizational structures are required to co-ordinate production, particularly in the commonly found case of unclear and uncertain user requirements.

The chapter is structured as follows. We describe the basic principles underlying an evolutionary approach to problem-solving behavior (PSB) in firms, contrasting these with the dominant (incentive-centred) formulation of agency in organizations. Next we present the building blocks of an evolutionary theory of PSB and firm organization, representing PSB as a form of complex design activity. The model – spelled out in more detail in Marengo (1999) and Marengo et al. (1999) – expands upon a "Simonian" representation of PSB grounded on the notions of combination of elementary physical and cognitive acts, and de-composability of firm behavior and structure in relation to particular product or process outcomes (Simon, 1981, 1991).

We apply the conceptual framework to CoPS found in sectors such as aerospace, information systems, many utilities, engineering construction, military systems, transportation, and telecommunications. Then we compare some properties of different organizational set-ups within multi-firm CoPS projects and their implications for innovative PSBs. Next we draw upon the organizational behavior literature to provide a practical set of heuristics for gathering "benchmark" data for complex non-routine projects: in the language we shall introduce below, such heuristics entail procedures for re-shaping "problem representations" and "problem decompositions". Some examples of the application of these concepts for the purposes of business improvement in CoPS are touched upon.[4]

## An Evolutionary Approach to Problem-solving Behavior in Firms

Before presenting the basic building blocks of an evolutionary theory of PSB it is useful to briefly recall the governing principles behind the dominant agency approach. As known, agency theory identifies efficient incentive mechanisms for the coordination of decisions (see e.g. Tirole, 1986; Grossman and Hart, 1986; Laffont and Tirole, 1986), while implicitly assuming that PSB structures and search heuristics exist from the outset. Within firms, people are postulated to play extremely sophisticated games according to rules designed to prevent them from doing much harm to others (and indirectly to themselves). Neither the complexity of the task itself, nor the product of the firm or the production technology have much, or any, bearing on the subject at hand. The main aim is to generate admissible incentive-compatible procedures based, when taken at face value, on hyper-rational agents.[5]

Relatedly, individuals within organizations are assumed to hold the entire plan of what to do, possibly akin to a well-functioning computer model. The issue of firm competence and its relationship with performance does not arise, except for problems of the misrepresentation of "intrinsic" individual abilities and adverse selection, or incentive misalignment in eliciting effort from individuals. Within the firm, as a first approximation, the social division of tasks is irrelevant to practice and performance. In the extreme, according to the mainstream approach, given the "right" incentives, any firm can make any product as well as any other firm (e.g. microprocessors as well as Intel or bioengineering products as well as Genetech).[6]

By contrast, at its most general level, the evolutionary approach sees economic organizations as problem-solving arrangements, viewing the different observed institutional set-ups in the real world as reflecting the complexity of the tasks and objectives faced by the firm (March and Simon, 1958; Nelson and Winter, 1982; Dosi and Marengo, 1994). In the world of non-trivial, complex, and uncertain tasks, governance arrangements and search heuristics play a central part in determining which eventual solutions are considered as possibilities, tested, and ultimately selected. Relatedly, a key evolutionary proposition is that in making decisions, firms and individuals and groups within them, confront extremely large, computationally intractable search "spaces" to choose from. Therefore the particular organizational arrangements and approaches, skill and experience in proceeding, shape and define the distinctive competence of individual firms.[7]

As can be formally demonstrated, the design of suitable organizational arrangements tends to be even more computationally complex than finding an optimal solution to the problem itself (Marengo et al., 1999). To the extent that this is a correct representation of real world decision-making, this implies that it is not sensible to assume that problem-solvers operate within ex ante established organizational structures, governance arrangements, and PSB routines. Indeed, organizational form has to be established as part of, and alongside, the problem-solving activity. Within this co-evolution of PSBs and organizational arrangements, individuals, groups and entire firms are far from having perfect knowledge or foresight, but "bounded rationality," broadly defined, is the rule (Simon, 1981; Dosi and Egidi, 1991; Dosi et al. 1996).[8]

To resolve highly complex dynamic problems, boundedly rational individuals and groups within firms (as with the firm itself) are highly likely to adopt problem decomposition procedures, (for a thorough illustration, see among others, the example of aeronautical engineering in Vincenti, 1990). Here and throughout this work, largely in tune with Herbert Simon's perspective on problem-solving, by "decomposition" we mean the identification of ensembles of tasks or "sub-problems" whose solution is meant to yield also to the solution of the overall problem. So, for example, if the general problem is the development and construction of an airplane with certain technical characteristics, "decompositions" might involve the identification of "sub-problems" concerning e.g. engine thrust, wing loads, aerodynamic shapes of the body, and so on. Over time, decomposition heuristics and routines are likely to evolve differently in different firms as they learn to reduce the dimensions of search space through experience. As a result, not all decomposition strategies are necessarily successful (or equally successful), and no selection mechanism or process of choice (e.g. incentives) necessarily exists to ensure an optimum solution to product, process, or organizational problems.

Consequently it is reasonable to assume that the problem-solving abilities of firms are nested within a "ubiquitous sub-optimality." Intra-firm learning patterns and inter-organizational selection processes need initially to be considered as evolutionary processes, even neglecting, in a first approximation, the diverse incentive-driven behaviors which different organizational forms elicit.[9]

These propositions are naturally consistent with an emerging evolutionary approach to "what business firms are and do" (e.g. Nelson and Winter, 1982; Winter, 1982, 1988; Dosi, 1988, Teece et al., 1994; Dosi and Marengo 1994; Marengo, 1996) and are largely overlapping and complementary with the view expressed by Simon (1991), March and Simon (1958) and Radner (1992) among others.

In this approach, the product in question clearly matters (e.g. steel, computers, or polypropylene) as does the great diversity in processes and organizational arrangements deployed to make a particular product. No single individual knows the entire production plan and, within both the management of business-as-usual and in the search for new product designs and efficient processes, organisations display an ensemble of routine procedures, through which organizations often manage to coordinate their tasks well enough to deliver a coherent set of processes and products. In contrast to the "optimal machine" analogy, the firm can be viewed as an intelligent but fallible "organism" trying to adapt imperfectly and path-dependently to a changing environment shaped also by other organisms (including competitors, suppliers, and buyers).

In the evolutionary view, the basic units of analysis for PSBs are, on the one hand, elementary physical acts (such as moving a drawing from one office to another) and elementary cognitive acts (such as a simple calculation) on the other. Problem-solving can then be defined as a combination of elementary acts within a procedure, leading eventually to a feasible outcome (e.g. an aircraft engine or a chemical compound). Or, seen the other way round, given the possibly infinite set of procedures leading to a given outcome or product, it is possible to decompose these procedures into diverse series of elementary cognitive and physical acts of varying lengths which may be executed according to various possible execution architectures (e.g. sequential, parallel, or hierarchical).

PBSs straightforwardly link with the notion of organizational competencies and capabilities. First, a firm displays the operational competencies associated with its actual problem-solving procedures (in line with the routines discussed by Nelson and Winter, 1982 and Cohen et al., 1996). Second, the formal and informal organizational structure of the firm determines the way in which cognitive and physical acts are distributed and the decomposition rules which govern what is and what is not admissible within a particular firm (providing a route into the analysis of incentive structures and processes). Third, the organization shapes the search heuristics for, as yet, unresolved problems, thereby governing creative processes within the firm.

This theoretical approach to PSB within the firm also corresponds closely to empirical accounts of firm behaviour from the economics of innovation (Freeman, 1982; Dosi, 1988; Pavitt, 1999). Moreover, it has the benefit of being applicable both to the analysis of intra-firm structures and to the analysis of the boundaries between firms and the market. Indeed, such boundaries can be seen as particular patterns of decomposition of an overall problem-solving task. In other words, the boundary of the firm is shaped, in part, by the problem to be solved, often corresponding to the product to be created (e.g. a car or a piece of steel). Particular decomposition strategies will range from the totally centralized and autarkic types (with no decomposition at all) to the equivalent of a pure market, where one person acts on each task with market-like transactions linking each elementary act.

From an empirical perspective, it then becomes important to ask whether and under which circumstances "markets" (i.e. complete decentralized distributions of knowledge) have problem-solving advantages over more centralized, "hierarchical" forms of decomposition. The next section presents some simple conceptual building blocks for analyzing this type of question.

## Products, Tasks, and Organizations as Problems of Design

It is helpful to think of complex problem-solving activities as problems of design: the design of elaborate artefacts and the design of the processes and organizational structures required to produce them. In turn, these processes require the design of complex sequences of moves, rules, behaviors and search heuristics involving one or many different actors to solve problems, create new "representations" of problems themselves and ultimately to achieve the techno-economic goals at hand. Common to all these design activities is that they involve search in large combinatorial spaces of "components" (as defined above in terms of elementary physical and cognitive acts) which have to be closely coordinated. To complicate matters still further, the functional relations among these elements are only partly understood and can only be locally explored through a process of trial-and-error learning, often involving also the application of expert, partly tacit knowledge.

For example, the design of a complex artefact such as an aircraft or a flight simulator requires the co-ordination of many different design elements, including engine type and power, wing size, and shape and other materials. The interaction between each of the sub-systems and components is only partly understood and each comprises many smaller components and sub-systems (Miller et al., 1995; Prencipe, 1997). The interactions between the elements of the system can only be partly expressed by general models and have to be tested through simulation, prototype building, and trial-and-error moves where learning and tacit knowledge play an important part. Producing an effective solution, such as a new aircraft, involves a long sequence of moves, each of which is chosen out of an enormous set of possibilities. In turn, the relations among the moves in the sequence can only be partly known as a full understanding would (impossibly) require the knowledge of the entire set of possibilities. The likelihood of combinatorial explosion within the search space presents a computationally intractable task for boundedly rational agents. As Metcalfe and de Liso (1995) argue, the beliefs and routines of the firm act as a focusing device, indicating where to search in order to produce functioning artefacts: "Paradoxical though it may seem, to make progress it is necessary to limit progress" (p. 21). In that, also the "culture" of the firm acts as an interpretative system grounded in the community of practice of the firm, which allows progress and learning under conditions of extreme uncertainty and vast opportunities for design choice.

Business firms as well as collaborative ventures among them can therefore be seen as complex, multi-dimensional bundles of routines, decision rules, procedures and incentive schemes, whose interplay is often largely unknown both to the managers of the organization and also to managers, designers, and engineers responsible for single projects. Of course, over time many repeated technical and business activities become routinized and codified, allowing for stable, formal structures and established codified routines as, for example, in the volume production activities of automobiles or commodity chemicals. In these circumstances, some sort of "steady state" problem decomposition becomes institutionalized, also allowing the establishment of neat organizational structures, and, together, the exploitation of economies of scale and scope. The "Fordist" and "Chandlerian" archetypes of organization are the classic examples. This is also the organizational arrangement which most forcefully highlights potential advantages (and also the in-built rigidities) of division of labor and specialization. However, even in this stable case there remain many non-routine, complex activities within the firm, including new product design, research and development, new marketing programmes, and so on. In these areas the foregoing properties of search for new PSBs continue to apply and organizational forms take a variety of shapes in relation to these tasks. In addition, under conditions of rapid market and technological change even stable ("Fordist") organizations are often forced to re-assess and re-constitute their structures in order to respond to new market demands and to exploit new technical opportunities (see, for example, the related discussions by Coriat and by Fujimoto in Dosi et al., (2000), on Japanese – "Toyotist" – organizational arrangements and routines).

During the multi-stage product design task, the basic elements to be co-ordinated are characterised by strong interdependencies which create many local optima within the search space. For instance, adding a more powerful engine could lead to a reduction in the performance of an aircraft or prevent it from flying altogether if the other sub-systems and components are not simultaneously adapted. Similarly, at the organizational level, the introduction of new routines, practices, or incentive schemes which have proven superiority in another context, could also prove counter-productive if other elements of the organization are not appropriately adapted to suit the new inputs (Dosi et al., 2000).

A helpful "reduced form" metaphor of the complex task problem is presented in Kauffman's (1993) model of selection dynamics in the biological domain with heterogeneous interdependent traits. Kauffman considers a model of the selection mechanisms whereby the units of selection are complex entities made of several non-linearly interacting components. Units of selection are combinations of N elementary components (genes or morphological or behavioral traits) which can assume one of an finite number of states and a fitness value is exogeneously assigned to each "gene" producing a fitness landscape on the space of combinations, reflecting the interdependencies among the constituent elements. His model shows that as the number of interdependent elements increases the fitness landscape presents an exponentially increasing number of local optima. In the presence of strong interdependencies (as occurs in many complex products, see part III) the system cannot be optimized by separately optimizing each element it is made of. Indeed, in the case of strong interdependencies it might well be the case that some, or even all, solutions obtained by tuning "in the right direction" each component yield a worse performance than the current one.

In the presence of strong interdependencies the problem cannot therefore be decomposed into separate sub-problems which could be optimized separately from the others (Marengo, 1999). However, as argued by Simon (1981) problem-solving by boundedly rational agents must necessarily proceed by decomposing a large, complex and intractable problem into smaller sub-problems which can be solved independently. Within the firm this is equivalent to a division of problem-solving labor. However, the extent of the division of problem-solving labor is limited by the existence of interdependencies. If, in the process of sub-problem decomposition, interdependent elements are separated, then solving each sub-problem interdependently does not allow overall optimization. As Simon (1981) also points out, since a perfect decomposition, which isolates in separate sub-problems all and only the elements which are interdependent to each other, can only be designed by someone who has perfect knowledge of the problem, boundedly rational agents will normally try to design "near-decompositions". The latter are decompositions which try to isolate the most performance relevant interdependencies into separate sub-problems.

Unlike the biological analogy above, the design space of a problem faced by an engineer or a firm is not given exogenously but, rather, is constructed by them as a subjective representation of the problem itself where, in practice, much of the search takes place. If the division of problem-solving labor is limited by interdependencies, the structure of the latter, in turn, depends on how the problem is framed by the problem-solvers. Sometimes with major innovations, problem-solvers are able to make important leaps forward by re-framing the problem itself in a novel way. For example, in the accounts of wireless communications development provided by Levinthal (1998) and the Polaris missile system by Sapolsky (1972) various known system elements were combined and re-combined in creative new ways.

In short, the representation of the problem itself plays a crucial part in determining its complexity. By acting on its representation, decision-makers can make a problem more or less decomposable. The division of problem-solving labor is therefore very much a question of how the problem is represented and its elements encoded.

Given the limits that interdependencies pose to the division of problem-solving labor, an important part of the representation is how agents evaluate the "goodness" of solutions. As already mentioned, the problem of interdependencies amount to a problem of misalignment of local vs. global performance signals: local moves in the "right direction" may well decrease overall performance if particular elements are not properly adjusted to the moves. Thus there is room for the design of many alternative methods of performance assessment. In the formal model presented elsewhere (Marengo et al., 1999), for every problem of a given class there can be different performance assessment schemes, providing a set of payoffs to variations of components of the solution which allow for maximum decomposition. This form of performance assessment makes local adaptation and decentralized trial-and-error search effective as strategies.

During the design of PSBs and in the long-term building of the distinctive competence of firms, the architecture of the firm co-evolves with its decomposition schemes. Indeed, any organizational hierarchy may be seen, from a problem-solving perspective, as entailing particular decompositions into blocks of elements (sub-problems and organizationally admissible behaviors and tasks assigned to them) which, together make the overall configuration of the PSBs and organizational governance of the firm. In complex tasks, firms continue to go through step-by-step experiments with groups of elements in order to improve the performance of the overall system. In some cases, activities are more or less decomposable (e.g. finance and manufacturing, or a mechanical and electrical system). Here the firm is able to rapidly find an appropriate "robust" decomposition.

However, in many cases (e.g. product design and systems integration) notwithstanding the ubiquitous search for "modularity," tasks are highly interdependent, leading to indeterminacy in PSBs and governance arrangements and many different solutions to chose from. When building a decomposition scheme, firms might ideally search for perfect decomposability, so that all groups of elements can be optimized in a totally independent way from the others. However, near-decomposability is more common as many problems cannot be divided into neatly isolated groups of components which can all be solved independently.

Problem-solving design does not only involve search within a given space but also, and very importantly, a re-framing of the problem itself by the agents within the firm. Changing the frame or representation of the particular problem is a powerful form of PSB. Indeed, as argued in Marengo (1996), the establishment of collectively shared representations and problem-solving frames is one of the fundamental roles of top management. Equally important, when the organizational architecture allows it, groups within the firm, by experimentation, are able to collectively evolve new representations, possibly yielding more effective decompositions. In the formal model presented by Marengo et al. (1999) the construction of shared representations allows for the simplification of complex problems, offering a more powerful strategy than attempting to optimize any particular given representation. Experience and learning provide the agents with knowledge of probable viable decompositions as well as probably "well-behaved representations."

In the real world of decision-making, agents rarely hold a full representation of the overall problem and can only control a limited number of elements involved. Firms have to proceed by roughly defining an architecture for various blocks of elements to be integrated (e.g. electronic hardware and software systems), assigning the blocks to individuals and groups, co-ordinated by a project manager or equivalent. This way they try to achieve decomposability and, where not possible, effective communications and interactions between agents across the various blocks of sub-tasks. Note that top-down assignments of sub-problems and formal tasks rarely match perfectly the actual decompositions achieved via "horizontal" self-organizing adjustments (for a fascinating longitudinal story of these dynamics throughout the establishment of a major telecom company see Narduzzo, et al. 2000). Indeed, the mismatches between "formal" representations and decompositions and actual (emergent) ones, are at the same time a major drawback on organizational performances but also a potential source of organizational learning. These processes are endemic to most activities involved in the production of CoPS, as discussed in the following sections.

## PSBs in Complex Products and Systems

Complex product systems (CoPS) are high value artefacts, systems, sub-systems, software packages, control units, networks and high technology constructs.[10] As high technology customized capital goods, they tend to be made in one-off projects or small batches. The emphasis of production is on design, project management, systems engineering and systems integration. Examples include telecommunications exchanges, flight simulators, aircraft engines, avionics systems, train engines, air traffic control units, systems for electricity grids, offshore oil equipment, baggage handling systems, R&D equipment, bio-informatics systems, intelligent buildings and cellular phone network equipment.

There are many different categories of CoPS, ranging from relatively traditional goods (e.g. train engines) to new IT networks (e.g. internet super-servers) to established goods which have been radically transformed by IT (e.g. integrated mail processing systems and printing press machinery). They can be categorized according to sector (e.g. aerospace, military and transportation), function (e.g. control systems, communications and R&D), and degree of complexity (e.g. as measured by the number of tailored components and sub-systems, design options and amount of new knowledge required).

The physical composition and production processes of most CoPS have changed due to the diffusion of IT and embedded software. As software becomes a core technology, many CoPS are becoming more complex and difficult to produce, partly as a result of the human, craft design element involved in software development.[11] Technical progress, combined with new industrial demands have greatly enhanced the functional scope, performance and complexity of CoPS throughout, from jet engines to nuclear power simulation systems.

CoPS have at least three defining characteristics which distinguish them from mass produced goods. First, as high cost, capital goods they consist of many interconnected, often customized elements (including control units, sub-systems and components), usually organized in a hierarchical manner and tailored for specific customers and/or markets. Often their sub-systems (e.g. the avionics systems for aircraft) are themselves complex, customized and high cost. Second, they tend to exhibit emergent properties during production, as unpredictable and unexpected events occur during design and systems engineering and integration (Boardman, 1990; Shenhar, 1994). Emerging properties also occur from generation to generation, as small changes in one part of a system's design often call for large alterations in other parts, requiring the addition of more sophisticated control systems and, sometimes, new materials (e.g. in jet engines). Third, because they are high value capital goods, CoPS tend to be produced in projects or in small batches which allow for a high degree of direct user involvement, enabling business users to engage directly into the innovation process, rather than through arm's length market transactions, as normally the case in commodity goods.

There are many different dimensions of product complexity, each of which can confer task complexity and non-routine behavior to production and innovation tasks. These dimensions include the numbers of components, the degree of customization of both system and components, multiple design choices, elaborate systems architectures, breadth and depth of knowledge and skill required, and the variety of materials and information inputs. Users frequently change their requirements during production, leading to unclear goals, uncertainty in production and unpredictable, unquantifiable risks. Managers and engineers often have to proceed from one production stage to the next with incomplete information, relying on inputs from other suppliers who may be competitors in other multi-firm projects. Project management often involves negotiating between the competing interests, goals and cultures of the various organizations involved in production.

Many CoPS are produced within projects which incorporate prime contractors, systems integrators, users, buyers, other suppliers, small and medium sized enterprises and sometimes government agencies and regulators. Often, these agents collaborate together, taking innovation (e.g. new design) decisions in advance of and during production, as in the case of flight simulators (Miller et al., 1995). Projects consist of temporary multi-firm alliances where systems integration and project management competencies are critical to production. The project represents a sort of focusing device which enables the problems of design and production to be addressed. It is also responsible for realizing the market, coordinating decisions across firms, enabling buyer involvement, and matching technical and financial resources through time. Because production is oriented to meet the needs of large business users, the project management task is fundamentally different from the mass production task. As Joan Woodward (1958:23) already put it in her research into UK project-based companies in the 1950s:

> Those responsible for marketing had to sell, not a product, but the idea that their firm was able to produce what the customer required. The product was developed after the order had been secured, the design being, in many cases, modified to suit the requirements of the customer. In mass production firms, the sequence is quite different: product development came first, then production, and finally marketing.

## Designing Organizational Forms for CoPS

Although vast and diverse bodies of literature exist on organizational forms, there are not many studies which examine in any depth the project-based organization or forms suited to CoPS.[12] Certainly, the relation between organizational form and the problem solving nature of the firm is at the heart of "competence-based" and, largely overlapping, evolutionary perspectives (e.g. Dosi et al., 2000; Dosi and Marengo, 1994; Kogut and Zander, 1992, 1996; Nelson and Winter, 1982; Nelson, 1991; Teece, Pisano and Schuen, 1994; Teece et al, 1994; Conner and Prahalad, 1996; Leonard-Barton, 1995; Winter, 1988). The competence view in fact focuses on organizations as repositories of problem-solving knowledge and analyzes some salient properties of knowledge accumulation and the ways the latter co-evolve with organizational structures and practices (including, of course, routines but also managerial heuristics and strategies).

Organizational specificities and persistently different revealed performances, are thus interpreted also on the grounds of path-dependence in knowledge accumulation and inertial persistence of organizational traits. Bounded rationality, in its broadest meaning, is the norm. Its general sources include the "complexity" and procedural uncertainty associated with problem-solving procedures and the intrinsic "opaqueness" of the relationship between actions and environmental feed-backs, so that it is seldom obvious, even ex post, to state how well one did and why (March, 1994).

Taking all that as a (quite sound, in our view) point of departure, one must acknowledge, however, that one is still far from having comprehensive taxonomies mapping discrete *organizational types* into diverse forms of knowledge distributions and problem-solving behaviours, even if one finds suggestive exercises in this direction. So, for example, Mintzberg (1979), partly building on the work of Burns and Stalker (1961) attempts to derive a classification contingent on the nature of markets, tasks and technologies. (A somewhat extreme notion of "contingency" of organizational forms upon environmental characteristics is, of course, in Lawrence and Lorsch, 1971.

Mintzberg describes five basic organizational forms: (1) the "machine bureaucracy" with highly centralized control systems, suited to a stable environment; (2) the divisional form suited to mass production efficiency; (3) the professional bureaucracy made up of flat organizational structures, useful for delegating complex, professional tasks (e.g. in universities); (4) the simple or entrepreneurial structure, valuable for its informality and flexibility; and (5) the "adhocracy," which is a temporary project-based design, suited to complex tasks and turbulent and uncertain markets. Somewhat similarly largely building upon a competence-based view of organisations, Teece (1996) proposes six categories of firm: (1) stand-alone entrepreneur inventor; (2) multiproduct integrated hierarchy; (3) high flex, Silicon Valley type; (4) "virtual" corporation; (5) conglomerate; and (6) alliance enterprise.[13] Other observers of organization form (e.g. Galbraith 1971, 1973; Larson and Gobeli, 1987, 1989) describe a range of alternatives from pure functional form through to pure "product form," where management structures are centered upon each product.

A general conjecture lurking through many such taxonomic efforts is the positive relation between some form of organizational flexibility, on the one hand, and complexity and variability of tasks, on the other. In that vein, Burns and Stalker (1961) make the famous distinction between "organic" and "mechanistic" organizational types. They argue that the latter is more suited to stable environments and routine PSB, taking advantage of, for example, clearly defined job description, stable operational boundaries and tayloristic work methods. Conversely, they suggest, under rapidly changing technological and market conditions, open and flexibile ("organic") styles of organization make for easier coordination between different organizational functions – such as R&D and marketing, etc.

The spirit of most of the foregoing studies tend to be either *prescriptive* (that is, focused on how to design suitable organizations) or *cross-sectionally* descriptive (comparing different sectors, technologies, etc.). That makes an interesting contrast with long-term historical studies, *in primis* the path-breaking investigations by Chandler (1962), highlighting a secular trend from the rather simple owner/manager firms of the eighteenth century, all the way to the twentieth-century divisionalized/matrix form. This is not to say that the two views are necessarily at odds with each other. For example, it could well be that profound inter-sectoral variations (nested into different problem-soling tasks, as mentioned) happened to go together with an overall average increase in organizational complexity.[14] We cannot tackle the issue here. Let us just mention that such "cross-sectional" and "historical" patterns are all nested into diverse forms of division of cognitive and manual labour which in turn is reflected in diverse PSB and learning patterns. In the perspective of the interpretation outlined above in this work, diverse organizational forms map into diverse

1   problem *representations,*
2   problem *decompositions,*
3   task *assignments,*
4   *heuristics for* and *boundaries to exploration and learning.*
5   *mechanisms for conflict resolution over interests,* and, equally important, over *alternative cognitive frames* and *problem interpretations.*

With respect to these dimensions, to repeat a telegraphic caricature we are rather fond of, one might think, at one extreme, of an archetype involving complete, hierarchical, ex ante representations, precise task assignments according to well defined functions/tasks, quite tight boundaries to exploration – "learning" being itself a specialized function – and, if all that works, no need for ex post conflict resolution.

The opposite extreme archetype might be somewhat akin to university departments, with a number of representations at least as high as the number of department members, fuzzy decompositions, little task assignments, and loose boundaries to exploration, fuzzy conflict resolution rules, and so on. clearly, Taylorist/Fordist organizational forms tend to be nearer the former archetype, which, to repeat, are not appropriate for CoPS, for all the reasons mentioned above. However, they do display a quite large variety of arrangements, and with that equally diverse PSB.

Figure 11.1 provides a description of six ideal-type organizational forms ranging from the pure functional form (type A) to pure product/project form (type F).[15] The various functional departments of the organization (e.g. marketing, finance, human resources, engineering, R&D, and manufacturing) are represented by F1 to F5, while notional CoPS projects are represented by P1 to P5. Type B is a functionally oriented matrix, with weak project coordination. Type C is a balanced matrix with stronger project management authority. Type D is a project matrix, where project managers are of equal status to functional managers. Type E, is a "project-led organization," in which the needs of projects outweigh the functional influence on decision-making and representation to senior management, but weak coordination across project lines occurs. Finally, type F is the pure project-based form where there is no formal functional coordination across project lines and the entire organization is dedicated to one or more CoPS projects.

The positioning diagram helps to contrast many of the various forms of organization available for dealing with complex tasks, accepting that a mixed organizational structure is possible even within a single business unit. Forms A to C tend to be unsuitable for CoPS, because they are inappropriate for performing non-routine, complex project tasks in an uncertain and changing environment. CoPS projects typically require "super-heavyweight" professional project managers (or directors), capable of integrating both commercial and technical business functions within the project and building strong lines of external communication both with the client (often the source of the innovation idea) and other collaborating companies. The collaborators may well have different goals, structures and cultures and the task of the project director is to skilfully negotiate a path towards successful completion.

The pure project form (F) appears to be well suited for large innovative projects and single project firms, where resources have to be combined and shared with other firms in the project (i.e. a large multi-firm project such as the English–French Channel Tunnel). The project form is suitable for responding to uncertainty and changing client requirements, coping with emerging properties and learning in real time. By contrast, the project form is weak where the functional and matrix structures are strong: in coordinating resources and capabilities across projects, in executing routine production and engineering tasks and achieving economies of scale for mass markets.

To illustrate the problem-solving advantages of the project-based form for CoPS,

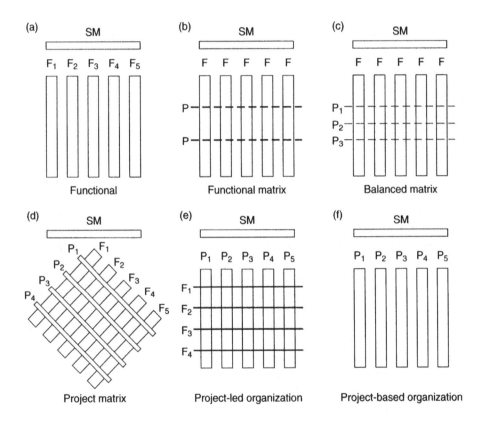

**Key**

* $F_1$-$F_5$ = various functional departmentss of the organization (e.g. marketing, finance, human resources, engineering, manufacturing, R&D)

* $P_1$-$P_5$ = major projects within the organization (e.g. CoPS projects)

* SM = senior management

**Figure 11.1:** Positioning the project-based organization

figure 11.2 contrasts the project management task within a functional matrix (type B) with that of a pure project form (type F). Figure 11.2(a) shows the position of the "weak" project manager within the functional matrix, involving multiple lines of communication, control and command, and the sub ordination to various department managers. Here project coordination embodies a linear or sequential model of project management, in which the project passes through various stages and departments in turn. Client and suppliers are external to the project and the project manager has to perform a highly complex internal task of balancing various internal interests and meeting different demands (e.g. in terms of reporting and quality control) of the departments. There are many lines of communication with project team members (TM 1 to TM 6) who also report to functional or departmental managers (FM 1 to FM 6) to whom they owe their career allegiance.

Throughout the problem-solving process, project managers in the functional and matrix forms also face many difficulties in external co-ordination. To reply to customer requests they often have to gain information and commitments from engineering, purchasing, and planning departments. The larger and more complex the project, the more difficult the task of keeping the client informed and responding to requests for changes.

By contrast, figure 11.2(b) shows the position of the project managers in a project-based organization in relation to the specialist functions within the project. The project manger is the main channel of communication and can exercise control to coordinate and integrate specialist functions, focusing on the needs of each project. Because there are few internal lines of command and communication to interfere with project objectives, the internal coordination task becomes simpler and the ability to react to emerging properties is enhanced.

Similarly on the external front, clear strong lines of command and communications can be built up with the client (figure 11.2(c)). In principle, the project manager is able to quickly assess and react to changes in client needs and learn from feedback from the client and major component suppliers (S 1 to S 5). The project manager has both the responsibility and power to react to unexpected events, negotiate changes with the client and, if necessary, put suppliers of sub-systems together with the customer to resolve difficult problems.

The project-based organization embodies a concurrent model of project management in which tasks are integrated as required by the project. In principle, the project-based form boasts several advantages over the functional and matrix forms for CoPS. Producing a CoPS is often a creative task, requiring innovation at both the product and organizational levels. Production typically involves many knowledge-intensive, non-routine tasks and decision-taking under conditions of uncertainty. These uncertain processes cannot easily be codified within routine procedures as learning during production is required to complete the task. Because the project-based form is able to create and re-create organizational structures and processes around the needs of each product (and customer) it contrasts sharply with the anti-innovation bias which are likely to be displayed by large functional organizations with their semi-permanent departments and rigid processes. The challenge of managing CoPS is one of ensuring responsiveness to the changing needs of customers, and dealing with the emerging properties which arise in production. It is

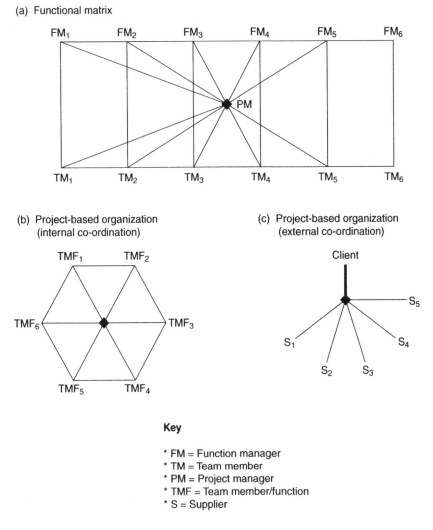

(a) Functional matrix

(b) Project-based organization
    (internal co-ordination)

(c) Project-based organization
    (external co-ordination)

**Key**

* FM = Function manager
* TM = Team member
* PM = Project manager
* TMF = Team member/function
* S = Supplier

**Figure 11.2:** Comparing the project-management function in functional and project-based organizations

also a challenge of anticipating future client needs and convincing buyers of the firm's competence to deliver new systems in the future. On the other hand, the looser the structure is, the more difficult it is also to codify past learning achievements into some organizational memory; the informal mobility of employees is usually the chief method of building organizational capabilities and performances. There are indeed subtle trade-offs in all the foregoing organizational arrangements – and unexploited learning opportunities – of which most often the actors involved are only partly aware. Symmetrically, "diagnostic" techniques and heuristics for organizational design might be surprisingly effective in the improvement of decision-making processes and PSB.

## Heuristics for Organizational Design and Collective Action in Complex Task Environments

In this respect, let us briefly report on how the foregoing framework on problem-solving can be combined with work from the organization development field to produce a method to assist in the real world of problem-solving, at least in the case of the design and the production of complex products and systems. We have been discussing above, from a theoretical point of view, the crucial step of *decomposition* of complex problems into nearly independent sub-problems and the difficulties thereupon. Indeed, a first operational task in a practical, diagnostic, exercise is to help identify alternative representations and, relatedly, decompositions of the problem at hand. Second, the exercise ought to be aimed to elicit the differences between formal vs. informal processes (and structures) for each project. Third, and relatedly, it provides mechanisms for a sort of *endogenous benchmarking*. This technique avoids the need for conventional benchmarking which, in any case, cannot be applied to one-off, non-routine tasks, but rather tries to elicit the very representation of such a benchmark and feeds back this data to the "actors" in a structured manner in order to help them design and develop the complex product and ensure an appropriate organizational structure. The outcome tends to be a re-combination of tasks and structures in the companies in which the intervention was made and, in general, a reduction of the difficulties inherent in complex one-off tasks, through a narrowing of the gap between formal and actual practices and processes.

To operationalize the theory, an experimental attempt was made to develop and apply an action research technique to collective decision-making in six large multi-project CoPS suppliers in Europe.[16] The approach is partly based on intervention techniques developed within the field of organization development (a sub-field of organizational behavior), which spans both management strategy and implementation (Schein, 1990; Mullins, 1994; Handy, 1993; French and Bell, 1973; Tyson and Jackson, 1992), and tends to treat strategy, management, learning and innovation as iterative processes rooted in working practices, which are "crafted", informal and sensitive to organizational forms (Mintzberg, 1989; Seeley Brown and Duguid, 1996). Using research data, selective outside interventions can sometimes be helpful in surfacing issues, identifying problems, and stimulating new working practices (French and Bell, 1973).

The method was initially developed for the analysis and improvement of PSBs in complex software projects in collaboration with process analysts in a large French corporation. The purpose of the method (or "tool") is to assist collective decision-making in order to arrive at effective PSBs and appropriate organizational forms for projects and specific tasks within projects (e.g. design, bidding, and sub-contractor management), in the common situation where each product and project is different and processes are, to a large extent, uncodifiable.[17] The method involves generating benchmark data on behaviors, routines, and structures and feeding this back to company teams in real time in order to assist problem-solving under conditions of bounded rationality and task complexity, by promoting more effective collective action by "shining a mirror" on the organization.

A distinctive feature of the method is that it focuses on the tacit, informal side of the PSB and informal organizations, comparing these systematically with formal processes and organizational structures. In other words it compares "what should be and what should happen" with real, actual practices ("what actually happens"), in order to identify variance (for explanation and discussion) problems, their causes and strategies for improvement. The tool complements other formal procedures which exist in most large firms by delivering a "bottom up" practitioner view of real processes in action.

The method is applied by decomposing the CoPS project roughly into tasks, which include not only the main technical activities, but other functions such as finance, manufacturing, and scheduling. To carry out a minimalist intervention in a large firm, typically two projects are identified, to allow for comparability and contrast. Within (and above) the projects, twelve or so individuals at three or four levels of seniority are selected across the project tasks. The researchers then carry out the intervention with the members of the "slice group" for each project, according to five standard steps, each with more detailed sub-processes and outputs (Hobday and Brady, 1998).

Step 1 involves agreeing with management and practitioners the scope, aims, outputs and timing of the exercise, and identifying the slice group of interviewees (this focuses especially on practitioners who understand best the informal project processes). In step 2 data is collected on formal codified practices as usually contained in toolkits, manuals, flow charts, formal procedures (and a few interviews with senior managers), on how the process "should" proceed. If the firm does not have formal codified procedures for the project, then senior management views or any "best practice" model of project management can be used.[18] Using a standard questionnaire, qualitative data is gathered from practitioners on how processes actually proceed in the two projects and in the wider organization (inputs, activities, and outputs are described and informal flow charts are drawn). Step 3 involves comparing the formal ("should be") practices with informal, uncodified activities to generate key differences (e.g. by comparing formal and informal flow charts). This represents a rapid form of real-time benchmarking (comparing actual with codified practices) for complex tasks.[19]

Variances tend to fall into two categories: major problem areas and best practices (or solutions to problems). Often solutions consist of engineers resolving problems caused by the formal processes! In step 4 the findings are presented back to practitioners for verification, which involves feedback on the accuracy of the data collected, omissions, the extent and depth of problems identified and the nature of the solutions. At this stage, quantitative data can be gathered if needed (using Likert scales, for example, on the extent of particular problems in the organization). Step 4 also includes an analysis of the causes of problems, a discussion of possible solutions and proposals for implementation, as applied both to project processes (including PSBs) and organizational structures. Step 5 involves reporting back to senior management (who have agreed to act on the findings) and the agreement of a plan for improvement. The actual format depends on the culture of the company. In some, the practitioners are happy to have senior managers involved closely in all steps. In others practitioners are inhibited in the presence of functional and project managers. The five basic steps of the process analysis and improvement method are as follows:

1   *Set up programme*; identify structured group for interviews and workshops;
2   *Data collection*: codified processes (management) *vs* actual informal processes (practitioners);
3   *Benchmark analysis*: identify key variances (a) problem areas (b) best practices – prepare workshop 1;
4   *Workshop 1*: (a) verification, (b) establish causes of problems, (c) identify solutions, (d) proposals on implementation;
5   *Workshop 2*: report back to senior management – agree actions/support for implementation.

Although the method was initially developed for complex software projects, it has subsequently been modified and applied to other domains and other non-routine, complex processes. However, the approach remains the same – the application of an outside intervention to benchmark codified against actual processes in order to provide data to question, assess and sometime re-compose organizational structures and processes. The following six examples give some idea of the scope of the intervention technique.

Company A is a producer of complex embedded software for flight simulators. Here, the purpose was to improve software processes within a new change programme. The group discussions led to the questioning of (redundant) software tools and a reconfiguration of parts of the software process, contributing to an upgrading of the latter according to the official international quality standard "CMM." The intervention enabled software practitioners to shape work processes by contributing new more appropriate tools and training programmes aligned with real, rather than formal work processes, with the consequence of reducing also variances between initial software estimates and actual outcomes in terms of budget and costs. In the language introduced above, the objective was achieved by the identification of a closer alignment between formal problem decompositions/task assignments and actual, "informally learned," ones.

Company B is a supplier of components for naval equipment organized along lines established in the 1960s. The task was the improvement of product development processes for a new generation of nuclear submarine cores. The two main technical groups involved – design engineering and manufacturing engineering – organized separately along traditional lines, were brought together during the intervention, enabling them to analyze, question, and reconfigure the "normal" linear sequence of design and production. By introducing more concurrency into the design-build cycle, re-work was reduced as a result of closer engineering-manufacturing integration: more "fuzzy" decompositions, broader "spans of exploration" and faster information exchange cycles have been key organizational modifications.

Company C is a producer of synchrotron particle accelerators and large-scale magnetic equipment for scientific research. This intervention focused on the assessment of the relative merits of two different organizational structures (one project based and one functionally based) in the company. The data gathered from practitioners during the interviews showed that the functionally based structure was generally unsuitable for large one-off projects, although it operated well for batch production and standard product lines with little new technology. By contrast, the project-based structure revealed a close matching between formal and informal processes and an ability to cope with emerging properties in design and production, by virtue of project team coherence and strong leadership. The data were used to design and implement a new project-based structure for all major projects as an alternative to the functionally based system. Some functional coordination was also introduced to promote learning and technical leadership along the lines of the project-led organization (see figure 11.1).

Company D is a producer of base stations for mobile phone systems. The intervention focused on the installation and extension of new turnkey systems for a mobile telecommunications network. The work, which compared formal project management processes with what actually occurred during the first implementation phase, captured major problems in the formal project management procedures and revealed many differences between formal and actual practices – some of which hindered the project, others which helped. The data were used by the company to develop a "best practice" "Turnkey Project Start-up Guide" which formally embodied many of the informal practices and excluded unnecessary procedures. This was placed on the company intranet to be updated with new experiences as learning occurred in new projects.

Company E is a large telecommunications service provider introducing a new business line of "integrated system and service solutions," involving several areas of network technology new to the company. The intervention helped practitioners decide which new processes and routines would be needed in bidding for new business contracts and which were only appropriate for traditional business lines. Eventually, this led to the setting up of, first, a consultancy wing of the company and, then, a new projects division, largely independent of the main organization. This recomposition of the organization turned out to be a valuable way of capturing and accelerating learning and rapidly expanding the new business.

Company F is a supplier of high value equipment for monitoring and measuring large-scale (rolling mill) steel production. The intervention, which focused on both research and the development of prototypes for in-house use and for sale to external users, revealed that the main total quality program (TQP) in place was suited to routine manufacturing activities, but unsuitable for the needs of R&D. In this case, the intervention was a rare opportunity for R&D staff to review internal procedures and external relations with university and sub-contractor partners. Eventually, the TQP was modified to recognize the uncertainties involved in R&D and the emerging properties expected in prototype development. Some modifications were made to the formal systems to bring them closer in line with real practices especially where sub-contractors and universities needed to be more closely integrated into the project teams.

To sum up, the diagnostic and benchmarking technique helped to analyze and recombine processes and structures for one-off, non-routine activities. In terms of scope, as the above cases indicate, the method has been applied to various complex tasks, cutting across sectors, technologies and different stages of the project life cycle, contributing to project processes and wider organizational structures. The above examples cover R&D, prototype development, design, engineering, production, and installation of CoPS, as well as bid phase and new business development activities. In describing impacts and benefits, it is important to emphasize that the cases above represent experimental, small-scale interventions and that much depended on management follow-through and, in some cases, on the success of the wider change programmes in which the interventions were embedded. It is also difficult to disentangle the effects of the interventions from the impact of other changes taking place (for example, three companies underwent mergers and restructuring during our work). However, each of the firms claimed that the decomposition and questioning of processes and structures, based on the foregoing heuristics had a significant impact on organizational learning and performances.

## Conclusion

In this work, we have proposed and tried to make operational an evolutionary perspective for understanding firms as imperfect, collective problem-solving entities, suggesting an interpretative framework for the patterns by which firms deploy and match problem-solving activities with organizational structures. The chapter applied these concepts to a broad class of high value capital goods (or "complex product systems") which are inherently complex and non-routine in nature, conferring extreme task complexity throughout many stages of production and innovation.

The chapter focuses on the processes through which problem-solving and creative knowledge co-evolve with organizational form in complex, non-stable, non-routine and complex task environments. Following Simon (1981), problem-solving and organizational structure are viewed as a type of design activity, where elementary physical and cognitive acts (or "elements") are tested, combined, and recombined to arrive at solutions. Because of bounded rationality, firms de-compose problems into manageable, but interdependent, and most likely "sub-optimal" blocks of elements. Within the firm, this is equivalent to a division of problem-solving labour, where the extent of the division of problem-solving labour is limited by the existence of interdependencies. If, in the process of sub-problem decomposition, interdependent elements are separated, then solving each block interdependently does not allow overall optimization. Since perfect decompositions with perfectly independent sub-problems rarely exist, boundedly rational agents normally try to design "near-decompositions" which try to isolate the most performance relevant interdependencies into separate sub-problems. Problem-solving design does not only involve search within a given space but also, and very importantly, a re-framing of the problem itself by agents within the firm. By such re-framing the organization and groups within it arrive at more powerful representations, which often (but not always) allows also greater decentralization and decomposability.

While the approach was applied to non-routine complex tasks and environment, the "spirit" of the model also applies to routine, decomposable tasks. Here, however, the decomposition problem is, so to speak, resolved "once-and-for-all," as for example in the Fordist/Taylorist archetype where the organization is thoroughly designed and tasks are unequivocally assigned. Notice however that, even here, many activities remain by nature non-routine and complex, including strategy formulation, R&D, marketing, and new product design and the decomposition approach to PSB and organizational governance is likely to apply. Furthermore, even the Fordist archetype eventually confronts technological and market changes which force organizational and task re-composition.

The application of the approach to complex products and systems showed how the various dimensions of product complexity can confer extreme task complexity and difficult problems of organisational design. For CoPS, one highly innovative form is the project-based organization. While traditional functional and matrix structures embody a linear or sequential model of project management, the project form provides a concurrent model for integrating various complex technical and marketing functions under conditions of high uncertainty, emerging properties, and changing user requirements.

To operationalize these ideas, an experimental attempt was made to facilitate collective decision-making for the purposes of process and structure analysis and re-composition in six large multi-project firms supplying CoPS in Europe. The method used is partly based on intervention techniques from the field of organization development, which tends to treat problem-solving as iterative processes rooted in both formal and informal working practices and structures. The intervention method was designed to assist firms re-frame problems using research data which compares formal, codified processes with "real"/informal ones. The aim was to re-compose PSBs and structures to arrive at more appropriate organizational forms at the levels of projects and specific sub-tasks within projects (e.g. design, engineering, production, bidding, sub-contractor management, etc.), and wider organizational arrangements.

The apparent success of such heuristics – notwithstanding their simplicity and subject to the caveats mentioned above – is in our view an encouraging evidence of the rich *operational* implications of an evolutionary view of organizations centered on their changing problem-solving capabilities. Adding more explicitly incentive – and power – related dimensions will certainly refine the analysis. However, as we tried to show, disentangling the processes of knowledge generation within firms is an activity of paramount importance in its own right – at both levels of theory and managerial practices. And one is only at the beginning of such an enterprise.

## Acknowledgement

Paper prepared for Dynacom Project (European Union, TSER, DGXII) in collaboration with the UK Complex Product Systems Innovation Centre (ESRC funded). Comments by Connie Helfat and Keith Pavitt helped in improving various drafts of the work.

## Notes

1  The terms organizational form, structure, and governance arrangements are used interchangeably in this chapter.
2  The chapter builds on previous works by Marengo (1999) and Marengo, et al. (1999), which provide a formal mathematical treatment of the approach presented here.
3  Many CoPS confront extreme task complexity because they embody a wide variety of distinctive skills and types of knowledge, and involve large numbers of firms or organizational units in their production. In the past 20 years or so, CoPS have been transformed by software and information technology (IT), leading to new levels of risk and uncertainty in

design and production. See Hobday (1998) for definition and discussion of CoPS as an analytical category, and also Miller et al. (1995) for an application to the flight simulation industry.

4    For more details see Hobday and Brady (2000).

5    Curiously, in the field of software engineering a vaguely similar approach (actually called "rational") dominates and is defended as a practical way of producing complex software systems (Parnas and Clements, 1986). See Hobday and Brady (1998) for a critique.

6    Although, as presented here, this "rational" incentive-based view is a caricature, it does help convey the nature of the major difference between the latter view of economic behaviour in organizations and the problem-solving evolutionary perspective suggested in the following.

7    With roots in the earlier contributions of Penrose (1958), Chandler (1962) and Richardson (1972), a growing literature is exploring the nature of organizations in terms of "competencies" and "capabilities": see, among others, Teece, Pisano, and Schuen (1994), Teece et al. (1994), Barney (1991) and the contributions in Dosi et al. (2000).

8    Problem-solvers in firms most likely include engineers, designers, or project managers, but also, in different ways, most other employees. This applies in particular to CoPS projects, wherein each worker or "practitioner" (e.g. a software writer or draftsperson) is an "intelligent agent" responsible for managing his or her task and interfacing with other individuals and groups working on different aspects of the same product or problem (Hobday and Brady, 1998).

9    A comprehensive account of economic behavior of firms should, of course, account for incentives as well as the co-evolution of PSBs and governance arrangements, as argued by Coriat and Dosi (1998) and Dosi and Marengo (1994). However, a second point of departure is given by the understanding of the diverse PSBs of firms, and then proceeding to assess the ways in which incentive structures co-evolve with PSBs.

10   This section draws from Hobday (1998). The term CoPS is used, as "capital goods" fails to capture the diversity and range of systems involved. CoPS are, in fact, a subset of capital goods (and might eventually include sophisticated consumer goods). Somewhat similar issues, related to the variety and complexity of knowledge emerge in connection with products which are relatively simple as such but require complex search procedures to be discovered. Pharmaceutical are an archetypical example: cf. Orsenigo et al. (1999).

11   The effect of software can be interpreted as shifting the emphasis of production from a relatively predictable "engineering" task to a much more imprecise design-intensive "development" process, increasing the degree of uncertainty and learning involved in the production of each system.

12   Works germane to our analysis include Gann and Salter (1998) who provide a rare account of how project processes relate to wider organizational activities within a project-based organization, and Middleton (1967) on the establishment of projects within functionally based organizations. See also Miller et al. (1995). Research on new product development and project success factors also illustrates the importance of the project form (Clark and Wheelwright, 1992; Pinto and Prescott, 1988; Shenhar, 1993).

13   On this see also Miles and Snow (1986), whose formulation of network brokers and partners is similar to Teece's virtual firm and alliance enterprise respectively.

14   And some scholars further speculate that the future "archetypical" firm might be somewhat different from the classic "M-form": cf. among others, Miles et al. (1997) on the prediction of "cell-based" organizational structures.

15   This section draws heavily on Hobday (2000).

16   This work is carried out by one of us (M. H.) within the CoPS Innovation Centre at SPRU. Hobday and Brady, (1998, 2000) provide full details of the method, one in-depth case

study, and the results of the six applications mentioned briefly below.
17 In such cases, firms cannot apply normal benchmarking or improvement techniques (e.g. total quality management, continuous improvement, statistical process control or business process re-engineering) as these presume routine codifiable procedures, determinate tasks and established forms (usually departments), rather than temporary project forms.
18 Formal procedural models are presented in many project management and software engineering texts (including Boehm, 1988, 1989; Kellner, 1996), most of which are rationalist in that they do not recognize or deal with informal processes, structures or emerging properties.
19 The aim is not to gather comprehensive data, but sufficient information to run the verification and improvement workshops.

# References

Argyris, C. and Schön, D. A. (1996) *Organisational Learning*. Reading, MA: Addison-Wesley.
Barnard, C. I. (1938) *The Functions of the Executive*. Cambridge, MA: Harvard University Press.
Barney, J. (1991) Firm resources and sustained competitive advantage, *Journal of Management*, 17(1), 99–120.
Bennis, W. G. (1966) *Changing Organizations: Essays on the Development and Evolution of Human Organizations*. New York: McGraw-Hill.
Boardman, J. (1990) *Systems Engineering: An Introduction*. New York: Prentice Hall.
Boehm, B. W. (1988) A spiral model of software development and enhancement; *IEEE Computer*, May, 61–72.
Boehm, B. W. (1989) *Software Risk Management*. Washington, DC: IEEE Computer Society Press.
Burns, T. and Stalker, G. M. (1961) *The Management of Innovation*. London: Tavistock.
Chandler, A. D. Jr. (1962) *Strategy and Structure: Chapters in the History of Industrial Enterprise*. Cambridge, MA: MIT Press.
Clark, K. B. and Wheelwright, S. C. (1992) Organizing and leading "Heavyweight" Development Teams, *Californian Management Review*, 34(3), 9–28.
Cohen M. D., Burkhart, R., Dosi, G., Egidi, M., Marengo, L., Warglien M. and Winter S. (1996) Routines and other recurring action patterns of organizations: contempory research issues, *Industrial and Corporate Change*, 5, 653–98.
Conner, K. R. and Prahalad, C. K. (1996) A resource-based theory of the firm: knowledge vs. opportunism, *Organization Science*, 7, 477–501.
Coriat, B. and Dosi, G. (1998) Learning how to govern and learning how to solve problems. In A. D. Chandler, P. Hagstrom and O. Solvell (eds). *The Dynamic Firm: the Role of Technology, Strategy, Organization and Regions*. Oxford: Oxford University Press.
Davis, S. M. and Lawrence, P. R. (1977) *Matrix*. Reading, MA: Addison-Wesley.
Dosi, G. (1988) Sources, procedures and microeconomic effects of innovation, *Journal of Economic Literature*, 26, 1120–71.
Dosi, G. and Egidi, M. (1991) Substantive and procedural uncertainty: an exploration of economic behaviours in complex and changing environments, *Journal of Evolutionary Economics*, 1, 145–68.
Dosi, G. and Marengo, L. (1994) towards a theory of organisational competencies. In R. W. England (ed.), *Evolutionary Concepts in Contemporary Economics*. Ann Arbor, MI: Michigan University Press.
Dosi, G., Marengo, L. and Fagiolo, G. (1996) Learning in evolutionary environments, University of Trento, CEEL working paper.

Dosi, G., Nelson, R., and Winter, S. G. (eds) (2000) *The Nature and Dynamics of Organisational Capabilities*. Oxford: Oxford University Press.

Freeman, C. (1982) *The Economics of Industrial Innovation*. London: Frances Printer, 2nd edn.

French, W. L. and Bell, C. H. (1973) *Organization Development: Behavioural Science Interventions for Organization Improvement*. New York: Prentice Hall, 2nd edn

Galbraith, J. (1971) Matrix organizational designs: how to combine functional and project forms, *Business Horizons*, February, 29–40.

Galbraith, J. R. (1973) *Designing Complex Organizations*. Reading, MA: Addison-Wesley.

Gann, D. and Salter, A. (1998) Learning and innovation management in project-based, service-enhanced firms, *International Journal of Innovation Management*, 2(4), 431–54.

Grossman, S. and Hart, O. (1986) The costs and benefits of ownership: a theory of vertical and lateral integration, *Journal of Political Economy*, 94, 691–719.

Handy, C. (1993) *Understanding Organizations*. London: Penguin Books, 4th edn.

Hobday, M. (1998) product complexity, innovation and industrial organisation, *Research Policy*, 26, 689–710.

Hobday, M. (2000) The project based organizations: an idial form for managing complex problems and systems *Research Policy*, 29, 871–93.

Hobday, M. and Brady, T. (1998) Rational *vs* soft management in complex software: lessons from flight simulation, *International Journal of Innovation Management*, 2(1), 1–43.

Hobday, M. and Brady, T. (2000) A fast method for analysing and improving complex software processes, *R&D Management* 3, 1–21.

Kauffman, S. A. (1993) *The Origins of Order*. Oxford: Oxford University Press.

Kellner, M. I. (1996) *Business Process Modeling: Lessons and Tools from the Software World*. Software Engineering Institute, Carnegie Mellon University.

Kogut, B. and Zander, U. (1992) Knowledge of the firm, combinative capabilities and the replication of technology, *Organization Science*, 3, 383–96.

Kogut, B. and Zander, U. (1996) What do firms do? Coordination, identity and learning, *Organization Science*, 7, 502–17.

Laffont, J. J. and Tirole, J. (1986) the dynamics of incentive contracts: *Econometrica*, 94, 1153–75.

Larson, E. W. and Gobeli, D. H. (1987) Matrix management: contradictions and insights: *Californian Management Review*, 29(4), 126–38.

Larson E. W. and Gobeli, D. H. (1989) Significance of project management structure on development success, *IEEE Transactions on Engineering Management*, 36(2), 119–25.

Lawrence, P. and Lorsch, J. (1971) *Organization and Environment*. Cambridge, MA: Harvard University Press.

Leonard-Barton, D. (1995) *Wellsprings of Knowledge: Building and Sustaining the Sources of Innovation*, Boston, MA: Harvard Business School Press.

Levinthal, D. (1998) The slow pace of rapid technological change: gradualism and punctuation in technological change, *Industrial and Corporate Change*, 7, 217–47.

March, J. G. (1994) *A Primer on Decision Making: How Decisions Happen*, New York: Free Press.

March, J. G. and Simon, H. A. (1958) *Organizations*, New York: Wiley.

Marengo, L. (1996) Structure, competencies and learning in an adaptive model of the firm. In G. Dosi and F. Malerba (eds), *Organisation and Strategy in the Evolution of the Enterprise*. London: Macmillan.

Marengo, L. (1999) *Decentralisation and market mechanisms in collective problem-solving*. Mimeo, University of Teram.

Marengo, L., Dosi, G. Legrenzi, P. and Pasquali, G. (1999) The structure of problem-solving knowledge and the structure of organizations. Paper prepared for the conference "The

Roots and Branches of Organizational Economics," SCANCOR, Stanford University, September.

McKelvey, B. (1982) *Organisational Systematics*, Berkeley CA: University of California Press.

Metcalfe, J. S. and de Liso, N. (1995) Innovation, capabilities and knowledge: the epistemic connection. Mimeo, University of Manchester, England.

Middleton, C. J. (1967) How to set up a project organization, *Harvard Business Review*, March–April, 73–82.

Miles, R. E. and Snow, C. C. (1986) Organizations: new concepts for new forms, *Californian Management Review*, 28(3).

Miles, R. E., Snow, C. C., Mathews, J. A., Miles, G. and Coleman, H. J. (1997) Organizing in the knowledge age: anticipating the cellular form, *Academy of Management Executive*, 11, (4), 7–24.

Miller, R., Hobday, M., Leroux-Demers, and Olleros, X. (1995) innovation in complex systems industries: the case of flight simulation, *Industrial and Corporate Change*, 4(2), 363–400.

Mintzberg, H. (1979) *The Structuring of Organizations*. Englewood Cliffs New Jersey: Prentice Hall.

Mintzberg, H. (1989) *Mintzberg on Management: Inside Our Strange World of Organisation*, New York: The Free Press.

Morgan, G. (1986). *Images of Organization*. London: Sage.

Mullins, L. J. (1994) *Management and Organisational Behaviour*. London: Pitman Publishing, 3rd ed.

Narduzzo, A., Rocco, E., and Warglien, M. (2000) Talking about routines in the field: the emergence of organizational capabilities in a new cellular phone network company, in Dosi, G., Nelson, R. R. and Winter S. G. (2000).

Nelson, R. R. (1991) How do firms differ, and how does it matter? *Strategic Management Journal*, 12, 61–74.

Nelson, R. and Winter, S. (1982) *An Evolutionary Theory of Economic Change*. Cambridge, MA: Harvard University Press.

Orsenigo, L., Pammolli, F., and Riccaboni, M. (1999) Learning, market selection and the evolution of industrial structures. S. Anna School, Pisa, Italy, working paper.

Parnas, D. L. and Clements, P. C. (1986) A rational design process: how and why to fake it, *IEEE Transactions on Software Engineering*, Vol. SE-12, February, 251–7.

Pavitt, K. (1999) *Technology, Management and Systems of Innovation*. Cheltenham: Edward Elgar.

Penrose, E. T. (1958) *The Theory of the Growth of the Firm*. New York: Wiley.

Pinto. J. K. and Prescott, J. E. (1988) Variations in critical success factors over the stages in the project life cycle, *Journal of Management* 14(1), 5–18.

Prencipe, A. (1997) Technological competencies and product's evolutionary dynamics: a case study from the aero-engine industry, *Research Policy*, 25(8), 1261–76.

Radner, R. (1992) Hierarchy: the economics of managing, *Journal of Economic Literature*, 30, 1382–15.

Richardson, G. B. (1972) The organization of industry, *Economic Journal*, 82, 883–96.

Sapolsky, H. M. (1972) *The Polaris System Development: Bureaucratic and Programmatic Success in Government*. Cambridge, MA: Harvard University Press.

Sayles, L. R. (1976) Matrix management: the structure with a future, *Organization Dynamics*, autumn, 2–17.

Schein, E. H. (1990) Organizational culture, *American Psychologist*, 45(2), 109–19.

Seeley Brown, J. and Duguid, P. (1996) Organizational learning and communities of practice: towards a unified view of working, learning, and innovation. In M. D. Cohen and L. S. Sproull (eds), *Organizational Learning*, Thousand Oaks, CA: Sage Publications, Chapter 3.

Shenhar, A. J. (1993) From low- to high-tech project management, *R&D Management*, 23(3), 199–214.

Shenhar, A. (1994) Systems engineering management: A framework for the development of a multidisciplinary discipline, *IEEE Transactions on Systems, Man, and Cybernetics*, 24(2), 327–32.

Simon, H. A. (1981) *The Sciences of the Artificial*. Cambridge, MA: MIT Press.

Simon, H. A. (1991) Organizations and markets, *Journal of Economic Perspectives*, 5, 25–44.

Teece, D. J. (1996) Firm organization, industrial structure, and technological innovation, *Journal of Economic Behaviour & Organization*, 31, 193–224.

Teece, D. J., Pisano, G. and Shuen, A. (1994) Dynamic capabilities and strategic management. CCC Working Paper 94–9, Berkeley, University of California.

Teece, D. J., Rumelt, R. Dosi, G and Winter, S. G. (1994) Understanding corporate coherence: theory and evidence. *Journal of Economic Behaviour & Organization*, 23, 1–30.

Tirole, J. (1986) Hierarchies and bureaucracies: on the role of collusion in organizations, *Journal of Law, Economics and Organisations*, 2, 181–214.

Tyson, S. and Jackson, T. (1992) *The Essence of Organizational Behaviour*. New York: Prentice Hall.

Vincenti, W. G. (1990) *What Engineers Know and How They Know It. Analytical Studies from Aeronautical History*. Baltimore, MD: Johns Hopkins University Press.

Winter, S. G. (1982) An essay on the theory of production. In H. Hymans (ed.), *Economics and the World around It*, Ann Arbor: University of Michigan Press, 55–93.

Winter, S. G. (1988) On Coase, competence and the corporation, *Journal of Law, Economics and Organisation*, 4, 181–97.

Woodward, J. (1958) *Management and Technology*. London: Her Majesty's Stationery Office, London.

# CHAPTER TWELVE

# Product Sequencing: Co-evolution of Knowledge, Capabilities, and Products

## Constance E. Helfat and Ruth S. Raubitschek

### Introduction

Why are firms different? This is one of the fundamental questions in strategic management, because the sources of firm heterogeneity underlie competitive advantage (Rumelt, Schendel, and Teece, 1994). The resource-based view (Barney, 1991; Peteraf, 1993; Wernerfelt, 1984) and knowledge management approaches (Grant, 1996) suggest that capabilities and knowledge form the basis for differential firm performance. But how do successful firms get to the point where they have superior resources and knowledge, and how do firms maintain this superiority through time? Dynamic capabilities that enable firms to introduce new products and processes and adapt to changing market conditions play an important role (Teece, Pisano, and Shuen, 1997; Helfat, 1997). But exactly how do firms build and deploy capabilities? We provide a conceptual model that explains how organizations can successfully build and utilize knowledge and capabilities, over long time spans, in single and multiple product markets, for continuing competitive advantage. The model further highlights the importance of products, supported by vertical chains of complementary assets and activities, to the development and exploitation of capabilities and knowledge. That is, we bring the role of products back into the analysis of resources, capabilities, and knowledge. We also provide an explicitly dynamic framework that tracks stages of organizational evolution through time, across markets, and in the context of products and vertical chains. This in turn yields a model of the *coevolution* of knowledge, capabilities, and products.

At the heart of the model are sequences of products within and across vertical chains, supported by an underlying system of knowledge and systems of learning. At any given point in time, an organization's portfolio of products serves as a platform for future product sequences. These product platforms evolve over time in concert with knowledge and capabilities, and provide opportunities for competitive advantage through the strategic linkage of products up, down, and across vertical chains.[1]

The paper proceeds as follows. We first set up some basic building blocks for the model. Next we explain the components of the model: the *system of knowledge* that underpins vertical chains of activities, and supports *product sequencing* within and across vertical chains over time, based on *systems of learning*. Then we present three company case histories that illustrate the model. The paper concludes with an explanation of the contributions of the model to several related literatures, including the resource-based view, dynamic capabilities, and knowledge management.

## Basic Setting and Building Blocks

The model applies to technology-intensive companies, and to firms that require complex coordination of knowledge and activities more generally. Such firms include those in high-technology industries, as well as businesses that are not considered to be high-technology but require complex or technologically sophisticated knowledge in order to design and operate plant, equipment, and services. For example, an oil refinery consists of many complex, interrelated pieces of equipment requiring substantial technological know-how to design, build, and deploy. Our analysis also applies to companies that rely heavily on information technology, even if the companies themselves are not in high-technology industries (e.g., retailers such as Wal-Mart). Additionally, the analysis encompasses service businesses that make less use of information technology, but nevertheless require complex coordination of activities (e.g., financial services prior to the widespread use of computers). Thus, the model applies to a wide range of companies.

Within this setting, we focus on *organizational* knowledge and its relation to *organizational* capabilities, activities, and products. Tacit knowledge, for example, has the characteristic that it is not easily communicated in words, numbers, or pictures, but instead requires people, and often teams of people – that is, organizations – to effect knowledge transfer and utilization (Winter, 1987; Leonard and Sensiper, 1998). The creation of tacit organizational knowledge also generally requires repeated interactions between people over time. Because we are interested in organizational knowledge and capabilities, we do not analyze the sort of knowledge that can be easily transferred independent of people. Thus, we do not seek to explain phenomena such as the decoupling of semiconductor chip design and manufacturing fabs, enabled by the codifiability of chip designs.[2] We do, however, analyze more complex coordination of codified knowledge that requires organizational mechanisms.[3]

The product sequencing model utilizes two well-established concepts. The first is that of complementary assets and resources surrounding a core technology (Teece, 1986). The second closely related concept is that of a value chain (Porter, 1985). Teece (1986) points out that capturing value from what he terms "core technological know-how" frequently requires complementary assets that reside in different stages of a vertical chain, such as finance, manufacturing, and marketing. A separate literature on vertical chains is associated with Porter (1985) in particular, who focuses on the "value chain" within firms.[4] The stages of the value chain are "activities" such as manufacturing and marketing, and we adopt that terminology here.

The basic unit of analysis in our model is a vertical chain in combination with the product it supports.[5] To simplify the exposition, we use the term "product" to denote either a product or a service. We do not analyze the internal workings of individual stages in a vertical chain (e.g., research, manufacturing) or factors related to design of the product, nor do we deal with issues of organizational design. Additionally, we abstract from boundary of the firm issues. Our analysis requires only a long-term relationship between stages of vertical (or horizontal) chains, in order to build and utilize knowledge, regardless of whether this takes place in a single firm or in multiple firms (see, for example, Dyer and Singh, 1998). Figure 12.1 provides an overview of the model.

To begin the analysis, we describe the *system of knowledge* that underlies a set of activities and products in a vertical chain. Then we analyze *product sequencing* within and across vertical chains, as well as the required *systems of learning*.

## System of Knowledge

The system of knowledge[6] in our model is composed of *core knowledge* and *integrative knowledge*. A more detailed explanation of each follows.

### Core knowledge

In technology-intensive industries, a fundamental resource of the firm is its technology base.[7] We define *core knowledge* as knowledge – often scientific or technological – that is at the heart of, and forms the foundation for, a product or service. Core knowledge also is specific to a particular vintage of technology or state of knowledge development. For example, knowledge of integrated circuit technology formed the basis for semiconductor chips beginning in the 1960s. This vintage of electronics technology was preceded by transistors, and vacuum tubes before that.

Henderson and Clark (1990) note that an individual product consists of multiple components, each of which has a separate "component knowledge" consisting of the basic knowledge underlying the component. In order to talk about basic knowledge for a product rather than a component, we focus on the critical aspects of the knowledge underlying a particular product. Such aspects of core knowledge for a product frequently relate to technology, and may include component knowledge underlying

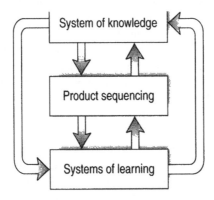

**Figure 12.1** Product sequencing model

critical components of the product, as well as architectural knowledge that links components.

Core knowledge in vertical chains has the following characteristic:

> Proposition 1: Core knowledge can form the foundation for multiple products and stages not only in different vertical chains, but also within vertical chains.

The logic behind this proposition is similar to the rationale for related diversification, involving expansion into different product-markets (and vertical chains) based on shared knowledge, resources, and capabilities (see, for example, Montgomery, 1994). As an example of this phenomenon within a vertical chain,[8] rather than across vertical chains as in related diversification, consider the relationship between refined oil products and basic petrochemicals (Helfat, 1988). A basic petrochemical plant converts a refined oil or natural gas product into ethylene, propylene, and by-products. The core knowledge underlying both refined oil products and basic petrochemicals has to do with the process technologies used to refine crude oil and to process refined oil products into petrochemicals, respectively. In particular, production of basic petrochemicals utilizes a refining process that relies on technological knowledge similar to that used to refine crude oil. Additionally, both oil refineries and petrochemical plants consist of complex, interrelated pieces of equipment (no two oil refineries are exactly alike) that require considerable tacit knowledge in order to operate the equipment together smoothly. As this example demonstrates, oil refining and basic petrochemicals production take place within a vertical chain, yielding separate products that rely on similar core technological knowledge and core capabilities.

### Integrative knowledge

In addition to core knowledge, we define *integrative knowledge* as: knowledge that integrates, or knowledge of how to integrate, different activities, capabilities, and products in one or more vertical chains. Integrative knowledge enables organizations to coordinate activities within a vertical chain or across vertical chains, to obtain market feedback from customers about products, and to obtain feedback either from within vertical chains or from external markets regarding technology.[9]

The nature of coordination within and across vertical chains depends in part on the sorts of knowledge that must be coordinated, such as tacit vs. codified knowledge. For example, Monteverde (1995: 1629) refers to "unstructured technical dialog" involving the "unstructured, uncodifiable, generally verbal, and often face-to-face communication demanded by integrated project management" of product design and manufacturing (see also Wheelwright and Clark, 1992). In this situation, coordination of tacit knowledge that resides in multiple stages of a vertical chain requires somewhat tightly coupled organizational mechanisms.[10]

In contrast, the product and organizational design literature on modularity (Baldwin and Clark, 2000; Sanchez and Mahoney, 1996) suggests that coordination often can take place via standardized rules when the knowledge in different activities that must be coordinated is codified and well understood. Coordination of codified knowledge, however, does not necessarily preclude the need for integrative knowledge. As an example, consider "just-in-time" manufacturing and distribution of goods to final sales outlets that requires close coordination between suppliers, manufacturers, and distributors (Flaherty, 1996). Although the information that flows between the various stages of the supply chain is largely codified (e.g., number of widgets needed), the complexity of coordinating these information flows may require integrative organizational mechanisms and knowledge. More generally:

> Proposition 2: Integrative knowledge is required not only for coordination of tacit knowledge, but also for complex coordination of codified knowledge, within and across vertical chains.

As an example, consider the ways in which Wal-Mart uses information technology to help integrate multiple stages of a vertical chain (Bradley and Ghemawat, 1995). The company obtains daily information from its stores about shelf-stocking needs (derived from cash register scanner information), which it then relays to its suppliers, who deliver the requested goods to Wal-Mart warehouses within 24 hours. Then a portion of the supplier delivered goods is immediately cross-docked directly onto company trucks for store delivery, without any holding of inventory in Wal-Mart warehouses. All of this greatly reduces inventory costs at Wal-Mart stores and warehouses, and improves customer satisfaction (and presumably leads to repeat customers) because store shelves are more fully stocked.

Wal-Mart's system, which requires underlying knowledge of how to integrate activities and sales in a vertical chain, has several aspects that merit attention. First, the system involves complex coordination of codified information. Second, the system has feedback from customers built into it, in the form of daily information about what consumers are buying at each store. Third, information about the "product" itself (i.e., retail sales) affects other activities in the chain. Fourth, Wal-Mart gains valuable information that it can use to forecast future coordination needs and consumer buying for its complete network of suppliers, distribution centers, and stores. Finally, Wal-Mart provides an example of how integrative knowledge can be embodied in organizational mechanisms and routines – in this case, facilitated by the use of information technology – that link activities and products.

Many other companies have made similar use of information technology to coordinate multiple stages of a vertical chain, including Federal Express (Rivkin, 1998) for example. We note that Wal-Mart and Federal Express are service companies. Their core products are retail sales and express delivery service respectively, and therefore the core knowledge underlying these products has to do with the attributes of the products themselves (e.g., knowledge of customer needs). But in addition, integrative knowledge and integrative capabilities allow the companies to more cost effectively deliver their products and to gain more information about their customers' needs, which the companies can then use to improve their core knowledge.

## Product Sequencing

Both core and integrative knowledge can lead to economies of scope. Core knowledge reduces joint costs of production via sharing of intangible assets such as technological know-how (Bailey and Friedlander, 1982; Teece, 1980), not only across product-markets (in different vertical chains) as in related diversification, but also across product-markets within a single vertical chain. Integrative knowledge also reduces joint costs of production between stages of a single vertical chain and across vertical chains via improved coordination and consequent cost reductions, as illustrated by Wal-Mart's lower inventory costs.[11] But perhaps more importantly, in the spirit of Penrose (1959), firms can utilize core and integrative knowledge to introduce sequences of new products that in turn may provide new bases for economies of scope and platforms for future expansion.

> Proposition 3: A system of core and integrative knowledge provides the basis for a matrix of product-market expansion paths, traced out by a series of new product introductions which we term product sequencing.

We classify product sequencing strategies into the following types: (1) new generations of an existing product, (2) replacement products, designed to partially or fully supplant customer usage of a company's prior product, (3) horizontal expansion (e.g., related diversification), (4) vertical expansion, and (5) complex sequences that combine two or more of the prior sequencing strategies.

The simplest product sequencing strategy involves new generations of a product, in the same product-market, generally using the same vertical chain. This strategy builds most directly on prior core knowledge, and likely requires the least alteration of the associated activities and integrative knowledge in the vertical chain. Manufacturing techniques frequently are similar, the distribution channels often remain the same, and marketing usually occurs to similar groups of customers. Additionally, integrative knowledge that links activities in the vertical chain facilitates the launching of new product generations in an organization's current market.

Like new generations of a product, some replacement products may be introduced in an organization's current market. Other sorts of replacement products, however, may be introduced in a separate market, essentially involving horizontal expansion. For example, the market for televisions differs from the market for radios, which televisions partially replaced. As this example also makes clear, a replacement product need not fully displace the prior product. Although replacement products may utilize previous core knowledge, they also may require new core knowledge and may require changes in manufacturing techniques. Distribution, marketing and sales, and customer service also may require changes to accommodate new customers and ways to reach them. Integrative knowledge in turn may need to adapt as well.

Opportunities for product sequencing in markets new to the organization encompass not only some forms of replacement product sequencing, but also horizontal expansion, as in related diversification, as well as product expansion up or down a vertical chain.[12] Consistent with Proposition 1, vertical product sequencing generally extends core knowledge underlying a product in one stage of a vertical chain to the introduction of a product in another stage of the same vertical chain. Horizontal product sequencing also extends core knowledge to another market, but across vertical chains. Like replacement product sequencing, both vertical and horizontal product sequencing may entail changes to integrative knowledge as well.

At some point of course, organizations may reach limits of integrative knowledge to coordinate across vertically and horizontally related markets, potentially with multiple generations of products in each. Moreover, expansion into new product-markets, including perhaps different customers, may require additions to core and integrative knowledge.[13] Additions to knowledge in this system, and product sequencing based on the system of knowledge, require learning, as we next explain.

## Systems of Learning

> Proposition 4: Accumulation of core and integrative knowledge can be conceptualized as consisting of two systems of learning that run in parallel, each linked to one another and to the current system of knowledge and portfolio of products. The first system involves incremental learning, and the second system involves what we term step function learning.

We next explain the two systems of learning in more detail.[14]

### Incremental learning

Incremental learning improves upon but does not fundamentally depart from current knowledge. Incremental learning in core knowledge may underpin new product generations, as in, for example, Sony's continual introduction of new Walkman and Discman models. These new models involved incremental improvements in the underlying technological knowledge of personal tape recorder and CD player technology and hardware design.[15] Incremental extensions of core knowledge also can involve new product development in another stage of a vertical chain, or in closely related horizontal markets.

Incremental learning also applies to integrative knowledge. As an example, consider Wal-Mart's addition of cross-docking (the unloading of supplier deliveries directly onto Wal-Mart store delivery trucks) to its distribution system. The integrative mechanisms linking supplier and company trucks changed, since Wal-Mart required greater coordination between supplier deliveries and store deliveries.

Rosenberg (1982: chapter 6) focuses on two forms of incremental learning: learning by doing and learning by using. The learning curve, where production costs decline as cumulative volume increases, typifies learning by doing in manufacturing. Additionally, learning by doing about productive processes can lead to alterations in the design of the product (Monteverde, 1995). In this instance, integrative knowledge that links manufacturing and product design activities facilitates incremental learning in core knowledge of the product.

With regard to learning by using, customer experience with a product can provide information about the relationship between specific product characteristics and product performance. Firms then can incorporate this information into design modifications (Rosenberg, 1982), including in new models or generations of a product (Von Hippel, 1976, 1986). Here again, incremental learning in core knowledge benefits from integrative knowledge, in this case involving feedback from customers that is linked to product design.

Incremental learning by doing and using is cumulative (Cohen and Levinthal, 1990) and also relies on local search for new knowledge in the neighborhood of existing knowledge. In general, cumulative learning combined with local search creates path dependence in the direction of organizational learning (Nelson and Winter, 1982; Helfat, 1994). Incremental learning therefore is path dependent, as are the product sequences that result. For example, as new generations of a product evolve, learning becomes more engineering and user oriented and specific to the particular product (Rosenberg, 1982: 122). Improvements typically require familiarity with the product (Gomory, 1987; Gomory and Schmitt, 1988). Thus, incremental learning, the knowledge underlying the product, and the product itself are inextricably linked to one another, and to the history of product sequencing over time.

### Step function learning

In contrast to incremental learning, what we term "step function learning" involves fundamental changes to core or integrative knowledge. Step function learning presents difficult challenges for organizations, and the literature is replete with examples of firms that failed because they could not adapt to new technologies in particular. But some firms have successfully managed to accomplish step function learning, with regard to both core knowledge and integrative knowledge, using processes that we next describe.

Step function learning at a minimum requires ongoing feedback about products, markets, and technologies that points to the need for new and different knowledge. For example, Kao, a leading Japanese household and chemical products maker, has developed what it calls the ECHO system for processing and analysis of customer questions and complaints about Kao products (Nonaka and Takeuchi, 1995). Phone operators in Kao's customer service organization enter customer questions and complaints into a computer system that in turn generates reports used in various activities throughout the vertical chain. Kao also uses this feedback system directly in product refinement, involving incremental learning in core knowledge. But in addition, Kao obtains information regarding shifts in customer desires (Quinn, Baruch, and Zien, 1997), which provides a basis for step function learning in core knowledge and for new product development.[16]

As with core knowledge, step function learning in integrative knowledge requires ongoing feedback mechanisms that point to the need for new knowledge. Benchmarking of competitors, for example, can provide feedback such that wide gaps in performance may signal the need for a major rethinking of integrative mechanisms.

In addition to recognizing the need for fundamentally new knowledge, organizations must acquire and learn to utilize the knowledge. This may require teams and organizational units dedicated specifically to the learning effort. For example, with regard to core knowledge, when Sony decided to develop what became the Trinitron color TV, the firm set up a team of researchers focused on this effort.[17] As an example involving integrative knowledge, the opportunity for GM to learn from Toyota about just-in-time supply chains came about through a new organizational unit in the form of the NUMMI joint venture between the two companies (Badaracco, 1988).[18]

**Product sequencing and linked systems of learning**

The product sequencing strategies outlined earlier rely on incremental and step function systems of learning, upon which the system of core and integrative knowledge is built. Not only are the systems of incremental and step function learning linked to the current system of knowledge, but also the two systems of learning are linked to one another in the following ways. First, incremental learning is likely to build upon step function learning. For example, incremental learning in core knowledge that leads to new generations of a product builds upon step function learning in core knowledge embodied in the initial product. Additionally, step function learning may build upon prior incremental learning. For example, although Sony required new core knowledge to develop the Trinitron color TV tube, which differed fundamentally from black-and-white TV tubes, Sony also adapted the new tube to the company's prior TV design, which embodied incremental learning related to black-and-white TVs.

By employing the two parallel linked systems of incremental and step function learning, organizations learn to effectively manage the product sequencing process within markets, as well as up, down, and across vertical chains and productmarkets, based on a system of core and integrative knowledge. The systems of learning create an understanding of the potential as well as the limitations of core and integrative knowledge, of the nature of the family of products that can be developed using the underlying system of knowledge, and of the markets for these current and potential products. Products are linked to one another at a point in time in different markets and through time, and coevolve with the underlying knowledge and capabilities.

## Product Sequencing and Competitive Advantage

The system of knowledge and portfolio of products, in combination with the two systems of learning, provide "real options" (Kogut and Kulatilaka, 1997: Brown and Eisenhardt, 1997) for future product sequences. As Bowman and Hurry (1993: 762) state, "options come into existence when existing resources and capabilities allow preferential access to future opportunities." In creating access to new opportunities, however, the history of product sequencing also constrains options for future product sequences.[19] More specifically, creation of new products and new knowledge depends on existing products, along with the underlying path-dependent knowledge and capabilities. This dependence on history matters not only for incremental (and hence, path-dependent) learning and the products it supports, but also for step function learning. For example, integrative mechanisms in the current system of knowledge often alert the organization to the need for step function learning: existing integrative knowledge therefore shapes the direction of step function learning. Moreover, step function learning in turn may build on some aspects of existing core knowledge.

Over time, a system of core and integrative knowledge may generate more real options than an organization has the organizational, productive, and financial resources to pursue.[20] Managers must make choices of paths to pursue and place bets (Raubitschek, 1988a), and the choices made will alter the options for future product sequencing, due to built-in path dependence. There is no certain "right" path to future success, since feedback that occurs in the process of developing, making, and selling each new product is not known ahead of time.

The product sequencing model implies differential firm success and competitive advantage. Different organizations rarely enter a market at the same time with the exact same initial sets of knowledge, products, and systems of learning, nor do these organizations necessarily make the same choices of product sequences over time. Therefore, due to path dependence, organizations will evolve different systems of knowledge, systems of learning, and portfolios of products. Furthermore, successful bets on products provide a richer set or real options and product platforms upon which to base future product sequences than do unsuccessful bets. Success may breed success and failure may make future success more difficult. And superior systems of learning that form the basis for continued product sequences can turn short-term competitive success into longer-term advantage.

## Examples of Product Sequencing Strategies

To illustrate the product-sequencing model, we next provide abbreviated histories of new product introductions over time in three technology-intensive Japanese firms: Sony, Canon, and NEC. These histories rely on publicly available sources of information and, as a result, the histories contain more information about core than integrative knowledge. Where possible, we identify the types of knowledge (core or integrative) and learning (incremental or step function) in the product sequences. Following the three histories, we discuss their implications as a group for the product sequencing model.

### Sony[21]

When incorporated as Tokyo Telecommunications Engineering Corporation (also called Totsuko) in 1946, Sony repaired radios and made radio upgrade kits that converted AM radios into short-wave receivers, among other products. By 1950, Sony produced magnetic audio tapes as well as tape recorders (step function learning related to audio magnetic recording for the company). Like radios, tape recorders were electromagnetic audio devices with mechanical parts.

In 1953, Sony licensed the basic technology underlying transistors from Bell Laboratories, and building on this technology developed a high-frequency transistor for radios (step function learning in electronics for the company). Sony went on to introduce the first Japanese transistor radio in 1955 (horizontal product sequencing from audio tapes and recorders into radios), as well as a "pocket-size" transistorized radio in 1957. Then in 1958, after having further developed transistors so that radios could receive FM signals, Sony introduced the first portable AM/FM transistor radio (replacement product sequencing in radios). For both its radios and the transistor inputs (vertical product sequencing), Sony utilized and extended its core knowledge of electronics. Additionally, with its transistor radios, Sony developed core knowledge involving miniaturization of electronic products.

Continuing its transistor research, in 1958 Sony developed a portable transistorized video tape recorder (VTR) (horizontal and vertical product sequencing), followed by new lower-priced VTR, models throughout the next decade (new-generation product sequencing). With the VTR, Sony added to its core knowledge of electronics and also fundamentally extended its knowledge of audio magnetic recording to video magnetic recording (step function learning).

Then extending its research in transistors even further,[22] Sony developed a semiconductor type of television receiver. Sony combined this development with its core knowledge of miniaturization, and by 1960 introduced the first all-transistor, black-and-white, portable, small-screen television set (horizontal product sequencing into TVs and vertical product sequencing of semiconductor inputs for TVs, based on core knowledge of electronics). Then in 1969 Sony introduced its extremely successful Trinitron color TV (replacement product sequencing in televisions), which produced a superior picture due to its unique technology. In order to develop a color TV, Sony had initially licensed a new TV tube technology based on the work of Nobel Prize-winning physicist O. E. Lawrence, but its efforts to commercialize the technology were unsuccessful. These efforts, however, aided Sony in its subsequent development of the Trinitron technology (step function learning), which the company also combined with its knowledge of TV design from black-and-white TVs (incremental learning). While Sony's first Trinitron TV was again a small set, utilizing its core knowledge of miniaturization, this product was extremely successful, and Sony subsequently introduced a series of new models with larger screens (new-generation product sequencing).

In 1971, building on its experience with televisions, video recording, tapes, radios, and semiconductors, Sony developed a video recorder that played bulky video cassettes (replacement product sequencing for reel-to-reel VTRs). This "U-Matic" machine became the standard format in the institutional market,[23] and formed the basis for Sony's subsequent Betamax video cassette recorder (VCR) and for competing VHS machines, both sold to the home market. Sony introduced its Betamax type VCR in 1975, and in 1976 JVC introduced the VHS-type VCR, which was not compatible with Betamax and had a longer recording time. This began the Betamax–VHS video war, which lasted until the early to mid-1980s, when VHS emerged as the industry standard (Cusumano et al., 1992).

Sony's failure with Betamax provides a cautionary tale that core technological knowledge alone cannot support effective product sequencing. Early on, JVC worked to line up other consumer electronics firms that would sell VHS-format VCRs. JVC's partners, especially its parent Masushita, provided technical feedback and assistance to JVC during development of the VHS machine, which led to improvements in product features such as longer recording and playback time (suggestive of integrative knowledge). Masushita also pursued large market share for the VHS format in order to obtain economies of scale, and therefore produced VCRs for other consumer products companies to market using their own brand names – which Sony refused to do. Additionally, Masushita held a dominant share of the retail appliance store market in Japan, giving the company guaranteed distribution outlets for its VCRs.

Masushita's large share of retail outlets in Japan also provided the company with good information about consumer reaction to its VCRs. In addition, JVC and Masushita, through their partners, gained early knowledge of the evolving importance to consumers of compatible prerecorded video software. JVC and Masushita had several partners in Europe, where video rentals become popular more quickly than in the United States. And one of Masushita's earliest partners in the United States was RCA, which saw consumer video software as important due to its videodisk business. As demand increased for prerecorded video tapes, consumers purchasing VCRs had to choose between two different video tape formats, and constraints on shelf space made stores reluctant to carry both formats. Masushita sped acceptance of the VHS format as a standard not only by manufacturing VCRs for other consumer electronics companies, but also by developing high-speed VHS video tape duplication equipment that it supplied at low cost to producers of prerecorded video tapes, which in turn increased availability of VHS tapes in stores.

In summary, throughout its history, Sony established strong links among its products based on core technological knowledge. With the VCR, however, Sony lagged JVC and Masushita in understanding customer needs and building market share in a market with network externalities, where small players often lose. Here we see the importance of feedback from consumers, feedback from partner companies, and integrative knowledge that facilitates this.

## Canon[24]

Founded in 1933 as the Precision Optical Research Laboratories, Canon relied on core technologies of precision optics (involving the grinding of lenses to exact specifications) and mechanics to produce mechanical cameras.[25] During the next half century, Canon introduced new camera models and further accumulated skills in precision optics and mechanics (incremental learning and new-generation product sequencing).

One of Canon's relatively early ventures beyond mechanical cameras involved photocopiers, which essentially are cameras that take a picture in a different way. To introduce its first copier in 1965 (horizontal product sequencing), Canon used technology licensed from RCA. Then in 1968 Canon announced that, based on its own research on plain paper copiers, it had developed a new process technology that provided the first alternative to Xerox's patented technology (step function learning). This new process reflected Canon's development of core knowledge in chemicals, which the company combined with its core knowledge of precision optics and mechanics to introduce a copier with dry toner in 1970 (replacement product sequencing). Canon then introduced a second-generation copier with liquid toner in 1972 (new-generation product sequencing) and a color copier in 1973. Because Canon lacked strong industrial marketing, the company licensed the technology to Japanese and foreign competitors. While providing royalty income, licensing inadvertently strengthened the competition, which gained manufacturing experience and brand recognition.

During the same time period, Canon entered the calculator business. In 1964, Canon introduced the world's first 10-key pad electronic desk calculator, which utilized the company's core knowledge of mechanics and which contributed to the development of core knowledge of electronic circuitry. Then in the early 1970s, Canon introduced hand-held electronic calculators, but was bested by Sharp's superior "thin" calculator, which it could not quickly duplicate. Nevertheless, with its hand-held calculator initiative, Canon developed knowledge of miniaturized electronic circuitry that contributed to the company's platform for future product sequencing, as we next explain.

In 1976, Canon revolutionized the 35   mm camera market by introducing the AE-1 camera – the world's first electronically controlled, fully automatic, single-lens reflex (SLR) camera with a built-in microprocessor unit (replacement product sequencing in cameras). In developing the AE-1, Canon combined its core knowledge of precision optics and mechanics (from cameras) with that of miniaturized electronic circuitry (from hand-held calculators) in a completely new way, to essentially put an electronic brain into what previously were mechanical cameras (step function learning).[26]

Improving on its marketing performance with copiers, Canon spent over a million dollars for a spectacular promotion on American television to introduce the AE-1 camera – the first time that 35mm cameras were advertised on TV. Canon also priced the camera at more than $100 below other cameras. Relying on experience gained in producing electronic calculators, the AE-1 used 20 percent fewer parts than conventional SLR cameras, resulting in significant cost reductions. In addition, Canon drew on knowledge it had gained in manufacturing mechanical cameras to construct new automatic equipment that helped to lower production costs. This learning in manufacturing from electronic calculators and mechanical cameras, and learning from copiers about the need for effective marketing, suggests that Canon may have had integrative mechanisms to facilitate knowledge transfer. The AE-1 became the world's best-selling 35   mm SLR camera, which Canon followed with new models that continued to attract consumer interest for many years (incremental learning and new-generation product sequencing).

Following the AE-1, Canon again hit the jackpot, this time with a personal copier introduced in 1979 and sold to the office market (replacement product sequencing in copiers). Canon had developed a new photocopying process, which the company did not license, and which it incorporated into the typewriter-size copier (step function learning). Then, in 1982, Canon introduced another personal copier (replacement product sequencing) that combined its new copying process with a disposable cartridge that incorporated the toner, developing assembly, and photoconductive drum, thus utilizing the company's core knowledge of chemicals. The cartridge eliminated the need for Canon to build a service network, a major barrier to entry in this market, by putting all parts that are likely to break down into a disposable cartridge.

To market the copier, Canon expanded its distribution channels and launched a major marketing campaign resembling its previous successful campaign for the AE-1 (suggestive of integrative knowledge in marketing across products). The company set a low price for the copier as well, relying in part on cost reductions obtained from redesign of the copier production line. These cost reductions in turn benefited from integrative mechanisms that facilitated knowledge transfer, in that Canon's copier product development group worked closely with the production engineering unit to utilize its camera-manufacturing know-how. Over time, Canon introduced new generations of personal copiers with features never before offered in the low-end price segment (new-generation product sequencing).

As yet another example of Canon's complex product sequencing strategy, in the early 1980s the company introduced a personal printer for desktop computers (horizontal product sequencing) that had higher speed and better quality text and graphics than existing daisywheel and dot matrix printers. Canon's personal printer relied on a copier-like printer engine and, like the copier, used a disposable cartridge. Canon offered the printer engine to other (original equipment) manufacturers of printers at a price such that, when configured with the necessary control electronics, the printers were priced competitively with the inferior daisywheel and dot matrix machines. Canon achieved this price breakthrough by using its experience in high-volume manufacturing of small copiers, and by employing common components in its copiers and printers, again suggestive of integrative knowledge across products in manufacturing. The Canon printer engine became an industry standard, used by many original equipment manufacturers including Apple and Hewlett-Packard.

In summary, Canon evolved from a simple new-generation product sequencing strategy in mechanical cameras to a complex product sequencing strategy in many markets. To introduce new products, Canon built on and extended its core knowledge of precision optics and mechanics, and developed completely different areas of core knowledge in electronics and chemicals (step function learning). Additionally, the evidence suggests that integrative knowledge across products in marketing and manufacturing may have played an important role in Canon's product sequencing strategy.

### NEC Corporation[27]

NEC was formed in 1899 as a joint venture between Japanese investors and Western Electric, the manufacturing arm of AT&T, to produce telecommunications equipment in Japan. In its long and complicated history, NEC also enjoyed strong ties to ITT and Sumitomo.

Using Western Electric technology, NEC initially built telephone communication equipment and later using this expertise entered radio communication systems (horizontal product sequencing). Both sets of products relied on electromagnetic waves, although at different frequencies with different carrying mediums, and utilized electronics technology. Subsequently, NEC integrated backwards into vacuum tubes (step function learning in electronics), an important input to its telephone and radio broadcasting equipment (vertical product sequencing based on core knowledge of electronics). NEC also established its own radio research unit, and later began research on microwave communication systems. Over time, the company grew to the point where toward the end of the Second World War, it was a major producer of radio equipment, vacuum tubes, telephone equipment, and telephone carrier transmission equipment (complex vertical and horizontal product sequencing). At the conclusion of the war, however, NEC's operations came to a standstill due to bombing of its facilities and severe shortages of personnel and materials.

Following the war, Japan enacted two reforms aimed at restructuring and remaking its communication infrastructure, which allowed NEC to quickly rebuild. One reform permitted commercial broadcasting, and the resulting boom in broadcasting created a huge demand for broadcasting equipment. The other reform created Nippon Telegraph and Telephone Public Corporation (NTT) as the monopoly provider of domestic telecommunications in Japan, although NTT was not allowed to manufacture its own equipment.

NEC reentered the communications business, providing broadcasting equipment and telephone communication systems, and became NTT's lead supplier. By 1950, NEC had begun research on transistors (the semiconductors of the time) out of concern that the transistor would replace the vacuum tube. After the war, NEC also resumed work on microwave communication technology involving extremely high-frequency transmissions used in both telephone and broadcasting systems. And in 1954, the necessity for complex calculations in telecommunications spurred NEC to enter computer research.

All of these efforts converged as follows. In 1958, NEC began mass production of transistors, primarily for industrial applications with some internal consumption (step function learning in electronics and replacement product sequencing whereby transistors replaced vacuum tubes). This advance in transistor development benefited in part from NEC's R&D and production of silicon diodes for its microwave communication systems. And NEC's advances in transistors further enabled the company by 1959 to develop the first Japanese transistorized computer targeted for the general public (step function learning, resulting in complex vertical and horizontal product sequencing involving core knowledge of electronics).

During this period, again building on core knowledge of electronics, NEC in 1955 invented a method for improving the FM receiver threshold. This led to over-the-horizon microwave communications systems used to connect telephone networks, which NEC produced in 1959, and ultimately to NEC's highly successful entry into satellite communication systems (horizontal product sequencing), which essentially involve microwave relay links in space.

In 1960, NEC also began development of integrated circuits, the vintage of semiconductors that followed transistors. By 1962, NEC had developed its own integrated circuits (step function learning in electronics for the company and replacement product sequencing in semiconductors), and over a period of two decades the company introduced a series of semiconductor devices (new-generation product sequencing). By the mid-1980s, NEC was the world's biggest producer of semiconductors.

NEC continued its development of computers as well. In 1965, NEC unveiled the Series 2200 family of computer systems sharing a common hardware and software architecture, which made it easy for users to connect the machines to one another and to trade up to more expensive machines. With these products, each linked to one another at a point in time and over time, NEC became a major computer manufacturer in its domestic market. Then, in 1972, NEC became the first Japanese company to develop a microcomputer (horizontal product sequencing), utilizing its semiconductors as inputs (vertical product sequencing based on core knowledge of electronics), and which it followed with even more powerful versions (new-generation product sequencing).

In the early 1970s, NEC also increased its output of consumer electronics products, building on an electrical household appliance business originally established in the 1950s. Once again, NEC employed vertical product sequencing in electronics, incorporating microelectronic control functions into new consumer products, such as a color TV set with an electronic tuning system introduced in 1973.

In 1977, Koji Kobayashi, then Chairman of the board of NEC, expressed the concept behind the strategy that NEC pursued through the 1980s. He called it C&C – integration of computers and communications. Kobayashi early on recognized trends whereby advances in semiconductors supported the development of computers and communications networks throughout the world. NEC, with its strong presence and core knowledge of electronics in all three markets, could utilize the company's knowledge and product base to capitalize on integration of these markets and technologies. By the mid-1980s, NEC was the only company in the world to achieve the "Triple Crown" in electronics. NEC alone ranked among the top 10 companies in the world in the three most important markets of the electronics industry: semiconductors, computers, and telecommunications.

## Discussion

The histories of Sony, Canon, and NEC highlight several aspects of the product sequencing model. First, per Proposition 1, NEC's and Sony's core knowledge provided the foundation for upstream as well as downstream products in vertical chains. For example, core knowledge of electronics underlay NEC's businesses in vacuum tubes (upstream) and telephone and radio communication systems (downstream). NEC also utilized core knowledge of a later vintage of electronics to produce semiconductors (upstream) as well as computers, consumer electronics, and telecommunication and broadcast systems (downstream). Similarly, Sony's core knowledge of electronics underlay semiconductors (upstream) and radios, VTRs, VCRs, and TVs (all downstream).

The company histories also demonstrate the importance of integrative knowledge, per Proposition 2. For example, Canon's copier product development group worked closely with the camera production engineering group to redesign the copier production line. Canon also benefited from learning across products in manufacturing and marketing for its electronic cameras and printers, suggestive of integrative knowledge. Sony's failure and Masushita's success in VCRs points to the importance of integrative knowledge as well.

Per Proposition 3, each of the companies' product sequences traces out a matrix of product-market expansion paths across or within vertical chains, building on previous core and integrative knowledge. For example, knowledge of audio and video technology, combined with core knowledge of electronics and miniaturization, are key links in Sony's horizontal product sequencing in radios, VTRs, TVs, and VCRs, supplemented by vertical integration into semiconductors. Canon built on its initial core knowledge of precision optics and mechanics in mechanical cameras, and combined this knowledge with core knowledge of electronics and chemicals to develop calculators, electronic cameras, copiers, and printers. And NEC's expansion based on core knowledge of electronics made it a leading player in the markets for semiconductors, computers, and communications.

Step function learning, per Proposition 4, also plays an important role in the product sequences. We see the importance that being in a market and making a product had in pointing to opportunities for related products and to the need to deal with emerging technologies. For example, by virtue of being in the markets both for vacuum tubes and for downstream communication systems that used vacuum tubes, NEC understood the threat posed by transistors. As a result, NEC undertook semiconductor research and made the leap from vacuum tubes to transistors.

Also with regard to step function learning, the desire to make a new type of product sometimes led the companies to combine previous areas of core knowledge and extend them in fundamentally new ways. For example, Canon's development of the electronically controlled AE-1 camera combined and extended the company's prior knowledge of precision optics and mechanics and electronic circuitry in a fundamentally new way. We also see how companies learned from their mistakes, as in Canon's ill-fated hand-held calculator initiative. From this endeavor, Canon gained a great deal of knowledge regarding miniaturized electronic circuitry, which it then employed in its highly successful AE-1 electronic camera.

Finally with regard to step function learning, we see how firms adapted to radical changes in technology and markets, and also shaped the evolution of products and markets. For example, NEC successfully managed the transition from vacuum tubes to transistors, a "radical" shift in technology and the underlying core knowledge. And Canon's development of the AE-1 camera, along with its aggressive marketing, shifted the consumer camera market away from mechanical cameras to electronically controlled cameras.

A critical element in the product sequencing of these companies, but not brought out in the histories, has to do with the role of top management. In Sony, the founders Morita and Ibuka often initiated and played a large role in decisions regarding product sequencing and acquisition of any new knowledge required. In NEC, Kobayashi was critical to the company's product sequencing strategy involving integration of computers and communications. Notably, these leaders played important integrative roles within their organizations, as well as scanning the environment for new technologies and generating new ideas.

Overall, the product sequencing histories illustrate the continued coevolution of knowledge and products through time, involving both incremental and step function learning. We also see how these systems of learning essentially constitute dynamic capabilities that enabled the firms to continually introduce new products and adapt to changing technological and market conditions.

## Conclusion

The product sequencing model provides a dynamic framework that enables us to track, step by step, how knowledge, capabilities, activities, and products coevolve over time and across markets. Admittedly, this is a large undertaking, and the model is a first step in unpacking the evolution of capabilities and products.

The model has several features that differ somewhat from existing models. As noted previously, the concept of knowledge shared across products is a well-known explanation for related diversification, but is not usually applied to vertical expansion. The oil-petrochemical example used earlier, as well as the histories of the electronics companies, suggest that not only does core knowledge form the foundation for multiple products and stages in a vertical chain, but it also applies to industries that contribute large shares to the world economy and that can be highly profitable. With regard to integrative knowledge, although the concept has been applied to linkages of activities within a vertical chain (e.g., Armour and Teece, 1980; Clark and Fujimoto, 1991; Iansiti and Clark, 1994), it has not been applied frequently to expansion into new product-markets either vertically or through diversification across vertical chains. More generally, the literatures on diversification and product development have not focused on the dynamic aspects of how expansion into new product-markets unfolds over time,[28] or on the importance of product platforms.

The product sequencing model has implications for several closely related literatures, including the resource-based view, knowledge management, dynamic capabilities, organizational learning, firm and industry evolution, and business history. First, the model highlights the importance of products to the resources and capabilities of firms. The analysis also helps to make the idea of resource and activity bundles (Rumelt, 1984; Conner, 1991) more concrete,[29] particularly with regard to knowledge and learning. The model further draws attention to the role of knowledge as a resource that supports capabilities, activities, and products, and that in turn arises from experience gained in making and selling products. Additionally, the model relates specific types of knowledge in specific ways to vertical chains of activities, and further suggests that it is useful to characterize the evolution of firms and industries in terms of vertical chains and products.[30] Thus, we may be able to gain greater understanding of changes in scale and scope (Chandler, 1990) over the course of business history by asking questions about exactly what types of knowledge and systems of learning formed the basis for expansion, and how these were linked to specific products. We also can examine deficiencies in knowledge and learning over the course of history.

With regard to change over time, the product sequencing model extends the analysis of dynamic capabilities as well. As noted earlier, the parallel systems of learning in the model are prime examples of dynamic capabilities (Teece et al., 1997), since these systems are fundamental to the ability of organizations to innovate and to adapt to changes in technology and markets, including the ability to learn from mistakes. We also bring in the role of products that coevolve with, and contribute to, specific systems of knowledge and learning.

With regard to organizational learning and innovation more generally, step function improvement in integrative knowledge is akin to architectural innovation (Henderson and Clark, 1990), but at the firm rather than the product level. The model also contributes to the limited literature that points to the possibility that firms can achieve both evolutionary and revolutionary change (Tushman and O'Reilly, 1996). Our analysis highlights the dual systems of incremental and step function learning that facilitate evolutionary and revolutionary change, respectively.

The product sequencing model does not necessarily yield generic predictions about the appropriate direction of expansion for broad categories of firms.[31] As an example, consider the costs of learning required for product sequencing. These costs depend in part on how "close" the new knowledge that must be acquired is to current knowledge, as well as on the extent of technological opportunity (or opportunity for knowledge advancement more generally) in a particular market. Although in general we would expect lower costs for incremental than step function learning, it is not clear *a priori* whether horizontal or vertical expansion, for example, will have lower costs of incremental learning, since both forms of expansion may build on current core and integrative knowledge. Nor is it clear *a priori* whether step function learning is less costly for vertical or horizontal expansion. Instead, costs of learning depend on the situation of the individual firm, and more specifically on how "close" the knowledge base required for a product expansion is to the current knowledge base of the firm, regardless of the direction of expansion.

In focusing on the knowledge bases and product sequencing of individual firms, the model alerts managers to factors to consider when making decisions regarding innovation, new product introduction, and market entry. Managers must consider the firm's core technological knowledge, as well information regarding the likely future trajectories of technologies and markets (gained from integrative knowledge), the firm's learning capabilities (systems of learning), and any new knowledge and capabilities the firm may need to acquire. Given this information, managers in essence place bets on product sequences, and scenario analysis can help managers plan in such situations (Raubitschek, 1988b).

In addition, using the model retrospectively, we can trace the progression of organizational knowledge and products through time using both qualitative historical analysis and statistical techniques if we can obtain appropriate data. The model predicts that, for each individual firm, successful product sequencing builds on and also augments the knowledge and capability base of the firm. More generally, we can start to unpack the evolution of firms (and other long-term organizational arrangements), and by implication the evolution of industries, into the evolution of the underlying systems of knowledge and learning, capabilities, and products.

## Acknowledgements

This paper has benefited from discussions with Paul Almeida, Betsy Bailey, Therese Flaherty, Rob Grant, Quintus Jett, Bruce Kogut, Dan Levinthal, Marvin Lieberman, David Mowery, Yiorgos Mylonadis, C. K. Prahalad, James Brian Quinn, Dick Rosenbloom, Lori Rosenkopf, Nicolaj Siggelkow, Harbir Singh, and Sid Winter. We also benefited from presenting the paper at the 1999 annual meetings of the Academy of Management and INFORMS, the Tuck/CCC conference on the Evolution of Firm Capabilities, and the Helsinki School of Economics and Business Administration. The views expressed herein are not purported to represent those of the US Department of Justice.

## Notes

1  Kim and Kogut (1996) use the term "platform technologies" to denote technologies that form the basis for diversification over time. The product platforms in our model serve a related purpose.
2  Grant (1996: 330) notes that more advanced chips require closer coordination of design and fabrication, which has reversed some of the separation of the design and fab stages.
3  Moreover, simply because knowledge is codified does not mean that it is necessarily well understood by all recipients of such knowledge. For example, most nonphysicists would have difficulty understanding a highly technical physics journal article. We thank Bruce Kogut for pointing this out. See also Zander and Kogut (1995) on the transfer of knowledge.
4  In operations management, a vertical chain is referred to as a "supply chain" that may

involve more than one firm (Flaherty, 1996).

5   Our analysis is in the spirit of Porter's (1996) recent focus on the entire activity system, with multiple linkages between different stages of the vertical chain. Fine (1998) also refers to "capability chains."

6   Leonard and Sensiper (1998: 121) refer to "system knowledge" as "collective tacit knowledge . . . developed communally, over time, in interactions among individuals in the group." Our use of the term "system of knowledge" also incorporates an important role for tacit knowledge between individuals, in our case involving stages of vertical chains that support specific products.

7   For this reason, Teece (1986) makes "core technological know-how" the centerpiece of his wheel of complementary assets, although he doesn't explicitly define the term.

8   Argyres (1996) refers to the idea of shared knowledge that is common to adjacent stages of a vertical chain but does not elaborate on the concept.

9   Integrative knowledge, as defined here, is in part a firm-level analogue to architectural knowledge (Henderson and Clark, 1990) that links components of a product.

10   We note that "learning by monitoring" (Helper, MacDuffie and Sabel, 1999) can mitigate pitfalls of tightly coupled systems. Learning by monitoring includes simultaneous engineering across groups (e.g., sharing of designs in real time), as well as error detection and correction systems (e.g., stopping the assembly line when a worker spots a defect). These continuous adjustments prevent problems in one part of the chain from continually causing problems throughout the chain. Additionally, greater experimentation can take place, because the system provides a means of resolving potential consequences of experimentation in one stage of a chain for other stages in the chain.

11   For products in two contiguous stages of a vertical chain, economies of scope occur when: $C(y_i, y_j) < C(y_i,0) + C(0, y_j, p_i) - p_i y_i(y_j,p^\star)$, where $y_i$ = upstream output, $y_j$ = downstream output, $p_i$ = market price for the intermediate product, $y_i(y_j,p^\star)$ = derived demand for the intermediate product, and $p^\star$ = vector of all input prices at the downstream stage (including $p_i$). This formula comes from Kaserman and Mayo (1991), who focused on avoidance of transactions costs and of monopoly pricing mark-up as an explanation of vertical integration, rather than on core and integrative knowledge.

12   Winter (1993) briefly discusses the possibility that knowledge may form the basis for the growth of firms via vertical integration.

13   We note also that integrative knowledge itself can provide the basis for horizontal product-market expansion. Federal Express, for example, is developing a new business as a logistics supplier, based on integrative knowledge developed in its express mail business (Smart, 1999).

14   The concepts of incremental and step function learning are similar to March's (1991) exploitation and exploration in organizational learning, respectively.

15   This statement is based on information in Patton (1999).

16   Kao's use of its customer service organization provides an example of Christensen's (1997) point that information from companies' less attractive customers (such as those that complain) may point to the need for what we term step function learning.

17   We are grateful to James Brian Quinn for suggesting the Trinitron TV example. The references for the Sony example here and elsewhere in the paper are given at the end of the paper.

18   GM, however, had difficulty taking full advantage of the opportunity NUMMI presented. For example, GM had difficulty transferring knowledge gained at the NUMMI plant throughout the rest of the company (Badaracco, 1988).

19   Ghemawat et al. (1999) make the more general point that investments in resource commitments and capabilities are often irreversible.

20   An essential element of options is that less promising options can be allowed to expire.
21   The sources for this history of Sony are: Bartlett (1992), *Broadcasting* (1983), Browning (1986), Burgess (1999), *Business Week* (1987), Cieply (1983), Cusumano, Mylonadis, and Rosenbloom (1992), *Economist* (1982, 1983a, 1983b), Gerson (1978), Ibuka (1975), Lyons (1976), Morita, Reingold, and Shimomura (1986), Nathan (1999), Pollack (1999), Rosenbloom and Cusumano (1987), Rubinflen, Ono, and Landro (1988), and Smith (1987).
22   Semiconductors, made of substances that are between conductors and insulators, are the class of devices that replaced the use of vacuum tubes. Transistors were the first generation of semiconductor microelectronics technology.
23   In 1970, Sony, Masushita, and JVC entered into a cross-licensing agreement for video recording patents that allowed the U-Matic to be adopted by all three companies as the standard for institutional use.
24   The sources for this history of Canon are: Beauchamp (1988), Blum (1978), Cavuoto (1984), Canon, Inc. (2000), *Economic World* (1976), *Electronic Business* (1984), Heller (1983), Helm (1985), Hof and Gross (1989), Ishikura and Porter (1983a, 1983b), Johansson (1986), Kraar (1981), Meyer (1985), Moore (1982), Port (1987), Sutherland (1988), Trachtenberg (1987), and Yamanouchi (1989).
25   This abbreviated history includes many but not all of Canon's product areas. The history does not, for example, cover Canon's optical products (semiconductor production equipment, broadcasting equipment, and medical equipment), which also utilize Canon's core knowledge.
26   This provides an excellent example of the power of combinative capabilities (Kogut and Zander, 1992).
27   The sources for this history of NEC are: Browning (1985), *Business Week* (1982), *Economist* (1984, 1986), Hayashi (1987), IEEE spectrum (1986), Joseph (1986), Kobayashi (1986), Mead (1985), NEC (1984), Smith (1984), and Sullivan (1988).
28   Teece et al. (1994) and Kim and Kogut (1996) are notable exceptions.
29   As an alternative approach with a somewhat different focus, Milgrom and Roberts (1990) provide a model of strong complementarities between groups of activities. See also Cockburn, Henderson, and Stern (1999).
30   Thus, the model adds a dynamic element to the literature on activity systems and value chains, which heretofore have often been analyzed in static terms (with notable exceptions of Ghemawat et al., 1999; McKelvey, 1999; and Siggelkow, 1999).
31   In this, we depart from Teece et al. (1994). We also differ somewhat from them in our explanation of vertical linkages.

# References

Argyres, N. 1996. Evidence on the role of firm capabilities in vertical integration decisions. *Strategic Management Journal* 17(2): 129–150.
Armour, H. and Teece, D. I. 1980. Vertical integration and technological innovation. *Review of Economics and Statistics*. 62: 470–474.
Badaracco, I. L. Jr. 1988. *General Motors' Asian Alliances*. Harvard Business School: Boston, MA, Case no. 9–388–094.
Bailey, E. E. and Friedlander, A. 1982. Market structure and multiproduct industries. *Journal of Economic Literature* 20: 1024–1048.
Baldwin, C. Y. and Clark, K. B. 2000. *Design Rules: The Power of Modularity*. MIT Press: Cambridge, MA.

Barney, J. B. 1991. Firm resources and sustained competitive advantage. *Journal of Management* 17: 99–120.

Bartlett, C. A. 1992. *Phillips and Masushita: A Portrait of Two Evolving Companies.* Harvard Business School: Boston, MA, Case No. 9–392–156.

Beauchamp, M. 1988. From Fuji to Everest. *Forbes* 2 May: 35–36.

Blum, E. 1978. Japan's camera makers wage fierce battle in U.S. SLR boom. *Economic World* September: 4–11.

Bowman, E. H. and Hurry, D. 1993. Strategy through the option lens: an integrated view of resource investments and the incremental-choice process. *Academy of Management Review* 19: 760–782.

Bradley, S. P. and Ghemawat, P. 1995. *Wal-Mart Stores, Inc.* Harvard Business School, Boston, MA, Case No. 9–794–024.

*Broadcasting*, 1983. Sony nearly 40 years of making it better and/or smaller. 104(20): 51–56.

Brown, S. I. and Eisenhardt, K. M. 1997. The art of continuous change: linking complexity theory and time-paced evolution in relentlessly shifting organizations. *Administrative Science Quarterly* 42: 1–34.

Browning, E. S. 1985. NEC's telephone products, computers hit trouble: but it keeps on trying. *Wall Street Journal* March 25: A1.

Browning, E. S. 1986. Sony's perseverance helped it win market for mini-CD layers. *Wall Street Journal* 27 February: A1.

Burgess, J. 1999. Sony's co-founder Akio Morita dies *Washington Post* October 4: A1, A14.

*Business Week* 1982. NEC's solo strategy to win the world. 2746 (July 5), 79–80.

*Business Week* 1987. Sony' challenge. 3001 (June 1) 64–69.

Canon, Inc. 2000. The Canon Story/Canon Fact Book http://www.canon.co.jp/story-e/fact/fact01.html [January 6, 2000].

Cavuoto, J. 1984. Laser printers: a status report. *Laser: and Applications* October: 69–72.

Chandler, A. D. 1990. *Scale and Scope: The Dynamic: of Capitalism.* Harvard University Press: Cambridge, MA.

Christensen, C. M. 1997. *The Innovator's Dilemma When New Technologies Cause Great Firms to Fail* Harvard Business School Press: Boston, MA.

Cieply, M. 1983. Sony's profitless prosperity. *Forbes* October 24: 128–134.

Clark, K. B. and Fujimoto, T. 1991. *Product Development Performance: Strategy, Organization, and Management in the World Auto Industry.* Harvard Business School Press: Boston, MA.

Cockburn, I., Henderson, R., and Stern, S. 1999. Exploring the diffusion of science driven drug discovery in pharmaceutical research. Working paper, MIT.

Cohen, W. M. and Levinthal, D. A. 1990. Absorptive capacity: a new perspective on learning and innovation. *Administrative Science Quarterly* 35: 128–152.

Conner, K. R. 1991. A historical comparison of resource-based theory and five schools of thought within industrial organization economics: do we have a new theory of the firm? *Journal of Management* 17: 121–154.

Cusumano, M., Mylonadis, Y., and Rosenbloom, R. 1992. Strategic maneuvering and mass market dynamics: the triumph of VHS over Beta. *Business History Review*, 66: 51–94.

Dyer, J. and Singh, H. 1998. The relational view: cooperative strategy and sources of interorganizational competitive advantage. *Academy of Management Review* 23: 660–679.

*Economic World*. 1976. Canon AE-1 breaks price barrier for electronic SLRs, September: 56–57.

*Economist*. 1982. The giants in Japanese electronics, 282 (February 20): 80–81.

*Economist*. 1983a. Sony and JVC: video wars, 288 (July 9): 66–69.

*Economist*. 1983b. Sony: Beta minus, 289 (24 December): 75–76.

*Economist*. 1984. NEC: a lightning semiconductor, 292 (7372): 84–85.

Fine, C. H. 1998. *Clockspeed: Winning Industry Control in the Age of Temporary Advantage*. Perseus: Reading, MA.

Flaherty, M. T. 1996. *Global Operations Management*. McGraw-Hill: New York.

Gerson, R. 1978. 1978 marks year of recovery for Sony. *Economic World*, May: 26–29.

Ghemawat, P., Collis, D. J., Pisano, G. P., and Rivkin, J. W. 1999. *Strategy and the Business Landscape: Text and Cases*. Addison-Wesley: Reading, MA.

Gomory, R. E. 1987. Dominant science does not mean dominant product. *Research and Development* 29: 72–74.

Gomory, R. E. and Schmitt, R. W. 1988. Science and product. *Science* 240: 1131–1204.

Grant, R. M. 1996. Toward a knowledge-based theory of the firm. *Strategic Management Journal* Winter Special Issue 17: 109–122.

Hayashi, A. 1987. NEC takes the Triple Crown in electronics. *Electronic Business* September 15: 40–48.

Helfat, C. E. 1988. *Investment Choices in Industry*. MIT Press. Cambridge, MA.

Helfat, C. E. 1994. Evolutionary trajectories in petroleum firm R&D. *Management Science* 40: 1720–1747.

Helfat, C. E. 1997. Know-how and asset complementarity and dynamic capability accumulation: the case of R&D. *Strategic Management Journal* 18(5): 339–360.

Heller, R. 1983. What makes Canon boom. *Management Today* September: 62–71.

Helm, L. 1985. Canon: a dream of rivaling Big Blue. *Business Week* May 13: 98–99.

Helper, S. MacDuffie, J. P., and Sabel, C. 1999. The boundaries of the firm as a design problem. Working paper, The Wharton School, University of Pennsylvania.

Henderson, R. and Clark, K. 1990. Architectural innovation: the reconfiguration of existing product technologies and the failure of established firms. *Administrative Science Quarterly* 35: 9–30.

Hof, R. and Gross, N. 1989. Silicon Valley is watching its worst nightmare unfold. *Business Week* September 4, 63: 67.

Iansiti, M. and Clark, K. 1994. Integration and dynamic capability: evidence from product development in automobiles and mainframe computers. *Industrial and Corporate Change* 3: 557–606.

Ibuka, M. 1975. How Sony developed electronics for the world market. *IEEE Transactions of Engineering Management* Em-22 (February): 15–19.

*IEEE Spectrum* 1986. Assessing Japan's role in telecommunications. 23(6): 47–52.

Ishikura, Y. and Porter, M. E. 1983a. *Canon, Inc.* Harvard Business School, Boston, MA: Case No. 9–384–151.

Ishikura, Y. and Porter, M. E. 1983b. *Note on the World Copter Industry in 1983*. Harvard Business School, Boston, MA: Case No. 9–384–152.

Johansson, J. K. 1986. Japanese marketing failures. *International Marketing Review* 3(3): 33–46.

Joseph, J. 1986. Japan begins forging dominion in optical communications. *Data Communications* 15(4): 66–68.

Kaserman, D. L. and Mayo, J. W. 1991. The measurement of vertical economies and the efficient structure of the electric utility industry. *Journal of Industrial Economics* 39: 483–502.

Kim, D., and Kogut, B. 1996. Technological platforms and diversification. *Organization Science* 7: 283–301.

Kobayashi, K. 1986. *Computers and Computers: A Vision of C&C*. MIT Press: Cambridge, MA.

Kogut, B. and Kulatilaka, N. 1997. Capabilities as real options. Paper prepared for the conference on Risk, Managers, and Options, The Wharton School, University of Pennsylvania.

Kogut, B. and Zander, U. 1992. Knowledge of the firm, combinative capabilities, and the replication of technology. *Organization Science* 3: 383–397.

Kraar, L. 1981. Japan's Canon focuses on America. *Fortune*. January 12: 82–88.

Leonard, D. and Sensiper, S. 1998. The role of tacit knowledge in group innovation. *California Management Review* 40: 112–132.

Lyons, N. 1976. *The Sony Vision*. Crown: New York.

March, J. G. 1991. Exploration and exploitation in organizational learning. *Organization Science* 2: 71–87.

McKelvey, B. 1999. Avoiding complexity catastrophe in coevolutionary pockets: strategies for rugged landscapes. *Organization Science* 10: 294–321.

Mead, T. 1985. Patience pays off for NEC America. *Electronic Business* February 1: 56–62.

Meyer, M. 1985. Can anyone duplicate Canon's personal copiers' success? *Marketing and Media Decisions* Spring: 97–101.

Milgrom, P. and Roberts, J. 1990. The economics of modern manufacturing: technology, strategy and organization. *American Economic Review* 80: 511–528.

Monteverde, K. 1995. Technical dialog as an incentive for vertical integration in the semiconductor industry. *Management Science* 41: 1624–1638.

Montgomery, C. A. 1994. Corporate diversification. *Journal of Economic Perspectives* 8: 163–178.

Moore, T. 1982. Canon takes aim at the snapshooter. *Fortune*, 106(2): 38–39.

Morita, A. (with Reingold, E. M. and Shimomura, M.). 1986. *Made in Japan: Akio Morita and Sony*. Signet: New York.

Nathan, J. 1999. *Sony: The Private Life*. Houghton-Mifflin: New York.

NEC. 1984. *NEC Corporation: The First 80 Years*. NEC Corporation: Tokyo.

Nelson, R. R. and Winter, S. G. 1982. *An Evolutionary Theory of Economic Change*. Harvard University Press: Cambridge, MA.

Nonaka, I. and Takeuchi, H. 1995. *The Knowledge-Creating Company*. Oxford University Press: New York.

Patton, P. 1999. Humming off key for two decades. *New York Times*, July 29: E1.

Penrose, E. T. 1959. *The Theory of the Growth of the Firm*. Wiley: New York.

Peteraf, M. A. 1993. The cornerstones of competitive advantage: a resource-based view. *Strategic Management Journal* 14(3): 179–191.

Pollack, A. 1999. Akio Morita, co-founder of Sony and Japanese business leader, dies at 78. *New York Times*, October 4: A28–29.

Port, O. 1987. Canon finally challenges Minolta's mighty Maxxum. *Business Week*, 2987 (March 2, 89–90.

Porter, M. E. 1985. *Competitive Advantage: Creating and Sustaining Superior Performance*. Free Press: New York.

Porter, M. E. 1996. What is strategy? *Harvard Business Review* 74(6): 61–78.

Quinn, J. B., Baruch, J. J., and Zien, K. A. 1997. *Innovation Explosion: Using Intellect and Software to Revolutionize Growth Strategies*. Free Press: New York.

Raubitschek, R. S. 1988a. Hitting the jackpot: product proliferation by multiproduct firms under uncertainty. *International Journal of Industrial Organization* 6: 469–488.

Raubitschek, R. S. 1988b. Multiple scenario analysis and business planning. In *Advances in Strategic Management*, Lamb, R., Shrivastava, P. (eds). Vol. 5: JAI Press: Greenwich, CT: 181–205.

Rivkin, J. 1998. *Airborne Express (A)*. Harvard Business School, Boston, MA, Case no. 9–798–070.

Rosenberg, N. 1982. *Inside the Black Box: Technology and Economics*. Cambridge University Press: Cambridge, UK.

Rosenbloom, R. S. and Cusumano, M. A. 1987. Technological pioneering and competitive advantage: the birth of the VCR industry. *California Management Review* 22: 51–76.

Rubinflen, E., Ono, Y., and Landro, L. 1988. A changing Sony aims to own the 'software' that its products need. *Wall Street Journal* December 3, A1.

Rumelt, R. P. 1984. Towards a strategic theory of the firm. In *Competitive Strategic Management*, Lamb B (ed.). Prentice-Hall: Englewood Cliffs, NJ; 556–570.

Rumelt, R. P., Schendel, D. E., and Teece, D. J. 1994. Fundamental issues in strategy. In *Fundamental Issues in Strategy: A Research Agenda*, Rumelt, R. P., Schendel, D. E., and Teece, D. I. (eds). Harvard Business School Press: Boston, MA; 9–53.

Sanchez, R. and Mahoney, J. T. 1996. Modularity, flexibility, and knowledge management in product and organization design. *Strategic Management Journal* Winter Special Issue 17: 63–76.

Siggelkow, N. 1999. Change in the presence of fit: the rise, the fall, and the renaissance of Liz Claiborne. Working paper, The Wharton School, University of Pennsylvania.

Smart, T. 1999. Delivering packages, partnerships. *Washington Post*, May 2: H1 and H8.

Smith, L. 1984. Japan's two-fister telephone maker. *Fortune* 109(13): 30–36.

Smith, L. 1987. Sony battles back. *Fortune* 111(8): 26–38.

Sullivan, K. 1988. Key word at NEC: applicability. *Business Month* 131(3): 48–49.

Sutherland, D. 1988. Still video: anything there for marketers? *Business Marketing* 73(10): 64–70.

Teece, D. J. 1980. Economies of scope and the scope of the enterprise. *Journal of Economic Behavior and Organization* 1: 223–247.

Teece, D. J. 1986. Profiting from technological innovation: implications from integration, collaboration, licensing and public policy. *Research Policy* 15: 285–305.

Teece, D. J., Pisano, G., and Shuen, A. 1997. Dynamic capabilities and strategic management. *Strategic Management Journal* 18(7): 509–534.

Teece, D. J., Rumelt, R., Dosi, G., and Winter, S. 1994. Understanding corporate coherence: theory and evidence *Journal of Economic Behavior and Organization* 23: 1–30.

Trachtenberg, J. A. 1987. I am betting my destiny. *Forbes* 139(5): 66.

Tushman, M. I. and O'Reilly, C. A. 1996. The ambidextrous organization: managing evolutionary and revolutionary change. *California Management Review* 38: 8–30.

Von Hippel, E. 1976. The dominant role of users in the scientific instrument innovation process. *Research Policy* 5: 212–239.

Von Hippel, E. 1986. Lead users: a source of novel product concepts. *Management Science* 32: 791–805.

Wernerfelt, B. 1984. A resource-based view of the firm. *Strategic Management Journal* 5(2): 171–180.

Wheelwright, S. and Clark, K. B. 1992. *Revolutionizing Product Development*. Free Press: New York.

Winter, S. G. 1987. Knowledge and competence as strategic assets. In *The Competitive Challenge: Strategies for Industrial Innovation and Renewal*, Teece DJ (ed.). Ballinger: Cambridge, MA; 159–184.

Winter, S. G. 1993. On Coase, competence, and the corporation. In *The Nature of the Firm: Origins, Evolution, and Development*, Williamson OE, Winter SG (eds). Oxford University Press: New York: 179–195.

Yamanouchi, T. 1989. Breakthrough: the development of the Canon personal copier. *Long Range Planning* 22(5): 11–21.

Zander, U. and Kogut, B. 1995. Knowledge and the speed of the transfer and imitation of organizational capabilities: an empirical test. *Organization Science* 6: 1–17.

# CHAPTER THIRTEEN

# Path-dependent and Path-breaking Change: Reconfiguring Business Resources Following Acquisitions in the US Medical Sector, 1978–1995

## Samina Karim and Will Mitchell

This paper studies how firms use acquisitions to reconfigure their business resources. Reconfiguration involves the retention, deletion, and addition of resources (Capron, Dussauge, and Mitchell, 1998). We view acquisitions as a key mechanism through which firms attempt to change their businesses (Capron and Mitchell, 1999). Our immediate conceptual goal is to study acquisitions as means of attempting to change both targets and acquires. This study is a step towards understanding the broader issues surrounding successful and failed business change.

The conceptual base for the study derives from what we refer to as a routine-based perspective on strategy, drawing on Williamson (1999). As we describe below, this perspective views firms as bundles of routines, which both provide firm value and create constraints on how businesses change their resources (Mitchell, Dussauge, and Garrette, 1999). Recent research in the strategy field has focused on how acquisitions provide a means by which firms attempt to overcome the constraints on change that existing routines create (Singh and Zollo, 1997; Capron and Mitchell, 1998; Capron, Mitchell, and Swaminathan, 1999). The research suggests that acquisitions help firms to overcome failures of discrete resource exchange that arise due to opportunism and coordination issues surrounding tacit resources. Key open issues remain in this perspective. First, it is not clear whether acquisitions tend to provide greater opportunities for changing resources than other modes of change. Second, the research has not yet determined whether acquisitions serve primarily to deepen firms' existing resource bases or whether acquisitions also provide a means by which firms can extend their activities into areas that require substantially different resources.

This study examines reconfiguration of product lines as a form of resource change, using a sample of more than 3000 US health sector firms that operated during the 1978–95 period. We test several sets of hypotheses. First, we compare product line retention and addition by acquirers and by target businesses. We expect targets to change more than acquirers. Second, we compare product line change of acquirers to those businesses that do not undertake acquisitions. We expect acquirers to change more than firms that do not participate in acquisitions. Third, we attempt to determine whether acquisitions tend to lead primarily to changes in which firms retain target resources that are similar to their own, or whether acquisitions also provide common means by which firms retain new types of resources and thereby undertake resource extension. We expect path-dependent resource deepening to be more common than path-breaking resource extension, but also identify situations in which acquisitions provide a means of undertaking path-breaking change.

The paper proceeds as follows. The first section outlines the conceptual basis and reviews relevant literature. We next develop specific hypotheses concerning acquisitions and business change. We then describe the data and methods that we use in the study. The following sections report the results and conclude the paper.

## Motivation

### Conceptual basis

Our conceptual goal is to help understand causes and processes of business change. Research in strategy, economics, and organizational theory during the past 20 years and more has identified barriers to change. Nonetheless, many businesses do change successfully. Firms use multiple methods to attempt to change. Some changes involve focused methods such as internal development and discrete market exchange, particularly when firms seek specific new resources. Other changes involve interorganizational methods, such as alliances or acquisitions, which require further interaction with other organizations (Capron, Mitchell, and Oxley, 1999). This paper focuses on acquisitions as a mode of changing business resources.

We begin by briefly outlining a framework for a theory of the firm with which we can study these changes. Table 13.1 reviews the basic assumptions concerning this framework.

**Table 13.1** Routine-based perspective assumptions

| Elements of theory | Assumptions |
| --- | --- |
| 1 Behavioral assumptions | Bounded rationality, with firm-specific foresight; potential self-interest |
| 2 Units of analysis | Routines (tacit, co-specialized, organizationally embedded), which combine to form resources. Use of resources generates value Production costs are outcomes of resources |
| 3 Description of the firm | Structure for governing routines and resources. Governance includes coordination, creation, and protection |
| 4 Purposes served | Economizing on the sum of production costs and governance costs. Multifaceted cost dimensions create substantial ambiguity concerning, economizing choices and scope for self-interested choices |
| 5 Efficiency criterion | Relative efficiency of current and future use of overall set of firm resources, based on feasible alternatives |

Williamson (1999) argues that a theory of the firm must specify five conceptual elements, including behavioral assumptions, units of analysis, description of the firm, purpose of the firm, and efficiency criteria. Our behavioral assumptions include potential self-interest plus bounded rationality with firm-specific foresight. We assume that economic actors have the capacity to look ahead and recognize opportunities and risks, but that a firm's experience shapes its foresight. This assumption of firm-specific foresight suggests that firms commonly recognize potential opportunities to gain efficiencies with existing resources or create new resources via acquisitions or divestitures, but that different firms will have different expectations about the potential outcome of acquisition activity.

Our fundamental unit of analysis is the routine, which in turn closely relates to the concept of resources. Routines are identifiable patterns of activity embodied in human or capital assets (Nelson and Winter, 1982; Winter, 1990; Dosi, Marengo, and Fagiolo, 1996). Several routines combine together to create particular resources. Resources, which we view as synonymous with the term capabilities, are stocks of knowledge, skills, financial assets, physical assets, human capital, and other tangible and intangible factors (Wernerfelt, 1984; Grant, 1996a; Amit and Schoemaker, 1993). Resources tend to be only semi-decomposable into their underlying routines, so that resources provide relevant units of analysis as well as their underlying routines. We will use product lines as the operational measure of resources in our discussion of acquisitions, as we discuss later in the paper, with the assumption that different product lines require different sets of routines.

We will discuss routines and resources in additional detail later in the paper. For the moment, we will note here that routines contain much of the knowledge of what a firm is able to accomplish (Hannan and Freeman, 1989). Routines consist of multiple related transactions that take place over time either within a firm or via interaction with external parties. Routines are often tacit, either because they are intrinsically uncodifiable or because they require the interactive participation of multiple people. Routines also tend to be co-specialized with other routines and to be embedded in broader organizational contexts. Routines and the resources that they create are often firm-specific and imperfectly tradable, owing to their tacitness, co-specialization, and organizational embeddedness.

The need for acquisitions arises from the imperfect tradability of routine and resources. That is, firms often need to acquire other businesses in order to extract value from underutilized resources the firms possess, either through more efficient use of existing resources or through the creation of new resources. By merging, firms may pool similar resources in order to gain greater efficiency, so long as increased economies of scale more than outweigh the governance costs of acquisitions. In addition, acquisitions may allow firms to combine the routines that underlie different types of resources in order to create valuable new resources, again including governance costs.

Our description of the firm and our view of the purpose of the firm both involve assumptions concerning the role of the firm in governing resources. We describe a firm as a governance structure, where governance includes coordinating the use of existing resources, creating new resources, and protecting the value of resources. This view closely follows Coriat and Dosi (1998), who argue that a firm is a particular set of routines that result from the co-evolution between corporate patterns of knowledge distribution and mechanisms of governance. Governance mechanisms include formal and informal incentive and control systems, legal regimes, organizational structures, and corporate cultures. Governance mechanisms will often be shaped by path dependency and local search, which arise from the tacitness, co-specialization, and organizational embeddedness of routines (Kogut and Zander, 1992; Capron and Mitchell, 1999). In turn, the purpose of the firm is to economize on the combination of production costs and governance costs. A key implication of our approach is that production costs are partly an endogenous outcome of firm-specific resources and governance mechanisms. That is, production costs vary depending on the nature of a firm's resources and the effectiveness with which a firm governs the use and creation of resources.

Our efficiency criterion is of the best available value of current and future use of routines, by which we mean that a firm seeks the best available mechanisms to jointly protect, coordinate, and create resources. In this paper, our emphasis will be on factors that differentiate the types of resources that firms use from acquisitions that create either efficiency or expansion opportunities, along with the protection mechanisms that the firms use to protect the value of the resources.

Overall, our conceptual approach combines the protection emphasis of governance perspectives such as transaction cost economics (Williamson, 1999) with the coordination emphasis of routine-based research. The fundamental difference between our approach and protection perspectives is that we focus on routines rather than individual transactions. In turn, this leads us to emphasize firms' coordination and creation governance roles in addition to their protection role. This combined emphasis on protection, coordination, and creation credits the firm with a critical role in both enhancing the value of existing resources and creating new resources. Our focus on routines as the fundamental units brings our approach close to that of evolutionary economics (Nelson and Winter, 1982). Our immediate goal is to study acquisitions as means of changing the capabilities of targets and acquirers, that is, of reconfiguring the resources that firms must create, coordinate, and protect.

## Literature review

Many studies in economics, organizational theory, and strategic management address the subjects of acquisition and change. Despite the extensive study, though, there is little consensus between theories and empirical works. Below we highlight several perspectives and their insights into acquisitions and change.

### Acquisition causes and effects

Economic theories addressing acquisitions highlight market power, efficiency, and risk as factors leading to a diversification strategy. Industrial organization economic theory focuses on environmental factors influencing firms and proposes that firms may pursue acquisitions in order to increase their current market power, consolidate an industry's businesses, avoid high barriers to entry, or change supply chain relationships (Bain, 1956; Caves, 1981). Transaction cost economics highlights internal efficiencies of scope and scale, and hypothesizes that related diversification can improve allocative efficiency in the sense that diversification establishes an internal capital market

(Williamson, 1975; Teece, 1982). The financial economics literature hypothesizes that diversification may stem from "free cash flow" (Jensen, 1986), from managers' assumptions that compensation is a function of organizational size instead of profits (Teece, 1982), or as a mechanism in the market for corporate control to replace inefficient management with more competent managers (Jensen and Ruback, 1983). Diversification may have positive outcomes including lowering of systematic risk (Jensen and Ruback, 1983; Lubatkin, 1987; Chatterjee and Lubatkin, 1990), increasing leveraging potential, and creating more stable cash flows (Amit and Livnat, 1988), but may also result negatively in the cross-subsidization of low-performing, unrelated segments (Jensen, 1986; Berger and Ofek, 1995). Therefore, there is no consensus about acquisitions in the economic literature.

In the organizational literature, the resource dependence perspective and institutional theory focus on organizations' influences upon one another. From a resource dependence perspective, which views the environment as full of resource exchange relationships and dependencies which distribute social power and create business constraints, acquisitions may allow organizations to change their relationships and, in turn, their environment (Pfeffer and Salancik, 1978). Institutional theory hypothesizes that organizations become similar due to institutional pressures of legitimacy and isomorphism, a process that makes organizations resemble other units facing similar environmental conditions (DiMaggio and Powell, 1983). In times of uncertainty or change, an organization may mimic another firm's acquisition strategy if it views that firm to be more legitimate or successful. The population ecology perspective highlights the strong environmental influences upon organizations and stresses that different organizational forms arise more from environmental selection than from organizational adaptation (Hannan and Freeman, 1984, 1989). Ecological studies have studied divestitures and show that they differ empirically from dissolutions, but without providing a clear conceptual rationale for the differences.

Although literature from economics and organizational theory provide insight into reasons that firms pursue acquisitions, they tend to focus rearward, emphasizing use of acquisitions to correct past mistakes or to increase the efficiency of existing operations. In addition to such rearward activities, though, organizations must engage in ongoing changes of their operations and strategic positions due to changing competitive environments. In this forward-looking view, acquisitions are a means of pursuing potential future competitive advantages. We continue with a review of the literature from the field of strategic management that has addressed this outlook.

The traditional strategy literature emphasized understanding the process of economic efficiency. This work focuses on resource-based causes of acquisition activity and studies acquisition performance outcomes. Penrose (1959) hypothesized that a business's resource base influences its diversification pattern. Related and unrelated diversification may depend on the types of excess resources that are available (Chatterjee and Wernerfelt, 1991). Studies on performance outcomes of acquisitions have mixed results. Some studies find that target shareholders tend to fare better than acquirer shareholders (Bradley, Desai, and Kim, 1988). Studies have found gains from related diversification (Singh and Montgomery, 1987; Wernerfelt and Montgomery, 1988), gains from unrelated acquisitions (Chatterjee, 1986), and no significant differences in returns to the bidding firm between related and unrelated acquisitions (Lubatkin, 1987; Lubatkin and O'Neill, 1988). Research on acquisition process and performance has highlighted the importance of targeting and integration (Porter, 1987; Hunt, 1990; Datta, 1991), including the value of employee retention (Walsh, 1988; Cannella and Hambrick, 1993) and knowledge transfer (Ranft, 1997). Capron (1999) shows that performance tends to increase with postacquisition reconfiguration of targets and acquirers. Overall, there is no empirical consensus on the expected returns from acquisitions. One reason for the lack of consensus stems from the need to understand more about the role of acquisitions in obtaining new resources, as opposed to emphasizing gains from more efficient use of existing resources.

*The market for firms*
Increasingly, the strategy literature has begun to consider how firms restructure to maintain a competitive advantage in changing environments. Researchers have spent much time developing the concept of intangible assets and their failure in markets for discrete resource exchange. Market failure in the exchange of tacit resources stems partly from potential opportunism and partly from knowledge and learning limitations within organizations. Theorists have developed a theory of economic organization that argues that in the case of tacit resources the market for firms is often more robust than the market for resources.

Obtaining tacit resources is often a goal of acquisitions. The evolutionary perspective on strategy theorizes that tacit resources such as knowledge and organizational memory reside in an organization's structure via the routines that the organization maintains (Cyert and March, 1963; Nelson and Winter, 1982). Routines include norms, procedures, and conventions around which an organization functions (Levitt and March, 1988). The embeddedness of routines supports acquisition; routines may remain intact and personnel with critical experience may transfer to the new organization. Acquisitions may serve to minimize issues of bounded rationality and time compression diseconomies that constrain the content and speed at which people learn (Simon, 1945; Dierickx and Cool, 1989), making acquisitions preferred to internal development. Exchange of information, which tends to be a tacit resource, often fails in the market for discrete exchange. Not only is information often tacit and uncodifiable, it also suffers from appropriability issues: first, exchange opportunities may be limited due to protecting the knowledge resource, and second, information acts as a public good and has severe impactedness problems (Teece, 1980, 1986; Grant, 1996b). These arguments all suggest that acquisition of tacit resources through the buying and selling of firms or business units may be more robust than the market for discrete exchange.

Studies on restructuring and post-acquisition change of targets and acquirers have provided empirical evidence of the market for firms. In their study of Swedish firms, Granstrand and Sjolander (1990) showed that large firms developed and exploited their technological capabilities by trading small firms. More recently, Capron et al. (1998) studied the redeployment of resources between target and acquiring businesses following horizontal acquisitions and confirmed that redeployment was more intense for resources that faced greater market failure. Thus, recent focus has turned to view acquisitions as mechanisms of change used to reconfigure targets and acquirers. Much of this research now emphasizes postacquisition analysis and the redeployment of resources between organizations.

*Long-term reconfiguration*

The empirical studies we reviewed above tend to focus on near-term acquisition activities and changes. At the same time, though, the theoretical perspectives, particularly those that focus on the presence of routines and resources, suggest that post-acquisition activities and implications will tend to take place over periods of years. Our interests lie in observing long-term effects of reconfiguration within acquirers and targets. This section addresses longer-term reconfiguration implications of acquisitions.

Longer-term reconfiguration requires changing businesses' resources. Resources have sometimes been defined as tangible and intangible assets that are tied semipermanently to the firm (Wernerfelt, 1984). Competitive pressures require that organizations change their mix of resources to create new opportunities (Penrose, 1959; Porter, 1979). Resources may provide many services to an organization. Penrose noted that "Services yielded by resources are a function of the way in which they are used . . .", so that resources consist of a bundle of potential services. She continues, "it is largely in this distinction that we find the source of the uniqueness of each individual firm" (Penrose, 1959: 25).

In this study, we use product lines, including both physical goods and nonphysical services, as measures of resources. As we noted above, Penrose (1959) argues that firms may use resources in different ways and this ultimately provides firms with their uniqueness. We believe this difference in resource use is evident from the unique product lines and services that the firms offer. Recall that our theory states that routines combine together to create resources. Different resources may involve the use of different routines or a different combination of similar routines. Based on our theory, a firm producing two different product lines is either using two different sets of routines, where some of the routines may be common to both product lines, to create those product lines or similar sets of routines that are combined differently. In the latter case, routines may have different linkages between them that create the combinations. If two firms produce the same product line, we assume that there is substantial similarity in the routines that underlie the product line. We further assume that there is more similarity between routines of the same product lines from different firms as compared to different product lines from different firms. We believe that the product lines of business organizations are an appropriate measure of firms' resources.

Several studies that have studied the market for firms have used the terms restructuring and redeployment as forms of reconfiguration. Restructuring means the buying or selling of businesses within an organization (Porter, 1987; Bowman and Singh, 1993). Resource redeployment means "the use by a target or acquiring business of the other business' resources" (Capron et al., 1998: 635). At the most general level, we define reconfiguration to be the change of resources within an organization. In this study, we consider reconfiguration to be greater when organizations retain fewer product lines and/or add more product lines over time.

In studying how acquirers reconfigure, we develop resource retention arguments below that differentiate between resource deepening and resource extension. We define resource deepening as the retention of product lines that overlap with current product lines. Conversely, resource extension involves retaining product lines that are distinct from a firm's current product lines. Resource deepening represents path-dependent change, while resource extension represents path-breaking change.

## Hypotheses

Our hypotheses investigate two aspects of reconfiguration through acquisitions. First, we are interested in acquisitions as mechanisms for change. We hypothesize about the change of targets and acquirers vs. businesses that do not undergo or undertake acquisitions. Second, for businesses that participate in acquisitions, we predict the forms of change and resource retention an acquirer will achieve.

### Baseline reconfiguration comparisons

Acquisitions behave as mechanisms for change in the sense that they provide a target and acquirer with new resources and opportunities. Penrose (1959) described a firm as basically a collection of resources. The evolutionary perspective and knowledge-based theories of firms have stressed the importance of tacit resources such as knowledge and memory that reside in routines in the structures of organizations (Nelson and Winter, 1982; Levitt and March, 1988). Organizations also hold values, norms, and culture that are difficult to imitate in different contexts. Barney describes such features as socially complex resources that contribute to competitive advantage. Barney states, "understanding that . . . an organizational culture with certain attributes . . . can improve a firm's efficiency and effectiveness does not necessarily imply that firms without these attributes can engage in systematic efforts to create them . . . Such social engineering may be . . . beyond the capabilities of most firms" (Barney, 1991: 110). If resources are tacit or socially complex, organizations may be unable to develop them internally and may procure them through acquisitions.

By obtaining resources through the process of acquisitions, organizations may open doors to new opportunities. Strategists who studied restructuring have shown how firms created new opportunities because of changes in their business lines (Porter, 1987; Hoskisson and Johnson, 1992; Singh, 1993). Firms may use acquisitions to pursue opportunities that allow for shared activities or the transfer of skills (Porter, 1987). Post acquisition, recombination provides opportunities for change. Schumpeter (1934) viewed innovations as new combinations of knowledge and learning. In their dynamic perspective on learning. Kogut and Zander (1992) also view new opportunities and capabilities as the result of combining new skills and resources. Acquisitions also allow for opportunities to enter new industries. Penrose summarized:

> Acquisition can be a means of obtaining the productive services and knowledge that are necessary for a firm to establish itself in a new field, and the addition of new managerial and technical services to the firm's internal supply of productive services is often far more important than the elimination of competition and the reduction of the costs of entry. For this reason acquisition is often a peculiarly suitable means of becoming acquainted with the techniques and problems of a new field when a firm wants to decide whether expansion in that field is an appropriate use of its own resources. (Penrose, 1959: 126)

Organizations may revert to acquisition strategies because of impediments of internal development. Not only may internal growth require a long time for the accrual of returns, but also its incremental nature may be more expensive than purchasing an ongoing business (Singh and Montgomery, 1987). Huber (1991: 97) also noted that in cases of imperfect imitability or time pressures "sometimes grafting-on of carriers of new knowledge is done on a large-scale basis, as in the case of an acquisition of a whole organization by another." Empirical work has also shown that acquisitions can serve as an alternative to internal investment in R&D since they offer immediate entrance to a new market or a larger share of an existing market presence (Hitt, Hoskisson, and Ireland, 1990). They argue that "the outcomes are more certain and can be estimated (or forecasted) more accurately with acquisitions than with internal development." "Therefore, acquisitions may serve as a substitute for innovations" (Hitt et al., 1990: 31). Capron et al. (1998: 631), meanwhile, found that "firms often use acquisitions in order to reconfigure the acquiring or target businesses as part of the process of commercial change." In comparing targets to continuing businesses, Granstrand and Sjolander (1990) found that acquired firms grew faster after acquisition than nonacquired firms. We believe that participants in acquisitions will have more opportunities available to them because of the presence of new resources. These opportunities may result in organizational change. Thus, we hypothesize that acquisition participants will change more than non-participants.

Hypothesis 1a: Acquired businesses change more than continuing businesses.

Hypothesis 1b: Continuing businesses that acquire targets change more than continuing businesses that do not acquire targets.

## Post-acquisition resource retention: alternatives

Firms participating in acquisitions face the issue of what to do with a target's resources. Acquirers may choose to retain the target's lines or divest them. We are interested in reconfiguration: the degree of retention as compared to addition of new lines. Acquirers may retain product lines that are similar to their own or distinct from their current collection. In the hypotheses below, we present resource retention questions that address resource deepening vs. resource extension.

### Resource deepening: path-dependent change

We view firms that retain resources that are similar to the firms' existing resources as pursuing path-dependent change. Firms accumulate resources as a result of path-dependent actions of learning, investments, and other organizational activities the firms take over time (Dierickx and Cool, 1989). Acquirers will commonly build on current capabilities instead of exploring new areas. Organizations may pursue a strategy to develop and effectively exploit a core competence (Andrews, 1987; Prahalad and Hamel, 1990). Prahalad and Hamel (1990) describe core competencies as the collective learning of the organization. Core competencies are the "complex harmonization of individual technologies and production skills" (Prahalad and Hamel, 1990: 83). This harmonization and learning may be more effective if similar resources are retained.

Theorists commonly argue that learning and the accumulation of knowledge possess path-dependent traits. Knowledge includes information (who knows what) and know-how (how to do something) (Kogut and Zander, 1992). von Hippel (1988) notes that know-how is the accumulated practical skill or expertise that allows one to do something smoothly and efficiently. Skills and experience condition the alternatives that management is able to perceive. "Where a firm can go is a function of its current position and the paths ahead. Its current position is often shaped by the path it has traveled" (Teece, Pisano, and Shuen, 1997: 522). Positions and paths are affected by learning processes (Teece et al., 1997). The absorptive capacity perspective highlights that the ability to learn is a function of what is already known (Cohen and Levinthal, 1990). Helfat (1994), for instance, shows that path-dependent routines shape firm investment. Similarly, the knowledge-based view of the firm acknowledges that the "capacity for aggregation" is important for recipients to be able to add new knowledge to existing knowledge (Grant, 1996a).

Along with sheer resource accumulation, the relatedness or commonality of resources may determine whether firms observe opportunities for learning. "Learning is cumulative, and learning performance is greatest when the object of learning is related to what is already known" (Cohen and Levinthal, 1990; 131). Prior knowledge enhances learning because memory is developed by associative learning (Fiol and Lyles, 1985; Huber, 1991). Kogut and Zander (1992) note that firms learn in areas closely related to their existing practice because the sharing of a common stock of knowledge facilitates the transfer of knowledge within groups.

Although related resources have benefits, several drawbacks also arise. First, the lack of balance between exploration and exploitation of current capabilities and resources can be self-destructive for an organization (March, 1991). Firms also need to be concerned about falling into competency traps where routines or actions that led to good performance in the past are used repeatedly even though they may be far from optimal (Levitt and March, 1988).

Based on the benefits and channels of related resources, we hypothesize that acquirers are more likely to retain targets' resources that are common to their own and pursue path-dependent change than retain distinct resources.

> Hypothesis 2a (resource-deepening argument): The greater the overlap of acquirer and target resources, the more likely that acquirers will retain targets' resources and their own resources.

### Resource extension: path-breaking change

The previous hypothesis proposed that acquirers are most likely to pursue path-dependent change and retain targets' resources that overlap with their existing resources. Nonetheless, the resource retention argument further expects that path-breaking change may occur in cases where expansion incentives and competitive pressures outweigh path dependence. Path-breaking change occurs when acquirers retain targets' resources that are distinct from their own.

Acquirers often have incentives to retain distinct resources in changing environments. Earlier we noted that resources provide firms with new opportunities. Distinct resources may provide an organization with potential competitive advantages in the future. In times of change, firms can create new advantages by having innovative responses (Teece et al. 1997). Theorists sometimes refer to this as a dynamic capabilities perspective. Prahalad and Hamel stress the importance of being a dynamic organization that builds core competencies. "Core competencies are the collective learning in the organization, especially how to coordinate diverse production skills and integrate multiple streams of technologies' (Prahalad and Hamel, 1990: 81). They state that "a company that has failed to invest in core competence building will find it very difficult to enter an emerging market" (Prahalad and Hamel, 1990: 84). Retaining distinct resources forces an organization to pursue greater degrees of coordination and integration, and such an organization may thus develop greater core competencies and dynamic capabilities.

Firms may also retain distinct resources if they provide a unique competitive advantage. Teece (1986) notes the importance of complementary assets that can be utilized in conjunction with other capabilities or assets and may be needed for the successful commercialization of an innovation. Complementary assets may come in the form of distinctive resources.

Resources have different value for different buyers depending on the potential synergy that they believe will come from owning the assets (Wernerfelt, 1984). Barney (1988) has stressed that acquisitions will create value when there are private and uniquely inimitable cash flows between the acquiring and target firm. By private and unique, he means that other buyers could not realize the potential synergies that may be created and, even if they did, they could not duplicate the synergy. Based on Barney's theories of unique synergies, Harrison, Hitt, and Ireland (1991) proposed that firms can create uniquely valuable synergy when differences exist in resources. They tested differences in resource allocations and found that differences did contribute significantly to performance.

Although dominant theories predict that similarities in resources create value and are most likely, acquirers may pursue path-breaking change and retain resources that are distinct from their own. These resources may help an organization further develop its core competencies and dynamic capabilities, or provide competitive advantage through unique synergies with existing resources. Wernerfelt (1984: 179; *italics in original*) reminds us that "candidates for products or resource diversification must be evaluated . . . in terms of their long-term capacity to function as *stepping stones* to further expansion." Thus we hypothesize:

> Hypothesis 2b (resource extension argument): Acquirers tend to retain target resources that are distinct from the acquirer's preacquisition resources.

In summary, we have developed two sets of hypotheses. The first set of hypotheses compares targets, acquirers, and nonacquirers. We expect target businesses to change more than acquirers and also expect acquirers to change more than nonacquirers. The second set of hypotheses addresses the impact of resource overlap of targets and acquirers on resource retention. A resource-deepening argument suggests that greater similarity will lead to greater retention, while a path-breaking argument suggests that greater difference will lead to greater retention. We expect the resource-deepening result to be the more common than resource-extension, but we want to explore situations in which resource extension also occurs.

## Data and Methods

### Data

The study uses data from several editions of the *Medical & Healthcare Marketplace Guide*, published in 1975, 1978, 1983, 1986, 1989, and each year thereafter.[1] The guides include information concerning US and non US firms operating in the US medical sector, including information concerning what product lines they offer each year. The guides include information about almost all medical sector firms of any appreciable size, including firms that focus on the medical sector (e.g., Medtronics, Inc.) and companies with extensive nonmedical activities (e.g., General Electric, Inc.), and also contain information about many smaller medical sector businesses. We gathered initial information concerning more than 2500 medical sector firms. We examined panel data for firms operating in 1978 and 1983. Of those firms operating in 1978 and 1983, we found which had pursued acquisitions, which had been acquired, and which continued onwards without acquisition activity by 1995. We chose the 1978 and 1983 panels as baselines for the study, using information from the 1975 guide to provide data concerning prior characteristics of the firms. The firms in the 1983 panel are companies that entered the guides after 1978, either because they were new entrants to the health sector or because the guide did not record information for them in 1978.

For each panel, we noted the product lines the firms offered in that year. We further categorized these product lines into broader sectors of more distinct sets of resources, including medical devices, dental devices, ophthalmic devices, pharmaceutical products, and healthcare services. By tracking firms and their acquirers and then recording their product lines in 1995, we identified which product lines the firms had dropped, retained, or added. The data base also provided data on firms' attributes such as public or private ownership, sales levels, founding date, site locations, profitability, top officers, subsidiaries, and a brief review of a firm's history. Overall, we had data on 1244 firms and 3387 firm-product line combinations in the 1978 panel, plus 2237 firms with 5421 firm-product line combinations in the 1983 panel. Of the firms in the 1978 panel, 853 also operated in 1983, so that we have a total of 2628 unique firms in the two panels. We also gathered product line and firm characteristic data for 437 firms that acquired participants of the 1978 and 1983 panels, gathering information from the time of acquisition and from the end of the sample periods for each of the acquirers.

To study the change in targets, acquirers, and nonacquirers, we compared the changes in product lines of the firms. We calculated the relative reconfiguration of targets, acquirers, nonacquirers, and continuing businesses from 1983 to 1995.

### Statistical methods

We used logistic regression for the empirical analysis of the resource retention questions (Pindyck and Rubinfeld, 1981; Menard, 1995; Greene, 1997). We are interested in the likelihood that a business retains a product line from 1978 or 1983 in 1995. Because our dependent variable is a dichotomous variable, we were unable to use a linear probability model. A logit model ensures that the probabilities will be within the [0,1] range. We estimated the logit model using a maximum-likelihood estimation procedure which results in parameter estimates that are consistent and asymptotically efficient for large samples. We test the significance of the entire logit model with the model log likelihood chi-square, which is analogous to the multivariate F-test in linear regression testing the null hypothesis that all coefficients are zero. Further, for each estimate, we conduct a two-tailed significance test of the Wald statistic, which is the ratio of the estimated coefficient to its estimated standard error and follows a chi-square distribution.

**Variables and expected outcomes**

Our dichotomous dependent variable in this study was the retention or disposal of a target's product line by the acquirer. For every acquisition case in our sample of firms operating in 1978 and/or 1983, we observed the product lines belonging to the target immediately prior to the acquisition and coded them 0 or 1 depending on whether the acquirer retained the lines in 1995. If the initial acquirer was acquired, in turn, we determined whether the ultimate acquirer retained the lines in 1995.

Table 13.2 lists the independent variables. We first discuss the focal variables, which we use to study the retention of product lines based on target and acquirer resource overlaps and distinctions. Table 13.2 lists these as variables for *Target – acquirer resource overlap and distinction*. Three variables address resource deepening. *Focal line overlap* captures whether or not an acquirer possessed the product line before the acquisition, *Complementary line overlap* is the number of lines shared by acquirer and target (excluding any focal overlap), and *Category overlap* records the number of overlapping categories (excluding the focal category). Our expectation, based on Hypothesis 2a, is that the overlap variables will result in positive relationship with line retention. Four variables address resource extension: *Target line distinction* and *Acquirer line distinction* record the number of nonoverlapping lines at the target and at the acquirer, while *Target category distinction* and *Acquirer category distinction* record the number of nonoverlapping categories at the target and acquirer. Although we expect resource extension to be less common than resource deepening, we do expect to find evidence of extension. Thus, based on Hypothesis 2b, we expect variables measuring distinction will have positive estimates but will be smaller relative to those of deepening.

The distinction between product lines and categories helps explore the different incentives and abilities to undertake resource deepening and extension. New product lines within existing categories represent incremental expansion, while new categories represent more path-breaking expansion. Firms can often undertake incremental expansion via internal development rather than through the more complex mode of acquisitions, but will tend to find internal path-breaking expansion into new categories to be much more difficult. Therefore, it is possible that postacquisition product line resource extension retention may be more common for new categories extension than for new lines within existing categories.

We also introduce control variables that may account for why firms retain certain product lines. As table 13.2 notes, we include controls for industry factors, medical category dummies, target attributes, and acquirer attributes.

**Table 13.2** Variables and expected relationship with resource retention

| Variable | Expected |
|---|---|
| **Industry factors** | |
| 1 No. of firms with product line before acquisition | + |
| 2 No. of firms with line increased, post acquisition | + |
| 3 Line was new to industry: introduced after 1978 | ? |
| | |
| **Medical category dummies** ("Medical devices" is the baseline category) | |
| 4 Category: healthcare services | − |
| 5 Category: dental devices | . |
| 6 Category: ophthalmic devices | . |
| 7 Category: pharmaceutical products | + |
| | |
| **Target attributes** | |
| 8 Medical sales (in $ millions) | + |
| 9 Non-medical corporate sales (in $ millions) | − |
| 10 Target age (log years) | + |
| 11 US target | ? |
| 12 Target profitability (ROS) | + |
| 13 Established line at target (exists in prior panel) | + |
| 14 Target business has single product line | + |
| 15 No. of product lines at target business | − |
| | |
| **Target-acquirer resource overlap and distinction** | |
| Resource-deepening variables | |
| 16 Focal line overlap: acquirer had line before acquisition | + |
| 17 Complementary line overlap: no. of non-focal shared lines | + |
| 18 Category overlap: no. of non-focal shared categories | + |
| Resource extension variables | |
| 19 Target line distinction: no. of non-overlapping lines at target | + |
| 20 Acquirer line distinction: no. of non-overlapping lines at acquirer | + |
| 21 Target category distinction: no. of non-overlapping categories at target | + |
| 22 Acquirer category distinction: no. of non-overlapping categories at acquirer | + |
| | |
| **Acquirer attributes** | |
| 23 Target was divested as a stand-alone business | − |
| 24 Acquirer preacquisition sales (In $ millions) | + |
| 25 Acquirer age | + |
| 26 Acquirer was US firm | + |
| 27 Acquisition year | + |
| 28 No. of times pursued acquisitions, 1983–95 | − |
| 29 Selection equation probability (see below) | − |

Selection equation: logit using log age, log medical sales, and number of lines as independent variables and 1995 continuation or acquisition as the dependent variable.

Table 13.2 lists three industry factors. As industrial organization economics suggests, firms may base their strategies on competitors' actions. We control for the number of firms in the medical sector that possessed the product line prior to the acquisition and the number of firms that increased their product line after the year in which the acquisition occurred; we expect both coefficients to be positive. We also consider whether a line had only recently appeared in the healthcare sector, with introduction after 1978, but it is unclear in which direction it will have effect.

Table 13.2 lists the medical sector categories. We categorized product lines as belonging to five broad categories: medical devices (187 lines), healthcare services (46 lines), dental devices (5 lines), ophthalmic devices (7 lines), and pharmaceutical products (16 lines). In our analysis, we omitted the medical device category from the list of dummy variables to avoid perfect collinearity between categories. In comparing the other categories to the medical device category, we expect healthcare services may be easier to change and less likely to be retained whereas pharmaceuticals are less easily reconfigured and more likely to be retained. Owing to their common status as devices, it is difficult to distinguish the attributes of dental, ophthalmic, and medical devices.

Table 13.2 also lists variables describing target and acquirer attributes. For both targets and acquirers, we recorded corporate age and whether the firms were based in the United States. Acquirers, as they age, gain experience and routines that may help them to integrate the target and retain product lines. We also expect older targets to be retained as a result of having greater experience and routines. We expect that US-based acquirers will tend to possess wider ranges of US market-specific routines than firms based in other countries, so that US acquirers may be able to retain a greater variety of product lines. How US-owned vs. foreign ownership of targets might influence the likelihood of an acquirer retaining a targets' lines is unclear.

Other attributes of targets in the model include their level of medical and nonmedical sales, their profitability measured as return on sales, if a product line is the only line that they possess, their total number of product lines, and whether a product line was an "established" line. "Established" line refers to a product line having been present at the firm in the former temporal panel. Having an established line, greater medical sales, greater profitability, and fewer lines reflect dedicated routines and we expect that retention is likely. Greater nonmedical sales and number of product lines implies greater fragmentation of investment and less likelihood of retention.

Under acquirers' attributes, we also include in the model their preacquisition level of total sales, the acquisition year, whether or not the target was later divested as a stand-alone business, and the number of times the acquirer undertook acquisitions between 1983 and 1995. Retention is less likely if the target was later divested as lines tend to move with the target, and also if an acquirer pursues many acquisitions and is pursuing a reconfiguration strategy. Retention is more likely for recent acquisitions having had less time for reconfiguration, and also for larger sales acquirers who may be more capable of maintaining and supporting a product line.

Finally, we include the output of a selection equation as an independent variable in our model. The selection equation refers to the likelihood that a firm will become acquired, which we modeled as a logistic regression based on a firm's age, medical sales, and number of product lines. Recall that in our Hypotheses 1a and 1b we predict that acquisitions act as mechanisms for change and reconfiguration. Acquirers may pursue acquisitions to gain targets' resources and then reconfigure their product lines. Based on this theory, we expect that the greater the likelihood that a firm becomes a target, the less likely that its product lines will be retained.

In summary, we have operationalized the focal variables for our study, which emphasize target–acquirer resource overlap and distinction. We have also measured control variables concerning industry, product, target, and acquirer firm attributes that the economic, organizational theory, and strategy literatures suggest will influence postacquisition resource retention, along with a selection equation for acquisition likelihood. We next report the tests of our hypotheses.

## Results

### Baseline reconfiguration comparisons

We predicted that targets would change more than continuing businesses, and also that continuing businesses that participated in acquisitions would change more than those that did not. To test our hypotheses, we examined product lines of firms operating in 1983 and compared them to their state in 1995. Table 13.3(a) reports the comparison of reconfiguration of targets, acquirers, and non-acquirers between 1983 and 1995.

Hypothesis 1a predicted that targets would change more than continuing firms. Table 13.3(a) reports that 2237 firms operated in 1983 with 5421 product lines, with about half (1117 firms) continuing in 1995. These firms that continued dropped 28 percent of their lines, retained 72 percent, and added 97 percent new lines. Thus, continuing firms reconfigured 134 percent (97 percent over 72 percent) of their businesses. Of the 2237 firms of 1983, 377 became targets before 1995. These targets had held 1171 lines in 1983. By 1995, acquirers had dropped 49 percent of the targets' lines and retained 51 percent. Moreover, when we consider the targets' preacquisition lines in concert with the 1995 lines of their acquirer, we find that the targets had gained access to line addition of 263 percent. Thus, targets' product lines had less retention (51 percent vs. 72 percent) and greater overall reconfiguration (520 percent vs. 134 percent) than continuing businesses, consistent with Hypothesis 1a.

Hypothesis 1b predicted that acquirers would change more than nonacquirers. As table 13.3(a) shows, of the 1117 firms from 1983 that remained in 1995, 98 (9 percent) pursued acquisitions and 1019 (91 percent) did not. The 98 acquirers had possessed 641 product lines prior to 1983. By 1995, these firms that were active in the acquisition market had dropped 33 percent of their 1983 lines, retained 67 percent, and added 125 percent new lines. Thus, acquirers reconfigured 187 percent (125 percent over 67 percent) of their businesses. The remaining 1019 continuing firms that did not partake in acquisitions held 2323 product lines in 1983. By 1995, they had dropped 27 percent of these lines, retained 73 percent, and added 89 percent. Thus, continuing firms that did not participate in acquisitions reconfigured 121 percent (89 percent over 73 percent). These results imply that acquirers change more than nonacquirers, both by adding more new lines and dropping more old lines, supporting Hypothesis 1b.

Table 13.3b reports similar figures for the 1978–83 period, which reinforce the conclusions that we draw from table 3a for the comparison of targets and continuing

**Table 13.3** Resource reconfiguration

| | Firms in 1983 | Lines in 1983 | Mean lines in 1983 | Firms in 1995 | Lines in 1995 | Mean lines in 1995 | Lines dropped, 1983–95 | Lines retained, 1983–95 | Lines added, 1983–95 | Lines added/ retained |
|---|---|---|---|---|---|---|---|---|---|---|
| **(a) Resource reconfiguration: product line retention and addition, 1983–95** | | | | | | | | | | |
| Total firms and lines in 1983 | 2237 | 5421 | 2.4 | 3868 | 12,926 | 3.3 | | | | |
| A. Continue in 1995 | 1117 | 2964 | 2.7 | 1117 | 4,996 | 4.5 | 832 28% | 2132 72% | 2864 97% | 134% |
| A1. Acquirers | 98 | 641 | 6.5 | 98 | 1,235 | 12.6 | 210 33% | 431 67% | 804 125% | 187% |
| A2. Non-acquirers | 1019 | 2323 | 2.3 | 1019 | 3,761 | 3.7 | 622 27% | 1701 73% | 2060 89% | 121% |
| B. Became targets before 1995 | 377 | 1171 | 3.1 | | | | 579 49% | 592 51% | 3081 263% | 520% |
| C. Shut before 1995 | 743 | 1286 | 1.7 | | | | | | | |

| | Firms in 1978 | Lines in 1978 | Mean lines in 1978 | Firms in 1983 | Lines in 1983 | Mean lines in 1983 | Lines dropped, 1978–83 | Lines retained, 1978–83 | Lines added, 1978–83 | Lines added/ retained 1978–83 |
|---|---|---|---|---|---|---|---|---|---|---|
| **(b) Resource reconfiguration: product line retention and addition, 1978–83** | | | | | | | | | | |
| Total firms and lines in 1978 | 1244 | 3387 | 2.7 | 2237 | 5421 | 2.4 | | | | |
| A. Continue in 1983 | 853 | 2468 | 2.9 | 853 | 2949 | 3.5 | 767 31% | 1701 69% | 1248 51% | 73% |
| A1. Acquirers | 73 | 502 | 6.9 | 73 | 790 | 10.8 | 134 27% | 368 73% | 422 84% | 115% |
| A2. Non-acquirers | 780 | 1966 | 2.5 | 780 | 2159 | 2.8 | 633 32% | 1333 68% | 826 42% | 62% |
| B. Became targets before 1983 | 187 | 555 | 3.0 | | | | 245 44% | 310 56% | 1801 325% | 581% |
| C. Shut before 1983 | 202 | 364 | 1.8 | | | | | | | |

firms. Targets both drop (44 percent) and add (325 percent) more lines. The comparison of new lines added by continuing firms that undertook acquisitions to those that did not undertake acquisitions also is similar, with acquirers adding more lines than nonacquirers (84 percent vs. 42 percent). The comparison of dropped lines by acquirers and nonacquirers differs somewhat, however, as acquirers drop fewer lines than nonacquirers in table 13.3b (27 percent vs. 32 percent), opposite to the comparison in table 13.3a. The difference in the comparison of dropped lines likely reflects the different time periods, with 12 years in table 13.3a and only 5 years in table 13.3b. This suggests that firms that are active in the acquisition market may pare their lines more actively than non-acquirers, but that the line paring tends to take place over a relatively long period. Overall, the results in table 13.3b again are consistent with Hypotheses 1a and 2b, that targets change more than acquirers which change more than non-acquirers.

When we gathered the firm-level data for the study, we also found that the number of product lines in the medical sector is growing, as firms introduce new products to the market. The number of unique product lines increased from 230 in 1983 to 258 in 1995. We were curious about which companies offered these new industry product lines in 1995. Such firms demonstrate evidence of being able to stay abreast of industry innovation.

Table 13.4 reports the distribution of the post-1983 new-to-industry lines. We first compared continuing 1983 firms to post-1983 entrants and found that on average they were responsible for roughly equal numbers of new lines per firm. Post-1983 firms (2751 firms) possessed 604 of the total 887 new product lines in 1995, and thus on average 0.22 lines per entrant. The 1117 continuing firms from 1983 into 1995 possessed 283 new lines, and thus on average 0.25 lines per continuing firm. These results imply that incumbents and entrants possess, on average, similar numbers of new product lines.

Table 13.4 next compares acquirers vs. nonacquirers within the 1117 continuing firms for possession of new product lines in the industry. Acquiring firms (98 firms) possessed 80 of the 283 new product lines, and thus on average 0.82 lines per acquirer. The 1019 nonacquirer firms possessed 203 new lines, and thus on average 0.20 lines per non-acquirer. These results indicate that acquirers possess more of the new product lines that are in the industry than do nonacquirers. This finding aligns with the earlier results that supported Hypotheses 1a and 1b, when we consider that acquisitions act as mechanisms for change, reconfiguration, recombination, and potential innovation. If innovation is often a recombinative process, as Schumpeter (1934) argued, it is reasonable that firms that attain new resources through acquisitions possess greater number of new lines in the industry.

**Post-acquisition resource retention**

*Path-dependent change*

Table 13.5 and 13.6 report the results of the resource retention analysis. We coded the dependent variable for the logistic regression analysis as 0 or 1 depending on whether the ultimate acquirer retained the product line in 1995. The first set of models (table 13.5) involves the product lines of all targets operating in 1978 or 1983, totaling 564

Table 13.4 Possession of new product lines in the medical industry, 1983–1995[a]

| Firms | No. of firms | Post-1983 product lines (new-to-industry lines) | No. of new-to-industry lines (total for all firms) | Average new-to-industry lines per firm |
|---|---|---|---|---|
| **(a) All participants in 1995: possession of new-to-industry lines in 1995** | | | | |
| No. of 1995 firms | 3868 (100%) | No. of new-to-industry lines in 1995 | 887 (100%) | |
| No. of post-1983 entrants | 2751 (71%) | No. of new-to-industry lines held by post-1983 entrants | 604 (68%) | 0.22 |
| No. of 1983 continuing firms | 1117 (29%) | No. of new-to-industry lines held by 1983 continuing firms | 283 (32%) | 0.25 |
| **(b) Continuing 1983 participants: possession of new-to-industry lines in 1995** | | | | |
| No. of continuing 1983 firms | 1117 (100%) | No. of new-to-industry lines held by 1983 participants | 283 (100%) | |
| No. of continuing acquirers | 98 (9%) | No. of new-to-industry lines held by continuing acquirers | 80 (28%) | 0.82 |
| No. of continuing non-acquirers | 1019 (91%) | No. of new-to-industry lines held by continuing non-acquirers | 203 (72%) | 0.20 |

[a] There were 230 product lines in 1983 and 258 lines in 1995; i.e., firms introduced 28 new-to-industry lines in the industry between 1983 and 1995

targets with 1843 product line cases. The second set of models (table 13.6) involves recursively smaller subsets of the data, based on the degree of overlap of target and acquirer resources.

We start with table 13.5, which reports the results for the full data set. Model 1 includes only the control variables for industry factors, category dummies, target attributes, and the selection equation. The second model adds the acquirers' attributes and the independent variables regarding product line overlap/nonoverlap. In regression three we added the independent variables regarding category overlap and distinction. We test the significance of each logit model and find each model log-likelihood ratio, following a chi-square distribution with $k$ (number of variables in equation excluding the constant) degrees of freedom, to be statistically significant. In comparing the three models, we find that most results are similar in both magnitude and significance, and are highly robust.

The results in Models 2 and 3 of table 13.5 provide strong support for the resource-deepening argument of Hypothesis 2a. Focal line overlap has a significant positive coefficient in both models. That is, acquirers that had the product line before the acquisition are likely to retain resources similar to their initial resources. Additional support for the hypothesis support arises from the significant positive impact of complementary overlap of non-focal product lines in Models 2 and 3, and also by category overlap in Model 3. The greater the degree of commonality in lines and categories between the acquirer and target, the more likely that an acquirer will retain a given product line of the target. Thus, path-dependent resource deepening appears to be a common outcome of postacquisition reconfiguration.

Model 3 of table 13.5 also sheds light on the resource extension argument of Hypothesis 2b. Three results are important here. First, greater target line distinction leads to lesser retention. That is, acquirers often shed targets' lines when there is substantial difference between the targets' sets of product lines and those of the acquirer. The likely cause of this result is that such targets possess very different routines from those of the acquirer, which create substantial integration difficulties. Instead, if a firm wishes to offer such lines, it will often be more feasible and efficient to do so internally. Second, though, in striking contrast, greater target category distinction leads to greater retention. Here, the likely cause is that acquirers could not undertake such path-breaking changes through internal development, so that it becomes increasingly worthwhile to undertake the investment of time and money that they need to retain such expansion opportunities. Third, neither acquirer line distinction nor acquirer category distinction affects retention, suggesting that most benefits and problems posed by disparate routines tend to arise from the new routines of the target firm, rather than from the routines that the acquirer already possesses and understands.

Thus, the resource extension argument of Hypothesis 2b also receives support, but for more substantial expansion into new product categories rather than for incremental changes into new product lines. The most likely cause of this distinction is that acquisitions create sufficient postacquisition costs and difficulties that undertaking integration of new resources is more worthwhile when the resources are far from a firm's existing set of resources and, therefore, tend to be beyond the firm's ability to undertake via internal development. This result suggests that acquisitions often provide means of undertaking substantial changes, while internal development is more likely to serve for incremental changes.

Most relationships between our control variables and product line retention emerge much as we expected. The number of firms that possessed a product line before an acquisition and the number of firms that increased their lines after the acquisition both increase the likelihood of retention in all three models. We conclude that industry factors, particularly when other firms invest more into a product line, play significant roles in resource retention. Compared to the medical device category, the healthcare services category had a consistent significant influence on the likelihood of retention. This influence was negative and significant across all regressions, as we expected. The result suggests that services are more fungible and reconfigurable than devices. As we expected, targets that invested highly in nonmedical industries are significantly less likely to retain their medical product lines. Also, acquirers tended to retain lines for targets that held only one product line. We found some support in the first model for our belief that acquirers will tend to retain lines of older targets. We also found weak

**Table 13.5** Logistic regression estimates of resource deepening and extension influences on target product line retention by acquirers (all targets; positive coefficient indicates acquirer was more likely to retain line in 1995)

| *Variables* | *1* | *2* | *3* |
|---|---|---|---|
| **Industry factors** | | | |
| 1 No. of firms with product line before acquisition | 0.005*** | 0.004** | 0.004** |
| 2 No. of firms with line increased, post-acquisition | 0.51*** | 0.37** | 0.31** |
| 3 Line was new to industry: introduced after 1978 | -0.55 | -0.80* | -0.76* |
| **Categories** (omitted is "medical devices") | | | |
| 4 Category: healthcare services | -0.36** | -0.45** | -0.61*** |
| 5 Category: dental devices | -0.49 | -0.35 | -0.50 |
| 6 Category: ophthalmic devices | 0.06 | -0.05 | -0.19 |
| 7 Category: pharmaceutical products | 0.35*** | 0.18 | 0.06 |
| **Target attributes** | | | |
| 8 Medical sales (in $ millions) | 0.13 | 0.10 | 0.08 |
| 9 Non-medical corporate sales (in $ millions) | -0.09*** | -0.09*** | -0.09*** |
| 10 Firm age (log years) | 0.35*** | 0.23* | 0.21 |
| 11 US firm | -0.07 | -0.01 | 0.03 |
| 12 Established line at target (exists in prior panel) | 0.22** | 0.15 | 0.22** |
| 13 Target business has single product line | 0.74*** | 0.61*** | 0.63*** |
| 14 No. of product lines at target business | -0.02*** | | |
| **Target-acquirer resource overlap and distinction** | | | |
| 15 Focal line overlap: acquirer had line before acquisition | | 1.27*** | 1.29*** |
| 16 Complementary line overlap: no. of non-focal shared lines | | 0.10*** | 0.11*** |
| 17 Category overlap: no. of non-focal shared categories | | | 0.49*** |
| 18 Target line distinction: no. of non-overlapping lines at target | | -0.04*** | -0.07*** |
| 19 Acquirer line distinction: no. of non-overlapping lines at acquirer | | -0.002 | 0.00 |

| | Model 1 | Model 2 | Model 3 |
|---|---|---|---|
| 20 Target category distinction: no. of non-overlapping categories at target | | 0.31*** | |
| 21 Acquirer category distinction: no. of non-overlapping categories at acquirer | | −0.03 | |
| **Acquirer attributes** | | | |
| 22 Target was divested as a stand-alone business | | −0.39* | −0.28 |
| 23 Acquirer preacquisition sales (in $ millions) | | 0.01 | 0.003 |
| 24 Acquirer age | | −0.01 | 0.002 |
| 25 Acquirer was US firm | | 0.27 | 0.19 |
| 26 Acquisition year (of first acquisition) | | 0.07*** | 0.07*** |
| 27 No. of times pursued acquisitions, 1983–95 | | −0.12 | −0.13 |
| 28 Selection equation probability (see below) | −4.04 | −2.23 | −1.86 |
| 29 Intercept | −0.63*** | −6.76*** | −6.67*** |
| Number of product line cases (53 percent retained in 1995) | 1843 | 1843 | 1843 |
| Number of target firms | 564 | 564 | 564 |
| Model log-likelihood chi-square | 2363 | 2179 | 2146 |
| Log-likelihood ratio | 230.2 | 368.6 | 401.5 |

Selection equation: logit (log age, log medical sales, no. of lines) on acquisition prior to 1995. Significant estimates (two-tailed tests): $*p < 0.1$; $**p < 0.05$; $***p < 0.01$.

**Table 13.6** Logistic regression estimates of resource-deepening and extension influences on target product line retention by acquirers (subsamples restricted in target-acquirer overlap; positive coefficient indicates acquirer was more likely to retain line in 1995)

| Variables | 4<br>No focal overlap | 5<br>No line overlap | 6<br>No category overlap |
|---|---|---|---|
| **Industry factors** | | | |
| 1 No. of firms with product line before acquisition | 0.003** | 0.002 | -0.0005 |
| 2 No. of firms with line increased, post acquisition | 0.29* | 0.27 | 0.31 |
| 3 Line was new to industry: introduced after 1978 | -0.94** | -0.84 | -0.57 |
| **Categories** (omitted is "medical devices") | | | |
| 4 Category: healthcare services | -0.61*** | -0.67*** | -0.71*** |
| 5 Category: dental devices | -0.56 | -0.59 | -0.30 |
| 6 Category: ophthalmic devices | 0.02 | -0.15 | 0.22 |
| 7 Category: pharmaceutical products | 0.03 | 0.05 | 0.24 |
| **Target attributes** | | | |
| 8 Medical sales (in $ millions) | 0.11 | 0.10 | -0.05 |
| 9 Nonmedical corporate sales (in $ millions) | -0.09*** | -0.06*** | -0.03 |
| 10 Firm age (log years) | 0.21 | 0.19 | -0.02 |
| 11 US firm | -0.04 | -0.31 | -0.49* |
| 12 Established line at target (exists in prior panel) | 0.22* | 0.29** | 0.52*** |
| 13 Target business has single product line | 0.72*** | 0.66*** | 0.44** |
| 14 No. of product lines at target business | | | |
| **Target-acquirer resource overlap and distinction** | | | |
| 15 Focal line overlap: acquirer had line before acquisition | 0.10*** | | |
| 16 Complementary line overlap: no. of non-focal shared lines | 0.58*** | | |
| 17 Category overlap: no. of non-focal shared categories | | 0.65*** | |
| 18 Target line distinction: no. of non-overlapping lines at target | -0.07*** | -0.09*** | -0.10*** |
| 19 Acquirer line distinction: no. of non-overlapping lines at acquirer | -0.01 | -0.02 | -0.08 |
| 20 Target category distinction: no. of non-overlapping categories at target | 0.31*** | 0.42*** | 0.34*** |
| 21 Acquirer category distinction: no. of non-overlapping categories at acquirer | -0.01 | 0.09 | -0.20 |

**Acquirer attributes**

| | | | |
|---|---|---|---|
| 22 Target was divested as a stand-alone business | -0.26 | -0.15 | -0.08 |
| 23 Acquirer preacquisition sales (in $ millions) | 0.01 | 0.003 | 0.03 |
| 24 Acquirer age | -0.01 | 0.09* | 0.06 |
| 25 Acquirer was US firm | 0.24 | 0.58** | 1.13*** |
| 26 Acquisition year (of first acquisition) | 0.06*** | 0.10*** | 0.11*** |
| 27 No. of times pursued acquisitions, 1983–95 | -0.11 | -0.01 | 0.19 |
| 28 Selection equation probability (see below) | -2.42 | -1.96 | 1.30 |
| 29 Intercept | -6.38*** | -10.28*** | -11.04*** |
| Number of product line cases (retained in 1995) | 1560 (48%) | 1203 (45%) | 903 (43%) |
| Number of target firms | 498 | 401 | 277 |
| Model log-likelihood chi-square (log-likelihood ratio) | 1926 (233.2) | 1461 (195.9) | 1077 (158.8) |

Selection equation: logit (log age, log medical sales, no. of lines) on acquisition prior to 1995. Significant estimates (two-tailed tests): * $p < 0.1$; ** $p < 0.05$; *** $p < 0.01$.

support for established lines at the target having greater retention likelihood. The number of product lines at the targets negatively influenced retention. Acquirer attributes were mostly insignificant, except for year of acquisition, which had the expected positive influence on retention. The selection equation had no significant effect on the likelihood of product line retention.

### Path-breaking change

The analyses in table 13.5 included all targets from our sample. Although we found support in regressions two and three for both Hypotheses 2a and 2b, we conducted more stringent tests to gain further insight into the resource extension arguments for path-breaking change. Table 6 reports a second set of models, each involving a subsample of our original targets with diminishing amounts of overlap with acquirer resources, as we eliminate cases with focal line overlap, then with any line overlap period, and finally with category overlap. These subsamples focus attention on opportunities for resource extension.

Model 4 of table 13.6 consists of 498 targets with 1560 product lines that did not have focal line overlap. That is, the acquirers did not already offer the observed product line of the target, although the acquirer and target may have other overlapping lines. We continue to find strong support for the resource-deepening argument, with complementary line overlap and category overlap both having positive influences on retention. The resource extension variables have similar impact on retention as in Model 3 of table 13.5: nonoverlapping categories at the target are highly positive, while nonoverlapping lines at the target have a small negative effect.

The robustness of the results in table 13.6 is striking. We find similar estimates in Model 5 (401 targets, 1203 lines) and Model 6 (277 targets, 903 lines), as the sample declines in the amount of overlap between the target and acquirer. In Model 6, acquirers become more likely to retain a target's product line as the target's categories grow more distinct. Moreover, once again, distinction of target product lines within a category reduces the likelihood of retention. The results provide at least suggestive evidence that acquisitions provide opportunities for path-breaking changes that are well beyond an acquirer's existing resources.

The control variables in table 13.6 have two main differences from table 13.5. First, industry factors lose their significance in the final two models of table 13.6, possibly due to the reduction in sample size. Second, whether or not the acquirer is a US firm becomes significantly positive in the constrained sample. This result may indicate an interaction effect where the markets in which a firm operates affect the likelihood of retaining lines from distinct categories. A US acquirer may be more likely to retain a distinct line than a foreign acquirer if the US acquirer is more confident that there is a potential market demand in the United States for the distinct line.

Overall, we find strong and robust support for the resource-deepening arguments and also find robust support for resource extension arguments when resource extension opportunities offer opportunities for path-breaking change. The degree of overlap in resources between acquirers and targets makes retention of similar product lines most likely. However, if product lines are in categories that are highly distinct, there is also a possibility of retention. Path-breaking change reflects larger-scale adjustments in product categories than a finer-grained adjustment of product lines.

## Conclusion

We set out to investigate how acquisitions affected business change. We wanted to determine whether firms participating in acquisitions changed more than firms that did not undertake acquisition activity. We also wanted to determine whether changes reflected resource deepening, in which firms followed path-dependent opportunities, or resource extension, in which firms use acquisition as a means of pursuing path-breaking opportunities.

As expected, we found that acquisition participants, including both targets and acquirers, tend to change substantially more than nonparticipants. Over the course of several years, acquirers and targets tend both to add more new lines and drop more old lines than nonacquirers, resulting in major differences in business reconfiguration. We also observed that acquirers were more likely than nonacquirers to possess resources that have only recently entered the industry. The results support our argument that acquisition activity is a key mechanism by which firms change their mix of business resources.

We also found striking evidence of both resource deepening and resource extension. Resource deepening, as firms retained target resources that built on their existing set of capabilities, was the most common outcome. This result is highly consistent with arguments concerning the role of existing absorptive capacity in shaping a firm's on-going changes. At the same time, though, the results show that acquisitions often provide means for undertaking path-breaking changes, by stretching beyond existing absorptive capacity and seeking targets that offer resources that differ markedly from a firm's existing skills. Together, the results imply that acquirers tend to use acquisitions either for close reinforcement of existing skills or for substantial jumps into new skills sets. By contrast, acquisitions may play less of a role for incremental movement away from existing skills, when internal development and discrete exchange of resources may be more prominent.

Several avenues for research seem fruitful. First, simply observing that acquisition-active firms are more likely to possess resources that are new to the industry, as we reported in table 13.4, does not disclose how the firms obtained the resources, whether by acquisition or by internal development. That is, the firms may tend to expand into the new areas primarily by acquiring resources from other firms or might be using acquisitions to support active internal development efforts. Second, it would be useful to determine the causes of cases in which acquirers retain targets' product lines, even after divesting a target to a new buyer. In other words, under what conditions is an acquirer able to learn enough from its target to be able to integrate the target's skills in other organizational units? Third, we have considered only the retention and dropping of new resources, without addressing the implications of business changes on firm survival and financial performance. We believe that firms that engage in acquisition activity will be more likely to survive than those that do not. Nonetheless, acquisitions may at least temporarily create risks of failure or divestiture. Moreover, resource deepening and resource extension may well involve different degrees of risk, with resource deepening seeming more likely to cause problems that could threaten business existence or independence.

We believe that this study helps show how acquisitions serve as means by which firms attempt to change their ability to create, coordinate, and protect resources. We hope the work leads to better understanding of the broader issues of successful and failed business change.

## Appendix 13.1. Medical Sector Categories and Product Lines

### A. Healthcare services

Ambulatory (Holter) Monitoring Services
Ambulatory Care Facility Management Services
Biomolecular Research and Development
Clinical Laboratory Testing Services
Consulting and Planning Services
Contract Research Services; Medical R&D Services
Dental Facility Management Services
Dental Laboratory Services
Diagnostic Imaging Services
Disinfection Services, Equipment, and Supplies
Emergency Medical Services
Employment Services
Environmental Testing Services
Food Service and Catering Operations
Health Care Cost Management
Health Maintenance Organization (HMO) Management Services
Home Health Care Services
Hospital Department Management Services
Hospital Management Services
Hospital Supplies Distribution
Hospital/Medical Facility Financing, Planning, and Construction
Housekeeping and Laundry Services
Instrument Refurbishing and Reconditioning Services
Instrument Repair and Maintenance Services
Laboratory Animals
Leasing and Rental Services
Medical and Health Insurance
Medical Clinic Management Services
Medical Data Processing Services
Medical Educational and Training Services
Nephrology Treatment Services
Nursing Home Management Services
Optometric Services
Other Medical Services
Outpatient Facility Management
Outpatient Medical and Surgical Services
Packaging Services
Pharmaceutical Services

Preferred Provider Organization (PPO) Management
Radiological Monitoring Services
Radiological Testing Services
Rehabilitation Services
Respiratory Therapy Services
Sterilization Services
Transtelephonic Electrocardiogram Analysis Services
Waste Disposal Services, Equipment and, Supplies

## B. Ophthalmic devices

Contact Lenses
Eyeglass Frames and Lenses
Intraocular Lenses
Ophthalmic Diagnostic Equipment
Ophthalmic Supplies and Accessories
Optical Products
Opticians' Apparatus

## C. Pharmaceutical products

Animal Products
Biochemicals, Chemicals, and Related Medical Chemicals
Biologicals
Biomaterials
Blood and Blood Products
Consumable Products
Chemicals
Dietary, Nutritional, and Vitamin Supplements
Drug Delivery Systems
Parenteral and Irrigating Solutions
Pharmaceutical Apparatus and Supplies
Pharmaceuticals, Drugs, and Medicines
Radioisotopes
Radiopaque Contrast Media
Radiopharmaceuticals
Veterinary Products

## D. Dental devices

Dental Equipment
Dental Products
Dental Prosthetics
Dental Supplies
Dental X-Ray Apparatus

## E. Medical devices

Ambulatory (Holter) Monitoring Equipment
Analytical Balances
Analytical Imaging Equipment
Analytical Instrument Data Systems
Analytical Instruments
Anesthesia Equipment and Accessories
Animal Equipment and Supplies
Anti-Embolism Devices
Appliances and Utility Equipment
Arterial Grafts
Artificial Voice Devices
Auditory Testing Equipment
Automated Cell Sorters
Automated Chemistry Analyzers
Automated Immunoassay Systems
Automated Liquid Chromatography Analyzers
Automated Microbiology Analyzers
Automatic Slide Stainers
Biofeedback Equipment
Blood Collection Supplies
Blood Flowmeters
Blood Gas Analyzers and Monitors
Blood Pressure Measuring Equipment
Blood Processing Equipment
Calibration and Test Equipment
Cardiac Assist Equipment
Cardiac Pacemakers
Cardiopulmonary Diagnostic Equipment
Cardiovascular Accessories
Cell Culturing Systems
Centrifuges
Clinical Laboratory Products
Coagulation Testing Equipment
Computed Tomography (CT) Scanners
Contraceptive Devices
Cryosurgical Equipment
Culture Media
Defibrillators
Diagnostic Imaging Products
Diagnostic Reagents and Test Kits
Digital Subtraction Radiography Equipment
Dilutors and Dispensers
Dressings and Bandages
Electrocardiographs
Electrochemical/Biochemical Sensors
Electrodes, Cables, Leads, and Gels
Electroencephalographs
Electrolyte Analysis Equipment
Electromedical Apparatus

Electromyographs
Electron Microscopes
Electronic Blood Cell Counters
Electronic Thermometers
Electrosurgical Instruments and Accessories
Emergency Medical Products
Endoscopes, Arthroscopes and Related Products
Enteral and Parenteral Hyperalimentation Products
Environmentally Controlled Enclosures
Evacuation and Filtration Equipment
Fermenters, Freeze-Dryers/Processing Equipment
Fiberoptic Examining Scopes
Freezers and Refrigeration Equipment
Furniture and Casework
Gamma Cameras
Gas Chromatographs
General Disposables
Hearing Aid Accessories
Hearing Aids
Heart Valves
Heart/Lung Machines
Home Care Equipment and Supplies
Hyperbaric Chambers
Hypo/Hyperthermia Therapy Equipment
Image Recording Systems
Immunohematological Testing Instrumentation
Implantables
Incontinence Products
Infection Control Products
Infusion Devices
Injectors
Kits and Trays
Laboratory Data Processing Equipment
Laboratory Equipment/Supplies
Laboratory Glass and Plastic Ware
Laboratory Incubators
Laboratory Ware
Laminar Flow Stations
Lamps and Lighting Equipment
Lasers
Life Support Systems
Lithotripters
Lung Function Testing Equipment
Magnetic Resonance Imaging (MRI) Equipment
Manikins
Mass Spectrometers
Materials Handling Systems
Medical Communications Systems
Medical Data Processing Equipment
Medical Data Processing Software Systems

Medical Educational and Training Products and Supplies
Medical Electronic Diagnostic Equipment
Medical Equipment Power Sources
Medical Gasses and Equipment
Medical Linens and Apparel
Medical Transportation
Medical/Surgical Gloves
Medical/Surgical/Hospital Supplies
Microbiological and Serological Testing Equipment
Microporous Membrane and Other Filters
Microscopy Accessories
Microtomes
Neonatal Incubators
Neurostimulators
Nuclear Diagnostic Equipment
Nuclear Instruments
Nuclear Supplies and Accessories
Nucleic Acid/Peptide Synthesizers
Neonatal Care Products
Operating Tables
Optical Microscopes
Orthopedic Devices and Appliances
Orthopedic Instruments
Ostomy Appliances and Supplies
Other Medical Equipment
Oxygen Therapy Equipment
Pacemaker Accessories
Pathology Tissue Processors
Patient Comfort Aids and Appliances
Patient Identification Products and Services
Patient Monitoring Equipment and Accessories
Patient Restraint Products
Patient Transport Systems
Patient Weighing Equipment
Penile Prosthetic Devices
Physical Therapy and Rehabilitation Equipment
Physicians' Aids
Physicians' Office Testing Equipment
Physiological Testing Equipment and Recorders
Physiological Therapeutic Equipment
Prosthetic Devices
Pulmonary Function Testing Equipment
Pumps
Radiation Therapy Equipment
Radioimmunoassay Test Kits
Radiological and Nuclear Equipment
Radiology/Nuclear Laboratory Data Systems
Recorder Paper Charts and Records
Renal Dialysis Equipment
Renal Dialysis Supplies

Renal Dialyzer Reprocessing Equipment
Respiratory Gas Analyzers
Respiratory Therapy Equipment
Scintillation Counting Equipment
Separation Products; Chromatography & Electrophoresis Equip.
Special Medical Vehicles
Specialty Beds
Specialty Tables and Chairs
Spectrophotometers, Colorimeters, Fluorometers, and Nephelometers
Sterile Packaging Materials
Sterilizing Equipment and Supplies
Suction Machines
Supply and Other Carts and Cabinets
Surgical and Obstetric Drapes
Sutures and Fasteners
Syringes and Needles
Staining Machines
Telemetry Equipment
Thermographic Diagnostic Equipment
Thermometers
Tubings, Tubes and Catheters
Ultrasonic and Other Transducers and Accessories
Ultrasonic Diagnostic Equipment
Ultrasonic Instrumentation
Urological Equipment
Water Treatment Equipment
Wheelchairs, Manual
Wheelchairs, Motorized
X-Ray Apparatus
X-Ray Developing Solutions Recovery Equipment
X-Ray Film
X-Ray Film Loading, Processing, and Handling Equipment
X-Ray Record Storage and Retrieval Equipment
X-Ray Supplies and Accessories
X-Ray Tables

## Notes

1   *The Medical & Healthcare Marketplace Guide* was published by International Bio-Medical
    Information Services, Inc. (Acton, MA, and Miami, FL; edited by Adeline B. Hale and
    Arthur B. Hale) in 1975, 1978, 1983, 1986, and 1989. Subsequent editions have been
    published by MLR Publishing Company (Philadelphia, PA) and by Dorland's Biomedical
    Publications (Philadelphia, PA).

## References

Amit, R. and Livnat, J. 1988. Diversification strategies, business cycles and economic perform-
    ance. *Strategic Management Journal* 9(2): 99–110.
Amit, R. and Schoemaker, P. J. H. 1993. Strategic assets and organizational rents. *Strategic
    Management Journal* 14(1): 33–46.

Andrews, K. R. 1987. *The Concept of Corporate Strategy*. Irwin: Homewood, IL.

Bain, J. S. 1956. *Barriers to New Competition*. Harvard University Press: Cambridge, MA.

Barney, J. 1988. Returns to bidding firms in mergers and acquisitions: reconsidering the relatedness hypothesis. *Strategic Management Journal* Summer Special Issue 9: 71–78.

Barney, J. 1991. Firm resources and sustained competitive advantage. *Journal of Management* 17(1): 99–120.

Berger, P. G. and Ofek, E. 1995. Diversification's effect on firm value. *Journal of Financial Economics* 37: 39–65.

Bowman, E. H. and Singh, H. 1993. Corporate restructuring: reconfiguring the firm. *Strategic Management Journal* Summer Special Issue 14: 5–14.

Bradley, M., Desai, A. and Kim, E. H. 1988. Synergistic gains from corporate acquisitions and their division between the stockholders of target and acquiring firms. *Journal of Financial Economics* 21: 3–40.

Cannella, A. A. and Hambrick, D. C. 1993. Effects of executive departures on the performance of acquired firms. *Strategic Management Journal* Summer Special Issue 14: 137–152.

Capron, L. 1999. The long-term performance impact of horizontal acquisitions. *Strategic Management Journal* 20(11): 987–1018.

Capron, L. and Mitchell, W. 1998. Bilateral resource redeployment following horizontal acquisitions: a multi-dimensional study of business reconfiguration. *Industry and Corporate Change* 7: 453–484.

Capron, L. and Mitchell, W. 1999. The impact of relevant resources and market failure on modes of business change. Working paper. University of Michigan.

Capron, L., Dussauge, P. and Mitchell, W. 1998. Resource redeployment following horizontal acquisitions in Europe and North America, 1988–1992. *Strategic Management Journal* 19(7): 631–661.

Capron, L., Mitchell, W. and Oxley, J. 1999. Four organisational modes of business change. *Financial Times* series on Mastering Strategy 29, November: 8–10.

Capron, L., Mitchell, W. and Swaminathan, A. 1999. Post-acquisition resource redeployment and asset divestiture: an evolutionary view, Working paper, University of Michigan.

Caves, R. D. 1981. Diversification and seller concentration: evidence from change, 1963–1972. *Review of Economics and Statistics* 63: 289–293.

Chatterjee, S. 1986. Types of synergy and economic value: the impact of acquisitions on merging and rival firms. *Strategic Management Journal* 7(2): 119–140.

Chatterjee, S. and Lubatkin, M. H. 1990. Corporate mergers, stockholder diversification, and changes in systematic risk. *Strategic Management Journal* 11(4): 255–268.

Chatterjee, S. and Wernerfelt, B. 1991. The link between resources and type of diversification: theory and evidence. *Strategic Management Journal* 12(1): 33–48.

Cohen, W. and Levinthal, D. A. 1990. Absorptive capacity: a new perspective on learning and innovation. *Administrative Science Quarterly* 35: 128–152.

Coriat, B. and Dosi, G. 1998. Learning how to govern and learning how to solve problems: on the co-evolution of competences, conflicts, and organizational routines. In *The Dynamic Firm*, Chandler A, Hagstrom, P, Solwell, O. (eds). Oxford University Press: Oxford; 103–133.

Cyert, R. M. and March, J. G. 1963. *A Behavioral Theory of the Firm*. Prentice-Hall: Englewood Cliffs, NJ.

Datta, D. K. 1991. Organizational fit and acquisition performance: effects of post-acquisition integration. *Strategic Management Journal* 12(4): 281–297.

Dierickx, I. and Cool, K. 1989. Asset stock accumulation and sustainability of competitive advantage. *Management Science* 35: 1504–1510.

DiMaggio, P. J. and Powell, W. W. 1983. The iron cage revisited: institutional isomorphism and collective rationality in organizational fields. *American Sociological Review* (April) 48: 147–160.

Dosi, G., Marengo, L. and Fagiolo, G. 1996. Learning in evolutionary environments, Working paper, University of Rome.

Fiol, C. and Lyles, M. 1985. Organizational learning. *Academy of Management Review* 10(4): 803–813.

Granstrand, O. and Sjolander, S. 1990. The acquisition of technology and small firms by large firms. *Journal of Economic Behavior and Organization* 13: 367–386.

Grant, R. M. 1996a. Towards a knowledge-based theory of the firm. *Strategic Management Journal* Winter Special Issue 17: 109–122.

Grant, R. M. 1996b. A knowledge based theory of interfirm collaboration. *Organization Science* 7: 375–387.

Greene, W. H. 1997. *Econometric Analysis*. Prentice-Hall: Upper Saddle River, NJ.

Hannan, M. T. and Freeman, J. 1984. Structural inertia and organizational change. *American Sociological Review* 49(2): 149–164.

Hannan, M. T. and Freeman, J. 1989. *Organizational Ecology*. Harvard University Press: Cambridge. MA.

Harrison, J., Hitt, M. A. and Ireland, R. D. 1991. Synergies and post-acquisition performance: differences versus similarities in resource allocations. *Journal of Management* 17(1): 173–190.

Helfat, C. 1994. Evolutionary trajectories in petroleum firm R&D. *Management Science* 40: 1720–1747.

Hitt, M. A., Hoskisson, R. E. and Ireland, R. D. 1990. Mergers and acquisitions and managerial commitment to innovation in M-form firms. *Strategic Management Journal* Summer Special Issue 11: 29–47.

Hoskisson, R. E. and Johnson, R. A. 1992. Corporate restructuring and strategic change: the effect on diversification strategy and R&D intensity. *Strategic Management Journal* 13(8): 625–634.

Huber, G. P. 1991. Organizational learning: the contributing processes and the literatures. *Organization Science* 2(1): 88–115.

Hunt, J. W. 1990. Changing pattern of acquisition behavior in takeovers and consequences for acquisition processes. *Strategic Management Journal* 11(1): 69–77.

Jensen, M. C. 1986. Agency costs of free cash flow, corporate finance, and takeovers. *American Economic Review* 76: 323–329.

Jensen, M. C. and Ruback, R. 1983. The market for corporate control: the scientific evidence. *Journal of Financial Economics* 11: 5–50.

Kogut, B. and Zander, U. 1992. Knowledge of the firm, combinative capabilities, and the replication of technology. *Organization Science* 3(3): 383–397.

Levitt, B. and March, J. G. 1988. Organizational learning. *Annual Review of Sociology* 14: 319–340.

Lubatkin, M. H. 1987. Merger strategies and stockholder value. *Strategic Management Journal* 8(1): 39–53.

Lubatkin, M. H. and O'Neill, H. M. 1988. Merger strategies, economic cycles, and stockholder value. *Interfaces* 18(6): 65–71.

March, J. G. 1991. Exploration and exploitation in organizational learning. *Organization Science* 2(1): 71–87.

Menard, S. (ed.). 1995. *Applied Logistic Regression Analysis: Quantitative Applications in the Social Sciences*, Sage: Thousand Oaks, CA.

Mitchell, W., Dussauge, P. and Garrette, B. 1999. Creating and protecting resources: scale and link alliances between competitors in the telecom-electronics industry and other sectors,

Working paper, University of Michigan.

Nelson, R. R. and Winter, S. G. 1982. *An Evolutionary Theory of Economic Change.* Belknap Press: Cambridge, MA.

Penrose, E. T. 1959. *The Theory of the Growth of the Firm.* Wiley: New York.

Pfeffer, J. and Salancik, G. 1978. *The External Control of Organizations: A Resource Dependence Perspective.* Harper & Row: New York.

Pindyck, R. S. and Rubinfeld, D. L. 1981. *Econometric Models and Economic Forecasts.* McGraw-Hill: New York.

Porter, M. E. 1979. How competitive forces shape strategy. *Harvard Business Review* 57(2): 137–145.

Porter, M. E. 1987. From competitive advantage to corporate strategy. *Harvard Business Review* 65(3): 43–59.

Prahalad, C. K. and Hamel, G. 1990. The core competence of the corporation. *Harvard Business Review* 68(3): 79–91.

Ranft, A. L. 1997. Preserving and transferring knowledge-based resources during post-acquisition implementation, Doctoral dissertation. Kenan-Flagler School of Business, Chapel Hill, University of North Carolina.

Schumpeter, J. A. 1934. *The Theory of Economic Development.* Transaction Publishers: New Brunswick, NJ.

Simon, H. A. 1945. *Administrative Behavior: A Study of Decision-Making Processes in Administrative Organization.* Free Press: New York.

Singh, H. 1993. Challenges in researching corporate restructuring. *Journal of Management Studies* 30(1): 147–172.

Singh, H. and Montgomery, C. 1987. Corporate acquisition strategies and economic performance. *Strategic Management Journal* 8(4): 377–386.

Singh, H. and Zollo, M. 1997. Knowledge accumulation and the evolution of post-acquisition management practices, Paper presented at the Academy Management Conference, Boston, MA.

Teece, D. J. 1980. Economies of scope and the scope of the enterprise. *Journal of Economic Behavior and Organization* 1: 223–247.

Teece, D. J. 1982. Towards an economic theory of the multiproduct firm. *Journal of Economic Behavior and Organization* 3: 39–63.

Teece, D. J. 1986. Profiting from technological innovation: implications for integration, collaboration, licensing, and public policy. *Research Policy* 15: 285–305.

Teece, D. J., Pisano, G. and Shuen, A. 1997. Dynamic capabilities and strategic management. *Strategic Management Journal* 18(7): 509–533.

von Hippel, E. 1988. *The Sources of Innovation.* MIT Press: Cambridge, MA.

Walsh, J. P. 1988. Top management turnover following mergers and acquisitions. *Strategic Management Journal* 9(2): 173–183.

Wernerfelt, B. 1984. A resource-based view of the firm. *Strategic Management Journal* 5(2): 171–180.

Wernerfelt, B. and Montgomery, C. A. 1988. Tobin's q and the importance of focus in firm performance. *American Economic Review* 78(1): 246–250.

Williamson, O. E. 1975. *Markets and Hierarchies: Analysis and Antitrust Implications.* Free Press: New York.

Williamson, O. E. 1999. Strategy research: governance and competence perspectives. *Strategic Management Journal* 20(12): 1087–1108.

Winter, S. G. 1990. Survival, selection, and inheritance in evolutionary theories of organization. In *Organizational Evolution: New Directions*, Singh JV (ed.), Sage: Newbury Park, CA; 269–296.

# CHAPTER FOURTEEN

# Commentary on: Karim–Mitchell and Helfat–Raubitschek Chapters

## James Brian Quinn

The Karim–Mitchell and Helfat–Raubitschek chapters are both very well done and suggest some interesting lines for further research. Many of the classic models of both innovation and acquisition are breaking down as the technology and the pace of world-wide change advances exponentially. It is significant that two of the most important (scientific and economics) papers of the century – Einstein's (on special relativity) and Markowitz's (on "efficient markets") had *no* footnotes. They indicated a major break with past theory and an introduction to a whole new realm of thought of the sort we are encountering in management today. Totally new models will be needed to guide further management action.

Until the last few years, strategic studies did not deal very often with services, technology, intellect, and software – the drivers of the new economy. As Helfat and Raubitschek suggest, old models of deepening versus broadening strategies tend to be less meaningful under conditions in which intellectual core competencies dominate. Such competencies allow both deepening and broadening simultaneously, just as technologies supporting such strategies optimize costs and flexibilities simultaneously. This is a common feature of technology-based service strategies – like those used in banking, financial services, wholesaling, retailing, communications, entertainment, and transportation. An effective core competency develops both "best-in-world" depth in some set of activities important to customers and a flexible "platform" for future innovations – as did Sony's best-in-world capabilities in innovating and introducing small electro-mechanical products for consumer and institutional markets or StateStreet Boston's capabilities for handling and innovating custodial account services.

As I found out when I did my first papers on technology and services in the early 1980s there were neither data nor references that were relevant. We found no directly useful references at the intersection of the words "innovation" and "services." The data that were available were so plagued with definitional problems that they were useless for many purposes. For example, the national accounts data on IT productivity in services did not collect the software portion of IT investment, and measures of services output (particularly quality) were notoriously inaccurate. Many a services industry's output was measured by its cost inputs. In other cases, the benefits of increased service productivity had to be passed on to customers because of intense competition. The result was that there appeared to be no productivity increase in services; while (perversely) vastly decreased costs of communications, transportation, distribution, software, accounting, other professional services (etc.) showed up as productivity improvements in their customers' industries. New data and new models were needed. This is why I was particularly impressed by the careful use and development of data by Karim–Mitchell in their chapter. We are going to have to develop entire new databases and measurement techniques for this entirely new economy we are entering.

All historical models of innovation and acquisition are breaking down in the face of new capabilities. Improved software provides for rapid, integrated innovation, and improved management of outsourced processes without ownership. Often, all sought-after benefits can be obtained without the direct capital outlays and inflexibilities of ownership. As Lord Keynes said, "Capital decisions, once made, create a new environment with no opportunity to replay [others]." Dell (computers), Nintendo (video games), America Online (connectivity), Millennium (pharmaceuticals), Wal-Mart (distribution), or StateStreet (custodials) – as well as many Internet companies provide instructive models. In each case, technological advances are moving so fast that no company can dominate the entire value chain or afford investment in a full enough range of support technology to justify integration or acquisition. The possible combinations of interactions among technologies, component designs, system configurations, and customer desires in advanced fields often render traditional targeted R&D or product-marketing strategies useless. Total unpredictability (not probabilistic outcomes) dominate. For example, 15 discrete software elements or genetic reactants can be combined in up to 10 trillion different ways, making outcomes impossible to predict or to defend as intellectual property. The bits on a single hi-density diskette can be combined in many more ways than there are identified celestial bodies in the heavens, offering as many potential outcomes.

When one multiplies such potentials by the number of ways customers (unpredictably) might want to utilize these outcomes, one is well into a realm of unknowability that is compounded by the further advances that the sum of all new (yet untapped) innovations might achieve in customer, supplier, or competitor situations. It has been estimated that two billion new minds will be connecting into "our" and other "international" marketplaces over the next fifteen years or so. One company cannot out-invent all those minds. It has to tap into them, to have information or position values to trade, combine its own and others' solutions to problems, and move quickly onto other problems. In an unknowable world, those who attempt to build large plants and fixed systems will frequently find them obsolete before payback occurs. Iridium is an interesting current example.

How does one deal with such unknowability? Helfat and Raubitschek properly look to highly developed special core intellectual competencies as one key. They also properly focus on "activities" – interfunctional clusters of tasks necessary to achieve a result – as the basis for such competencies. Such "platforms" provide endless possibilities for future connections, products, and services. I would hope that the authors would add that, for success, one element of such competencies must always connect directly to customer needs or perceptions.

Another developing element is leveraging interconnection of these competencies

internally and externally through software and outsourcing to achieve maximum innovation and impact. In cases to date, properly developed software-based innovation has
allowed the reduction of innovation costs and investments by 60–90 percent, cycle
times by an equal amount, risks by two-thirds, and improvement of impact (through
customer interactions) by orders of magnitude. The combination changes all the base
parameters of older innovation paradigms.

Rather than internally focused acquisition-innovation strategies, many of the most
rapidly growing new technology companies find that interactive mutually beneficial
collaboration among numerous quasi-independent internal and external groups is a
key to best resource allocation. Each group concentrates on what it does best – most
efficiently or with highest value – coordinating its activities through software or communications interfaces (not ownership or line authority) with the user. The company
coordinating innovation in this milieu provides sufficient access to its model – as
Aerospatiale, Nike, MCI, Nintendo, Millennium, or Ford do – to allow suppliers to
innovate independently, yet coordinate their activities toward system goals. Many enterprises in the telecommunications, genetic, entertainment, news, publications, investments, computer, professional services, software, or other services activities now
perform this way. By strategic outsourcing, the coordinating company avoids the investments and risks of involvement in all competing alternatives, combines solutions
for its specific customers, and services them through its core competencies. Solutions
"emerge" rather than being designed through "strategic choices" or through "critical
path sequences." The secret to the re-emergence of GE, IBM, AT&T, Harley Davidson,
Enron, and many others has been such "core-competency-with-outsourcing" strategies. Solutions emerge faster, cheaper, and in a more customer tailored fashion than
ever before. Both the quality and rapidity of innovation has exploded as a result.

This is the true meaning of incrementalism in strategy for today's world. With so
many options and unknowables in the knowledge, technology, supplier, competitive,
and user marketplaces, it is ever more risky to develop heavy investment positions and
seek traditional economies of scale. The keys to strategy are: creating an exciting vision
that attracts top quality people; developing to "best-in-world levels" an intellectually
based core competency of importance to customers in the long run; consciously structuring flexibility and entrepreneurial incentives for employees and suppliers; getting as
close to customers as possible; establishing an interactive open system to tap into ideas
from the supplier, technology, and customer communities; managing a software system that provides the central discipline to coordinate disparate providers' and customers' ideas; creating the flexibility to adapt both the system and its outputs as innovations
appear; and decentralizing both knowledge and performance groups to the "minimum replicable unit of activity." Such strategies allow the maximum combination of
information sources, customer knowledge, and entrepreneurial motivation to create
customer value. Such have been the keys for success in many of today's most progressive companies – like Dell, Amgen, Disney, Merrill Lynch, Wal-Mart, StateStreet Bank,
Microsoft, Lakeland Hospital, Sony, Kyocera, or Ford. Yet few measures exist for how
well these are performed.

The interaction of these elements and their management deserves much further
attention and research. One of the key missing links in the strategy literature today is
how to develop and manage the software systems that are the core of most innovative,

adaptive strategies in successful companies. Another is developing the new measurement techniques and reporting systems needed to measure performance in highly outsourced activities. In some current papers, we are trying to demonstrate how to develop anticipatory strategic control systems for outsourced activities, how to develop "figures of merit" to ensure that core competencies are truly achieved, and how to measure and manage outputs from intellectual processes. Properly developed software and support systems can avoid the need for expensive risky acquisitions, cumbersome internal bureaucracies and procedures for innovation, and the slow moving integration and top-down "command-and-control" structures that traditional internally focused strategies tend to bring with them.

# CHAPTER FIFTEEN

# The Relational Organization: From Relational Rents to Alliance Capability

## Harbir Singh

As firms increasingly find themselves in an interconnected set of strategic relationships, a question arises: how can they get the most out of their alliances and network relationships? Although at the time of formation, decision-makers can see the possibility of forging useful relationships with firms with complementary capabilities, the process of managing them and generating desired outcomes falls considerably short of expectations. What factors drive the formation of relational capabilities? Do firms need to actively create a function that manages such relationships and put in place specific mechanisms to achieve the desired goals from their alliances? To what extent can these processes be put in place in anticipation of engaging in a variety of strategic partnerships? These are some of the questions we will address in this commentary.

A related theme is: where do capabilities come from? This has been a question that has intrigued strategy researchers since the early 1990s. As capabilities gained salience following the rise of the resource-based view, it became increasingly clear that not enough was known about their origins and the mechanisms needed to develop, nurture and reinvest in them. We will discuss the issues of capability development in the context of the relational organization, as this may be a good testing ground for understanding how firms may develop these new capabilities.

## The Relational Perspective of the Firm: How Relational Rents can be Earned

Dyer and Singh (1998)[1] introduced the relational perspective of the firm as a way of understanding how firms earn rents from their strategic alliances and network relationships. Integrating prior theoretical and empirical work, they identified four factors that drive rents from interfirm relationships. These factors were: interfirm asset specificity, complementary capabilities, interfirm knowledge-sharing routines, and effective governance.

*Interfirm asset specificity* refers to the extent to which trading partners in the relationship customize their assets to the partner, so that the combination of assets is idiosyncratic in a value enhancing way. Such customization would be necessary also to create some barriers to imitation by competitors. On the other hand, this customization would also result in exposure to hold up, or to the costs of redeploying the assets to the second-best application. On balance, however, partnering firms would need to increase their interfirm asset specificity to get the most out of their relationships. Asset specificity can take several forms including site specificity, physical asset specialization, and human asset specificity. Human co-specialization allows partners to work together more efficiently and effectively, reducing communication errors and increasing the quality of the output of the relationship (Asanuma, 1989; Dyer, 1996).

*Complementary assets* have been advanced by several scholars as a driver of strategic partnerships, most visibly by Teece (1987). The argument is quite intuitive: firms create greater relational rents when they find highly complementary strategic partners.

An often overlooked aspect of complementary is that there are also degrees of misfit in combinations between real organizations. Thus, the search for complementarity capabilities also entails a careful look at the areas in which the relationship actually has some level of misfit. As in the world of acquisitions, an alliance partner that has several positive complementarities also has negative complementarities, or misfits in critical areas. Frequently, there may be complementarity in assets, but a lack thereof, in terms of organizational processes of communication or decision-making. Firms with greater relational capabilities have alliance screening processes that assess both positive and negative complementarities. We will elaborate on these capabilities later in this comment.

*Interfirm knowledge sharing routines* have, until recently, not received enough attention in the world of strategic partnering. Yet, there is evidence that in many cases, the most important source of new ideas is the firm's alliance partner. Transfer of these ideas is facilitated by knowledge sharing routines. We define knowledge sharing routines as a regular pattern of firm-level interactions that permit the transfer, recombination or creation of knowledge (Grant, 1996). For effective knowledge transfer, interfirm processes need to be developed and then institutionalized.

A firm's ability to absorb knowledge from a partner depends upon prior related knowledge or "absorptive capacity" (Cohen and Levinthal, 1990). Cohen and Levinthal define absorptive capacity as the firm's ability to recognize and assimilate new knowledge, and apply it to commercial ends.

From a relational perspective, absorptive capacity can be conceptualized as a function of the source as well as the recipient. Accordingly, Dyer and Singh (1998) suggest that partner-specific absorptive capacity is an important contributor to knowledge sharing in alliances. Using the logic underlying absorptive capacity in general, partner-specific absorptive capacity will depend upon two factors: the extent to which their knowledge bases overlap to lend a basic compatibility, and the extent to which they have developed effective routines of interaction. Partner-specific absorptive capacity is enhanced as individuals on each side of the interface learn more about the nature of critical expertise within the other firm.

Besides the factors that address the generation of mutual benefit, there are contractual, ownership and monitoring issues related to alliances. Dyer and Singh propose that *effective governance* is a fourth element driving relational rents. Part of the argument is very consistent with traditional transactions cost explanations: governance of the alliance must be done through contracts or ownership structures that effectively protect each side from opportunistic behavior of the other. Thus, formal contracts should effectively protect the interests of each side, and there is a greater likelihood of equity-based relationships when there are high levels of asset specificity on each side. The new element of effective governance is the importance of informal safeguards in protecting the interests of each side against opportunism. Evidence from supplier relationships in asset intensive businesses in Japan has underscored high levels of effectiveness of informal safeguards (trust, reputation) in controlling opportunistic behavior in alliance relationships (Dyer, 1996; Gulati, 1995). Effective governance entails the choice of the appropriate mix of formal and informal safeguards to govern the partnering relationship.

The four factors driving relational rents: interfirm asset specificity, complementary capabilities, interfirm knowledge-sharing routines, and effective governance constitute a different, relational, perspective on sources of returns than the resource-based view. From a relational perspective, the firm earns rents from assets it does not control in the legal sense of having majority equity ownership. In an interconnected industry (industries do vary in their levels of interconnection between firms), the pursuit of relational rents is a primary motive for building relationships. A question arising from this discussion is: are there some specific factors that distinguish firms that are effective in pursuing relational rents, and if so, what are they? We address this question in the next section.

## Relational Capability and the Role of the Alliance Function

In further exploration of the process by which firms extract gains from their alliance relationships, Kale, Dyer, and Singh (2002), find that knowledge accumulation is at the core of the creation of relational capability in the firm. The relational capability of the firm is strongly rooted in the alliance function: whether it exists explicitly, and if so, the processes it coordinates. According to Kale, Dyer, and Singh, the alliance function has four important activities: improving knowledge management, providing internal coordination, facilitating intervention and accountability, and increasing external visibility.

### Knowledge management processes

Our foregoing discussion of relational rents indicates that interfirm knowledge-sharing routines are one source of such rents. Implicit in our discussion was the point that firms differ in these knowledge-sharing routines. However, an interesting question is: how do firms develop such routines, and are they aware of their origins? Our discussion of knowledge-management processes underlying relational capability will address new research on how these processes actually develop and are managed in organizations.

Alliance capability has been referenced frequently as a driver of alliance success. Yet, there has been limited work on the actual components of alliance capability. In research both based on field work and on surveys of a large sample of alliances, Dyer,

Kale, and Singh (2001) find that firms that had an *alliance function* with very specific activities perform significantly better than those without such functions. The success rates (in terms of achievement of long-term goals), is 63 percent for firms with an alliance function, and only 49 percent for those without a function. Although this difference may not appear to be high, it should be noted that it is very significant, statistically, and that this finding is obtained after controlling for all assets involved in the alliance. This underscores the importance of skills, processes and templates, all of which are essentially intangible, in predicting performance. In addition, firms that have an alliance function as a focal point for accumulating knowledge and experience in alliance management create an average of $75 million in shareholder value at the time of announcement of the alliance, versus an average of $20 million for firms without such a function. It should also be noted that the long-term success rate (measured through survey responses by managers) is significantly and positively correlated with archivally obtained abnormal returns at the time of announcement of the alliance (0.33).

There are four processes identified as part of the alliance management function: improving knowledge management, providing internal coordination, facilitating accountability, and increasing external visibility. These processes are inter-related, but different in their foci and locus of activity.

*Improving knowledge management* is a fundamentally important part of the alliance function. As noted by several scholars working with the knowledge-based perspective of the organization, knowledge tends to be diffused and fragmented within the organization. Alliances tend to occur at a relatively low frequency, and the low comparability of transactions makes the learning process more difficult. The alliance function acts as a storehouse for knowledge on managing various stages of the process: screening, negotiation, initial launch, alliance management, and assessment and evaluation.

Part of the knowledge management function consists of the development of codified explicit knowledge about managing various stages of evolution of an alliance. Firms have tended to do this by creating both print and online documents detailing steps to be taken in such transactions, and the types of interventions needed to address various difficulties that may emerge as the alliance is run. Other companies create various tools, templates and processes to manage a particular decision or stage in the alliance's evolution. For instance, in high-technology industries, some companies have created a map of their industry in which they have charted the domain knowledge of various firms to determine who might be interesting alliance partners.

*Providing internal coordination* is a very important element within an alliance function. There are many examples of failed alliances that had the right vision, but were undone by poor coordination between partners. The flow of information within each partner firm may be very different based on its organizational structure, information systems, degree of centralization, and culture. If the rules of engagement between managers on each side of the interface are not anticipated and developed, it is likely that coordination will be very difficult. The alliance function helps the firm develop a set of processes that can be used for communication both within its own boundaries, but also across boundaries to the other firm. If both partners have a well developed alliance function, protocols of communication can be developed to overcome incompatibilities present as a result of differences in organizational structure.

Internal coordination presupposes effective communication, which in turn is influenced by the activities related to the alliance function. Communication here refers to dissemination of information concerning alliance related initiatives developed on each side, as well as early warning signals of tension or conflict. Kale, Singh, and Perlmutter (2000) found that alliance success was significantly related to the presence of effective conflict resolution mechanisms, a critical aspect of the internal coordination function.

*Facilitating Intervention and Accountability* is another important part of the alliance function. Only 30 percent of firms that do not have an alliance function have formal metrics for measuring alliance performance, while 70 percent of firms with an alliance function use formal metrics. Both of these percentages are low, because a lack of formal metrics for measuring alliance success would naturally result in a lack of attention to the indicators of performance that are unique to an alliance. The alternative would be the firm's default performance measures for its ongoing businesses, which would not necessarily provide the right performance information. The managers working in the alliance functions of the more sophisticated firms have developed extensive scorecards consisting both of qualitative and numerical measures of performance.

Accountability is an important element of relational capability. As firms have developed networks of relationships, ambiguity of authority has severely increased. As a result, there are significant problems of accountability. Clarifying accountability of key decision-makers, once the metrics are in place, is an important part of relational capability.

*Maintaining external visibility* is the fourth element of the alliance function. For firms involved in multiple strategic relationships, it is very important to have high visibility for its alliance function. The alliance function serves as a highly visible initial point of contact of firms seeking relationships with the organization. Another important part of the function is to maintain visibility with the investment community. In light of the statistically significant and positive impact of alliance announcements in the stock market, it is clear that analysts follow alliances and attempt to assess their income implication. Kale, Dyer, and Singh find in their fieldwork that firms place a significant value on coordinating their dissemination of information about their alliances with external agents, including the investment community and regulators.

## Discussion

There has been extensive discussion of the poor track record of strategic alliances. This poor record is often attributed to a lack of understanding of the sources of success in alliances, or to a lack of alliance capability. Yet, in our research, we have observed that firms differ systematically in their ability to manage alliances. These differences are directly related to the extent to which decision-makers understand the sources of relational rents they may earn, and to the presence of systematic alliance management processes to earn these rents. Relational organizations are those in which both elements of success in managing alliances are present.

We began our discussion by highlighting the four sources of relational rent. We then discussed how firms can manage knowledge to build alliance capability. From empirical research (Kale, Dyer, and Singh, 2002; Dyer, Kale, and Singh, 2001) briefly reported in this article, we pointed out that firms differ quite significantly in their ability to manage alliances. These differences can be traced to firm-specific capabilities. The creation of an alliance function is an important step in marshalling the resources and corporate commitment needed for firms to be successful in these transactions. Besides the creation of an alliance function, we have also found that there are distinct processes to be managed to build relational capabilities.

There are broader implications of these issues for the discussion on the origins of firm capabilities. Our work suggests that, alliance capabilities are built through conscious efforts to learn from prior experience and develop tools and templates to address repeatable challenges. Particularly in situations with a low frequency and a high degree of variation (alliances), there are significant gains to be had from systematizing the process of learning within the organization. Taking alliance capability as one of many possessed by the organization, one can conclude that there are applications of these findings to other capabilities as well. The larger point, however, is that such learning processes are more likely to be put in place by decision-makers who understand how capabilities are built in their organizations, and that the process is incremental but cumulative. Additionally, the intangible nature of knowledge assets related to alliance capability can be deceptive: too often, firms undo what they have learned, as they restructure their organizations without adequate attention to the impact such moves will have on the underlying, intangible, knowledge base driving their relational capabilities. In the end, this may explain why it is difficult to create the relational organization.

## Notes

1   In the interest of brevity, we will not refer to the extant literature underlying each concept discussed in this comment. The references provided here attempt to comprehensively cover the underlying literature.

## References

Asanuma, B. (1989) Manufacturer–supplier relations in Japan and the concept of relationship-specific skill, *Journal of Japanese and International Economies*, 3, 1–30.

Cohen, W. M. and Levinthal, D. A. (1990) Absorptive capacity: a new perspective on learning and innovation, *Administrative Science Quarterly*, 35 (1), 128–52.

Dyer, J. H. (1996) Specialized supplier networks as a source of competitive advantage: evidence from the auto industry, *Strategic Management Journal*, 7 (4), 271–91.

Dyer, J. H. and Singh, H. (1998) The relational view: cooperative strategy and sources of interorganizational advantage, *Academy of Management Review*, 23 (4), 660–79.

Dyer, J. H., Kale, P., and Singh, H. (2001) How to make strategic alliances work, *Sloan Management Review*, 42 (4), 37–43.

Grant, R. (1996) Toward a knowledge based view of the firm, *Strategic Management Journal*, Winter Special Issue 17, 109–22.

Gulati, R. (1995) Does familiarity breed trust? The implications of repeated ties for contractual choice in alliances, *Academy of Management Journal*, 38, 85–112.

Kale, P., Dyer, J. H., and Singh, H. (2002) Alliance capability, stock market response, and long-term alliance success: the role of the alliance function, *Strategic Management Journal*, 23, 747–67.

Kale, P., Singh, H., and Perlmutter, H. (2000). Learning and protection of proprietary assets in strategic alliances: building relational capital, *Strategic Management Journal*, 21 (3), 217–27.

Teece, D. J. (1987) Profiting from technological innovation: implications for integration, collaboration, licensing, and public policy. In D. J. Teece, ed. *The Competitive Challenge: Strategies for Industrial Innovation and Renewal*. Cambridge, MA: Ballinger, 185–219.

# CHAPTER SIXTEEN

# Innovative Routines in Large Firms: What the Evidence Suggests

## Keith Pavitt

One of the major contributions of evolutionary theory has been to highlight the importance of firm-specific "routines" in dealing with a complex and fast-changing world (Nelson and Winter, 1982). One of the additional challenges to those of us concerned with public and corporate policies for science and technology has been to give operational meaning to what remains an abstraction. How do we recognize an innovative "routine" when we see one? Most progress has been made by mainly management researchers who have consistently found that the successful implementation of innovation is strongly associated with strong "horizontal" linkages between R&D and other functional departments (especially marketing), thereby confirming the insights first presented by Burns and Stalker some forty years ago. Otherwise, the consensus on what we know is rather thin. In particular, there is little agreement on whether or not routines in large established firms are effective vehicles for exploiting radically new technologies. On the one hand, the notion of scale advantages and increasing returns supports established firms. On the other, the notion of core rigidities supports entrants. Evidence can readily be assembled to support either position.

I argue here that the notion of corporate capabilities can help us resolve this dilemma, once we recognize that they consist of both specialized and professionalized technological skills and competencies, coupled with the *organizational* capabilities to combine them effectively. The emergence of major technological opportunities is the main driver for change. But the main difficulties in corporations are in the matching of changing technology with changing markets and changing organizational practices. This conclusion emerges (but is not completely based upon) research on the measurement of the *technological* capabilities of large firms,[1] using data on their patenting activity broken down according to technological fields.[2]

### "Core" and "background" competencies

It emerges that large firms typically have technological capabilities spread across a wide range of fields, and are more diverse in technologies than in their product range. These capabilities are composed of "core" competencies which give sustainable competitive advantage, and "background" competencies necessary for the assimilation of technologies developed mainly elsewhere – mainly amongst suppliers of components, materials, sub-systems, production machinery, and software services.[3] The accumulation of core technological competencies requires formal, professionalized and equipment-intensive R&D activities and therefore creates high barriers to entry. They are typically found in firms in the transportation, chemical, and electrical-electronic industries, where they generate both new families of products for existing markets, as well as new product markets. The acquisition of corporate background competencies is targeted both at the coordination and management of change in the supply chain, and at the use of "pervasive" technologies, such as production machinery and control instrumentation, with applications over a wide range of industries. Pervasive technologies can experience periods of rapid improvement in performance per unit cost, and thereby open up major new technological and market opportunities. But given relatively low barriers to entry, they are rarely by themselves a source of sustainable competitive advantage in large firms. In this context, we should note the high rates of increase across industries since 1970 in the number of large firms with active competencies in materials and computing technologies, which are emerging as pervasive. E-commerce is a very recent manifestation, following the progressive spread of software applications in administration, production, design, and distribution.

### Technological and market proximity

It also emerges that corporate mixes of fields of technological competence are very different according to the broad (two-digit) product markets in which they produce and sell. These differentiated competencies change very slowly over time, and the directions of technological search are heavily influenced by the fields of corporate competence already accumulated. The constrained patterns and paths of the corporate accumulation reflect the importance of domain-specific knowledge, and underlines the importance of technological and market proximity in the changes that large firms achieve.

### Organizational not technological diversity in competition

Finally, it emerges that large firms within the same sector have very similar mixes of technological competencies, and that the degree of similarity is highest in the sectors with the highest rates of technological change (pharmaceuticals and computers). This shows that common bodies of technological understanding underlay firms with competing and similar products. What differs amongst them are the organizational practices that link these technological capabilities with products and markets. Some of the relevant domains of organizational practice emerge from the above discussion: in particular, judgments and practices about the nature and extent of technological opportunities, about distinguishing core from background technologies, and about coping with technological and market proximities. Others emerge from one of the major properties of technological knowledge production and use that explains many of the characteristics of corporate technological activities described above, namely the increasingly specialized nature of its production and use.

## Increasing specialization in knowledge production and use

Adam Smith's identification of the benefits of specialization in the production of knowledge has been amply confirmed by experience. Professional education, the establishment of laboratories, and improvements in techniques of measurement and experimentation have progressively increased the efficiency of discovery, invention, and innovation. Increasingly difficult problems have been tackled and solved.[4] These increasingly specialized disciplines have become useful over a growing range of applications, so that products incorporate a growing number of technologies: compare the eighteenth-century loom with today's equivalent, with modern fluid flow, electrical, electronic, and software elements improving the efficiency of its mechanical functions. In other words, products are becoming increasingly "multi-technology," and so are the firms that produce them. Each specific body of technical knowledge consequently cannot be associated uniquely with a single, specific class of product. One of the main tasks of technology management therefore becomes the promotion of various forms of co-ordination and integration: between specialized knowledge sources within the firm and those outside; and inside the firm, between various technological specialisms, and between technological and other functional specialisms.

## The elements of innovative routines

We can now begin to identify those elements that make up the large firm's innovative routines, and that condition whether or not it succeeds in exploiting radical new technologies successfully.

| Technologies | Product markets | Organizational practices |
| --- | --- | --- |
| ● Recognizing opportunities | ● Technological proximity | ● External links |
| | ● Customer proximity | ● Internal links |
| ● Core or background? | | ● Core rigidities |
| | | ● Incentives to explore opportunities (options) |
| | | ● Degree of centralization of decisions (cost of experiments) |

What emerges is that the capacity to identify technological opportunities is only a small part of the story. The outcome from exploiting these opportunities will depend on whether they can lead to a sustainable technological advantage (core technology) or not (background technology), on their proximity to the firm's accumulated knowledge of technologies and customers, and the effectiveness of linkages amongst specialized professional and functional groups within and outside the firm.

In regimes with normal rates of technical change, outcomes can – at least to some extent – be anticipated and planned for. At times of rapid and radical technical change, anticipation and reasoned action become more difficult. The aura of excitement surrounding revolutionary technologies tempts firms to treat them as potentially core technologies when they can never be: competencies in new technological fields may need to be acquired, new markets and customers may emerge unexpectedly and far distant from the firm's established experience, and new linkages may need to be made between professional and functional groups within and outside the firm. In addition, radically new technologies may render established competencies obsolescent, so that they become core rigidities that resist change. And changes in the range of technological opportunities and in their scale requirements may require radical changes in practices in resource allocation and the degree of centralization of decision-making.

Small wonder, then, that established firms have greater difficulties in dealing with radically changing technologies than incrementally evolving ones: both the level of uncertainty and the degree of change required in established habits are greater. But, as the evidence shows, failure to exploit radically changing technology is not preordained, and a consideration of the elements in the above table may help to explain why: the greater the number of above routines that require change, the greater the risks for established firms. Given the high levels of uncertainty, it is often difficult or impossible to identify and predict beforehand the precise nature and extent of these changes: one can be wise only after the event. And one can only offer practitioners a checklist of innovative routines which may require radical change. Thereafter, they can exercise their judgement, and learn from subsequent experience. This – as much as the willingness to take risk – defines what is successful entrepreneurship.

## Notes

1   See, in particular, Granstrand et al. (1997), Patel and Pavitt (1994, 1997), Pavitt (1998).
2   The advantages and drawbacks of the patent measure has been discussed extensively elsewhere. (See, for example, Griliches, 1990; Patel and Pavitt, 1995.) For our purposes, its main drawback is the inadequate measurement of advances in software technology.
3   The classic background technologies are production machinery and measurement and control instrumentation (see Patel and Pavitt, 1994). It is probable that software and e-commerce will increasingly become so in future.
4   The classic texts on this are Rosenberg (1974), de Solla Price (1984) and Mowery and Rosenberg (1989). For recent research on increasing specialization in invention in the nineteenth century, see Lamoreaux and Sokoloff (1999).

## References

Burns, T. and Stalker, G. (1961) *The Management of Innovation.* London: Tavistock (republished in 1994 by Oxford University Press).

Granstrand, O., Patel, P. and Pavitt, K. (1997) Multi-technology corporations: why they have "distributed" rather than "distinctive core" competencies, *California Management Review*, 39, 8–25.

Griliches, Z. (1990) Patent statistics as economic indicators, *Journal of Economic Literature*, 28, 1661–1707.

Lamoreaux, N. and Sokoloff, K. (1999) Inventive activity and the market for technology in the USA. NBER Working paper 7107, National Bureau of Economic Research, Inc., Cambridge, MA.

Mowery, D. and Rosenberg, N. (1989) *Technology and the Pursuit of Economic Growth*. Cambridge: Cambridge University Press.

Nelson, R. and Winter, S. (1982) *An Evolutionary Theory of Economic Change*. Cambridge, MA: Belknap.

Patel, P. and Pavitt, K. (1994) The continuing, widespread (and neglected) importance of improvements in mechanical technologies, *Research Policy*, 23, 533–46.

Patel, P. and Pavitt K. (1995) Patterns of technological activity: their measurement and interpretation. In P. Stoneman (ed.), *Handbook of the Economics of Innovation and Technical Change*. Oxford: Blackwell, 14–51.

Patel, P. and Pavitt, K. (1997) The technological competencies of the world's largest firms: complex and path-dependent, but not much variety, *Research Policy*, 26, 141–56.

Pavitt, K. (1998) Technologies, products and organisation in the innovating firm: what Adam Smith tells us and Joseph Schumpeter doesn't, *Industrial and Corporate Change*, 7, 433–52.

Price, D. de Solla (1984) The science/technology relationship, the craft of experimental science, and policy for the improvement of high technology innovation, *Research Policy*, 13, 3–20.

Rosenberg, N. (1974) Science, invention and economic growth, *Economic Journal*, 84, 333.

# CHAPTER SEVENTEEN

# The Evolutionary Roots of Resource-based Theory

## Jay B. Barney

Resource-based theory has, since the 1990s, become an important part of the strategic management literature. Several authors have articulated the basic assumptions and propositions of this theory concerning the relationship between firm resources and capabilities and performance (Wernerfelt, 1984; Rumelt, 1984; Barney, 1986, 1991; Helfat, 1991). This theoretical work has generated several testable hypotheses that have been empirically examined using increasingly sophisticated methods (e.g., Henderson and Cockburn, 1994; Miller and Shamsie, 1996). Resource-based theory has also been extended to develop propositions that compete with transactions cost economics in explaining firm boundaries (Conner and Prahalad, 1996) and with agency theory to explain managerial decision-making (Helfat, 1991). The emphasis in re-source-based theory on knowledge as a particularly important intangible asset has led to an explosion in theoretical and empirical work on the impact of knowledge on firms (Spender, 1996; Liebeskind, 1996).

While many of these developments in resource-based theory are important contri-butions to the field of strategic management, most of them fail to fully appreciate the relationship between resource-based theory and evolutionary theories of the firm. This failure has limited the development of resource-based theory. The purpose of this chapter is to more fully articulate the relationship between resource-based theory and evolutionary theory, and to show how an understanding of this relationship can en-hance research in resource-based theory.

All evolutionary theories draw on a common logic that emphasizes the importance of variation, selection, and retention (Ulrich and Barney, 1984). As applied to organi-zations, variation suggests that, for any of a variety of reasons, firms can differ along numerous competitively relevant dimensions. Selection suggests that some of these firm attributes will be more consistent with a firm's environment than others, while retention suggests that those firm attributes that are more consistent with a firm's environment are more likely to survive in the long run than firm attributes that are less consistent with a firm's environment.

Given this general theoretical framework, it is clear that resource-based theory is, in fact, a special case of an evolutionary theory of the firm. The variation requirement in evolutionary theory is equivalent to the assumption of firm heterogeneity in resource-based logic (Barney, 1991, 1997). Competition is the primary selection mechanism in resource-based theory. And retention in evolutionary theory is equivalent to the assumption of imperfect mobility in resource-based theory (Barney, 1991, 1997). In resource-based theory, it is the assumed that firm differences can be very stable over time, especially if those differences are path dependent, causally ambiguous, or socially complex (Deirickx and Cool, 1989; Barney 1999). This can be true, even if firms without certain resources consistently outperform firms with these resources.

What can be gained by recognizing that resource-based theory is actually just a special case of evolutionary theory? At least three possibilities present themselves.

First, evolutionary theory recognizes the importance of randomness and luck in explaining differential firm performance more completely than resource-based theory. While luck was an important explanatory variable in some earlier resource-based theories (e.g., Rumelt, 1984; Barney, 1986), luck has not remained a prominent part of the theory as it has evolved in the field of strategic management. This is probably because of the bias, in this field, towards developing theories that have implications for managerial decision-making. However, evolutionary theory tells us that if luck has an important impact on firm performance, then, in fact, luck can have important managerial implications. For example, if a firm's superior performance is based entirely on good luck, efforts to replicate this performance in other settings seem misguided, at best. Also, just because a firm's superior performance might depend on its good luck, significant managerial efforts need to be expended in taking advantage of that good luck. Thus, one thing evolutionary theory can teach resource-based theorists is to not be afraid of luck as an explanation of superior firm performance.

Second, resource-based theorists have an underdeveloped theory of selection. The process by which the value of a firm's resources and capabilities are estimated is not well described in resource-based theory. Evolutionary theory, on the other hand, has a richer description of this process. Nelson and Winter (1982), for example, explicitly model differences in firm production functions, and how these differences compete with each other in an explicit environmental context. In an important sense, Nelson and Winter (1982) are able to introduce some of the rigor and precision of neoclassical price theory into understanding the selection process, without having to adopt the numerous limiting assumptions of this theory. Resource-based theory could use a similar modeling approach. This, of course, would help avoid the tautology problem that has afflicted less sophisticated versions of resource-based theory.

Third, there is a huge body of empirical methods that have been developed to test evolutionary theories. This is especially true for testing population ecology versions of evolutionary theory (e.g., Barnett, Greve, and Park, 1994). By recognizing the link between evolutionary theory and the resource-based view of the firm, it may be possible to leverage these important methodological developments in testing resource-based theory.

The first draft of one of the earliest resource-based theory papers was originally subtitled "An evolutionary theory of competitive advantage." Since then, evolutionary and resource-based theories have developed along separate paths. By recognizing that resource-based theory is actually just a special case of evolutionary theory, it is possible that both evolutionary theory and resource-based theory will be significantly enhanced.

# References

Barnett, W. P. Greve, H. R., and Park, D. Y. (1994) An evolutionary model of organizational performance, *Strategic Management Journal*, 15, 11–28.

Barney, J. B. (1986) Organizational culture: can it be a source of sustained competitive advantage?, *Academy of Management Review*, 11(3), 656–65.

Barney, J. B. (1991) Firm resources and sustained competitive advantage, *Journal of Management*, 17(1), 99–120.

Barney, J. B. (1997) *Gaining and Sustaining Competitive Advantage*. Reading, MA: Addison-Wesley.

Barney, J. B. (1999) How a firm's capabilities affect boundary decisions, *Sloan Management Review*, 40 (3), 137–45.

Conner, K. R. and Prahalad, C. K. (1996) A resource based theory of the firm: knowledge versus opportunism, *Organizational Science*, 7(5), 477–501.

Dierickx, I. and Cool, K. (1989) Asset stock accumulation and the sustainability of competitive advantage, *Management Science*, 35 (12), 1504–11.

Helfat, C. E. (1991) Managerial resources and rents, *Journal of Management*, 17(1), 155–71.

Henderson, R. M. and Cockburn, I. (1994) Measuring competence? Exploring firm effects in pharmaceutical research, *Strategic Management Journal*, 15, 63–84.

Liebeskind, J. P. (1996) Knowledge, strategy, and the theory of the firm, *Strategic Management Journal*, 17 (winter special issue), 93–107.

Lippman, S. A. and Rumelt, R. R. (1982) Uncertain imitability: an analysis of inefficiency under competition, *Bell Journal of Economics*, autumn (13), 418–53.

Miller, D. and Shamsie, J. (1996) The resource-based view of the firm in two environments: the Hollywood film studies from 1936–1965, *Academy of Management Journal*, 39(3), 519–43.

Nelson, R. R. and Winter, S. G. (1982) *An Evolutionary Theory of Economic Change*. Cambridge: Harvard University Press.

Rumelt, R. R. (1984) Towards a strategic theory of the firm. In R. Lamb (ed.), *Competitive Strategic Management*, Englewood Cliffs, NJ: Prentice-Hall.

Spender, J. C. (1996) Making knowledge the basis of a dynamic theory of the firm, *Strategic Management Journal*, 17 (winter special issue), 109–22.

Ulrich, D. and Barney, J. B. (1984) Perspectives in organizations: resource dependence, efficiency, and population, *Academy of Management Review*, 9, 471–81.

Wernerfelt, B. (1984) A resource-based view of the firm, *Strategic Management Journal*, 5 (April–June), 171–80.

# Dealing with Radical Change

# CHAPTER EIGHTEEN

# The Satisficing Principle in Capability Learning

## Sidney G. Winter

## Introduction

Perhaps there are some cases where the state of an organization's ability to accomplish some specific desired result $R$ could be adequately represented by a single dummy variable: either the organization can do it ($X_R = 1$) or it can't ($X_R = 0$). In the former case, we would say that the organization has the $R$ capability, while in the latter case we would say that it lacks such a capability. In such cases, if they exist, the question of what it means to "have" the capability has a sharp answer that is quite distinct from the question of how the capability is created. In all other cases, the two questions are entangled: the statement that an organization "has" a certain capability is of meager import by itself; it generally needs to be followed by the words "in the sense that . . ." followed by a list of key criteria, values of performance measurements, and so forth. These details vary over time, generally in the direction of improvement, as the capability develops.

I doubt that examples of the dummy variable type actually do exist. Isn't it always the case that there is more than one significant performance dimension, and that some significant dimensions are appropriately represented by continuous variables, or at least ones that are not binary? True, it does matter whether our flight actually reaches its destination or not, and a safe arrival certifies, in a limited way, the airline's possession of a capability to mount such a flight. But *"almost on time"* beats *"hours late because of an equipment problem identified at the departure gate,"* which in turn beats *"hours late because of the emergency landing en route"* – and, come to think of it, there are also significant differences within the $X_R = 0$ category: *"canceled"* beats *"crashed."*

In any case, this essay deals with capability learning situations in which the outcome variable for an individual exercise of the capability is multidimensional and on some dimensions non-perfectible – i.e., performance could always be made at least a little better, perhaps because performance varies continuously in some dimensions and cannot realistically be driven to an ideal limit value, if such exists. These situations pose the questions of what it means for an organization to "have" the capability, how the details of performance come to be determined, and what organizational learning has to do with the latter question. Consideration of these issues leads to an ecological and evolutionary perspective on organizational capabilities and capability learning. It is ecological in the sense that the simple notion of "having" a capability is seen as meaningful only in relation to a particular competitive context at a particular time, and evolutionary in the sense that changes in competitive standards, and learning responses to those changes, are seen as key drivers of long-term change in capabilities. It is evolutionary, also, in the sense that its basic answer to the question of "Where did all of these intricate and marvelously designed production capabilities come from?" parallels the biologist's answer to the corresponding question about advanced life forms: they evolved out of the similar but somewhat less marvelous instances of the recent past, which in turn, . . ., and so on. (In the capabilities case, at least, we can often identify origins that weren't all that marvelous in terms of quality of design.)

In the following section, I address conceptual issues involving the terms in my title and give a stylized description of the learning process and the end of what I call "overt" learning. The third section examines the influences on the performance levels that an organization aspires to as it attempts to acquire a capability. In the final section, the analysis is employed as a perspective on organizational crises and on the quest for "continuous improvement." First, however, I review a relatively familiar example of a specific organizational capability and its acquisition, for the sake of establishing one specific reference point for the subsequent discussion.

### Nucor adopts compact strip production[1]

In 1983, the steel producer Nucor Corporation initiated a search for a casting technology that would permit it to enter the flat-rolled sheet segment of the steel market. Like other minimill producers, Nucor had concentrated on "low-end" steel products, such as structural shapes, where the usefulness of the output was more robust to the quality problems caused by the impurities in the steel scrap that fed the minimills' electric furnaces. The best margins in the steel business went to firms who could meet the quality standards of the high end of the flat steel market. At the time, only the large integrated mills were in that group. In contemplating entry to the flat-steel segment, Nucor faced not only the challenges of acquiring new capabilities and of the quality problem but also a substantial scale economy barrier associated with the conventional casting technology.

In 1986, Nucor decided to become the first adopter of a new steel-shaping technology called compact strip production (CSP), which was being marketed by the German equipment manufacturer SMS Scholemann-Siemag. This was one of several potentially viable but unproven technologies for casting steel in thin slabs, thus reducing the difficulty and cost of further processing the steel into flat sheets. It reduced the indivisibility challenge because an efficient plant could be built at a capacity equal to about one-third of that of a conventional plant. The central innovative element in the CSP process was a lens-shaped mold in which the steel cooled. While this may suggest a modest technical challenge, the opposite is suggested by the fact that prior to Nucor more than 100 companies are said to have sent representatives to observe the SMS pilot operation, but did not sign on.[2] Or at least, the challenges must have seemed large relative to the estimated economic advantages, which were significant but not overwhelming.

Steel making and casting is a batch production process. In a minimill, one "heat" of steel results when an electric furnace is charged with scrap steel which is then melted over a period of 5–10 hours. The entire heat of molten steel goes from the furnace to a ladle, from which it is poured into the molds and then cools into solid form. There are various ways in which this process can fail. A particularly spectacular failure is a "breakout" – a rupture of the partially solidified skin of the emerging steel strand that allows molten steel to escape and run through the machinery, welding parts together. Less spectacular problems in the casting, rolling, and coiling of the steel may cause the finished steel to be deficient in quality or unusable.

In 1988, Nucor initiated construction of its Crawfordsville, Indiana, plant implementing the CSP technology. The first attempt to use the new caster was made in June of 1989. The following months were "a roller coaster of success and failure, with breakouts and breakdowns occurring daily" (Rosenbloom, 1991: 6). In spite of the difficulties, the Crawfordsville plant pulled ahead of the planned production ramp-up schedule after a few months of operation. The quality of the steel was not sufficient to make it possible to serve the high end of the flat steel market as originally contemplated, but there was more than adequate demand for the plant's products. The level of success achieved, if not 100 percent, was high enough so that Nucor soon began expanding its thin-slab capacity.

## Conceptual Groundwork

### What is a capability?

Given the fact that there is a rather thick terminological haze over the landscape where "capability" lies, it may be helpful to begin with an attempt at definition.[3] *An organizational capability is a high-level routine (or collection of routines) that, together with its implementing input flows, confers upon an organization's management a set of decision options for producing significant outputs of a particular type.* This definition takes the notion of routine as a primitive, and can be explicated by identifying the ways in which capabilities differ from routines in general. First, whereas routines can be of any size and significance, capabilities are substantial in scale and significance. A capability is reflected in a large chunk of activity that enables outputs that clearly matter to the organization's survival and prosperity. Second, whereas routines are sometimes entirely invisible and unknown to the management, capabilities are necessarily known at least in the minimal sense that the control levers and their intended effects are known. The "set of decision options" language emphasizes this managerial control aspect and the fact that a capability is deployable in various directions. By contrast, many routines are "wired directly to the environment" and get invoked in response to external stimuli without managerial choice. Finally, the reference to "implementing input flows" is a reminder that is as relevant for routines in general as for capabilities, but perhaps more significant in the context of capabilities. It is a reminder that the coordinating information flows and information processing of a capability are only its nervous system; producing output requires actual input services from its bones and muscles.

Also, the focus here is on the learning that yields, for a business firm, the capability to produce marketable output. That learning may itself reflect a *dynamic capability* (Teece, Pisano, and Shuen, 1997) of the organization, if its approach to learning is a systematic and persistent feature of the organization (Zollo and Winter, 2002). Thus, for example, Nucor learned the capability to produce marketable steel with the CSP technique. The pace at which it accomplished that learning arguably reflected persistent features of the organization, some of them also the result of learning, that collectively endowed it with a dynamic capability for innovation in steel making – a dynamic capability whose "output" is not steel but new capabilities for making steel. The creation of such dynamic capabilities is, however, a subtle matter, and one that is not necessarily within the scope of the satisficing logic discussed here.

The notion of "learning" itself has some substantial ambiguities, and might be thought to require careful definition. In fact, few of the puzzles that can arise with the broad concept are actually relevant here. What counts as learning for purposes of this analysis is, at least for the most part, what counts as learning for the managers involved in the process.

### What is satisficing?

As classically expounded by Simon (1955, 1956), satisficing is a theory of choice focused on the process by which alternatives are examined and assessed. As such, it contrasts with optimization theory. Simon has explained that the contrast is between "looking for the sharpest needle in the haystack" (optimizing) and "looking for a needle sharp enough to sew with" (satisficing) (Simon, 1987: 244). Under many circumstances (e.g., a large haystack containing a substantial number of heterogeneous needles, many sharp enough to sew with), the costs of the satisficing process are radically lower than those of optimizing, and this is put forward as the central appeal of the satisficing approach to the decision-maker – and hence, indirectly, to the decision theorist. The example makes clear the following related points about this classic formulation: (1) the discovery of a satisficing alternative ends the assessment process; (2) assessment of alternatives precedes action; (3) the search process explores a well-defined set of preexisting alternatives, i.e., alternatives are discovered rather than created; (4) the defining criteria of a satisficing alternative are static. Although less evident in the example, it is also true in the classic formulation that (5) the costs of assessment are conceived, primarily if not exclusively, as computation costs.

Later work involving the satisficing principle has often embedded it in some formal model of decision, and has generally given it a more expansive and dynamic interpretation (Winter, 1971; Levinthal and March, 1981; Nelson and Winter, 1982). A *search* for alternatives may be conceived as involving creation, rather than mere discovery and assessment of alternatives that are in some sense preexisting.[4] The principle may govern not merely the termination of search, but also its initiation or its *resumption*, if the criteria characterizing a satisficing alternative are subject to change. Some action precedes assessment in the sense that search typically departs from a working *status quo* alternative rather than from a null alternative. It may be that the most important costs arise not from computation in any narrow sense, but from the fact that alternatives must first be created and then can be effectively assessed only *on-line* – the only cost-effective way to assess the performance of an alternative is to implement it.[5] When the necessity for online assessment is joined with the common circumstance that performance is affected by a multiplicity of contingencies, both systematic and random, it becomes clear that assessment is likely to be both costly and time-consuming. When the new alternative displaces the *status quo* alternative, rather than being implemented in parallel to it, the costs of the experiment include opportunity costs, the foregone benefits of operating with the status quo alternative. Finally, and for present purposes very importantly, the dynamic adjustment of *aspirations* modifies the criteria for a satisficing alternative. As March has observed, "discussions of search in the limited rationality tradition emphasize the significance of the adaptive character of aspirations themselves" (March, 1991: 72).

To illuminate capability learning, it is the more expansive and dynamic version of the satisficing principle that will prove useful. It is first necessary to locate the role of satisficing by describing the capability-learning situation in the terminology of the choice-theoretic framework. Broadly speaking, an "alternative" here is a way of doing things; in particular, an *ex ante* plausible way of *attempting* to accomplish the end result at which the capability aims. To create a significant new capability, an organization must typically make a set of specific and highly complementary investments in tangible assets, in process development, and in the establishment of relationships that cross the boundaries of the organizational unit in which the process is deemed to reside. Although significant learning can certainly occur with respect to other investments, a learning perspective is most obviously relevant to process development. It is natural to focus on the process because the success of the process in achieving the desired output is the operational test for the other investments as well as for process learning proper.

### A stylized view of learning

For analytical purposes, it is helpful to schematize process learning as occurring in a series of (on-line) trials, interspersed or alternated with variable periods of off-line deliberation and analysis.[6] That learning has such a discrete trials structure is clearly a common feature of reality. For example, in the case of CSP, there is a trial at the level of a single "heat" – that volume of molten steel is either converted successfully to product or not. All "batch production" processes obviously have such a discrete trials structure; in other contexts the key value creation events are trips, system conversions, consulting assignments, acquisitions, construction projects, store openings, lawsuits, *trials*, and so forth. In still others, cycles induced by clocks and calendars introduce a behavioral punctuation that structures the learning process into discrete episodes, even when the underlying work has no such character – for example, the process is periodically shut down for routine maintenance. Finally, there are admittedly cases in which production truly occurs continuously under normal conditions, but even in these there are typically episodic interventions to adjust the process – and such interventions produce precisely the sort of structure that the present stylization of capability learning presumes.

The important point for the application of the satisficing framework is that the end of a trial affords an opportunity to examine output, assess process performance, and consider various types of adjustments to the process – all in ways that are not similarly available during a trial. The focal decision is the decision on whether to make (deliberate) adjustments to the process or not; the latter choice deems the current way of doing things "a needle sharp enough to sew with;" it satisfices, at least for the time being. Adjusting the process is looking at another needle. The question is what considerations govern the choice. For simplicity of exposition, I assume that the organization contains an effective decision locus for this choice, a "unitary actor" who makes these particular choices.

Given this framing, it is clear that the satisficing principle does not govern all of the learning that takes place as trial follows trial; much less does it govern all the change in the process. In particular, some organizational learning is largely driven by task repetition and can occur without conscious awareness; this is particularly true when the organizational learning reflects skill learning at the individual level. Also, some change in the process occurs because of fluctuations in the context, and some "within-trial" learning occurs as responses to such fluctuations are improvised and then practiced as similar situations recur. Further, what is identified as a "trial" at one level of analysis may be a complex behavioral pattern involving multiple repetitions of tasks at a lower level; the sort of satisficing-governed learning described here may occur at the lower levels within a single trial of the higher-level process. There are many ways to get down the learning curve of a complex process, and those just described can easily produce measurable learning within the framework of a "way of doing things" that is constant in the sense that no deliberate process innovation is made.[7] The relevant managers would probably say, "We are just getting better at it." The "covert" learning that happens in these ways is unintended or at least unplanned by top management; some part of it may even be outside the conscious awareness of all participants. Its mechanisms leave their observable traces primarily in data that support performance comparisons over substantial time intervals. Its costs, if any, typically leave no trace at all, but are hidden in the costs attributed to production.

By contrast, overt learning efforts are undertaken when the current way of doing things does not satisfice. There is (by definition) a perceived need in the organization to improve the process. Such a perception typically leads to activities and resource deployments that are observable, though perhaps only to observers who have appropriate vantage points on the scene. An organization that is creating an entirely new capability is obviously particularly likely to display such overt activity, since early trials are likely to yield results that are unsatisfactory, often dramatically so. The first question to be confronted by the satisficing analysis is when and under what circumstances that sort of observable activity disappears and the adequacy of the by-then-established way of doing things begins to be taken for granted. In more concise form, the question is, "When does overt learning stop?"[8]

## "Optimal" capability learning?

A brief digression into a normative perspective may serve to illuminate the interest of this question. Learning *should* stop when the incremental costs of pursuing it further begin to exceed the incremental benefits derived from it. There are, however, significant obstacles in the way of a precise weighing of this balance. Considered in fine detail, overt learning efforts have the character of investment projects under uncertainty. Some costs are incurred in the form of deliberation, training, and physical adjustments to the process; then the adjusted way of doing things is given a trial, results are observed, and the desirability of the changes is assessed *ex post* – when it is too late to avoid the costs. Thus, *ex ante* uncertainty about the benefits of further effort implies that even "optimal stopping" cannot stop learning at the point an omniscient observer would pick. At best, optimality implies the maximization of expected benefits, calculated with reference to some probability distribution. But there are significant obstacles standing in the way of successful completion of this decision-theoretic program.

Especially in complex production systems, the possible combinations of adjustments that might be considered are enormous in number, and deficits of understanding and imagination prevent a skillful selection of the specific adjustments to be attempted (von Hippel and Tyre, 1995). Further, such systems are generally characterized by multiple strong interactions among the components, implying that simultaneous adjustments of a small number of parameters might have major effects, but also that *ex ante* assessment of such effects is difficult. The significance of this point has been illuminated by simulation studies based on Kauffman's "$NK$" model (Kauffman, 1989, 1993; Levinthal, 1997). The more numerous the interactions ($K$) among the available policy parameters ($N$), the more the performance measure forms a "rugged landscape" over the policy space. Such a landscape displays a multiplicity of local maxima, defined as positions where it is impossible to improve performance further by adjusting any single policy parameter in isolation. Learning based on local search can, at best, reach such a local peak. Only a comprehensive understanding, of a sort that would ordinarily make search unnecessary in the first place, can clearly reveal the distant peaks and the path to them.[9] The theoretical metaphor provided by the $NK$ model makes it easier to understand why boundedly rational managers might extrapolate from the experience of dwindling returns to local search and underestimate the expected returns to search in general. Finally, assessment of the consequences of specific adjustments may be difficult or slow even *ex post* if there is substantial random variation in trial outcomes.

All of the foregoing is particularly relevant in the early stages of capability learning, when accumulated data are particularly sparse and causal understanding particularly weak. Such a situation presents maximal obstacles to accurate estimation of both the actual benefits of a particular adjustment and the expected benefit of a population of adjustments. The implication is that, regardless of the subjective rationality of the participants, overt learning could easily stop at a point where a hypothetical omniscient observer could see that strong positive results were "just around the corner," or more accurately, just around a small number of corners. Although a small number of parameter changes might make a big difference, the diminutive number does not imply that it is easy to find those changes; there are many, many corners in such a high-dimensional space. Only an omniscient observer can easily see what a few turns in the right directions would reveal to the experimenters.

When the data that ideally would guide a decision are simply unavailable, the door is clearly open for strong influence from other considerations.[10] A number of these have been well described in the discussion of the imperfect balance that organizations tend to strike between exploration and exploitation (March, 1991; Levinthal and March, 1993). The main tendency of these influences is in the direction "exploitation drives out exploration." In the relatively specific context of the ending of capability learning, this translates as "overt learning tends to end too soon;" the above points suggesting why this might happen are akin to ones that have been made in the more general exploration/ exploitation discussion. For example, the idea that the benefits of a process adjustment can sometimes be assessed only by protracted on-line testing is an illustration of the general point that the benefits of exploration are often relatively remote in time from those of exploitation (understood as satisficing on the unadjusted process).

More specific insight into the suspension of overt learning can be derived by using the satisficing framework to interpret key features of the capability-learning context. That framework offers the determination of aspiration levels as a principal channel through which a number of considerations enter the picture. Some candidate sources of these influences are discussed in detail in the following section.

To frame that discussion, consider how a higher or lower initial aspiration affects the situation, taking the dynamics of aspiration adjustment and a hypothetical improving trend of potential trial outcomes as given. Set aside for the moment the complication, discussed below, that there may be a minimum level of aspirations and trial outcomes might not reach it: assume they do. Then, low initial aspirations imply an early end to learning and a relatively inferior achievement in the capability initially accepted. Should the fire of learning subsequently be reignited, there would be abundant room for further progress. High aspirations imply the opposite: protracted learning, a stronger capability when overt learning ends, and reduced room for subsequent achievement. If this logic is correct, there are immediate implications concerning heterogeneity of organizational capabilities and performance. Consider the hypothetical situation of a group of organizations that are identically positioned initially with respect to a new capability and have identical learning capacity in the sense that they would generate equally satisfactory tracks for trial outcomes in a given period of overt learning activity. Among such organizations, those with aspirations that are initially high or particularly resistant to downward adjustment will persist longer in overt learning, ultimately satisficing at higher levels of performance. Those with lower aspirations will cease overt learning earlier – but will have more room to respond effectively to a subsequent "wake-up call," which could plausibly be generated either by the visible example of the superior performers or by the competitive stress that they generate. Thus, heterogeneity in aspirations and in aspiration adjustment speed is a force for heterogeneity in capabilities that exists independent of differences in (technical) initial position and learning ability, though it need not be strictly additive to those other forces when the two sets coexist.

## Determinants of Performance Aspirations

The prospects for deriving useful generalizations and explanatory power from the satisficing framework depend crucially on the ability to characterize the likely behavior of performance aspirations. In contrast to trial outcomes, which depend so heavily on the characteristics of the technology, the organization's initial knowledge endowment and its specific path of learning progress, aspirations are influenced by a set of consid-erations that are broadly relevant across learning situations. This makes it easier to formulate broadly relevant propositions linking characteristics of the aspiration con-text to learning outcomes and characteristics of the capabilities acquired.

The behavioral rule generally posited in the extended satisficing framework is that aspirations adapt to experience, adjusting downward when outcomes fall short of aspi-rations and upward when outcomes surpass expectations. Acceptance of this principle here is subject to the qualification that aspirations may in some circumstances remain unchanged in spite of discrepancies with realized outcomes. The downward adjust-ment of aspirations that typically ensues from repeated failure is a particularly signifi-cant theme in capability learning, for it must very often be the case that organizations emerge from initial learning episodes with capabilities that are useful, but not as useful as had been hoped. The following section remarks, however, that there often are prac-tical limits to the amount of downward adjustment that can be accepted.

**Threshold success**

In the Nucor example, one possible trial outcome is a "breakout." It seems very unlikely that a long series of breakouts could reduce aspirations for CSP steel production to the point where a breakout would be considered an acceptable outcome. In this case and many others there is a lower limit of technical success for a trial, beneath which failure is unequivocal and obvious even to casual observers.[11] A significantly higher standard must typically be achieved for a capability to actually play its intended role of contributing to the overall success of the organization. For example, in the Nucor case the basic promise of the CSP technology was that it would allow them to produce flat-rolled sheet at cost and quality levels competitive with rolled steel from integrated mills. This is clearly a more demanding standard than merely avoiding breakouts, but as a standard of success it lacks the sharpness that characterizes "no breakout." Indeed, Nucor's success with CSP was ambiguous by the higher standard just stated.

For analytical purposes, it is reasonable to assume that there is a minimum level of output achievement below which aspirations cannot be driven. Protracted failure to achieve at this threshold level drags aspirations down toward it, but leads eventually to the abandonment of the learning effort as aspirations become resistant to further re-duction. This threshold level is assumed to be at or above the threshold for technical success. An interesting question is whether it should also be assumed to be, in all cases, high enough to assure that the ongoing exercise of the capability at that level actually makes a positive contribution to the organization. The answer here is no: it is well known that a number of considerations can make it difficult for organizations to aban-don activities that are actually hazardous to their long-term health, and these same considerations suggest that an organization might satisfice initially at a level of capabil-ity learning that left the organization worse off than if it abandoned the effort. One reason for doing so might be the more-or-less rational belief that experience alone would ultimately lift performance far enough to make the capability a positive con-tributor. There is an aphorism for this attitude that is familiar in the context of defense systems procurement and perhaps elsewhere: "Buy it now, fix it later!"

Above the threshold success level, aspirations are adaptive. The overall aspiration level may be thought of as an aggregate of a number of different influences, which differ in origin, level, and firmness – the latter being defined as the tendency to persist in the face of results different from aspiration. Some major categories into which these influences might fall will now be discussed.

## "The Book"

Sometimes an organization seeking to build a new capability is following a well-traveled path. It may, for example, be learning to operate equipment or systems from a supplier who has supplied the same thing to other organizations. The supplier may offer instruction along with the equipment and, along with the instruction, definite aspirations based on the quantitative record of the experience of those other organizations. This sort of influence is likely to be important with respect to the level of initial aspirations, but it may not be very firm. Discrepancies can always be rationalized: "Our situation is different." But if the influence is firm, or situations tend not to be very different, the result can be a reasonable homogeneity of achieved performance.

## Needs, plans, and targets

Sometimes the circumstances of the learning organization establish some particular level of performance as critical. For example, although there proved to be some "give" in Nucor's aspirations, it would not likely have satisficed at a level of CSP performance significantly below what was required to sell the resulting steel products at a price in excess of variable cost. If (counter-factually) the company had been running a loss overall at the time of the CSP adoption, it might have "pinned its hopes" on the innovation and aspired to a greater success – a large enough profit to bring the company as a whole out of the red. More generally, the strategic objectives surrounding the effort to acquire particular capabilities may entail relatively firm performance aspirations related to those objectives. And, quite apart from objective considerations that might lend significance to a particular performance level, any performance estimate or target that gets developed early in the process is a candidate for becoming a "focal point" or "anchor" to which aspirations attach. Research in decision-making suggests that human beings are prone to establish anchors for their expectations even when the objective basis for the anchor value is very slim (Tversky and Kahneman, 1974), and many managers seem to believe in the value of establishing definite targets even when there is little basis for the specific target values set. These considerations suggest that decision processes that create performance estimates or targets at an early stage in the learning process may have a strong influence on aspirations, even though early trial outcomes deliver vastly more information about the actual possibilities than was available for the early estimates.

## Related experience

Ideas about what can be learned, and how fast it can be learned, are undoubtedly influenced by the organization's previous experience. This effect is presumably stronger when the new capability "closely resembles" something the organization attempted and learned previously. However, the problem of providing a nontautologous answer to "How close is close?" is a difficult one. In an information vacuum, remote analogies can seem persuasive. Assessing the strength of rival influences on aspirations may therefore be a more promising way to assess this factor than actually trying to calibrate the quality of the analogy to previous experience.

When it undertook the CSP innovation, Nucor had a good deal of experience with bringing other steel-making and steel fabrication plants on line, and those experiences endowed it not only with relevant capabilities and confidence, but also with ideas of what a successful start-up would be like. The extent to which that experience was "really" relevant to the CSP innovation is not easy to assess, but it certainly contributed some specific skills and some general confidence. Although Nucor experienced substantial difficulties in mastering the new technique, those difficulties were overcome more promptly than its plans anticipated.

### Vicarious experience

It may be that other organizations have undergone experiences that are more obviously analogous to the current one than anything in the organization's own past. If information about what the others achieved is available, it is likely to have a strong influence on aspirations. This is particularly true when the new learning effort is construed from the start as imitative of, or responsive to, the accomplishments of others, and still truer when those others are rivals and their achievements are relevant to the competitive threat they represent.[12] For example, the learning response of US automakers to the Japanese challenge in the 1980s was influenced at an early stage by independent assessments of the quality of Japanese cars, and then profoundly shaped by the example of the Japanese transplant assembly plants in the United States. Whereas the early information was subject to various forms of discounting and "denial", the transplants delivered a clear message about what was possible with "lean production" and quality management (MacDuffie, 1996; Pil and MacDuffie, 1999; Cole, 2000). As this example illustrates, the "firmness" of this sort of influence is affected by the amount and quality of the information available, including the degree to which comparison is complicated by contextual differences.

### Costs of learning

Since overt learning activity requires some deliberate resource allocation, its continuance involves at least a passive acceptance of the proposition that its likely benefits cover the costs of the resources devoted to it. Such costs are not strictly a determinant of aspirations as such, but they are a determinant of the satisficing level of performance: the higher they are, the lower the level of performance that is satisficing.[13] There are obvious costs to such learning activities as off-line analysis, consultations, experiments, or simulations, or making process adjustments that involve changes in equipment, training, or configuration and layout. Perhaps less obvious are the opportunity costs represented by downtime in the production process: a major reason to stop overt learning is to graduate to "real life," i.e., production. This factor obviously is not relevant when learning has not yet reached the technical success threshold; at that stage there is no output to forego. But when inter-trial pauses for learning mean foregoing a profitable output stream, that sacrifice has to be weighed against the benefit of cost reductions and the more conjectural benefit of further improvements in quality parameters. When the foregone sales also may mean the sacrifice of lead-time advantages and longer-term market share, the urgency of stopping the "tinkering" and getting on with production is even more apparent. Although this impatient viewpoint has at least a superficially rational basis, its advocates in an organizational context may be from higher organizational levels, or perhaps from marketing, and be uninformed or insensitive regarding both the shortcomings of the achieved performance and the promise of the remaining learning opportunities. They may also be frustrated because at this point the schedule has (most likely) already slipped a good deal. And their case is built on the usual argument for getting on with the "exploitation" – the benefits of the prospective sales are near term and relatively certain, while those of the learning are long term and conjectural. Thus, the superficial rationality of the impatient view should not lead us to imagine that it is always correct.

Subtler opportunity cost issues arise at the level of individual participants. Some members of the team assembled to support learning may not be hierarchical subordinates of the manager chiefly responsible for the progress of learning. They are *de facto* volunteers, either as individuals or because they have been "volunteered" by their bosses. Volunteer workers tend to disappear when other priorities seem more urgent to them (or their bosses). Thus, overt learning may falter, pause, or stop because of implicit cost–benefit calculations by individual participants – calculations that are partly based in considerations remote from the learning effort itself.

### "Stretch goals"

It is not a secret that high aspirations can often contribute to high achievement. Indeed, this observation has congealed into managerial doctrine, perhaps most obviously in the notion of "stretch goals" (Hamel and Prahalad, 1993), but also as "strategic intent" (Hamel and Prahalad, 1989) and in the high aspirations expressed in mission statements. Top managers differ in their devotion to these ideas. It is probably a reasonable conjecture that initial aspirations tend to be higher, other things equal, where leaders talk more about high aspirations. How firm this influence might be, especially when set against the costs of learning, is not so clear.

### Empirical evidence: "windows of opportunity"

An empirical study by Tyre and Orlikowski (1994) provides powerful examples of some of the foregoing points. Though focused at a more micro level than the learning of a capability (as defined above), it examines organizational events of much the same kind. The authors report on the adaptive activities that were undertaken in response to the introduction of new technology in three organizations, one of which was a manufacturer of precision metal components dubbed "BBA." Multiple projects were examined at each organization, including 41 examples of new process technology at BBA. Adaptation activity was found to be particularly intense for a period of a few months right after the change and declined thereafter, but was sometimes resumed in brief bursts. Four organizational forces were found to depress adaptation effort, each of which is illustrated here with one of the many striking quotations the authors report from their interviewees at BBA:

1   Pressure to produce instead of continuing adaptation. "Once we got the equipment into the factory, time to do important engineering work was squeezed out by everyday work to keep things running" (Tyre and Orlikowski, 1994: 107).
2   The tendency for patterns of use to congeal into routine operations in which users adapted themselves to the technology instead of the reverse. "The idea was that we would get back in later to do the fine tuning. But now the operators depend on the machine – it's built in, they don't want to change. So the fact is we haven't gone back" (Tyre and Orlikowski, 1994: 109).
3   The tendency for expectations to converge to actual achievement. In a project involving a high-end precision grinder, users were having trouble getting correct dimensional finishes. "But once we decided that the finish was OK as it was, then we figured that we need not and in fact could not improve beyond what we were getting!" (Tyre and Orlikowski, 1994: 110).
4   The tendency for the relevant teams to dissolve and lose momentum. "Since the major problems were solved, there was no impetus for engineering support to help on other improvements – and once (they) left, a lot of effort just never got done" (Tyre and Orlikowski, 1994: 111).

As this last comment indicates, it was not the case that adaptation efforts stopped because *all* of the problems had been solved. In fact, some of the things left undone were in some cases considered high priorities when the projects were initiated. Further, the BBA projects took an average of 14 months to get to the point where they produced parts on a consistent basis, and another 8 months to be "fully integrated" (Tyre and Orlikowski, 1994: 105). The authors do not indicate how much performance improvement and how much aspiration adjustment went on in the latter part of the 22-month period, but their data clearly indicate that the level of adaptation effort was low. The data also seem to suggest a role for the calendar in igniting bursts of renewed learning. Looking at it, one can almost hear someone saying, "Do you realize that it is almost (6 months, a year, 2 years) since we installed that equipment, and we still haven't straightened out the (whatever)?"[14]

### Review

Since the actual pay-off to continued investment in learning is unknown when the investment is made, there is no reason to expect overt learning to stop at the point that an omniscient observer would pick. The above discussion identifies a number of plausible influences on this decision that are not grounded in the specific reality of the learning effort but rather reflect contextual factors. In many cases, the influence of these factors is clearly mediated by contingencies of exposure to relevant information, by managerial judgements, and by organizational politics. Thus, there are sources of heterogeneity in achieved performance levels that have little to do with the technical difficulty of raising the capabilities to a higher level.

Although these various influences can push aspirations in different directions, there is one systematic tendency that is worthy of note. More radical advances, representing a greater disconnect with the previous activities of the focal organization and others, have a distinctive profile in terms of the level and firmness of the influences identified above. In such cases there is no "Book" and no comparable experience of other organizations, and any analogy with previous experience of the focal organization is remote. Thus, these influences are either nonexistent or soft. There may well be plans and targets for the learning effort, but the weakness of the factual basis is likely to soften these influences. In many cases, considerations of need and cost will begin to point to an early stop as soon as production and sale promise a return over variable cost, yielding some relief from cash flow problems. If the capability yields an innovative product that represents a sound concept for meeting a newly identified need, and the effort is appropriately directed toward a niche market that places a high value on the concept, revenue opportunities may be substantial even for primitive and costly versions of the product. Indeed, the "need" factor can take the form of a need for cash to continue the work, and the decision to satisfice temporarily on a primitive version of the product may coincide with the identification of a niche willing to put up with it (Levinthal, 1998).

Thus, the satisficing principle helps to explain why new capabilities are so often born in forms that are primitive (and thus more easily achieved) and improve from there. At a finer level of analysis, it suggests the sorts of capabilities for which this is likely to be true, or what attributes are particularly likely to appear in primitive form. At one level, of course, the explanation is the obvious technical one, a matter of "not knowing how to do it better." But more learning would generate more knowing, and the question of how much of the learning gets done before any output appears needs an answer.

As a sobering exercise, consider what this sort of analysis implies for the significant performance attributes associated with the capability of operating a nuclear reactor to generate electricity, in the historical context in which such operations developed in the United States. The signal virtue of nuclear power is its very low variable cost. Therefore, to leave an operable reactor shut down is to incur a large opportunity cost. The context was one in which government policy strongly supported and promoted the nuclear power technology, but did very little to subsidize individual reactor projects or otherwise soften the market test that the innovating utilities faced from established modes of power generation – thus leaving the utilities to bear the full weight of the opportunity cost of an idle reactor. Neither did the government complement its R&D on nuclear power with comparably serious efforts on safe reactor designs, human factors analysis, and other components of the safety problem. Viewed against the ominous potentials of that background, the Three Mile Island episode looks like good luck.

## Re-igniting Learning: Crisis Response and Continuous Improvement

For simplicity, the above discussion has proceeded as if, in the learning of a given capability, overt learning would ordinarily stop once and for all. This is certainly not the case. Even when there is a single major transition from a learning mode to a routinized production mode, the transition is not likely to be very sharp. A more plausible pattern is one of waning efforts and gradually lengthening pauses. The satisficing principle suggests that such pauses are likely to be systematically related to performance fluctuations, being triggered by episodes of relatively good performance and terminated with the recurrence of difficulty. There may be no identifiable decision that marks the transition as routines stabilize; learning may simply fade away. Difficulties with the process may continue to occur and be dealt with, but the manner of dealing with them no longer produces a trend of improvement in the process. Alternatively, a more decisive end to the "tinkering" may occur in response to the difficulty of maintaining coordination among different parts of the process when they are in constant flux, or to the need for standardization of the output.

There are a number of reasons why the learning flame might be re-ignited at some later date, after it had definitely been out for a substantial period. The categories identified in the previous section remain relevant; they suggest the sorts of events that might produce an up-tick in performance aspirations that would lead to a renewal of overt learning efforts. New targets may appear when customers express unusual output demands, requiring that some performance attributes take on values not attainable with the capability in its previously stabilized form. New personnel may introduce new sources of vicarious experience, leading to the importation of higher performance standards from other organizations. New problem-solving resources may be acquired, suggesting that advances can be made more speedily and hence that the opportunity costs of learning have fallen.

A general issue that is particularly significant here is the degree of specificity or localization of these sorts of effects on aspirations. An organization may command several major capabilities, which in turn can be thought of as a hierarchically organized structure that is decomposable into routines, subroutines and so on. The stylization of the learning process introduced earlier in this paper is relevant at multiple levels of this hierarchy, and so are the various influences on aspirations. For a performance improvement to register at a given level of the hierarchy, there generally has to be improvement in some of the constituent processes at a lower level.[15] Hence, whatever the hierarchical level at which a particular influence on aspirations makes its initial impact, it tends to "decompose" and trickle down the hierarchy of routines from there. For example, aspirations affecting learning in Nucor's implementation of CSP might reflect influences relating to casting specifically, or alternatively to the trickle-down of strategic aspirations relating to the quality of Nucor's flat steel sheet. The latter aspirations, however, could equally well be "allocated" to the operations of the rolling mill. In the absence of specific information linking the higher-level aspirations to potentials for improvement in a particular constituent routine, the effect of the higher-level aspiration tends to be diffused across the lower levels. This likely means that the effect on a particular lower-level routine tends to be soft, i.e., aspirations will reconverge with actual performance if improvement is not quickly forthcoming. Influences specific to a particular subprocess would tend to create firmer aspirations there; a perceived shortfall in the operations of the caster implies a quest for improvement there, not elsewhere.[16]

The possibility of the converse pattern is also worth remarking. If prevailing ways of doing things are satisficing at a higher level, there are no unattained aspirations trickling down from there. In fact, satisfaction at the higher level may even reduce the salience of influences that suggest shortfalls in particular constituent processes, softening the aspirations induced by those influences. This can readily happen when the performance criterion in focus at the higher level is one to which the constituent processes relate in an additive way, such as unit cost or overall return.[17]

Two major classes of scenarios for the re-ignition of learning provide contrasting illustrations of the observations just made about specificity. The first class involves cases where the organization is in a crisis induced by sustained competitive pressure. There is a clear "need" for better performance; the survival of the organization, or at least top managers' jobs, may be at stake. This influence relates to the overall performance of the organization and thus impinges on the structure of capabilities and routines from the top; it relates to the big "how we make a living" capability of the organization as whole. Such an influence is not (as such) diagnostic of any particular shortcoming; it is entirely nonspecific. It may raise aspirations for constituent processes temporarily, but the effect tends to be soft and temporary because the hypothesis that "the real problem lies elsewhere" is available everywhere. For renewed learning to make a contribution to the resolution of the crisis, it is generally necessary for the survival threat to be supplemented by influences that are more diagnostic of specific and correctable deficiencies. Numerous examples suggest that the search for a diagnosis can be protracted, and of course the crisis tends to deepen while it goes on. It can be particularly protracted when the basic problem is that a needed function or capability is entirely absent – higher-level aspirations then have no helpful place to which they can trickle![18]

The quality management doctrine of continuous improvement (*kaizen*) illustrates the opposite class of scenarios. The practice of continuous improvement amounts to an effort to re-ignite learning so frequently that the flame burns pervasively and, so to speak, continuously. A key part of this effort is the institutionalization of multiple means of strengthening influences that create higher and firmer aspirations for specific processes. Benchmarking, for example, is a method for accomplishing this by drawing more systematically on vicarious experience; internal benchmarking does the same thing with respect to the organization's own experience. (Of course, benchmarking efforts seek to transfer know-how as well as aspirations – but without the heightened aspirations, the chances of effective utilization of the know-how would be slim.[19]) Similarly, efforts to attend closely to the sources of defects and difficulties, as in root-cause analysis, can be viewed as an active promotion of the influence of "the process when it is working well" on aspirations for its average performance (MacDuffie, 1997; Flaherty, 2000).

Thus, analysis based on the satisficing principle makes a dual contribution to understanding of why and when quality management efforts make sense.[20] Its implications for the cessation of overt learning help to explain why valuable opportunities to renew learning can be abundant. And, as just explained, many of the specific techniques of quality management can be broadly understood as involving efforts to strengthen types of influences on aspirations that are generally operative, creating higher and firmer aspirations as a result.

## Summary and Conclusion

As they learn new capabilities, organizations draw on the society around them for both means and ends. The means include the multiple sources of knowledge that are drawn upon in solving the long series of individual problems that arise in the course of such an effort – the technical training of employees, the sophisticated equipment, the more-or-less accurately perceived solutions that other organizations have developed for similar problems. The ends include, at the highest level, socially legitimated organizational goals. But the ends also include more proximate aspirations that guide learning and define its "success," both for process details and for the capability as a whole. Heterogeneity in aspirations thus joins many other causes as a potential explanation for why organizations wind up doing similar things in different ways and with different effectiveness. Other things equal, low aspirations mean an early halt to overt learning and more improvement opportunities "left on the table," while high aspirations imply the opposite. But covert learning likely continues after overt learning stops; besides that, the opportunities "table" tends to be refilled from external sources while overt learning is halted.

The perspective offered by the satisficing analysis of capability learning has broad and profound implications for the conceptualization of production methods. In mainstream economics, the standard conceptualization of production ignores the fact that production methods have emerged from a historical process and presumes that the limits of the feasible are sharply defined.[21] Ignoring the historical origins is viewed as a legitimate simplification, while the idea that technical feasibility is sharply defined is taken very seriously – probably because it is necessary to the conception of optimal behavior, which itself is taken very seriously. The foregoing analysis shows, however, that these two aspects of the standard conceptualization are closely connected. Acknowledging the historical and evolutionary origins of capabilities leads us to consider what is happening in real settings when overt learning stops. Such consideration reveals that the sharp edge of the technically feasible world is a myth; what the explorers discover is not an edge but a gradually thickening fog bank. When the fog is discouragingly thick, exploration stops – but it might resume later either because the fog lifts or because the incentives to press further increase. This means that subsequent analysis – for whatever descriptive or normative purpose at whatever level, from the shop floor to national economic policy – cannot safely assume that prevailing routines mark the edge of the feasible. They only mark the place where learning stopped, and perhaps it stopped only temporarily.

When viewed in a broad historical context, the plausible range of aspirations for a given organization at a given point of time seems quite narrow. When Boeing developed its 247 aircraft in the 1930s, it could not plausibly have come up with the 707 or the 747 just by raising its sights. In a more microscopic view, however, significant ranges of discretion appear. At a particular time and place, an incremental dose of resources devoted to learning would ordinarily (or on the average) produce an increment of learning and a superior capability. (If the 247 could not have been the 707, it might plausibly have been sufficiently better than it was to earn the accolades that history instead bestows on its rival, the DC-3) In their role as regulators of learning investments in the small, performance aspirations partially determine the new capabilities that emerge. By many branches from that early path, they influence the levels of performance aspirations a bit farther down the road, both in the same organization and elsewhere. In the evolving capabilities of the social system, therefore, what it is possible to accomplish is much more responsive to what people are generally trying to accomplish than might appear at first sight.

It has been well said (by Keith Pavitt), that "Nobody wants to fly the Atlantic in a socially constructed airplane." On the other hand, we can be grateful that the social mechanisms governing aspirations for such flights have helped to move the available capabilities beyond the performance level of the *Spirit of St Louis*.

## Acknowledgements

This paper was prepared for the conference on Evolution of Firm Capabilities held at the Amos Tuck School of Business Administration, September 24–25, 1999. I am indebted to Connie Helfat, Richard Rosenbloom, John Paul MacDuffie, and Dan Raff for helpful comments on an earlier draft.

## Notes

1   This account is drawn from Ghemawat (1992, 1997), and especially from Rosenbloom (1991).
2   Ghemawat (1992) and Rosenbloom (1991) seem to diverge on the innovativeness of CSP, with Ghemawat tending to downplay it.
3   The terminological problems are discussed at some length in the Introduction to *The Nature and Dynamics of Organizational Capabilities* (Dosi, Nelson, and Winter, 2000).
4   Of course, at the philosophical level there is always the ontological option of assuming that all feasible alternatives are preexisting from time immemorial. This often seems unnatural at the conceptual level, though convenient for modeling purposes.
5   Gavetti and Levinthal (2000) have recently proposed and analyzed the distinction between "experiential" and "cognitive" search. While "cognitive" search can be conducted off-line in the sense that new alternatives can be generated and assessed without actually changing the process, choice and implementation of an alternative lead to the more conclusive type of assessment that can only be accomplished on-line.
6   What is here called "off-line" deliberation is concerned with the generation of alternatives and with evaluation up to the point of choice of a specific alternative; the actual value of adjustments introduced as a result of such choice can only be assessed in additional trials.
7   On the other hand, it is clear that empirical learning curves typically describe situations where the way of doing things is not at all constant in that sense, and where deliberate change efforts persist. See Sinclair, Klepper, and Cohen (1998); Argote (1999); Mishima (1999).
8   I assume for the time being that there is one significant stopping point for overt learning of a particular capability. This assumption is relaxed in the final section of the paper.
9   Gavetti (2000) explores how a less comprehensive cognitive understanding can usefully complement local "experimential" search in the *NK* context.
10   I do not suggest that these other considerations are necessarily "irrational." For example, it is arguably rational to be guided by a remote analogy between the present situation and one previously encountered, if no better guidance is available. The point is that the tenuous relationship to what the decision-maker really needs to know renders the rationality issue moot.
11   Adner and Levinthal (2001) make a similar point about the "minimal threshold of functionality for a technology" and offer the following in explication: "A horseless carriage that is likely to break down after a quarter of a mile is a novelty, not a substitute for a horse."

12  This influence differs from that of "The Book," in which there is not only extensive experience elsewhere, but a codification of that experience. The competitive threat of rivals supports the informational influence of rival experience with a "need" influence.

13  This is fully consistent with the modeling of satisficing as a rational search or "optimal stopping" problem (Simon, 1955: appendix). (As discussed above, that model misleads to the extent that it suggests that the data required for the optimality analysis are available.)

14  The four points above illustrate previous remarks about opportunity costs at the organization level (1), at the individual level (4), and the related facts that aspirations adjust and overt learning ends with visible lines of improvement still visible ((2) and (3)).

15  An exception might be when improvement at the original level can be achieved by improving, at that same level, the coordination of constituent routines, without affecting their inner workings significantly.

16  The foregoing paragraph is essentially a variation on the insight-laden theme that Cyert and March introduced under the name "problemistic search" (Cyert and March, 1963).

17  Tyre and Orlikowski mention an example of this kind where one project engineer confidently declared, "The fact that this is an optimized system was proved by the corporate post-project audit – it showed that we are getting 138 percent payback." This, notwithstanding the fact that one system originally considered a major feature of the new tool had not been debugged and was not in use (Tyre and Orlikowski, 1994: 110) – the major misunderstanding of the concept of optimality implied here is commonplace. In fact, this "optimized system" is about as clear an example of Simon's "needle sharp enough to sew with" as one could imagine.

18  One of the crisis situations described in Starbuck, Greve, and Hedberg (1978) is of just this kind. Kalmar Verkstad, a Swedish manufacturer of railroad rolling stock, almost succumbed due to the misperception that it needed new product lines when it fact it needed a competent sales capability for the products it had.

19  Recent empirical work by Szulanski (2000) generally confirms the positive role of motivation in facilitating internal transfers – with the interesting exception that the *lack* of motivation in the recipient significantly facilitates the "ramp-up" phase of the transfer. This is consistent with other evidence suggesting that too much eagerness in the recipient can cause problems.

20  I have explored this at greater length in Winter (1994).

21  Winter (1982) provides a more extended analysis of the impact of a knowledge/learning viewpoint on the standard economic theory of production and offers suggestions for reform. These objections to standard production theory are a key issue for the evolutionary theory that I developed in collaboration with Richard Nelson (Nelson and Winter, 1982).

## References

Adner, R. and Levinthal, D. 2001. Demand heterogeneity and technology evolution: implications for product and process innovation. *Management Science* 47(5): 611–628.

Argote, L. 1999. *Organizational Learning: Creating, Retaining and Transferring Knowledge*. Kluwer: Boston, MA.

Cole, R. E. 2000. Market pressures and institutional forces: the early years of the quality movement. In *The Quality Movement & Organization Theory*, Cole, R. E. Scott, W. R. (eds). Sage: Thousand Oaks, CA; 67–87.

Cyert, R. M. and March, J. G. 1963. *A Behavioral Theory of the Firm*. Prentice-Hall: Englewood Cliffs, NJ.

Dosi, G., Nelson, R. R., and Winter, S. G. 2000. *The Nature and Dynamics of Organizational*

*Capabilities*. Oxford University Press: New York.

Flaherty, M. T. 2000. Limited inquiry and intelligent adaptation in semiconductor manufacturing. In *The Nature and Dynamics of Organizational Capabilities*, Dosi, G., Nelson, R. R., Winter, S. G. (eds). Oxford University Press: New York.

Gavetti, G. 2000. Cognition, capabilities and corporate strategy making, Working paper, The Wharton School, Philadelphia.

Gavetti, G. and Levinthal, D. 2000. Looking forward and looking backward: cognitive and experiential search. *Administrative Science Quarterly* forthcoming.

Ghemawat, P. 1992. Nucor at a crossroads. Harvard Business School, Case 9–793–039.

Ghemawat, P. 1997. *Games Businesses Play: Cases and Models*. MIT Press: Cambridge, MA.

Hamel, G. and Prahalad, C. K. 1989. Strategic intent. *Harvard Business Review* 67: 63–76.

Hamel, G. and Prahalad, C. K. 1993. Strategy as stretch and leverage. *Harvard Business Review* 71(2): 75–84.

Kauffman, S. 1989. Adaptation on rugged fitness landscapes. In *Lectures in the Sciences of Complexity*, Stein D (ed.). Addison-Wesley: Reading, MA; 517–618.

Kauffman, S. 1993. *The Origins of Order*. Oxford University Press: New York.

Levinthal, D. 1997. Adaptation on rugged landscapes. *Management Science* 43: 934–950.

Levinthal, D. 1998. The slow pace of rapid technological change: gradualism and punctuation in technological change. *Industrial and Corporate Change* 7(2): 217–247.

Levinthal, D. and March, J. G. 1981. A model of adaptive organizational search. *Journal of Economic Behavior and Organization* 2(4): 307–333.

Levinthal, D. A. and March, J. G. 1993. The myopia of learning. *Strategic Management Journal*, Winter Special Issue 14: 95–112.

MacDuffie, J. P. 1996. International trends in work organization in the auto industry: national-level vs. company-level perspectives. In *The Comparative Political Economy of Industrial Relations*, Wever, K., Turner, L. (eds). Industrial Relations Research Association: Madison, WI; 71–113.

MacDuffie, J. P. 1997. The road to "root cause": shop floor problem-solving at three automotive assembly plants. *Management Science* 43(4): 479–502.

March, J. G. 1991. Exploration and exploitation in organizational learning. *Organization Science* 2: 71–87.

Mishima, K. 1999. Learning by new experiences: revisiting the Flying Fortress learning curve. In *Learning by Doing in Markets. Firms and Countries*. Lamoreaux, N. R., Daniel, R., Temin, M. G., Temin, P. (eds.). University of Chicago Press: Chicago, IL; 145–179.

Nelson, R. R. and Winter, S. G. 1982. *An Evolutionary Theory of Economic Change*. Harvard University Press: Cambridge, MA.

Pil, F. K. and MacDuffie, J. P. 1999. Transferring competitive advantage across borders: a study of Japanese auto transplants in North America. In *Remade in America: Transplanting and Transforming Japanese Production Systems*. Liker, J., Fruin, M., Adler, P. (eds). Oxford University Press: New York; 39–74.

Rosenbloom, R. S. 1991. Nucor: expanding thin-slab capacity, Harvard Business School, Case 9–792–023.

Simon, H. A. 1955. A behavioral model of rational choice. *Quarterly Journal of Economics* 69: 99–118.

Simon, H. A. 1956. Rational choice and the structure of the environment. *Psychological Review* 63: 129–138.

Simon, H. A. 1987. Satisficing. In *The New Palgrave: A Dictionary of Economics*, Eatwell, J., Millgate, M., Newman, P. (eds). Vol. 4: Stockton Press: New York: 243–245.

Sinclair, G., Klepper, S., and Cohen, W. 1998. What's experience got to do with it? Sources of cost reduction in a large specialty chemicals producer, Working paper, Carnegie Mellon

University, Pittsburgh.

Starbuck, W. H., Greve, A., and Hedberg, B. 1978. Responding to crises. *Journal of Business Administration* 9: 111–137.

Szulanski, G. 2000. The process of knowledge transfer: a diachronic analysis of stickiness. *Organizational Behavior and Human Decision Processes* 82(3): 9–27.

Teece, D., Pisano, G., and Shuen, A. 1997. Dynamic capabilities and strategic management. *Strategic Management Journal* 18(7): 509–533.

Tversky, A. and Kahneman, D. 1974. Judgement under uncertainty: heuristics and biases. *Science* 185: 1124–1131.

Tyre, M. J. and Orlikowski, W. J. 1994. Windows of opportunity: temporal patterns of technological adaptation in organizations. *Organization Science* 5(1): 98–118.

von Hippel, E. and Tyre, M. J. 1995. How learning by doing is done: problem identification in novel process equipment. *Research Policy* 24: 1–12.

Winter, S. G. 1971. Satisficing, selection and the innovating remnant. *Quarterly Journal of Economics* (May) 85: 237–261.

Winter, S. G. 1982. An essay on the theory of production. In *Economics and the World Around It*. Hymans S (ed.). University of Michigan Press: Ann Arbor, MI: 55–91.

Winter, S. G. 1994. Organizing for continuous improvement: evolutionary theory meets the quality revolution. In *Evolutionary Dynamics of Organizations*. Baum, J. A. C., Singh, J. V. (eds). Oxford University Press: New York; 90–108.

Zollo, M. and Winter, S. G. 2002. Deliberate learning and the evolution of dynamic capabilities. *Organization Science* 13(3): 339–351.

# CHAPTER NINETEEN

# Untangling the Origins of Competitive Advantage

## Iain M. Cockburn, Rebecca M. Henderson, and Scott Stern

### Introduction

> Strategy studies . . . . is systematic, like the system of touts at the race track.
> [Stinchcombe, 2000]

What are the origins of competitive advantage? Although this question is fundamental to strategy research, it is one to which we lack a clear answer. As strategy researchers we believe that some firms consistently outperform others, and we have some evidence consistent with this belief (Rumelt, 1991; McGahan and Porter, 1997). We also have a number of well-developed theories as to why, at any given moment, it is possible for some firms (and some industries) to earn supranormal returns. As of yet, however, we have no generally accepted theory – and certainly no systematic evidence – as to the origins or the dynamics of such differences in performance. We know, for example, why high barriers to entry coupled with a differentiated product positioning obtained through unique organizational competencies may provide a firm with competitive advantage. But we know much less about how barriers to entry are built: about why this firm and not that one developed the competencies that underlie advantage, and about the dynamic process out of which competitive advantage first arises and then erodes over time.

This conceptual ambiguity has always been problematic for many economists, who have tended to view persistent differences in performance as a function of "unobserved heterogeneity" (Mundlak, 1961; Griliches, 1986). For example, empirical work in industrial organization routinely controls for "firm fixed effects." These are usually statistically significant and often account for a substantial fraction of the total variation in firm productivity or performance. Whereas strategy researchers tend to emphasize the degree to which these kinds of results offer support for the importance of "capabilities" or "positioning" (Rumelt, 1991; Henderson and Cockburn, 1994; McGahan and Porter, 1997; Lieberman and Dhawan, 2000), economists tend to emphasize the possibility that fixed effects are simply controlling for a series of much more mundane measurement problems, ranging from the difficulty of computing appropriately depreciated capital stocks and of measuring firm-specific input and output price schedules, to the problem of controlling for difficult-to-observe factors such as worker effort or worker quality. In short, the evidence which strategy researchers view as the motivation for their intellectual agenda are interpreted by many economists in terms of "nuisance" parameters – things which must be controlled for but which are not of intrinsic interest.

This implicit critique has been reinforced by theoretical and empirical research in the tradition of population ecology (see, for example, Hannan and Freeman, 1989). In summarizing the contributions of this literature and its application to strategy, Stinchcombe (2000) charges that the preponderance of strategy scholars have simply failed to understand (and certainly to systematically account for) the implications of population dynamics for performance heterogeneity. Stinchcombe suggests that if superior performance arises from the degree to which a firm's resources and/or strategy "match" the competitive environment, and if resources are randomly distributed at "birth" (or if the environment which firms face at the time strategies are chosen and resource investments are made is sufficiently uncertain), then performance heterogeneity simply reflects the fact that the realized competitive environment favors some strategies and some resource bundles over others. Such a critique implies that the cases which motivate so much of strategy research, and indeed even some of our theoretical frameworks, are roughly equivalent to *ex post* accounts of the way in which a winning gambler chose to put her money on red rather than on black at the roulette table.

In this paper we argue that grappling with this problem should be of central concern to strategy researchers: that while many of us are aware of the issue that Stinchcombe raises, without a more detailed understanding of the origin and dynamics of the development of competitive advantage we run the grave risk of meriting Stinchcombe's taunt that we are indeed "touts at the racetrack." We suggest that empirical strategy researchers need to move beyond studies of differential performance to more integrated studies which not only identify those factors that are correlated with superior performance but also attempt to explore the origins and the dynamics of their adoption.

We begin the paper with a brief literature review. By and large, Stinchcombe's critique – and population ecology more generally – suggests that most performance differentials, particularly differences in the probability of survivorship, can be explained by differences in a firm's initial conditions, and, moreover, that differences in initial conditions are largely the result of difficult-to-explain (and even harder-to-measure) differences in each firm's initial allocation of resources and capabilities. In contrast, strategy is centrally concerned with the process of how firms and managers *respond* to and exploit environmental signals. For example, there has been an explosion of powerful frameworks for evaluating the determinants of differential performance, from Porter's five forces framework to the resource-based view to transaction-cost economics. While each of these frameworks offers a somewhat different explanation for heterogeneous performance, all share two assumptions: that competitive advantage arises through earlier or more favorable access to resources, markets, or organizational opportunities; and that exploiting such opportunities reflects some degree of active interpretation of internal and external environmental signals by managers. Indeed, we argue that these literatures often share the implicit view that the *origins* of competitive advantage lie in the unusual foresight or ability of the firm's managers.

Of course, this characterization of the two schools of thought is unrealistically stark: population ecologists recognize the possibility that firms may be able to adapt to their environment and their competitive experience (Barnett and Hansen, 1996), and strategy researchers understand that firm strategy and capabilities are subject to powerful inertial forces (Christensen and Bower, 1996). But as we discuss in some detail in the next section, substantial differences in focus do exist: while population ecology is principally focused on exploring the performance implications of strong organizational inertia, one of the core agendas of strategy is understanding which organizational structures allow firms to first identify and then exploit opportunities offered by their environment and so (potentially) overcome organizational constraints.

We then turn to a discussion of an empirical methodology that might enable us to explore the relative importance of initial conditions and strategic choice in shaping competitive advantage. Our goal is to lay out an empirical framework that might allow us to compare and contrast the distinctive implications of the strategic perspective alongside the predictions of the population ecology literature, and thus to both offer a preliminary response to Stinchcombe's critique and to begin disentangling the origins of competitive advantage.

We begin by distinguishing between differences among firm in terms of their "initial conditions" vs. differences in the rate at which they adopt a particular performance-enhancing practice (or strategy) that has been linked to superior performance. Using Stinchcombe's analysis, we would expect the primary determinant of each firm's degree of adoption at any particular point in time to be the initial condition or founding state of that firm. This is not to imply that Stinchcombe's analysis suggests that firms cannot change, only that we believe that in general he would argue that change will not be systematically tied to the kinds of environmental cues which would be readily amenable to empirical analysis by strategy researchers.

We contrast this hypothesis with two explanations for diffusion which are consistent with a strategic perspective, and which are more difficult to reconcile with Stinchcombe's hypothesis. First, a strategic orientation would suggest that, in the absence of organizational failure, those firms whose early history places them in a particularly unfavorable position will tend to be the firms that respond most aggressively in terms of the rate at which they adopt particular performance-enhancing practices or strategies. We label this the "convergence" hypothesis, under which the key empirical question is not so much whether differences between firms will persist but how long they take to erode. From this perspective, the dynamics of competitive advantage are driven by two distinct processes: the exploitation of particularly favorable combinations of practices and/or market positions by firms whose initial positions "match" their environment, and the erosion of these rents as competitors "catch up" by mimicking the successful strategies of market leaders.

Second, we suggest that, beyond initial conditions and the process of convergence, adoption rates may be associated with environmental cues which are more intensively experienced by some firms rather than others. Firm strategy may thus be responsive to factors which provide information about a distinctive opportunity to invest in resources or strategies which will ultimately be associated with competitive advantage. For example, if firms are in different "niche" markets during the early stage of an industry, then the information these firms will possess about the future evolution of the industry may be different and their strategy should in principle respond to these signals. From an empirical perspective, this hypothesis suggests that strategy will be a function of the firm's *current or recent* environment; of course, a second issue exists as to whether we should focus on environmental cues which tend to be associated with internal (organizational) factors, external (market) factors, or both.

To illustrate these ideas, we apply this empirical framework to an evaluation of the adoption and diffusion of one particular strategy – the use of science-driven drug discovery – in the context of the worldwide pharmaceutical industry. We begin by briefly motivating the study of the adoption of science-driven drug discovery as a useful context in which to think about the origins of competitive advantage, and then turn to a discussion of our data sources and variable construction. We explore the measurement of both initial conditions and convergence, and then use our qualitative knowledge of the industry to identify five distinct "environmental cues" that might drive "strategic" adoption: a firm's distance from public science, whether or not the CEO is a scientist, its accumulated stock of scientific knowledge, its market position, and the composition of its sales portfolio.

Our analysis is by no means definitive. We offer it as a preliminary descriptive analysis of a complex phenomenon that raises as many questions as it answers. However, we believe that it illustrates concretely one approach to taking Stinchcombe's hypothesis seriously while also evaluating the origins of competitive advantage in a systematic manner.

Our findings are consistent with a perspective in which both population ecology and strategy have an important role to play in explaining patterns of organizational heterogeneity. On the one hand, "initial conditions" – or the position of each firm at the beginning of the period covered by our data – play an important role. Firms differ very significantly in the degree to which they had adopted the techniques of science-driven drug discovery in the first years of our period, and these differences persisted for many years. But there is also evidence for a powerful convergence effect, with the firms which were furthest from best practice at the beginning of the period moving most aggressively to adopt it. Finally, after controlling for initial conditions and convergence, additional time-varying characteristics of the firm play a modest role in explaining patterns of diffusion: both the composition of the firm's sales portfolio and its market share are significantly correlated with the rate at which the practice of science-driven drug discovery is adopted by the firm. Our results therefore provide substantial support for both Stinchcombe's view of the sources of competitive advantage and for a more traditional, "strategic" view, the implications of which are addressed in the conclusion.

## The Origins of Competitive Advantage

Early studies of competitive advantage were rooted firmly in historical analyses and careful qualitative research. This work could be interpreted as suggesting that competitive advantage was a complex phenomenon, that depended crucially on the active presence of superior leadership (Andrews, 1971; Selznick, 1957; Chandler, 1962). For example, Chandler's early work can be read as implying that those firms who adopted the new M-form before their competitors gained a strategic advantage, and, moreover, that the choice to adopt the new organizational form reflected the structure and leadership qualities of a company's top management. Through the 1960s and 1970s, the study of "strategy" was thus the study of what general managers or "leaders" should do and it was generally assumed that doing these things would make a difference: firms with better leaders would make better choices and would ultimately do better than their competitors.

Porter turned this paradigm on its head (Porter, 1980). In transforming the study of "imperfect competition" into the analysis of "competitive advantage," Porter shifted the focus of strategy research *outward*, towards the analysis of the firm's microeconomic environment. Porter's approach yielded sharply defined tools for understanding exactly why some firms (and industries) were likely to be more profitable than others. A "five forces" analysis is essentially a structural map of the underlying economics of an industry: a map of the degree to which competitors, entrants, substitutes, and vertical bargaining power exert pressure on the margins of a firm in a particular industry. A firm operating in an industry in which there are substantial returns to scale coupled with opportunities to differentiate, that buys from and sells to perfectly competitive markets and that produces a product for which substitutes are very unsatisfactory (e.g., the US soft drink in the 1980s), is likely to be much more profitable than one operating in an industry with few barriers to entry, and a large number of similarly sized firms who are reliant on a few large suppliers and who are selling commodity products to a few large buyers (e.g., the global semiconductor memory market).[1]

Structural analysis is a powerful tool for understanding why a particular strategic action (e.g., branding or investment in complementary product areas) may be associated with supranormal returns, but in and of itself says nothing about the role of senior management – or the process of strategic choice – in determining profitability. Consider the case of Crown Cork and Seal.[2] This classic HBS case describes the metal can industry: an industry that has a classically unfavorable structure and in which, in consequence, the vast majority of firms are relatively unprofitable. A structural analysis provides concrete insight into why it is so difficult for most firms to make supranormal returns in steel can production. In addition, the case can be read as suggesting that Crown itself earns supranormal returns because it has developed unique capabilities that have allowed it to differentiate its product in a way that is difficult for competitors to imitate. Does the case therefore imply that Crown was particularly well managed or that it had chosen a "good" strategy? Analogously, does it also imply that those metal can producers that are not performing forming well are managed by "bad" managers who have chosen "bad" strategies? Certainly this is the way that the case is often taught: as if the vision and determination of John Connelley, who developed Crown's strategy, was a critical determinant of its success. To take Stinchcombe's critique seriously, however, is to wonder whether Crown was simply lucky: whether it happened to be managed by Connelley, who happened to be obsessed with customer service. Stinchcombe forces us to ask: would Connelley have been as successful, as "visionary," in choosing a strategy in another environment?

Porter's analysis was fundamentally agnostic on this point, but a simplistic interpretation of his work seemed to imply that structural analysis could be used prospectively: that doing strategy was about "choosing good industries" or "rebuilding industry structure." The literature filled up with "five force analyses", and it was tempting to use them prescriptively: build these kinds of barriers to entry, structure rivalry along these lines, and your firm and perhaps your industry would become more profitable. Notice that at its roots this stream of work returns to the founding assumption of the field: good strategy is about leadership, about foresight. Managers who are smart enough to understand the implications of structural analysis and to make the commitments that it requires are likely to outperform those who do not (Ghemawat, 1991; Shapiro and Varian, 1998). Certainly it is the case that most teaching in strategy (at least implicitly) assumes this to be true. We act as if we believe that if we teach our students to analyze industry structure they will be better positioned to allocate resources into the "right" industries, or to influence industry structure in favorable directions. But we should recognize that while a variety of field studies certainly suggest that this is the case, there is, at least to our knowledge, no compelling quantitative evidence supporting this view: no broad-based statistical study showing that firms in which senior management actively used analytical tools to understand industry structure outperformed those that did not.

It was against this background that the "resource-based view" of the firm emerged (Wernerfelt, 1984; Barney, 1991; Peteraf, 1993). At one level, the resource-based view (hereafter "RBV") is simply a reinterpretation of the environmental perspective. Where the latter describes analytically why a differentiated position within an industry coupled with high entry barriers can lead to profitability, the former redirects attention towards the underlying heterogeneity making such a position sustainable. For example, while early environmental analyses seemed to suggest that competitive advantage arose from purely technological factors (such as economies of scale) or from unique assets (such as a brand name reputation), the RBV emphasized the idea that these technological or market positions reflect internal organizational capabilities, such as the ability to develop new products rapidly, to understand customer needs profoundly, or take advantage of new technologies cheaply. Proponents of the RBV suggested that strategic investments directed towards these *internal* activities might be of equal (or even greater) importance in generating supranormal returns.

More importantly, however, the RBV deepened the discussion of causality by focusing attention on two key insights about the sources of competitive advantage. First, in many cases, an industry's "structural" features are the result of the organizational capabilities of its constituent firms: a powerful brand name, for example, may reflect years of successful new product introduction and superb (and unique) marketing skills. Second, there are good reasons for thinking that the market for organizational capabilities may be imperfect in exactly the kinds of ways likely to lead to the existence of supranormal returns. In part because of these two insights (which are implicit but not always manifest in environmental analyses), the RBV is often positioned as an "alternative" to the environmental perspective. In our view, such a positioning reflects a significant misconception, since the RBV and the environmental perspective are complementary in many important respects. Each proposes a model of why firms may sustain superior performance, but the two models are not mutually exclusive, at least in terms of their empirical predictions: while the environmental view focuses attention on external industry structure, the RBV directs us towards the fact that internal capabilities and investments provide the instruments and tools to shape this external environment.[3]

Moreover, both literatures offer a similar theory about the process of strategic choice. In the case of environmental analysis, while economics is used to explain what kinds of strategic positions are likely to be most profitable, the theory is essentially agnostic as to how firms come to assume them. Firms can be lucky, they can be fast, or they can be far sighted: as long as they deal with the "five forces" they will be profitable, and the power of the tools lies in explaining exactly what these forces are and what kinds of mechanisms will help a firm deal with them. At least at some level, many (perhaps most) empirical treatments within the RBV tradition follow a similar logic, with the caveat that rather than emphasizing the fact that one firm rather than another "chose" a particular market position or production technology, the analyses focus on the fact that one firm "chose" to develop a certain set of internal capabilities or unique organizational assets (see, for example, Henderson and Clark, 1990; Clark and Fujimoto, 1991; Eisenhardt and Tabrizi, 1995).

At a more subtle level, however, the RBV literature begins to address causality and the ultimate origins of competitive advantage more deeply. It has implicit within it a significantly different view of the dynamics of strategic advantage, and, in particular, of exactly what managers can and cannot do. While the canonical reference for the RBV literature is usually taken to be Penrose (1959), the RBV perspective on the strategy *process* seems to be influenced more by Stinchcombe (1965), on the one hand, and Nelson and Winter (1982), on the other. Specifically, RBV scholars often seem to suggest that organizations are fundamentally different from each other for reasons that may have very little to do with any kind of "strategic logic," and that they can only change through limited, local search. To the extent that competencies are built on organizational routines that are only tacitly understood – indeed if tacit understanding and complexity are a prerequisite for any competence to be a source of competitive advantage – then there may exist a fundamental tension between the fact that competencies lie at the heart of competitive advantage and the use of this insight to guide strategy choice (Leonard-Barton, 1998). From this perspective, the simple observation that competencies may lead to advantage is only half the battle: the other half is understanding where competencies come from.

The theoretical RBV literature thus makes explicit a view of "strategy" that has long been latent – the sense that strategy is not all, or not only, about the cognitive ability of the senior management and their ability to make the "right" decisions, but also about their ability to work creatively with the raw material presented by their firm and their environment (Quinn, 1978; Mintzberg, 1987); to respond appropriately when their firm's organizational structure finds "good" strategies (Burgelman, 1994); and to create decision structures and procedures that allow a firm to respond to its environment adaptively (Bower, 1974; Levinthal, 1997). In short, in focusing on the dynamics of competence and resource creation, the RBV is centrally concerned with the degree to which successful firms are indeed "lucky" – since it suggests that many of the competencies underlying advantage are the result of investments made under a heavy cloud of uncertainty and that they are subject to local but not globally adaptive evolution.

This approach promises a bridge between the insights of those who stress "luck" or "initial heterogeneity" in shaping firm performance and the central insight of the strategy field: that what managers do matters. But we believe that these implications have not been fully worked out. Most importantly, the RBV has not generated the kinds of empirical studies of adoption that are crucial both to fleshing out a full response to Stinchcombe's critique and to building a richer understanding of the origins of competitive advantage. While there are studies suggesting that the possession of unique organizational competencies is correlated with superior performance (Henderson and Cockburn, 1994; Powell, Koput, and Smith-Doerr, 1996), and others suggesting that competitive advantage may be heavily influenced by conditions at a firm's founding (Holbrook et al., 2000; Eisenhardt, 1988; Eisenhardt and Schoonhoven, 1990), so far as we are aware there are few careful studies of the hypothesis that successful strategy is the successful management of the evolution of organizational skills and its changing environment.[4] Indeed, some of the most elegant and widely cited studies of the diffusion of organizational innovation do not control for firm founding conditions (see, for example, Davis, 1991). At its worst, just as overenthusiastic readings of Porter led to the prescription "choose a good industry," overenthusiastic readings of the RBV have had the flavor of "build the right resources/competencies." Even Barney's original piece has something of this tone, as for example when he suggests that:

> To be a first mover by implementing a strategy before any competing firms, a particular firm must have insights about the opportunities associated with implementing a strategy that are not possessed by other firms in the industry, or by potentially entering firms. (Barney, 1991: 104)

Such an analysis clearly places the source of competitive advantage in the insight of the firm's managers, and leaves unanswered the critical empirical question: *how does one know?* Is the success of Sony in introducing the Playstation the result of a strategic competence possessed by Sony's senior managers? Or is it the result of a complex history, an evolutionary process by which Sony was "lucky" enough to be in the right place at the right time? In short, what are the concrete and distinct implications of Stinchcombe's and Nelson and Winter's insights for our understanding of strategy?

## Empirical Methodology

In the remainder of this paper, we begin to address the implications of these questions for empirical research in strategy, at least in a preliminary way. Distinguishing between alternative theoretical perspectives in evaluating the origins of competitive advantage is a massive and difficult task. The empirical work in the remainder of this paper should thus be interpreted as outlining one type of empirical approach which might yield fruitful analysis of the origins of competitive advantage rather than as a definitive test of one particular theory in the specific context that we examine.

Our empirical analysis is designed to tease apart the issues that we identified above. We identified two core hypotheses: on the one hand, the view that competitive advantage is largely determined by factors put in place at the organization's founding; and, on the other, the view that competitive advantage results from a firm's "strategic" response to changes in this environment or to new information about profit opportunities. We believe that one way in which one might plausibly begin to separate these two effects is to identify an organizational practice that is closely associated with competitive advantage, and then to explore the determinants of the diffusion of this practice across a population of firms.[5]

To do this, we build on a long tradition of modeling the process of diffusion of new technologies. Our analysis consists of the estimation and interpretation of a "diffusion equation" $y_{j,t} = f(I_{j,0}, Z_{j,t}, t, \Omega)$, where $y_{j,t}$, our dependent variable, is a measure of the extent to which firm $j$ has adopted the practice as of time $t$, and the explanatory variables are chosen to illuminate the competing hypotheses. $I_{j,o}$ is a measure of the initial, or founding conditions of firm $j$, while $Z_{j,t}$ is a vector of variables which reflect the opportunities and environmental conditions affecting firm $j$ at time t, and thus highlight the existence of potential sources of differences across firms. For example, $Z_{j,t}$ might include measures of the nature of firm decision-making, of absorptive capacity or other strategies associated with seeking external sources of knowledge, of market position, or of the talent or focus of managers in the firm. Time, $t$, plays a critical role as an explanatory variable here, since it allows us to capture the *rate* of diffusion of the practice, and so allows us to test whether firms in alternative environments tend to have faster or slower rates of adoption of the practice in question. $\Omega$ is the vector of parameters to be estimated.[6]

Within this general framework, choices about functional form or about which of these explanatory variables to include correspond to different perspectives on the sources of competitive advantage. Three possibilities are of particular interest. First, perhaps the simplest model one can imagine would be to regress $y_t$ on a favored set of $Z_t$'s, from which one might conclude that the level of adoption of the practice was satisfactorily "explained" by the $Z$'s, providing support for a "strategic response" perspective.

Alternatively a second approach would be to regress $y_t$ on $I_0$ by itself, perhaps to test the conclusion that "it's all initial conditions." Finally, our focus on diffusion allows us to evaluate a third (somewhat more subtle) implication of the "environmental" perspective, namely that firms who find themselves to have chosen strategies or organizational practices which are particularly *unfavorable* will be likely to have a higher rate of adoption than firms who are near the "frontier" of profitability. In other words, even if the level of $y_t$ is positively associated with $I_0$ (there is "persistence" in the impact of initial conditions), a strategy-oriented perspective suggests that $y_t$ will be *negatively* associated with $I_0 \times t$. That is, firms which begin at the "lowest" level will have the highest rate of increase. This strategic response, if it occurs, will manifest itself in the data in the form of *convergence* over time among (surviving) organizations in terms of the organizational practices which they exhibit – the laggards will "catch up" with firms who were "lucky" enough to have chosen favorable practices at their founding (or at the beginning of the observed sample period).

To assess the relative salience of "initial conditions" and environmental heterogeneity in driving patterns of adoption of a performance-enhancing practice, we require an empirical model of the dynamics of diffusion which allows for both effects to work factor simultaneously. We therefore specify a model which includes a firm's initial conditions, $I_0$, a firm's environment and opportunity set at a given point in time, $Z_t$, and interactions between each of these elements and time, t.

$$y_t = \alpha + \beta t + \gamma I_0 + \delta I_0 \cdot t + \varphi Z_t + \rho Z_t \cdot t \qquad (1)$$

The parameters of this model nest a number of key hypotheses about the determinants of $y_t$ which can be formulated as restrictions on the parameters.[7] For example, a naive reading of population ecology would suggest that, beyond a firm's initial conditions, there should be no systematic pattern to diffusion relating to the firm's changing environmental circumstance: some firms will be able to execute the practice as a function of their founding conditions and others will not. Thus for a given set of firms, current levels of adoption should be a function only of initial conditions, implying that $\varphi = \rho = \delta = 0$.

Conversely, the simple environmental or "strategic" hypothesis implies that $yt$ should also be driven by $Z_t$: firms may change their behavior in response to changes in the environment with levels of adoption not wholly determined by a firm's starting position. This would imply $\varphi \neq 0$ and/or $\rho \neq 0$. For example, we believe that one could interpret a finding that $y_t$ was correlated with the current market position of the firm as suggesting it is indeed reacting to exogenous shocks in its environment, independent of its founding conditions. Similarly a finding that $y_t$ was correlated with the experience of the firm's CEO would suggest that the firm is changing its strategy as it develops new capabilities.

Finally, the "convergence" hypothesis suggests that, in addition to a firm's initial conditions, and its responsiveness to objective measures of its environment, firms who face unfavorable initial conditions may be those who are most likely to have the highest rate of adoption, that is, $\delta < 0$. This would imply that initial conditions are important in shaping strategy, though hardly in the way that Stinchcombe hypothesized.

Before turning to the data, two further modeling issues must be addressed. The first is that of functional form: if we interpret $y_t$ as "fraction adopted" then it would be appropriate to follow the diffusion literature in recognizing that the diffusion of most practices or technologies follows an S-shaped (or sigmoid) pattern through time. There are a variety of functional forms which allow for this type of nonlinear time path, but the simplest transformation involves taking the log-odds ratio $(\log(y_t/(1 - y_t))$ of the dependent variable measuring the extent of adoption (Griliches, 1957). On the other hand, if $yt$ is a more general indicator of the use of a practice, then theory offers us little guidance as to functional form.[8]

A second issue relates to the measurement of initial conditions, $I_0$. Two possibilities present themselves: either to take on the formidable task of identifying and explicitly measuring all the relevant aspects of heterogeneity in firm capabilities, or, more straightforwardly, to capture their empirical content with $y_0$ – the presample value of $y_t$. This second option is attractive not just because it is easy to implement, but also because it allows us to be agnostic about the precise nature of the initial characteristics of firms which drive their subsequent evolution.[9] Actual estimation of these models therefore requires data only on $y$ and $Z$. We now turn to our specific application of this framework, the diffusion of science-driven drug discovery in the worldwide pharmaceutical industry.

## Data and Variable Construction

### Competitive advantage from science-driven drug discovery

We focus here on the adoption of "science-driven drug discovery" as a primary strategy in the management of pharmaceutical research. As we have laid out in a number of papers, prior to the late 1970s pharmaceutical research was conducted largely through a process of so-called "random" search (see, for example, Henderson, Orsenigo, and Pisano, 1999, and papers referenced therein).[10] From the late 1970s on, firms began to respond to the acceleration in the growth of publicly available biological knowledge by adopting a new mode of so-called "science-driven" drug discovery. This move appears to have been tightly associated with the creation of competitive advantage: those firms adopting the new techniques appear to have been significantly more productive (Gambardella, 1995; Henderson and Cockburn, 1994) in an industry in which the introduction of blockbuster drugs is a source of tremendous value (Grabowski and Vernon, 1990).[11]

Despite the power of this strategy, its diffusion across the industry was surprisingly slow. As late as 1991, some firms continued to view scientific publication and participation in the broader community of public science – a key requirement for the full adoption of science-driven drug discovery – as a diversion from the more "important" business of finding drugs. As the research manager at one of these companies put it:

> Why should I let my people publish? It's just a waste of time that could be spent in the search for new drugs. (quoted in Henderson, 1994)

Here we argue that exploring the factors that drove these differences in the rate of adoption across firms not only concretely illustrates the difficulty of distinguishing between explanations, but also serves as a springboard for thinking through the relationship between theories of adoption and theories of the source of strategic advantage. The remainder of this section describes the sources of the data from which we construct our empirical tests, our alternative measures of the practice itself, $y_t$, and measures associated each firm's environment at a given point in time, $Z_t$.

### Data sources and sample construction

We draw on two primary data sets. The first contains detailed qualitative data and quantitative data for 10 major pharmaceutical firms for the period 1965–90. These data formed the basis for our previous work and are described in detail there (Henderson and Cockburn, 1994, 1996). The second data set consists of a sample of 16 large research-oriented pharmaceutical firms for the period 1980–97.[12] Overall the average firm in both samples is somewhat larger than the average publicly traded pharmaceutical firm. While they do not constitute a random sample in a statistical sense, they are reasonably representative of the larger pharmaceutical firms who invest substantially in original research and comprise a substantial portion of the industry (the firms in the sample account for approximately 50 percent of US pharmaceutical sales in 1993). While we were able to obtain detailed, internal data for the first sample, the second relies on comprehensive data collected from secondary sources, including information on the composition and background of senior management, firms' geographical location and patenting activity, scientific papers, and product sales compiled at the therapeutic class level (e.g., cardiovascular therapies, antiinfectives, or cancer). Data about senior management were collected from annual reports, while geographical data were derived from the publication record of each firm. Our source for patent data is Derwent Inc.'s *World Patent Index*; scientific publications are drawn from ISI's *Science Citation Index* and *Web of Science*. Sales data are from various publications of IMS America, a market research firm.

### Measuring the adoption of "science-driven drug discovery" ($y_t$)

A quantitative analysis of the adoption of science-driven drug discovery requires the construction of a reliable measure of the extent to which firms are engaged in the practice.

Our initial measure of this practice, PROPUB, identifies the degree to which researchers were given incentives to establish standing in the scientific public rank hierarchy. In prior work (Cockburn and Henderson, 1998; Cockburn, Henderson, and Stern, 1999b), we have argued that the extent to which a firm has adopted this practice is an indicator of how thoroughly they have embraced the techniques of science-driven drug discovery.[13] This measure was derived from detailed qualitative interviews conducted within 10 major pharmaceutical firms. While it has the great virtue of being a direct measure of the organizational practice in which we are interested, it unfortunately suffers from two important limitations. First, it was derived from qualitative interviews conducted by a single researcher, which may raise questions as to its reliability and replicability. Second, PROPUB is not currently available beyond 1990 or for the 11 firms in the sample that were not included in our earlier data collection efforts.

We therefore also evaluate the diffusion of science-based drug discovery using three quantitative measures derived from public sources. These variables all draw on bibliographic information collected for every paper published in the journals indexed in the Institute for Scientific Information's *Science Citation Index* between 1980 and 1994 for which at least one author's address was at one of our sample of firms. The most straightforward, PAPERS, is a simple publication count: the number of papers published in any given year for which at least one author was affiliated with our sample firms. As prior research has established, pharmaceutical companies publish heavily, with annual counts of papers comparable to the output of similarly sized universities and research institutes (Koenig, 1982; Hicks, 1995). Publication counts are clearly an important indicator of research activity, and have been previously interpreted as capturing the level of investment in "basic science" (Gambardella, 1995). Of course, since the volume of publication activity may simply reflect the scale of the firm's research effort, when we use any of these measures as a dependent variable we control for size by including total US pharmaceutical sales in the regression.[14]

While PAPERS has several attractive properties in terms of capturing the degree to which firms have adopted the science-based drug discovery techniques, PAPERS is also fundamentally an output measure, and may therefore also measure factors such as the success of the firm's research program: the discovery of interesting compounds also generates interesting papers. Using the same data, we therefore constructed AUTHORS: a variable which identifies the number of science-oriented researchers at each firm. AUTHORS is a count of the number of distinct individuals publishing at the firm in any given year. We hypothesize that at those firms in which the scientists face high-powered incentives to raise their standing in the public eye the marginal incentives to publish will be higher and the "marginal" scientist will make more of an effort to get their name on the papers to which they have contributed.[15]

Although counting authors may give us a better measure of the adoption of the new practice than a raw publication count, it remains an output measure. Our preferred measure of the degree to which the firm has adopted propublication incentives is PUBFRAC: the fraction of individuals whose names appear on a patent who also appear as an author on papers published within 2 years of the patent application. By explicitly tying publishing and patenting together, this measure incorporates the degree to which a firm is encouraging those researchers who are directly involved in the firm's drug discovery process to participate in scientific publication. In addition, since this is measured as a share rather than an absolute number of papers or authors, in principle it captures the *propensity* to publish, independent of the scale of the firm, either in terms of sales or number of employed scientists.[16]

Table 19.1 provides summary statistics and the correlation coefficients for these four variables. In addition to the relatively high levels of objective measures such as PAPERS and AUTHORS, it is worth noting that all four of the measures are quite closely correlated. The time path of these variables indicates the gradual diffusion of the practice across the industry over time. Table 19.2 shows the evolution of both the mean values and the coefficient of variation (standard deviation/mean) for each of our four measures of science-driven drug discovery. Not only does the mean level of each measure rise, but the coefficient of variation steadily falls, suggesting that there was considerable "convergence" towards a common level of intensity of use of the practice at the same time that its average level increased. Note that this diffusion is not driven primarily by the exit of firms from the sample.[17] In itself, this immediately raises questions about the extreme form of Stinchcombe's hypothesis: the firms in the sample appear to be actively adopting the practice of science-driven drug discovery over the period covered by our data, an observation which suggests that there is more going on than a simple initial random distribution of capabilities followed by an exogenous environmental shock. Indeed, it is consistent with a "strategic" view in which managers gradually recognize the opportunities presented by the new techniques and move to adopt them. These simple statistics highlight the empirical salience of the convergence hypothesis: that initial conditions engender persistence over the medium term, but that laggard firms aggressively more to adopt these techniques, erasing the importance of the past in the long term.

### Measuring initial conditions, $I_0$

As discussed above, rather than attempt to characterize initial conditions directly, we use $y_0$, or the firm's initial level of adoption of the practice of science-driven drug discovery, as the summary statistic for its initial condition. This is calculated from average level of $y$ in the 2 years preceding the sample period.

**Table 19.1** Descriptive statistics for alternative dependent variables

*(a) Summary statistics*

|  | N | Mean | S.D. |
|---|---|---|---|
| PROPUB | 83 | 3.6 | 1.3 |
| AUTHORS | 153 | 854 | 550 |
| PAPERS | 153 | 299 | 189 |
| PUBFRAC | 153 | 0.65 | 0.14 |

*(b) Correlation coefficients*

|  | PROPUB | PUBFRAC | AUTHORS |
|---|---|---|---|
| PUBFRAC | 0.11 | | |
| AUTHORS | 0.56 | 0.42 | |
| PAPERS | 0.55 | 0.38 | 0.35 |

## Defining Z: measures of firm heterogeneity

We draw on the literature and on our qualitative data to construct six distinct measures of heterogeneity in the environment and opportunity sets of each firm. Some of these focus on general characteristics of the firm: others focus on the role of cardiovascular therapies – a leading application for science-driven drug discovery – in the firm's research and sales portfolio and on the firm's share of the market for cardiovascular therapies. This list of variables includes both factors that might "rationally" drive differences in the diffusion of science-driven drug discovery – including the firm's closeness to public science and its technological experience and market position – and factors that might shape the attention of senior managers, including whether the firm's CEO has a scientific background and the composition of its sales portfolio. Our discussion here focuses largely on the qualitative and theoretical evidence that motivates each variable. Full details of the ways in which each was operationalized are included in the appendix. Table 19.3 presents descriptive statistics for these variables.

### Scientis–CEO

Qualitative interviews with senior industry participants often explained variations across firms in the rate at which they moved to science-driven drug discovery in terms that resonate deeply with a "strategic" picture of adoption.[18] Our informants suggested that differences in "leadership" or "vision" across firms had a very significant effect on the decision to adopt the new mode of research. One senior researcher remembered:

> We spent most of the seventies going to T groups. It was fun, but we didn't get much science done . . . The managers of the firm were largely focused on using the cash generated by the pharmaceuticals group to look for diversification opportunities.

**Table 19.2** Means and coefficients of variation over time, alternate dependent variables

| | *PROPUB* | | *PAPERS* | | *AUTHORS* | | *PUBFRAC* | |
|---|---|---|---|---|---|---|---|---|
| *Year* | *Mean* | *CV* | *Mean* | *CV* | *Mean* | *CV* | *Mean* | *CV* |
| 1976 | 2.40 | 0.71 | | | | | | |
| 1977 | 2.40 | 0.71 | | | | | | |
| 1978 | 2.50 | 0.66 | | | | | | |
| 1979 | 2.70 | 0.55 | | | | | | |
| 1980 | 2.70 | 0.55 | | | | | | |
| 1981 | 3.10 | 0.51 | 182.4 | 0.63 | 393.6 | 0.60 | 0.54 | 0.30 |
| 1982 | 3.30 | 0.43 | 197.2 | 0.65 | 431.7 | 0.61 | 0.58 | 0.24 |
| 1983 | 3.30 | 0.43 | 210.1 | 0.67 | 478.3 | 0.64 | 0.53 | 0.31 |
| 1984 | 3.40 | 0.42 | 199.3 | 0.69 | 489.9 | 0.66 | 0.56 | 0.29 |
| 1985 | 3.40 | 0.42 | 252.0 | 0.74 | 615.8 | 0.68 | 0.58 | 0.25 |
| 1986 | 3.50 | 0.41 | 257.9 | 0.67 | 656.3 | 0.62 | 0.66 | 0.18 |
| 1987 | 3.50 | 0.41 | 283.9 | 0.67 | 746.3 | 0.55 | 0.68 | 0.17 |
| 1988 | 3.60 | 0.37 | 279.8 | 0.68 | 800.1 | 0.59 | 0.67 | 0.21 |
| 1989 | 3.67 | 0.36 | 309.1 | 0.50 | 913.9 | 0.46 | 0.64 | 0.16 |
| 1990 | 4.00 | 0.23 | 370.6 | 0.46 | 1128.8 | 0.38 | 0.68 | 0.13 |
| 1991 | | | 376.8 | 0.47 | 1230.1 | 0.41 | 0.68 | 0.16 |
| 1992 | | | 452.5 | 0.46 | 1436.0 | 0.45 | 0.73 | 0.12 |
| 1993 | | | 460.1 | 0.49 | 1553.9 | 0.45 | 0.80 | 0.13 |

Managers in firms that failed to adopt the new techniques looked back on their failure as an embarrassment:

> By now you will have worked out that we didn't really do any real research in the eighties. We talked about it, but X didn't understand what it required. We kept doing what we had always done.

The decision to invest in the science-driven approach was often identified with the hiring of key individuals:

> Oh, that's when we hired Y. He built a completely new research facility and started to hire aggressively. He had a fundamental belief that if we did leading edge science we would find breakthrough drugs.

Capturing this insight empirically is a challenging task. One option is to explore the correlation between changes in research strategy and changes in senior management personnel. Unfortunately we have not yet been able to collect this information in rich enough detail for our full sample. Here we use a binary variable (Scientist–CEO) measuring whether or not the firm's CEO has a scientific background as a first attempt at capturing the idea. We hypothesize that firms with scientifically trained CEOs will be more likely, all else equal, to adopt the techniques of science-driven drug discovery. While the classical environmental approach implicitly suggested that top managers

**Table 19.3** Descriptive statistics for independent variables

| Variable | Mean | SD | Min. | Max. |
|---|---|---|---|---|
| Cardiovascular patents share of firm patents (%) | 12.47 | 4.40 | 5.18 | 27.98 |
| Cardiovascular therapies as share of firm sales (%) | 18.54 | 19.50 | 0 | 73.78 |
| Share of firm in US cardiovascular market (%) | 5.27 | 8.71 | 0 | 44.92 |
| Total firm sales ($ million) | 938.8 | 701.1 | 99.9 | 3653.7 |
| Scientist–CEO | 0.065 | 0.248 | 0 | 1 |
| Distance from science | 0.363 | 0.515 | 0.001 | 2.290 |

150 observations.

who can deeply understand the value associated with novel strategies is important, the RBV literature has placed much greater emphasis on these kinds of factors.

*Cardiovasculars as a share of total firm sales*
Our qualitative evidence suggests that the speed with which the new techniques were adopted was a function of the balance of power within the firm. Those firms whose sales portfolios were dominated by therapeutic classes in which the new techniques were likely to be particularly important – particularly by sales of cardiovascular drugs – appear to have become convinced that the new techniques were likely to be important much faster than managers in those firms in which sales were much more heavily concentrated in therapeutic areas for which the new techniques were much less useful. Thus we hypothesize that firms whose sales are dominated by cardiovascular therapies will adopt the new techniques faster than their rivals.

Notice that because of the very long lead times characteristic of the pharmaceutical industry, share of the sales portfolio is *not* highly correlated with share of the patent portfolio. Thus we interpret any effect of the share of sales portfolio on the diffusion of science-driven drug discovery as a reflection of the focus of attention of senior management attention, rather than as a response to any difference in the firm's research base.[19] It may also, of course, reflect the presence of marketing and sales assets.

*Distance from public science*
Our qualitative evidence suggests that differences in geographic location may also have had systematic effects on the decision to adopt the new research techniques since the benefits of adopting the new approach may well have been significantly higher (and the costs significantly lower) for those firms whose research laboratories were located in reasonably close proximity to large communities of publicly funded researchers. Close proximity not only made it easier to attract the best-quality researchers, but probably also made it much easier to maintain close connections to the public sector once these researchers had joined the firm (Jaffe, 1986; Zucker et al., 1998). Indeed, both the classical environmental perspective and the RBV have emphasized the role of geographic location in shaping the ability of firms to more aggressively adopt practices associated with superior performance. We have developed a measure, DISTANCE, of the geographical position of a firm's research activities using the publications data from ISI.

*Knowledge capital: cardiovascular patents as a percentage of total firm patents*
One of the key claims of the RBV is that a firm's particular experience with specific technologies or technological trajectories provides it with a firm-specific capital stock which it can both exploit as well as providing a mechanism to draw upon outside knowledge. In the current context, the techniques of science-driven drug discovery were not immediately applicable to all areas of drug research. In the late 1970s and early 1980s, for example, many scientists believed that the new techniques would be much more useful in the search for cardiovascular therapies than they would be in the search for new anti-infective drugs. Scientific understanding of cardiovascular disease was much further advanced, and it was thought that this understanding would provide a particularly rich basis for drug discovery. Firms with more experience in cardiovascular therapies might therefore have expected to benefit disproportionately from adoption of the new techniques. Thus, in the RBV tradition, we hypothesize that adoption will be positively correlated with experience in cardiovascular disease.

*Market position: share of the cardiovascular market*
Following the classical environmental perspective, we also expect a firm's position in the product market to have an effect on its decision to adopt the new techniques. A large literature in economics links the degree to which a firm possesses monopoly power in the product market to its decision to adopt an innovation (Gilbert and Newbery, 1982; Reinganum, 1981; Fudenberg and Tirole, 1985; Henderson, 1993; Karshenas and Stoneman, 1993). Unfortunately this literature yields no very clear predictions – under some circumstances monopolists appear to have incentives to adopt innovations *before* entrants; under others they have an incentive to wait. Moreover, it has not directly addressed the question of the drivers of adoption of a research technique, as opposed to the adoption of a new product. Nonetheless, we believe that in this context the most plausible interpretation of this literature is that firms with monopoly power in the relevant product market will have higher incentives to adopt the new techniques, since they are more likely to benefit from them. Thus, consistent with an externally oriented environmental perspective, we evaluate whether firms that have a high share of the cardiovascular market will adopt the new techniques faster than others.

*Firm sales*
Finally, total US sales is included to control for the fact that there may be economies of scale in the adoption of the new techniques. Zucker and Darby (1997) found evidence for economies of scale in the adoption of the techniques of biotechnology, and to the degree that "science-driven" drug discovery also takes advantage of scientific resources that can be maintained centrally and exploited throughout the organization one would expect economies of scale to be important in this case as well. Indeed, one of the key tenets of most strategy perspectives (either the classical environmental perspective or RBV) is that *scale matters*, if only in terms of having sufficient liquidity or slack resources to aggressively adopt performance-enhancing organizational practices.

## Other potential sources of heterogeneity

This list of variables could be expanded almost indefinitely. We do not explore, for example, the degree to which either a firm's position in its network or wider institutional context determines adoption. Determining the network position of a major pharmaceutical firm turns out to be an exceptionally difficult undertaking[20] and, while we are sure that the wider institutional context plays a role in shaping the adoption of science-driven drug discovery, distinguishing between the effects of institutional isomorphism or management fashion and the simple effects of time and convergence turns out to be very difficult. We also do not address the extent to which governance structures and incentive systems at the most senior levels of the firm affect adoption decisions. While this is an intriguing hypothesis, preliminary analysis highlighted both the difficulty of constructing consistent measures of governance problems across national boundaries and the fact that they appeared to be only very weakly correlated, if at all, with the firm's choice of research technique.

## Results

In this section we discuss the results from two sets of regression models. The first set focuses on the "initial conditions" and convergence model. The second set brings in the measures of environmental heterogeneity.

Our analysis begins by considering a simple model of the adoption of science-driven drug discovery which focuses exclusively on the dynamic impact of "initial conditions":

$$y_t = \alpha + \beta t + \gamma y_0 + \delta y_0 \cdot t + \varepsilon_t$$

This equation is estimated using each of our alternate measures of the extent of diffusion of science-driven drug discovery (with the appropriate functional forms for each measure). Table 19.4 presents the results, which we find quite striking. In the first place, they show that at any point in time the degree to which a firm has adopted the techniques of science-driven drug discovery is to a very great extent a function of the firm's position at the beginning of the period. The estimated coefficient on the initial value of the dependent variable is large and very significant in all of the regressions. Second, the highly significant *negative* coefficient estimated for the interaction of $y_0$ with time provides evidence in favor of the convergence hypothesis. The firms that were "furthest away" from best practice (with lower initial levels of the dependent variable) moved *fastest* to adopt. However, while convergence seems to be an important aspect of these data, the coefficient estimates imply a relatively slow diffusion process: 10 years or more for the laggard firms to catch up with the leaders.

These results are important. They illustrate concretely a model of competitive advantage that is implicit in much of our teaching and research but that is rarely demonstrated. Understanding the origins of competitive advantage requires a focus on two distinct processes: *creation*, the means whereby first adopters develop and exploit new techniques or strategies; and *imitation*, whereby laggard firms respond to their unfavorable positions and move to imitate market leaders.

**Table 19.4** Initial conditions and convergence at the determinants of the adoption of science driven drug discovery

| Dependent variable: N | Log-odds (PROPUB) 135 | Ln (PAPERS) 150 | Ln (AUTHORS) 150 | Log-odds (PUBFRAC) 150 |
|---|---|---|---|---|
| PROPUB₀ | 1.00** | | | |
| | (0.08) | | | |
| PROPUB₀* time | −0.04** | | | |
| | (0.01) | | | |
| Ln(PAPERS₀) | | 1.02** | | |
| | | (0.07) | | |
| Ln(PAPERS₀) * time | | −0.05** | | |
| | | (0.01) | | |
| Ln(AUTHORS₀) | | | 1.04** | |
| | | | (0.05) | |
| Ln(AUTHORS₀)* time | | | −0.04** | |
| | | | (0.01) | |
| PUBFRAC₀ | | | | 3.57** |
| | | | | (0.71) |
| PUBFRAC₀* time | | | | −0.29** |
| | | | | (0.11) |
| Intercept | −3.87** | −1.03* | −0.85* | −2.45** |
| | (0.61) | (0.04) | (0.40) | (0.60) |
| Time | 0.18** | 0.32** | 0.35** | 0.26** |
| | (0.03) | (0.06) | (0.05) | (0.06) |
| Ln (Fmsales) | 0.21* | 0.15** | 0.10** | 0.09 |
| | (0.10) | (0.05) | (0.03) | (0.08) |
| Adj. R² | 0.75 | 0.82 | 0.91 | 0.38 |

*$p<0.05$; **$p<0.01$.

Note that at one level these results are consistent with a Stinchcombian view of the sources of competitive advantage. Early movers, who happen to be endowed with the "right" set of organizational practices, reap the returns from being in the right place at the right time. Laggards manage to change, but changing does not create advantage, it merely re-levels the playing field. At another level, though, convergence provides evidence for a more "strategic" perspective on the dynamics of competitive advantage. Competitive advantage is as much about responding to unfavorable positioning as it is about exploiting those opportunities which present themselves. As such, aggressive imitation by those who are initially positioned most unfavorably is consistent with a process whereby thoughtful managers actively interpret their environment and use their discretion to implement a *strategic* response.

Table 19.5 builds on this analysis and develops evidence relating to the full diffusion model following equation 1. Each column includes either (a) only variables associated with initial conditions (5.1), (b) only variables associated with time-varying environmental heterogeneity ((5.2) through (5.4)), or (c) both types of variables (5.5). For

**Table 19.5** Initial conditions and contemporaneous heterogeneity; dependent variable: log-odds (PUBFRAC), 150 observations throughout

|  | (5.1) | (5.2) | (5.3) | (5.4) | (5.5) |
|---|---|---|---|---|---|
| $PUBFRAC_0$ | 3.57** |  |  |  | 7.11** |
|  | (0.71) |  |  |  | (0.92) |
| $PUBFRAC_0$ * time | −0.29** |  |  |  | −0.79** |
|  | (0.11) |  |  |  | (0.15) |
| Scientist–CEO$_{(t-1)}$ |  | 0.84 |  | 0.87 | 0.33 |
|  |  | (0.53) |  | (0.54) | (0.46) |
| Scientist–CEO$_{(t-1)}$ * time |  | −0.07 |  | −0.07 | −0.01 |
|  |  | (0.13) |  | (0.13) | (0.11) |
| Share of cardiovasculars in firm sales$_{(t-1)}$ |  | −0.00 |  | 0.00 | 0.05** |
|  |  | (0.01) |  | (0.01) | (0.01) |
| Share of cardiovasculars in firm sales$_{(t-1)}$ * time |  | 0.00 |  | 0.00 | −0.006** |
|  |  | (0.00) |  | (0.00) | (0.001) |
| Distance from science$_{(t-1)}$ |  |  | 0.20 | 0.29 | −0.60* |
|  |  |  | (0.26) | (0.27) | (0.25) |
| Distance from science$_{(t-1)}$ * time |  |  | −0.01 | −0.02 | 0.08 |
|  |  |  | (0.04) | (0.04) | (0.04) |
| Share of cardiovasculars in firm patents$_{(t-1)}$ |  |  | 0.01 | 0.00 | −0.03 |
|  |  |  | (0.03) | (0.03) | (0.03) |
| Share of cardiovasculars in firm patents$_{(t-1)}$ * time |  |  | 0.00 | 0.00 | 0.01 |
|  |  |  | (0.01) | (0.01) | (0.01) |
| Share of US cardiovascular market$_{(t-1)}$ |  |  | −0.03 | −0.03 | −0.12** |
|  |  |  | (0.02) | (0.02) | (0.02) |
| Share of US cardiovascular market$_{(t-1)}$ * time |  |  | 0.004* | 0.01* | 0.02** |
|  |  |  | (0.002) | (0.00) | (0.00) |
| Intercept | −2.45** | −1.22** | −1.43* | −1.52 | −4.99** |
|  | (0.60) | (0.56) | (0.74) | (0.83) | (0.83) |
| Time | 0.26** | 0.08** | 0.04 | 0.03** | 0.44** |
|  | (0.06) | (0.02) | (0.07) | (0.07) | (0.10) |
| Ln(total firm sales$_t$) | 0.09 | 0.21* | 0.23* | 0.24* | 0.22* |
|  | (0.08) | (0.09) | (0.11) | (0.12) | (0.10) |
| Adj. $R^2$ | 0.38 | 0.28 | 0.28 | 0.33 | 0.51 |

*$p<0.05$; **$p<0.01$.

each regression, the dependent variable is PUBFRAC.[21] The environmental variables are lagged by one period to allow time for firms to adjust their level of PUBFRAC, and each regression includes both a time trend and the log of total firm sales as control variables.

After replicating the "initial conditions plus convergence" result in (5.1) for easy reference, we present our initial analysis of the impact of environmental heterogeneity by dividing the explanatory variables into two groups corresponding to "behavioral" and "economic" hypotheses about the drivers of adoption. The two "behavioral" variables are Scientist–CEO and the within-firm share of cardiovascular drugs, which are included by themselves in (5.2). The "economic" variables are those measuring the firm's distance from science, its knowledge capital, and its competitive positioning, which are included by themselves in (5.3). (5.4) includes both the behavioral and economic variables together but still does not include initial conditions. These results are quite weak. Among the 11 explanatory variables (including firm sales), the only (marginally) significant coefficients are associated with firm sales and the interaction between the firm's market position in cardiovasculars and TIME; the small positive parameter suggests faster "catch-up" for firms with a larger share of the cardiovascular market.

However, we believe that each of the first four regressions in table 19.5 are likely misspecified. For example, by excluding the impact of initial conditions in (5.2) through (5.4), we introduce a great deal of noise into the regression, likely limiting our ability to distinguish the "true" impact of the environmental drivers. Model (5.5) therefore includes both the initial conditions and environmental heterogeneity variables, with a dramatic impact on the explanatory power of the regression and on the coefficient estimates. For example, the regressions suggest that, after controlling for initial conditions and convergence (the coefficients for which remain large and significant as in earlier regressions), those firms whose sales were concentrated in cardiovascular therapies were associated with higher levels of PUBFRAC (though their *rate* of adoption was slower) and firms more distant from scientific centers are associated with lower levels of PUBFRAC. Those firms that had a larger share of the cardiovascular market were also faster to adopt the new techniques (though the impact on the level is negative (in contrast to our initial hypotheses)). Finally, the measures of Scientist–CEO and knowledge capital (share of firm patents associated with cardiovascular therapies) remain insignificant, perhaps due to the noisy nature of each of these proxy measures and their imperfect correlation with the underlying concepts they are associated with. More generally, (5.5) suggests that the inclusion of variables to incorporate the impact of initial conditions and convergence allows for a more precise and systematic evaluation of the impact of environmental heterogeneity on the diffusion process, as well as providing an important confirmation for our earlier results about the impact of initial conditions and convergence.

The alternative specifications offered in table 19.5 also provide some evidence about the relative importance of initial conditions vs. environmental heterogeneity, at least in terms of goodness-of-fit. Of course evaluating the differences in $R^2$ from each regression is of only limited value since it cannot provide evidence for how a change in one of the explanatory variables changes the expected value of the dependent variable. However, this comparison does suggest two things in the current context. First, the regressions which focus on the firm's initial conditions explain a significantly higher share of the overall variance than the regressions which evaluate environmental heterogeneity by itself. Second, and perhaps more importantly, initial conditions and environmental heterogeneity are complementary in their explanatory power – there is over a 33 percent increase in adjusted $R^2$ in the combined model (5.5) compared with either (5.1) or (5.4).

## Conclusions and Implications for Further Research

These results are intriguing. At face value, table 19.5 appears to offer support for Stinchcombe's critique, in that initial conditions play a very important role in explaining the diffusion of science-driven drug discovery.[22] However, by developing a dynamic model of adoption which allows for both convergence and change associated with local environmental cues, our results suggest that conscious strategic adjustment is also quite important for understanding the dynamics of competitive advantage: convergence is a key factor in explaining the overall pattern of adoption, many of the "strategic" variables are significant after controlling for initial conditions, and the explanatory power of the diffusion model substantially improves when all of the effects are included simultaneously.

In other words, our results imply that – at least in this context – Stinchcombe's hypothesis is powerful but not all encompassing. One of the most striking features of our data is *convergence*: firms that were initially "behind" at the beginning of the period move more rapidly to "catch up" to their more advanced competitors. While associated with the same "initial conditions" that Stinchcombe emphasizes, the process of convergence and imitation is nonetheless interestingly different from a simple model of competition in which competitive advantage reflects the failure or exit of those firms that are not initially well positioned. Our results also suggest that, after controlling for initial conditions, variables traditionally associated with "strategic intent" are important determinants of the level and rate of adoption. While Stinchcombe's hypothesis is well worth taking seriously (and we would encourage future researchers to be careful to control for it), it seems to us that there is sufficient evidence here to suggest that firms can and do change in purposeful ways in response to exogenous shocks. For example, convergence suggests that managers who are initially associated with poorly positioned firms may be the most proactive in altering their practices and strategies. In other words, there seems to be a clear role for understanding the processes of strategic adjustment which occur in response to the internal and external environmental cues. In this sense, our framework and results provide evidence consistent *both* with Stinchcombe's hypothesis that competitive advantage is importantly driven by exogenous initial variation and with the more "rational" or "strategic" perspective that views firms as responding with foresight to changes in their environment.

Of course, as we have emphasized several times, our empirical results are quite preliminary, and perhaps raise as many questions as they answer. Indeed the statistical analysis is largely descriptive, and we have tried to highlight throughout the paper some of the difficult and interesting statistical questions that are raised by the attempt to distinguish among the central hypotheses. Our paper also highlights the need for richer longitudinal data. One could plausibly argue, for example, that the significance of initial conditions in our results is simply a consequence of "left truncation:" that if we knew more about the history of the firms in our sample – about the origins of each firm's "initial conditions" – we might be able to uncover additional evidence for the importance of managerial vision and action in shaping competitive advantage. For example, we know from a number of early histories of the industry that pharmaceutical firms differed enormously in the extent to which they invested in basic or scientific research in the 1940s and 1950s. Some firms, such as Parke-Davis, Lilly, and Merck, made early and extensive commitments to pure research, while other firms delayed making these investments for many years (Parascandola, 1985). Perhaps extending our empirical study of this industry further back in time would allow us to conclude that the adoption of science-driven drug discovery stemmed from far-sighted decisions made decades before the practice became widespread.

This suggestion brings us back to the discussion with which the paper began. During the 1980s, firms that used science-driven drug discovery techniques outperformed those that did not. As such, one might be tempted to conclude that adopting this practice was a "good" strategy that led, through the creation of unique capabilities, to significant competitive advantage in the sense of superior ability to generate new drug products. We have, ourselves, recommended to pharmaceutical firms that they adopt these techniques and the managers of many firms have by and large agreed with us. But one of the key conclusions to be drawn from our analysis here is that positively responding to such a recommendation is only half the battle. Incorporating best practice is necessary, but imitation based on the experience of rivals can usually only level the playing field, and in this case, at least, imitation took many years. While key aspects of the adoption process – in particular firms' rate of convergence to best practice – reflected purposive "strategic" responses to a changing environment, these responses were greatly constrained by factors that were in place long before many of these firms even began to think seriously about the issue. The RBV has emphasized the importance of long-lived "sticky" assets, and the powerful influence of historical circumstances seen here indicates that these can be very long lived and very sticky indeed.

The advent of science-driven drug discovery had a dramatic impact on the innovation process in the pharmaceutical industry. The basis of competitive advantage was changed in important ways, and firms in the industry responded to this shock by making appropriate changes to their internal structure, and by investing in the necessary capabilities and resources. But some firms entered this period of transition much better equipped than others to exploit the potential of the new techniques. Were they lucky or were they smart? The difficulty of answering this question empirically points to a deeper research agenda. We believe that a fuller appreciation of the origins of competitive advantage is to be found in a better analytical and empirical understanding of the types of managerial processes which allow some firms to be ahead, and stay ahead, of the game. *Ex post*, it is clear that some firms actively identify, interpret, and act upon early signals from their internal and external environment, and so position themselves to effectively exploit these opportunities well in advance of others' demonstration of the pay-off from the strategies which emerge later on as "best practice." These firms are *creating* new sources of competitive advantage. Understanding how they organize *ex ante* to do this is, in our view, a central question for strategy research.

## Appendix 19.1

### Data appendix: construction of our measures of $Z$

*Scientist–CEO*
Scientist–CEO is a binary variable set to 1 if the firm's CEO has a scientific background. We constructed this variable by systematically checking the Annual Report of each company in our

sample for the title or background of the CEO. Those CEOs who were listed as having either a PhD or an MD were coded as scientists.

### Distance from science

For any single paper, ISI lists the addresses of each author. From these data we constructed a count of the paper authorships by city for each firm for each year. We designated every city that constituted more than 2 percent of all the firm's authorships over the entire period a "research node" for the company, and obtained its longitude and latitude. We then weighted each node by the fraction of authorships it hosted relative to all authorships attributed to the company that year. These data gave us a good sense of the changing geographical location of the firm's research over time.

In order to measure the degree to which the firm was "close" to publicly funded science we needed to construct a weighted measure of the location of publicly funded research. This is difficult to do without full data on public spending by geographical location across the world, and data for Europe and Japan are relatively difficult to obtain. As a first approximation we constructed a data set consisting of the addresses of all those authors who coauthored papers with NIH researchers over our period. We designated each city listed in these data that constituted over 2 percent of total NIH coauthorships an NIH node, and obtained its latitude and longitude. We weighted these nodes using two schemes: as the fraction of NIH coauthorships that they obtained in a given year and as a rank from 1 to 10 on the basis of the scientific reputation of each node.

A firm's "closeness to science" was then calculated as: $\Sigma_{ij} w_i * w_j * 1/d_{ij}$, where $d_{ij}$ is the distance from each firm node $_i$ to NIH node $_j$, $w_i$ is the weight assigned to the company node and $wj$ to each node.

### Firm sales

Firm sales are measured as total pharmaceutical sales in the United States, as reported to IMS. We excluded sales of OTC or "over-the-counter" medications that can be obtained without a prescription. Note that the United States is only about 50 percent of the world pharmaceutical market, and that many of the firms in our sample have substantial global sales. U.S. sales are thus a rather noisy measure of total sales.

### Knowledge capital: share of patents in cardiovascular therapies

We used Derwent patent data to construct a measure of the firm's experience or "knowledge capital" in cardiovasculars. For all of the firms in our data set, Derwent generously donated to us complete data about each patent family granted to each firm over our period. Each patent family includes complete information about the patents granted to the firm across the entire world and a complete set of Derwent "manual codes."[23] For each patent that had been granted in two out of three major world markets (Japan, the United States, and Europe) we used the "manual codes" to assign patents to particular therapeutic areas. We then calculated a "knowledge stock" in the standard manner assuming a 20 percent deprecation rate.

### Market position: share of the cardiovascular market

We measure share of sales using detailed data at the product level obtained from IMS America. Note that the pharmaceutical market is a global one. The U.S. market represents roughly 50 percent of the world market, and nearly every firm in our sample has extensive global operations.

Unfortunately our share measures will be distorted by the fact that the distribution of sales across therapeutic classes is *not* uniform across the world.

*Managerial attention: cardiovascular therapies as a share of the sales portfolio*
We measure cardiovascular sales as a share of total firm sales using IMS America data. Note that it is subject to the same source of error as our measure of market position, above.

## Acknowledgements

This study was funded by POPI, the Program for the Study of the Pharmaceutical Industry at MIT and by the MIT Center for Innovation in Product Development under NSF Cooperative Agreement Number EEC-9529140. Stern completed this paper while a Health and Aging Fellow at the National Bureau of Economic Research. Their support is gratefully acknowledged. Jeff Furman and Pierre Azoulay provided outstanding research assistance, and we would also like to thank Bob Gibbons, Connie Helfat, David Hounshell, Zvi Griliches, and participants at the Dartmouth conference focused on this special issue for their many helpful comments.

## Notes

1  Structural analysis has, of course, moved much beyond Porter's original book, and we do not even attempt to summarize this literature here. For some recent contributions, see Brandenberger and Nalebuff (1998) and Besanko, Dranove, and Shanley (2000).

2  HBS : 9-378-024.

3  For example, from an environmental perspective, the pharmaceutical industry has historically been profitable because buyers and suppliers are weak, entry is costly and difficult, and substitutes and rivalry are quite muted. At least in part, this structure reflects external forces, such as the fact that the industry's products can be securely protected through patents, and so is not the result of a specific organizational competence on the part of a particular firm. But the industry's attractiveness also reflects the unique competencies developed by the larger pharmaceutical firms, including, among other factors, their years of investment in sophisticated research capabilities, their knowledge of regulatory systems around the world, and their extensive distribution and physician networks.

4  There is of course a powerful literature demonstrating that changes in top management team compensation are correlated with major strategic reorientations (see, for example, Fletcher and Huff, 1990, and work by Tushman and his collaborators, including Murmann and Tushman, 1997). While this literature is suggestive, in general it leaves the question of causality unaddressed.

5  Note that our focus on diffusion contrasts with the traditional emphasis on explaining *performance* as a function of initial conditions, environmental factors, or strategic choices.

6  In the remainder of this discussion we suppress the firm-specific subscript $j$ on all the variables.

7  Note that this is very much a "reduced form" model of adoption. It is not our goal (at least in this paper) to develop or estimate a fully specified structural model of optimizing adoption behavior. Indeed, given the diverse set of plausible hypotheses about the drivers of adoption behavior, it is not clear that estimating such a model is currently feasible without preliminary empirical work, which substantially narrows down the potential range of theo-

ries to be accommodated. Consequently, we confine ourselves here to identifying the principal covariates of adoption, recognizing that adoption is a dynamic process. Distinguishing the relative empirical salience of competing hypotheses may provide an initial guide to specifying a more fully articulated structural model.

8   Our empirical results are surprisingly robust to variation in the functional form imposed on the adoption-intensity variable. Our robustness checks (not presented here, but available on request) included using the level of adoption intensity as well as the natural logarithm.

9   Conditioning on the starting value of the dependent variable (or some function of it) is a well-understood procedure in the econometrics literature on dynamic panel data models (see, for example, Arellano and Bond, 1991). This also allows us to understand the implications of our results in the framework of the heterogeneity/state dependence distinction used by econometricians (see Heckman, 1991).

10  Notice that this terminology can be deceptive. The major pharmaceutical firms began investing in fundamental science after the First World War, and by the 1950s many of them employed significant numbers of well-trained scientists (Parascandola, 1985). "Random" drug discovery was "random" in that while research was often guided or informed by fundamental science, the precise mechanism of action of many drugs was not understood, and new compounds were screened against animal models rather than against particular disease pathways (Henderson, 1994; Henderson, Orsenigo, and Pisano, 1999).

11  The question of just *why* "science-driven drug discovery" should be a major source of competitive advantage is a fascinating one. The interested reader is referred to our related work (Henderson, Orsenigo, and Pisano, 1999; Cockburn and Henderson, 1998; Cockburn, Henderson and Stern, 1999a, 1999b; Stern, 1999). There are, of course, other sources of competitive advantage in the pharmaceutical industry, including the possession of strong regulatory capabilities, an extensive distribution network, or well-developed marketing capabilities.

12  The firms are: Abbott, Bristol-Myers Squibb, Burroughs-Wellcome, Ciba-Geigy, Glaxo, Fujisawa, Hoechst, Hoffman La-Roche, Lilly, Merck, Pfizer, Sandoz, Searle/Monsanto, SmithKline Beecham, Takeda, and Upjohn. Nine of these firms are also included in the earlier sample: the remainder were selected to include the industry's leading R&D performers and to obtain worldwide geographical representation.

13  In the ideal case we would like to be able to use a measure based on the actual nature of the science conducted within each firm over time: in the absence of reliable longitudinal survey data about research methodology this is impossible to construct from secondary sources. Instead we use here a number of measures derived from the publication behavior and incentives provided by research-oriented pharmaceutical firms.

14  Total spending on research would clearly be preferable, but for the complete sample we have only data on total R&D expenditures. This measure is very noisy in that it includes development expenditures in addition to discovery expenditures, and we know from our prior work that the ratio of discovery to development spending is not constant across firms. It is a particularly noisy measure when the firm is diversified beyond the pharmaceutical industry.

15  Another possibility would be to count "stars": the number of individuals in a firm who publish prolifically. Zucker, Darby, and Brewer (1998) have suggested that this "higher standard" is critical for understanding successful performance in, at least, biotechnology firms. In preliminary work we have found that this variable performs much like AUTHORS.

16  Constructing PUBFRAC was far from straightforward. For each firm in the sample, we first identified all papers (a) which were published between 1980 and 1994 in journals indexed by the *Science Citation Index* and (b) in which the name of the firm, or one of its subsidiaries, appears in at least one of the authors' addresses. We had then to attempt to

match the names of many thousands of individuals across two different data sets and consistently apply rules for ambiguous cases. Much of this matching was accomplished straightforwardly in software, but a number of difficulties did induce some measurement error into the process. These included typographical errors in the source data, and differences across papers by the same author in the use of initials, surnames, and given names; extensive hand-coding was necessary to complete the task. A consistent matching procedure was applied to all firms, and so we are reasonably confident that bias in the measurement of PUBFRAC is limited to differences across firms in the severity of these problems.

17   Of our original sample of 10 firms, two exited through merger. Of our later sample of 19, only two have (at the time of writing) exited through merger.

18   In order to assist us in framing our hypotheses, between September 1998 and April 1999 we conducted interviews at seven pharmaceutical firms. All but one were based in the United States. The interviews were loosely structured discussions that explored, first, whether it was plausible that the adoption of science-driven drug discovery had significant effects on research productivity and, second, why it might have been the case that despite their plausible impact on productivity many firms were slow to adopt them.

19   Share of the sales portfolio might also shape the choice of research technique if firms have specialized marketing or distribution assets. These assets certainly exist – Eli Lilly, for example, has historically had a very strong position in the distribution and marketing of treatments for diabetes. However, we believe that in the majority of cases they are relatively fungible.

20   To begin with, there is the question of which network to focus on. In the context of a single industry study, it does not make sense to focus on the degree to which there is interlock across the board of directors, for example, since within a single industry directors are forbidden from serving on multiple boards to avoid potential conflicts of interest. We explored the degree to which we could use patterns of joint publication to construct a plausible network, but discovered that constructing such a network requires the collection (and coding) of data about hundreds of thousands of papers and would result in an intractably large network containing thousands of nodes. We are currently exploring whether we can usefully construct such a network by tracing the movement of senior executives across the industry.

21   We have experimented extensively both with PUBFRAC as well as our other measures of the intensity of science-driven drug discovery (PUBFRAC, PAPERS, and AUTHORS). Overall, the key results as they relate to distinguishing between alternative sources of competitive advantage are robust.

22   One possibility, of course, is that $y_0$ is capturing not the characteristics of the firm's founding, but a complex (unobserved) history of strategic adjustment. As a very preliminary cut at whether this is plausibly the case, we compared the usefulness of our measures of heterogeneity as measured at the beginning of the period, $Z_0$, as explanatory variables for $y$. The regression performed quite poorly, with an even lower proportion of the variance in the dependent variable explained than in the regressions that included contemporaneous measures of heterogeneity.

23   The U.S. patent office classifies pharmaceutical patents largely on the basis of chemical structure: a classification that contains very little information about therapeutic intent. The Derwent manual codes are assigned by specialists in the field who classify each patent on the basis of its therapeutic implications.

# References

Andrews, K. R. 1971. *The Concept of Corporate Strategy*. Dow-Jones Irwin: Homewood, IL.

Arellano, M. and Bond, S. 1991. Some tests of specification for panel data: Monte Carlo evidence and an application to employment equations. *Review of Economic Studies* 58(194): 277–320.

Barnett, W. P. and Hansen, M. T. 1996. The Red Queen in organizational evolution. *Strategic Management Journal* 17: 139–158.

Barney, J. 1991. Firm resources and sustained competitive advantage. *Journal of Management* 17(1): 99–120.

Besanko, D., Dranove, D., and Shanley, M. 2000. *Economics of Strategy*. 2nd edn, Wiley: New York.

Bower, J. L. 1974. *Managing the Resource Allocation Process*. Harvard Business School Press: Boston, MA.

Brandenberger, A. and Nalebuff, B. 1998. *Co-opetition*. Harvard Business School Press: Boston, MA.

Burgelman, R. A. 1994. Fading memories: a process study of strategic business exit in dynamic environments. *Administrative Science Quarterly* 39(1): 24–56.

Chandler, A. 1962. *Strategy and Structure*. MIT Press: Cambridge, MA (reprinted January 1990).

Christensen, C. M. and Bower, J. L. 1996. Customer power, strategic investment, and the failure of leading firms. *Strategic Management Journal* 17(3): 197–218.

Clark, K. B. and Fujimoto, T. 1991. *Product Development in the World Automobile Industry*. Harvard Business School Press: Boston, MA.

Cockburn, I. M. and Henderson, R. M. 1998. Absorptive capacity, coauthoring behavior, and the organization of research in drug discovery. *Journal of Industrial Economics* 46(2): 157–182.

Cockburn, I. M., Henderson, R. M., and Stern, S. 1999a. Balancing incentives: the tension between basic and applied research. NBER working paper no. 6882, January.

Cockburn, I. M., Henderson, R. M., and Stern, S. 1999b. The diffusion of science driven drug discovery: organizational change in pharmaceutical research. NBER working paper no. 7359, December.

Davis, G. 1991. Agents without principles? The spread of the poison pill through intercorporate networks. *Administrative Science Quarterly* 36: 583–613.

Eisenhardt, K. M. 1988. Agency- and institutional-theory explanations: the case of retail sales compensation. *American Management Journal* 31(3): 488–511.

Eisenhardt, K. M. and Schoonhoven, C. B. 1990. Organizational growth: linking founding team, strategy, environment, and growth among U.S. semiconductor ventures, 1978–1988. *Administrative Science Quarterly* 35: 504–529.

Eisenhardt, K. M. and Tabrizi, B. N. 1995. Accelerating adaptive processes. *Administrative Science Quarterly* 40(1): 84–110.

Fletcher, K. and Huff, A. S. 1990. Strategic argument mapping: a study of strategy reformulation at AT&T. In *Mapping Strategic Thought*, Huff AS (ed). Wiley: New York: 165–194.

Fudenberg, D. and Tirole, J. 1985. Pre-emption and rent equalization in the adoption of new technology. *Review of Economic Studies* 52: 383–401.

Gambardella, A. 1995. *Science and Innovation in the US Pharmaceutical Industry*. Cambridge University Press: Cambridge, UK.

Ghemawat, P. 1991. *Commitment: The Dynamics of Strategy*. Free Press: New York.

Gilbert R. J. and Newbery, D. M. 1982. Pre-emptive patenting and the persistence of monopoly. *American Economic Review* 514–595.

Grabowski, H. G. and Vernon, J. M. 1990. A new look at the returns and risks to pharmaceutical R&D. *Management Science* 36(7): 804–821.

Griliches, Z. 1957. Hybrid corn: an exploration in the economics of technical change. *Econometrica* 25(4): 501–522.

Griliches, Z. 1986. Data problems in econometrics. In *Handbook of Econometrics*, Intriligator, M. and Griliches, Z. (eds). North-Holland: Amsterdam; 1466–1514.

Hannan, M. T. and Freeman, J. H. 1989. *Organizational Ecology.* Harvard University Press: Cambridge, MA.

Heckman, J. J. 1991. Identifying the hand of the past: distinguishing state dependence from heterogeneity. *American Economic Review* 81(2): 75–79.

Henderson, R. M. 1993. Underinvestment and incompetence as responses to radical innovation: evidence from the semiconductor photolithographic alignment equipment industry. *Rand Journal of Economics* 24(2): 248–270.

Henderson, R. M. 1994. The evolution of integrative competence: innovation in cardiovascular drug discovery. *Industrial and Corporate Change* 3(3): 607–630.

Henderson, R. M. and Clark, K. B. 1990. Architectural innovation: the reconfiguration of existing product technologies and the failure of established firms. *Administrative Science Quarterly* 35: 9–30.

Henderson, R. M. and Cockburn, I. M. 1994. Measuring competence? Exploring firm effects in pharmaceutical research. *Strategic Management Journal*, Winter Special Issue 15: 63–84.

Henderson, R. M. and Cockburn, I. M. 1996. Scale, scope and spillovers: the determinants of research productivity in drug discovery. *Rand Journal of Economics* 27(1): 32–59.

Henderson, R. M., Orsenigo, L., and Pisano, G. 1999. The pharmaceutical industry and the revolution in molecular biology: interactions among scientific, institutional and organizational change. In *The Sources of Industrial Leadership*, Mowery, D. and Nelson, R. (eds). Cambridge University Press: New York: 267–311.

Hicks, D. 1995. Published papers, tacit competencies and corporate management of the public/private character of knowledge. *Industrial and Corporate Change* 4(2): 401–424.

Holbrook, K., Cohen, W. M., Hounshell, D. A., and Klepper, S. 2000. The nature, sources and consequences of the early history of the semiconductor industry. *Strategic Management Journal.* 21(10–11): 1017–1041.

Jaffe, A. B. 1986. Technological opportunity and spillovers of R&D: evidence from firms' patents, profits and market value. *American Economic Review* 76(5): 984–1001.

Karshenas, M. and Stoneman, P. 1993. Rank, stock, order and epidemic effects in the diffusion of new process technologies: an empirical model. *Rand Journal of Economics* 24(4): 503–528.

Koenig, M. 1982. A bibliometric analysis of pharmaceutical research. *Research Policy* 12: 15–36.

Lieberman, M. B. and Dhawan, R. 2000. Assessing the resource base of U.S. and Japanese auto producers: a stochastic production frontier approach. Mimeo, UCLA Anderson School of Management, February.

Leonard-Barton, D. 1998. *Wellsprings of Knowledge: Building and Sustaining the Sources of Innovation.* Harvard Business School Press: Boston, MA.

Levinthal, D. A. 1997. Adaptation on rugged landscapes. *Management Science* 43: 934–950.

McGahan, A. M. and Porter, M. E. 1997. How much does industry matter, really? *Strategic Management Journal*, Summer Special Issue 18: 15–30.

Mintzberg, H. 1987. Crafting strategy. *Harvard Business Review* 65(4): 66–75.

Mundlak, Y. 1961. Empirical production function free of managerial bias. *Journal of Farm Economics* 43: 44–56.

Murmann, P. and Tushman, M. L. 1997. Impacts of executive team characteristics and organization context on organization responsiveness to environmental shock. In *Technological*

*Innovation: Oversights and Foresights*, Garud, R., Nayyar, P., and Shapira, Z. (eds). Cambridge University Press: New York; 260–278.

Nelson, R. R. and Winter, S. G. 1982. *An Evolutionary Theory of Economic Change*. Harvard University Press: Cambridge, MA.

Parascandola, J. 1985. Industry research comes of age: the American pharmaceutical industry, 1920–1940. *Pharmacy in History* 27(1): 12–21.

Penrose, E. T. 1959. *The Theory of the Growth of the Firm*. Wiley: New York.

Peteraf, M. A. 1993. The cornerstones of competitive advantage: a resource-based view. *Strategic Management Journal* 14(3): 179–191.

Porter, M. E. 1980. *Competitive Strategy*. Free Press: New York.

Powell, W. W., Koput, K. W., and Smith-Doerr, L. 1996. Interorganizational collaboration and the locus of innovation: networks of learning in biotechnology. *Administrative Science Quarterly* 41(1): 116–145.

Quinn, J. B. 1978. Strategic change: logical incrementalism. *Sloan Management Review* 20(1): 7–23.

Reinganum, J. F. 1981. Market structure and the diffusion of new technology. *Bell Journal of Economics* 12: 618–624.

Rumelt, R. P. 1991. How much does industry matter? *Strategic Management Journal* 12(3): 167–185.

Selznick, P. 1957. *Leadership in Administration: A Sociological Interpretation*. Harper & Row: New York.

Shapiro, C. and Varian, H. R. 1998. *Information Rules*. Harvard Business School Press: Boston, MA.

Stern, S. 1999. Do scientists pay to be scientists? NBER working paper no. 7410, October.

Stinchcombe, A. L. 1965. Social structure and organizations. In *Handbook of Organizations*, March J (ed). Rand-McNally: Chicago, IL; 142–193.

Stinchcombe, A. L. 2000. Social structure and organizations: a comment. In *Economics Meets Sociology in Strategic Management: Advances in Strategic Management*, Baum J, Dobbin F (eds). JAI Press: Greenwich, CT.

Wernerfelt, B. 1984. A resource-based view of the firm. *Strategic Management Journal* 5(2): 171–180.

Zucker, I. G. and Darby, M. R. 1997. Present at the revolution: transformation of technical identity for a large incumbent pharmaceutical firm after the biotechnological breakthrough. *Research Policy* 26(4): 429–447.

Zucker, L. G., Darby, M. R., and Brewer, M. 1998. Intellectual human capital and the birth of U.S. biotechnology enterprises. *American Economic Review* 88(1): 290–306.

# CHAPTER TWENTY

# Strategy and Circumstance: The Response of American Firms to Japanese Competition in Semiconductors, 1980–1995

## Richard N. Langlois and W. Edward Steinmueller

### Introduction

The transistor was an American invention, and American firms led the world in semiconductor production and innovation for the first three decades of that industry's existence. In the 1980s, however, Japanese producers began to challenge American dominance. Shrill cries arose from the literature of public policy, warning that the American semiconductor industry would soon share the fate of the lamented American consumer electronics business. Few dissented from the implications: the only hope for salvation would be to adopt Japanese-style public policies and imitate the kinds of capabilities Japanese firms possessed.[1]

But the predicted extinction never occurred (see figure 20.1). Instead, American firms surged back during the 1990s, and it now seems the Japanese who are embattled. This remarkable American turnaround has gone largely unremarked upon in the public policy literature. And even scholarship in strategic management, which thrives on stories of success instead of stories of failure, has been comparatively silent.[2]

This essay attempts to collect some of the lessons for strategy research of the American resurgence.[3] We argue that, although some of the American response did consist in changing or augmenting capabilities, most of the renewed American success is in fact the result not of imitating superior Japanese capabilities but rather of taking good advantage of a set of capabilities developed in the heyday of American dominance. Serendipity played at least as important a role as did strategy.

### The Origins of American Capabilities

For a variety of reasons, both political and strategic, AT&T chose to offer easy intellectual-property access to what is perhaps the most important and fertile commercial

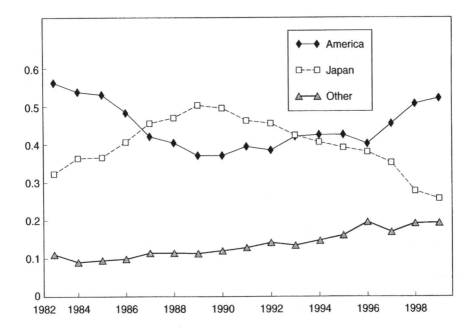

**Figure 20.1** Worldwide semiconductor market share (%), 1982–98. Source of data: Semiconductor Industry Association.

invention of the century. Firms of all shapes, sizes, and national origins were able to license the transistor for a nominal fee. Bell Labs even provided some early seminars and technical assistance in producing the device. Perhaps most important, Bell Labs personnel soon found themselves in demand from companies wishing to develop transistor technology, and their departure initiated the pattern of defection and spin-off that continues today in the United States.

For example, William Shockley left Bell Labs in the early 1950s for the San Francisco peninsula, where he founded Shockley Semiconductor Laboratories. Although his enterprise was never a commercial success, eight of Shockley's team defected in 1957 to found the semiconductor division of Fairchild Camera and Instrument Corporation, an organization of seminal importance in the industry. Largely through the efforts of Jean Hoerni, one of the eight defectors, Fairchild developed the planar process, a technology that allowed large-scale batch production of transistors. Almost immediately, Hoerni's colleague and fellow defector Robert Noyce would extend the planar process to the fabrication of multi-transistor devices – integrated circuits (ICs). By 1968, Noyce and others had left Fairchild to found the next generation of semiconductor firms.[4]

A significant feature of the transition from discrete transistors to the IC was the disappearance of the vertically integrated American electronics companies that had led in the production of vacuum tubes and that had been able to stay in the race during the discrete semiconductor era. The market shares of those firms declined in the face of new entrants and the growth of relatively specialized manufacturers like TI, Fairchild, and Motorola. By 1965, the vertically integrated systems firms had fallen from the top five slots in American semiconductor sales, and by 1975 all but RCA had fallen off the top-ten list (see table 20.1).

Why did the vertically integrated electronic system firms do so poorly in this era? Wilson, Ashton, and Egan (1980) point out that the new leaders were either specialized startups or multi-divisional firms (like TI, Fairchild, and Motorola) in which the semiconductor division dominated overall corporate strategy and in which semiconductor operations absorbed a significant portion of the attention of central management. By contrast, the semiconductor divisions of the integrated system firms were a small part of corporate sales and of corporate strategy, thereby attracting a smaller portion of managerial attention and receiving less autonomy.

This is consistent with the literature of management strategy urging corporations to cultivate their "core competences" and to recognize that deviation from these competences is risky (Teece, 1986; Prahalad and Hamel, 1990). Indeed, recent evidence suggests that specialized competence is important not so much in the core technology itself as in the complementary activities necessary to transform the technology into highly demanded products (Christensen and Rosenbloom, 1995). Granstrand, Patel, and Pavitt (1997) argue in general that firms should not try to limit their core competences but rather should strive to widen those competences while retaining focus in complementary and downstream activities. Gambardella and Torrisi (1998) show that electronics firms in the 1980s did better when they narrowed their product focus while expanding their technological competences. Such product specialization is arguably of even greater value when market and technological opportunities are expanding rapidly along a well-defined trajectory (Patel and Pavitt, 1997: 153). American merchants in the integrated-circuit era arguably followed this advice: they expanded their technological competence in semiconductor design and fabrication while limiting their product diversification (relative to the large system houses) in a way that was shaped by the pattern of end-use demand. As we will see presently, however, the product diver-

**Table 20.1** Leading US merchant semiconductor manufacturers, 1955–1975

| 1955<br>*Transistors* | 1960<br>*Semiconductors* | 1965<br>*Semiconductors* | 1975<br>*Integrated circuits* |
|---|---|---|---|
| Hughes | Texas Instruments | Texas Instruments | Texas Instruments |
| Transitron | Transitron | Motorola | Fairchild |
| Philco | Philco | Fairchild | National |
| Sylvania | General Electric | General Instrument | Intel |
| Texas Instruments | RCA | General Electric | Motorola |
| General Electric | Motorola | RCA | Rockwell |
| RCA | Clevite | Sprague | General Instrument |
| Westinghouse | Fairchild | Philco-Ford | RCA |
| Motorola | Hughes | Transitron | Signetics (Phillips) |
| Clevite | Sylvania | Raytheon | American Microsystems |

*Source*: Mackintosh (1978: 54).

sity of American merchants did grow over time, to an extent that was to make them vulnerable to a challenge from even more narrowly focused Japanese firms wielding wide technological capabilities.

The price advantage of the integrated circuit compared with transistors assured a relatively rapid diffusion of the new technology. It did not, however, immediately create major shifts in the electronic-system industries. During the first half of the 1960s, the methods for IC manufacturing were still under development and the technical characteristics of the ICs were limited, particularly for use in analog circuits.[5] But the technical capabilities of ICs were ideal for digital circuits, the major customers for which were the military and the computer industry. Early military and space procurement hastened American firms down the slopes of their learning curves.[6] And the government insistence on second sourcing sped the diffusion of IC technology. As IC prices fell, however, civilian uses, especially for the computer, quickly came to dominate government procurement (see table 20.2).

The 1960s was a period of rapid growth for the American computer industry. The leading firm, IBM, had built up its position during the 1950s by relying heavily on outside suppliers. By 1960, however, IBM had created its own components division, which geared up to make semiconductors for the phenomenally successful IBM 360 Series, announced in 1964. By the 1970s, IBM's dominance in computers had made it the world's largest producer of ICs. Thus the vertical division of labor in the United States became markedly different from, and more diverse than, that in Europe and Japan.[7] Many small, highly specialized merchant firms dealing with relatively autonomous systems companies stood alongside a handful of large, vertically integrated captive producers.[8]

Merchant semiconductor firms faced basically two options. One class of product strategies involved making high-volume standard products, notably memories. Despite IBM's moves to convert from ferrite core to semiconductor memory, this market continued to be relatively small until 1972. In that year, Intel's 1003 DRAM became the best-selling IC in the world, accounting for more than 90 percent of the company's $23.4 million in revenue (Cogan and Burgelman, 1989). The other class of product strategies involved attempting to use the rapidly growing complexity of ICs to create differentiated products. For a time, American firms were able to do well with both sets of strategies.

**Table 20.2** End use shares of total US sales of integrated circuits and total market value, 1962–1978

| Markets | 1962 | 1965 | 1969 | 1974 | 1978 |
|---|---|---|---|---|---|
| Government | 100% | 55% | 36% | 20% | 10% |
| Computer | 0 | 35 | 44 | 36 | 38 |
| Industrial | 0 | 9 | 16 | 30 | 38 |
| Consumer | 0 | 1 | 4 | 15 | 15 |
| Total US domestic shipments (millions) | $4 | $79 | $413 | $1204 | $2080 |

*Source*: Borrus, et al. (1983: 159).

## The Japanese Challenge

During the 1970s, the integrated circuit reinforced American dominance of the international market for semiconductors. The United States held a two-to-one overall advantage over Japan in market share in semiconductors and a better than three-to-one advantage in integrated circuits (Braun and Macdonald, 1982: 153). A decade later, as figure 20.1 suggests, Japan had overtaken the United States in semiconductor market share.

The loss of American dominance is striking. How and why did this happen? The answer is to be found in the dynamics of competition between American and Japanese companies in the new generations of IC products introduced beginning in the late 1970s. This competition involved issues of productive efficiency, investment rates and timing, and design strategy. The success of Japanese companies was aided by the nature of end-use markets in Japan, the timing of market developments, and the patterns of investment by American and Japanese companies.

The vitality of the American IC industry during its period of dominance was its intense technological competitiveness, supported by its industrial structure. That structure was one in which relatively small, often vertically specialized firms played a major role. Among the benefits of this structure were flexibility, focus, and the ability to take advantage of the "external economies" of participation in technological and geographic networks like Silicon Valley (Saxenian, 1994; Langlois and Robertson, 1995). Almost from its origins, the industry had been oriented toward growth rather than toward profit margins. Indeed, the profitability of the industry collectively ran below the average for American manufacturing.[9] The industry maintained prosperity through the growth of product markets, a process that required continual investment in physical capacity and in research and development. This meant that American IC companies could not generate large cash reserves from retained earnings; moreover, as these companies were not typically divisions of larger organizations, they could not benefit from intraorganizational transfers of capital. The result was that, during periodic industry downturns, the industry reduced investment spending and laid off workers; in the upturns, the industry delayed in committing to new plant, which led to capacity shortages.[10] In Japanese firms, IC production occurred within a vertically integrated structure that allowed Japanese firms to mobilize internal capital resources to make investments in the IC industry in a way that U.S. companies could not.

In addition, the very wealth of product possibilities offered by the rich technological trajectory of the IC and the planar process meant that American firms rationally directed their energies as much – or more – to product innovation as to process innovation. By focusing on the task of reducing the process specification for the next stage in the industry's technological trajectory while selecting a mass-produced and potentially standard product, a potential challenger could make significant gains.

The structure and capabilities of Japanese industry thus led naturally to a two-pronged strategy for challenging American dominance: investment in capacity and investment in manufacturing quality. This left the problem of identifying which products were vulnerable to a challenge. Hindsight makes it obvious that the emerging dynamic random-access memory (DRAM) of the early to mid-1970s was the most attractive market to challenge. At that time, Japanese producers could certainly have concluded that the DRAM market would be suited to the Japanese approach to manufacturing. The potential for the DRAM to become a standardized, mass-produced product had already been demonstrated by Intel's 1003, the 1K DRAM that established the market.

American firms continued to dominate in the early – 1K and 4K – DRAM markets. But an industry recession delayed the American "ramp-up" to the 16K DRAM, which appeared in 1976. Aided by unforeseen production problems among the three leaders, Japanese firms were able to gain a significant share of the 16K market. By mid-1979, 16 companies were producing DRAMs, and Japanese producers accounted for 42 percent of the market (Wilson *et al.*, 1980: 93–94) (see table 20.3). The opportunity opened for Japanese producers in the 16K DRAM market had proven sufficient for them to advance to a position of leadership in the 64K DRAM. Their success relied upon manufacturing advantage and price-cutting. The Japanese fixed early upon a conservative design for their 64K DRAMs, which allowed them simply to scale up existing process technology. By contrast, the American firms insisted on radical new designs and new process technology, which increased development times and startup problems (Borrus, 1988: 144). As a result, Intel, Mostek, and National encountered production difficulties, giving Japanese firms a head start down the experience curve.

Japanese dominance accelerated in the 256K (1982) and 1-megabit (1985) generations. The scale-up of 64K DRAM production had caused a very rapid reduction in price, which, combined with the general recession in the U.S. industry in 1985, caused all but two American merchant IC companies to withdraw from DRAM production[11] (Howell, Bartlett, and Davis, 1992: 29). In 1990, American market share had fallen to only 2 percent of the new generation 4-megabit DRAMs[12] (see table 20.3).

As had been the case in the rise of the American semiconductor industry, the pattern of end-use demand was crucial in shaping the bundle of capabilities that Japanese industry possessed – as well as in narrowing and limiting the choices the Japanese firms had open to them. In this case, that end-use demand came largely from consumer electronics and, to a somewhat lesser extent, from telecommunications. Consumer demand helped place the Japanese on a product trajectory – namely CMOS ICs – that

**Table 20.3** Maximum market share in DRAMs by American and Japanese companies, by device

| Device | Maximum market share (percent) | |
|---|---|---|
| | United States | Japan |
| 1K | 95 | 5 |
| 4K | 83 | 17 |
| 16K | 59 | 41 |
| 64K | 29 | 71 |
| 256K | 8 | 92 |
| 1M | 4 | 96 |
| 4M | 2 | 98 |

*Source*: Dataquest, cited in Methé (1991: 69).

turned out eventually to have much wider applicability. And NTT's demand for high-quality memory chips for telecommunication switching systems helped nudge the industry into a strategy of specialization in high-volume production of DRAMs.

Japan was without a significant military demand that could provide a market to support specialized high-performance devices. Japanese computer manufacturers had attained a moderate success, with 1973 production of ¥472 billion ($2.15 billion). Nonetheless, the consumer electronics market of that year was far larger at ¥1685 billion ($7.66 billion). Consumer electronics accounted for one half of all electronic equipment production in Japan in 1973, a share that was to remain almost constant throughout the 1970s despite a 50 percent growth in the overall size of production.

The particular consumer product of greatest relevance in the early years was the desktop (and eventually hand-held) calculator. Although this product may seem mundane, it created a very large demand for ICs: in the early 1970s, nearly 50 percent of the Japanese IC market went for desktop calculators (Watanabe, 1984: 1564). Calculators thus provided Japanese firms with a "product driver" that could be used to fund large-scale production of ICs (Borrus, 1988: 124). More significantly, perhaps, the calculator market started Japanese firms down the technological trajectory of CMOS production.[13] American firms favored the alternative NMOS technology for the early generations of DRAMs, largely because of its (initially) lower cost and because of conservatism about the technological risks of CMOS. Japanese firms chose to develop expertise in CMOS because its lower power consumption – useful in portable devices – had offsetting benefits in calculators and other consumer applications. But a technological change in the lithography process canceled out the cost advantage of NMOS, and CMOS turned out to have a steeper learning curve. By 1983–4, the cost of CMOS had fallen below that of NMOS, and CMOS quickly became the clear technological choice for almost all applications. The Americans thus found much of their previous experience with NMOS had become obsolete, and that they lagged behind the Japanese in CMOS.

## The American Resurgence

The American resurgence reflects a combination of several factors of varying importance. These include:

- a renewed emphasis on manufacturing and some success in improving productivity;
- organizational innovation and specialization, allowing the American industry to take advantage both of its own structural advantages and of global manufacturing capabilities; and, relatedly and most significantly,
- a favorable shift in the importance of those products in which American firms have specialized.

As we saw, Japanese firms had been nudged by the character of the demand they faced onto the technological trajectory of CMOS – a technology that was to prove superior in cost and performance dimensions in most applications. In 1988, CMOS represented about 40 percent of the value of IC production; by 1994, it was responsible for 80 percent of production value (ICE, 1995). Because American firms had concentrated on NMOS technology, they lagged in converting to CMOS, which meant that the American companies were engaged in a process of "catch-up" with their Japanese competitors in process technology. This seemed an insurmountable problem, as most American companies feared that DRAM production was the only means of improving or "driving" the state of the art in CMOS technology. In the end, however, this fear proved groundless. American companies were able to make CMOS circuits with sufficient quality, performance, and transistor counts to meet the competition using experience with logic chips and specialized memory devices such as SRAMs.[14]

What evidence is there that American firms improved their manufacturing productivity significantly? One piece of indirect evidence is that American firms were able to hold their market shares in a number of product segments, including application-specific integrated circuits (ASICs), where American and Japanese companies compete nearly head-to-head.[15] There is also more direct evidence.[16] One of the factors driving the success of Japanese firms in memory products in the early 1980s was the higher quality of the chips they produced. For Japanese chips, defect rates – the fraction of chips that prove to be defective – were probably half to one tenth the rates for American products. By the second half of that decade, however, American firms had dramatically increased expenditures for quality control, imitating Japanese practices such as Total Quality Management (TQM), greater attention to preventive maintenance, and automated process control and monitoring. By the early 1990s, American manufacturers had probably begun to match the defect levels of their Japanese counterparts. Intel reportedly reduced its defect rate by a factor of 10 (Helm, 1995). There is also evidence that American firms have improved manufacturing yield rates and direct labor productivity since the early 1990s.[17] This represents a closing of the gap, but it doesn't mean that American fabs have reached the levels of Japanese or even Taiwanese fabs, in part because American fabs operate at smaller scales on average and cannot take as much advantage of the economies of large production runs.

Nonetheless, the Americans' improved manufacturing capabilities were more than adequate in view of favorable structural changes and demand shifts. The abandonment of the DRAM market by most American firms – including Intel – was a dark cloud with a bright silver lining. When Intel led the world industry in almost all categories, it and many of its American counterparts faced a full plate of product alternatives. With the elimination of mass memory as a viable market, these firms were impelled to specialize and narrow their focus to a smaller subset of choices. As we saw earlier, a relatively narrow product focus coupled with a deepening technological competence can be an extremely successful strategy, as it arguably was in the early days of the industry. It is also, indeed, the strategy that Japanese firms leveraged to success in DRAMs.

The areas in which American firms concentrated can generally be described as higher-margin, design-intensive chips. For such chips, production costs would not be the sole margin of competition; innovation and responsiveness would count for more. And innovation and responsiveness were arguably the strong suit of the "fragmented" American industry. As Nelson and Winter (1977) and others have argued, a decentralized structure permits the trying out of a wider diversity of approaches, leading to

rapid trial-and-error learning. And the independence of many firms from larger organizations permits speedier realignment and recombination with suppliers and customers. Building on existing competences in design (especially of logic and specialty
circuits) and close ties with the burgeoning American personal computer industry,
American firms were able to prosper despite the Japanese edge in manufacturing technology.

Product design has once again become a major determinant of competitive outcomes. This is true not only in the area of custom logic chips and ASICs but – perhaps
most importantly – in microprocessor unit (MPU) and related segments, also called
the microcomponent (MCU) segment.[18] Between 1988 and 1994, a period in which
merchant IC revenues grew by 121 percent, MPU revenues grew much faster than did
memory revenues (ICE, 1998). This evolution of the product mix in the industry has
strongly favored American producers. In the microcomponent portion of the chip
market, American companies accounted for 72 percent of world production in 1996,
compared with a 21 percent share for Japanese companies (see figure 20.2).

The importance of the microprocessor segment has meant that a single company,
Intel, is responsible for much of the gain of American merchant IC producers. In
1996, Intel accounted for 43 percent of world output in the microcomponent market,
led by its strong position in microprocessors (see figure 20.2). Intel's strategy for
recovery, begun in the 1980s, has proven remarkably successful (Afuah, 1999). In the
late 1980s, the firm consolidated its intellectual-property position in microprocessors
by terminating cross-licensing agreements with other companies and, more importantly, began extending its first-mover advantage over rivals by accelerating the rate of
new product introduction. These developments pushed Intel into the position of the
largest IC producer in the world, with 1998 revenues of $22.7 billion – more than the
next three largest firms combined (see table 20.4). Although Intel dominates the microprocessor market, it is not entirely without competitors; and it is significant that its
principal competitors are also American companies.

The success of American firms in microprocessors and related chips has been reinforced by trends in end-use demand. In 1989, computer applications took 40 percent

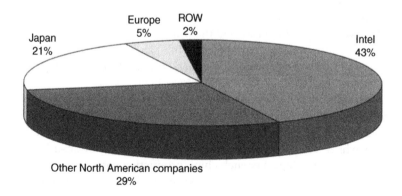

**Figure 20.2** 1996 MOS, MPU, MCU, and peripherals production (%). Source of data:
ICE (1998)

**Table 20.4** Estimated 1998 semiconductor revenues ($ million)

| Company | Revenues |
| --- | --- |
| Intel | 22,675 |
| NEC | 8,271 |
| Motorola | 6,918 |
| Toshiba | 6,055 |
| Texas Instruments | 6,000 |
| Samsung | 4,752 |
| Hitachi | 4,649 |
| Philips | 4,502 |
| STMicroelectronics | 4,300 |
| Siemens | 3,866 |
| Fujitsu | 3,866 |

*Source*: Dataquest, cited in *Electronics Times*, January 11, 1999: 3.

of merchant IC sales, followed by consumer and automotive applications at 28 percent.[19] By 1996, the respective shares were 50 percent for computer and 23 percent for consumer and automotive applications. The worldwide changes have led to increasing specialization. Between 1989 and 1994, North American use of ICs for computer applications soared from 15 to 24 percent of the total value of world merchant sales, while the Japanese IC market for consumer applications fell from 13 percent to 10 percent of world merchant sales. Thus, in contrast to rough parity (15 vs. 13 percent) in 1989, an enormous gap has opened between IC demand for consumer and computer applications in the Japanese and American markets. Keep in mind that these figures are in terms of revenue, not physical units, and much of the reversal of American fortunes has to do with the high value per component of microprocessors and other design-intensive chips, as against the low value per unit of the mass-produced DRAMs on which Japanese firms long rested their strategies.

Another aspect of specialization that benefited the American industry was the increasing "decoupling" of design from production. Such decoupling is in many respects a natural manifestation of the division of labor in growing markets (Young, 1928); in this case, it was abetted by the development of computerized design tools (Hobday, 1991) and the standardization of manufacturing technology (Macher et al., 1999). On the one hand, this allowed American firms to specialize in design-intensive chips, taking advantage of an American comparative advantage that arguably arises out of the decentralized and "fragmented" structure of that country's industry.[20] On the other hand, it also allowed many American firms to take advantage of growing production capabilities overseas.

"Globalization" has long been a trend in the semiconductor industry (Langlois et al., 1988), and American firms had long used "offshore" production as a strategy for cost reduction, beginning with outsourcing of assembly and packaging stages. But the decoupling of design from production has enabled American firms to benefit from globalization without investing large amounts of their own money overseas. These "fabless" semiconductor firms are able to contract out production to "silicon foundries" around the world, especially in the Far East.

As globalization (broadly understood) has bolstered the fortunes of American firms, it has eroded those of the Japanese. Japanese firms were not the only ones who could understand the economics of capacity investment or productivity in manufacturing, and they were soon joined by Korean semiconductor producers and by larger American companies who matched Japanese productivity by the simple expedient of establishing Japanese plants. The result is a dilution of the control of capacity investment by Japanese producers. By the mid-1990s, a Korean firm had displaced Japanese firms as the leading producer of DRAMs in the world, and two other Korean firms had joined the top 10 (see table 20.5).

## Conclusions

For a number of reasons, including the early pattern of military, space, and computer demand in the United States, American semiconductor firms developed a distinctive set of capabilities and a distinctive industrial structure. Because of the richness of the technological paradigm opened up by the integrated circuit, and the planar process that underlay it, American firms in the 1970s and 1980s began to broaden not only their technological capabilities but also the menu of product alternatives the integrated circuit had made possible. By concentrating narrowly on specific products, Japanese firms were able to challenge American dominance in the 1980s, taking advantage of their own distinctive capabilities in high-quality manufacturing and of the benefits that their own industrial structure conferred on them for capital-intensive mass production.

In part, the more recent American resurgence was the result of imitating these Japanese capabilities, notably by improving semiconductor manufacturing. In the large, however, that resurgence reflects a renewed focus on what had long been distinctive American capabilities in design-intensive chips, especially logic chips. It also reflects a

**Table 20.5.** Worldwide merchant-market sales of DRAMs ($ million)

| Company | Country | 1995 | 1996 |
|---|---|---|---|
| Samsung | Korea | 6462 | 4805 |
| NEC | Japan | 4740 | 3175 |
| Hitachi | Japan | 4439 | 2805 |
| Hyundai | Korea | 3500 | 2300 |
| Toshiba | Japan | 3725 | 2235 |
| LG Electronics | Korea | 3005 | 2005 |
| Texas Instruments | US | 3200 | 1600 |
| Micron | US | 2485 | 1575 |
| Mitsubishi | Japan | 2215 | 1400 |
| Fujitsu | Japan | 2065 | 1350 |
| Others | | 4999 | 1880 |

*Source*: ICE (1998).

favorable shift in end-use demand that gave advantage to those American capabilities and to the American industrial structure that had grown up in the period of America's early dominance.

What lessons does this episode provide for research on corporate strategy? The American response to Japanese competition is not essentially about the ability of firms to "reengineer" themselves or their capabilities in the face of change. American firms certainly did build capabilities in response to the Japanese challenge. But, as Penrose (1959) taught, the pattern of capabilities or resources available to a firm evolves slowly out of earlier patterns, largely in response to the opportunities the world presents. Strategy is not a matter of creating capabilities out of whole cloth but rather of picking and choosing among existing capabilities from a menu that circumstance dictates. And even that choice is often constrained and shaped by conditions outside the control of managers.

## Acknowledgements

This paper was presented at the Tuck/CCC Conference on the "Evolution of Capabilities: Emergence, Development, and Change," September 24–5, 1999, Hanover, New Hampshire. Langlois is grateful for financial support from the Center for International Business Education and Research (CIBER), School of Business Administration, University of Connecticut. Much of Steinmueller's work on this project was accomplished while he was Professor of the Economics of Technological Change at the Maastricht Economic Research Institute on Innovation and Technology (MERIT) at University of Maastricht, The Netherlands.

## Notes

1   A contemporary exception is Langlois et al. (1988).
2   The exceptions include Macher, Mowery, and Hodges (1998) and Afuah (1999).
3   This essay concentrates on the roles of capabilities and strategies. For more on the role of government policy, see Langlois and Steinmueller (1999).
4   As Saxenian (1994) and others have argued, the localization of many of these firms on the San Francisco Peninsula created the kind of industrial district discussed by Alfred Marshall (1961), generating a self-reinforcing system of external economies.
5   Analog circuits involve the continuous variation of current or voltage, in contrast to the on-or-off character of digital circuits.
6   Along with Westinghouse and RCA. Texas Instruments participated in the Minuteman II Program, the first major military use of ICs (Kleiman, 1966: 195; Levin, 1982: 62). And, while shunning military markets, Fairchild was the major IC vendor to NASA for the Apollo Project (Levin, 1982: 62).
7   As Gavin Wright (1999: 317) has argued, the "coexistence and complementarity of large and small technology-based firms has been a persistent feature of the US in major twentieth century industries."
8   The other major American captive producer was AT&T. These two American captives also behaved differently from their integrated counterparts overseas in that they generally refrained from selling on the merchant market at all – because of legal constraint in the case of AT&T and of company policy in the case of IBM.

9   See Braun and Macdonald (1982: 148) for net earnings after tax as a percent of sales for 1967–77.

10  American firms did, of course, have recourse to the arm's length capital markets. And most economists would see this chronic "undercapitalization" of the industry as a sign that capital markets had "failed." In fact, of course, arm's length capital markets and the internal capital markets of multi-divisional firms are both institutions with pluses and minuses, and neither is sensibly judged against an abstract ideal standard. As we will see, the decentralization and independence of American firms served the industry well in many circumstances, both early and late in our story. But, because of what one might generally view as transaction-cost problems, arm's length financing may be less adept in smoothing cyclical fluctuations than is internal financing. We include in this venture-capital financing, which is, in any case, typically used for startup capital rather than for ongoing capitalization of mature businesses.

11  The exceptions were Texas Instruments, which produced in Japan, and Micron Technology, which produced in Idaho.

12  These figures do not take into account the sizable captive production at IBM and AT&T.

13  The remainder of this paragraph follows Ernst and O'Connor (1992: 66).

14  In part, the claim that the production of DRAMs was necessary as a process driver confused the properties of DRAMs with the fact of volume production. As microprocessors and other non-memory chips began to be produced in greater volume (because of the growth of the personal computer industry), those devices were able to serve as process drivers (Robertson, 1997). Indeed, microprocessor chips are in many ways more complicated than RAMs. They typically require more layers, which helped give American firms, and their American equipment suppliers, advantage in (among other things) the complex technology of interconnecting levels (Langlois, 2000).

15  Even here, American firms tend to specialize in the standard-cell approach to ASICs, which is more design intensive and less manufacturing intensive than the linear and gate arrays favored by the Japanese. Between 1989 and 1994, however, this specialization diminished somewhat as American firms lost two percentage points of share in standard cells but gained a point in linear and gate arrays (ICE, 1990, 1995).

16  The remainder of this paragraph follows Macher, Mowery, and Hodges (1999).

17  According to one study, the yields of American firms increased from 60 percent in 1986 to 84 percent in 1991. The yields of Japanese firms increased over the same period from 75 percent to 93 percent, implying that American firms narrowed the gap in yield rates from 15 percent to 9 percent. (U.S. General Accounting Office, 1992).

18  This segment includes not only microprocessors, but also microcontrollers (less sophisticated microprocessors that are used in embedded applications) and related "support" chips, such as memory controllers, that are necessary to assembling a microprocessor system.

19  These and succeeding figures in this paragraph are from ICE (1990), ICE (1995), and ICE (1998).

20  Perhaps surprisingly, the mid-1980s – that dark period for American fortunes – was actually the most fertile period in history for the startup of new semiconductor firms, by a large margin. Most of these new firms were involved in design-intensive custom devices and ASICs (Angel, 1994: 38).

## References

Afuah, A. 1999. Strategies to turn adversity into profits. *Sloan Management Review* 40(2): 99–109.

Angel, D. P. 1994. *Restructuring for Innovation: The Remaking of the U.S. Semiconductor Industry*. Guilford Press: New York.

Borrus, M. G. 1988. *Competing for Control: America's Stake in Microelectronics*. Ballinger: Cambridge, MA.

Borrus, M. G., Millstein, J. E., and Zysman, J. 1983. Trade and development in the semiconductor industry: Japanese challenge and American response. In *American Industry in International Competition: Government Policies and Corporate Strategies*, Zysman, J. and Tyson, L. (edn). Cornell University Press: Ithaca, NY; 142–248.

Braun, E. and Macdonald, S. 1982. *Revolution in Miniature*. 2nd edn, Cambridge University Press: Cambridge, UK.

Christensen, C. M. and Rosenbloom, R. S. 1995. Explaining the attacker's advantage: technological paradigms, organizational dynamics, and the value network. *Research Policy* 24(2): 233–257.

Cogan, G. W. and Burgelman, R. A. 1989. Intel Corporation (A): the DRAM decision. Stanford Business School Case II-10. (Reprinted in *Strategic Management of Technology and Innovation*. (2nd edn) 1996, Burgelman, R. A., Maidique, M. A., and Wheelwright, S. C. (eds). Irwin: Chicago, IL; 314–339.

Ernst, D. and O'Connor, D. 1992. *Competing in the Electronics Industry: The Experience of Newly Industrialising Economies*. OECD: Paris.

Gambardella, A. and Torrisi, S. 1998. Does technological convergence imply convergence in markets? Evidence from the electronics industry. *Research Policy* 27(5): 447–465.

Granstrand, O., Patel, P., and Pavitt, K. 1997. Multi-technology corporations: why they have "distributed" rather than "distinctive core" competencies. *California Management Review* 39(4): 8–25.

Helm, L. 1995. In the chips. *The Los Angeles Times* March 5,: D1.

Hobday, M. 1991. Semiconductor technology and the newly industrializing countries: the diffusion of ASICs (Application Specific Integrated Circuits). *World Development* 19(4): 375–397.

Howell, T. P., Bartlett, B., and Davis, W. 1992. *Creating Advantage: Semiconductors and Government Industrial Policy in the 1990s*. Semiconductor Industry Association and Dewey Ballantine: Cupertino, CA and Washington, DC.

Integrated Circuit Engineering Corporation (ICE). Various years. *Status of the Integrated Circuit Industry*. ICE: Scottsdale, AZ.

Kleiman, H. S. 1966. *The Integrated Circuit: A Case Study of Product Innovation in the Electronics Industry*. DBA dissertation, George Washington University.

Langlois, R. N. 2000. Capabilities and vertical disintegration in process technology: the case of semiconductor fabrication equipment. In *Resources, Technology, and Strategy*, Foss N. J. and Robertson, P. L. (eds). Routledge: London; 199–226.

Langlois, R. N., Pugel, T. A., Haklisch, C. S., Nelson, R. R., and Egelhoff, W. G. 1988. *Microelectronics: An Industry in Transition*. Unwin Hyman: London.

Langlois, R. N. and Robertson, P. L. 1995. *Firms, Markets, and Economic Change: A Dynamic Theory of Business Institutions*. Routledge: London.

Langlois, R. N. and Steinmueller, W. E. 1999. The evolution of competitive advantage in the worldwide semiconductor industry, 1947–1996. In *The Sources of Industrial Leadership*, Mowery, D. C. and Nelson, R. R. (ed.). Cambridge University Press: New York; 19–78.

Levin, R. C. 1982. The semiconductor industry. In *Government and Technical Progress: A Cross-Industry Analysis*, Nelson, R. R. (eds.). Pergamon: New York; 9–100.

Macher, J., Mowery, D. C., and Hodges, D. 1998. Reversal of fortune? The recovery of the U.S. Semiconductor industry. *California Management Review* 41(1): 107–136.

Macher, J., Mowery, D. C., and Hodges, D. 1999. Performance and innovation in the U. S.

Semiconductor industry, 1980–1996. In *U.S. Industry in 2000: Studies in Competitive Performance*, Mowery, D. C. (ed.). National Academy Press: Washington, DC; 245–286.

Mackintosh, I. M. 1978. Large-scale integration: intercontinental aspects. *IEEE Spectrum* 15(6): 51–56.

Marshall, A. 1961. *Principles of Economics*. Ninth (Variorum) Edition, Vol. 1. Macmillan: London.

Methé, D. T. 1991. *Technological Competition in Global Industries: Marketing and Planning Strategies for American Industry*. Quorum: Westport, CT.

Nelson, R. R. and Winter, S. G. 1977. In search of more useful theory of innovation. *Research Policy* 5: 36–76.

Patel, P. and Pavitt, K. 1997. The technological competencies of the world's largest firms: complex and path-dependent, but not much variety. *Research Policy* 26: 141–156.

Penrose, E. T. 1959. *The Theory of the Growth of the Firm*. Basil Blackwell: Oxford.

Prahalad, C. K. and Hamel, G. 1990. The core competence of the corporation. *Harvard Business Review* 68(3): 79–91.

Robertson, J. 1997. http://www.semibiznews.com/pub/0397/story2.html [Semiconductor Business News, March].

Saxenian, A. L. 1994. *Regional Advantage: Culture and Competition in Silicon Valley and Route 128*. Harvard University Press: Cambridge, MA.

Teece, D. J. 1986. Profiting from technological innovation: implications for integration, collaboration, licensing, and public policy. *Research Policy* 15: 285–305.

US General Accounting Office. 1992. *Federal Research: Sematech's Technological Progress and Proposed R&D Program*. US GAO: Washington, DC.

Watanabe, M. 1984. Semiconductor Industry in Japan: past and present. *IEEE Transactions on Electron Devices* ED31(11): 1562–1570.

Wilson, R. W., Ashton, P. K., and Egan, T. P. 1980. *Innovation, Competition, and Government Policy in the Semiconductor Industry*. DC Heath: Lexington, MA.

Wright, G. 1999. Can a nation learn? American technology as a network phenomenon. In *Learning by Doing in Markets, Firms, and Countries*, Lamoreaux, N. R., Raff, D. M. G., and Temin, P. (eds). University of Chicago Press: Chicago, IL; 295–331.

Young, A. A. 1928. Increasing returns and economic progress. *Economic Journal* 38: 523–542.

# CHAPTER TWENTY-ONE

# Dynamic Capabilities: What Are They?

## Kathleen M. Eisenhardt and Jeffrey A. Martin

The resource-based view of the firm (RBV) is an influential theoretical framework for understanding how competitive advantage within firms is achieved and how that advantage might be sustained over time (Barney, 1991; Nelson, 1991; Penrose, 1959; Peteraf, 1993; Prahalad and Hamel, 1990; Schumpeter, 1934; Teece, Pisano, and Shuen, 1997; Wernerfelt, 1984). This perspective focuses on the internal organization of firms, and so is a complement to the traditional emphasis of strategy on industry structure and strategic positioning within that structure as the determinants of competitive advantage (Henderson and Cockburn, 1994; Porter, 1979). In particular, RBV assumes that firms can be conceptualized as bundles of resources, that those resources are heterogeneously distributed across firms, and that resource differences persist over time (Amit and Schoemaker, 1993; Mahoney and Pandian, 1992; Penrose, 1959; Wernerfelt, 1984). Based on these assumptions, researchers have theorized that when firms have resources that are valuable, rare, inimitable, and nonsubstitutable (i.e., so-called VRIN attributes), they can achieve sustainable competitive advantage by implementing fresh value-creating strategies that cannot be easily duplicated by competing firms (Barney, 1991; Conner and Prahalad, 1996; Nelson, 1991; Peteraf, 1993; Wernerfelt, 1984, 1995). Finally, when these resources and their related activity systems have complementarities, their potential to create sustained competitive advantage is enhanced (Collis and Montgomery, 1995, 1998; Milgrom, Qian, and Roberts, 1991; Milgrom and Roberts, 1990; Porter, 1996).

Recently, scholars have extended RBV to dynamic markets (Teece et al., 1997). The rationale is that RBV has not adequately explained how and why certain firms have competitive advantage in situations of rapid and unpredictable change. In these markets, where the competitive landscape is shifting, the dynamic capabilities by which firm managers "integrate, build, and reconfigure internal and external competencies to address rapidly changing environments" (Teece et al., 1997: 516) become the source of sustained competitive advantage. The manipulation of knowledge resources, in particular, is especially critical in such markets (Grant, 1996; Kogut, 1996).

Despite the significance of RBV, the perspective has not gone unchallenged. It has been called conceptually vague and tautological, with inattention to the mechanisms by which resources actually contribute to competitive advantage (e.g., Mosakowski and McKelvey, 1997; Priem and Butler, 2000; Williamson, 1999). It has also been criticized for lack of empirical grounding (e.g., Williamson, 1999; Priem and Butler, 2000). And, particularly relevant here, sustained competitive advantage has been seen as unlikely in dynamic markets (e.g., D'Aveni, 1994).

The purpose of this paper is to extend our understanding of dynamic capabilities and in so doing enhance RBV. Since dynamic capabilities are processes embedded in firms, we assume an organizational and empirical lens, rather than an economic and formal modeling one (Barney, 1991; Peteraf, 1993). We examine the nature of dynamic capabilities, how those capabilities are influenced by market dynamism, and their evolution over time.

We have several observations. First, dynamic capabilities consist of specific strategic and organizational processes like product development, alliancing, and strategic decision-making that create value for firms within dynamic markets by manipulating resources into new value-creating strategies. Dynamic capabilities are neither vague nor tautologically defined abstractions. Second, these capabilities, which often have extensive empirical research streams associated with them, exhibit commonalities across effective firms or what can be termed "best practice." Therefore, dynamic capabilities have greater equifinality, homogeneity, and substitutability across firms than traditional RBV thinking implies. Third, effective patterns of dynamic capabilities vary with market dynamism. When markets are moderately dynamic such that change occurs in the context of stable industry structure, dynamic capabilities resemble the traditional conception of routines (e.g., Cyert and March, 1963; Nelson and Winter, 1982). That is, they are complicated, detailed, analytic processes that rely extensively on existing knowledge and linear execution to produce predictable outcomes. In contrast, in high-velocity markets where industry structure is blurring, dynamic capabilities take on a different character. They are simple, experiential, unstable processes that rely on quickly created new knowledge and iterative execution to produce adaptive, but unpredictable outcomes. Finally, well-known learning mechanisms guide the evolution of dynamic capabilities and underlie path dependence.

Overall, our work attempts to contribute to RBV by explicating the nature of dynamic capabilities in a way that is realistic, empirically valid, and non-tautological. Our work also attempts to clarify RBV's logic of dynamic capabilities, resources, and competitive advantage. We argue that, since the functionality of dynamic capabilities can be duplicated across firms, their value for competitive advantage lies in the resource configurations that they create, not in the capabilities themselves. Dynamic capabilities are necessary, but not sufficient, conditions for competitive advantage. We also argue that dynamic capabilities can be used to enhance existing resource configurations in the pursuit of long-term competitive advantage (RBV's logic of leverage). They are, however, also very frequently used to build new resource configurations in the pursuit of temporary advantages (logic of opportunity). Most significant, we suggest a boundary condition. RBV breaks down in high-velocity markets, where the strategic challenge is maintaining competitive advantage when the duration of that advantage is inherently unpredictable, where time is an essential aspect of strategy, and the dynamic capabilities that drive competitive advantage are themselves unstable processes that are challenging to sustain.

## Dynamic Capabilities

Resources are at the heart of the resource-based view (RBV). They are those specific physical (e.g., specialized equipment, geographic location), human (e.g., expertise in chemistry), and organizational (e.g., superior sales force) assets that can be used to implement value-creating strategies (Barney, 1986; Wernerfelt, 1984, 1995). They include the local abilities or "competencies" that are fundamental to the competitive advantage of a firm such as skills in molecular biology for biotech firms or in advertising for consumer products firms. As such, resources form the basis of unique value-creating strategies and their related activity systems that address specific markets and customers in distinctive ways, and so lead to competitive advantage (e.g., configurations, Collis and Montgomery, 1995, 1998; Porter, 1996; core competencies, Prahalad and Hamel, 1990; lean production, Womack, Jones, and Roos, 1991).

Dynamic capabilities are the antecedent organizational and strategic routines by which managers alter their resource base – acquire and shed resources, integrate them together, and recombine them – to generate new value-creating strategies (Grant, 1996; Pisano, 1994). As such, they are the drivers behind the creation, evolution, and recombination of other resources into new sources of competitive advantage (Henderson and Cockburn, 1994; Teece et al., 1997). Similar to Teece and colleagues (1997), we define dynamic capabilities as:

> The firm's processes that use resources – specifically the processes to integrate, reconfigure, gain and release resources – to match and even create market change. Dynamic capabilities thus are the organizational and strategic routines by which firms achieve new resource configurations as markets emerge, collide, split, evolve, and die.

This definition of dynamic capabilities is similar to the definitions given by other authors. For example, Kogut and Zander (1992) use the term "combinative capabilities" to describe organizational processes by which firms synthesize and acquire knowledge resources, and generate new applications from those resources. Henderson and Cockburn (1994) similarly use the term "architectural competence" while Amit and Schoemaker (1993) use "capabilities."

### Dynamic capabilities as identifiable, specific processes

Dynamic capabilities are often described in vague terms such as "routines to learn routines" that have been criticized as being tautological, endlessly recursive, and non-operational (e.g., Mosakowski and McKelvey, 1997; Priem and Butler, 2000; Williamson, 1999). Yet, dynamic capabilities actually consist of identifiable and specific routines that often have been the subject of extensive empirical research in their own right outside of RBV.

Some dynamic capabilities integrate resources. For example, product development routines by which managers combine their varied skills and functional backgrounds to create revenue-producing products and services (e.g., Clark and Fujimoto, 1991; Dougherty, 1992; Helfat and Raubitschek, 2000) are such a dynamic capability. Toyota has, for example, used its superior product development skills to achieve competitive advantage in the automotive industry (Clark and Fujimoto, 1991). Similarly, strategic decision -making is a dynamic capability in which managers pool their various business, functional, and personal expertise to make the choices that shape the major strategic moves of the firm (e.g., Eisenhardt, 1989; Fredrickson, 1984; Judge and Miller, 1991).

Other dynamic capabilities focus on reconfiguration of resources within firms. Transfer processes including routines for replication and brokering (e.g., Hansen, 1999; Hargadon and Sutton, 1997; Szulanski, 1996) are used by managers to copy, transfer, and recombine resources, especially knowledge-based ones, within the firm. For example, at the premier product design firm, IDEO, managers routinely create new products by knowledge brokering from a variety of previous design projects in many industries and from many clients (Hargadon and Sutton, 1997). Resource allocation routines are used to distribute scarce resources such as capital and manufacturing assets from central points within the hierarchy (e.g., Burgelman, 1994). At a more strategic level, coevolving involves the routines by which managers reconnect webs of collaborations among various parts of the firm to generate new and synergistic resource combinations among businesses (e.g., Eisenhardt and Galunic, 2000). Disney, for example, has historically excelled at coevolving to create shifting synergies that drive superior performance (Wetlaufer, 2000). Patching is a strategic process that centers on routines to realign the match-up of businesses (i.e., add, combine, and split) and their related resources to changing market opportunities (Eisenhardt and Brown, 1999). Dell's constant segmentation of operating businesses to match shifting customer demands is an example of a superior patching process (Magretta, 1998).

Still other dynamic capabilities are related to the gain and release of resources. These include knowledge creation routines whereby managers and others build new thinking within the firm, a particularly crucial dynamic capability in industries like pharmaceuticals, optical disks, and oil where cutting-edge knowledge is essential for effective strategy and performance (e.g., Helfat, 1997; Henderson and Cockburn, 1994; Rosenkopf and Nerkar, 1999). They also include alliance and acquisition routines that bring new resources into the firm from external sources (e.g., Capron, Dussauge, and Mitchell, 1998; Gulati, 1999; Lane and Lubatkin, 1998; Powell, Koput, and Smith-Doerr, 1996; Ranft and Zeithaml, 1998; Zollo and Singh, 1998). Cisco Systems has, for example, a very effective acquisition process by which managers have assembled a changing array of products and engineering know-how that drive superior performance. Similarly, biotech firms with strong alliancing processes for accessing outside knowledge achieve superior performance (Powell et al., 1996). Finally, although often neglected, exit routines that jettison resource combinations that no longer provide competitive advantage are also critical dynamic capabilities as markets undergo change (Sull, 1999a, 1999b).

The identification of particular processes as dynamic capabilities has several implications. For one, it opens up RBV thinking to a large, substantive body of empirical research that has often been neglected within the paradigm. This research on capabilities such as product development and alliance formation sheds light not only on these specific processes, but also on the generalized nature of dynamic capabilities. So, contrary to the criticism that dynamic capabilities lack empirical grounding (Williamson,

1999), dynamic capabilities as specific processes often have extensive empirical research bases and management applicability.

More significant, the identification of specific routines in terms of their relationship to altering the resource base addresses the tautology which arises when the value of dynamic capabilities is defined in terms of their effects on performance (e.g., Priem and Butler, 2000; Williamson, 1999). That is, when the VRIN resources that drive competitive advantage are identified by observing superior performance and then attributing that performance to whatever unique resources the firm appears to possess, the theory becomes tautological. In contrast, by defining dynamic capabilities in terms of their functional relationship to resource manipulation, their value is defined independent of firm performance. This enables empirical falsification.

### Commonalities in key features, idiosyncrasy in details

Dynamic capabilities are often characterized as unique and idiosyncratic processes that emerge from path-dependent histories of individual firms (Teece et al., 1997). Yet, while dynamic capabilities are certainly idiosyncratic in their details, the equally striking observation is that specific dynamic capabilities also exhibit common features that are associated with effective processes across firms. These commonalities arise because there are more and less effective ways of dealing with the specific organizational, interpersonal, and technical challenges that must be addressed by a given capability. In other words, just as there are better and worse ways to hit a golf ball or ski a mogul field, there are more and less effective ways to execute particular dynamic capabilities such as alliancing, strategic decision -making, and knowledge brokering. In popular parlance, there is "best practice."

Take, for example, the product development process, an important dynamic capability that has been extensively researched (see Brown and Eisenhardt, 1995, for a review). Effective product development routines typically involve the participation of cross-functional teams that bring together different sources of expertise. These sources of expertise are essential for superior products because each addresses a unique aspect of product quality or related production. For example, Imai, Ikujiro, and Takeuchi (1985) studied seven product development efforts in five Japanese companies operating in several industries. The products included the Fuji-Xerox FX-3500 copier, the City box-car by Honda, and the Canon Sureshot camera. Performance was measured in terms of the speed and flexibility of development. The findings indicated that cross-functional teams were essential for superior performance. The use of these teams enhanced the range of information that was available, and eased the coordination and overlap of manufacturing, marketing, and design tasks during the course of the process.

Effective product development processes also involve routines that ensure that concrete and joint experiences among team members, such as working together to fix specific problems or participating in brainstorming sessions occur. Such experiences enhance innovation by breaking down the thought worlds that arise because people with different expertise not only know different things, but know those things differently. Concrete experiences with others on the development team create a common experience base and language that facilitates communication among functionally distinct people. Dougherty (1992), for example, studied 18 product development projects in five well-established US firms including Kodak and Campbell Soup. She found that common customer visits and feedback were essential for an effective product development process. Simply having liaisons between groups was not enough to ensure effective communication.

Effective product development processes also have extensive external communication that is often facilitated by strong or "heavyweight" team leaders. For example, Ancona and Caldwell (1992) found that successful product development processes were characterized by extensive communication links outside of the group, particularly when those links were used by project team leaders to buffer the group from outside influences and to garner resources. Clark and Fujimoto (1991) similarly found that heavyweight leaders who engaged in significant external communication and vision setting led more productive product development projects.

Commonalities that are related to more effective routines exist for other dynamic capabilities as well. For example, successful acquisition processes are characterized by preacquisition routines that assess cultural similarity and consistency of vision (e.g., Larrson and Finkelstein, 1999) and postacquisition routines that pay particular attention to the speed of integration (Graebner, 2000) and the strategic redeployment of assets across the two firms (Capron et al., 1998; Graebner, 1999, 2000). Similarly, effective routines for coevolving in order to capture synergies among resources located in different parts of the organization typically have common features. These include routines to ensure that business heads develop social bonds with one another, and surprisingly that the business heads are rewarded for individual, not collective success (Christensen, 1997; Eisenhardt and Galunic, 2000).

The existence of common features among effective dynamic capabilities does not, however, imply that any particular dynamic capability is exactly alike across firms. Take, for example, knowledge creation processes, a crucial dynamic capability especially within high-technology firms. A common feature across successful knowledge creation processes is explicit linkage between the focal firm and knowledge sources outside the firm. In the pioneering research of Allen and colleagues (e.g., Allen, 1977; Allen, Piepmeier, and Cooney, 1971; Katz and Tushman, 1981), these linkages were a small number of "gatekeepers" within the firm. These individuals maintained active communication with scientists at other firms, government laboratories, and universities. Similarly, Henderson and Cockburn (1994) found that external linkages were crucial to effective knowledge creation processes in their extensive study of the pharmaceutical industry. These linkages, however, took the form of propublication incentives by which scientists were rewarded for maintaining external links to the wider scientific community through the use of publication in scientific journals as a promotion criterion. Similarly, Powell et al (1996) found that knowledge creation processes that included external linkages in the form of significant alliance relationships led to superior R&D performance within biotech firms. So, while external linkages are necessary for effective knowledge creation, those linkages can take varied forms including informal personal relationships, relationships driven by promotion criterion, and formal alliances.

Commonalities across firms for effective specific dynamic capabilities have several implications. First, they imply equifinality. That is, managers of firms that develop an effective dynamic capability such as patching, knowledge creation, or alliancing processes very probably begin the development of that capability from different starting points, and take unique paths. Yet, since they end up with capabilities that are similar in terms of key attributes, there are multiple paths (equifinality) to the same dynamic capabilities.

A recent study by Cockburn, Henderson, and Stern (2000) illustrates this phenomenon. These authors studied the emergence of propublication incentives (as noted above, a common feature of effective knowledge creation processes in the pharmaceutical industry). They found that managers began at different starting points and traveled different paths before adoption of these incentives. By happenstance, managers at some firms were already rewarding scientists for their publications at the start of the study. Some adopted the practice sooner than others because cutting-edge research was more relevant in their particular areas of therapeutic emphasis, or because they were located near major research universities where firms were more influenced by the norms of academic institutions. Still others adopted the practice when senior leadership changed. Firms began with different initial conditions and propensities for adoption, and followed different adoption paths. But eventually managers at most firms adopted propublication incentives for their scientists.

Second, commonalities in key features of effective dynamic capabilities imply that these routines are more substitutable and fungible across different contexts than current theory suggests. In the case of substitutability, as our example of knowledge creation processes suggests, effective dynamic capabilities can differ in form and details as long as the important commonalities are present. In the case of fungibility, commonalities imply the efficacy of particular dynamic capabilities across a range of industries.

Third, commonalities imply that dynamic capabilities per se are not likely to be sources of sustained competitive advantage. The thinking is as follows. According to the logic of RBV, sustained competitive advantage occurs when capabilities are not only valuable and rare, but also inimitable, immobile, and nonsubstitutable. Dynamic capabilities are typically valuable. They may be rare or at least not possessed by all competitors equally, as is apparent in much of the empirical research. Sustainability, however, breaks down for the latter conditions. Equifinality renders inimitability and immobility irrelevant to sustained advantage. That is, firms can gain the same capabilities from many paths, and independent of other firms. So, whether they can imitate other firms or move resources is not particularly relevant because managers of firms can discover them on their own. Dynamic capabilities are substitutable because they need to have key features in common to be effective, but they can actually be different in terms of many details. This suggests that dynamic capabilities per se can be a source of competitive, but not sustainable, advantage.

Finally, commonalities suggest that the scale of "idiosyncratic firm effects" in the empirical literature (Brush, Bromiley, and Hendrickx, 1999; McGahan and Porter, 1997; Roquebert, Phillips, and Westfall, 1996; Schmalensee, 1985; Wernerfelt and Montgomery, 1988) is probably overstated. Simply using dummy variables for firms leads to underspecified models that cannot capture key organizational attributes of dynamic capabilities as drivers of performance. Table 21.1 contrasts our view with previous ones.

**Table 21.1** Contrasting conceptions of dynamic capabilities

|  | *Traditional view of dynamic capabilities* | *Reconceptualization of dynamic capabilities* |
|---|---|---|
| Definition | Routines to learn routines | Specific organizational and strategic processes (e.g., product innovation, strategic decision-making, alliancing) by which managers alter their resource base |
| Heterogeneity | Idiosyncratic (i.e., firm specific) | Commonalities (i.e., best practice) with some idiosyncratic details |
| Pattern | Detailed, analytic routines | Depending on market dynamism, ranging from detailed, analytic routines to simple, experiential, ones |
| Outcome | Predictable | Depending on market dynamism, predictable or unpredictable |
| Competitive advantage | Sustained competitive advantage from VRIN dynamic capabilities | Competitive advantage from valuable, somewhat rare, equifinal, substitutable, and fungible dynamic capabilities |
| Evolution | Unique path | Unique path shaped by learning mechanisms such as practice, codification, mistakes, and pacing |

## Market dynamism: moderately dynamic to high-velocity markets

The pattern of effective dynamic capabilities depends upon market dynamism. In particular, dynamic capabilities vary in their reliance on existing knowledge. Moderately dynamic markets are ones in which change occurs frequently, but along roughly predictable and linear paths. They have relatively stable industry structures such that market boundaries are clear and the players (e.g., competitors, customers, complementers) are well known. In these markets, effective dynamic capabilities rely heavily on existing knowledge. Managers analyze situations in the context of their existing tacit knowledge and rules of thumb, and then plan and organize their activities in a relatively ordered fashion (Burns and Stalker, 1966). They can develop efficient processes that are predictable and relatively stable with linear steps, beginning with analysis and ending with implementation (Helfat, 1997).

For example, Pisano (1994) studied the development of new manufacturing processes in a sample of 23 process development projects in chemical- and biological-based pharmaceutical companies. In the moderately dynamic chemical industry where there is deep theoretical and practical knowledge, the routines for developing new manufacturing processes were more effective when they involved a structured and analytic process. Termed by the author "learning before doing", managers relied on analyzing the situation to come up with an appropriate manufacturing process, and then implementing that process within the factory.

Similarly, Fredrickson (1984) examined strategic decision-making in the paint industry, a slowly evolving industry. He found that more effective decision-making processes were linear. These effective processes were characterized by a sequence of problem solving steps that began with comprehensive collection of data, followed by development of alternatives, extensive analysis of those alternatives, and choice.

In some situations, existing tacit knowledge is further codified into detailed routines that precisely specify steps and subdivide activities among different individuals. Such routines deepen the memory of firms for the routine (Argote, 1999) and enhance the predictability of the process (Nelson and Winter, 1982). A good example is Eisenhardt and Tabrizi's (1995) study of 72 product development projects in the computer industry. In the moderately dynamic mainframe sector, more effective product development processes were characterized by a linear progression through progress gates, from specification through prototype to design, test and finally manufacturing ramp-up. Tasks within the development process were distributed among suppliers and focal firms, which permitted the overlap of different process steps without requiring extensive communication during the process.

In contrast, when markets are very dynamic or what is termed "high velocity" (e.g., Eisenhardt, 1989), change becomes nonlinear and less predictable. High-velocity markets are ones in which market boundaries are blurred, successful business models are unclear, and market players (i.e., buyers, suppliers, competitors, complementers) are ambiguous and shifting. The overall industry structure is unclear. Uncertainty cannot be modeled as probabilities because it is not possible to specify a priori the possible future states. In these markets, dynamic capabilities necessarily rely much less on existing knowledge and much more on rapidly creating situation-specific new knowledge. Existing knowledge can even be a disadvantage if managers overgeneralize from past situations (Argote, 1999).

Effective dynamic capabilities in high-velocity markets are simple, not complicated as they are in moderately dynamic markets. Simple routines keep managers focused on broadly important issues without locking them into specific behaviors or the use of past experience that may be inappropriate given the actions required in a particular situation. Often these routines consist of a few rules that specify boundary conditions on the actions of managers or indicate priorities, important in fast-moving markets where attention is in short supply.

Eisenhardt and Sull (2000) discussed the use of simple routines in high-velocity markets. They described, for example, how Yahoo's very successful alliancing process is largely unstructured, consisting of a two-rule routine that sets the boundary conditions for mangers wishing to forge alliances. The rules are: no exclusive alliance deals and the basic service provided by the deal (e.g., online greeting cards, party planning services, etc.) must be free. There is little else to the routine. These rules set the boundary conditions within which Yahoo managers have wide latitude for making a variety of alliancing deals.

Similarly, Burgelman's (1994, 1996) study of Intel's resource allocation process illustrates a simple routine, in this case one that specifies priorities. At a time of extreme volatility in which Asian manufacturers disrupted world markets with severe price cutting and accelerated technological improvements, Intel managers followed a simple production rule, "margin-per-wafer-start" that determined the resource allocation for manufacturing capacity (Burgelman, 1996: 205). Accordingly, as margins for memory chips decreased and margins for microprocessors increased, Intel began producing proportionally more microprocessors. By following this simple prioritization, Intel managers flexibly allocated resources and ultimately morphed into a microprocessor company well before senior managers recognized the transition.

While dynamic capabilities are simple in high-velocity markets, they are not completely unstructured or "organic" (e.g., Burns and Stalker, 1966; Lawrence and Lorsch, 1967). Indeed, if there were no structures, these processes would fly out of control and exhibit no coherence. Therefore, simple routines provide enough structure (i.e., semistructure) so that people can focus their attention amid a cacophony of information and possibilities, help provide sense making about the situation, and be confident enough to act in these highly uncertain situations where it is easy to become paralyzed by anxiety.

Brown and Eisenhardt's (1997) study of multiple product development processes is an illustration. The authors found that firms with highly structured processes such as extensive gating procedures produced new products quickly, but that those products often were not well adapted to market conditions. But, firms without some simple rules were equally ineffective. Developers at these firms had difficulty delivering products on time to hit market windows, and consistently reinvented technical solutions. In contrast, firms with the most successful product development processes relied on limited routines for priority setting, a business vision that bounded possible products, and adherence to deadlines, but little else in the way of routines.

In high-velocity markets, absence of detailed, formal routines is not indicative of extensive use of tacit knowledge or complex social routines that cannot be codified, although these may be present. Rather, dynamic capabilities strikingly involve the creation of new, situation-specific knowledge. This occurs by engaging in experiential actions to learn quickly and thereby compensating for limited, relevant existing knowledge by rapidly creating new knowledge about the current situation. So, dynamic capabilities often use prototyping and early testing to gain new knowledge quickly. Such actions create rapid learning through small losses and immediate feedback (Argote, 1999; Sitkin, 1992). Dynamic capabilities in these markets proceed in at iterative fashion. As managers adjust to new information and changing conditions, they engage in more recycling through steps such as developing alternatives and implementation that would be linear in less dynamic markets. Dynamic capabilities also rely more on real-time information, cross-functional relationships and intensive communication among those involved in the process and with the external market. Real-time information alerts people early on to the need to adjust their actions since problems and opportunities are spotted more quickly than when individuals were more distant from information. Real-time information also builds intuition about the marketplace such that managers can more quickly understand the changing situation and adapt to it (Eisenhardt, 1989). Finally, dynamic capabilities in these markets are characterized by parallel consideration and often partial implementation (e.g., prototyping) of multiple options. Such options provide fallback positions, which are useful since situations can change rapidly.

They also give mangers a sense of confidence to act quickly. The emotional inability to cope with uncertainty is a major factor that slows down mangers in high-velocity markets (Eisenhardt, 1989).

Pisano's (1994) study of the process to develop new manufacturing procedures in chemical- and biological-based pharmaceutical firms mentioned above, is consistent with this thinking. The author found that "learning-by-doing" (as contrasted with "learning-before-doing" described above) was advantageous in the more rapidly changing biotech industry. In this context, it was effective to engage in greater experimentation and prototyping with early testing of processes. Similarly, studies of strategic decision processes (e.g., Eisenhardt, 1989; Judge and Miller, 1991; Wally and Baum, 1994) found that experiential actions like creating multiple alternatives (in addition to actions such as using real-time information) was related to more effective strategic decision-making processes in high-velocity markets. These findings contrasted significantly with the linear, analytic process that Fredrickson (1984) found in the less dynamic paint industry. Finally, Eisenhardt and Tabrizi (1995) found that more and earlier testing, and more prototypes were features of effective product development processes in the fast-paced work station and personal computing markets. These experiential processes contrasted with the detailed, linear processes that were effective in the less dynamic, mainframe sector. Taken together, these studies support the view that effective dynamic capabilities in high-velocity markets are experiential with extensive and frequent use of prototyping, real-time information, experimentation, and multiple alternatives.

While dynamic capabilities in high-velocity markets consist mostly of simple rules and real-time knowledge creation, they may have detailed routines to deal with aspects of the process where prior knowledge and/or codification are particularly useful. Very often, this more detailed scripting exists at the end of a process where such scripting helps to ensure fast, coordinated execution of complex details.

For example, Terwiesch, Chea, and Bohn (1999) examined the process of developing manufacturing processes in the disk drive industry. They found that, while most of the process involved prototyping a variety of manufacturing alternatives, once decided, implementation of the chosen approach occurred in a highly scripted fashion. Adler's (1999) study of developing manufacturing processes in the automotive industry had similar results for the importance of experimentation followed by highly rationalized implementation of the chosen option. Brown and Eisenhardt's (1998) study of multiple product development also indicated that most of the process was experiential except for a highly scripted roll-off routine to move developers from the end of one project to the beginning of the next.

The effects of market dynamism on dynamic capabilities have several implications. One is that sustainability of the capabilities themselves varies with the dynamism of the market. In moderately dynamic markets, dynamic capabilities resemble the traditional conception of routines (Cyert and March, 1963; Nelson and Winter, 1982; Zollo and Winter, 1999). That is, they are complicated, predictable, analytic processes that rely extensively on existing knowledge, linear execution and slow evolution over time. As managers continue to gain experience with these routines, they groove the processes more deeply such that they become easily sustained and even inertial. Codification of the routines through the technology or formal procedures enhances that sustainability (Argote, 1999). Therefore, the capabilities become robust.

In contrast, in high-velocity markets, dynamic capabilities take on a different character. They are simple (not complicated), experiential (not analytic), and iterative (not linear) processes. They rely on the creation of situation-specific knowledge that is applied in the context of simple boundary and priority-setting rules. But since these routines are simple, there is little structure for mangers to grasp and so they become easy to forget (Argote, 1999). This tendency to forget is exacerbated by the high turnover and rapid growth that often accompanies firms in high-velocity markets. In more technical terms, these improvisational processes are dissipative, meaning that they require constant energy to stay on track (Prigogine and Stengers, 1984). They are in the continuously unstable state of slipping into either too much or too little structure that is sometimes termed the "edge of chaos" (Kauffman, 1995). What is challenging to manage then is the optimal amount of structure (Eisenhardt and Bhatia, 2000). Therefore, dynamic capabilities themselves become difficult to sustain in high-velocity markets. In moderately dynamic markets, competitive advantage is destroyed from outside the firm. In high-velocity markets, the threat to competitive advantage comes not only from outside the firm, but also more insidiously from inside the firm through the potential collapse of dynamic capabilities.

The following quotes from several managers in the computing industry capture this instability. As one manager described, "We do everything on the fly . . . I've done some things at IBM and other companies where there is a very structured environment–these companies are failing and we're leading the way. I'm not comfortable with the lack of structure, but I hesitate to mess with what is working." At the other extreme, another manager described, "It is real easy for the division to just sort of put its head down in blinders and just go run forward and implement . . . We've got to force ourselves to step back" (Brown and Eisenhardt, 1997: 28).

A second implication is that causal ambiguity of dynamic capabilities varies with market dynamism. In moderately dynamic markets, dynamic capabilities are causally ambiguous because they are complicated and difficult to observe (Simonin, 1999). In contrast, in high-velocity markets, dynamic capabilities are causally ambiguous because they are simple. The extensive, experiential activity of effective dynamic capabilities in high-velocity markets obscures the fundamental commonalities that drive the effectiveness of the capability. So, it is difficult to isolate causality from the extensive, but unimportant idiosyncratic details. Sometimes even the managers themselves do not know why their dynamic capabilities are successful. For example, the CEO of a major biotech firm told one of the authors, "We have the best research process in the industry, but we don't know why." Further, many managers have a tendency to imitate more than is appropriate in the mistaken belief that more detailed processes are better. Indeed, the counterintuitive insight is that the complicated, highly adaptive moves required by high-velocity markets are driven by simple rules. Table 21.2 links characteristics of dynamic capabilities with market pace.

### Evolution of dynamic capabilities

The literature characterizes dynamic capabilities as complicated routines that emerge from path-dependent processes (Nelson and Winter, 1982; Teece et al., 1997; Zollo and Winter, 1999). However, while path dependence appropriately emphasizes the

Table 21.2 Dynamic capabilities and types of dynamic markets

|  | *Moderately dynamic markets* | *High-velocity markets* |
| --- | --- | --- |
| Market definition | Stable industry structure, defined boundaries, clear business models, identifiable players, linear and predictable change | Ambiguous industry structure, blurred boundaries, fluid business models, ambiguous and shifting players, nonlinear and unpredictable change |
| Pattern | Detailed, analytic routines that rely extensively on existing knowledge | Simple, experiential routines that rely on newly created knowledge specific to the situation |
| Execution | Linear | Iterative |
| Stable | Yes | No |
| Outcomes | Predictable | Unpredictable |
| Key to effective evolution | Frequent, nearby variation | Carefully managed selection |

encoding of inferences from the unique histories of firms into distinctive routines, path dependence is more accurately described in terms of learning mechanisms that have been identified principally within the psychological literature (Argote, 1999). These learning mechanisms guide the evolution of dynamic capabilities.

For example, repeated practice is an important learning mechanism for the development of dynamic capabilities. Practice helps people to understand processes more fully and so develop more effective routines. The efficacy of such experience has been demonstrated in numerous empirical studies, including the vast literature on learning curves in manufacturing (Argote, 1999). Similarly, Zollo and Singh's (1998) research on bank acquisitions illustrates the role of repeated practice. The authors found that integration, relatedness and acquisition experience led to increased performance. Specifically, repeated practice with homogeneous acquisitions (i.e., those in the related markets) was positively associated with the accumulation of tacit and explicit knowledge about how to execute acquisitions and achieve superior acquisition performance.

While repeated practice per se can contribute to the evolution of dynamic capabilities, the codification of that experience into technology and formal procedures makes that experience easier to apply and accelerates the building of routines (Argote, 1999; Zander and Kogut, 1995). For example, Kale, Dyer and Singh (1999), in a cross-industry study of alliances, found that concentrating alliance experience in a dedicated alliance function was a more powerful predictor of alliance success than experience alone. They suggest that a dedicated alliance function provides an important formalization mechanism through which alliancing know-how (e.g., routines) can be articulated, codified, shared and internalized within the organization.

Mistakes also play a role in the evolution of dynamic capabilities. Small losses, more than either successes or major failures, contribute to effective learning (Sitkin, 1992). Success often fails to engage managers' attention sufficiently so that they learn from their experience. Major failures raise defenses that block learning. In contrast, small failures provide the greatest motivation to learn as such failures cause individuals to pay greater attention to the process, but do not create defensiveness that impedes learning.

The effects of mistakes were examined by Hayward (2000) in his study of 241 acquisitions in 120 US firms in six market sectors. He found that a moderate number of small mistakes led to superior acquisition skills. Similarly, Eisenhardt and Sull (2000) recounted how Yahoo managers developed one of their rules for alliancing, described above, from a mistake. Yahoo managers formed an exclusive relationship with a major credit card firm. Shortly, they recognized that this alliance restricted flexibility, especially with regard to retailers, and terminated it at great expense. The "no exclusive deals" rule emerged from this mistake. Similarly, in a study of long-term development of capabilities, Kim (1998) noted the importance of crises, both contrived and real, for developing dynamic capabilities. In his investigation of the long-term building of Hyundai's organizational competencies in their automotive business, Kim (1998) found that the internal generation of a sense of failure (which he termed "constructed crisis") was essential to the motivation of the internal learning environment. These crises created greater engagement in the situation, and so increased learning within Hyundai.

The evolution of dynamic capabilities is also affected by the pacing of experience. Experience that comes too fast can overwhelm managers, leading to an inability to transform experience into meaningful learning. Similarly, infrequent experience can lead to forgetting what was learned previously and so result in little knowledge accumulation as well (Argote, 1999). For example, in the study mentioned earlier, Hayward (1998) found that timing had an inverted "U"-shaped shaped relationship with acquisition performance. Too many acquisitions done too frequently impaired managers' ability to absorb the lessons of any particular acquisition. They needed time to consolidate their learning. Yet, when there were too few acquisitions spaced too far apart, managers did not have enough opportunities to hone their skill.

While basic learning mechanisms such as those noted above underlie the evolution of dynamic capabilities, crucial aspects of that evolution also depend upon market dynamism. In moderately dynamic markets, experience in closely related, but different situations, is particularly effective in sharpening dynamic capabilities. Frequent, small variations help managers to deepen capabilities by elaborating them in current situations and extending them to related new ones. The result is efficient, robust routines that keep pace with changing markets and broaden opportunities for growth.

For example, Haleblian and Finkelstein (1999), in their study of 449 acquisitions, explored the relationships between acquisition experience and acquisition performance. Using the theoretical frame of learning theory, the authors found that mangers with extensive experience were able to discern similarities and differences between current and previous acquisitions, and so apply their acquisition skills in a more discriminatory manner that was associated with superior performance. In contrast, managers with moderate experience had less nuanced acquisition capabilities. Similarly, Hayward (2000) found that moderate levels of prior acquisition similarity were positively related to the development of acquisition capability. Managers appeared to create superior skill when they both reinforced their existing knowledge and yet also extended their experience into new types of acquisitions.

In contrast, in high-velocity markets, the more crucial aspect of evolution is selection, not variation. Variation happens readily in such markets. In contrast, selection is difficult because it is challenging to figure out which experience should be generalized from the extensive situation-specific knowledge that occurs. Which of the many experiences should be incorporated into the ongoing routines for the capabilities and which should be forgotten? The temptation is to generalize too quickly, and so to churn capabilities too often on the basis of idiosyncratic events (Gersick, 1994; Sastry, 1999).

Finally, the order of implementation of dynamic capabilities is consequential. That is, dynamic capabilities are often combinations of simpler capabilities and related routines, some of which may be foundational to others and so must be learned first. Brown and Eisenhardt (1997) termed this property "sequenced steps." In their study of multiple product development processes in six firms in the computer industry, they observed that multiple product development required the combination of three simpler dynamic capabilities: single product development, probing the future and linking routines from one product development project to the next. Managers who built an effective dynamic capability to develop multiple products did so according to "sequence steps" that had to be executed in the proper order. Single product development skills needed to come first to provide the platform for future products, then skills related to probing the future for new product opportunities, and finally time-pacing skills to create a product development rhythm connecting current products to future ones. Similarly, in his study of Hyundai, Kim (1998) found an appropriate sequencing of the learning of capabilities from the simpler and more predictable capabilities around manufacturing process creation to the more improvisational design ones in the development of design routines. Thus, effective implementation requires knowing both the ingredients (i.e., key commonalities of capabilities) and the recipe (i.e., order of implementation).

## Discussion

The purpose of this paper is to explore dynamic capabilities and more generally, RBV. In addressing this agenda, we focused on the nature of dynamic capabilities, the impact of market dynamism, and their evolution. Our observations link to several research areas.

Our work suggests reframing the concept of dynamic capabilities. Dynamic capabilities are not tautological, vague, and endlessly recursive as some have suggested (e.g., Priem and Butler, 2000; Williamson, 1999). Rather, they consist of many well-known processes such as alliancing, product development, and strategic decision-making that have been studied extensively in their own right, apart from RBV. Their value for competitive advantage lies in their ability to alter the resource base: create, integrate, recombine, and release resources.

Dynamic capabilities also exhibit commonalities across firms that are associated with superior effectiveness. So while the specifics of any given dynamic capability may be idiosyncratic to a firm (e.g., exact composition of a cross-functional product development team) and path dependent in its emergence, "best practice" exists for particular dynamic capabilities across firms. These commonalities imply that dynamic capabilities are equifinal such that firms can develop these capabilities from many starting points and along different paths. They are also more homogeneous, fungible, and substitutable than is usually assumed. Overall, these observations suggest a modified conception of dynamic capabilities.

Our work also suggests an expanded view of routines (Cyert and March, 1963; Nelson and Winter, 1982; Winter and Szulanski, 1999). We argue that, in moderately dynamic markets, routines in the form of dynamic capabilities are embedded in cumulative, existing knowledge. They involve analysis using existing knowledge and rules of thumb, followed by implementation. When this existing knowledge is codified, the resulting routines are often detailed and specific with predictable outcomes (Helfat, 1997; Nelson and Winter, 1982). Therefore, in moderately dynamic markets, dynamic capabilities exhibit the properties suggested in the traditional research where effective routines are efficient and robust processes (Cyert and March, 1963; Nelson and Winter, 1982).

In contrast, in high-velocity markets, dynamic capabilities rely extensively on new knowledge created for specific situations. Routines are purposefully simple to allow for emergent adaptation, although not completely unstructured. Since new knowledge must be rapidly gained in each new situation, experiential activities such as prototyping, real-time information, multiple options, and experimenting that generate immediate knowledge quickly replace analysis. In order to adapt to changing information, routines are iterative and cognitively mindful, not linear and mindless. Although there may be pockets of detailed routines where existing knowledge is relevant, dynamic capabilities are strikingly simple. Therefore, in high-velocity markets, effective routines are adaptive to changing circumstances. The price of that adaptability is unstable processes with unpredictable outcomes. Overall, this points to a richer conception of routines that goes beyond the usual view of efficient and robust processes (Cyert and March, 1963; Nelson and Winter, 1982) to include these more fragile, "semistructured" ones that are effective in high-velocity markets.

Our work also addresses the evolution of dynamic capabilities. We observe that, while the evolution of dynamic capabilities occurs along a unique path for any given firm, that path is shaped by well-known learning mechanisms. Repeated practice, for example, accelerates the formation of dynamic capabilities (Argote, 1999). Small losses (Sitkin, 1992), crises (Kim, 1998), and paced experience (Hayward, 2000) can motivate more rapid evolution. In moderately dynamic markets, small and frequent variations through related experience deepen capabilities (Haleblian and Finkelstein, 1999). In high-velocity markets where learning can be too rapid, selection of what to keep from experience is more crucial (Gersick, 1994). Finally, the order of implementation can be critical in dynamic capabilities that are composed of several distinct capabilities (Brown and Eisenhardt, 1997). Taken together, these insights open the "black box" of path dependence to reveal that the evolution of dynamic capabilities is guided by well-known learning mechanisms.

### Towards a new perspective on the resourcebased view

Most significant, our work addresses the logical links among dynamic capabilities, resources, and competitive advantage, a problematic area within RBV (Priem and Butler, 2000). We have three points. First, the argument that VRIN dynamic capabilities are themselves the source of long-term competitive advantage in dynamic markets misidentifies the source of that advantage. As noted earlier, effective dynamic capabilities have commonalites across firms in terms of key features (popularly termed, "best practice"). Therefore, they violate the RBV assumption of persistent heterogeneity across firms. So, while firms with more effective dynamic capabilities such as superior product innovation and alliancing processes are likely to have competitive advantage over firms with less effective capabilities, dynamic capabilities are not themselves sources of long-term competitive advantage.

So where does the potential for long-term competitive advantage lie? It lies in using dynamic capabilities sooner, more astutely, or more fortuitously than the competition to create resource configurations that have that advantage. So, for example, the acquisition capability of GE Capital is well known, and competitors can readily copy it or independently develop it themselves. But what is far more difficult to duplicate is the resource base of already acquired companies and the related synergies among them that GE Capital has achieved and continues to build. This advantage is particularly enhanced when the related resource configurations are combinations of tightly woven, synergistic activities (Collis and Montgomery, 1995; Milgrom and Roberts, 1990; Porter, 1996; Prahalad and Hamel, 1990). Therefore, long-term competitive advantage lies in the resource configurations that managers build using dynamic capabilities, not in the capabilities themselves. Effective dynamic capabilities are necessary, but not sufficient, conditions for competitive advantage.

Second, RBV thinking overemphasizes the strategic logic of leverage. While certainly some resource configurations do lead to long-term competitive advantage and some situations such as those with significant scale economies or network effects favor the emergence of such advantages, long-term competitive advantage is infrequently achieved in dynamic markets. Rather, the reality is that competitive advantage is often short term. In these situations, it makes sense for managers to compete by creating a series of temporary advantages. Their strategic logic is opportunity (Lengnick-Hall and Wolff, 1999).

For example, D'Aveni (1994) described the Coke vs. Pepsi duopoly in which the competitors leapfrogged one another for decades with temporary advantages in new products, technical and organizational innovations, and advertising. Neither firm could consistently gain the upper hand. Rather, each prospered by rapidly moving into new sources of advantage. Similarly, Roberts' (1999) study of the pharmaceutical industry indicated that persistent high performance was driven by temporary advantages in the form of new products. More successful firms appeared to possess a product development dynamic capability that led to a superior product flow, but one that only rarely led to long-term positional advantage. In both of these situations, creating a series of moves and counter-moves to out-maneuver the competition and build temporary advantage led to superior performance (D'Aveni, 1994).

Overall, dynamic capabilities are best conceptualized as tools that manipulate resource configurations. Sometimes it is effective to use these tools to enhance existing resource configurations and to strengthen current position using RBV's path-dependent strategic logic of leverage. Here, the goal is long-term competitive advantage. More frequently, in dynamic markets, it makes sense to use dynamic capabilities to build new resource configurations and move into fresh competitive positions using a path-breaking strategic logic of change (see also Karim and Mitchell, 2000). Here, the goal is a series of temporary competitive advantages. The broad point is that a blend of strategic logics makes sense in dynamic markets.

Finally, high-velocity markets are a boundary condition for RBV, a much needed addition to the theory (Lengnick-Hall and Wolff, 1999; Priem and Butler, 2000). In such markets, firm managers must cope not only with the external challenge of competition, but also with the internal challenge of potentially collapsing dynamic capabilities. As significant, RBV's path-dependent strategic logic of leverage not only lacks a logic of change that is crucial in dynamic markets, but also underplays the difficulty of predicting the length of current advantage and the sources of future advantage. Intel is a terrific example. Although the firm dominated its market for over a decade, its managers operated as if its competitive advantage could end at any time. Indeed, their slogan was "only the paranoid survive."

Similarly, RBV's assumption of the organization as a bundle of resources breaks down in high-velocity markets. In these situations, resources are added, recombined, and dropped with regularity (Galunic and Eisenhardt, 2000; Galunic and Rodan, 1998). Being tightly bundled is usually problematic. RBV's emphasis on long-term competitive advantage is often unrealistic in high-velocity markets. Short-term, unpredictable advantage is the norm. Growth is a more useful performance metric than profit. Finally, RBV misses the strategic role of time. Understanding the flow of strategy from leveraging the past to probing the future and the rhythm of when, where, and how often to change is central to strategy in high-velocity markets (Brown and Eisenhardt, 1998). Overall, while RBV centers on leveraging bundled resources to achieve long-term competitive advantage, strategy in high-velocity markets is about creating a series of unpredictable advantages through timing and loosely structured organization. The strategic logic is opportunity and the imperative is when, where, and how often to change.

## Conclusion

This paper explores dynamic capabilities and, more broadly, RBV. Based on the sometimes neglected insights of organizational theory and empirical research, we conclude with what we hope is a more realistic, theoretically valid, and empirically accurate view. Dynamic capabilities include well-known organizational and strategic processes like alliancing and product development whose strategic value lies in their ability to manipulate resources into value-creating strategies. Although idiosyncratic, they exhibit commonalities or "best practice" across firms. Their broad structural patterns vary with market dynamism, ranging from the robust, grooved routines in moderately dynamic markets to fragile semistructured ones in high-velocity ones. They evolve via well-known learning mechanisms.

More broadly, we conclude that long-term competitive advantage lies in resource configurations, not dynamic capabilities. In moderately dynamic markets, RBV is enhanced by blending its usual path-dependent strategic logic of leverage with a path-breaking strategic logic of change. Finally, RBV encounters a boundary condition in high-velocity markets where the duration of competitive advantage is inherently unpredictable, time is central to strategy, and dynamic capabilities are themselves unstable. Here, the strategic imperative is not leverage, but change.

## Acknowledgements

An earlier version of this paper was presented at the September 1999 Tuck/Consortium on Competitiveness and Cooperation (CCC) conference on the Evolution of Firm Capabilities. We appreciate the helpful comments of Anil Gupta, Connie Helfat, Cynthia Montgomery, Filipe Santos, and the consortium participants.

## References

Adler, P. S. 1999. Flexibility versus efficiency? A case study of model changeovers in the Toyota production system. *Organization Science* 10(1): 43–68.

Allen, T. J. 1977. *Managing the Flow of Technology: Technology Transfer and the Dissemination of Technological Information within the R&D Organization*. MIT Press: Cambridge, MA.

Allen, T. J., Piepmeier, J. M., and Cooney, S. 1971. *Technology Transfer to Developing Countries: The International Technological Gatekeeper*. Massachusetts Institute of Technology: Cambridge, MA.

Amit, R. and Schoemaker, P. J. H. 1993. Strategic assets and organizational rent. *Strategic Management Journal* 14(1): 33–46.

Ancona, D. G. and Caldwell, D. F. 1992. Bridging the boundary: External process and performance in organizational teams. *Administrative Science Quarterly* 37(4): 634–665.

Argote, L. 1999. *Organizational Learning: Creating, Retaining, and Transferring Knowledge*. Kluwer Academic: Boston, MA.

Barney, J. B. 1986. Organizational culture: can it be a source of sustained competitive advantage? *Academy of Management Review* 11(3): 656–665.

Barney, J. B. 1991. Firm resources and sustained competitive advantage. *Journal of Management* 17(1): 99–120.

Brown, S. L. and Eisenhardt, K. M. 1995. Product development: past research, present findings and future directions. *Academy of Management Review* 20(2): 343–378.

Brown, S. L. and Eisenhardt, K. M. 1997. The art of continuous change: linking complexity theory and time-paced evolution in relentlessly shifting organizations. *Administrative Science Quarterly* 42(1): 1–34.

Brown, S. L. and Eisenhardt, K. M. 1998. *Competing on the Edge: Strategy as Structured Chaos*. Harvard Business School Press: Boston, MA.

Brush, T. H., Bromiley, P., and Hendrickx, M. 1999. The relative influence of industry and corporation on business segment performance: an alternative estimate. *Strategic Management Journal* 20(6): 519–547.

Burgelman, R. A. 1994. Fading memories: a process theory of strategic business exit in dynamic environments. *Administrative Science Quarterly* 39(1): 24–56.

Burgelman, R. A. 1996. A process model of strategic business exit. *Strategic Management Journal*, Summer Special Issue 17: 193–214.

Burns, T. and Stalker, G. M. 1966. *The Management of Innovation*. 2nd edn., Associated Book Publishers: London.

Capron, L., Dussauge, P., and Mitchell, W. 1998. Resource redeployment following horizontal acquisitions in Europe and North America, 1988–1992. *Strategic Management Journal* 19(7): 631–661.

Christensen, C. 1997. *Managing Innovation at NYPRO, Inc. (A) (B)*. Harvard Business School Publishing: Boston, MA.

Clark, K. B. and Fujimoto, T. 1991. *Product Development Performance: Strategy, Organization, and Management in the World Auto Industry.* Harvard Business School Press: Boston, MA.

Cockburn, I., Henderson, R., and Stern, S. 2000. Untangling the origins of competitive advantage. *Strategic Management Journal.*

Collis, D. J. and Montgomery, C. A. 1995. Competing on resources. *Harvard Business Review* 73(4): 118–128.

Collis, D. J. and Montgomery, C. A. 1998. Creating corporate advantage. *Harvard Business Review* 76(3): 70–83.

Conner, K. R. and Prahalad, C. K. 1996. A resource-based theory of the firm: knowledge versus opportunism. *Organization Science* 7(5): 477–501.

Cyert, R. M. and March, J. G. 1963. *A Behavioral Theory of the Firm.* Prentice-Hall: Englewood Cliffs, NJ.

D'Aveni, R. A. 1994. *Hypercompetition: Managing the Dynamics of Strategic Maneuvering.* Free Press: New York.

Dougherty, D. 1992. Interpretive barriers to successful product innovation in large firms. *Organization Science* 3: 179–202.

Eisenhardt, K. M. 1989. Making fast strategic decisions in high-velocity environments. *Academy of Management Journal* 32(3): 543–576.

Eisenhardt, K. M. and Bhatia, M. M. 2000. Organizational complexity and computation. In *Companion to Organizations,* Baum, J. A. C. (ed.). Blackwell: Oxford, UK.

Eisenhardt, K. M. and Brown, S. L. 1999. Patching: restitching business portfolios in dynamic markets. *Harvard Business Review* 77(3): 72–82.

Eisenhardt, K. M. and Galunic, D. C. 2000. Coevolving: at last, a way to make synergies work. *Harvard Business Review* 78(1): 91–101.

Eisenhardt, K. M. and Sull, D. 2001. What is strategy in the new economy? *Harvard Business Review.*

Eisenhardt, K. M. and Tabrizi, B. N. 1995. Accelerating adaptive processes: product innovation in the global computer industry. *Administrative Science Quarterly* 40(1): 84–110.

Fredrickson, J. W. 1984. The comprehensiveness of strategic decision processes: extension, observations, future directions. *Academy of Management Journal* 27(3): 445–467.

Galunic, D. C. and Eisenhardt, K. M. 2000. Architectural innovation and modular corporate forms. Working paper, 1–41. INSEAD/Stanford University, Fontainebleau and Stanford, CA.

Galunic, D. C. and Rodan, S. 1998. Resource recombinations in the firm: knowledge structures and the potential for Schumpeterian innovation. *Strategic Management Journal* 19(12): 1193–1201.

Gersick, C. J. G. 1994. Pacing strategic change: the case of a new venture. *Academy of Management Journal* 37(1): 9–45.

Graebner, M. 1999. A review of recent research on mergers and acquisitions. Working paper, Stanford University, Stanford, CA.

Graebner, M. 2000. Acquisitions of entrepreneurial firms. Working paper, 1–85. Stanford University, Stanford, CA.

Grant, R. M. 1996. Toward a knowledge-based theory of the firm. *Strategic Management Journal,* Summer Special Issue 17: 109–122.

Gulati, R. 1999. Network location and learning: the influence of network resources and firm capabilities on alliance formation. *Strategic Management Journal* 20(5): 397–420.

Haleblian, J. and Finkelstein, S. 1999. The influence of organizational acquisition experience on acquisition performance: a behavioral learning perspective. *Administrative Science Quarterly* 44(1): 29–56.

Hansen, M. T. 1999. The search-transfer problem: the role of weak ties in sharing knowledge across organization subunits. *Administrative Science Quarterly* (March) 44: 82–111.

Hargadon, A. and Sutton, R. J. 1997. Technology brokering and innovation in a product development firm. *Administrative Science Quarterly* 42(4): 716–749.

Hayward, M. L. A. 1998. Is learning loopy? Evidence of when acquirers learn from their acquisition experiences. Working paper (LRP WP45/1998), London Business School, London.

Hayward, M. L. A. 2000. Acquirer learning from acquisition experience: evidence from 1985–1995. Working paper, London Business School, London.

Helfat, C. E. 1997. Know-how and asset complementarity and dynamic capability accumulation. *Strategic Management Journal* 18(5): 339–360.

Helfat, C. E. Raubitschek, R. S. 2000. Product sequencing: co-evolution of knowledge, capabilities and products. *Strategic Management Journal* 21(10–11): 961–979.

Henderson, R. and Cockburn, I. 1994. Measuring competence? Exploring firm effects in pharmaceutical research. *Strategic Management Journal*, Winter Special Issue 15: 63–84.

Imai, K., Ikujiro, N., and Takeuchi, H. 1985. Managing the new product development process: how Japanese companies learn to unlearn. In *The Uneasy Alliance: Managing the Productivity-Technology Dilemma*, Hayes, R. H., Clark, K., and Lorens, J. (eds.). Harvard Business School Press: Boston, MA; 337–375.

Judge, W. Q. and Miller, A. 1991. Antecedents and outcomes of decision speed in different environments. *Academy of Management Journal* 34(2): 449–464.

Kale, P., Dyer, J. H., and Singh, H. 1999. Alliance capability, stock market response, and long term alliance success. Working paper, University of Michigan: Ann Arbor, MI.

Karim, S. Z. and Mitchell, W. 2000. Path-dependent and path-breaking change: reconfiguring business resources following acquisitions in the U.S. medical sector 1978–1995. *Strategic Management Journal* 21 (10–11): 1061–1081.

Katz, R. and Tushman, M. L. 1981. An investigation into the managerial roles and career paths of gatekeepers and project supervisors in a major R&D facility. *R&D Management* 11(3): 103–110.

Kauffman, S. A. 1995. *At Home in the Universe: The Search for Laws of Self-Organization and Complexity*. Oxford University Press: New York.

Kim, L. 1998. Crisis construction and organizational learning. *Organization Science* 9(4): 506–521.

Kogut, B. 1996. What firms do? Coordination, identity, and learning. *Organization Science* 7(5): 502–518.

Kogut, B. and Zander, U. 1992. Knowledge of the firm, combinative capabilities, and the replication of technology. *Organization Science* 3: 383–397.

Lane, P. J. and Lubatkin, M. 1998. Relative absorptive capacity and interorganizational learning. *Strategic Management Journal* 19(5): 461–477.

Larrson, R. and Finkelstein, S. 1999. Integrating strategic, organizational, and human resource perspectives on mergers and acquisitions: a case survey of synergy realization. *Organization Science* 10(1): 1–26.

Lawrence, P. R. and Lorsch, J. W. 1967. *Organization and Environment; Managing Differentiation and Integration*. Division of Research Graduate School of Business Administration Harvard University: Boston, MA.

Lengnick-Hall, C. A. and Wolff, J. A. 1999. Similarities and contradictions in the core logic of three strategy research streams. *Strategic Management Journal* 20(12): 1109–1132.

Magretta, J. 1998. The power of virtual integration: an interview with Dell Computer's Michael Dell. *Harvard Business Review* 76(2): 72–84.

Mahoney, J. T. and Pandian, J. R. 1992. The resource-based view within the conversation of strategic management. *Strategic Management Journal* 13(5): 363–380.

McGahan, A. M. and Porter, M. E. 1997. How much does industry matter, really? *Strategic Management Journal*, Summer Special Issue 18: 15–30.

Milgrom, P., Qian, Y., and Roberts, J. 1991. Complementarities, momentum, and the evolution of modern manufacturing. *American Economic Review* 81(2): 84–88.

Milgrom, P. and Roberts, J. 1990. The economics of modern manufacturing: technology, strategy, and organization. *American Economic Review* 80(3): 511–528.

Mosakowski, E. and McKelvey, B. 1997. Predicting rent generation in competence-based competition. In *Competence-Based Strategic Management*, Heene A, Sanchez R (eds.). Chichester: Wiley; 65–85.

Nelson, R. R. 1991. Why do firms differ, and how does it matter? *Strategic Management Journal*, Winter Special Issue 12: 61–74.

Nelson, R. and Winter, S. 1982. *An Evolutionary Theory of Economic Change*. Belknap Press: Cambridge, MA.

Penrose, E. T. 1959. *The Theory of the Growth of the Firm*. Wiley: New York.

Peteraf, M. A. 1993. The cornerstones of competitive advantage. *Strategic Management Journal* 14(3): 179–191.

Pisano, G. P. 1994. Knowledge, integration, and the locus of learning: an empirical analysis of process development. *Strategic Management Journal*, Winter Special Issue 15: 85–100.

Porter, M. E. 1979. How competitive forces shape strategy. *Harvard Business Review* 57(2): 137–145.

Porter, M. E. 1996. What is strategy? *Harvard Business Review* 74(6): 61–78.

Powell, W. W., Koput, K. W., and Smith-Doerr, L. 1996. Interorganizational collaboration and the locus of innovation. *Administrative Science Quarterly* 41(1): 116–145.

Prahalad, C. K. and Hamel, G. 1990. The core competence of the corporation. *Harvard Business Review* 68(3): 79–91.

Priem, R. L. and Butler, J. E. 2000. Is the resource-based "view" a useful perspective for strategic management research? *Academy of Management Review*.

Prigogine I. and Stengers I. 1984. *Order Out of Chaos: Man's New Dialogue with Nature*. Bantam Books: New York.

Ranft, A. L. and Zeithaml, C. P. 1998. Preserving and transferring knowledge-based resources during post-acquisition implementation: a study of high-tech acquisitions. Working paper, College of Business and Economics, West Virginia University, Morgantown, WV.

Roberts, P. W. 1999. Product innovation, product-market competition and persistent profitability in the U.S. pharmaceutical industry. *Strategic Management Journal* 20(7): 655–670.

Roquebert, J. A., Phillips, R. L. and Westfall, P. A. 1996. Markets vs. management. *Strategic Management Journal* 17(8): 653–664.

Rosenkopf, L. and Nerkar, A. 1999. Beyond local search: boundary-spanning, exploration and impact in the optical disc industry. Working paper, The Wharton School, University of Pennsylvania, Philadelphia, PA.

Sastry, M. A. 1999. Managing strategic innovation and change. *Administrative Science Quarterly* 44(2): 420–422.

Schmalensee, R. 1985. Do markets differ much? *American Economic Review* 75(3): 341–351.

Schumpeter, J. A. 1934. *The Theory of Economic Development*. 7th edn (transl. Opie, R.) Harvard University Press: Cambridge, MA.

Simonin, B. L. 1999. Ambiguity and the process of knowledge transfer in strategic alliances. *Strategic Management Journal* 20(7): 595–623.

Sitkin, S. B. 1992. Learning through failure: the strategy of small losses, In *Research in Organizational Behavior*, Staw BM, Cummings LL (eds.). Vol. 14: JAI Press: Greenwich, CT; 231–266.

Sull, D. N. 1999a. The dynamics of standing still: Firestone tire & rubber and the radial revolution. *Business History Review* 73 (Autumn): 430–464.

Sull, D. N. 1999b. Why good companies go bad. *Harvard Business Review* 77(4): 42–52.

Szulanski, G. 1996. Exploring internal stickiness: impediments to the transfer of best practice within the firm. *Strategic Management Journal*, Winter Special Issue 17: 27–43.

Teece, D. J., Pisano, G., and Shuen, A. 1997. Dynamic capabilities and strategic management. *Strategic Management Journal* 18(7): 509–533.

Terwiesch, C., Chea, K. S., and Bohn, R. E. 1999. An exploratory study of international product transfer and production ramp-up in the data storage industry. Report 99–02, Information Storage Industry Center, Graduate School of International Relations and Pacific Studies, University of California at San Diego, La Jolla. CA.

Wally, S. and Baum, J. R. 1994. Personal and structural determinants of the pace of strategic decision-making. *Academy of Management Journal* 37(4): 932–956.

Wernerfelt, B. 1984. A resource-based view of the firm. *Strategic Management Journal* 5(2): 171–180.

Wernerfelt, B. 1995. The resource-based view of the firm: ten years after. *Strategic Management Journal* 16(3): 171–174.

Wernerfelt, B. and Montgomery, C. 1988. Tobin's q and the importance of focus in firm performance. *American Economic Review* 78(1): 246–250.

Wetlaufer, S. 2000. Common sense and conflict: an interview with Disney's Michael Eisner. *Harvard Business Review* 78(1): 114–124.

Williamson, O. E. 1999. Strategy research: governance and competence perspectives. *Strategic Management Journal* 20(12): 1087–1108.

Winter, S. G. and Szulanski, G. 1999. Replication as strategy. Working paper, University of Pennsylvania, Philadelphia, PA.

Womack, J. P., Jones, D. T., and Roos, D. 1991. *The Machine that Changed the World: The Story of Lean Production*. HarperCollins: New York.

Zander, U. and Kogut, B. 1995. Knowledge and the speed of the transfer and imitation of organizational capabilities. *Organization Science* 6(1): 76–92.

Zollo, M. and Singh, H. 1998. The impact of knowledge codification, experience trajectories and integration strategies on the performance of corporate acquisitions. Academy of Management Best Paper Proceedings. San Diego, CA.

Zollo, M. and Winter, S. 1999. From organizational routines to dynamic capabilities. Working paper WP 99–07, University of Pennsylvania, Philadelphia, PA.

# CHAPTER TWENTY-TWO

# Leadership, Capabilities, and Technological Change: The Transformation of NCR in the Electronic Era

## Richard S. Rosenbloom

The "digital revolution" pervades current headlines as "e-business" transforms commercial practices and reshapes major industries. But the wellsprings of today's digital technologies surfaced more than a half-century ago, stimulating successive waves of change that repeatedly threatened the survival of well-established firms in home entertainment, electronic components, communications services, data processing, and related fields. Even the most dominant firms in the information industries have found themselves challenged to develop new strategies and new capabilities to cope with the incursions of new rivals exploiting new technologies.

The academic literature on innovation has repeatedly observed that mature, successful firms often fail to adapt successfully to revolutionary changes in technology (Cooper and Schendel, 1976; Foster, 1986; Christensen, 1997). Rather than analyzing patterns of failure, however, this paper traces the means by which one prominent firm – national Cash Register Company (NCR) – coped with radical changes in technology over four decades. We will examine in detail how NCR addressed the introduction of electronics to the field of business equipment and the advent of digital computers to widespread use. NCR not only survived but eventually prospered in the face of these powerful forces of change. Through this account of NCR's history from 1938 to 1978, we hope to illuminate the processes by which other firms threatened by similar fundamental change might cope successfully with the emergent threats.

## Academic Perspectives

Scholars have advanced various theories to explain the failure of market leaders in the face of technological change. One theme that is prominent in the literature is that the prospects for incumbents are contingent on the inherent nature of the technology and the proximate consequences of its innovative use. Studies have shown that "architectural" changes in design and "competency-destroying" innovations will be problematic for established leaders (Henderson and Clark, 1990; Tushman and Anderson, 1986). A web of implicit and explicit social commitments to employees, customers, and communities also can also impede adaptation to change (Sull, Tedlow, and Rosenbloom, 1997). Other studies suggest that when the greatest opportunities inherent in a new technology lie in novel "value propositions" directed at new customers, its effects will be most disruptive to established leaders (Christensen, 1997). Economists have stressed the consequences of the asymmetry of incentives among differing sorts of firms facing the same technological opportunities (Henderson, 1993). They argue that small incumbents and new entrants will have a smaller stake in the current technology than will large incumbents, and therefore have less to lose from cannibalization of the established technology by the new. Similar logic leads to emphasis on the effect of irreversible resource commitments leading to persistence of strategies over time (Ghemawat, 1991).

In today's world, it seems inevitable that a firm will eventually encounter new technology that is disruptive in one or more respects and that its responses may be limited by financial disincentives and established managerial commitments. Some argue, nevertheless, that firms should be able to adapt successfully if they possess sufficient "dynamic capabilities." Dynamic capabilities are what enable a firm "to integrate, build, and reconfigure internal and external competences to address rapidly changing environments" (Teece, Pisano, and Shuen, 1997: 516). Teece and Pisano (1994) suggest that a firm's dynamic capabilities are determined by three classes of factors:

- *processes*: managerial and organizational "routines";
- *positions*: current endowments of technology, customer bases, and suppliers;
- *paths*: available strategic alternatives.

The ability to achieve new forms of competitive advantage is the essence of a dynamic capability. In the following account of NCR's history we shall seek to identify the extent to which its successes can be attributed to dynamic capabilities, and to characterize just what seems to constitute a dynamic capability.

## National Cash Register: Origins and Transformation

NCR was founded in 1884 by John H. Patterson, a legendary salesman and business leader. A titan of early 20th-century industry, Patterson was an autocrat, paternalist, showman, and innovator (Friedman, 1998). Patterson created a multinational industrial giant that dominated its field. By 1911, NCR was selling 95 percent of the world's cash registers. The heart of the company lay in a sprawling complex of buildings on a huge site in Dayton, Ohio.

### Building competitive advantage

Technological prowess was a part of NCR's competitive strength. In 1900, Patterson hired Edward A. Deeds, a pioneering electrical engineer and inventor who later became a national figure in industry and aviation. In 1904 Deeds hired Charles Kettering to work in the "Inventions Department." Before leaving NCR in 1909 to concentrate on inventions for the automobile industry, Kettering's biggest contribution to NCR was to invent, at the prodding of Deeds, a practical electrical cash register.

John Patterson died in 1922, to be succeeded as president by his son Frederick, who left the running of the company in the hands of general manager John H. Barringer, a stellar salesman. Comptroller Stanley Allyn, a protégé of the senior Patterson, had been elevated to top management and a seat on the Board in 1917 at the tender age of 26.

NCR's scale advantages in manufacturing and selling protected it from attack in its base business while Barringer and Allyn broadened the product line to include accounting machines and adding machines. With the company in financial difficulty in the Depression, Patterson dismissed Barringer in 1931 and brought Deeds back as chairman, president, and chief executive. Deeds appointed Allyn to the number two spot, with the title of executive vice president, and enlisted Charles Kettering as a member of the board of directors. In 1940, when Deeds turned 66, he passed on the title of president to Stanley Allyn. Although Deeds gradually withdrew to "the perimeter of operations" he remained chairman until 1957 (Allyn, 1967: 67).

## Research in Electronics

The transition to electronics at NCR began in 1938 with the establishment of an electronics research activity in the Dayton engineering organization. The initial commitment, sponsored by Deeds, who was being strongly encouraged by Kettering, had no immediate commercial motive. Deeds sensed that electronics would become important in the future of the business. Joseph R. Desch, who had worked on radio at General Motors, was hired to lead the effort. Robert E. Mumma, a younger colleague from GM, joined the company early in 1939.

The work of Desch's small group positioned NCR among the pioneers in computational research in the United States. Mumma soon designed a small machine that could add and subtract and started to develop a calculator that could also multiply and divide. He had figured out the design of the latter machine by mid-1941 and demonstrated its operation for addition, subtraction, and multiplication on April 24, 1942. As the nation began to prepare for war in 1941, the National Defense Research Council (NDRC) turned to NCR, along with Radio Corporation of America and Bell Telephone Laboratories, to apply its electronics capabilities to military fire control devices.

In 1942 NCR suspended all commercial activity to devote its resources entirely to wartime needs. The Naval Computing Machine Laboratory (NCML), established to design and build top-secret devices capable of breaking German codes, was located at NCR's facilities in Dayton, with Joseph Desch as its head. This decision by the government suggests the depth of NCR's prowess in computing at that early date. At the end of the war, the Navy wanted to continue the work of NCML, but NCR's management chose to focus entirely on reviving its commercial activities. Although Deeds and Kettering continued to encourage pioneering work in electronics, NCR's operating management dedicated itself to the task of meeting the pent-up postwar demand for its traditional mechanical products.

While NCR's earlier work earned it recognition as a technical leader in computational devices, its management did not seize the opportunity to define strategic directions responsive to the opportunities implied by the postwar emergence of the digital computer. Mumma's electronics group worked mainly on features – like punched-tape output – that could be added to traditional designs, and on printers and data storage devices that would later emerge as "peripherals" for computer systems. As Mumma later characterized it, "We were still considered outsiders in a mechanical factory" (Mumma, 1984: 18).

## Developments in Computing

Early commercial progress in computers was stimulated by a few small entrepreneurial ventures, including the Eckert-Mauchly Computer Corporation (EMCC) in Philadelphia, founded by the principal designers of ENIAC, the first electronic computer in the United States, Electronic Research Associates (ERA) in Minnesota, and a few West Coast ventures associated with aviation and defense contracting. While the scientific value of digital computers was becoming clear, the cost-effective business applications of these expensive and bulky devices were far from obvious. Late in 1949, EMCC, fast running out of cash, sought to sell itself to one of the leading business equipment producers. NCR sent a delegation of seven men to visit EMCC in December, 1949, but wasn't prepared to move swiftly enough to meet the struggling firm's pressing needs; on February 1, 1950, EMCC accepted a buyout offer from Remington Rand.

The business machine industry in the postwar years was highly concentrated, with more than 70 percent of industry revenues garnered by the four dominant firms: IBM, NCR, Remington Rand, and Burroughs. Despite the prewar stresses of depression and the postwar revolution in technology, industry structure remained highly stable. The four postwar leaders had been the largest and most profitable in 1928 and all would continue to rank among the top six in the computer industry in 1973. In 1949, NCR ranked second in revenues, close behind IBM and twice the size of fourth-ranked Burroughs (Cortada, 1993: 256, 258).

## NCR's Postwar Strategy

In early 1950, despite the development of significant new capabilities in electronics and a fourfold increase in revenues, NCR was essentially the same company it had been a decade earlier. Three product lines still formed the core of National Cash Register's business: the eponymous cash register line, accounting machines, and adding machines. These products were all standalone electromechanical machinery, some quite complex in design and manufacture, made primarily in highly integrated facilities in Dayton, Ohio, and sold to users by a large and highly effective field sales force supported by a large service organization. The company's leadership, its culture, and its operating methods had changed little since the 1930s and would remain intact for another decade.

The requirements of marketing differed among the various lines. While cash registers faced little competition, accounting machines competed against similar devices offered by

Burroughs, Remington, and Underwood, and also against the punched-card systems of IBM. More sophisticated salesmen, organized separately, sold the accounting machines. With the introduction of a new line in 1950, accounting machine revenues grew rapidly and NCR pulled ahead of Burroughs to lead the market (W. Anderson, 1991: 165–166).

Although it was an early mover in research on electronics for computing, NCR was the last of the "big four" to choose a strategic path toward the new era, making what was in many ways the most cautious commitment. In 1947, Burroughs had launched a major research effort in electronics aimed at transforming its product line. In 1949, in a speech to IBM salesmen that also was circulated widely among customers, Thomas Watson Jr. had asserted that all of IBM's products would come to be "based on electronics" within a decade (Usselman, 1993). Within a year, IBM was committed to market the Model 701 computer. Remington, having acquired EMCC in 1950, was the first to sell computers commercially.

In 1952, NCR management set its course for the transition to electronics. Allyn made an entrepreneurial commitment to add a fourth product line – digital computers – while defining the strategic guidelines that would govern the adaptation of the established lines to electronics. He declared that electronics should lead to "evolutionary" change in the company's standalone products, which would increasingly be called upon to serve as data-entry devices for electronic data-processing (EDP) systems in which the newly emerging computer products functioned as a central element.

Although the investments in electronics R&D at Dayton were intensified to support movement along this new strategic pathway, no changes were made in the structure or work processes of the organizational units that developed, made, and sold NCR's core products. It remained the role of the Product Development Department to tell Research and Engineering "what types of products are wanted" (National Cash Register Company, 1953: 1–3).

The contemporary reader, in an environment in which computers are ubiquitous, may find it difficult to grasp how speculative and uncertain the commercial prospects for digital computing appeared in 1952. The first commercial stored program computer, the UNIVAC, built by the Eckert-Mauchly division of Remington Rand, began operations for the US Census in mid-1951; IBM's first computer, the Model 701, was announced in May 1952. These leaders in business data-processing systems using punched cards were natural first movers, IBM using internal capabilities and Remington relying on its acquisition of EMCC and later, in mid-1952, of ERA. The ultimate market potential for these "giant brains" – room-sized and costing millions – was generally reckoned to be limited to a few dozens or, possibly, hundreds of installations. The first half-dozen UNIVACs and the full run (16) of the IBM 701 systems went to scientific users, mainly government agencies or defense contractors. It was not until September 1953 that IBM announced the Model 702 designed for business use and 1954 when the first commercial installations of UNIVAC occurred (Campbell-Kelly and Aspray, 1996).

## Entering the Computer Market

In 1952, Stanley Allyn, strongly encouraged by Joseph Desch, committed NCR to a new strategic direction by entering the nascent computer industry through acquisition of the Computer Research Corporation (CRC), located in Hawthorne, California. CRC was one of the handful of companies founded soon after the war to turn the new computer technology into a business; all of them soon were driven, like CRC, into the arms of a larger firm seeking to expand its capabilities.

The founders of CRC had worked at Northrop Aviation, where they had designed a Magnetic Drum Digital Differential Analyzer in 1949. The MADDIDA was a special-purpose compact computer intended to solve differential equations for airborne guidance applications. When top management at Northrop, struggling with financial woes, did not support continuation of their efforts, the group struck out on its own, incorporating CRC on July 13, 1950. As one of the founders later described it, "this wasn't a 'sandbox' for engineers; we were trying to build a computer business" (H. Sarkissian, personal interview, Newport Beach, CA, March 7, 1998).

The young firm attracted attention in the military services, hungry to exploit the nascent computer technology. One of the research contracts thus ensuing, from the Air Force's Cambridge (Massachusetts) Research Center, led to the design of CRC's first general-purpose computer, dubbed the CRC 102. Installed in Cambridge in January 1952, the 102 proved reliable and effective. Meanwhile, CRC's engineers adapted the design to create a standardized product, the Model 102-A, a general-purpose computer designed for volume production. Donald Eckdahl, one of the founders, was assigned to head manufacturing operations as well as engineering. He hired most of his staff from the aircraft industry, where learning curve effects dominated manufacturing practices. He later said that "I learned manufacturing management mainly by doing it and from the people I hired" (D. E. Eckdahl, personal interview, Colton, CA, March 19, 1998).

But finding capital was an obstacle – today's robust venture capital industry did not exist – and prospective investors generally believed that there was a limited market for computers. In mid-1952, the founders of CRC – then primarily an engineering research and manufacturing organization employing 150 people – sold the business to NCR. Stanley Allyn intended that CRC's research activities should be integrated with those at Dayton, "within the framework of [NCR's] overall product development program" (National Cash Register Company, 1953: 3). As new products emerged, Dayton would manufacture them.

Looking back on these choices, some four decades later, William Anderson, who became NCR's CEO in 1972, concluded that it had been an "error" to assume "that the computer business would simply be another 'layer' on the cash register, accounting machine, and adding machine 'cake'. The theory was that to NCR's three departments . . . a fourth would be added . . . Seen by only a few was that eventually all of these businesses would tend to merge" (W. Anderson, 1991: 170).

## Evolution in the Core Business

NCR's *Annual Report* for 1953 devoted two pages (24–25) to defining the company's position in electronics. Three themes pervaded that statement and subsequent acts and utterances of management. The first was the company's commitment to participate in providing all elements of "systems" for commercial record-keeping. With it came, as a second theme, management's conviction that changes in practice would come by "evolution," not revolution. Finally, they had a firm belief in the competitive advantages that NCR would enjoy in the new marketplace.

In the view of NCR's leaders, "Most of the records business management requires are secured from an analysis of the many individual sales or other transactions." Computers could process data at blinding speed, but were limited in productivity by constraints on input and output. Thus NCR was seeking "to make the cash register or accounting machine the 'input' mechanism," transforming it into a "link in an over-all electronic system rather than a machine which could be bought and used as a unit." Hence, NCR was "working toward an integrated system which will ultimately provide the three necessary elements . . . input, computation, and output" (NCR *Annual Report*, 1953: 25).

Realization of this sweeping vision was believed to lie in the distant future since the utility of established products was expected to dominate for some time. As management repeatedly cautioned the shareholders:

> new developments are expected far too quickly . . . The only sound development is that which moves forward step by step. (NCR *Annual Report*, 1953: 25)

> it becomes increasingly clear that the development of an electronics system will be more evolutionary than revolutionary . . . Important as electronics will be to the future of the business we must realize that there will always be a place for machines based on mechanical principles. (NCR *Annual Report*, 1955: 15)

Allyn and his associates approached the electronics era with confidence in NCR's advantages. Those included capabilities already in place in Dayton's research and engineering, and in 500 field sales and service locations. More fundamentally, they believed that NCR "knew the needs of business from a systems standpoint." Additionally, the "long line of cash registers, accounting machines, and adding machines [could be] converted [by electronics] into ideal input devices" (NCR *Annual Report*, 1955: 15).

The effect of this new doctrine was to map a specific strategic pathway based on "evolutionary" application of electronics to enhance its traditional products and to suit them to serve as input devices for computer systems employed by established customers. The organizational vehicles for this strategy were those already established in Dayton. Development and production of the traditional product line, and of the evolving electronic enhancements to it, remained in the hands of existing groups, which were dominated by staff whose experience was rooted in electromechanical technologies.

The differences implied by electronics technology were little noted. The implications for sales and marketing were challenging. NCR's established business was based on selling many thousands of units at prices ranging from one to a few thousand dollars each. The new computer business, in contrast, was based on selling small numbers of systems at prices measured in hundreds of thousands of dollars. While the pace of change accelerated in the new marketplace, NCR's product development organizations retained the leisurely habits of an earlier era, in which they had set the pace (W. Anderson, 1991: 171).

The existing products were often very complex; the simplest register contained 1500 parts; some accounting machines used more than 20,000. Because NCR was a highly integrated producer, fabricating all required parts from metal stock, labor represented 80 percent of manufacturing costs (NCR *Annual Report*, 1956). The proportions were reversed in manufacture of most electronic machinery, for which components had to be purchased from specialized vendors. In the early 1950s, half of the company's 45,000 employees worldwide worked in manufacturing. Conversion to electronics would hold ominous implications for most of them.

In support of the new thrusts into electronics, management increased the intensity of R&D spending from a mere 1 percent of revenues in 1950 to a peak of 3.9 percent in 1958. Most of the increase was spent on evolutionary improvement of the traditional product lines and on creating the wholly new EDP line. But Allyn's actions to integrate computer research with product planning in Dayton and to press them to stay in touch with the expressed wants of customers, few of whom could have any sense of what electronics and computers could offer, would have the effect of limiting the pace of NCR's innovations in the new field.

The advent of electronics in the core business was signaled by the introduction of "Sales-Tronic" and "Post-Tronic" product lines. The latter was an accounting machine that could "pick up" prior balances encoded in magnetic stripes on the back of a ledger card.[1] By 1954, Dayton engineering had developed a series of engineering models for the Post-Tronic in great secrecy. Although the product was straightforward technically, requiring a modest amount of electronic circuitry to add "memory" to a standard electromechanical product, the weight of opinion in management was against commercialization. Some argued that it would soon be made obsolete by computers; others believed that cautious bankers would hesitate to adopt so novel a concept. Nevertheless, the head of sales for accounting machines decided to show the Post-tronic to some customers, whose enthusiastic response settled the issue. Sales of the machine surpassed $100 million within a few years; the resultant strong cash flow cushioned the burden of the costly venture into computers (Allyn, 1967: 159). The Sales-Tronic was a cash register that recorded transactions on punched paper tape that could be fed as input to central computers. Dayton also developed and sold optical scanners to read the punched paper tapes produced by Sales-Tronic registers.

NCR's early movement toward evolutionary change in established products proved a successful strategic choice. For more than a decade, the company profited from evolutionary and incremental adaptation and enhancement of standard products, without any evidence of opportunities lost for failure to move more aggressively to innovate in the core product lines.

## First Moves in Computers

In contrast to NCR's initial success with evolutionary change in the core, it proved to be difficult to find the right strategic pathway into the computer business and to create the organizational capabilities required to pursue it. The first approach was to let CRC follow its own path, although soon after the acquisition Allyn had replaced its president with an NCR sales and product planning executive, Robert Pierson, from Dayton. CRC had strong technological capabilities but lacked experience in marketing and administration.

CRC was an early leader in the design of inexpensive machines using magnetic drum memories. As noted earlier, while continuing to ship scientific computers and some peripherals, largely to government contractors and industrial research organizations, CRC's founders had developed the Model 102-A as a standard product intended for volume production. The new design, like its competitive counterparts, was compact and relatively inexpensive; sales prices – generally under $100,000 – were equivalent to only a few months rental for the UNIVAC or IBM 701 computer systems then reaching the market. In late 1952, four of the other six firms marketing small drum memory computers were business machine producers.[2]

The drum machines competed in the markets for engineering and business applications with the IBM Card Programmed Calculator (CPC), introduced in 1949. In 1953 IBM announced the Model 650 magnetic drum computer, whose superior performance backed by IBM's marketing prowess eventually made it the dominant computer product of the 1950s.

The binary arithmetic and limited input-output (I/O) capabilities of the 102-A were well suited to scientific use, but appeared to the people in Dayton as obstacles to business application. As a senior engineer commented, "when you talked about a binary machine, you scared our salesmen" (Rench, 1984: 26). There was also a certain disdain for the use of punched cards for I/O. IBM was anathema among managers in Dayton, who went to great lengths to avoid employing its products. Under pressure from Dayton, CRC designed the 102-D, using decimal arithmetic and punched paper tape for input and output.

The first unit of the 102-A was shipped to a customer in February, 1954; by August, a dozen systems had been shipped, with another 14 or so lined up for shipment in the next 12 months. By that date, CRC's staff had grown to 360 employees, 85 in engineering research and design, and 156 in manufacturing operations.

## Second Thoughts about Computers

In mid-1954, as CRC was building momentum in manufacture of its first standard product, and IBM and Univac were opening up the business market for computers, NCR's top management in Dayton was rethinking its strategy in the field. According to Donald Eckdahl, Allyn seemed to want CRC to produce "business machines" – i.e., devices for a specified business function – in the tradition of the parent company's established strengths. CRC's principals perceived that he was "afraid of electronics" (D. E. Eckdahl, personal interview, Colton, CA, March 19, 1998). Allyn chafed at the CRC engineers' commitment to building "general-purpose" devices and they believed he failed to understand their utility. Allyn also seemed to expect that CRC could quickly become a profitable subsidiary. When losses persisted he began to get "cold feet." Abruptly, in mid-1954 he recalled General Manager Pierson to Dayton and instructed CRC to terminate production operations. All personnel in the manufacturing organization were laid off, some founders left the company, and the subsidiary was reconstituted as the Electronics Division of NCR, with Eckdahl as General Manager.

In one move, CRC's engagement with users was quenched and its manufacturing capability extinguished. What remained was an engineering organization skilled in the design of general purpose computers. They soon designed the Model 303, a small general-purpose digital computer still using vacuum tubes and drum memory – basically an improved version of the 102. An early version of the 303 was installed in a department store, but technical progress rapidly overtook the design. Progress in silicon transistor technology led to a decision to shelve the 303 and develop a version using semiconductor circuits and ferrite core memory – features soon to become universal. For the first time, product planners in Dayton collaborated closely with Eckdahl and his engineers to define specifications for what would emerge as the Model 304. A prototype was fully operational in 1956 and was displayed in the Division's Lobby in Hawthorne.

Electronics Division staff also collaborated with engineers in Dayton to design an accounting machine that fulfilled Allyn's vision of evolutionary adaptation. A console adapted from the Class 31 electromechanical accounting machine served as the interface for a small computer designed in Hawthorne that could serve a myriad of accounting applications. Known for a while internally as the National Electronic Accounting Machine, and finally introduced as the Model 390 in 1959, the machine sold well.

## Alliance with General Electric

Meanwhile, Allyn struggled with NCR's options for entry into the mainstream of the computer industry. While management in Dayton had retained tight control of product planning for computers, and Hawthorne clearly was the only place where they could be designed, choosing the location for computer manufacture was vexing. Allyn's original idea that manufacture could take place in Dayton had quickly been seen as impractical. But he was reluctant to rebuild the capability in Hawthorne. Another senior executive later explained that Allyn lacked confidence in the company's ability to cope with production of such advanced technology (W. S. Anderson, personal interview, New York, January 19, 1989).

At the time, NCR was involved in computer innovation in banking because it had developed the technology for magnetic ink encoding (MICR), adopted by the American Banking Association to enable machine sorting of checks. As a consequence, NCR was drawn into the ERMA project, the first major bank automation endeavor at Bank of America. ERMA's computers were to be built by General Electric, then entering the computer industry. Allyn approached Ralph Cordiner, GE's chairman, to discuss what would now be called a "strategic alliance." What emerged was an agreement under which GE would build the central processor and memory units for both companies, and would buy high-speed card-readers, printers, and other peripherals produced in Dayton by NCR. The 1956 *Annual Report* (p. 13) cited the complementary nature of GE's experience in electronics and NCR's skills "in the field of business systems."

Announcement of this move stunned the staff in Hawthorne. Eckdahl recalled that "that was as close as I ever came to quitting." In his view the 304 – then operating on display in the lobby – could have been put directly into production without further engineering refinement. Although GE did a "good job" of production engineering, the real benefit of that was open to question in view of the small number of units to be produced. Furthermore, in his view, this decision by Allyn set NCR back 2–3 years in developing its own capabilities as a manufacturer of digital computers (D. E. Eckdahl, personal interview, Colton, CA, March 19, 1998).

The 304 design was released to GE in 1957. In the course of production engineering, according to D. E. Eckdahl (personal interview, Colton, CA, March 19, 1998), the Electronics Division "taught GE everything it knew about computer design." NCR began shipping 304 systems to government and retail customers in 1960. In that year, the Sales Division also opened Data Centers in New York and other major cities to train customer personnel, test software, and, as service bureaus, to process the punched tapes being produced by the new models of NCR cash registers and accounting machines. A modular mid-size system, the 315, was announced by NCR in 1960. Design and engineering for the 315 followed work on the 304 at Hawthorne, and this time Allyn authorized the Electronics Division to handle production engineering and manufacture. First units of the 315 were shipped in 1962.

In 1962, 60 percent of the company's 2000 R&D professionals worked in Dayton. Even then, a decade after the company had entered the computer industry, the R&D effort remained centered amidst the traditions of 80 years of mechanical engineering. Although a small "advanced development" group under Joseph Desch worked in Dayton on computer development, research and design for CPUs and mass storage was mainly at Hawthorne. In the late 1950s, to support expected applications for online transaction-oriented systems, the Hawthorne engineers developed a random access memory unit based on magnetic cards. The Card Random Access Memory (CRAM) functioned effectively in several bank installations in the early 1960s, but lost out to the disk drive design invented by IBM, which became dominant in the industry (Rench, 1984: 28). Nevertheless, NCR persisted in its aggressive stance toward the leading edges of computer technology. For example, NCR began development of integrated circuits in 1963 in order to be able to develop proprietary "application-specific" integrated circuits (ASICS) and was an early user of metal oxide (MOS) technology (NCR Corporation, 1984: 20–24).

## Gaining a Foothold in Computers

NCR had been a few years late in entering the market for computer systems and somewhat hesitant about its strategy. But it had the advantage of established relationships with numerous customers in the market segments it chose to address. The 304 and 315 systems successfully positioned the company as a supplier of small and medium-size systems used primarily by retailers and banks for recording transactions and issuing payrolls. RCA and GE, which had also entered late, chose to go head-to-head with IBM across a broad market, and failed. NCR's timing was not necessarily a handicap in its niches. While the potential opportunity for bank automation was large, it was not realized substantially until the late 1960s. In 1963, fewer than 20 percent of the nation's 14,000 banks reported that they either already used computers or had plans to automate. Even by 1969, barely 1000 had their own computers, and 6700 still had no plans to automate (Phister, 1979: Table II.3.11.6).

Computer sales grew slowly and were persistently unprofitable for NCR, as they were then for most computer manufacturers. In 1962, a decade after the decision to enter the business, NCR's computer revenues were only 2 percent of the company's total (NCR Corporation, 1984: 4). Because the Model 304 was a high-cost design, production was stopped after only 36 of the systems were sold.[3] The more successful Model 315 was eventually placed in more than 1000 installations.

The belief in "systems" remained strong. NCR's display at the 1964 New York World's Fair featured the theme: "NCR Total Systems – from original entry to final reports." The view in technical circles, however, was that the words were not matched by deeds in marketing. As one manager noted:

> NCR's strength in the marketplace and (sales force) was deeply imbedded in the knowledge that the company had in selling accounting machines and cash registers in a distributive sense rather than in a systems sense. So the strength of the company might have been its weakness in its marketing efforts. (Rench, 1984: 22)

By 1963, NCR was shipping enough systems to place it in the middle of the "seven dwarfs," as the press came to call the group battling for the 30 percent of the market not claimed by IBM in the burgeoning new marketplace.[4] According to one analyst, the value of NCR's shipments that year represented 3 percent of the market, a level that would persist, with modest variations up and down, for a decade (Phister, 1979: Table II.1.31.1).

## Management Succession

A new generation of top management took command as NCR moved into the EDP market, but it brought no change to the traditions of its predecessors. Stanley Allyn, who had been catapulted into top management by John Patterson in 1917, retired as chairman on the last day of 1961. His successors were selected in much the same way as Allyn had been – chosen at a relatively young age and then groomed for the top. The first of them, Robert S. Oelman, was a native of Dayton and a *summa cum laude* graduate of Dartmouth College. After a year of graduate work in law and economics in Vienna, he had joined the company in 1933 as a file clerk. He moved rapidly into sales promotion and advertising responsibilities. In 1942, when Deeds and Allyn were looking for someone "intelligent and of distinctly contagious personality and political astuteness" to understudy Allyn, they chose Oelman and brought him into the executive office (Allyn, 1967: 185). By 1950 he was executive vice president and was named president in 1957, succeeding Allyn as chairman in 1962.

Oelman's understudy was R. Stanley Laing. Trained in Mechanical Engineering at the University of Washington, Laing earned an MBA at Harvard in 1947. Allyn hired him that year as an assistant in the executive suite, and then moved him into a series of staff jobs in finance. By 1954, he was controller and in 1960 was named vice president, finance. In 1964, Oelman named him president.

Both Oelman and Laing were perceived as extremely intelligent, but with differing management styles. William Anderson, who succeeded Oelman as chairman, described him as "essentially a consensus-type leader . . . [who] always went out of his way to avoid conflicts and bruised egos." Laing, in contrast, often seemed "authoritarian," inclined toward a style that implied "this is what I've decided and this is what I want you to do" (W. Anderson, 1991: 217).

## Corporate culture

Despite differences in style, both Oelman and Laing were products of a strong corporate culture, shaped a half-century earlier by John Patterson and sustained by Deeds and Allyn. The prevailing style was described as "formalistic and procedural" by a senior consultant who worked there in 1971. As he described it thus:

> If product development needed to coordinate with manufacturing engineering, a meeting would be scheduled, agendas prepared, notes taken, and yet often little would happen. There was no notion of teams. (S. P. Kaufman, personal interview, Melville, NY, December 17, 1998)

A senior manager who spent most of his career outside Dayton described the organization structure as a "Byzantine labyrinth." Management procedures lacked the "give and take discussions" and formal checks and balances that would limit errors and excesses (W. Anderson, 1991: 180). Executives spent their careers within a single department, like manufacturing engineering; there was no tradition of rotation.

Nevertheless, as a reporter noted in 1962, "NCR has long been noted for the togetherness of its executive family. Oelman and many of his top aides live in Oakwood, a Dayton suburb just beyond the NCR plant, and except on the coldest days of winter they meet on corners to walk in groups down the short hill to the plant" (*Business Week*, 1962: 106). Senior executives lunched together daily at the same table in the "Horseshoe Room," established in the 1930s as a common venue for managers and factory supervisors. Service began promptly at noon and a short educational or inspirational film was screened regularly at 12:40. The chumminess of this group bred what was later noted as a "Dayton mentality" in which NCR staff in other locations were referred to as "outsiders." The press would later speculate that a certain myopia about electronics had been fostered by the daily sight of massive factories with their workers and machines chugging mightily to fabricate the familiar mechanical products.

## Core rigidities

In the 1960s, NCR's Dayton manufacturing organization, once a pillar of its competitive advantage, was turning into a handicap, mired in high costs and inflexibility. This was one of several instances in which long-standing core capabilities evolved into core rigidities as NCR faced the need for fundamental change (Leonard-Barton, 1992). Some 15,000 manufacturing workers and engineers worked at the massive Dayton facility. Labor costs were high; wages for relatively unskilled personnel were then three times the level at the Electronics Division in Hawthorne. Factory workers in Dayton were organized by a strong independent union, which followed the lead set by the local General Motors contracts. A piecework compensation system installed by NCR early in the century still governed factory operations. In combination with a strict union contract, it hobbled efforts to improve methods and productivity. Many managerial practices were obsolete. Few in manufacturing management were university-trained; one executive later commented that NCR at that time "did not have manufacturing managers; it had manufacturing supervisors" (W. Anderson, 1991: 184). Inventory, scheduling, and control systems were antiquated; foremen had wide discretion in determining parts quantities in any batch. Manual systems persisted in part because of management antagonism toward IBM punched card systems, which had long been used at Hawthorne (W. Anderson, 1991: 183). In contrast to the "experience curve" doctrine advocated by Eckdahl in California, managers and cost estimators in Dayton assumed that costs would rise continually with inflation. The policy of vertical integration was carried to an extreme; NCR even made its own fasteners (with nonstandard threads). Costs of most components were eventually discovered to be as much as double what vendors would have charged (D. E. Eckdahl, personal interview, Colton, CA, 19 March 1998).

In the mid-1960s, NCR was still pouring money into the old technologies. Pride in mechanical prowess was a strong element of the Dayton culture. When Charles Exley, then a vice president of arch-rival Burroughs, visited NCR in the late 1960s, he was shown around the plant and told proudly about plans to expand facilities like the automatic screw machine department, which was already the largest in the world. On his return to Burroughs, he told the chairman "You can stop worrying about NCR. They're making more and more commitments to mechanical technology" (W. Anderson, 1991: 183). The new Class 5 cash register, first marketed in 1967, was an engineering triumph and an economic flop. It anticipated the imminent functionality of programmable logic in electronic point-of-sale equipment in the design of an electromechanical product that could be produced in hundreds of configurations through selective combination of thousands of standard parts. But the engineers' vision that salesmen would master the art of programming these devices to adapt to the customer's unique needs could not be realized in practice.

## The End of an Era

In hindsight, it is clear that the 1960s were the twilight years of the age of electromechanical technology for information processing. At the time, however, the signals were more confusing. Demand for mechanical cash registers was remarkably strong; steady 12 percent annual growth in volume throughout the 1960s was fueled by the sustained expansion of the American economy and enhanced by the rapid spread of suburban shopping malls. But, by the mid-1960s, the retail marketplace was rife with speculation about a revolution on the horizon: point-of-sale terminals, all electronic, and online.

### A retail revolution

In 1964, Singer Sewing Machine Company began to look for a vendor who could provide point-of-sale terminals for its retail stores. Told by NCR that neither the economics nor the technology would support such a product in the foreseeable future,

Donald Kircher, Singer's CEO, gave the task to the Friden Company, a venerable producer of mechanical calculators that Singer had recently acquired. While Friden's engineers were fully as skeptical as NCR's, they couldn't refuse their new CEO.

Top management at some of the largest customers began to express their interest in machines that would feed data directly to their new computer systems. In 1965, a new entrant made the first move: Uni-Tote (a subsidiary of General Instrument Corporation) introduced the first electromechanical cash register with "online" computer capability. In 1966, Remington Rand also introduced an "online" product, the Point-O-S-Recorder. By 1970, Friden was marketing an electronic Modular Data Transaction System.

In the late 1960s, with multiple vendors in the marketplace, Penney, Sears, and other chains began to experiment with point-of-sale equipment, often with initially discouraging results. *Datamation* magazine (1966) advised retailers to wait for the price of point of sale [POS] machines and computers to drop in half before considering their purchase. In 1968, American Regitel Corporation, a start-up later acquired by Motorola, introduced an electronic cash register system for medium-sized and large department stores. By 1969, other competitors were field testing all-electronic machines for the retailing industry, notably Alpex (later acquired by Pitney Bowes), General Electric, and Singer's Friden Division. NCR responded to the POS challenge of new rivals by upgrading its Sales-Tronic line, promoting new optical scanning wands and decoders for input, and designing a special line of low-cost electromechanical registers for retail use.

Critics would later fault NCR's management for its hesitant response. For example, a 1975 article in *Fortune* asserted: "big retailers – J. C. Penney, Singer, Sears, Kroger – were pounding on NCR's door trying to get the company to experiment with computerized point-of-sale systems . . . NCR failed to listen" (Martin, 1975). But in 1970 the signals from the marketplace remained very mixed. Corporate executives at the major chains foresaw the coming transition and pressed for action; but at the store level, operating executives – NCR's immediate customers – still preferred to buy the familiar (and still cost-effective) older products. Stanley Laing, NCR's president, speculated (in 1970) that "cash registers will be around for some time to come . . . Five years from now, maybe even ten, even the most advanced department stores will still be in the process of automating" (*Dun's*, 1970: 29) This, of course, was what customers were then telling NCR's salesmen (W. S. Anderson, personal interview, New York, January 19, 1989). According to a consultant who worked with NCR in 1971, its managers believed strongly even then that electronic registers would "always" be too costly for the low end of the line (S. P. Kaufman, personal interview, Melville, NY, December 17, 1998). Laing believed that NCR had already accomplished a tremendous change with its new emphasis on entire business systems rather than individual business machines (*Dun's*, 1970).

Product development began in the late 1960s for a line of fully electronic terminals, targeted for market launch in the early 1970s. This was a challenging task. Engineers made the risky decision to base the line on MOS integrated circuitry, then still commercially unproven. In the end this yielded cost advantages over competitive bipolar designs, but the choice led to problems in development and schedule slippage of almost 2 years. As Carl Rench, head of engineering and product planning in Dayton, later said, this development required that they "architect a whole new family of products from the ground up," including design of ancillary elements such as printers, displays, keyboards, and communication devices (Rench, 1984: 58).

### EDP systems

Two fateful events signaled the future of the computer market in 1964: IBM introduced the 360 series, which set the pattern for mainframes and cemented its dominance of the field; and tiny Digital Equipment Corporation marketed the PDP-8, sparking the emergence of a distinct minicomputer segment. RCA responded by marketing a series of "clone" systems to compete head-on with IBM at lower prices and GE differentiated its line by pioneering in time-sharing technology. Both strategies failed and the giants of electronics were forced to exit. The remaining "Dwarfs," now termed the BUNCH (Burroughs, Univac, NCR, Control Data, and Honeywell) sought security in niches in the few market spaces left open by IBM. NCR's intended niche was described by Stanley Laing as follows:

> We didn't want to be in the computer business just to sell computers, as IBM basically did. We wanted to sell terminal-oriented computer systems, because our two biggest clients were retailing and finance. We wanted to develop terminals whose outputs would be the inputs to the computers. We would basically offer a total system from input at the terminal level to output at the computer printer level. (R. S. Laing, interview, Delray Beach, FL May 3, 1999)

In 1966, the NCR Electronics Division, still headed by Donald Eckdahl, was renamed the Data Processing Division. NCR spent $150 million to develop a third-generation computer system, the Century Series, introduced in 1968. Like IBM's System 360, the series featured a scalable design for the CPU, permitting users to upgrade readily as their needs increased. Unlike IBM, NCR's offerings would serve only a segment of potential users. At first, NCR offered Models 100 and 200, at the low end of the line; later a mid-range model, the 300, was added. In search of performance and cost advantage, NCR introduced highly innovative design features in the Century, including novel plated rods for main memory, to permit automated assembly, and a mass storage system using disk drives with a radically different head design. The new line made a strong debut in the marketplace; domestic orders for computers in 1968 were double those of the preceding year and, for the first time, exceeded those for either cash registers or accounting machines. But the Century's memory and disk drive technologies had not been perfected. Customers became irate over repeated breakdowns. Over the years from 1968 to 1972, the Century series would drain another $150 million from NCR for redesign and repair.

The market for EDP systems, while growing rapidly throughout the 1960s, was also changing in character. One significant trend was the increasing importance of peripherals as a component of system cost. As demand grew, an OEM market for peripherals developed to serve the needs of the "Dwarfs" and a "plug-compatible" market emerged among IBM customers. NCR did not enter the plug-compatible segment and, despite its early moves (in the 1950s) to develop peripherals technology, failed to establish a strong position as an OEM supplier.

## Pressure on management

Throughout the 1960s, Stanley Laing struggled with sustaining NCR's profits in the face of adverse trends. As he described it:

> We had the P&L impact of the conversion to the rental business – the more we produced, the more we rented. It took a whack at our gross margins at the time when we couldn't afford to do it. And simultaneously, we were faced with a huge R&D problem of developing not only mainframes, but a huge array of peripheral gear which imposed a very substantial financial impact. (R. S. Laing, interview, Delray Beach, FL, May 3, 1999)

To alleviate these stresses, Laing initiated discussions with William Norris, head of Control Data Corporation (CDC) to explore cooperative measures in development and manufacture of peripherals. Relationships between the companies were warm, going back to wartime friendship between Joseph Desch and Norris (Rench, 1984: 45). CDC, like NCR, was under increasing financial pressure. In February 1972, the companies announced a broad cooperative program to coordinate their mainframe product lines and to rationalize development and manufacture of peripherals. CDC purchased NCR's disk drive engineering and manufacturing facility at Hawthorne and would supply NCR's needs for disk products. The companies formed a 50/50 joint venture to develop and produce other peripherals, including magnetic tape drives, punched-card equipment, and high-speed printers. NCR would supply CDC's needs for serial printers. In future CPU development, the companies would seek to achieve

> a high degree of compatibility . . . between future small and medium-size computers developed by NCR and future large computers developed by Control Data . . . NCR will be able to offer its customers an easy transition to more powerful systems. (*NCR Annual Report*, 1971: 5)

The task of selling the computer products created stresses for the field sales force, the heart of the company's traditional competitive strength. In NCR's early days in the computer field, the Model 315 had been marketed by a small cadre of people based in Dayton, assisted by a few specialists operating from the branch offices. As the business grew, instead of recruiting experienced computer salesmen, NCR retrained its own force and assigned both accounting machines and complete EDP systems to the same staff. In 1970, 80 percent of the staff selling the Century series were former cash register or accounting machine salesmen (*Dun's*, 1970). But it was hard to find a compensation scheme that worked well for both large systems and stand-alone machines. As one salesman grumbled, "computers took 75 percent of your time and would bring in 25 percent of your income" (NCR Corporation, 1984: 5).

Top management debated alternative approaches to selling computers, especially the idea of "vocationalizing" the sales force-to create teams specialized according to the customer industry rather than NCR product. In 1965, top management went so far as to "recommend" that foreign subsidiaries restructure along those lines. In Japan, William S. Anderson, who also initiated the development of an all-electronic cash register for his local market, implemented the idea in 1967. In 6 years, NCR's sales in Japan tripled with only an 11 percent increase in the sales force (*Business Week*, 1973).

One executive pointed to customer loyalty as the main factor behind the company's ability to succeed. He commented:

> We had amazing customer loyalty. Nobody had a longer history of caring for customers ... sons of customers remember us. We did everything for our customers. We sold a *system* to the customer, not just a machine. We became part of the customer's organization. They were reluctant to abandon us. (W. S. Anderson, personal interview, New York, January 19, 1989)

## Crisis and Response

The cross-currents of a technological watershed buffeted NCR's performance throughout the 1960s. Returns fell as assets grew more rapidly than revenues and productivity growth was sluggish (see figure 22.1). Yet revenues nearly tripled over the decade as the computer business achieved significant scale and demand for traditional products boomed in the United States and abroad (see figure 22.2). NCR expanded facilities while payrolls swelled; employment doubled, peaking at 102,000 in 1969. By 1968, EDP systems still accounted for only 11 percent of corporate revenues, but the installed base of systems represented 25 percent of assets on the balance sheet. The cash drain of leasing computers drove the debt/equity ratio steadily upward. In the late 1960s, NCR reaped an average of only $12,000 in revenue per employee (equivalent to $56,000 in 1999) – about two-thirds the comparable measure for Burroughs and half that for IBM. Internal controls were strained, and margins were squeezed as costs rose throughout the decade.

At the end of the decade, NCR was under attack in all its core businesses. By 1969, Burroughs Corporation, NCR's chief rival in the banking marketplace, had completed the transition from electromechanical to electronic machines, and was gaining market share. Revenues from accounting machine sales started to fall in 1970, declining by 16 percent between 1970 and 1972, but the company was slow to introduce new systems to halt the advance by Burroughs (Martin, 1975). In the retail market, although NCR was losing share, the buoyant market brought ever-increasing revenues through 1972. Despite success in selling the Century series of computers, NCR was still losing money in the EDP market. For the first time since 1962, profits declined substantially in 1970, a recession year, and then, burdened by a costly strike, NCR barely broke even in 1971. In the meantime, Friden had taken first place in the market for electronic cash registers, followed by Pitney Bowes-Alpex. IBM had an electronic register in field test, while both Litton's Sweda and Retail Systems divisions, as well as TRW, had development projects well under way.

In 1972, NCR began to ship its new electronic terminals: the 270 bank terminal and the 280 for retail point-of-sale. Encouraged by an order from Montgomery Ward for 1500 of its 280s, William Harris, NCR's director of department store marketing, predicted that NCR would have an 80 percent share of the market based on the strength of knowing their customers on a first name basis and understanding their problems. Harris also predicted that the market wouldn't begin to grow rapidly until 1973, so "it doesn't make sense to push a product until you can get sufficient volume to support a

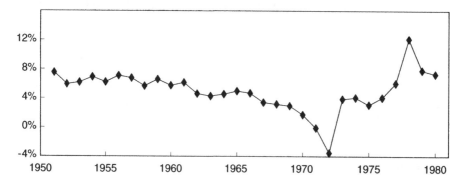

**Figure 22.1** NCR return on total assets, 1951–1980

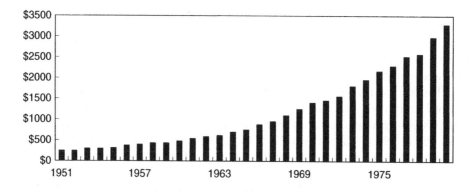

**Figure 22.2** NCR revenues (in millions), 1951–1980

low price" (*Dun's*, 1971). The business press was calling the new market a four-way race between Singer's Friden, NCR, Litton's Sweda and Pitney Bowes-Alpex.

By 1972, Singer controlled 50 percent of the electronic point of sale market, followed in second place by Pitney Bowes-Alpex, with NCR third (*Wall Street Journal*, 1972: 1). The average price of an electronic cash register had declined, as *Datamation* had predicted, so that an electronic register, typically selling for $3400, cost only $200 more than an electromechanical model. The press forecast they would cost less than $3000 by 1976 (*Business Week*, 1972). NCR introduced two new models of freestanding electronic cash registers: the NCR 250 and NCR 230.

### Facing realities

In 1970, Donald Eckdahl was appointed vice president of operations for the corporation and moved to Dayton. Stanley Laing, he found, was well aware of the need to do something radical about the Dayton operation, but seemed unaware of the extent to which costs were out of line and management methods behind the times. In mid-year, Laing assigned Eckdahl to study potential uses for Dayton's three million square feet of factory space and nearly 15,000 production people as NCR moved from high-labor-content mechanical products to electronic technologies. With the aid of consultants from McKinsey & Company (and other firms), Eckdahl explored several options, some quite far from NCR traditions. The possibility, for example, of diversifying into the automotive aftermarket was discarded when studies showed that NCR's costs to make parts would be double those of other shops in Dayton. Analysis cast strong doubt on the feasibility of changing the structure, philosophy, and culture of manufacturing in NCR's Dayton operations to meet the needs of the future. The conclusion was that, despite their deep reluctance to do so, NCR management would have to let Dayton operations wither away, while building new capabilities in other locations.

Stanley Laing had recognized for some time that wrenching changes in manufacturing, engineering, and sales would be required to reverse the slide in NCR's fortunes. In the late 1960s, despite pressures on profits, he had increased investments in training and had moved to recruit MBAs to bring modern ideas into management. Eckdahl was moved from California for the same purpose. But Laing also believed that a number of senior people were unlikely to adapt and would have to be replaced. Oelman, loyal to his subordinates, resisted these moves and, in Laing's view, slowed down the pace of change (R. S. Laing, interview, Delray Beach, FL, May 3, 1999).

Battered by a strike and increasing competition in computers, terminals, and accounting machines, NCR saw its profits vanish in 1971, forcing the Board to cut the dividend in February 1972. The outside members of the Board of Directors had become increasingly concerned about the company's performance and its leadership and direction. One director, with a high opinion of Laing's intelligence and abilities, believed that he was more open to change than Oelman, who was more of a traditionalist (anonymous interview). But even this person believed that no one with deep roots in Dayton would have been able to implement the necessary cutbacks there. According to another account, "also disturbing were reports that the relationship between the chairman and the president had become so strained that they were scarcely speaking to each other" (W. Anderson, 1991: 210). According to R. S. Laing (interview, Delray Beach, FL, May 3, 1999), he himself made the move that broke the stalemate at the top, going to Oelman to tell him "that I just didn't think he knew where we were going and I thought he ought to step down," adding "if you don't step down, I'm going to leave." Oelman's response precipitated Laing's resignation, effective May 17, 1972.

### A new leader

Meanwhile, the outside directors had concluded that new leadership was in order for the company. With Oelman's participation, they chose William S. Anderson, an Englishman born in China and educated in Shanghai, who had started his career with NCR in Hong Kong and eventually rose to become head of its large subsidiary in Japan. Although Anderson had spent his career with NCR outside the United States, he knew the country; he had married an American woman and had visited the United States annually since 1951. Anderson moved rapidly to take charge, arriving in Dayton in June 1972. Oelman remained as chairman until 1974, and served as a director and chairman of the Executive Committee until retirement in 1980.

The board had looked for a market-oriented man to take NCR through what looked to be tough years of transition ahead. Charles A. Anderson, who had joined the Board in 1969, described William Anderson as "smart and courageous . . . a consummate salesman very good at high-level customer relationships" (C. A. Anderson, personal interview, Palo Alto, CA, January 28, 1999). Another director, asked to characterize William Anderson, mentioned "a wonderful personality for meeting people" and a style that could be "stern, very determined." Overall, he found him "straight-forward, very honest, very open, a wonderful executive" (C. H. Hardesty, personal interview, Myrtle Beach, FL, May 4, 1999).

By 1972, NCR's previous strengths in sales and manufacturing had turned into obstacles to progress (see Leonard-Barton, 1992). Anderson quickly set out to break up the "Dayton mentality," reshuffling most of top management and restructuring manufacturing and marketing. He also attended to some necessary symbolic changes, including a new name – NCR Corporation – and a new corporate headquarters building. He quickly communicated the direction NCR was to take: "The NCR of 1982 will be primarily an electronics company" he told the employees. "Our principal products will be complete information processing systems" (National Cash Register Company, 1972: 16).

Anderson understood that the changes that NCR must make would have severe consequences for its employees in Dayton. Early on he told the Board that he was sure to experience severe pressure both from the union and from the Dayton civic leaders. To persevere he would need assurance of the directors' support. As one outside director said: "The Board gave him that support; it was critical that they stood solidly behind him" (C. A. Anderson, personal interview, Palo Alto, CA, January 28, 1999).

*Restructuring*

As Anderson was taking charge, Donald Eckdahl was working out the final elements of his plan for a radical restructuring of manufacturing operations. He would recommend the establishment of a series of self-contained, small to medium-sized plants across the country, each with its own general manager, engineering, finance, information systems, human resource management, quality control, and purchasing. All products currently made in Dayton would remain there; the transition to electronics in the marketplace would rapidly phase out those activities. Products still in development would be moved, with their engineering staffs, to the new locations where they would be produced. The new operations would be primarily for assembly and test. Most components would be purchased, reversing historic practices.

Anderson accepted the plan immediately, telling Eckdahl that it should be presented at the next board meeting. At the conclusion of the presentation, the directors applauded – "not for the presentation, but with relief" D. E. Eckdahl (personal interview, Colton, CA, March 19, 1998) recalled. As the product mix shifted, manufacturing at the Dayton plant was rapidly reduced from 80 percent of NCR's domestic production to 30 percent. NCR had been Dayton's second largest employer, after General Motors, employing approximately 15,700 factory workers at its peak in 1969. By 1976, NCR would have only 2000 factory workers remaining in Dayton. Throughout the company, the number of employees dropped from a 1969 high of 103,000 to 90,000 at the end of 1973. Within two more years, manufacturing had metamorphosed from being a high-precision mechanical parts fabricator and assembler to a high-quality assembler of purchased components.

Anderson shook the marketing organization from top to bottom, restructuring it along the vocational lines that had worked so well in Japan. All marketing and sales staff were identified with one of four "vocational" customer segments: retailing, financial, commercial/industrial, and medical/educational/government. A shake-up among the senior marketing and sales managers occurred as promotions were made to new vocational vice president and regional director positions. A New York securities firm estimated that attrition from the restructuring might result in a 10–12 percent reduction in NCR's sales force. A new training program was established and backed by a 20 percent increase in the training budget to implement the restructuring (*Business Week*, 1973). NCR's marketing efforts became heavily dependent on the field engineering force, so that by 1975 one in every four employees (18,000) was a field engineer.

Senior management was completely transformed. Five top executives took early retirement while another seven found new jobs outside of NCR. Seven more vice presidents were demoted or had their organizations eliminated. But almost all of the new appointees were also NCR veterans. Only two top spots, in R&D and finance, were filled from outside. The new chief financial officer was nearly an insider; Donald Macintosh had worked with the company for 11 years as the audit partner for Price Waterhouse. In 1973, when Anderson selected the marketing vice president from the Atlanta region to become senior vice president of marketing, non-Dayton people were in all the key spots in manufacturing, R&D, finance and marketing.

In NCR'S 1972 *Annual Report*, in contrast to the earlier emphasis on evolution, management noted:

> A technological revolution is now impacting on other types of free-standing business machines including the cash register, providing dramatic improvements in performance and flexibility. The transition of the business equipment industry into what will soon be essentially an all-electronic industry has presented many challenges.

The result of Anderson's immediate changes were write-offs of $135 million and an earnings deficit in 1972 of $59.6 million. Macintosh summed up the problem as follows: "We didn't recognize early enough that market demand was moving much more rapidly than anticipated toward electronics. So we were caught two years behind the market" (*Forbes*, 1973a).

## Resurgence

NCR delivered thousands of its new electronic cash registers in 1973 and was poised to introduce a new machine once the food industry officially adopted the new Universal Product Code standards. At this point, all but one major NCR plant was producing the new generation of electronic equipment. NCR believed that it was "neck-and-neck with Singer" in the point of sale market (*Datamation*, 1973). A significant market development occurred when Pitney Bowes-Alpex withdrew from the POS market, citing losses of $28 million over the previous 3 years. By 1974, capitalizing on the exit of Pitney Bowes-Alpex and with a new product line, NCR had captured 50 percent of the electronic cash register market; Singer was now second. By 1975, when NCR had a complete line of integrated point-of-sale systems, its market share rose to 61 percent, despite the added competition created by IBM's entry into the retail POS marketplace (*Forbes*, 1976). By the end of 1975, Singer, Bunker-Ramo and MSI Data had dropped out of the electronic cash register market.

NCR, having at last gone electronic in cash registers, had triumphed because of the power of its reputation and relationships, strengthened by the scope of its product line and the new systems orientation of its marketing force. As *Forbes* (1973b) reported, "Customers would rather have a single manufacturer responsible for the entire system." In 1973, NCR's revenues from computer systems and services ranked it last among the "Bunch" but, for the first time, it earned a profit on system sales. The five firms then chasing IBM in computers were "bunched" closely in revenues in 1973. NCR's $726 million was not far behind the $1.1 billion of Honeywell and Burroughs, the largest of the five (Flamm, 1988: 102).

Nineteen seventy-five marked the last year that NCR produced mechanical cash registers in the United States. The market had evaporated with stunning speed. Stand-alone electromechanical products represented only 7 percent of equipment shipments in 1976, down from 66 percent 4 years earlier, while electronic terminals rose from 9 percent to 55 percent and computer systems from 25 percent to 39 percent. Equipment sales and rentals represented about 55 percent of total revenues – service and supplies providing the balance – in this period. NCR's revenues from traditional products (electromechanical registers and accounting machines) fell from nearly 40 percent of total revenues in 1972 to only 4 percent 5 years later (NCR, *Annual Report*, 1976; Foster, 1986: Figure 18).

By 1978 NCR had completed its transition from the age of mechanical registers to that of electronic systems. Revenues zoomed upward and profitability returned to peaks the company had last enjoyed in the gravy days of the early 1950s. And to lead it into the 1980s, NCR had a new Chief Executive: Charles Exley Jr, a 22-year veteran of Burroughs Corporation recruited by Anderson to succeed him in 1976 as president and later as chief executive.

## Discussion

The history of NCR is the story of only one organization among the many that were transformed in the mid-20th century by the gales of creative destruction that accompanied the coming of electronics to the office products industry. There are obvious limits to what can be inferred from analysis of a single historical case. But, the richness of detail available in this extended case should enable us to seek insights into some of the general propositions about adaptation to technological change that have gained currency in academic discourse.

As we noted at the outset, the thrust of most academic discussion of the impact of transforming technological change is to explain why it leads to the failure of dominant incumbent firms. NCR serves well as a counter-example; it was one of the dominant firms in its industry in 1948, and it unquestionably did not "fail" – in 1978 it maintained leadership in its principal market segments and was highly profitable (see figure

22.1).[5] Yet, while it was not a "failure," neither would it be judged by most observers as a "success" in these transitions. The company did not exploit computer opportunities as fully as might have been done and it endured a painful crisis in the adaptation of its core product line. But it survived, and even regained its prosperity, with a significant position in computers and a leading position in transaction terminals by the late 1970s. Survival in the face of a technological transition as strong as this one is no small achievement; many firms that had strong positions in specialized fields of business equipment in the 1950s were severely diminished or had vanished from the scene by 1975–e.g., Smith-Corona (typewriters), Marchant and Monroe (calculators), and Addressograph-Multigraph (reprographics).

Given this detailed, complex, and decades-long story of adaptation and survival, different readers will undoubtedly come to different interpretations about its larger meaning. The author's view is that this story offers qualified support for each of the varied theoretical perspectives identified at the outset. Incremental change in product designs, competence destruction, new value propositions, and threats to long-standing social commitments all appear as consequences of new technologies deployed by NCR and as factors shaping its behavior. Each of the propositions about the significance of such characteristics of an innovation is useful in explaining part of NCR's experience in the transition to electronics.

For example, the successful "Post-tronic" accounting machine enhanced the value to users of existing designs through incremental design changes that built on established competencies. In contrast, inherent in the technology of the Model 102-A drum computer, launched in the same year, but later aborted by Stanley Allyn, was an opposite set of consequences. Implicit in the emergence of small general-purpose computers in the 1950s was a wholly different value proposition, at first not well understood by either producers or users, but potentially a replacement for accounting machines and hence destructive of those established competencies. In the first case electronics was sustaining and enhancing; in the second it would be disruptive and destructive. One was embraced by top management, the other rejected.

The logics of economics do not help to justify some of the most important investment decisions in this story. The foundations of the requisite new technical capabilities in electronics were laid down by Desch and his associates, beginning in 1938, and by the acquisition of CRC in 1953. The first of these investments was made nearly 20 years before NCR's first electronic products reached customers. Net profits from the second were not realized until the 1970s.

In the postwar years, the founders of the entrepreneurial start-ups were probably more highly motivated to invest in computers than were the established leaders in office equipment, but IBM, Remington, Burroughs, and NCR were not unwilling to invest and were better able to access the requisite capital. Financial constraints appear more evident in the 1960s, when the continuing squeeze on margins did limit NCR's investments in its computer line. Furthermore, the reluctance to restructure ("vocationalize") the field sales organization, or to change its incentive system, was clearly rooted in the concern that change might disrupt the flow of current revenues and profits.

Several other kinds of commitments stand out as influential in NCR's story. The company's manufacturing prowess and heavy investment in people and equipment would be rendered null by a "revolutionary" (as opposed to "evolutionary") shift to electronics technology. Management's long-standing commitment to the masses of factory workers and to the city of Dayton hindered the implementation of changes that were essential to adaptation. On the other hand, another longstanding commitment – to help customers meet their needs – served the company well in making the transition to the new era.

As the foregoing indicates, the established theoretic perspectives do offer some explanatory power when applied to specific aspects of the story. The necessary qualification, however, is that no single theoretical perspective is sufficient to "explain" the path of NCR's behaviour in a more general sense. Neither specification of the characteristics of specific innovations, nor generalization about asymmetric incentives, social commitments, and the like, will by itself sum up the story. Hence we conclude by raising some broader questions which might be addressed in future research.

## Waves of change

As is evident in the story, the task facing NCR's management was not simply one of coping with a particular innovation; the company participated in a revolution in technology that played out over decades and comprised multiple innovation opportunities within two major waves of change. The first wave led to the practical possibility of using electronics, rather than mechanics, to register and to process financial information; the second led electronics into the age of semiconductor integrated circuitry. Each of these waves presented the potential for numerous innovations with varied consequences.

Seminal inventions, like ENIAC or the first integrated circuits, open new frontiers of technological opportunity. Pioneering investments to develop their capabilities and explore their applications are usually required before significant innovations can be commercialized. NCR's stance on the frontiers of technology changed over time. In the 1930s, it was a technological pioneer in electronic calculation but it was not among the first to bring the technology to market. In the 1960s, it was an early mover in the applications of semiconductor technologies pioneered by others. The company, however, survived both waves of change; its revenues grew consistently and, although profitability suffered during the 1960s and it endured an acute crisis in the early 1970s, it emerged in the mid-1970s more profitable than ever. This suggests that it would be useful to formulate and test theories that can explain the changes in the fortunes of firms in the face of aggregate changes in technology, as well as with respect to specific innovations.

## Dynamic capabilities

Looking at the NCR story from the "dynamic capabilities" perspective, the significance of organizational processes stands out. Organizational processes within NCR were strong, in the sense that they were long-standing, robust, and influential. Yet they were weak in the sense that they proved to be poorly suited to the new era. The established processes for product development, product delivery, and marketing were hierarchical, ineffective at integration, and slow. They had been sufficient to sustain a near-monopoly position in markets where needs and technologies changed slowly – even encouraged by that environment. But electronics changed all that, destroying entry barriers and creating rapid change in the customers' sense of their information needs and in the products available to them. New processes were required to integrate marketing and product development, so that the latter could be driven by customer needs rather than the preferences of "expert" product planners. Teamwork was needed to bridge formal boundaries and speed response to change. The established culture was a barrier to meeting these new needs. Learning was not an inherent element of processes at NCR. The company had had no experience with reconfiguration or transformation of structure and processes in what was until 1972, a highly centralized organization.

### The role of leadership

NCR regained prosperity when new leadership provided the impetus for a required transformation whose nature was clear to all whose vision was not clouded by commitments to an earlier order of things. Because it possessed strong capabilities in the new technologies plus strengths in sales and distribution that could serve well, with some adaptation, to bring new products to old customers, the organization was able to move rapidly in the new directions. But the value of these capabilities would have been dissipated without the action of leaders to enable the transforming changes that made that possible.

The central role of NCR's leaders over the decades was both to make new commitments and to break old commitments. Hesitancy in both respects acted to limit success. Creation of new capabilities, by Deeds in 1938, by Allyn in 1952, and by Anderson in 1972, were essential to the long-run outcome. On the other hand, the postwar decision to focus on core products and restrict electronics work to "research" foreclosed strategic paths that might have been open to NCR. For example, in a retrospective on the early days of the industry, a computer historian speculated on what he called "an intriguing industrial 'might-have-been.'" Noting the prewar inventions at NCR, he suggested that

> this machine could have become the first commercial electronic computer had the company wished to pioneer in this field. However, NCR management was not interested in automatic computing, *per se*, but only in improving its existing line of office equipment. (Tropp, 1974: 76)

In 1954, another strategic path was closed off by the decision to shut down drum computer sales by CRC.

The *position* of a business can be partly defined, as Teece and Pisano suggest, by the firm's current "endowments," but it also is determined by choices made about which *paths* to follow. Important choices of strategic *direction* were effected by Deeds' decision to invest in electronics research and Allyn's acquisition of CRC. But the capabilities thus added to NCR's endowment left open a range of opportunities along a range of potential strategic paths. The more concrete choices to pursue certain pathways and eschew others were more determinative of long-run results.

What stands out is that creation of some essential capabilities implied a corresponding willingness to break commitments and take risks. Anderson criticized his predecessors for treating computers as "a fourth department", in effect, assuming that new paths could be followed successfully without transforming the old ones. The leader's main role, perhaps, is to own responsibility for the breach of commitments.

This brings us to our final observations, on the role of leadership. One dimension that was conspicuously influential in the NCR story, individual leadership, is rarely mentioned in the academic sources cited at the beginning of this paper. It deserves closer examination and may well be a central element in dynamic capability.

Some organizations may have the capacity to transform themselves to adapt to changes in strategy or in the environment. Robert Burgelman (1994) has described how Intel's established processes for resource allocation redistributed the application of its critical assets from memory to microprocessors, a move eventually ratified by its top executives. Early in this century, as Alfred Chandler (1962) has shown, middle-level executives at DuPont took the lead in moving the organization to a decentralized structure as a creative adaptation to the requirements of a new strategy of diversification. At NCR, which lacked the culture of learning and adaptation, decisive action by the top executive was necessary to resolve the problems that arose in the 1960s. The roles and functions of the Chief Executive should probably figure more prominently in our theorizing about adaptation to change.

## Acknowledgements

This article benefited from comments by participants in the June 1997 Conference on the History of Computing sponsored by the IEEE History Center; the Business History Seminar at Harvard Business School, November 1998; and the Conference on the Evolution of Firm Capabilities at the Amos Tuck School, September, 1999. Special thanks to: William Aspray, Clayton Christensen, Walter Friedman, Thomas McCraw, Frederick Nebeker, Richard Nelson, Gary Pisano, and Emerson Pugh. Baker Library was an invaluable source of information. The Division of Research at Harvard Business School provided generous financial support. Finally, my unbounded thanks to the several former executives of NCR who graciously spent time speaking with me about their experiences and offered helpful comments on my drafts.

## Notes

1   In the days before computers, account transactions were posted to unit records called "ledger cards," which maintained a running balance in the account. For example, to record a deposit to a bank account, a clerk would read the prior balance on the card, enter it into the accounting machine, enter the deposit amount, and then have the machine update the balance and print it on the card. To ensure accuracy, some banks would have each transaction recorded twice by different clerks.

2   These were: Marchant Calculator, Monroe Calculator, Remington Rand (ERA Division), and Underwood (typewriters). A fifth, Electrodata, was acquired in 1956 by Burroughs (Pugh and Aspray, 1996).

3 The initial commitment to GE had been for 24 systems; under pressure from the field, management in Dayton authorized another dozen, even though costs exceeded revenues (W. Anderson, 1991: 172).
4 The "Dwarfs," in order of size in 1963, were Univac, Burroughs, Control Data, NCR, Honeywell, RCA, and GE (Phister, 1979: Table II.1.31.1).
5 Anita McGahan (1999: 78) shows that this kind of turnaround from chronic low profitability is a rare event.

# References

Allyn, S. C. 1967. *My Half Century with NCR*. McGraw-Hill: New York.
Anderson, W. S. 1991. (with Truax C) *Corporate Crisis: NCR and the Computer Revolution*. Landfall Press: Dayton, OH.
Burgelman, R. A. 1994. Fading memories: a process theory of strategic business exit in dynamic environments. *Administrative Science Quarterly* 39: 24–56.
*Business Week*. 1962. Making up for a late start in computers, August 4: 103–106.
*Business Week*. 1972. The retailers go electronic. August 19: 38.
*Business Week*. 1973. NCR's radical shift in marketing tactics, December 8: 103.
Campbell-Kelly, M. and Aspray, W. 1996. *Computer: A History of the Information Machine*. Basic Books: New York.
Chandler, A. D. 1962. *Strategy and Structure: Chapters in the History of the Industrial Enterprise*. MIT Press: Cambridge, MA.
Christensen, C. M. 1997. *The Innovator's Dilemma: When New Technologies Cause Great Firms to Fail*. Harvard Business School Press: Boston, MA.
Cooper, A. C. and Schendel, D. E. 1976. Strategic responses to technological threats. *Business Horizons*, February: 61–69.
Cortada, J. W. 1993. *Before the Computer: IBM, NCR, Burroughs, and Remington Rand and the Industry They Created, 1865–1956*. Princeton University Press: Princeton, NJ.
*Datamation*. 1966. Is retailing ready for "on-line, real-time"? August: 38–39.
*Datamation*. 1973. Spice leaves POS market. December: 101.
*Dun's*. 1970. The moment of truth for NCR? January: 29–31.
*Dun's*. 1971. Three-way free-for-all. September: 68–69.
Flamm, K. 1988. *Creating The Computer: Government, Industry, and High Technology*. Brookings Institution: Washington, DC.
*Forbes*. 1973a. The numbers game: NCR's new math. July 15: 49–50.
*Forbes*. 1973b. Can NCR come back? 1 March: 56.
*Forbes*. 1976. Back in the running. April 1: 36.
Foster, R. N. 1986. *Innovation: The Attacker's Advantage*. Summit Books: New York.
Friedman, W. 1998. John H. Patterson and the sales strategy of the National Cash Register Company, 1884 to 1922. *Business History Review*, Winter: 552–584.
Ghemawat, P. 1991. *Commitment: The Dynamic of Strategy*. Free Press: New York.
Henderson, R. 1993. Underinvestment and incompetence as responses to radical innovation: evidence from the photolithographic alignment equipment industry. *Rand Journal of Economics* 24: 248–270.
Henderson, R. and Clark, K. B. 1990. Architectural innovation: the reconfiguration of existing product technologies and the failure of established firms. *Administrative Science Quarterly* 35: 9–30.
Leonard-Barton, D. 1992. Core capabilities and core rigidities: a paradox in managing new product development. *Strategic Management Journal*, Summer Special Issue 13: 111–126.

Martin, L. G. 1975. What happened at NCR after the boss declared martial law? *Fortune* September: 100–104.

McGahan, A. M. 1999. Competition, strategy, and business performance. *California Management Review* 41: 74–101.

Mumma, R. E. 1984. Interview by William Aspray, April 19, in Dayton, Ohio. Interview number 73, transcript. Oral Histories, Charles Babbage Institute: Minneapolis, MN.

National Cash Register Company. 1953. *NCR Factory News*, November.

National Cash Register Company. 1972. *NCR World*, September–October: 16.

NCR Corporation. 1984. *Celebrating the Future: A Centennial History*, Vol. 3, The Computer Era. The NCR Corporation: Dayton, OH.

Phister, M. Jr 1979. *Data Processing Technology and Economics*, 2nd edn. Digital Press: Santa Monica, CA.

Pugh, E. W. and Aspray, W. 1996. Creating the computer industry. *IEEE Annals of the History of Computing* 18: 7–17.

Rench, C. 1984. Interview by William Aspray, April 18, in Dayton, Ohio. Interview number 72, transcript. Oral Histories, Charles Babbage Institute: Minneapolis, MN.

Sull, D. N., Tedlow, R. S., and Rosenbloom, R. S. 1997. Managerial commitments and technological change in the U.S. tire industry. *Industrial and Corporate Change* 6(2): 461–501.

Teece, D. and Pisano, G. 1994. The dynamic capabilities of firms: an introduction. *Industrial and Corporate Change* 3: 537–556.

Teece, D., Pisano, G., and Shuen, A. 1997. Dynamic capabilities and strategic management. *Strategic Management Journal* 18(7): 509–533.

Tropp, H. 1974. The effervescent years: a retrospective. *IEEE Spectrum*, February, 70–79.

Tushman, M. L. and Anderson, P. 1986. Technological discontinuities and organizational environments. *Administrative Science Quarterly* 31: 439–465.

Usselman, S. W. 1993. IBM and its imitators: organizational capabilities and the emergence of the international computer industry. *Business and Economic History* 22: 1–35.

*Wall Street Journal*. 1972. The superregisters: computers handle checkout at many stores, November 20: 1.

# CHAPTER TWENTY-THREE

# Capabilities, Cognition, and Inertia: Evidence from Digital Imaging

## Mary Tripsas and Giovanni Gavetti

## Introduction

Organizational change is difficult. Even when established firms recognize the need to change in response to shifts in their external environment, they are often unable to respond effectively. Technological change has proven particularly deadly for established firms, with numerous examples of established firm failure in the face of radical technological change (Cooper and Schendel, 1976; Majumdar, 1982; Tushman and Anderson, 1986; Henderson and Clark, 1990; Utterback, 1994; Tushman and O'Reilly, 1996; Christensen, 1997). Existing explanations for failure to adapt to radically new technology have focused on the nature of a firm's capabilities.[1] In this paper we expand upon this work by examining how managerial cognition influences the evolution of capabilities and thus contributes to organizational inertia.

In the tradition of evolutionary economics, much research has focused on how existing technological capabilities, codified in the routines, procedures, and information processing capabilities of the firm, limit its adaptive intelligence (Arrow, 1974; Nelson and Winter, 1982; Teece, Pisano and Shuen, 1997). A firm's prior history constrains its future behavior in that learning tends to be premised on local processes of search (March and Simon, 1958; Levitt and March, 1988; Teece, 1988). When learning needs to be distant, and radically new capabilities need to be developed, firms often fall into competency traps, as core competencies become "core rigidities" (Leonard-Barton, 1992). A firm's nontechnological assets also influence the direction of its technological trajectory (Dosi, 1982). Firms are more likely to develop technologies that can utilize existing complementary assets – assets essential for the commercialization of the technology (Teece, 1986; Helfat, 1997). For instance, a firm's existing marketing capability, particularly its knowledge of customers, makes it more likely to develop technologies that appeal to existing customers as opposed to a new set of customers (Christensen, 1997).

Empirical evidence supports the importance of capabilities in explaining incumbent inertia and subsequent failure. When a new technology is "competence destroying" in that it requires mastery of an entirely new scientific discipline, established firms are more likely to fail (Tushman and Anderson, 1986). More subtly, when a new technology destroys the "architectural knowledge" of the firm – knowledge about interfaces among product components – established firms also suffer (Henderson and Clark, 1990). Finally, when technological change destroys the value of a firm's existing complementary assets, the firm is more likely to fail (Mitchell, 1989; Tripsas, 1997).

While most innovation scholars have emphasized the role of capabilities, others have focused on the role of cognition in explaining organizational inertia (Garud and Rappa, 1994). Since managers are boundedly rational, they must rely on simplified representations of the world in order to process information (Simon, 1955). These imperfect representations form the basis for the development of the mental models and strategic beliefs that drive managerial decisions. They influence the manner in which managers frame problems and thus how they search for solutions.

Cognitive representations are typically based on historical experience as opposed to current knowledge of the environment (Kiesler and Sproull, 1982). For instance, as senior managers work together over time they often develop a set of beliefs, or "dominant logic" for the firm based on their shared history (Prahalad and Bettis, 1986). These beliefs include a shared sense of who the relevant competitors are (Reger and Huff, 1993; Porac et al., 1995; Peteraf and Shanley, 1997). Firm founders also play a significant role in establishing beliefs, leaving their imprint on the organization long after their departure (Baron, Hannan, and Burton, 1999). Given the influence of the historical environment on the development of beliefs, in rapidly changing environments top managers often have difficulty adapting their mental models, resulting in poor organizational performance (Barr, Stimpert, and Huff, 1992; Brown and Eisenhardt, 1998).

Our goal in this paper is to explore how the combination of capabilities and cognition helps to explain organizational inertia in the face of radical technological change. We focus on cognition at the level of the senior management team given the critical influence of top management teams on strategic decision-making (Mintzberg, 1979; Hambrick and Mason, 1984). We examine how managerial cognitive representations may play a central role in terms of constraining organizational behavior, and ultimately, the development of a firm's capabilities (Zyglidopoulos, 1999; Gavetti and Levinthal, 2000). In order to explore the relationship between capabilities, cognition, and inertia, we perform an in-depth historical case study of a firm undergoing a radical transition. We analyze how the Polaroid Corporation has responded to the ongoing shift from analog to digital imaging.[2] The firm provides a particularly compelling example in that, despite early investments and leading-edge technical capability in areas related to digital imaging, the firm has so far not performed well in the digital imaging market. We explore why Polaroid has had difficulty, with an emphasis on understanding the role of both capabilities and cognition in explaining organizational inertia.

We find that by restricting and directing search activities related to technology development, managerial cognition influences the development of new capability. For instance, given Polaroid senior management's belief in pursuing large-scale "impossible" technological advances, the firm made significant investments in developing technical capability related to digital imaging. At the same time, their belief in a razor/blade business model delayed commercialization of a stand-alone digital camera product. Understanding processes of organizational change thus requires examining not only the central inertial forces associated with developing new capabilities, but also the impact that cognition has on such processes.

## Methods and Data

This research is based on an in-depth, inductive case study of the Polaroid Corporation's historical involvement in digital imaging. Given the open-ended nature of our questions regarding the relationship among capabilities, cognition, and inertia, we felt that this approach would be most useful for theory building (Glaser and Strauss, 1967; Miles and Huberman, 1994; Yin, 1984). In addition, by taking a long-term historical perspective we gain insight into the evolutionary nature of both capabilities and cognition. A combination of public data, company archives, and interview data were collected on the evolution of Polaroid's activities related to both digital imaging and the traditional instant photography business.

Publicly available data included a complete set of historical annual reports, financial analyst reports, prior studies of Polaroid's history, and business press articles on both Polaroid and the digital imaging industry. We were greatly aided by extensive prior historical work on Edwin Land and Polaroid's position in instant photography (McElheny, 1998). Company archives supplemented publicly available data. Historical strategic plans, organization charts, internal memos, and technical papers helped to document the evolution of the organization.

Finally, we interviewed a sample of current and ex-Polaroid employees. Our sample varied along three dimensions. First, it included individuals from multiple levels of the organizational hierarchy. We interviewed ex-CEOs, other senior managers, mid-level project managers, and first-line research scientists and marketing specialists. Second, we included individuals from multiple functional areas. Research and development, marketing, and manufacturing were all represented in our sample. Third, we included individuals present at different points in Polaroid's history in order to understand how the organization had evolved. In many cases this process involved interviewing retired employees as well as employees who had moved to other companies. We interviewed individuals present during the "Land era" (before 1980) as well as outsiders brought in at various points in time in order to facilitate digital imaging efforts. Every key manager involved in Polaroid's digital imaging efforts was contacted and interviewed. Some individuals were contacted multiple times as we worked through the iterative process of data collection and theory development. In total, we conducted 20 interviews with 15 individuals. We stopped interviewing/collecting material when a level of saturation was reached (Glaser and Strauss, 1967).

Interviews were open ended, but based on a common set of questions. Interviewees were first asked to discuss their specific role in the company, and how it changed over time. We then asked them to broadly discuss the evolution of digital imaging activities vis-à-vis the evolution of activities in the traditional instant imaging business. A third set of questions specifically dealt with the emergence of strategic beliefs in the digital competitive arena, and the factors that constrained or inhibited this process. Interviews lasted from 1 hour to all day.

Data collection, data analysis, and conceptualization have been iterative (Glaser and

Strauss, 1967). Analysis began with a cluster methodology (Aldenderfer and Blashfield, 1984) where each researcher identified common words and topics for clustering. Cluster labels included both firm capabilities and managerial beliefs/mental models. Researchers then met, compared differences, and repeated the clustering, resulting in a final set of groupings related to both capabilities and cognition.

## Polaroid in Digital Imaging

### Polaroid's foundations: 1937–1980

Polaroid was founded in 1937 by Edwin Land, based on his invention of light-polarizing filters. It was Land's work in instant photography, however, that made Polaroid a household word. Polaroid introduced the first instant camera, a 5-pound device that produced low-quality brown and white pictures, in 1948. From that point forward, Polaroid focused on making improvements to the instant camera. Through ongoing research, Polaroid was able to significantly improve the picture quality, decrease the development time required, introduce color, and enable one-step development (see table 23.1 for a list of major instant photography developments). Firm performance was exceptional, with average annual compounded sales growth of 23 percent, profit growth of 17 percent, and share price growth of 17 percent between 1948 and 1978.

This period of strong performance culminated in a clear set of firm capabilities and managerial beliefs resulting from both Land's imprint on the firm and years of innovation related to instant photography. We next review what these capabilities and beliefs were and how they influenced subsequent search activities related to digital imaging (see figure 23.1).

### Capabilities: 1980

As one would expect, Polaroid's capabilities centered around its dominant position in instant photography. The firm's knowledge of the technologies relevant to instant photography technology was unsurpassed in the industry. Land himself held over 500 patents. The firm's patent position was so strong that when Kodak entered the instant

**Table 23.1** Polaroid's major instant photography developments, 1948–80

| Year | Advance |
| --- | --- |
| 1948 | First instant camera: sepia (brown and white) film |
| 1950 | First black and white film |
| 1963 | First instant color print film |
| 1964 | Colorpack camera |
| 1965 | Polaroid Swinger, first low-priced camera (under $20) |
| 1972 | SX-70 (one-step developing with no waste) |
| 1978 | Sonar automatic focusing |

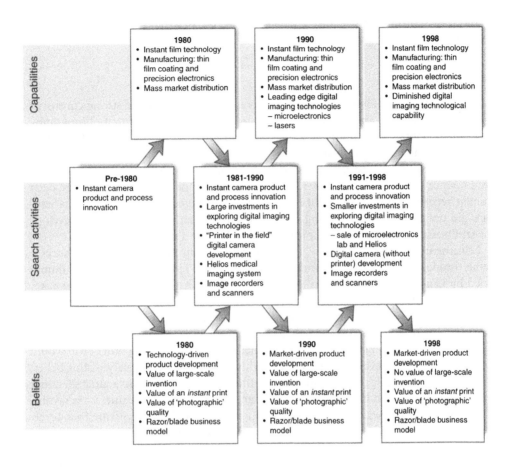

**Figure 23.1** The evolution of capabilities and beliefs at Polaroid

photography market in 1976 Polaroid successfully sued them for patent infringement and was able to exclude Kodak from the U.S. market.[3] Polaroid's knowledge included not only a strong understanding of silver halide chemistry, but also a foundation in optics and electronics. For instance, Polaroid spent over $2 million on the development of the eyepiece for the SX-70 camera in the mid-1970s. The firm also used sonar technology to add an autofocus feature to some of its cameras.

Manufacturing was another of Polaroid's strengths. While manufacturing of both cameras and film was originally subcontracted, at the end of the 1960s Land decided to bring manufacturing in-house. For this purpose, both a camera manufacturing plant and a color negative plant were built. The evolution of these plants over time resulted in two distinct manufacturing capabilities: one in precision camera assembly and another in thin film coating.

Finally, the firm had strong distribution through mass market retailers such as K-Mart and Wal-Mart. This innovative use of channels contributed to Polaroid's success. By avoiding direct competition with traditional cameras, which were sold primarily through specialized camera stores, Polaroid was able to establish a strong presence without inciting a competitive response.

## Beliefs: 1980

Land was a strong character, notorious for his autocratic manner and strong control of Polaroid as well as his absolute commitment to both science and instant photography (McElheny, 1998). His imprint can be codified in a number of beliefs that dominated the senior management team at the end of this period.

Polaroid was clearly a technology-driven, not market-driven company. Land considered science to be an instrument for the development of products that satisfy deep human needs–needs that could not be understood through market research. He therefore did not believe in performing market research as an input to product development; Polaroid's technology and products would create a market.

Consistent with this philosophy, Polaroid management firmly believed that success came through long-term, large-scale research projects. This philosophy was summarized by Land in the 1980 Annual Report's Letter to Shareholders, where he wrote, "Do not undertake the program unless the goal is manifestly important and its achievement nearly impossible. Do not do anything that anyone else can do readily." A member of senior management during that time commented in an interview, "What we were good at was major inventions. Large-scale, lengthy projects that other firms would hesitate to tackle." Several projects during this period were exemplary of this belief. For instance, in 1972, the firm announced the SX-70 instant camera after spending half a billion dollars on its development over an 8-year period. The camera was revolutionary in that it was waste free: after exposing the film, it ejected a picture that developed as the customer watched. The one-step SX-70 camera was a huge commercial success and served to reinforce the firm's belief in funding major inventions.

Another firmly held belief of management was that customers valued a physical instant print. For this reason, products such as video camcorders were not considered competition. As Land wrote to shareholders in 1981, "None of the electronic devices which prepare tapes or magnetic records to be viewed in television satisfied the conditions imposed by that early dream [of an instant print]." The success of the Polaroid instant camera was taken as prima facie evidence of this need.

Throughout this period there was also an obsession with matching the quality of traditional 35lmm prints, driven by a belief that customers required "photographic" quality. As the 1982 Annual Report's Letter to Shareholders stated, "Our research and engineering efforts continue to be challenged to bring our amateur systems to a level of performance consistent with the best in photography."

Finally, there was a strong belief in the razor/blade business model. While Polaroid had initially made money on both camera hardware and film in 1965 with the introduction of the "Swinger" model, a decision was made to adopt a razor/blade pricing strategy. The firm dropped prices on cameras in order to stimulate adoption and subsequent demand for film. Film prices and thus margins were then increased. This strategy was extremely successful, and over time a fundamental, commonly held belief developed: Polaroid could not make money on hardware, only software (i.e., film). In one of our interviews, an ex-CEO began his comments with the following:

One of the things that's terribly important, and I think most people understand it but maybe not as fully as they should, is that in the photographic business all the money is in the software, none of it's in the hardware . . . We were good at making hardware but we never made money on it . . . So the fundamental objective in these things was to find ways to advance products but that would be useful for improving the software sales.

## Beyond Instant Photography – Digital Imaging Search: 1981–89

The capabilities and beliefs articulated above had a profound influence on Polaroid's approach to digital imaging. These digital imaging search efforts were led by a new CEO, Bill McCune, who took over for Land in mid-1980. McCune, a Polaroid employee since 1939, had taken over the presidency in 1975 and was a long-time research colleague of Land's.

McCune began by committing substantial investment dollars to digital imaging technologies. An electronic imaging group was formed in 1981, and as part of this effort work began on a microelectronics laboratory. The microelectronics laboratory opened up in 1986 after a capital investment of about $30 million, and with an operating budget of about $10 million/year. By 1989, 42 percent of R&D dollars were devoted to exploring a broad range of digital imaging technologies. A 1981 strategic planning document identifies the following technological areas for exploration: microelectronics, IC design, advanced optical design, image processing, software design, PC board design, surface mount assembly, CAD/CAM/FEA design, and fiber optics.

While peripherally related to prior technical capabilities (e.g., to knowledge of electronics for instant cameras), these technologies primarily covered new scientific ground for Polaroid. For instance, about 90 percent of the employees in the microelectronics lab were newly hired. Developing radically new technical capability, however, was quite consistent with Polaroid's belief in the primacy of technology. As ex-CEO McCune stated in one of our interviews, "If you have good technical people you shouldn't be afraid of going into whole new technical areas." Similarly, one of the individuals involved in electronic imaging development commented, "We compared ourselves to Bell Labs. Our orientation was 'technical challenge – we can do it.' "

The Electronic Imaging group's exploratory efforts were guided by a desire to eventually develop an instant digital camera/printer product termed "PIF" for Printer In the Field. This product concept combined electronic semiconductor (CCD) sensors for image capture, software for image enhancement, and instant film for image output. As the 1984 Annual Report's Letter to shareholders stated, "We believe that there is considerable potential in developing new hybrid imaging systems that combine instant photography and electronics." This work culminated in a 1990 patent (U.S. 4,937,676) for an "electronic camera system with detachable printer."

The PIF concept built on both Polaroid's prior capabilities and beliefs. Since the output was to be on instant film, it leveraged the firm's strong film-manufacturing capabilities. It was also, however, consistent with the firmly held belief in a razor/blade model. Since the digital camera was bundled with instant film output, there was a clear consumable/software piece of the product. In addition, the product was consistent with the belief that consumers valued an instant physical print. Rather than provide customers with the capability to view images on something like an LED screen, they were provided with an immediate print.

The second major area of digital imaging investment during this period was in a medical system called Helios. Helios used a high-energy laser to expose a dry film material. It was targeted at radiologists as a higher-resolution substitute for X-rays. Like the PIF concept, the development of Helios was influenced by both prior capabilities and beliefs. Although the media was not instant film, its development still leveraged Polaroid's chemical knowledge base. In addition, manufacturing of the Helios media was quite consistent with the thin film coating capabilities utilized in the manufacture of instant film.

The Helios business model was also consistent with the belief in the razor/blade model used in instant imaging. The majority of the profit stream was to come from the sale of high-margin media following the sale of the hardware. In commenting on the broad support for Helios, one manager in the electronic imaging area told us, "[Helios] was not, in their [senior management] minds . . . an electronic imaging thing. It had an electronic front end, but it's a film product and you make the money on the film. So it fell into the conventional wisdom. This is why it was always well funded and well taken care of." A member of senior management at the time confirmed this perspective commenting, "I haven't found many people that can make a buck outside of the consumable area . . . and so I think that Helios was part of that same business model. It fit comfortably into it." Helios also fit the belief in large-scale invention. In reflecting on the large investments made in Helios, a senior manager said, "The technology . . . was too costly. It took us too long . . . but it did miracles . . . We were three years late, and we never got the hardware costs in line. But by God, we tried to bite off the whole world . . . new media, new lasers, new this, new that. And that goes back to doing the impossible."

In addition to working on PIF and Helios, a small number of electronic imaging products were developed and shipped during this period. A series of image recorders was sold, starting in 1983. These machines were used to print images from computer or video input onto instant film, slides or transparencies. Targeted at specialized vertical markets such as graphic arts, these machines were never sold in large quantities. These products were once again building on existing knowledge of chemistry for the output media, although the electronic front-end was clearly based on newly acquired knowledge. The potential for an ongoing stream of media sales also made these products consistent with the razor/blade business model.

While the beliefs of senior management clearly influenced search activities that did take place, they also had a direct influence on activities that did not take place. In particular, there were three important areas of capability that Polaroid did not invest in: low-cost electronics manufacturing capability, rapid product development capability, and new marketing and sales capability.

In order to compete successfully in the hardware arena using a business model different from the traditional razor/blade approach. Polaroid would have to have developed low-cost electronics manufacturing capability and rapid product development capability – two areas in which Polaroid was particularly weak. Strong, low-cost electronics manufacturing capability would have been fundamental to increasing the typically smaller margins in the hardware business. At the same time, fast product development capability would have been necessary to permit the timely introduction of innovative products in a market where product life cycles were measured in months, as opposed to the years Polaroid was accustomed to for its instant imaging products. Polaroid's weakness in product development was characterized by one digital imaging manager as follows: "Polaroid didn't have a sense of the distinction between research and product development. It was all mixed up. Many people were totally oblivious to what it means to get a product really developed and make it ready for the market place." Although it is unclear whether Polaroid could have been successful at developing either of these capabilities, senior management's belief in the razor/blade business model and their resistance to supporting activities that were not fully consistent with this view precluded any investment in them.

Senior management beliefs also influenced the evolution of marketing capability. Consistent with the belief that technology was dominant, Polaroid's top management viewed the transition to digital imaging through a technology-focused filter. Digital imaging was therefore viewed primarily as a technological, not a market shift, with the majority of digital imaging investment directed towards the development of new technical capabilities. As a consequence, the firm never invested in developing any sales or marketing capability specific to digital imaging. For instance, rather than establish new distribution channels, the existing sales force was chartered with selling electronic imaging products. This approach was taken despite the protests of those directly involved in digital imaging product development who were aware of the profound market differences between instant and digital imaging. As one member of the electronic imaging group in the mid-1980s told us, "We were not really happy about it, but there was not much else we could do."

### Resulting capabilities and beliefs: 1990

The actions taken from 1980 to 1989 were influenced by prior capabilities and beliefs, but also resulted in a gradual shift in those same capabilities and beliefs. By the end of 1989 Polaroid had not only continued to evolve its expertise in technologies related to traditional instant photography, but also the firm had developed leading-edge technical capability in a number of areas related to digital imaging. Whereas the percentage of the firm's patents related to electronics between 1976 and 1980 was only 6 percent, between 1986 and 1990 that had increased to 28 percent.

Polaroid's image sensor technology was particularly strong with a number of clear advantages over competing sensors. By producing a higher-quality raw input file, Polaroid's sensors were able to generate a resolution of 1.9 million pixels when the majority of the competition had sensors that generated only 480,000 pixels. Polaroid also held a patent on the ability to use rectangular rather than square pixels. This technology improved color recovery. Finally, whereas most compression algorithms resulted in loss of information and thus a decrease in image quality, Polaroid had developed proprietary lossless compression algorithms. Polaroid was therefore well positioned by 1989 to develop a leading-edge digital camera.

During this time period the composition of the senior management team remained relatively unchanged. In 1986 McCune stepped down as president and CEO (although he remained chairman) but his successor, MacAllister Booth, had been with Polaroid since 1958 and was a long-time member of senior management. In addition, seven of the nine officers on the Management Executive Committee in 1989 had been members in 1980. It is not surprising, therefore, that the overall beliefs of senior management remained relatively static during this period.

In particular, the belief in the razor/blade business model remained firmly ensconced. Clearly, this business model was still appropriate for the traditional instant photography business. It was also continuing to be applied to digital imaging. An employee who joined the firm's electronic imaging group in 1989 commented on what he found: "What's the business model? It's the razor/blade . . . so we make money with the film. They [senior management] wanted to duplicate that in the electronic domain. This idea was pervasive. It was an idea they could easily relate to because it was continuing the instant photography business model. Right?"

There was also still a strong sense that customers wanted instant prints. The 1985 Letter to Shareholders states, "As electronic imaging becomes more prevalent, there remains a basic human need for a permanent visual record." Similarly, an employee who joined the firm's electronic imaging area in 1990 commented, "another truth [I encountered] was that people really value an instant print. This was also an ontological truth."

Finally, there was still a strong emphasis on matching the quality of 35mm cameras, in both the instant and digital imaging domains. A number of new films for instant cameras were announced in the 1980s, including new high-contrast and high-speed films. The electronic imaging group was also working on developing a mega-pixel sensor that would enable a photographic-quality image to be produced from a digital camera. As one employee in the electronic imaging area commented, "Polaroid was always stung by the assessment that instant photography was really cool, too bad the quality stunk . . . the entire motivation as near as I could detect for the investments that they put into sensor technology and so on was to counteract the 35mm quality deficit."

The most significant change in senior management's beliefs was a shift away from being a purely technology-driven company. Polaroid faced stagnant growth for the first time in the 1980s with waning demand in the traditional instant photography market. After having achieved double digit annual sales growth for 30 years, total sales actually decreased between 1980 and 1985. Faced with this situation, management placed an increased emphasis on marketing, and a formal market research function was established. Market input also became an official part of the product development process. In the 1989 Letter to Shareholders Booth stated, "We have studied the needs of our customers in each market segment and those needs are driving the development of our new products." This statement is in direct contrast to the philosophy articulated by Land.

## Refocusing on Digital Imaging—Search Activities: 1990–98

In 1990, electronic imaging moved up in the corporate hierarchy as part of a major reorganization. Three market-focused divisions – Consumer, Business, and Scientific/ Technical Imaging were formed in addition to a fourth: Electronic Imaging Division. The Electronic Imaging Division was intended to feed products to each of the three market-focused divisions. At the same time, the exploratory investments of the 1980s were curtailed in 1990 when research into fiber optics, solar cells, and disk drives was cut. This decision was made in order to focus research efforts on those technologies directly related to products under development. In addition, in 1993 the Microelectronics Lab was sold to MIT, ending the majority of Polaroid's more basic research in microelectronics.

The composition of the electronic imaging group also changed dramatically after 1990. While a long-time Polaroid employee was initially in charge of the group, the majority of members were new hires with experience in digital imaging and other high-technology industries. Consistent with the new belief in being more market driven, an electronic imaging marketing group, comprised entirely of new hires, was established. This group was given the charter to develop a digital camera product concept. Once this concept was defined, a new hire was put in charge of the overall development project. And in 1994 another outsider was brought in to head up the entire group. This individual brought in yet more outsiders, assigning them to key strategic positions within the electronic imaging group.

Clearly, these new individuals, with no prior Polaroid experience, had a different perspective from that of senior management. The digital camera product concept developed by the group was therefore quite different from the prior PIF concept. While this digital camera could eventually be bundled with a Polaroid instant film printer, the initial concept included just a high-resolution camera, targeted at professionals in industries such as real estate that had a need for "instant verification," not necessarily an instant print. Given Polaroid's leading position in sensor technology development, the marketing group felt that Polaroid could offer a significant price/performance advantage over the competition. By 1992, there was a working prototype of the camera.

One can best characterize the period from 1990 to 1996 as one of cognitive dissonance between senior management and the newly hired members of the Electronic Imaging Division. This clash was driven by fundamentally different beliefs. First, there was disagreement about the appropriate business model for digital imaging. One of the newly hired individuals described to us the ongoing dialogue with senior management as follows:

> The catch [to our product concept] was that you had to be in the hardware business to make money. "How could you say that? Where's the film? There's no film?" So what we had was a constant fight with the senior executive management in Polaroid for five years . . . We constantly challenged the notion of the current business model, the core business, as being old, antiquated and unable to go forward . . . What was fascinating to me was that these guys used to turn their noses up at 38 percent margins . . . But that was their big argument, "Why 38 percent? I can get 70 percent on film. Why do I want to do this?"

Senior management, on the other hand, felt that the electronic imaging group did not understand the limitations of Polaroid's manufacturing and product development capabilities. As discussed earlier, given the strong belief in the razor/blade model, Polaroid had not invested in developing the manufacturing capability necessary to make money on "razors." In addition, the belief in large-scale projects with lengthy development cycles, had precluded investment in fast product development capability. Management did not, therefore, feel comfortable competing with firms that possessed these capabilities. As one senior manager noted, "We're not just going to be up against Kodak, Fuji, etc. We're going to be up against 30 consumer electronic companies – the Sonys, Toshibas, Hitachis, the Intels, etc. We need to have a unique idea that corresponds to our core capabilities and the way we relate to the marketplace." There was also concern about Polaroid's ability to simultaneously manage very different businesses as voiced by another senior manager: "Can we be a down and dirty manufacturer at the same time we're an innovator over here? Can you have two different philosophies running simultaneously in the company?"

As a result of this ongoing clash between senior management and the Electronic Imaging Division, there were continuous delays in development related to the digital camera, an inability to commit to relationships with potential strategic partners, and ultimately a lengthy delay in the commercialization of a digital camera product. Despite having a prototype in 1992, Polaroid did not announce its PDC-2000 megapixel camera until 1996. By that point in time there were over 40 other firms on the market selling digital cameras. The PDC-2000 received a number of awards for its technical achievement (the *Netguide Magazine* State-of-the-Art Award, *Publish* magazine's Impact Award, and the European Technical Image Press Association's Best Digital Product of 1996), but it did not do well in the market. Although Polaroid was more "market driven" in the sense of using customer needs as an input to development, senior management still did not perceive the need for different sales channels. The Electronic Imaging Division requested separate sales support for the PDC-2000, but was told that they had to use the instant photography sales force. As one frustrated individual commented, "We had products in the $1000 range and these people were used to going to K-Mart and WalMart." In 1997 a follow-on PDC-3000 was announced, after which development activity ceased. By this point in time, the majority of the individuals hired to staff the Electronic Imaging Division in the early 1990s had left Polaroid.

Other activities of the Electronic Imaging Division also encountered senior management resistance throughout the early 1990s. Given the belief in a razor/blade model, one obvious avenue for Polaroid to explore was the development of alternative hardcopy technologies, such as ink jet or thermal dye sublimation. The belief that consumers needed "photographic quality," however, kept senior management from committing to these alternatives. As one member of the Electronic Imaging Division commented, "We had the capability . . . but there was disbelief that ink jet could be near photographic quality. Mathematical models and demos couldn't convince people." A member of senior management explained their reluctance to accept a lower-quality ink-jet output as follows: "I spent an awful lot of my life, [Sr. Manager X] spent almost all of his life – a lot of us . . . [Sr. Manager Y] spent an awful lot of his life focusing on improving the quality of the instant image . . . So that was an every day, all day part of our lives . . . so that can't help but have been indelible in the DNA or something."

The one digital imaging product that received consistent, ongoing support throughout this period was the Helios medical imaging system. In fact, Helios was such a large project, with an annual investment of about $120 million in development (compared to $30–$40 million for the Electronic Imaging Division), that it was not organized as part of the Electronic Imaging Division, but was a separate group. As discussed earlier, Helios continued to receive such strong support because it was consistent with both Polaroid's capabilities and the beliefs of senior management. In addition a spin-off of the Helios technology, dry-output film for the graphic arts, also received support for the same reasons. Helios finally reached the market in 1993 after almost 10 years of development effort. Unfortunately, despite its technical achievement, Helios was not successful in the market. This failure was attributed to a number of factors including the lack of strength in distribution as well as misreading of the film size required by radiologists. Digital imaging losses of $180 million in 1994 and $190 million in 1995 were primarily attributed to Helios. In 1996 the Helios division was sold to Sterling Diagnostic, although Polaroid still provides the film and lasers.

The sale of the Helios group was just part of an overall decrease in commitment to internal development of digital imaging technologies. In 1996 a new CEO, Gary DiCamillo, succeeded MacAllister Booth. DiCamillo was the first outsider to hold this position, and he brought with him a new top management team. Of 25 directors listed in the 1998 annual Report, 15 had joined Polaroid after DiCamillo's arrival. With a background in consumer marketing, DiCamillo decreased the focus on technology even more. Soon after arriving at Polaroid he commented, "We're not in the business to get the most patents. We're not in the business to write the most research papers. And we're not in the business to see how many inventions we can come up with" (Convey, 1996). Consistent with this approach, research and development expenses were cut from $165.5 million in 1995 to $116.3 million in 1996. Not surprisingly, development of Polaroid's next-generation digital camera, the PDC-300 announced in 1997, was totally outsourced.

In conjunction with the decreased emphasis on technology, DiCamillo and his team placed renewed emphasis on marketing in both the instant photography and digital imaging domains. While the amount of money allocated to R&D decreased, the amount spent on advertising increased slightly from $124.1 million in 1995 to $134.6 million in 1996. Polaroid's marketing department created a new category called "photoplay," with products such as the Barbie instant camera introduced in 1998.

### Resulting capabilities and beliefs: 1998

The series of digital imaging disappointments combined with a new top management team resulted in the evolution of capabilities and beliefs. By 1998 Polaroid's earlier strength in digital imaging technologies had significantly diminished. The firm had about 50 internal employees devoted to digital imaging research as opposed to a high of about 300 in 1992. Consistent with this decrease, the belief in the value of large-scale invention had disappeared. Instead Polaroid was focused on rapid incremental product development. "We have announced our intention of becoming a new products company . . . to bring 20 to 40 new products to market each year," DiCamillo stated in the 1998 Annual Report. The transition from a technology-driven to a market-driven company also seemed complete with the "photoplay" category taking on increased strategic importance.

Some parts of the senior management belief system, however, were surprisingly similar. DiCamillo supported the razor/blade business model, stating in a 1997 interview, "In the digital world we believe that hard copy is required . . . Unless there is a consumable component, the business model falls apart. So we have to focus on what's consumable and what value-added we can provide that's unique" (Rosenbloom, 1997: 16). His commitment to photographic quality and therefore conventional film was also quite strong. "What are we? What are we good at? We're pretty good at creating images instantly. Not very many companies can do that . . . there's both a time and a skill required to take conventional film and make it look good. Substitute technology such as ink jet or thermal technologies are interesting, but they're not here yet" (Rosenbloom, 1997: 13).

Clearly the digital imaging market is still evolving, and it is uncertain what Polaroid's ultimate position will be. We believe it is fair to say, however, that having invested in and developed such strong technical capability in digital imaging in the 1980s it is disappointing that Polaroid was unable to capitalize on its technical position in the marketplace. In addition, despite its early technological lead, Polaroid is ultimately left with quite limited technical strength in this emerging market.

## Discussion and Conclusions

Our goal in this paper was to explore the relationship among capabilities, cognition, and inertia. While prior work in the evolutionary tradition has shown that failures to adapt to radical technological discontinuities often stem from the local nature of learning processes and, consequently, from the relative rigidity of organizational routines (Teece et al., 1994), little emphasis has been devoted, at least in this tradition, to understanding the role of managerial cognition in driving the dynamics of capabilities. Through the Polaroid story, we clearly demonstrate that search processes in a new learning environment are deeply interconnected to the way managers model the new problem space and develop strategic prescriptions premised on this view of the world.

From a strictly evolutionary point of view, one would expect Polaroid to have had difficulty developing new, unrelated digital imaging technologies. Instead, we find that the firm had little problem overcoming the path dependencies normally associated with knowledge evolution. Indeed, thanks to the early investments in electronic technologies, Polaroid was able to develop leading-edge capabilities in a broad array of technological areas related to digital imaging. For instance, by the time the market for digital cameras started to take off in the early 1990s Polaroid had a working prototype of a high-resolution, mega-pixel digital camera that was a step function improvement in price/performance relative to other products in the market. Similarly, Helios, a medical imaging system aimed at replacing X-ray technologies, although a commercial failure, was a major technological achievement. Despite these capabilities, Polaroid failed to adapt to the radical changes that had occurred in the imaging competitive landscape. Understanding this paradoxical behavior requires us to go beyond explanations focusing on the localness of learning processes and on the inertia of a firm's competencies.

We argue that only by considering the role of cognition and its implication in terms of the learning dynamics of the organization can one gain insights into this apparent inconsistency. As previously documented, a number of strong beliefs were deeply diffused in the top management of the company, and remained substantially unaltered during its entire history. During the Land era, the company was characterized by a solid belief in the primacy of technology, according to which commercial success could only come through major research projects. There is little doubt that Polaroid's early exploration of the electronic domain, the basis for its state-of-the-art technological competencies in digital imaging, was legitimated by this view of the world. Despite the absence of a market for digital imaging applications, during the 1980s the company kept allocating considerable resources to this technological trajectory. For at least a decade, resource allocation in digital imaging was totally disjointed from any notion of performance. To put it simply, Polaroid did not experience major difficulties searching in a radically new technological trajectory and developing new technological competencies, largely due to the consistency of this purely exploratory behavior with the belief in the primacy of technology.

A second commonly held belief was that Polaroid could not make money on the hardware, but only on consumables, i.e., the razor/blade model. This business model, successfully developed and adopted in the instant imaging business, was applied to the company's activities in digital imaging, and we believe was a main source of Polaroid's inertia. At the beginning of the 1990s, when a market for digital imaging applications slowly started to emerge, senior managers strongly discouraged search and development efforts that were not consistent with the traditional business model, despite ongoing efforts from newly hired members of the Electronic Imaging Division to convince them otherwise. Digital camera development efforts, for instance, were stalled given the inconsistency with a razor/blade business model. Similarly, Polaroid never attempted to develop the manufacturing and product development capabilities that would have been key had Polaroid decided to compete in digital imaging with a nonrazor/blade business model (e.g., as a low-cost/high-quantity hardware producer). In contrast, products such as Helios that were consistent with this view of the world received unconditional support on the part of senior managers.

In short, if on the one hand Polaroid's beliefs allowed the company to develop the necessary technological knowledge for competing in digital imaging, they became a powerful source of inertia when decisions were taken on how to further develop such knowledge in specific products and activities. This evidence points to the deep interrelationships between a manager's understanding of the world and the accumulation of organizational competencies. Although much current theorizing on the dynamics of capabilities emphasizes the inertial effects of the path dependencies associated with learning processes, we believe that understanding how capabilities evolve cannot neglect the role of managerial cognitive representations, especially in constraining and directing learning efforts. Importantly, emphasizing cognitive elements in the explanation of the genesis and evolution of capabilities raises both positive and normative issues that traditional explanations in the evolutionary realm largely overlook.

A particularly important issue is the question of how beliefs evolve within organizations. Can the top management team, for instance, simultaneously manage businesses with different dominant logics (Prahalad and Bettis, 1986)? In the Polaroid case, we find that senior management was able to develop new beliefs for digital imaging only as long as those beliefs were consistent with the instant photography business. For instance, they recognized the importance of being more market driven in both the instant photography and digital imaging domains. In contrast, they found it difficult to endorse a nonrazor/blade business model for digital imaging given that it was still the prevalent model for the instant photography business. In such situations Tushman and O'Reilly (1996) have found that successful organizations are "ambidextrous," simultaneously embracing multiple contradictory elements through an organizational architecture that combines a mix of autonomy and central control.

Turnover in the top management team is also an important driver of change. In particular, changes in both the CEO and executive team have been found to initiate discontinuous organizational change (Tushman and Rosenkopf, 1996). At Polaroid, the arrival of an outsider CEO, DiCamillo, combined with a new top management team, significantly changed elements of the belief system. The shift from lengthy, large-scale, technology-driven invention to rapid, incremental, market-driven product development is epitomized by Polaroid's new focus on products for the "photoplay" market. In rapidly changing environments, however, ongoing turnover of top management teams is likely to be impractical. In these situations, the development of "deframing" skills, the ability to question current strategic beliefs in an ongoing way, becomes increasingly important (Dunbar, Garud, and Raghuram, 1996).

These arguments suggest that a crucial challenge for organizations facing radical technological discontinuities is the ability to distinguish changes that require only the development of new technological capabilities from changes that also require the adoption of different strategic beliefs. For Polaroid, digital imaging represented an instance of the latter type of change: success in this new competitive landscape required fundamentally different strategic beliefs as articulated at the time by individuals in the digital imaging group. However, radical technological discontinuities do not always provoke mutations in the bases of competition. In fact, in some cases enduring belief systems can be a source of competitive strength (Collins and Porras, 1994; Porac and Rosa, 1996). In this situation, cognitive change can be highly dysfunctional for the organization, since strategic reorientations are costly and associated with high mortality rates (Tushman and Romanelli, 1985; Amburgey, Kelly, and Barnett, 1993; Sastry, 1997). In particular, changes in the basic strategic beliefs of a firm typically have short-term disruptive effects on organizational practices and routines (Gavetti and Levinthal, 2000). When environmental change does not render current strategic beliefs obsolete, the net effect of their modification is hardly positive for the organization.

A second issue that clearly emerges in this research is the role of hierarchy in cognition. Polaroid's difficulties in adapting to digital imaging were mainly determined by the cognitive inertia of its corporate executives. As we have documented, managers directly involved with digital imaging developed a highly adaptive representation of the emerging competitive landscape. They abandoned Polaroid's "software-oriented" view and adopted a "hardware-oriented" model that they were not free to put into practice. We speculate that the cognitive dissonance between senior management and digital imaging managers may have been exacerbated by the difference in signals that the two groups were receiving about the market. This evidence is suggestive not only of the presence of profound cognitive differences across hierarchical level, but also that there might be structural reasons underlying differences in cognitive adaptability across hierarchical levels (Gavetti, 1999).

Finally, this work raises important questions regarding the origins of both capability and cognition. The vast majority of research in each of these areas has focused on the capabilities and cognition of established firms, with limited understanding of their historical development. In the case of Polaroid it appears that Edwin Land, the founder, had a profound and lasting influence on the development of both capabilities and cognition. However, given that that not all founders are as memorable as Land, one might ask what other initial factors are important. Work on organizational imprinting has demonstrated that a broad range of environmental conditions at organizational founding (e.g., the social, economic, and competitive environments) have a lasting influence on organizational structure and culture (e.g., Stinchcombe, 1965; Kimberly, 1975; Boeker, 1988). How do these same environmental factors affect capabilities and cognition? By focusing future research efforts on start-up firms, in addition to established firms, we believe we can start to address these questions and significantly enrich our knowledge of both the origins and the evolution of firm capabilities and cognition.

## Acknowledgements

We are grateful to Hank Chesbrough, Connie Helfat, Dan Levinthal, Anjali Sastry, Mike Tushman, Steven Usselman, and the participants in the CCC/Tuck Conference on the Evolution of Capabilities for feedback on earlier versions of this paper. Financial support from the Huntsman and Reginald H. Jones Centers at the Wharton School is gratefully acknowledged.

## Notes

1   Since we are focusing on the distinction between capabilities and cognition, we use the term "capabilities" broadly to represent a number of noncognitive factors including capabilities, competencies, assets, and resources.

2   Digital imaging is the capture, manipulation, storage, transmission, and output of an image using digital technology. Digital imaging is competence destroying for analog photography firms in that it requires the mastery of new scientific domains such as semiconductors/electronics as well as the development of different distribution channels and new customer relationships. (For more detail on the technologies involved in digital imaging see Rosenbloom, 1997.) There is also a great deal of uncertainty about the digital imaging competitive landscape with firms from the photography, consumer electronics, computer and graphic arts industries all converging on the industry. While the first digital cameras arrived on the market in the late 1980s, only recently has consumer demand for digital imaging skyrocketed. As of the end of 1998 there were over 70 firms that had entered the digital camera market with over 250 models available. The industry is growing rapidly, and the worldwide digital camera market is expected to reach $10 billion by the year 2000 (*Future Image Report*, 1997).

3   After a lengthy court battle, in 1991 Polaroid was awarded $924.5 million in damages from Kodak.

# References

Aldenderfer, M. S. and Blashfield, R. K. 1984. *Cluster Analysis.* Sage: Beverly Hills, CA.

Amburgey, T., Kelly, D., and Barnett, W. 1993. Resetting the clock: the dynamics of organizational change and failure. *Administrative Science Quarterly* 38(1): 51–73.

Arrow, K. J. 1974. *The Limits of Organization,* Norton: New York.

Baron, J. M., Hannan, M. T., and Burton, M. D. 1999. Building the iron cage: determinants of managerial intensity in the early years of organizations. *American Sociological Review* 64: 527–547.

Barr, P. S., Stimpert, J. L., and Huff, A. S. 1992. Cognitive change, strategic action, and organizational renewal. *Strategic Management Journal,* Summer Special Issue 13: 15–36.

Boeker, W. 1988. Organizational origins: entrepreneurial and environmental imprinting at the time of founding. In *Ecological Models of Organizations,* Carroll, G. (ed.). Ballinger: Cambridge, MA; 33–51.

Brown, S. L. and Eisenhardt, K. M. 1998. *Competing on the Edge: Strategy as Structured Chaos.* Harvard Business School Press: Boston, MA.

Christensen, C. 1997. *The Innovator's Dilemma.* Harvard Business School Press: Boston, MA.

Collins, J. C. and Porras, J. I. 1994. *Built to Last: Successful Habits of Visionary Companies.* HarperCollins: New York.

Convey, E. 1996. Polaroid chief charting new course for R&D. *The Boston Herald* 26 March: 32.

Cooper, A. C. and Schendel, D. 1976. Strategic responses to technological threats. *Business Horizons.* 61–69.

Dosi, G. 1982. Technological paradigms and technological trajectories. *Research Policy* 11(3): 147–162.

Dunbar, R. L. M., Garud, R., and Raghuram, S. 1996. A frame for deframing in strategic analysis. *Journal of Management Inquiry* 5(1): 23–34.

*Future Image Report.* 1997. Gerard, A. (ed.). Future Image. Inc: San Mateo, CA.

Garud, R. and Rappa, M. 1994. A socio-cognitive model of technology evolution: the case of cochlear implants. *Organization Science* 5(3): 344–362.

Gavetti, G. 1999. Cognition, capabilities and corporate strategy making. Working paper, The Wharton School.

Gavetti, G. and Levinthal, D. 2000. Looking forward and looking backward: cognitive and experiential search. *Administrative Science Quarterly* 45: 113–137.

Glaser, B. G. and Strauss, A. L. 1967. *The Discovery of Grounded Theory,* Aldine: Chicago, IL.

Hambrick, D. C. and Mason, P. 1984. Upper echelons: the organization as a reflection of its top managers. *Academy of Management Review* 9: 193–206.

Helfat, C. E. 1997. Know-how asset complementarity and dynamic capability accumulation: the case of R&D. *Strategic Management Journal* 18(5): 339–360.

Henderson, R. M. and Clark, K. B. 1990. Architectural innovation: the reconfiguration of existing product technologies and the failure of established firms. *Administrative Science Quarterly* 35: 9–30.

Kiesler, S. and Sproull, L. 1982. Managerial response to changing environments: perspectives on problem sensing from social cognition. *Administrative Science Quarterly* 27: 548–570.

Kimberly, J. 1975. Environmental constraints and organizational structure: a comparative analysis of rehabilitation organizations. *Administrative Science Quarterly* 20(1): 1–9.

Leonard–Barton, D. 1992. Core capabilities and core rigidities: a paradox in managing new product development. *Strategic Management Journal,* Summer Special Issue 13: 111–126.

Levitt, B. and March, J. G. 1988. Organizational learning. *Annual Review of Sociology* 14: 319–340.

Majumdar, B. A. 1982. *Innovations. Product Developments and Technology Transfers: An Empirical Study of Dynamic Competitive Advantage. The Case of Electronic Calculators.* University Press of America: Washington, DC.

March, J. and Simon, H. 1958. *Organizations.* Wiley: New York.

McElheny, V. 1998. *Insisting on the Impossible: The Life of Edwin Land.* Perseus: Reading, MA.

Miles, M. B. and Huberman, A. M. 1994. *Qualitative Data Analysis: An Expanded Sourcebook.* 2nd edn, Sage: Thousand Oaks, CA.

Mintzberg, H. 1979. *The Structuring of Organizations.* Prentice-Hall: Englewood Cliffs, NJ.

Mitchell, W. 1989. Whether and when? Probability and timing of incumbents' entry into emerging industrial subfields. *Administrative Science Quarterly* 34: 208–234.

Nelson, R. and Winter, S. 1982. *An Evolutionary Theory of the Firm.* Harvard University Press: Cambridge, MA.

Peteraf, M. and Shanley, M. 1997. Getting to know you: a theory of strategic group identity. *Strategic Management Journal,* Summer Special Issue 18: 165–186.

Porac, J. and Rosa, J. A. 1996. In praise of managerial narrow-mindedness. *Journal of Management Inquiry* 5(1): 35–42.

Porac, J., Thomas, H., Wilson, R., Paton, D., and Kanfer, A. 1995. Rivalry and the industry model of Scottish knitwear producers. *Administrative Science Quarterly* 40: 203–227.

Prahalad, C. K. and Bettis, R. A. 1986. The dominant logic: a new linkage between diversity and performance. *Strategic Management Journal* 7(6): 485–501.

Reger, R. K. and Huff, A. S. 1993. Strategic groups: a cognitive perspective. *Strategic Management Journal* 14(2): 103–123.

Rosenbloom, R. 1997. Polaroid Corporation: digital imaging technology in 1997. Harvard Business School Case 9-798-013.

Sastry, A. 1997. Problems and paradoxes in a model of punctuated organizational change. *Administrative Science Quarterly* 42(2): 237–276.

Simon, H. A. 1955. A behavioral model of rational choice. *Quarterly Journal of Economics* 69: 99–118.

Stinchcombe, A. 1965. Social structure and organizations. In *Handbook of Organizations,* March, J. G. (ed.). Rand McNally: Chicago, IL; 153–193.

Teece, D. 1986. Profiting from technological innovation: implications for integration, collaboration, licensing and public policy. *Research Policy* 15: 285–305.

Teece, D. J. 1988. Technological change and the nature of the firm. In *Technical Change and Economic Theory,* Dosi, G., Freeman, C., Nelson, R., Silverberg, G., and Soete, L. (eds). Pinter Publisher: London; 256–281.

Teece, D. J., Pisano, G., and Shuen, A. 1997. Dynamic capabilities and strategic management. *Strategic Management Journal* 18(7): 509–553.

Teece, D. J., Rumelt, R., Dosi, G., and Winter, S. 1994. Understanding corporate coherence. *Journal of Economic Behavior and Organization* 23: 1–30.

Tripsas, M. 1997. Unraveling the process of creative destruction: complementary assets and incumbent survival in the typesetter industry. *Strategic Management Journal,* Summer Special Issue 18: 119–142.

Tushman, M. L. and Anderson, P. 1986. Technological discontinuities and organizational environments. *Administrative Science Quarterly* 31: 439–465.

Tushman, M. L. and O'Reilly, C. A. 1996. Ambidextrous organizations: managing evolutionary and revolutionary change. *California Management Review* 38(4): 8–30.

Tushman, M. L. and Romanelli, E. 1985. Organizational evolution: a metamorphosis model of convergence and reorientation. In *Research in Organizational Behavior,* Cummings, L. L., and Staw, B. M. (eds.). Vol. 7: JAI Press: Greenwich, CT; 171–222.

Tushman, M. L. and Rosenkopf, L. 1996. Executive succession, strategic reorientation and performance growth: a longitudinal study in the U.S. cement industry. *Management Science* 42(7): 939–953.

Utterback, J. 1994. *Mastering the Dynamics of Innovation.* Harvard University Press: Cambridge, MA.

Yin, R. K. 1984. *Case Study Research: Design and Methods.* Sage: Beverly Hills CA.

Zyglidopoulos, S. 1999. Initial environmental conditions and technological change. *Journal of Management Studies* 36(2): 241–262.

# CHAPTER TWENTY-FOUR

# Leadership and Cognition: Or, What Could Those Folks at the Top Have Been Thinking?
## Commentary on Chapters by Rosenbloom and Tripsas and Gavetti

## Steven W. Usselman

These two fine studies of corporate adaptation bear much in common. Each confronts a situation in which a respected firm operating within a solid established niche responded to the challenge of electronics. Each identifies a set of core capabilities residing within the firm at the start and proceeds to examine how those capabilities facilitated or impeded the transition to electronics. In this, the two chapters resemble the sorts of work we have come to expect from scholars interested in corporate response to technological change.

What distinguishes these papers from many others is their insistence upon moving beyond capabilities and considering more ephemeral matters. Tripsas and Gavetti make this clear from the start. They expressly set out to meld an analysis of Polaroid's capabilities with a discussion of its "cognition." As it turns out, this endeavor brings us pretty quickly to what I would term the "habits of mind" of upper management. Rosenbloom keeps his cards closer to his chest, but in the end he leaves us pondering much the same territory. The real key to the NCR story, he suggests, may lie in the struggles of its top management to see past established ways of thinking about the firm. Such an ability to envision new departures appears to be the key component in what Rosenbloom refers to as "leadership."

In venturing into these murky waters, these authors confront a major challenge for those of us who approach the subject of corporate change through an evolutionary framework. To the extent evolutionary thinking asks us to conceive of firms as highly structured routines embedded deeply within organizations, it directs our focus away from matters of strategy devised by a cadre of top managers who at least in theory operate at some remove from those routines. In its most rigid form, the evolutionary model situates the dynamic elements outside the firm, in the realm of technology and in the market. Though firms may have incorporated some capacity to learn into their routines, such abilities are circumscribed and confined. The market selects from a pool of firms whose capabilities are largely fixed.

One trouble with this way of thinking is that it does not easily account for firms that demonstrate an ability to negotiate significant transitions across time. Nor does it leave much room for activities carried out by those within firms, typically top management, who seek consciously to reorient activities. The authors of these papers, while respectful of the evolutionary approach, accept that firms at least have the potential to change quite significantly. Thus Rosenbloom speaks of "dynamic capabilities" and portrays NCR as an adaptive survivor, while Tripsas and Gavetti credit Polaroid with developing new capabilities that led to significant technological triumphs in the field of digital imaging. In assessing the dynamics occurring within these firms, moreover, the authors take seriously the thinking and behavior of upper-level management.

Some defenders of the evolutionary model may question these assumptions, especially in light of the decidedly mixed performance of the firms under study. I prefer to take a different tack. Sympathetic to their assumptions, to their research agenda, and to their interpretations in these cases, I would press the authors about how we might pursue the subject of leadership and cognition more rigorously. Tripsas and Gavetti offer a useful template, one which has the advantage of joining cognition with capabilities. But I wonder if they might not wish to tell us not just what management believed, but also how they came to believe it (or, perhaps more appropriately in this case, why they persisted in believing it). We have some sense of this, of course. Managers inherited much from the founder, and the persistently high returns from sales of film reinforced established thinking. Still, a study of cognition ultimately calls for closer attention to the flow of information into and within the firm. Cognition involves the gathering and dissemination of information, tasks which demand that managers read signals from many sources and manipulate symbols effectively. How did management at Polaroid go about this? What sources of information did they tap? Who got heard, and why? How might their routines of gathering and disseminating information have served to perpetuate the past?

Rosenbloom's account of NCR offers some insights along these lines. He is sensitive, for instance, to the possible influence of lunchtime habits. We sense that marketing structures closed NCR off from valuable input from customers. The geographic isolation of the computer development team appears to have impeded efforts to turn managerial rhetoric about systems into reality. Such observations point toward the importance of information flows. Can we pursue them further? Can we, for instance, get a better sense of how managers of the various product divisions interacted with one another and with top management? This would seem central to comprehending why management conveyed the goal of systems more effectively to stockholders through annual reports than it did internally to its own management.

By focusing more closely on matters of process and structure in communications, those who believe concepts such as leadership and cognition deserve a place in explaining corporate change can only grow more persuasive. Such an approach moves beyond the recollections of individual managers at specific firms and opens the opportunity for meaningful generalization about these elusive but essential features of corporate performance.

# CHAPTER TWENTY-FIVE

# Toward Developing an Organizational Capability of Learning from Mistakes

## Sydney Finkelstein

Every organization makes mistakes. This statement is intuitive, but is also consistent with a broad range of studies in the organizational literatures (e.g., Mintzberg, 1990; Hambrick and D'Aveni, 1988; Cameron, Kim, and Whetton, 1987; Levy and Merry, 1986). There is also an even larger body of literature that focuses on failures, and especially failures driven by external factors (e.g., Hannan and Carroll, 1992; Meyer, 1982). However, in spite of this work, it is rare for researchers to adopt an organizational learning perspective in examinations of corporate mistakes. Such a perspective focuses special attention on the role of management in both making the mistake, and in learning from it. In recent years there has been a renewed interest in studying organizational mistakes, but with few exceptions the development of a learning perspective has lagged (but see Shimuzu, 1999; Levinthal and March, 1993; Sitkin, 1992 for examples of studies that have tried to link learning and mistakes).

The purpose of this brief chapter is to suggest one approach to studying and learning from organizational mistakes. I do so by describing the experiences of Motorola in the cellular phone business. After presenting a mini-case that describes the mistake, I summarize the lessons learned and how Motorola is considering institutionalizing this learning within the organization. As such, the Motorola experience represents one example of an organization that is moving toward developing a capability of learning from its mistakes.

## Motorola and the Cell Phone Business in 1998

### Overview

> It's hard to imagine that 6 or 7 years ago Motorola was one of the most admired companies in the world. Now, you talk about Nokia and Ericsson and how they're eating Motorola's lunch.
> *Steven Goldman, Lehigh University professor and Motorola consultant, 1997[1]*

Motorola was one of America's most admired companies in the early 1990s. Its focus on high-technology markets and gold-plated quality symbolized by the 1988 Baldrige

Award and the company's famous Six-Sigma quality standard commanded respect in the eyes of the competition as well as the general public. As Motorola entered the 1990s with a clear lead in the booming cellular market, it seemed to be very well positioned for years of additional growth.

By the mid-1990s, the cellular telephony market was changing rapidly. The advent of digital technology and the prospects of "cellular for the masses instead of cellular for the classes" took Motorola by surprise, and the company that once seemed infallible was quickly losing market share to nimbler competitors such as Nokia, Ericsson, and Lucent.

## Cellular telephony dominance and six-sigma

> They [Motorola] were firing on all cylinders.
> *Ajay Diwan, Goldman Sachs analyst*[2]

Developed in the Bell Labs in the 1970s, cellular telephony became part of Motorola's high-tech focus in 1982 with the acquisition of Four-Phase Systems for $253 million.[3] The Information Systems Group was thus created, combining complementary product portfolios of Four-Phase (data processing) and Codex Corporation (a data communications equipment maker Motorola also acquired). Motorola's first cellular system, the Dyna-TAC, began commercial operation in 1983.[4]

By the mid-1980s, Motorola's success in cellular telephony prompted an aggressive price-cutting reaction by Japanese manufacturers. In 1986, however, the US commerce department shielded Motorola by declaring eight Japanese competitors guilty of dumping charges, providing Motorola with an additional competitive edge. Motorola thus became the world's top cell phone supplier.[5]

Internally, the overall quality of Motorola's products and operations was made a priority, leading to the adoption of TQM (total quality management) in a time of US manufacturing decline *vis-à-vis* the Japanese. Motorola's employee empowerment drives earned the admiration of analysts and competitors alike. These efforts culminated in 1988, as Motorola was the winner of the first Malcolm Baldridge National Quality Award, given by the US Congress to recognize and inspire the pursuit of quality in American business. In 1992, the company aimed for six-sigma quality, which statistically means less than 3.4 errors per million.

By 1990, Motorola's revenues surpassed $10 billion. Underway was the development of Iridium, a system of cellular communications owned 17.7 per cent by Motorola and based on an array of 66 small satellites in low-Earth orbit, with the goal to reach every point on the globe.[6] At this stage, Motorola dominated 45 per cent of the world cellular phone market as well as 85 per cent of the world's pager market.[7]

Motorola capitalized on the advent of cellular telephony. Initial cellular phone users were hardly price-sensitive; cellular phones were expensive, brick-like analog devices that appealed to businesspeople and professionals whose life depended on the ability to make and receive calls when a phone line was not at hand. In the mid-1980s, cellular phones were practically unknown; by 1996, some 85 million were in use worldwide, together with 90 million pagers and 44 million two-way radios.[8] There was little doubt that Motorola was well positioned in this business. As Robert Galvin Sr said

"We were the unbridled leader in analog devices around the world."[9] From 1992 to 1995, Motorola seemed to prove that even a huge company, if managed correctly, could rack up impressive growth, as revenues increased at an average of 27 percent to $27 billion in 1995, while net income surged 58 per cent a year over the same period, to $1.8 billion.[10]

### The advent of digital mobile telephony: a dramatic market shift

In 1994, as Motorola claimed 60 per cent of the US cellular market, an alternative technology to the incumbent analog cellular began catching the eye of wireless carriers such as Ameritech. The new technology was digital mobile telephony, which would be first available through so-called PCS (personal communications system).

Analog technology transmitted calls via sound waves. Signals were subject to interference, calls were frequently dropped, and it was easy for interlopers to eavesdrop.[11] On the positive side, since analog had been around for some time, area coverage was extensive.[12] Alternatively, PCS would translate calls into digital signals: interference could be programmed out, while security codes would be encrypted. On the negative side, PCS could not roam (search for calling signals) and coverage was simply non-existent as it was a brand new technology.[13]

The powerful underlying economics regarding digital technology would provide a means to support true mass-market subscriber populations for the first time. As a rule of thumb, digital networks could accommodate around ten times more subscribers than their analog counterparts for a given chunk of radio spectrum,[14] due to the easy-to-manipulate (and "compress") characteristics of digital technology. In essence, digital technology would spread fixed costs over a broader user base, making individual use cheaper.

For gear suppliers such as Motorola, such powerful technology economics would mean sailing into unchartered waters. The new consumer profile brought into the picture by digital technology was a type Motorola had limited experience dealing with. Unlike Motorola's usual analog cell client, such as successful businesspeople, digital consumers would be price-sensitive and less functionally and more aesthetically demanding. Additionally, distribution channels for the new, cheaper digital technology would be different from the incumbent ones.

### Focus on Analog Technology

> Forty-three million analog customers can't be wrong.
> *Motorola executive, February 1995*[15]

Motorola's cell phone business was headed by the senior executive who had been responsible for making it a success. In 1995, he believed that what most consumers wanted was a better analog phone, not a digital phone that would have to be bulky because the technology was so new.[16] Such was his power within the organization that the company narrowed its focus to the development of StarTAC, which was a design as small as a cigarette pack, but an analog phone. Such 'smaller and cuter phones' were technological marvels, but they were not digital.[17] Further delaying their entry to the digital arena were in-house analyses based on mathematical models show-ing that phone users would be better off carrying analog than digital equipment.[18] At the same time, Motorola decided to develop the chips necessary for digital cellular in-house instead of outsourcing, which resulted in a two-year effort.

Meanwhile, competitors had taken the digital lead as Motorola launched its own digital in 1997. To complicate matters further, there were three digital standards avail-able domestically: CDMA, TDMA, and GSM. By early 1998, Code Division Multiple Access (CDMA) offered six times the capacity of analog systems and accounted for 50 percent of the US market. Time Division Multiple Access (TDMA), which had three times the capacity, accounted for 25 percent of the market. Finally, Global Standard for Mobile Communications (GSM), with two to three times the analog capacity, claimed 25 percent of the US market and was the technology of choice in Europe and parts of Asia.[19]

Interestingly, Motorola had been aggressively developing digital products by 1995. However, the effort was on just one standard in the US: CDMA. As it turned out, that eliminated Motorola from 50 percent of the US market. Ironically, Motorola had been developing TDMA gear but abandoned it to focus on CDMA. The company, despite being ahead of the competition, dropped TDMA because it did not believe it had strong enough relationships with TDMA carriers to land deals.[20] In other words, Motorola had assumed that the carriers interested in TDMA would turn to alternative gear suppliers, and not Motorola, to develop TDMA equipment. Nevertheless, while Motorola did not introduce a digital cell phone for years, the company was still earn-ing royalties from several patents they held based on digital technologies.

In July 1996, Motorola's growth machine officially stalled. After reporting second-quarter results 22 percent below what analysts were expecting, Motorola sent other high-tech stocks and the entire market into a tailspin.[21] Analysts expected Motorola's domestic mobile telephony market share, including both analog and digital (PCS), to fall dramatically. Worse, it would be very difficult to displace rivals who were granted initial PCS contracts. Like an annuity, incumbent suppliers to carriers were almost assured of the add-on business,[22] because PCS are customized to individual carriers and are bound to high switching costs. (The analogy of mainframe computer suppliers being assured of maintenance contracts fits well.) In 1997, Motorola's share of the fast-growing PCS domestic market segment was 13 per cent, whereas Lucent had a 38 percent share.[23] Overall in the US mobile telephony market, including both analog systems and digital (PCS), Motorola's share peaked at 60 percent in 1994 only to dip to 34 percent in early 1998.[24]

## Motorola's cellular business: an analysis

There are three primary aspects of the Motorola story that provide opportunities for insights on learning from corporate mistakes. First is leadership. Motorola has tradi-tionally operated with a highly decentralized organizational structure. In fact, inter-views with several Motorola executives referred to the culture of "warring tribes" where each business unit would be totally focused on its own needs and would be given substantial autonomy to do so. Given this, the manager who ran the cell phone busi-ness was allowed tremendous autonomy to decide strategy and implement it. This person had built the cell phone business into a market leader, and had made Motorola dominant in analog phones. As a result, he was given free rein and his analysis of the market was above direct challenge. When asked to describe what the problem with the cell phone business was, a top manager at Motorola said, "the word you want to use is arrogance." He was referring to the inability and unwillingness of cell phone business unit managers to consider other perspectives. In analyzing what went wrong at Motorola, senior management repeatedly pointed out how sales people and other individuals with personal contact with customers came back with questions about when digital phones would come on line in the company. Questions were raised at managerial levels as well, but the power of the cell phone business head – derived from past success, personality, internal reputation, and a highly decentralized organizational structure – combined to effectively shut down internal dissent.

The second type of insight that comes from this case relates to strategy and market conditions. Motorola was well aware of the potential of digital phones and in fact was tracking sales of rivals very closely. As owners of some of the key digital technology patents, Motorola even earned royalties from sales of rivals' products, providing excellent information on sales trends. Yet with all this information, the company was slow to enter the market with a digital phone. As a senior Motorola executive admitted, "we improperly judged the pace of change from analog to digital. We were lulled into a situation of digital coming at the pace it did." Strategically, the company had always been an innovator, and in the case of digital they were in a position of strength because of patents and ongoing R&D, but they decided that the market was not yet ready for digital phones.

The final learning point is related to the first two, but provides an additional insight to the slow response of Motorola to changes in the marketplace. Along with a highly decentralized structure comes highly decentralized reward systems. Senior management in the cell phone business had been richly rewarded for their successes in analog, and may well have had a disincentive to risk the makeover to digital. Further, bringing digital online would entail considerable costs that were sure to affect the bottom line of the business unit. So, both the risk of changing from an older, but profitable, product and the real costs associated with such a shift seemed to play a role in the Motorola story. As a senior company executive from corporate noted, "their [business unit managers"] thinking was colored by the upfront costs they would entail by shifting from analog to digital." That there is a downside to a reliance on extensive business unit incentive compensation, particularly when there are major changes in the marketplace, is an interesting counterpoint to the prevailing thinking on reward systems in both academia and practice.

### Toward the development of an organizational capability of learning from mistakes

The Motorola case is of particular interest because of the opportunities it affords to consider how organizations can develop a capability of learning from mistakes. The mistakes at Motorola boil down to a combination of judgement, incentives, and structure.

How can organizations improve the judgement of their senior managers? In some ways, this question is analogous to asking how organization can ensure they have high quality management, since judgement is so central to what managers do. At Motorola, several changes are taking place. They are developing methods of measuring the quality of senior leadership in an attempt to test managerial thinking more precisely. For example, managers from different parts of the organization are forming teams to act as sounding boards for each other. Senior management is taking a more active role in reviewing not just the outcomes of business unit decisions, but the decisions themselves. There is a renewed interest in identifying what "legacy" a manager is leaving behind when s/he moves on in the organization. While the success of such efforts cannot be predetermined, these changes within the company suggest that they are trying to avoid the problem of the all-powerful senior manager who is above review. For changes such as these to become a "capability" of learning from mistakes, internal processes will need to become more established in the organization, perhaps even institutionalized as the way in which the company does business. The same is true for changes in structure and incentives, which at Motorola have proceeded at a much slower pace.

There is a big difference in an analytic sense between studying capabilities and their value on the one hand, and studying how capabilities are developed on the other. The literature in strategy is full of work on the first of these problems (e.g., Barney, 1991; Amit and Schoemaker, 1993). While there are still questions to be answered, we do have some clear notions on how to value capabilities, at least analytically. Much more complicated is how organizations actually develop such capabilities. It is this area of work that is truly in its infancy, but yet may hold the key to understanding which organizations will be successful and which will not. This research on corporate mistakes focuses on the development of one such capability.

## Notes

1  Crockett, Roger: "How Motorola lost its way," *Business Week*, 05/04/98, page 140.
2  Elstrom, Peter: "Did Motorola make the wrong call?" Business Week, 07/29/96, page 66.
3  *Company Histories* (St James's Press, Detroit, 1992): volume 11, page 327.
4  Motorola website, May 1998.
5  *Company Histories* (St James's Press, Detroit, 1992): volume 11, page 327.
6  Crockett, Roger: "How Motorola lost its way," *Business Week*, 05/04/98, page 140.
7  *Company Histories* (St James's Press, Detroit, 1992): volume 11, page 327.
8  Anonymous Writer: "Tough at the top", *The Economist*, 01/06/96, page 47.
9  Interview with Robert Galvin, Sr, former CEO, Motorola Corporation, May 21, 1999.
10  Elstrom, Peter: "Did Motorola make the wrong call?" *Business Week*, 07/29/96, page 66.
11  Arnst, Catherine: "Cell phones: more, better," *Business Week*, 05/26/97, page 174.
12  Elstrom, Peter: "Lost in the phone zone?" *Business Week*, 11/24/97, page 20.
13  Arnst, Catherine: "Cell phones: more, better", *Business Week*, 05/26/97, page 174.
14  Williamson, John: "Survey of mobile communications," *Financial Times*, 09/08/93, page 6.
15  Crockett, Roger: "How Motorola lost its way," *Business Week*, 05/04/98, page 140.
16  Crockett, Roger: "How Motorola lost its way," *Business Week*, 05/04/98, page 140.
17  Interview with Andrew J. Audet, General Manager, Cable Data Products, Motorola Corp., March 2, 1999.

18   Interview with Robert Galvin, Sr, former CEO, Motorola Corporation, May 21, 1999.
19   Crockett, Roger: "How Motorola Lost its Way," *Business Week*, 05/04/98
20   Crockett, Roger: "How Motorola Lost its Way," *Business Week*, 05/04/98
21   Elstrom, Peter: "Did Motorola Make the Wrong Call?" *Business Week*, 07/29/96, page 66.
22   Elstrom, Peter: "Did Motorola Make the Wrong Call?" *Business Week*, 07/29/96, page 66.
23   Crockett, Roger: "How Motorola lost its way," *Business Week*, 05/04/98, page 140.
24   Crockett, Roger: "How Motorola lost its way," *Business Week*, 05/04/98.

# References

Amit, R. and Schoemaker, P. J. (1993) Strategic assets and organizational rent, *Strategic Management Journal*, 14, 33–46.
Barney, J. B. (1991) Firm resources and sustained competitive advantage *Journal of Management*, 17, 99–120.
Cameron, K. S., Kim, M. U., and Whetton, D. A. (1987) Organizational effects of decline and turbulence, *Administrative Science Quarterly*, 32, 222–40.
Hambrick, D. C. and D'Aveni, R. A. (1988) Large corporate failures and downward spirals, *Administrative Science Quarterly*, 33, 1–23.
Hannan, M. T. and Carroll, G. R. (1992) *Dynamics of Organizational Populations: Density, Legitimation, and Competition*. Oxford: Oxford University Press.
Levinthal, D. A. and March, J. G. (1993) The myopia of learning, *Strategic Management Journal*, (special winter issue), 95–112.
Levy, A. and Merry, U. (1986) *Organizational Transformation: Approaches, Strategies, Theories*. New York: Praeger.
Meyer, A. D. (1982) Adapting to environmental jolts, *Administrative Science Quarterly*, 27, 515–37.
Mintzberg, H. (1990) *Mintzberg on Management*. Englewood Cliffs, NJ: Free Press.
Shimuzu, K. (1999) Imperfect learning: what does an organization learn from its mistakes? Paper presented at the National Academy of Management meetings, Chicago.
Sitkin, S. B. (1992) Learning through failure: the strategy of small losses. In B. M. Staw and L. L. Cummings (eds), *Research in Organizational Behavior*, Vol. 14. Greenwich, CT: JAI Press, 231–66.

# CHAPTER TWENTY-SIX

# Resources, Capabilities, Core Competencies, Invisible Assets, and Knowledge Assets: Label Proliferation and Theory Development in the Field of Strategic Management

## Jay B. Barney

Oliver had the kind of intellectual curiosity that only first-year strategic management Ph.D. students seem to possess. Indeed, while others viewed it as a chore, he took delight in preparing for each session of the strategic management seminar he was then taking.

Perhaps it was that preparation that led him to his discovery. Or maybe it was his inherent intellectual curiosity. Maybe he was just lucky – that he happened to be in just the right place at the right time to discover that which had eluded so many strategy scholars before him. Whatever the reason, the moment Oliver discovered the capability, his academic life changed forever.

The capability that Oliver found was on the side of the physics building, about 15 feet from the sidewalk. Hundreds of people walk by that location each day, but no one had yet noticed the capability. It was small, difficult to see. But if you knew what you were looking for – and Oliver did – you could find it. And then there it was, just the kind of intangible asset Oliver knew was at the core of several theories in strategic management.

Oliver also knew that finding capabilities was unusual. Once he spotted it, he quickly scooped it into a brown paper bag he found on the sidewalk. He wanted to share his discovery with his colleagues. He knew they – and the entire field of strategic management – would be just as excited as he to see, once and for all, a real capability.

He first took his capability to Art, the most senior Ph.D. student in the program. Art was finishing his dissertation and already had a job, and thus rarely even talked to first-year students like Oliver. But Oliver's natural reluctance to talk to Art was overcome by enthusiasm for his incredible discovery – he had found a capability! Holding his paper bag in front of him, like an empty bowl of gruel, Oliver interrupted Art's concentration.

"Art, guess what I have in this bag!"

"Your lunch?" Art responded with the smugness borne of employment.

"No, it was incredible. I was just walking across campus, next to the physics building, and I found a capability. It's right here in this bag."

"Oliver," Art replied with the intellectual confidence that would be dashed when he received his first reviews from SMJ. "You can't have a capability in that paper bag. Capabilities are intangible assets. You can't pick them up and put them in your bag!"

But Oliver was insistent. "Seriously Art, I do have a capability in this bag."

"All right," Art acquiesced. "Let's take your capability to Professor Sikes. Let's see what he has to say!"

As a first-year student, Oliver had never actually met Professor Sikes. But he had heard of him. Sikes had been hired two years earlier as an Assistant Professor in Strategic Management. He currently had several papers under review, and everyone thought his career was moving along well. Professor Sikes was particularly well known for his quantitative skills. If there was anyone equipped to evaluate whether or not Oliver actually had a capability in the bag, it was Sikes. Oliver noticed that even Art approached Professor Sikes' office with care and deference.

"Excuse me, Professor Sikes? Do you have a second to talk to Oliver and me?" Art asked.

"Sure, come in," said Professor Sikes, looking at Oliver's paper bag. "But please, call me Bill."

No one ever called Professor Sikes "Bill."

"What have you got there?" Professor Sikes continued.

"It's a capability!" Oliver cried out, barely able to control his enthusiasm.

"It can't be a capability, Oliver. Capabilities are intangible assets. You can't pick them up and put them in your bag!" Professor Sikes looked at Oliver with mild disgust. "When will these doctoral students ever learn about real quantitative methods?" Sikes mumbled to himself – only half heard by Oliver and Art.

But Oliver's enthusiasm was undaunted. "I know you're skeptical, but I really do have a capability in this bag!"

Oliver's enthusiasm shamed Professor Sikes. After all, it wasn't that long ago he too was a first-year Ph.D. student. "OK, Oliver. Why don't we take your capability to Professor Fagin?"

Now, everyone had heard of Professor Fagin. He was probably the best known strategic management scholar in the school, and had been a full professor for at least ten years. Dr Fagin was not only a well known scholar, but he had a very successful consulting practice. Oliver, Art, and Professor Sikes went upstairs to Dr Fagin's office. Much to everyone's surprise, Dr Fagin was actually in.

"Hi Bill, Art, and, uh, what was your name again?"

"Oliver, I am a first-year Ph.D. student."

"Oh yes. How do you do? So, Oliver, what do you have in that paper bag?" Dr Fagin asked with a curious grin.

"Why, it's the capability I found. By the physics building," Oliver replied confidently.

"Now Oliver. It can't be a capability. Capabilities are intangible assets. You can't pick them up and put them in your bag!" Dr Fagin was beginning to wonder why these three were wasting his time. But Oliver seemed remarkably confident.

"OK, Oliver, let's have a look at your capability."

Oliver gingerly gave his paper bag to Dr Fagin. Once Dr Fagin had a firm grasp on the bag, he turned to Oliver, Art, and Sikes.

"OK, let's all look into the bag at the same time. If anyone sees Oliver's capability, shout out!"

As the group gathered around the bag, an air of excitement descended on them. Was there really a capability in the bag? Would they be the first to ever see a capability? What would it look like? Thousands of questions – and potential SMJ articles – flashed through their minds in seconds.

And then, Dr Fagin opened the bag.

It was empty.

Art, Professor Sikes, and Dr Fagin looked at Oliver with a mixture of anger, disgust, and disappointment. And for a moment, Oliver too seem confused. He knew he had put the capability in the bag, but now it was empty. Where had it gone?

And then it became obvious what had happened to the capability, as Oliver triumphantly looked at his colleagues and announced,

"It was a dynamic capability!"

While Oliver's ability to quickly "explain" the fact that his capability was no longer in the bag speaks highly of his creativity and glibness, it also demonstrates a fundamental confusion that exists in a great deal of strategic management research. Oliver, like so many other strategic management scholars, seems to have confused the act of labeling a phenomenon with the act of developing a theory to understand that phenomenon.

Developing labels for phenomena can, of course, add value to a field of study. This occurs when a new label identifies either a new phenomenon worthy of incorporating into current theory, or a new variety of an already labeled phenomenon worthy of incorporating into current theory. Labeling a new phenomenon can even lead to the development of entirely new theory designed to understand the causes and consequences of that phenomenon. But labeling a phenomenon is not the same as developing theory to understand that phenomenon.

In the field of strategic management, the confusion between labeling a phenomenon and developing a theory to understand a phenomenon is most obvious in research that focuses on the organizational antecedents to sustained competitive advantage. A wide variety of labels have been developed to describe these organizational phenomena. Some have called them "resources" (Wernerfelt, 1984; Barney, 1991), others have called them "capabilities" (Stalk, Evans, and Shulman, 1992), or "dynamic capabilities" (Teece, Pisano, and Shuen, 1997), or "core competencies" (Prahald and Hamel, 1990), or "invisible assets" (Itami, 1987), or even "knowledge assets" (Grant, 1996). Some of these labels may turn out to be fruitful in the ways described earlier. That is, some of these labels may identify either new phenomena, or special cases of already identified phenomena, worthy of incorporating into existing theory. It may even be the case that some of these newly labeled phenomena will require the development of entirely new theories.

However, while these labels have proliferated, there has not been a corresponding proliferation of theory. Indeed, when these labels are used to develop theoretical arguments, those arguments all seem to have pretty much the same structure. They all adopt pretty much the same dependent variable – some way of characterizing firm competitive advantages. They all focus on independent variables that have numerous common attributes – they tend to be intangible, hard to buy and sell, and so forth. And most importantly, the hypothesized causal linkages between these independent and dependent variables seems remarkably consistent. This logic tends to emphasize the importance of firm heterogeneity, why that heterogeneity can last over time, and how it can generate competitive advantage in ways that are consistent with the earliest work in this area (e.g., Wernerfelt, 1984; Rumelt, 1984; Barney, 1986, 1991).

To me, all this suggests that while labeling these new phenomena can be very helpful in identifying ways in which a common theoretical perspective can be applied, these labels – per se – do not represent theoretical contributions to the field. Thus, while applying this common theoretical perspective to these newly labeled phenomena can be a fruitful enterprise, describing the resulting effort as a "new theory of competitive advantage" seems inappropriate. Rather, these are simply "new applications of the received theory of competitive advantage." These new applications can be very important contributions to the field of strategic management.

Of course, this does not suggest that it is not possible to develop what is, in fact, a "new theory of competitive advantage." And, it may be the case that some of the newly labeled phenomena listed above may ultimately require such new theories to understand their causes and consequences. However, to date, most of the debate among scholars that are pursuing these different research agenda does not focus on differences in the causal mechanisms of the proposed models, but on differences in how the independent variables are defined and measured and the relative impact of these different independent variables on competitive advantage.

Such debates are healthy and important. To the extent that they lead to rigorous empirical research, they will significantly benefit the field of strategic management. But such debates do not justify describing what is essentially the same theory as if it were multiple theories. In physics, the "law of gravity" is not relabeled every time it is applied to a different physical object. Neither should this common theory of competitive advantage be called a "competence-based theory of competitive advantage" when it is applied to competencies or a "knowledge-based theory of competitive advantage" when it is applied to knowledge assets. This can only cause confusion. These two theories of competitive advantage are essentially the same, although they may have been applied to different (but related) independent variables.

Of course, a practical problem remains: what do we call this common theory of competitive advantage? My choice has been to call it the "resource-based theory of competitive advantage." This is not because I believe the label "resource" is somehow empirically superior to other labels that have been suggested in the literature. Rather, I choose this term only because it was among the first labels proposed in the literature (Wernerfelt, 1984) and because its broad definition (Wernerfelt, 1984; Barney, 1991) seems likely to encompass most of the other organizational phenomena that may turn out to be of interest in understanding competitive advantages for firms.

At a recent academic meeting I overheard two young scholars debating about the empirical implications of the "resource-based view" and the "knowledge-based view." One of them was arguing that the "knowledge-based view" was a superior theory because it could be tested, while the "resource-based view" couldn't. The other was arguing that several excellent empirical tests of the "resource-based view" had already been published. When they noticed me listening to them, they asked for my opinion. I simply observed that one really good way to test the "resource-based view" was through the study of knowledge assets. They both looked confused.

The "twist" of this story is that both these academics were named Oliver.

## References

Barney, J. B. (1986) Strategic factor markets: Expectations, luck and business strategy, *Management Science*, 32, 1512–14.

Barney, J. B. (1991) Firm resources and sustained competitive advantage, *Journal of Management*, 17, 99–120.

Grant, R. M. (1996) Toward a knowledge-based theory of the firm, *Strategic Management Journal*, 17, Winter Special Issue, 109–22.

Itami, H. (1987). *Mobilizing Invisible Assets*. Cambridge, MA: Harvard University Press.

Prahalad, C. K. and Hamel, G. (1990) The core competence of the organization, *Harvard Business Review*, 90, 79–93.

Rurnelt, R. (1984) Toward a strategic theory of the firm. In R. Lamb (ed.), *Competitive Strategic Management*. Upper Saddle River, NJ: Prentice Hall.

Stalk, G., Evans, P., and Shulman, L. (1992) Competing on capabilities: the new rules of corporate strategy, *Harvard Business Review*, March–April, 57–69.

Teece, D. J., Pisano, G., and Shuen, A. (1997) Dynamic capabilities and strategic management, *Strategic Management Journal*, 18 (7), 509–33.

Wernerfelt, B. (1984) A resource-based view of the firm, *Strategic Management Journal*, 5, 171–180.

# Index

Figures are denoted by italic type. Where the reference is found in a note, this is shown by "n" after the numerals.

Printed and bound by CPI Group (UK) Ltd, Croydon, CR0 4YY

23/04/2025

14660966-0004